BLOOD OF THE PROPHETS

Brigham Young as governor of Utah, 1852. From Frederick Hawkins Piercy and James Linforth, *Route from Liverpool to Great Salt Lake Valley*, 1855. Courtesy Utah State Historical Society.

Blood of the Prophets

Brigham Young and the
Massacre at Mountain Meadows

WILL BAGLEY

UNIVERSITY OF OKLAHOMA PRESS : NORMAN

EDITED BY WILL BAGLEY

A Road from El Dorado: The 1848 Trail Journal of Ephraim Green

Frontiersman: Abner Blackburn's Narrative

West from Fort Bridger: The Pioneering of Immigrant Trails across Utah, 1846–1850, revised and updated with Harold Schindler from the first edition by Roderic Korns and Dale L. Morgan

This Is the Place: A Crossroads of Utah's Past, with Pat Bagley

The Pioneer Camp of the Saints: The 1846 and 1847 Mormon Trail Journals of Thomas Bullock

Scoundrel's Tale: The Samuel Brannan Papers

Army of Israel: Mormon Battalion Narratives, with David L. Bigler

Library of Congress Cataloging-in-Publication Data

Bagley, Will, 1950–
Blood of the prophets : Brigham Young and the massacre at Mountain
Meadows / Will Bagley.
p.   cm.
Includes bibliographical references (p.   ) and index.
ISBN 0-8061-3426-7 (hc: alk. paper)
1. Mountain Meadows Massacre, 1857.   2. Young, Brigham, 1801–
1877.   3. Mormons—Utah—History—19th century.   4. Mormons—
Utah—Biography.   5. Frontier and pioneer life—Utah.   6. Utah—
History—19th century.   I. Title.

F826 .B13 2002
979.2'47—dc21
2001057996

1   2   3   4   5   6   7   8   9   10

For David L. Bigler and Floyd A. O'Neil

Friends and Mentors

Dearly beloved, avenge not yourselves, but rather give place unto wrath: for it is written: Vengeance is mine; I will repay, saith the Lord. Therefore if thine enemy hunger, feed him; if he thirst, give him drink: for in so doing thou shalt heap coals of fire on his head. Be not overcome of evil, but overcome evil with good.

ROMANS 12:19–21

Truth will cut its own way.

JOSEPH SMITH, JR.

CONTENTS

ILLUSTRATIONS

MAPS

PREFACE

The first reliable report of the murder of more than one hundred men, women, and children in southern Utah on September 11, 1857, did not reach the American public until almost two years after the event. In an August 1859 article for *Harper's Weekly*, U.S. Army surgeon Charles Brewer described what he had seen and learned on a visit to the site. "I deem it proper to send you a plain and unvarnished statement of the affair as it actually happened," Brewer wrote, because no previous account could "in the slightest degree approximate to a description of the hideous truth."[1] Although the story contended for the epithet "crime of the century" in its time and scandalized the nation for decades, the "hideous truth" of this American drama remains elusive.

Early accounts called the Mountain Meadows massacre "the darkest deed of the nineteenth century." One man who saw the human remains scattered at the site in 1859 termed it "a crime that has no parallel in American history for atrocity." In the twentieth century, Joseph Fielding Smith, who served for some seventy years as historian and briefly as prophet of the Church of Jesus Christ of Latter-day Saints (LDS, or, popularly, the Mormons), denounced this "bloody and diabolical deed" as the most "horrible and shocking crime ever perpetrated" in Utah.[2] Practically every adult male in Utah's southern settlements was implicated in the killings, and the earliest investigators were convinced that orders for the mass murder had come directly from the highest levels of the LDS church. Yet only one man was punished for the crime, and that after a delay of twenty years. The story of the most violent incident in the history of America's overland trails remains among the West's most controversial historical subjects, yet even students of the American West have nearly forgotten the event. Most Americans, including many Utahns, have never heard of it.

The world should not forget the Mountain Meadows massacre. It raises hard questions and issues that echo in today's headlines. Acts of religious fury still make news. Mass murders in the Balkans and Africa and the inability of powerful nations to bring to justice men guilty of heinous war crimes offer grim reminders of this atrocity and its aftermath. Now, regrettably, another horrific September 11 has been added to the list of crimes against humanity. Like all such acts, the murders at Mountain Meadows raise larger questions about the human condition, particularly how decent men can, while acting on their best and firmest beliefs, commit a great evil.

I am not the first to ask these questions and attempt to answer them honestly. I happily acknowledge my immense debt to Juanita Leavitt Pulsipher Brooks, one of the West's best and bravest historians. No one could equal the insight, dedication, and courage Juanita Brooks brought to the story her son said she was born to tell. For fifty years her classic monograph, *The Mountain Meadows Massacre,* has been the definitive study. Her intimate connections to the Mormon frontier and her encyclopedic knowledge of southern Utah's history made Brooks the best-qualified historian of her generation to tell this story, and she told it with integrity and heart.

People often ask, "What is there to say about Mountain Meadows that Juanita Brooks hasn't already said?" This book is not a revision but an extension of Brooks's labors. In the past fifty years scholars have located and published an astonishing number of journals, letters, reminiscences, government documents, church records, newspaper accounts, tribal traditions and ethnography, graphic images, folk songs, and family legends concerning the West, Mormonism, and Mountain Meadows. These materials, and key documents she was never allowed to see, generally confirm Brooks's competence as a historian and verify the private conclusions found in her extensive research. Along with the papers of Brooks and her colleagues, these materials provide ample reason to take a new look at the subject.

Any historian must be careful not to let his or her fascination with a single subject obscure the larger picture. Mountain Meadows was only one event in the history of Mormonism and a single incident in the long career of Brigham Young. I have tried to avoid making more of the topic than the record justifies, but LDS scholars have dismissed early Mormon religious violence too blithely and have neglected the devastating impact the crime and its cover-up had on the LDS church and Brigham Young's reputation. His daughter Susa Young Gates noted in 1929, "Our father had his faults and failings, no doubt of that. There were plenty of people in his life-time, and there are people even today, who will tell you about that." Yet devout Mormon historians hesitate to acknowledge even the most minor imperfections in the great man and, like Mrs. Gates, prefer to ignore his failings: "His family and friends loved him so well they forget to remember anything about him but his shining virtues."[3] This is a disservice to Young and to history. A balanced assessment of this complex man must recognize his many achievements, but apologists have dismissed difficult questions about Young that a careful historian must consider. No one should attempt a credible evaluation of Young's life without mentioning Mountain Meadows (as several recent publications have), just as no one should write Richard Nixon's biography without noting Watergate or hope to understand modern German history without considering the Holocaust.

This book answers what may be the most frequently asked question about Mountain Meadows: What did Brigham Young know, and when did he know it? Almost to a man, federal officers were convinced that the Mormon prophet, then Utah Territory's governor and Indian superintendent, was directly responsible for the Mountain Meadows massacre, but the men who investigated the crime could not produce enough evidence to bring him to trial, let alone make their case in court. (Those who seek to "prove" that Young explicitly ordered the massacre should consider this fact.) Yet LDS apologists cannot explain why Brigham Young had to send orders to southern Utah *not* to massacre outsiders. They ignore the evidence that the Mormon leader was an accessory after the fact, which Brooks considered "abundant and unmistakable, and from the most impeccable Mormon sources."[4]

This work considers the massacre a watershed event and attempts to interpret the story's complex context in a broad historical perspective. Readers will find here neither a complete biography of Brigham Young nor a comprehensive history of the Latter-day Saints. Instead, it is an examination of a defining incident in Mormon history and a significant part of Brigham Young's life. To comprehend what is widely considered the darkest episode in Utah's history, this book examines the intertwined religious beliefs and political conditions that led to the crime. Believers looking for an inspirational recounting of LDS history will need to look elsewhere. My purpose is to examine how decent men, believing they were doing God's work, committed a horrific atrocity.

Despite volumes of fiery sermons in print and more troublesome material in manuscript records, some argue that Brigham Young did not actually mean what he said, that his verbal excesses were simply rhetorical. Down deep, this argument goes, Young was too sensitive to contemplate, let alone execute, the acts of violence so vividly evoked in his speeches. This book adopts a different approach. Like the faithful who sat through his fire-and-brimstone sermons, I believe Brigham Young meant exactly what he said.

As someone with a deep respect for the craft of history, writing this story has been like wrestling the devil with little prospect of victory. For six years I have attempted to discover what happened long ago at that isolated oasis in southwestern Utah and to understand why it happened. Rather than simply round up all the material that supported a preconceived theory, I sought to examine every available piece of evidence and establish a factual basis for the incident. Initial drafts of this work exhaustively evaluated all these sources and presented every interpretation, but to spare the reader I have replaced tedious debates with the simplest conclusions most consistently supported by the best accounts. Because the historical record is so bedeviled by contradictory sources and outright lies, I often explain why I accept one account over another, but I attempt to summarize all the evidence and arguments fairly. As a creature of chronology, I paid special attention to the sequence of events. I sought to tell a story that would make sense to a reasonable person and to avoid speculation beyond the facts, reserving my personal conclusions for the end of the book. By telling the story of *what* happened, I trust readers to form their own opinions about *why* it happened.

A veil of silence has shrouded the truth about Mountain Meadows, and its legacy of shame remains a powerful influence on the culture of southern Utah. Virtually every explanation of this episode has a distinct bias and can be challenged for one good reason or another. Historians must reconstruct this event from the testimony of children, murderers, and passersby, an immense technical challenge. None of the adult emigrants survived to describe what happened, since as Brigham H. Roberts put it, "all were killed who could have had any certain memory of the circumstances." A distinguished LDS scholar, Roberts defined the historian's problem when relying on Mormon sources: the emigrants' tale must be pieced together from the confessions of their murderers. These stories were told in despair or in revenge against those who had "betrayed the deed of blood."[5] The reminiscent accounts of the surviving children, subtly shaded by the passage of time and the influence of questionable histories, are problematic, but they are surprisingly reliable and consistent, especially when compared to the self-serving tales of the murderers that have long been used to tell the story. Although for almost one hundred fifty years few took the trouble to ask Southern Paiutes to tell the story, their tribal traditions provide useful insights and information.

Among the standard sources that richly document most LDS history—Mormon journals, letters, minutes, recollections, and reports—so little authentic material about the massacre survives that it suggests a concerted official effort to eliminate any mention of the subject in Mormon annals. More probably, this odd silence in the historical record reflects remarkable self-censorship. Missing or destroyed sources include John D. Lee's 1857 diary, the minutes of the Cedar City church meeting whose participants voted to kill the emigrants, correspondence between local militia commanders and Brigham Young, and pages ripped from dozens of 1857 journals. From the time the Fancher party left Salt Lake until all the adult emigrants were dead, there is hardly a single account of their journey and fate that does not pose serious problems in its fairness or reliability.

Reliable history requires accurate data. In the case of Mountain Meadows, we have a record irrevocably colored by dubious folklore and corrupted by perjury, false memory, and the destruction of key documents. Almost every acknowledged "fact" about the fate of these murdered people is open to question. The contradictory eyewitness reports of the massacre recount a nightmare whose precise details vary wildly, depending on the prejudices and perspectives of the narrator. Yet while many of the affair's incidental details are lost to history, the assault on the emigrants and its grim result are established historical facts. By applying the basic rules of the craft of history, I have rejected the most obvious myths and use common sense to reconstruct the event as accurately as the sources will permit.

These sources are vast but problematic. A few warnings about them are in order. I have made extensive use of long-ignored contemporary newspaper accounts that provide useful insights into the events of 1857. They often contain the earliest and most useful information on the subject and accurately represent the spirit of their time. Yet be forewarned: nineteenth-century newspapers were at least as fallible as their modern counterparts. I often note when information is drawn from reminiscent accounts or statements long after the fact, since such evidence is usually less reliable than contemporary reports. I occasionally use sources such as journalist John Hanson Beadle and apostate T. B. H. Stenhouse that are characterized and dismissed as "anti-

Mormon." I have tried to use such biased materials judiciously, often where Mormon accounts corroborate them. It is worth noting that these works have proven more reliable than virtually anything printed in official LDS sources until well into the twentieth century. Family traditions preserve much valuable historical information, but I have used these stories more for the deeper truths they hold about attitudes and beliefs than for their factual reliability. When I identify a source as folklore, readers should treat it as mythology and not as the gospel truth.

Mountain Meadows lures its chroniclers into a maze of duplicity built by men who lied to protect their very lives. In places, I use participant statements like Lee's without questioning their accuracy, even when they clearly contradict other accounts and even themselves. I leave it to the reader to discern the truth of such tales. The story of Mountain Meadows demonstrates that before trying their hands at murder, most killers are accomplished liars. Lee fabricated a variety of colorful, dramatic, detailed, and wildly inconsistent justifications of the massacre. He was a compelling storyteller with a brilliant talent for reconfiguring the past to suit the needs of the present, and he had great motivation to do so. Every trick of human memory—forgetfulness, invention, denial, repression, conflation, and distortion—acted upon the recollections of Lee and his companions. Lee's autobiography has long been used as a key source to reconstruct the massacre and its aftermath, but it contains perhaps the most suspect telling of this problematic event. Lee's diaries and the early chapters of his autobiography are among the most vivid and accurate accounts of early Mormonism, but his motives render his massacre accounts suspect. I have avoided relying on Lee unless the information is substantiated elsewhere, but occasionally he provides the only eyewitness account of critical events—and even when covering his tracks, John D. Lee knew how to tell a story.

Many LDS historians have a deep love for a religion they believe was revealed by God and passionately accept their roles as defenders of the faith. B. H. Roberts considered the massacre the most difficult of all the controversial subjects he had to cover in his six-volume history of Mormonism's first century. Regarding Mountain Meadows, he conceded that Latter-day Saints "have been naturally slow to admit all the facts that history may insist upon as inevitable."[6] In their desire to exonerate Brigham Young of any guilt, official Mormon accounts of the crime laid the blame on victims and Indians, a tradition that is alive and well today. I have made a special effort to set the record straight on these points. Mormons and emigrants undoubtedly did come into conflict in 1857, but beyond folklore there is no evidence to prove the Arkansans did *anything* to provoke the men who killed them: they were simply in the wrong place at the wrong time. The old story that vicious Southern Paiutes forced the outnumbered Saints to commit mass murder collapses under the most casual historical analysis. Mormon scholars, historian Kenneth M. Stampp concluded, have never adequately confronted this episode. "Local Indians were accomplices in the crime," he noted, "but not the instigators as some participants claimed in order to diminish their own guilt."[7]

History is story, and this work attempts to bring to life forgotten victims and heroes. Recent research by descendants has produced a wealth of detail about those who died and the lives of the children who survived. These memories humanize the once faceless victims, and the experiences of these families reveal surprising details of life on America's overland trails, which were torn by crime and violence executed more often than not by white criminals and not "red" warriors. This book tells the stories of the many Mormons who bravely resisted participating in this great evil or who refused to countenance its cover-up, often at great personal risk. The integrity and courage of Olive Coombs, Josiah Gibbs, John and William Hawley, George A. Hicks, William Laney, Laban Morrill, Joseph Walker, Charles W. Wandell, George Calvin Williams, and Juanita Brooks should not be forgotten or ignored.

I have tried to tell this American story so that it will make sense to thoughtful Americans. The massacre was not an isolated aberration. It was the logical culmination of a long process. These events took place in the context of a young republic torn by economic volatility, millennial strivings, riots, "mobbings," and civil outrages that often escaped punishment. Like many new faiths, nineteenth-century Mormonism had a dark side of violence and fanaticism. The devotion of early Latter-day Saints and their mix of politics and religion repeatedly provoked conflict with their neighbors. The Saints regarded such opposition as persecution of their righteousness, and battles with their neighbors drove them from Ohio, Missouri, Illinois, and finally into Mexico in 1847. Oblivious to the provocative nature of their more radical doctrines and their claim to being the only true church, early Mormons developed what two modern historians have called "the myth of persecuted innocence." Each new struggle generated further bitterness and zealotry, which in turn provoked more hostile resistance and opposition.[8] This vicious cycle inexorably fueled the fanaticism and emotions that led to Mountain Meadows.

Historians of the LDS faith often explain Mountain Meadows as an example of frontier violence. Yet the endorsement of such actions by a ruling elite made frontier violence in the Mormon West fundamentally different from the vigilantism and hooliganism that wracked western mining camps and boomtowns. Today the religion has abandoned its support of "holy murder" and virtually every practice—polygamy, theocracy, blood atonement, consecration, communalism, millennialism—that made it so provocative in the nineteenth century. Doctrines such as a belief in unquestioned obedience to the Lord's anointed persist, but the "old-time religion" described in this study has little relation to today's LDS church, which for a century has been firmly committed to becoming no more controversial than Methodism.

The modern LDS church wishes the world to simply forget the most disturbing episode in its history, and the institution does not conceal its resentment of anyone who stirs the darker ashes of its past. Although I am proud of my Mormon heritage, my duty as a historian obliges me to abide by the rules of my craft. It is simply beyond human understanding to identify the hand of God in history, and it is beyond the power of history to prove or disprove claims of faith: these are matters of the human heart. It is not my purpose to challenge anyone's personal beliefs but rather to tell the story of Mountain Meadows forthrightly. I hope the reception of this work will emulate the fate of Juanita Brooks's *The Mountain Meadows Massacre* and that the book will come to be appreciated as a service to my people and to history.

We must not forget that humanity is capable of both great evil and enlightened heroism—and we should note the conditions that inspire both. This work attempts to do just that, as honestly and accurately as possible. In this quest, I share the hope of my forebears: The truth is mighty and will prevail.

Editorial Note

Where necessary, I have added punctuation in quoted material and uppercased or lowercased the first word to conform to standard usage, but I have preserved misspellings and grammatical errors found in original sources. Some important sources are transcribed literally, with four spaces substituted for periods. All italicized text in quotations is italicized or underlined in the original. Strike-outs indicate that the material was originally crossed out in manuscript.

ACKNOWLEDGMENTS

The greatest reward of a historian's work is meeting the many dedicated people who work in libraries, archives, historical societies, and museums. I can only name a few of the many wonderful friends I have met in the course of this project.

I have identified sources once known to be located in various archives that cannot be found in current collections. As there are a variety of reasons documents "go missing" in archival collections, this is to identify possible problems with sources, not to imply any nefarious intent.

The staff of the Family and Church History Department of The Church of Jesus Christ of Latter-day Saints (formerly the Church Historian's Office or the Historical Department) have been extremely helpful in aiding my search for information. I have cited materials from the Archives of the Church of Jesus Christ of Latter-day Saints as "LDS Archives." The staff of the Utah State Historical Society has also been of invaluable assistance.

At Special Collections and Manuscripts, Marriott Library, University of Utah, I owe a great debt to director Gregory Thompson, Roy Webb, Madelyn Garrett, and the entire staff, especially Walter Jones. At Special Collections, Stewart Library, Weber State University, thanks to archivist John Sillito, assistant archivist Julie Middlemas, and student archivist Robb White. Utah State Archivist Jeffrey Johnson and Val Wilson provided copies of Jacob Forney's guardian petitions regarding the Mountain Meadows orphans and the opportunity to survey Nauvoo Legion militia records. Janet Seegmiller, Blanche Clegg, and Thomas Muir of Special Collections, Gerald R. Sherratt Library, Southern Utah University, helped to track down invaluable documents and photographs, especially in the William Rees Palmer and Kate Vilate Isom Palmer Western History Collection.

Archivist Ronald E. Romig, assistant archivist Barbara Bernauer, and librarian Sue McDonald of the Library and Archives of the Community of Christ (formerly the Reorganized Church of Jesus Christ of Latter Day Saints) in Independence, Missouri, offered invaluable assistance. Librarian Joseph F. Perry of the Database and Newspaper Center at the Free Library of Philadelphia copied the Brigham Young, Jr., 1869 interview with the *Morning Post*.

I must acknowledge the special help of librarians and archivists Bonnie Hardwick of the Bancroft Library, Terry Cook of the California State Archives, Patricia Keats of the California Historical Society, and Edith Menna of the Pioneer Memorial Museum of the International Society, Daughters of Utah Pioneers. My special appreciation to Gary F. Kurutz, John R. Gonzales, and Sibylle Zemitis of the California State Library and the entire staff at Special Collections and Manuscripts, Harold B. Lee Library, at Brigham Young University.

The staff of The Henry E. Huntington Library was extremely accommodating. Curators Peter J. Blodgett and Jennifer L. Martinez guided me through their Western Historical Manuscripts. Historians Martin Ridge and Andrew Rolle were generous with both their insights and their suggestions.

At the Library of Congress, I wish to thank Jeff Flannery, Fred Bauman, and Ruth and Daniel Boorstin. At the National Archives, I must express my gratitude to Ann Cummings, Mike Meier, Robert M. Kvasnicka, Richard Fusick, Matt Fulgham, Claire Prechtel-Kluskens, Fred J. Romanski, Aloha P. South, Ed Schamel, Kristen Wilhelm, and Robert Ellis.

Shirley Pyron very kindly opened the Carroll County Historical Society on a Monday and helped me to copy the Mountain Meadows material in its files. The staff of the Boone County Library in Harrison, Arkansas, allowed me to copy their clipping files and book collection. Deputy director Russell Baker and librarian Sheila Berrill of the Arkansas History Commission helped to quickly survey their Mountain Meadows materials and locate several significant newspaper accounts. Michael J. Dabrishus, Andrea E. Cantrell, and Cassandra McCraw of the Special Collections Division of the University of Arkansas Libraries found important items in their collection. Karen Mason and Lee Kruetzer of Capitol Reef National Park searched their archives for Charles Kelly photos and documents. Eric Moody and Martha M. Lauritzen helped me to track down material at the Nevada Historical Society.

The opportunity to work as a research associate in the Beinecke Library's Yale Collection of Western Americana allowed me to survey their magnificent Coe collection. I owe special thanks to Ralph Franklin, George Miles, and Howard Lamar for their help.

I wish to thank Scot Denhalter for his Spanish translations and Shannon Novak for permission to quote from her draft forensic report on the victims of Mountain Meadows. Blaine M. Simons shared the results of forty years' research on the subject—an amazing collection of source documents, interviews, books, and articles, including notes of his visit to northwestern Arkansas and his conversations with members of the Fancher family.

Gary Fancher, Sam Fancher, Paul L. Blair, Lora Blair and Roger P. Blair, M.D., Lesley Wischmann, and J. K. Fancher provided valuable information about the Fancher family. Paul Buford Fancher, author of *Richard Fancher's Descendants 1764–1992,* shared his insights into the family, as did Burr and Ada Fancher, who kindly welcomed me into their home for a weekend.

Karl Brooks spent a wonderful morning discussing his memories of his mother, the incomparable Juanita Brooks. Basil Parker descendant Shirley McFadzean supplied an astounding amount of information on the 1857 Arkansas wagon parties. John Fancher descendant Ronald E. Loving, who located the 1860 Arkansas depositions in the National Archives, shared a wealth of family information and his personal experiences working to create the 1990 monument at Mountain Meadows. With Verne R.

Lee, he has accomplished miracles. I owe both men a great debt, as does anyone interested in the event and its legacy. Southern Utah historian Morris Shirts kindly shared his insights shortly before his death, and Cedar City resident Alva Matheson told his stories and shared his collection of artifacts from the site. Bill Walker supplied information about his ancestor, miller Joseph Walker. Peter McAuslan descendant Polly Aird provided sources on George Hicks and much interesting family information.

Terry Del Bene and Russ Tanner of the Rock Springs, Wyoming, Bureau of Land Management office shared their extensive knowledge of the Utah War and overland trails. Durwood Ball of the University of New Mexico Press has been unstinting with his discoveries from the National Archives. Robert A. Clark and Hugh McKell of the Arthur H. Clark Company have provided invaluable insights. Robert Kent Fielding graciously shared his transcriptions of articles about the Lee trial from the *Salt Lake Daily Tribune.* Dave Rowan of KUTV and Janine Carter of KSL, Salt Lake City television stations, helped to locate archival videotape.

Gary Tom of the Paiute Indian Tribe of Utah arranged a meeting with tribal elder Clifford Jake. Marion "Omar" Jacklin, U.S. Forest Service archaeologist for the Dixie National Forest in Cedar City, shared her wide knowledge and unique professional insights. Anna Jean Backus, Robert Blake, Clive Burgess, Norman Eatough, John and Lori Huber, Karl Hugh, Glenn Lee, Glen Leonard, Judge Roger V. Logan, Jr., George P. Lytle, Stan Lytle, Clint Lytle, Kent Bylund, Joseph Platte, Sen. Frank E. Moss, Linda King Newell, Boyd Redington, Gordon Remington, and Rory Swenson have all made contributions to this work.

Historians Douglas D. Alder, John Alley, Alan Barnett, Lyndia Carter, D. Robert Carter, Lawrence Coates, Todd Compton, Chris Graves, Ralph Hafen, Steven Heath, Michael W. Homer, Kristin Johnson, Melvin C. Johnson, Edward Leo Lyman, Michael Marquardt, Ardis Parshall, Charles S. Peterson, Levi Peterson, John Peterson, D. Michael Quinn, Richard Roberts, and David Whittaker have shared their time and expertise. Melvin T. Smith provided key insights into southern Utah and Mormon culture. I owe a special thanks to Laura Bayer. Booksellers Curt Bench, Lyndon Cook, Joan Nay, Ken Sanders, Kent Walgren, and Sam and Tony Weller have generously assisted my search for information.

I am especially indebted to the scholars who patiently reviewed this manuscript in all its stages. Todd Berens contributed his wide-ranging knowledge of the history of the West and insights into the trail. With his wife, Betty, I spent three delightful days exploring southern Utah's emigrant roads and learning of their friendship with Juanita Brooks. Bishop Keith Irwin of San Jose has provided stern counsel and appreciated advice. Judith Freeman's many suggestions demonstrated her great skill as a writer. Will Rusho's editorial insights have substantially improved the narrative. William P. MacKinnon contributed his encyclopedic knowledge of the Utah War and his superlative editorial skills. Veteran journalist Bryce Nelson made valuable stylistic improvements. Elliott West and Gene Sessions provided helpful critiques of the manuscript.

As always, David L. Bigler's vision has had a profound impact on the way I look at Utah's history. I am not sure I would have found my way out of this particular thicket without his guidance. Perhaps our friend Harold Schindler could now explain it all. Floyd Alexander O'Neil has been a constant inspiration and guide who shared his wide-ranging knowledge of the National Archives. He has relentlessly exorcised bad history and unnecessary speculation from these pages, and the expertise of this great scholar and teacher informs much of this work.

The hard work and brilliant editing of Charles E. Rankin of the University of Oklahoma Press have made me a better writer and this a much better book.

I must finally acknowledge Frank James Singer and the able support of his executive assistant, Laura Buttrell, whose vision launched this project and whose generous financial support helped to make this book possible. Good luck Frank, wherever you are.

BLOOD OF THE PROPHETS

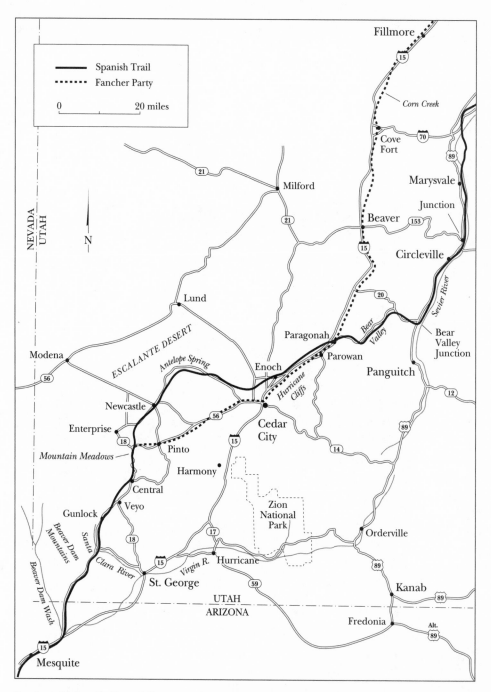

Southern Utah trails. From Fillmor , Utah, to Mesquite Nevada. Based on map courtesy Utah State
University Press.

Prologue

THE MOUNTAIN MEADOW

Beyond the Rocky Mountains in the vast reaches of the American West lies the Great Basin. On its arid southern rim three mountain ranges rise from the desolation of the Escalante Desert. To the north their peaks command the broken red rock country of Zion National Park; to the south they overlook the Mojave Desert of Nevada and the Sonoran ranges of the Arizona strip. These mountains shelter an alpine valley one mile wide and six miles long that is laden with snow in the winter and filled with grass and flowers in the spring. The barely perceptible ridge that divides these broad fields into separate meadows marks the rim of the Great Basin; the streams born in the northern fields disappear into the basin's playas, while those to the south flow to the Sea of Cortez and the Pacific. Perched more than a mile above sea level, this remote spot offers a refuge from the wide deserts that surround it. The valley narrows at its southern end, where a small creek breaks through a mountain wall to cut a tortuous canyon. Here beside a spring nestles a natural campsite.

For at least six hundred years the Nuwuvi (known today as Southern Paiutes) have roamed here, but their own traditions say this country has always been their home. The sites of their dwellings and storage pits still surround this sheltered bowl. For generations the Nuwuvi hunted rabbits and deer in the meadows, gathered pine nuts and grasses, and escaped the intense summer heat of the surrounding lowlands.[1]

Four hundred years ago, long before any Nuwuvi saw a European, bitter change disrupted their way of life. Unknown plagues and terrible pestilence took a mysterious toll on the people. In time powerful bands of their cousins the Utes preyed on the Paiutes, stealing their children and selling them as slaves in the new Spanish colonies to the south. The meadow later became a resting place for freebooters on their way to plunder the ranchos of California. By 1830 American fur trappers and Mexican mule traders from Taos and Santa Fe had followed Indian trails across the

Mojave Desert, blazing the Spanish Trail to the Pacific. Soon the annual caravans from New Mexico rested in the mountain cove. When Lt. John C. Frémont visited in 1844, he found "an extensive mountain meadow, rich in bunch grass and fresh with numerous springs of clear water, all refreshing and delightful to look upon." The oasis would soon be known as the Mountain Meadow, but the romantic explorer named it las Vegas de Santa Clara—the Meadows of the Santa Clara—at "the terminating point of the desert."[2] The Pathfinder told how the Paiutes "infested and insulted" his camp and murdered one of his herders, but he failed to count the Indians his men killed to avenge the murder. To survive this onslaught, the Paiutes struck like ghosts at the traders and raiders who crossed their country, furtively extracting a toll of livestock as some recompense for the havoc these animals wreaked on their lands.

The discovery of gold in California brought new significance to the meadow, for strategically it made the southern wagon road through Utah to Los Angeles practical. The valley let travelers rest (or as they said, "recruit") their teams and prepare for the arduous crossing of the Mojave. Emigrants brought the first wagons through the meadows in 1849 and soon returned every fall, praising the abundant springs and lush fields. There was "fine & tender grass enough growing on this Vegas," sojourner Orville Pratt wrote, "to fatten a thousand head of horses or cattle." But a day's march away, he noted, "the Piutes at this place are said to be the worst on the route."[3]

In 1850 Latter-day Saints came to explore and settle the Nuwuvi lands. The Mormons gave simple names to the ranges, calling them the Pine Valley, Red, and Beaver Dam Mountains. One of their scouts called this oasis "the most beautiful little valley that I have seen in the mountains south."[4] Unlike the traders and explorers who shot first and asked questions later, these whites befriended the Paiutes. The "Saints" believed they shared the blood of Israel with the beleaguered people they called Piedes and won the Indians' loyalty when they stopped the theft of their children. The Nuwuvi soon developed both respect for and fear of their new neighbors, whose powerful magic and weapons appeared to dominate both the material and spiritual worlds but whose demands for land, water, and grass were never-ending.

The Mormons taught the Paiutes to distinguish between them—the "Mormonees"—and Americans—the "Mericats." Non-Mormon wagon trains still came to the meadow every fall to recruit their outfits before heading south and west across the Mojave. When one such company with perhaps a thousand head of livestock camped at this remote spot in 1857, the Paiutes joined the Mormons in a ritual of blood and vengeance. As dawn broke on the first Monday in September, officers of the Utah Territorial Militia led warriors and settlers disguised as Indians in a devastating attack on the Fancher party, a wagon train from Arkansas. For five days forty men, thirty women, and seventy children fought for their lives. On Friday afternoon the party surrendered its arms to the Mormons in exchange for a promise of protection from the Indians.

The Mormon officers carefully segregated the emigrant families into three groups—men, women and children, and infants and wounded—and their supposed protectors marched them north from the camp. In early twilight at the rim of the Great Basin, the militia shot down the unarmed men. Young whites disguised in paint and feathers and a small band of native freebooters rushed from ambush to murder the terrified women and children. More than two dozen adult women and fifty children, ranging in age from infancy to eighteen years, died in the assault. The Mormons and their allies killed everyone except seventeen children, none over six years of age. Some of them were painfully wounded, but their "innocent blood" and presumed inability to tell their story spared them from the general slaughter.

The Nuwuvi recalled that the leader of the whites "was like a wild beast who had tasted of fresh blood. He was turned into a demon." At first light the next morning, the Paiutes watched the Mormons return, strip the bodies, toss the corpses into ravines, and cover the remains with a layer of dirt too thin to hide the dead from the wolves and coyotes that prowled the meadow.[5] As their Indian allies looted the wagons, the white men met in a great circle to swear a blood oath, vowing that their grim ritual would remain forever a secret.

In the wake of the killing, travelers called the campsite Murderers Spring, but the stream kept its Nuwuvi name, Magotsu Creek. Some cattle from the massacred party ran wild and gave their name to the Bull Valley Mountains, the range to the west of the haunted the place the Mormons called the Mountain Meadow.

1

Their Innocent Blood Will
Cry unto the Lord of Hosts

Eleanor Jane McComb was born in western Virginia in 1817. As a child, she followed her family down the great rivers of the American heartland to the Deep South. Her trials began when she wed Hector McLean at Greenville, Louisiana, in 1841.[1] The well-spoken but taciturn McLean was born in about 1815. His wife later described his "large forehead, very white, fair skin, very large straight nose keen gray eyes (most persons think them black) thin lips of a positive expression, and sharp chin."[2] Mrs. McLean, dark haired and well educated, was attractive and given to writing impassioned poetry. Both husband and wife came from "old and somewhat noted Presbyterian stock," but theirs was a troubled marriage.[3] Hector's drinking resulted in a separation in 1844 that led Eleanor to contemplate ending her life in "the smoothe current of the Mississippi." Hector confessed he had failed "to live soberly and righteously before God and men" and proposed they "seek an asylum among the people of God" to help save and reform him. By the early 1850s the troubled couple and their three children had moved to California to start a new life. McLean worked as a customshouse official and was a respectable citizen of San Francisco, but the gold rush metropolis was not a good refuge from the vices of the world.[4]

In the early 1850s San Francisco was notorious for its saloons, bordellos, and "gambling hells," yet it was also a center for a dynamic young American religion. Eleanor McLean had already encountered an unnamed missionary of the Church of Jesus Christ of Latter-day Saints while living in a port town on the Mississippi River. Even then perhaps she was "fascinated by the romance which the Mormon may have skillfully woven into his discourse." In November 1851 the McLeans took shelter from the rain at a Latter-day Saints service. She recalled, "From the time I heard the first sermon I never spoke except in defence of the 'Mormons' and their faith."[5]

The religion's devoted missionaries taught Mrs. McLean the story of their prophet, Joseph Smith, Jr. Very much a product of his time, Smith came of age in upstate New York among people devoted to unusual superstitions and religious beliefs. The fiery revivals that swept the region earned it the name "Burned-over District."[6] The young visionary claimed an angel had told him of an ancient record written on golden plates and hidden in a nearby hillside. Smith had been deeply involved in folk magic and arcane arts such as "glass-looking" using seer stones to divine secrets and "money-digging" for lost treasures, but by 1830 he had forsaken magic for religion. That year Smith published *The Book of Mormon*, which he said he had translated by divine inspiration from the gold plates. The book described the origin and history of the American Indians, a people it called Lamanites. On April 6, 1830, the twenty-four-year-old Smith founded a religion based on "a new and everlasting covenant."[7]

The compelling force of the young man's personality accounted for much of his remarkable success. On meeting him, Brigham Young knew Joseph Smith was a prophet and "felt his spirit to mingle with Joseph's as two drops of water," and he later said the experience burned "like a fire in [his] bones." John Taylor recalled how an electric current ran up his arm when the prophet grasped his hand.[8] Smith had definitive answers to life's most troubling questions and gave his followers a new identity, branding them a "peculiar people." The Saints believed they were literally the Children of Israel, the chosen people of God's new covenant, making early Mormonism very much an Old Testament religion. Mormonism's God was not an abstraction but a physical being who spoke directly to his people through the Prophet Joseph. Smith issued dozens of revelations beginning "Verily, thus saith the Lord" that addressed everything from church finances to the date of Christ's Second Coming. A living prophet capable of receiving divine instructions became one of the new religion's great attractions.

Early on, Smith introduced doctrines that inevitably generated conflict. His revelations on politics, Indians, blood atonement, consecration, and obedience became fundamental to nineteenth-century Mormon doctrine, but they provoked fear and hostility among those who rejected the prophet's claims. Mormonism adopted Old Testament models to reform such basic institutions as marriage and the economy and set out to restore primitive Christianity. *The Book of Mormon* described an orthodox trinity and explicitly denounced polygamy, but Smith's evolving theology soon abandoned two thousand years of monotheistic religious tradition. The Mormon scripture of the prophet's collected revelations, the *Doctrine and Covenants,* revealed a polytheism founded on immortal families. The practice of celestial marriage and the doctrine of eternal progression allowed the most ordinary backwoodsman to become a god and rule over worlds of his own creation with as many wives as his righteousness could sustain. As early as 1831 Smith secretly began to instruct his followers in "the eternity of the marriage covenant, as also [the] plurality of wives," which unbelievers labeled simply polygamy.[9]

Smith's economic policies were as provocative as his views on marriage. His vision of a communal society was tied to the millennial belief that the Second Coming of Christ would take place not within a lifetime but soon. The imminence of the end of time encouraged Smith's followers to dedicate their worldly possessions to God. In return the Lord gave them "the land of Missouri," which he "appointed and consecrated for the gathering of the saints," confirming their neighbors' fears.[10] Everywhere the chosen people answered their prophet's call to gather Israel, Smith's revolutionary beliefs brought his followers into conflicts with their neighbors, conflicts that would ultimately cost them their homes and their charismatic prophet his life.

THE BELOVED PARLEY

Like thousands of other troubled souls in nineteenth-century America, Eleanor McLean found spiritual consolation in Joseph Smith's doctrines. Hector McLean bitterly rejected her new beliefs, and his wife's intense faith accelerated the collapse of their marriage. He threatened to kill her and any man who baptized her if she became a Mormon, but she attended LDS services in San Francisco whenever she could. While she was at home one Sunday night singing from a Mormon hymnal, Hector ripped it from her hands, beat her, and threw her into the street, locking the door behind her. She eventually dropped charges of assault and battery and returned to her husband, but her heart "had died within her." She declared that she "*would no more be his wife,*" though she kept up appearances for the sake of her children. She never slept with McLean again.[11]

Shortly after William McBride baptized her in May 1854, Eleanor McLean met the charismatic Parley Parker Pratt, a remarkable man in a young religion awash in remarkable men. The Archer of Paradise, as he was known, was famous as a writer, publisher, theologian, overland captain, explorer, evangelist, and legislator. As one of the original twelve apostles of Mormonism, Pratt had preached from England to Chile and along the way had been indicted for murder, treason, and counterfeiting. He had converted hundreds of Saints and was personally known and loved by thousands more. His account of the Missouri troubles captured the bitterness the Latter-day Saints felt about their unrighteous persecution by a nation that had betrayed them. He was arguably the most popular man in Utah Territory, for Mormons respected Brigham Young but loved Parley Pratt.

Devoted to the teachings of Joseph Smith, Pratt had married eleven women in polygamy. The wife who came with him to San Francisco was a semi-invalid, and Eleanor McLean frequently brought food and clothing to their home. Pratt tried to reconcile Hector McLean to his wife, but this only increased the aggrieved husband's bitterness, which exploded when Pratt secretly baptized the couple's oldest boys. McLean tried to have his wife declared insane, and Pratt assigned Brigham Young's nephew John R. Young to help her. Young took a job in the McLean household, and his testimony helped to establish Eleanor's sanity. On learning his identity, McLean paid him a month's wages, fired him, and declared, "If you were not a child, I would kill you." Fearful his wife would abscond to Utah with his children, in January 1855 McLean smuggled his sons and daughter aboard the *Sierra Nevada,* sending them to their grandparents in Louisiana. He told Eleanor he had sent them "where [she] and the cursed 'Mormons' can never see them again!"[12]

McLean eventually relented and helped to pay for his wife's passage home. Their children reached New Orleans on February 13, 1855 and were taken to their mother's parents. Eleanor McLean arrived on March 2 and spent three months at her parents' home, "closely guarded at all times lest she should try to take the children." She successfully escaped with them for four days but could not get out of the city. Her parents concluded Eleanor was insane but ultimately gave her funds to travel to Utah, provided she leave her children behind. A Mormon emigration party hired her as a cook and "after incredible hardships and toils, [she] made her way to Great Salt Lake City," where she arrived on September 11, 1855. She found work in Parley Pratt's home as a schoolteacher. Without the benefit of a divorce, Brigham Young sealed Eleanor McLean to Pratt for time and all eternity on November 14, 1855, in Salt Lake's Endowment House as the apostle's twelfth wife.[13]

Eleanor McLean's profound faith in Mormonism may have destroyed her family and would cause her untold heartache, but like tens of thousands of her fellow believers, persecution only increased her devotion to her religion. Like many new faiths, Mormonism generated a fierce commitment among its adherents. The intensity of Mormon beliefs in ideals such as communalism and their total submission to a leader they considered ordained by God contradicted the young American republic's celebration of individuality and independence. Believers viewed the resulting conflicts as religious persecution, which in turn fueled a zealotry that generated deeper fear and opposition from their neighbors, creating a cycle of escalating violence. Within ten years of its founding, Mormonism had a celebrated tradition of strife and suffering.

A WAR OF EXTERMINATION

The odyssey of the Mormon people began with a move from New York to Kirtland, Ohio, not long after the founding of the church. Smith's charisma converted entire fundamentalist congregations and their influential preachers such as Sidney Rigdon and Parley Pratt, who brought formidable debating skills to the new religion. The move to Ohio was completed by May 1831, but almost immediately Smith directed his people to relocate in Missouri, the site of the Garden of Eden, which the Lord promised to "consecrate unto [his] people." Smith journeyed west that summer to Missouri, which he said the Lord had revealed as the land of promise. He designated "a spot for the temple which is lying westward, upon a lot which is not far from the court-house" in Independence.[14]

The land of promise, unfortunately, already was occupied by a people whose natural sympathies could hardly have been more different from those of the Mormons. Both parties made the same complaints. The Missouri settlers, mostly immigrants from the South, charged that their new Yankee neighbors came from the dregs of society and were "idle, lazy, and vicious" as well as poor. A century later the official history of the LDS church characterized the residents of Jackson County as alcoholic, violent, illiterate, lazy, narrow-minded, ferocious, and jealous of those "who aspired to something better in life."[15]

If the Yankee origins and abolitionist sentiments of many Mormons did nothing to endear them to their southern neighbors, then Joseph Smith's claim that the Indians would be the harbingers of the apocalypse was even more provocative. *The Book of Mormon* condemned the Lamanites as "a dark, and loathsome, and a filthy people, full of idleness and all manner of abominations," but it also predicted that the American Indians would unite with the Saints in the last days to destroy sinners and unbelievers. Soon after the organization of his church, Smith sent envoys to the "Lamanites in the west." Pratt joined them, and in fall 1830 the missionaries preached to the Delawares in the land of the Lamanites—the unorganized Indian country west of the Missouri frontier. The Mormons' activities aroused the suspicions of U.S. Indian agents, who ordered them to leave, and alarmed the settlers in the fifteen or twenty log cabins that made up Independence.[16]

Equally provocative was Mormon political and economic power. Although the Saints never constituted a majority in any of the states where they sojourned, their monolithic voting could determine the outcome of elections. Smith's ability to deliver his follower's votes in a bloc outraged non-Mormons of all political persuasions and provoked more hostility.

The prophet hoped to create utopian communities that took from members according to their ability and gave according to need. He directed several attempts to establish the Law of Consecration under which believers conveyed all their property to the Lord's agent.[17] Missourians disturbed by the Mormons' communal economic power were made even more uneasy by LDS scriptures in which God consecrated the property of his enemies and said he would "take when he please, and pay as seemeth him good." Smith's 1831 revelation that "the land of Zion shall not be obtained but by purchase or by blood" fed these concerns. In July 1832 the Mormon newspaper confirmed their fears when it published the Lord's statement that "I will consecrate the riches of the Gentiles [non-Mormons], unto my people which are the house of Israel."[18]

Mormon convert John S. Higbee, who settled in Jackson County in April 1833, soon learned the cost of this clash of cultures. He wrote that he "put in a good crop and Built . . . a good dwelling house," confident that his neighbors would not "drive [them] from [their] lands and homes Contrary to all law." When a mob destroyed a Mormon printing shop, Higbee described the act as "hellish designs" of "demons." Seeing the rage of the non-Mormons, he agreed to leave Jackson County with his aged parents and his wife, who had just given birth to a daughter, "she not Being able to set up." "But," he wrote, "go we must or suffer death immediately." Higbee's wife and child survived the ordeal, but the family spent the winter in a stable without doors or chimney. Higbee and his sons would later be driven from their homes in Missouri's Clay, Ray, and Caldwell Counties.[19]

Joseph Smith organized a relief effort in Ohio and marched to Missouri with Zion's Camp, an impromptu private militia, but the Mormons were driven from Jackson County in 1833. The Missouri legislature created Caldwell County as a refuge for the displaced citizens, and a brief idyll graced local relations. When the Saints began to expand outside of Caldwell County in 1838, however, the peace quickly deteriorated. Smith's intemperate second in command, Sidney Rigdon, gave a Fourth of July oration to the Mormon settlement at Far West. He vowed that if the mob attacked the Saints again, "it shall be between us and them a war of *extermination*, for we shall follow them *till the last drop of blood is spilled*, or else they will have to exterminate us."[20]

Despite previous disasters, Smith seemed oblivious to the provocative nature of his doctrines and actions. At the same time, he was obsessed with stifling dissent among his followers. When zealots called for the murder of traitors so they could not injure the church, cooler heads prevailed, but by the end of June 1838 there were calls to organize a band that would obey the prophet "in all things." "Whatever he requires," they directed, "you shall perform being ready to give up life and property for the advancement of The Cause." These men first took the name Daughters of Zion but eventually settled on a more masculine title, Sons of Dan, recalling Daniel's prophecies of the Last Days. When word of a Mormon secret police organization leaked out, Missourians were outraged. Although the formal Danite organization lasted only a few weeks, it created an enduring belief that the Mormons sponsored a secret brotherhood of religious terrorists.[21]

Smith also organized all adult Mormon males in Missouri into a private army known as the Host of Israel, further exacerbating the fears of "the gentiles," as the Mormons called their unbelieving neighbors. The bad blood came to a head at a Daviess County election on August 6, 1838, when three hundred Missourians confronted LDS voters at the small town of Gallatin. A Mormon gave the Danite sign of distress, and eight comrades grabbed oak-heart clubs and used them to beat the non-Mormons. "In the battle, which was spirited, but short in duration," John D. Lee wrote, "nine men had their skulls broken." Lee, a new LDS convert, said, "I felt the power of God nerve my arm for the fray. It helps a man a great deal in a fight to know that God is on his side." The triumphant Mormons voted and then dispersed.[22]

As tensions increased, the state issued a warrant for Joseph Smith's arrest for threatening a justice of the peace, and Gov. Lilburn W. Boggs called out five hundred militiamen to enforce it. In response, a Mormon raiding party seized a state supply wagon. Boggs declared a state of insurrection and issued orders to his commanders to crush the uprising. At dawn on October 25, the first battle of the Mormon War erupted at Crooked River, where LDS forces under Apostles David Patten and Parley Pratt captured the militia's camp and horses. Patten was killed in the fray and became his religion's first martyr, but exaggerated reports of the Mormon triumph prompted the governor to call two thousand men to arms and issue his notorious order: "*The Mormons must be treated as enemies, and must be exterminated or driven from the state.*"[23]

The outraged local militia acted on its own initiative. On the afternoon of October 30, 1838, three companies attacked Haun's Mill, a settlement swollen with Mormon refugees. Believing they had negotiated an armistice, the community's leaders begged for quarter as the militia followed its orders: "Shoot at everything wearing breaches, and shoot to kill." The militia murdered eighteen men and boys who sought refuge in an improvised log fort.[24] Isaac Leany, who was shot four times, recalled, "We could do no more than fire a few shots while the women and children made their escape." Among the dead were Revolutionary War veteran Thomas McBride, Benjamin Lewis, and a ten-year-old boy. When a Missourian tried to spare the child, William Reynolds shot him, saying, "Nits will make lice, and if he had lived he would have been a Mormon."[25] Survivors included Benjamin Lewis's brothers David and Tarlton, Isaac and William Leany, and Samuel Knight, all of whom would later be pioneers of southern Utah.[26]

Joseph Smith had prepared for war at Far West but surrendered on the morning of October 31. Charged with high treason, he narrowly escaped summary execution and was jailed at Liberty to await trial. His followers were forced to surrender their weapons and sign over deeds to their Missouri lands to pay for the war. All the Saints were ordered to leave the state by April 1, 1839.[27] Among the thousands of Mormons driven from Missouri was Jabez Durfee, who complained that "Governor Boggs authorized an armed force to drive me and others from the State." John W. Clark lost a forty-acre farm "in consequence of mobbery and [the] order of Governor Boggs." Enos Curtis fled from Clay to Caldwell County and then from the state. These men or their sons would seek to avenge the "Missouri persecutions" of the Saints in 1857.[28]

The First Law of Heaven

Joseph Smith preached obedience to priesthood authority as a fundamental LDS belief. Obedience in Mormon culture remains "the first law of heaven, the cornerstone on which all righteousness and progression rest," demanding "complete subjection to God and his commands." The story of Abraham's willingness to sacrifice his son Isaac became a model for unquestioning submission to divine authority. In a belief system based on a living prophet in direct communication with God, absolute obedience was a prerequisite. Mormon scripture made clear that to defy authority at any level was to rebel against God, who did not take such resistance lightly: "Behold, I, the Lord, utter my voice, and it shall be obeyed. . . . [L]et the rebellious fear and tremble . . . for the day of wrath shall come upon them as a whirlwind." The Lord distributed his blessings based on obedience to that law: "he that will not obey shall be cut off in mine own due time." When Smith failed to conquer Missouri in 1834, the Lord explained, "My people must needs be chastened until they learn obedience, if it must needs be, by the things they suffer."²⁹

It was a lesson Smith's followers learned well. The LDS church "*is not a democracy*," a modern apostle has written. "The Church is a kingdom. The Lord Jesus Christ is the Eternal King, and the President of the Church, the mouthpiece of God on earth, is the earthly king. All things come to the Church from the King of the kingdom in heaven, through the king of the kingdom on earth." The people have the democratic right to accept or reject the Lord's counsel, but "acceptance brings salvation; rejection leads to damnation." When early Mormons received "counsel," it was not simply advice: it was an order from God. Rejecting counsel was a sure sign of apostasy.³⁰

The citizens of Quincy, Illinois, had watched events in Missouri with horror and invited the Saints to settle in Illinois. The church's agents purchased land on both sides of the Mississippi, including a small village on the east bank named Commerce, and began again "to build up a city." Smith escaped after five months in a Missouri jail, and in April 1839 he arrived in Illinois. He changed the village's name to Nauvoo, which he said was Hebrew for "beautiful location," "carrying with it also the idea of rest." His followers drained the swamps, and he subdivided the acreage. Soon Nauvoo became a new gathering place for the Saints.³¹

The Mormons secured a charter from the Illinois legislature in 1840 that made Nauvoo virtually an independent city-state. The charter created autonomous courts and authorized the Nauvoo Legion, a local militia that received state arms and was directly under the control of the mayor, Joseph Smith. Prospects for a peaceful life in Illinois seemed bright, but Smith again failed to learn from the mistakes that had repeatedly brought his people into conflict with their neighbors. With warrants for his arrest still pending in Missouri, he became obsessed with security and tried to win a financial settlement from the federal government for Mormon losses. Failing at that, he supported criminal activities to punish the church's enemies. One of Smith's bodyguards, Orrin Porter Rockwell, even tried to assassinate Governor Boggs in 1842.³²

The Nauvoo Legion expanded the Mormon tradition of amateur militarism that had started with Zion's Camp, developed during Smith's service as commander of the Armies of Israel in Kirtland, and then evolved into the Host of Israel during the bloody Missouri war. On its founding in February 1841, the Nauvoo Legion elected Smith its lieutenant general, making him the first American to claim that rank since George Washington. The legion was two thousand strong in 1842 and by Mormon estimates swelled to about five thousand men in 1844, making it almost as large as the U.S. Army.³³ Smith cut a dashing figure in a blue-and-buff uniform topped with an ostrich feather. Although the legion never fired a shot in anger in Illinois, its members took seriously their role as the Army of Israel.

Nauvoo became one of the largest cities in Illinois and attracted a host of new Saints. With the startling success of Mormon missionaries in Britain, hundreds of English believers flocked to the new gathering place on the Mississippi. The town had about twelve thousand inhabitants when its population peaked in 1844. These converts brought an intense zeal to their new religion, and personal contact gave many of them a lifelong devotion to Joseph Smith. When Isaac Haight and his wife were baptized in New York in winter 1838, they had to break the ice on a creek. As Haight recalled, the cold was so severe "that our clothes froze stiff the moment we came out of the water yet our hearts were warm with the spirit of God." Along with fellow stalwarts, Haight became one of Smith's forty chosen men, who acted as his bodyguards and as Nauvoo's police force.[34]

Amid the peace and prosperity of Illinois, Joseph Smith began a reformulation of Mormon doctrine so controversial that he revealed it only to a small circle of intimates. The centerpiece of this revolutionary theology was the "new and everlasting covenant, including the eternity of the marriage covenant, as also the plurality of wives." In a radical departure from monotheistic Christianity, Smith taught that "as man is, God once was; and as God is, man may become." Believers in Smith's new order would "be gods, because they have no end; therefore, shall they be from everlasting to everlasting." The size of a man's family and the number of his wives and descendants would profoundly influence the degrees of glory he received in the next life. Men who achieved the highest exaltation would procreate with their wives to populate new worlds, while everyone else would be reduced to sexless angels and servants for those "worthy of a far more, and an exceeding, and an eternal weight of glory." Keepers of the covenant would have all their sins forgiven at the first resurrection, save one: "that ye shed innocent blood." Those who refused to accept the doctrine were damned—"for no one can reject this covenant and be permitted to enter into [God's] glory."[35] In the early 1840s the prophet also introduced the endowment, temple rites that symbolically represented Mormonism's dynamic theology. These rituals, which resembled Masonic rites, were required to seal polygamous marriages and eternal family relationships. The ceremony created a profound bond between the religion and its most devoted followers.

Rumors of adulterous affairs had followed Joseph Smith for years. "Whenever I see a pretty woman," the prophet may have admitted, "I have to pray for grace."[36] His bold new theology appeared to many to be a rationalization of his philandering. Whatever the source, these beliefs had sweeping consequences for his followers. Polygamy further alienated Mormons from American society and served to bind those who entered the covenant to the church. Beginning in 1842, Smith married dozens of women and personally initiated scores of confidants into polygamy. Almost all rejected it at first. Smith's legal wife later denounced the practice as a vile aberration introduced by Brigham Young, but Young recalled that when Smith revealed the doctrine to him, he "desired the grave, and I could hardly get over it for a long time."[37] Family tradition tells that Parley Pratt accepted plural marriage only after receiving a vision of his dead first wife, who told him that "by taking other wives he would be adding to his own glories in the next world and thus would make her a queen over the other wives."[38] The prophet, however, persuaded most of his colleagues that polygamy was ordained by God. Once converted to the practice, they followed it with remarkable enthusiasm.

The Mormons' provocative beliefs inevitably led to conflict. Smith himself had suffered the indignity of being tarred and feathered by a mob led by a disaffected follower. Such violence, plus the prophet's personal history of being attacked and arrested, helped him to portray the Saints as victims of unprovoked religious oppression and to view any opposition as persecution. "I should be like a fish out of water, if I were out of persecutions," he conceded. "The Lord has constituted me so curiously that I glory in persecution."[39] The more their prophet suffered at the hands of mobs and backsliders, the more his followers worshiped him.

MY BLOOD SHALL CRY FROM THE GROUND FOR VENGEANCE

Politics proved to be an even more dangerous field than theology for the prophet of the latter days. "It has been the design of Jehovah," Smith's newspaper announced in 1842, to "take the reins of government into his own hand."[40] In Nauvoo Smith proclaimed the political Kingdom of God, a theocratic state God had ordained to usher in the Second Coming and rule the earth in the Last Days. "I have the whole plan of the kingdom before me, and no other person has," he revealed in 1842.[41] He organized the Council of Fifty in March 1844 to implement the Kingdom of God. The council and its operations were cloaked in secrecy, and to this day the LDS church refuses to make its minutes public.[42]

Harking back to the Old Testament, Smith planned to set up "the kingdom of Daniel by the word of the Lord, and . . . to lay a foundation that will revolutionize the whole world." His theocratic state would govern both spiritual and temporal affairs. "Either God has something to do in our national affairs, or he has not," proclaimed the church newspaper at Nauvoo in March 1844. "God in ancient days had as much to do with governments, kings and kingdoms, as he ever had to do with religion." The same issue proposed that "Church must not triumph over State, but [must] actually swallow it up like Moses' rod swallowed up the rods of the Egyptians.—If this be not so, the kingdom of God can never come." One of the Council of Fifty's first acts was to petition Congress to authorize Joseph Smith to recruit one hundred thousand volunteers. This irregular army would protect Texas and Oregon and "prevent the crowned nations from encircling us as a nation on our western and southern borders, and save the eagle's talon from the lion's paw."[43]

The first Council of Fifty included senior apostles such as Brigham Young and the Pratt brothers, Smith's brothers and cousins, and hard cases such as Jedediah Grant, Porter Rockwell, and Edward Bonney. Historians have hotly debated the role of the council, which Brigham Young ignored after taking control of the church, but it bound the princes of Joseph Smith's Kingdom of God to his expansive political vision. These men would carry forward Smith's vision of theocracy for two generations.[44]

The organization of the Council of Fifty was another manifestation of the millennial hopes of the Saints. The very name of their religion, Latter-day Saints, expressed their belief in the imminence of the Second Coming. Smith's followers were not content simply to wait for Jesus to return: they believed the event depended on their faith and works to "prepare the way." Many of Brigham Young's most perplexing policies originated in his conviction that the Kingdom of God would roll on like the stone of Daniel's prophecy to fill the whole earth.[45] Young believed this was inevitable, but his Yankee theology inspired him to take active measures to usher in the Second Coming. The Mormons saw it as their solemn duty to create the conditions that would hasten Christ's return.

During the last months of his life, Smith acted with reckless abandon. In April 1844 the Council of Fifty acclaimed him "Prophet, Priest and King by Hosannas," which council member William Marks recalled as a coronation "in which Joseph suffered himself to be ordained a king." Two days later Smith "prophecied the entire overthrow of this nation in a few years." He became a candidate for the presidency of the United States and dispatched the apostles to campaign for him. He simultaneously plunged into new sealings to married women, their sisters, and very young girls, including Apostle Heber C. Kimball's fourteen-year-old daughter, Helen. His proposals to women whose husbands were absent on missions (such as Apostle Orson Pratt's wife) and to the daughters of close associates (such as Sidney Rigdon's daughter Nancy) had already created a host of defections, but Smith was undeterred.[46]

The prophet's willful conduct inevitably alienated men who knew too much about his secret doctrines, notably when he propositioned the wives of Dr. Robert Foster and William Law. After a secret council excommunicated them, they launched the *Nauvoo Expositor*, a newspaper created to expose Smith as a fallen prophet. In its first issue the *Expositor* denounced polygamy and "political schemes and intrigue" designed to Christianize the world. The editors pledged, "We will not acknowledge any man as king or lawgiver to the church" and promised in their next issue to "tell the whole tale" of Smith's political plans.[47]

There would be no more editions of the *Expositor*. Smith had survived such exposés before, but the newspaper's revelations meant someone in the Council of Fifty had betrayed his most dangerous secrets: his polygamous doctrines and theocratic political ambitions. The Nauvoo City Council accused the *Expositor*'s editors of seduction, pandering, counterfeiting, and thievery, and Mayor Smith ordered the press destroyed as a public nuisance. The Nauvoo Legion marched to the newspaper office, wrecked the press, and burned the remaining papers. For the prophet, it was a fatal mistake. The vandalism provoked outrage among the Mormons' neighbors, and Gov. Thomas Ford complained the act was "a gross outrage upon the laws and liberties of the people" that violated the constitution. When warned that his press would be destroyed, William Law wrote, "I could not even suspect men of being such fools." Law and Foster swore out warrants for Smith's arrest on a charge of riot.[48]

Resentment of Mormon political and economic power had long simmered in the river towns of northern Illinois, but when the Mormon prophet refused to submit to arrest, declared martial law, and mobilized the Nauvoo Legion, the hostility exploded into hysteria. "Such excitement I never witnessed in my life," a local militia officer recalled. "We all felt that the time had come where either the Mormons or old citizens had to leave." A Warsaw County newspaper denounced Smith as "a tyrant, who is the masterpiece of Hell's workmanship" and proclaimed, "War and extermination is inevitable!"[49]

In the midst of this firestorm, Joseph Smith seemed ready to abandon the Kingdom of God and the secret doctrines that were the foundation of his new theology. At midnight on June 22, 1844, he slipped across the flooded Mississippi in a leaky skiff, hoping to escape to Washington, D.C., or the Rocky Mountains. Smith's desertion threw his followers into a panic, and Emma Smith begged her husband not to abandon his people. Her messenger, Reynolds Cahoon, warned, "When the shepherd deserts his flock, who is to keep the wolves from devouring them?" Smith agreed to return, saying, "If my life is of no value to my friends it is of none to myself." He told his brother Hyrum, the church's patriarch and his fellow prophet, that they would be butchered if they returned to Illinois. Joseph wanted Hyrum to live to avenge his blood, but his brother refused to leave him. Before surrendering at Carthage jail, Smith said, "I am going like a lamb to the slaughter." He had a clear conscience and warned, "If they take my life I shall die an innocent man, and my blood shall cry from the ground for vengeance."[50]

Governor Ford pledged to protect the Mormon prophets, hoping they would escape and take their followers with them. Ford left Carthage on the morning of June 27, 1844, to visit Nauvoo, leaving two militia companies to guard the jail. He denied Smith's request to accompany him. That evening, after the militia disbanded, many of them joined a mob. Some two hundred men painted their faces black, stormed the jail, and rushed the stairs to the second floor. The Smiths put up a stout resistance, with the prophet emptying a six-shooter into the hallway as the other prisoners tried to bar the door. Guns blazing, the mob burst into the cell and Hyrum Smith fell dead, shot in the face. Apostle John Taylor collapsed with four bullet wounds, and Willard Richards was pinned by the door. Almost unscathed, Joseph Smith made his way to the jailhouse window, gave the Masonic sign of distress, and perhaps cried, "Oh Lord my God! Is there no help for the widow's son?" A volley from the jail yard answered him. He tumbled to the ground. The mob propped him up against a well and finished the work of death with bullets and bayonets.[51]

So died the Prophet and Seer of the Lord, who had finally "sealed his mission and his works with his own blood." The mob had destroyed the Smith brothers, but their martyrdom ensured the future of their church. "Their *innocent blood*," Mormon scripture promised, "will cry unto the Lord of Hosts till he avenges that blood on earth. Amen."[52]

BRIGHAM YOUNG AND THE GREAT WESTERN MEASURE

Temple guard Isaac Haight may have been the first man in Nauvoo to learn of Joseph Smith's murder. He was standing watch at 2:00 A.M. on June 28 when a messenger from Carthage told him "that Joseph and Hyrum were dead and the way they came to their death[s]." "My heart shrunk within me," he said, "and I felt to curse the purpetrator of that dark and diabolical deed." Porter Rockwell soon charged into Nauvoo shouting, "Joseph is killed—they have killed him! Goddamn them! They have killed him." The news sent the Mormon capital into shock. Thousands turned out to meet the bodies of the martyrs, and more than ten thousand people streamed through the prophet's mansion to view the dead. Dimick B. Huntington, Smith's brother-in-law, washed the bodies and that night helped to bury them secretly in the basement of an unfinished hotel.[53]

Brigham Young, president of the Quorum of the Twelve Apostles, abandoned his mission and returned to Nauvoo in August 1844, disheartened by the murder of his beloved friend but determined to carry on his legacy. One of the most remarkable Americans of any age, Young was born in Vermont in 1801 to a struggling farming family. By his own account he received only eleven days of formal schooling. At sixteen he began working as a carpenter, joiner, painter, and glazier. He learned of *The Book of Mormon* in 1830 but did not join the Saints until two years later. Young visited Kirtland in fall 1832 and met the Mormon prophet, who was chopping wood with his brothers. By the spirit of prophecy Young received a sure testimony that Joseph Smith "was all that any man could believe him to be, as a true Prophet."[54]

The convert moved to Kirtland in 1833 "and was ever afterward an important personage in the growth and development of that city." Captain Young served in Zion's Camp in 1834 and was among the first apostles called in 1835. He oversaw completion of the Kirtland Temple, served numerous missions, and stood by Smith during the Panic of 1837 when other apostles called for his overthrow. As Mormon chronicler Andrew Jenson noted, Elder Young "was obliged to leave Kirtland to escape the fury of the mob" in December 1837 and arrived at Far West the following March.[55] Under the direction of John Smith, Young helped to lead the evacuation of Missouri and demonstrated a talent for organization. The apostasies of Thomas Marsh and Orson Hyde raised Young to leadership in the Quorum of the Twelve Apostles, while the imprisonment of Smith and Rigdon in a Missouri jail meant that many churchly responsibilities fell to the apostles. When Smith called them to open a mission to Britain, Young helped to launch one of the Mormonism's most successful recruiting efforts in the desperately poor English midlands.[56]

Following the martyrdom of Joseph Smith, Brigham Young quickly bested Sidney Rigdon in the first battle for leadership of the LDS church, though the struggle to claim Smith's legacy would continue for decades. By the end of August 1844,

Young assumed command of the Nauvoo Legion as lieutenant general. Officially he was only first among equals as president of the Quorum of the Twelve Apostles, but by December 5, 1844, he was signing documents as president of the church.[57]

Brigham Young was just the man for the moment. Still in his early forties when he became leader of the Saints, he was youthful, handsome, and attractive: of middle height, clean shaven, a surprisingly dapper dresser, with shoulder-length sandy red hair. His lack of formal education made him contemptuous of intellectual pretensions, but his blue-gray eyes reflected a sharp, practical intelligence. Unlike the visionary Smith, he was not naturally charismatic, and his leadership was forceful and pragmatic: his only canonized revelation dictated the organization of the Mormon emigration. He was passionately devoted to the martyred prophet, and his life's work became carrying out the prophet's plans. Hoping to maintain a foothold in Illinois, Young struggled with growing anti-Mormonism and worked relentlessly to complete the Nauvoo Temple. He ultimately recognized that the Saints must leave the United States to survive, and in September 1845 he agreed to abandon Nauvoo to prevent a civil war.

The apostles now turned their attention to the Great Western Measure, their plan to establish the Kingdom of God in the isolation of the Rocky Mountains. Joseph Smith's erratic brother William told the *New York Sun* of Mormon plans "to set up an independent government somewhere in the neighborhood of the Rocky Mountains, or near California," which was exactly what Brigham Young intended to do. Apostle Orson Pratt announced that the Saints in New York had been given "the choice of death or banishment," and called on God "to deliver us out of the hands of the bloodthirsty Christians of these United States." To launch this plan, the apostles directed Samuel Brannan to go by sea to California. When some 230 Latter-day Saints sailed from New York in February 1846, Brannan and his compatriots were armed to the teeth and carried a banner to raise over the Mexican province they hoped to conquer.[58]

A MOST EXTRAORDINARY MAN: JOHN D. LEE

Meanwhile, in fall 1845 Brigham Young organized the Saints to travel overland to the Rocky Mountains, assisted by his able head clerk, John D. Lee, who had an office "in room number one, at President Young's apartment." Through the law of adoption, a temple ordinance since abandoned, virtually every priesthood member was adopted into the extended families of the Mormon authorities. Brigham Young was sealed to Joseph Smith as a son in December 1845. Young in turn had thirty-eight men sealed to him as sons, the second being John D. Lee. (Lee claimed he could have listed himself as Young's first adopted son but gave the honor to A. P. Rockwood.)[59] The practice had a powerful effect on its adherents, and Lee began signing his correspondence "J. D. L. Young."

Born in Kaskaskia, Illinois, in 1812, Lee was an exceptional man by any standard, but he was virtually a prototype of the early Mormon convert. His alcoholic father abandoned him to the care of a black nurse when his mother died in 1815. "What his fate was," the son recalled, "I never knew." The orphan came into the care of relatives, who raised him as a strict Catholic but robbed him of his inheritance. At sixteen Lee struck out on his own, learning the ways of frontier business as a courier and Mississippi riverboat fireman. He served in the Black Hawk War, married in 1833, and settled in Fayette County, Illinois. The night his daughter died of scarlet fever in 1837, Lee finished reading *The Book of Mormon*. "Everything but my soul's salvation was a matter of secondary consideration to me," he recalled. "I sold out and moved to Far West." There he met Joseph Smith, noting "something in his manner and appearance that was bewitching and winning."[60] Lee remained passionately devoted to the prophet for the rest of his life.

As religious civil war ignited in northwestern Missouri in 1838, the new convert witnessed Sidney Rigdon's Fourth of July tirade threatening a "war of extermination." By the end of the speech, Lee believed the Saints could resist the world. Like other true believers, Lee "felt that the Mormon Hosts of Israel were invincible" and blamed the Missouri disasters on "the brethren's refusal to obey the wishes of the prophet," especially their failure to consecrate their property to the church. Returning from battling Missouri mobs that winter, Lee found his new house in Caldwell County burned and his family huddled in a corner of the ruin. With 380 other Mormons, Lee signed a covenant "to stand by and assist each other to the best of our abilities, in removing from this state."[61]

During December 1838, Isaac Morley gave Lee a patriarchal blessing—a special benediction in which "the recipient's lineage from one of the tribes of Israel is usually declared, exhortations are given, and spiritual gifts and life-missions are specified." Lee's blessing predicted that kings and princes would call him father. It promised the homeless refugee "houses and habitations, flocks, fields, and herds." "Thy table shall be strewed with the rich luxuries of the earth, to feed thy numerous family and friends." Moreover, Lee would "have power over [his] enemies" and "understand the hidden things of heaven." If he lived a righteous life, he would come forth in the morning of the first resurrection. The blessing carried an odd qualifier: the only act that could prevent Lee's salvation was "the shedding of innocent blood or consenting thereto."[62]

John D. Lee was one of Joseph Smith's forty chosen men, though he was often sent on missions to Kentucky, Tennessee, and Arkansas. The eloquent Lee baptized entire families and congregations. (One of his converts was William "Bill" Hickman, later famous as "Brigham's Destroying Angel.") When Brigham Young reorganized the Kingdom of God in 1845, he dropped his opponents from the council and in their place installed his brothers and John D. Lee.[63]

At tremendous sacrifice, the Saints completed the Nauvoo Temple in December 1845 and quickly bestowed endowments on more than five thousand believers.[64] Lee was among the first to receive his washings and anointings in the Nauvoo Temple. He also received the "second anointing." This rite went far beyond the standard temple endowment to ensure exaltation and to "seal up" initiates from the consequences of any sin except the shedding of innocent blood. George Laub recalled his second anointing: "We was sealed up to Eternal Life to come forth in the morning of the first Resurrection and nothing Can prevent us from coming forth in the first Resurrection only the Sining against the holy Ghost which is the sheding of innocent Blood."[65]

Brigham Young added a new element to the temple endowment, the Oath of Vengeance. Initiates pledged, "I will pray, and never cease to pray, and never cease to importune high heaven to avenge the blood of the Prophets on this nation, and I will teach this to my children, and my children's children unto the third and fourth generations."[66] Lee heard Young "swear by the eternal Heavens," "I have unsheathed my sword, and will never return it until the blood of the Prophet Joseph and Hyrum, and those who were slain in Missouri, is avenged." All those who received their sacred endowments had the most sacred obligation, Lee said, "to avenge the blood of the Prophet, whenever the opportunity offered, and to teach their children to do the same."[67]

Lee was one of the most active participants in the pageantlike temple ceremonies, in which congregants played the roles of God, the Devil, Adam, and various angels. When the Saints arrived in Utah, they performed these rites in the Endowment House, a temporary location until a temple could be built. The Lee family preserves a tradition that his keen memory and intimate knowledge of the Nauvoo endowment led Mormon leaders in Utah to select him to write down the complete ceremony for the first time.[68]

In late 1845 Lee was engaged to marry the gentle and beautiful Louisa Free and her sister, Emmeline. "One day Brigham Young saw Emeline [sic] and fell in love with her," Lee recalled. He promised that if Lee would surrender the girl, he would uphold Lee "in time and in eternity & he never should fall," and he would sit at Young's right hand in his kingdom. The request tormented Lee, for he loved Emmeline dearly, but he agreed to resign his claim in Young's favor. Emmeline became one of Young's favorite wives and bore him ten children, but the bargain ignited an odd reaction in the explosive Lee. He later boasted to George Grant "he had frigged Louisa Free 20 times in one night." Grant did not believe him, but Lee "called God and Angels to witness that he told the truth." Grant told Lee he was a bigger fool than Grant thought he was "if he would allow his arse to run away with his head." Undeterred, Lee claimed "he went home . . . after frigging so often and frigged all the women he had in his house." Lee, Grant testified, "believed he had the Devil in him."[69]

OUR HOMES IN THE DESERT

Brigham Young launched the Mormon exodus to the Rocky Mountains on February 4, 1846. The great hegira began with the evacuation of Nauvoo and an arduous crossing of Iowa. Young hoped to send an expedition west that summer to locate a refuge outside the United States where the Saints could establish the independent Kingdom of God, but events disrupted his plans. The Mormons lacked the resources to cross the plains in 1846, and the declaration of war with Mexico in May further complicated their plans to leave the United States. To raise much-needed cash, Young enlisted five hundred of his followers in the U.S. Army as the Mormon Battalion, which marched to New Mexico and California. He wrote to President James K. Polk in August to inform him the Saints were bound for the Great Basin. Brigham Young asked "for a territorial Government bounded on the north by the British and on the south by the Mexican dominions; & east and west by the summits of the Rocky & Cascade mountains."[70]

Making the best of their circumstances, the Saints camped on the west bank of the Missouri River in Indian country at a ragged settlement called Winter Quarters. Of the six thousand refugees, six hundred died that bitter winter. Isaac Haight lost his infant son, and Apostle George A. Smith lost his third wife and four children to scurvy.[71] In spring 1847 Brigham Young led the vanguard of the emigration to the Great Basin and established Great Salt Lake City. More than one thousand miles from the Missouri frontier, the valley's isolation met Young's requirements perfectly. Here the Saints could build up the Kingdom of God, perfect their experiment in theocracy, and prepare for the battles that would soon usher in the millennium.

Young's brilliant leadership of the 1847 expedition and his mastery of the church's internal politics validated his claim to power. On his return to Winter Quarters in December 1847, he was at last sustained president of the church and formed his own First Presidency, the triumvirate that stood at the pinnacle of the Mormon hierarchy.

By the end of 1848, the second year of their great move west, some six thousand Mormons had arrived in the new Zion. Secure in the isolation of the Great Basin, Young proceeded to consolidate his power. In late 1848 or early 1849 the Council of Fifty ordained him Joseph Smith's successor, crowning him king and priest over the Kingdom of God. He became trustee-in-trust of the LDS church in April 1850, securing control of all its financial enterprises. A year later the annual church conference sustained Young as prophet, seer, and revelator.[72] Brigham Young had now acquired all the offices and powers of Joseph Smith.

The Saints fell in love with their new mountain home. They savored the irony that they had been driven into the wilderness among the Lamanites, the Indian people who shared the blood of Israel with the Mormons and were destined to assist them in the conflicts that would precede the return of Christ. "We are here!" Brigham Young rejoiced on reaching Utah again in 1848. "We are in the midst of the Lamanites!"[73] Surrounded by the Indian nations in the Rocky Mountains, the prophet and his people began to build the kingdom and prepare for the battles they believed would mark the end of time.

2

The Battle-Ax of the Lord

By the end of 1849 some ten thousand Mormons were living in the Great Basin, most of them clustered along the eastern shore of the Great Salt Lake. In their new mountain home, the Latter-day Saints never forgot they were refugees: they nurtured their bitterness, savored their isolation, and longed for the Lord to avenge their suffering. The Wasatch Mountains were ten-thousand-foot towers of granite and snow that stood as real and symbolic ramparts against the incursions of the Christian America the Saints had fled to the wilderness to escape. "We now choose to make our homes in the Desert among Savages rather than try to live in the garden of the world surrounded by Christian Neighbors," wrote John Pulsipher in 1848. "The Lord Almighty is preparing a scourage for this nation. The blood of the Saints is crying out from the ground for vengeance on that wicked nation. . . . We are glad the mountain valies are so far off as they are."[1]

In summer 1849 news of the discovery of gold at Sutter's Mill and the lure of a new El Dorado brought hordes of adventurous young men to shatter the pleasant but impoverished solitude of the Mormons. These vagabonds had all the traditional bad habits of youthful males and an unhealthy curiosity about Mormon marriage customs, but they provided financial salvation for the strategically located colony. They traded desperately needed food, clothing, wagons, tools, medicines, and even stoves for any animal that appeared strong enough to make the hard journey to California.

Seven hundred miles of unrelieved desolation separated Salt Lake from California, yet the influx of outsiders and the lure of gold challenged Brigham Young's efforts to keep his followers focused on building up the kingdom. As their prophet, he sought to bind his people more firmly to their religion, and as a political leader, he reconsidered his 1846 request for a territory with the right to select its own officers. The Mormons organized the state of Deseret and petitioned to be admitted to the Union. The borders of Deseret, whose *Book of Mormon* name meant "honeybee," encompassed virtually the entire Great Basin and extended to the Pacific Coast. The compromise of 1850 created Utah Territory, much smaller than Deseret (but still stretching from the crest of the Colorado Rockies to the Sierra Nevada) and entirely lacking the sovereignty of a state, an unhappy outcome for the Mormons. Territorial status put Utah under the control of officials and judges appointed by Congress and the president. To further complicate matters, the territory's organic act did not address the problem of land titles. Until they could settle the question of Indian lands, the Mormon settlers would hold nothing more than squatters' rights, a problem that exacerbated their contentious relations with Washington. To make the compromise palatable to the Saints, President Millard Fillmore named Brigham Young the territory's governor and Indian superintendent. Utah's first non-Mormon federal officers and judges soon learned Governor Young held complete power over his followers, who regarded outsiders with deep suspicion.

To secure their new kingdom, the Mormons quickly colonized every likely spot for settlement in the territory and beyond, founding towns at key points that gave them control of the Great Basin. In 1850 traders opened Mormon Station in Carson Valley at the gateway to the southern Sierra crossings. Peter Haws built a ranch on the Humboldt River at a choke point on the emigrant road. Parley Pratt led an exploring expedition to the south in late 1849 and discovered iron deposits. George A. Smith led settlers two hundred fifty miles south to establish the Iron Mission at Parowan in 1851, the first in a string of settlements on what became known as the "southern road." That year Amasa Lyman and Charles C. Rich took some five hundred Saints to southern California, where they founded the city of San Bernardino. These strategic colonies, often established by veterans of the Council of Fifty, gave the Mormons a virtual stranglehold on the overland trails to California.

LAMANITES

In the isolation of the Rocky Mountains, Brigham Young began to implement Joseph Smith's dream that the Saints could "form a Union with the Indians" in the West and then "move on the wicked world And put to flight those that have Oprest them."[2] The belief that they could use American Indians as instruments of vengeance complicated Mormon dealings with the outside world and led to a host of unforeseen consequences.

Of all the issues that inflamed their relations with the federal government during the Mormons' first decade in the West, only polygamy was as corrosive as the complicated relationship between the Latter-day Saints and the people they called the Lamanites.[3] The act creating Utah Territory specified that the governor would serve as ex officio superintendent of Indian affairs. The federal government appointed three agents in February 1851 to work under Young's supervision. They quickly grasped the

thrust of his Indian policy. The Mormons "at first conciliated the Indians by kind treatment; but when they once got a foothold, they began *to force their way*," subagent Jacob
H. Holeman wrote. "The consequence was a war with the Indians, and in many
instances, a most brutal butchery." As early as March 1852, Holeman reported that the
Mormons wanted "to form an alliance with the Indians to resist the government,
should it be determined to force authority in the territory." In addition, he charged
that Young made use "of his office as superintendent and the money of the government to promote the interest of his church." This practice, Holeman felt, dictated
"that no Mormon should officially have anything to do with the Indians."[4]

The corruption that riddled the management of Indian affairs in the West persisted in Utah, but with a twist. "Brigham Young never spent a dollar on the Indians
in Utah, while he was Indian Agent," John D. Lee claimed in his embittered memoir. "The only money he ever spent on the Indians was when we were at war with
them."[5] Young did spend money on the Indians, but as Holeman charged he spent it
to promote the interests of his church. U.S. Army lieutenant Sylvester Mowry traveled through southern Utah in 1855 and found that LDS missionaries had convinced
the Indians of "the inferiority and hostility of the Americans and the superiority and
friendship of the Mormons."[6] Many emigrants on the California Trail were certain
that Mormons led Indian raids on their stock, and even the most sympathetic observers
believed they were fencing stolen cattle. Elizabeth Brittain Knowlton recalled that in
1857 the "Mormon traders were after the money. They would induce [the Indians] to
drive off our stock and then they would get them and by so doing they made fortunes."[7] The Mormons, overlander P. H. Ferguson wrote from Fort Laramie in June
1857, were "a great deal worse than the Indians."[8]

Caught between the mystical view of the Lamanites enshrined in their scriptures and the realities of Indian life on the frontier, the Mormons faced no greater
challenge than that posed by their Ute, Paiute, Goshute, and Shoshoni neighbors.
The Mormons succeeded brilliantly at establishing their new homeland, but they
did so at great cost to the people who lived on the land in 1847. Brigham Young's
"regrettable strategy of selective extermination" ultimately challenged their very
survival. His Indian policy, which historian Howard Christy characterized as "open
hand and mailed fist," gave the Indians the choice of becoming enemies or depend-
ent clients of the Mormons.[9]

Young's Indian policy was founded on the special place of the Lamanites in Mormon theology. The stated purpose of the golden plates was to bring "the knowledge
of their fathers" to America's Indians, so they might "believe the gospel and rely upon
the merits of Jesus Christ." *The Book of Mormon* told that America's natives were actually Israelites who migrated to the Americas six centuries before Christ. They divided
into two groups, the righteous Nephites, who sought to keep the commandments of
God, and the Lamanites, "who were rebellious, whose minds were darkened by unbelief, who were apostates from the Church." To prevent intermarriage between the

two peoples, God "did cause a skin of blackness to come upon" the Lamanites—a curse that was to be removed if they repented and became righteous, when they would become "a white and delightsome people again."[10]

In their struggle to establish the Kingdom of God, the Mormons believed that America's Indian peoples, whom they called "Cousin Lemuel" and the "stick of Joseph," would be their most powerful allies and fearsome weapon—the battle-ax of the Lord. Brigham Young savored the irony that his enemies had driven the Mormons into Indian country. He recalled in 1857 that Joseph Smith's enemies had always surrounded him with a string of guards lest he should have "communion with the remnants of Israel who are wandering on the plains and in the kanyons of this country." God's enemies, he said, had "fought us, whipped us, killed our Prophets, and abused our community, until we are now driven by them into the very midst of the Lamanites. Oh, what a pity they could not foresee the evil they were bringing upon themselves, by driving this people into the midst of the savages of the plains."[11]

Young preached that the Indians "must be saved, for they are the children of Abraham."[12] Although *The Book of Mormon* condemned the Lamanites, Mormon belief gave American Indians a pivotal and violent role in the Last Days. Before the great day of the Lord, LDS scripture foretold, the Lamanites would blossom as the rose. As an essential precursor to the Second Coming, the redeemed tribes would unite with the Saints to destroy unbelievers. The war prophecy of the *Doctrine and Covenants* decreed "that the remnants who are left of the land will marshal themselves, and shall become exceedingly angry, and shall vex the Gentiles with a sore vexation."[13]

The Book of Mormon set the time for the overthrow of all "gentile governments of the American continent." The "way and means of this utter destruction" would be the remnant of the house of Jacob, which would "go through among the Gentiles and tear them in pieces, like a lion among the flocks of sheep" until "all their enemies shall be cut off." "This destruction includes an utter overthrow, and desolation of all our Cities, Forts, and Strong Holds—an entire annihilation of our race, except such as embrace the Covenant, and are numbered with Israel."[14]

Any alliance of whites and Indians was suspect on the frontier, but a religious doctrine that saw Indians as harbingers of the apocalypse was a prescription for bitter conflict. Joseph Smith had eventually realized that his Lamanite doctrines would not win friends in the West and had done his best to obscure the meaning of his Indian prophecies. Still, he had not been able to conceal the thrust of these doctrines from his enemies—or restrain rumors. Anti-Mormon George Davis of Illinois said the prophet claimed his wife Emma Smith was of Indian descent. "God had revealed to him," Davis wrote, "that the Indians and Latter Day Saints, under Joe as their King and Ruler, were to conquer the Gentiles, and that their subjugation to this authority was to be obtained *by the sword*!" Davis said it was "a fact, ascertained beyond controversy, that the Indian tribes of Sacs and Foxes, Siouxs and Potowattamies, were consulted, and their ascent obtained," before the Council of Fifty crowned Smith king of the Kingdom of God.[15] Joseph Smith had in fact met with "about one hundred chiefs and braves" of the Sac and Fox tribes at Nauvoo in August 1841. He instructed them "in many things," including "the promises that were made concerning them in the Book of Mormon."[16] Within six months of Smith's murder, the Saints developed a tradition that the Indians would play a key role in avenging their martyred prophets. One Nauvoo Mormon fantasized that "there is all ready ten hundred thousand of the lamanites baptized into the Church and they are waiting verry impatient to avenge the blood of Joseph and Hirum. We have to keep men among them to keep them back."[17]

Early in 1845 Parley Pratt wrote a proclamation to the rulers of the world from the twelve apostles. The Kingdom of God has come, it announced, "even that kingdom which shall fill the whole earth, and shall stand forever." Certain events would prepare the way for Christ's return. The Indians, "a remnant of the tribes of Israel, . . . are about to be gathered, civilized, and made *one nation* in this glorious land." The Saints must instruct the children of the forest to "refine, purify, exalt, and glorify them as the sons and daughters of the royal house of Israel and of Joseph." The Lord would make the Indians "a great, and strong, and powerful nation," crowning the despised and degraded sons of the forest with authority and power. Everyone would be required to take sides either for or against the Kingdom of God, and events would "reduce all nations and creeds to *one* political and religious *standard*." Those who received the Messiah would "dwell for ever under his peaceful government in this happy country." Those who opposed the work would be the Lord's inveterate enemies and would "soon perish from the earth, and be cast down to hell."[18]

Pratt's proclamation demonstrated the conviction that the Indians were one nation. In contrast to the Mormon belief that Indian culture was racial and unified, it was fragmented and tribal. Intertribal warfare was embedded in their cultures, which contained no concept of the Indians as a single people. Most tribes held that friendship meant "my enemy is your enemy," and they had no patience for whites who professed friendship but allied themselves with rival bands. The Mormons slowly grasped this, but their millennialistic beliefs convinced them the Last Days would transform the fragmented Indian tribes of the West into a single nation, the Lamanites.

LET THEM EAT THE CRICKETS

Shortly after arriving in the Salt Lake Valley, the Mormons witnessed the bloody resolution of a dispute between the two most powerful tribes of the Great Basin. A band of Shoshonis came to trade, and one of their warriors quarreled with a Ute and broke a gun over his head. Humiliated and angry, the Ute ran off one of their horses, and six Shoshoni warriors started across the plain in pursuit. They killed the Ute and returned to the pioneer camp "exhibiting fresh blood" on one of their rifles. This show of force warned their new neighbors not to trifle with the Shoshonis. Brigham Young appreciated the lesson, noting that the Indians "stole guns yesterday and had them under their blankets and if you don't attend to this you are heating a kettle of boiling water to scald your own feet. If you listen to council you will let them alone, and let them eat the crickets."[19]

Young hoped to do much more with Utah's tribes than simply let them alone. Four days after arriving in Salt Lake, he outlined his plans for the native peoples whose lands the Mormons must seize and occupy. He predicted "the Elders would marry Wives of every tribe of Indians," and "the Lamanites would become a White & delightsome people." He sounded themes of independence and vengeance that would recur again and again in the Mormons' first ten years in Utah. Young "hoped to live to lead forth the armies of Israel to execute the judgments & justice on the persecuting Gentiles." He promised "that no officer of the United States should ever dictate [to] him in this valley, or he would hang them on a gibbet as a warning to others." His people would "never have any commerce with any nation, but be Independent of all."[20]

Some twenty thousand Numic people lived in today's Utah in 1847 in loosely confederated tribes: Northern Shoshonis, Western Shoshonis, Goshutes, Utahs (today called Northern Utes), and Southern Paiutes. The Salt Lake Valley was a contested buffer zone between the Utes to the south and the Shoshonis to the north.[21] Based on past experience with white traders, the Indian nations assumed the Mormons were merely visitors who had not come to stay.[22]

The Utes stood directly in the path of Mormon expansion. Their homeland extended through most of present Utah and far into the mountains of Colorado and New Mexico. The Che-ver-ets, or Shiberetches, a roving band of Utes, dominated the Great Basin under the leadership of the legendary Wakara. The mastery of the horse let Wakara's nomads range from the Great Plains to California in search of grass, buffalo, slaves, and plunder.[23] In the Sevier River country of central Utah, the Pahvants, or "Bearded Utes" (a designation that perhaps reflected their long relations with Spanish and Mexican traders), acted as a porous buffer between the Utes and the Paiutes. The Mormons quickly replaced their belligerent leader, Chuick, with Kanosh, the "white man's friend," who had acquired a facility for language in the California missions. Believing it was pointless to resist white power, Kanosh became a valued ally of the Saints, and he was rewarded handsomely for his services.[24]

In the southern deserts, the Nuwuvi, or Southern Paiutes, ranged far into Nevada, Arizona, and even California. The Mormons called them Pah Utaus and Piedes. Most of Utah's Paiutes lived along the Virgin, Santa Clara, and Muddy Rivers, raising corn, squash, beans, melons, sunflowers, gourds, and "Piede wheat" in small irrigated plots. They lived in small bands composed of several families that ingeniously exploited every available food source in their harsh homelands, migrating with the seasons to hunt or harvest. They cooperated in hunting and gathering, but there was little or no tribal organization.[25] White experts later identified Paiute bands such as the Moapits, the Shivwits, and the Tonaquints (or Yannawants), usually named after their primary food source or a geologic feature of their homeland. Magotsu Creek, which flows through

Mountain Meadows, was named for the country of the Matooshats band, whose head-quarters were south of Mountain Meadows at a hot spring near present Veyo.[26]

Brigham Young adopted a pragmatic Indian policy based on frontier realities, but he never forgot the Indians' prophesied role in ushering in the millennium. He quickly gave up hope of reforming the adult Indians, for he believed they were hopeless cases who would die and be damned.[27] In a meeting of the Council of Fifty on May 12, 1849, Young announced that the present race of Indians would never be converted. It did not matter "whether they kill one another off or Some body else do[es] it," and as for "sending Missionarys amoung them to convert them, it is of no use." Young proposed instead to take their children and teach them "to love morality & then raise up seed amoung them & in this way they will be brought back into the presance & knowlege of God."[28] To redeem the Lamanites, he would raise the children in white homes and marry young Mormon men to Indian women. Hoping to resolve the problem completely, in 1850 Young instructed territorial representative John Bernhisel to work for the removal of Utah's Indians to a reservation, perhaps on the western slopes of the Sierra Nevada, far from the lands the Saints wanted to settle.[29]

A Most Brutal Butchery

As Joseph Smith's Indian doctrines ran into frontier realities in Utah, Mormon preachers and writers quit praising the children of the forest and began complaining about degraded savages. Utah's most powerful tribes had little interest in playing their prophetic role. For all the enlightened talk of the Saints, the tribes could see the devastating results as white encroachment on their land and food sources pushed them to the brink of starvation.

Once the Mormons began to expand to the south and build towns on the most important Indian campsites and water sources, conflict with the Utah bands became inevitable. Shortly after a fight at Battle Creek in March 1849, Young sent thirty-three settlers under John Higbee to colonize Utah Valley on a site at the mouth of the Provo River that happened to be the traditional Ute fishing grounds. Angatewats, a young warrior, met the settlers and blocked the trail with his horse. Dimick Huntington pleaded with the Utes "to try the emigrants for a while and see if they could not live in peace together." The skeptical Indians made Huntington "raise his right hand and swear by the sun that the white people would not drive the Indians away, or take from them any of their rights."[30]

Despite their promises, the settlers did just that. Tensions mounted during the winter and boiled over when several Mormons brutally murdered an Indian who had caught them poaching a deer. Local leaders believed they must abandon the settlement or fight the Utes. At a council held in Great Salt Lake City on January 31, 1850, Parley Pratt thought it best to kill the Indians. When the question was put to a vote of the settlers, according to Higbee, "every man and boy held up their hand to kill them off." Willard Richards expressed the conclusion of the council: exterminate them. "Take no hostile Indians as prisoners," militia commander Daniel Wells ordered, "and let none escape, but do the work up clean." In the subsequent battle at Fort Utah, the Saints suffered minimal casualties: Joseph Higbee peered over an embankment and took a fatal bullet, and the Utes wounded Jabez Nolan's most prominent feature, his nose. In the aftermath of the fight, the militia executed seventeen Ute prisoners on the ice of Utah Lake and enslaved their wives and children.[31]

Despite these stern measures, Brigham Young acknowledged that "We are on their land, for it belongs to them as much as any soil ever belonged to any man on earth; we are drinking their water, using their fuel and timber, and raising food from their ground." He realized the Saints had seized the tribes' birthright and were in their debt: "It is our duty to feed these poor ignorant Indians. We are living on their possessions and at their homes."[32] Young felt that in offering the Indians a choice between surrendering and being fed or resisting and being killed or starved, he was simply acknowledging frontier realities. However much he understood the Indians' plight, his sympathies did nothing to moderate his policies.

The South Part of the Mountains of Israel

Parley Pratt set out with fifty-two men, twelve wagons, a carriage, a brass cannon, and Indian trade goods in late 1849 to find a valley "for another settlement of the saints in the south part of the mountains of Israel." Interpreter Dimick Huntington and diarists Robert Lang Campbell and Isaac C. Haight accompanied the expedition. In San Pete Valley, Haight saw how Wakara's Utahs responded to a measles epidemic: "They shot a young Pah Utau boy as a sacrifice that the sickness may stop." Terrible weather transformed the journey into an ordeal. The explorers slogged through snowbound mountains and endured temperatures as low as 21 degrees below zero. Pratt led a small mounted contingent over the rim of the Great Basin into a country totally alien to anything the Mormons had experienced before. They crossed "a wide expanse of chaotic matter huge hills, Sandy deserts, cheerless, grassless, waterless plains, perpendicular rocks, loose barren clay, dissolving beds of Sandstone," Pratt wrote, "in short a country in ruins." The party ascended the Santa Clara River from its confluence with the Virgin to Mountain Meadows, where Pratt noted its fertile land, cedar for fuel, fine stream, and inexhaustible pastures. Haight called the area one of the loveliest places in the Great Basin.[33]

The Paiutes on the Virgin River struck Robert Campbell as "rude, dirty mean & filthy." Some said all their families had "died in sickness." The diarists recorded that the Paiutes repeatedly asked the Mormons to settle among them and help them raise corn, even though the explorers found dams, irrigated fields, and cornstalks eleven feet high. Dimick Huntington, whose grasp of Paiute was extremely limited, said they offered to "give us all the land round here for a knife," but the Indians probably would have been just as happy to trade the sky for such a valuable tool. Huntington informed the natives, "We [are] Mormons not Americans." The majesty of the landscape left the Mormons awestruck. Pratt made an optimistic assessment of the prospects of the country for settlement. In the mountains he had found "an almost inexhaustible supply of fuel which makes an excellent coal" and vast quantities of "the richest specimens of iron ore."[34]

Late in 1850 Brigham Young called one hundred twenty men, many of them British converts with experience as ironworkers, and sent them south to establish the Iron Mission under the command of thirty-three-year-old George A. Smith. A cousin of the prophet Joseph, Apostle Smith won the enduring love of the Mormon people at Winter Quarters when "the potato Saint" discovered that raw potatoes could prevent scurvy. Six feet tall and a "big, burly man," Smith was also bald, awkward, and generally weighed more than three hundred pounds. He accepted his comical appearance with self-deprecating humor, but he was an intensely partisan preacher whose fiery rhetoric could inflame the passions of a congregation. Although poorly educated, he served as church historian, chief justice of the state of Deseret, and colonel commanding the Nauvoo Legion in southern Utah, rising in 1866 to the rank of brigadier general despite his inability to mount a horse. "George A." was surprisingly vain, and bad taste led him to acquire outlandish clothes and ill-fitting red wigs.[35] According to legend, after watching him insert his false teeth, adjust his toupee, and put on his glasses, the Indians dubbed him "Man Who Comes Apart."

Young hoped to use the region's rich ore deposits to manufacture iron, increase Utah's economic autonomy, and, some said, cast cannons. Few of the settlers welcomed the assignment, but they followed the prophet's orders. Lee offered $2,000 to be released from the call, which Brigham Young declined.[36] The settlers arrived at the site of Parowan in the middle of January and quickly built Fort Louisa. By the end of the year they had discovered coal nearby and established Cedar Fort, present Cedar City. The colony produced a small sample of low-grade iron in 1852, and the Deseret Iron Company would struggle to produce pig iron for six more years under the direction of able but inexperienced leaders such as Isaac Haight. Despite an enormous effort, the pioneering ironworkers were unable to adapt smelting technology to the rigors of the frontier.[37] The Iron Mission, however, settled hundreds of Mormon families in the south and created a string of settlements along the southern road to California.

Although economic independence was the primary goal of the Iron Mission, it also brought the Mormons into close contact with the Piedes. The Southern Paiutes were the weakest of Utah's tribes and were delighted when the Saints stopped the relentless assaults of Mexican and Ute raiding parties. On a visit to the southern settlements in May 1851, Young advised his followers "to buy up the Lamanite children as fast as they could, and educate them and teach them the gospel, so that many generations would not pass ere they should become a white and delightsome people."

Young said, "[The Lord] could not have devised a better plan than to have put us where we were in order to accomplish that thing. I knew the Indians would dwindle away, but let a remnant of the seed of Joseph be saved."[38]

The Whites Want Every Thing: Wakara's War

His people called the great Ute warrior Wakara—or perhaps Wakarum, Yellow Man—but to the Mormons he was "Devil Walker, who held despotic sway over all the tribes between the Rocky and Sierra Nevada mountains, north from Provo waters and south to the great Colorado." Born about 1815, Wakara was already legendary as "the King of the Mountains" by the 1830s when he raided Mexican settlements at both ends of the Spanish Trail with mountaineers Thomas "Peg-leg" Smith and Jim Beckwourth. Plunder and tribute made Wakara wealthy. When the Mormons arrived he invited them to settle near him in San Pete Valley, but friendly relations did not last. One of the founders of Parowan recalled how the nervous settlers waited for Wakara's band to return "from the Spanish settlements where they had gone to steal, murder and plunder." The cry "Walker is coming!" inspired the Saints "to complete the fort in quick time." Among the mountaineers Wakara had a less imposing reputation, for they considered him a petty adventurer.[39]

The Mormons impressed Wakara with their power. They baptized and ordained him an elder, but by 1853 the relationship had collapsed. While Wakara was camped in Utah Valley in July, a settler killed a Ute and the Saints refused to turn over the man to the Utahs. This ignited the Walker War, which led to the deaths of some twenty whites and an unknown number of Utes. Brigham Young mobilized the territorial militia and ordered outlying settlements to consolidate and "fort up." Col. George A. Smith assumed command of all militia forces south of Salt Lake County, with orders to follow a defensive war policy that was despised in southern Utah. He also implemented Young's unpopular directive to concentrate the settlements and move all livestock to the Salt Lake Valley.[40]

Wakara eloquently stated Indian grievances in July 1853. "He said he has always been opposed to the whites settling on his lands, but the whites were strong and he was weak, and he could not help it." Mormon promises of lasting friendship endured only until "they became strong in numbers, then their conduct and treatment towards the Indians changed." Now they drove their neighbors "from place to place—settlements have been made on all their hunting grounds in the valleys, and the graves of their fathers have been torn up by the whites." The Utahs were forced to leave their homes or submit to the constant abuse of the whites, who "seemed never to be satisfied—the Indians had moved time after time, and yet they could have no peace." Wakara's fellow chiefs complained that "the whites want every thing, and will give the Indians nothing." The Utahs especially resented the false charge that they had murdered an Indian trader named Bowman.[41]

Wakara proved to be a better businessman than a general, for the war was "badly organized and conducted by the Indians, in spite of Wakara's vaunted fame."[42] After a year of raids and running battles, the Mormons and the Utes made peace on Chicken Creek, but they did not resolve the key question of landownership. Wakara died suddenly in January 1855, probably of pneumonia but perhaps from poison. His grieving followers sacrificed a number of Paiute slaves and horses to accompany their most renowned warrior to the great beyond.[43]

As Simple as Children: The Missions to the Lamanites

Mormon Indian policy in territorial Utah was a gauge of their millennial expectations. Brigham Young feared events would not let him wait for the unsalvageable older Indians to die off and be replaced by their virtuous children. In fall 1853 the LDS church took active measures to redeem the Lamanites. Young called Parley Pratt to lead the first wave of Indian missionaries, and twenty-five proselytizers headed south from Salt Lake on April 14, 1854, to found the Southern Indian Mission.[44] Young visited them in May and explained, "You are sent, not to farm, build nice houses & fence fine fields, not to help white men, but to save the red ones." Their first objective was to learn the native language, but the prophet found "Dymock, Geo. Bean & other interpreters much dificient in understanding what they say."[45]

Young's complaint underscored the difficulty of communicating with the Indians and reflected the problems Mormons had comprehending native cultures. Their interpreters were generally very young men, and few of them gained even a modest command of the complicated Numic dialects. George Brimhall, recalling his start as an interpreter, wrote, "I learned it very slowly, it being mixed with so many gesticulations of every conceivable position of body, arms, legs, feet, eyes and fingers. I despaired of ever learning the first lesson but with close application I did, and was soon ready for promotion." Brimhall never progressed much beyond his first lesson, for he failed to grasp the complexity of the language, which he said "consisted of about six hundred words and grunts, and as many monkeyings and figures."[46] Few of his colleagues did better.

Although he led the list of those whose language skills Brigham Young found much deficient, Dimick Huntington was the most important of the Mormon interpreters. His family joined the LDS church in about 1836. "In its New England origin and its history of sacrifice, devotion, and fanaticism," wrote Wallace Stegner, "the Huntington family is a compendium of early Mormonism."[47] Huntington had sealed two of his sisters to Joseph Smith despite their existing marriages to other men. After the prophet's death, the sisters married Brigham Young and Heber Kimball.[48] In 1857 Huntington was the official federal interpreter in Utah, a prized job that paid five dollars per day in gold.[49] Huntington was ordained patriarch to the Indians, and he led Dimick's Band, a popular Salt Lake fife-and-drum ensemble. The prophet trusted him to settle some of his "most dangerous and delicate" Indian problems and relied on him to translate his most important conversations with tribal leaders.[50]

The mission to the Southern Paiutes proved to be the most successful effort to convert territorial Utah's native peoples. The beleaguered Paiutes had good reason to welcome the Mormons. In 1851 Brigham Young began to move aggressively against slave traders from New Mexico. Utah's territorial legislature passed an act in 1852 "for the Further Relief of Indian Slaves and Prisoners" that regulated the trade to Mormon advantage by outlawing the removal of slaves from the territory and legalizing the raising of indentured Indian children in Mormon homes.[51] The Utes felt the Mormons had no right to stop the trade unless they bought the children themselves. Daniel W. Jones witnessed Arapeen's reaction to attempts to discourage the slave trade. He seized a child by the heels and "dashed its brains out on the hard ground, after which he threw the body towards us, telling us we had no hearts, or we would have bought it and saved its life."[52]

The obstruction of Wakara's slave trade had been a contributing cause of the Walker War, but it also provided the opening that led to the LDS church's only real success in recruiting Utah's Indians. The Paiutes rejoiced "that the Big Captain had told Walker to quit stealing their Squaws & children."[53] Finding them "naked, peaceful, and disposed to cultivate the arts of peace," Young sent the tribe a "small amount of plain clothing, cheap and substantial," using government funds to reinforce the efforts of the Southern Indian Mission.[54] The Mormons also promised to protect the Paiutes from emigrants on the California Trail, where the natives had provided target practice for Americans since fur trader James Ohio Pattie encountered a band in 1826. Apostle George A. Smith charged in 1844 Frémont's men "killed several Pah-Ute Indians near the Rio Virgin without any provocation."[55] When the gold rush ignited large-scale overland emigration, the argonauts' herds devastated native food sources. Indian agent Garland Hurt reported that the traffic had decimated the game, leaving the Paiutes nothing to eat but ground squirrels and "piss ants."[56]

Young sent Rufus C. Allen, president of the Southern Indian Mission, and Jacob Hamblin south from Harmony in 1854 to contact the Indians who lived on the Virgin and Santa Clara Rivers. By early winter Hamblin, Ira Hatch, Samuel Knight, Thales Haskell, and A. P. Hardy had built a dam on the Santa Clara and reported success among the Paiute bands. Hamblin moved his family and several neighbors, including his brother Oscar and Dudley Leavitt, from Tooele Valley to the Santa Clara, where they built a stone fort the Paiutes called "Jacob's Wikiup." Zadoc Judd recalled that the several hundred Indians on the river "carried on farming quite extensive for lamanites." Although "in their way they used all the water yet by the influence of the brethren[,] they were prepared to be a little more economical & let the missionaries have water."[57] Within a few years it was the Mormons who were allocating water to the Paiutes.

Superintendent Brigham Young appointed John D. Lee "Farmer to the Indians" for the Piedes on January 1, 1856. As Indian Farmer, Lee was a federal government agent whose job was to protect the Southern Paiutes and emigrants from each other, distribute goods to the Indians, and teach them to farm. The federal office came with a $600 annual salary, paid in gold, a fortune in poverty-stricken Utah.[58] The tribe consisted of at least sixteen major groups centered on food and water resources. Perhaps the largest band was the Tonaquints who lived on the Santa Clara River and numbered some eight hundred souls, mostly men and women, as many of their children had been stolen or traded away.[59] To his white neighbors, Tutsegabit appeared to hold supreme power over the Paiute bands, and Lee identified him as "Tatsegobbotts, the Head Chief of the Piedes in this range."[60] This reflected white views of authority more than tribal tradition, for a Paiute headman's power was more advisory than authoritative.[61]

Tribal and even band membership was more fluid than formal. Enos (also Eneis, Enis, and Enyos), "a young Indian living sometimes with the Pah-van-tes and at other times with the Piedes," provides a case study of native loyalties. Schoolteacher Marion J. Shelton called Enos an Indian freebooter. Pahvant leader Kanosh gave Enos twenty lashes in June 1856 for "the mean tricks he had been guilty of since he had been in the Southern country among the Piedes." In contrast to Enos, the Mormons considered Kanosh a model Indian and rewarded him with wives and property. Lee had Kanosh preach to the Indians at Harmony, describing their condition before the arrival of the whites and noting "the great change for the better with himself and his tribe, and the Utahs generally." He extolled "the benefits to be derived from raising their own grain and living like the whites," warning that if they did not stop stealing they would all fall sick and die. Kanosh did "much good among the Lamanites in this country, and behaved himself like a gentleman."[62]

The Paiutes, weak and disorganized, were plagued by brutal internal warfare. The Cedar bands mounted an expedition against the Muddy River Moapas in summer 1856. "We endeavored to make peace," Jacob Hamblin recalled, "but blood had been spilled, and nothing but blood would satisfy them." To avenge the killing of a Tonaquint woman, the Santa Clara band "took a Moapats woman, fastened her to a tree, and burnt her." Such atrocities led Hamblin to wish he would be called to labor among a higher class of people. Still, the buckskin apostle was extremely effective as an Indian missionary. One evening he made mush for the Moapas and "got them to dance by joining with them." (Catholic missionaries such as Pierre-Jean de Smet showed a gift for winning the affections of the Indians, but Protestants such as Marcus Whitman seldom made such intimate connections as did the Mormons.) The Saints felt they had established as good a government among the Paiutes as their circumstances would permit, but as Tutsegabit said, "We cannot be good, we must be Piutes. . . . [W]e want to follow our old customs."[63]

The intimacy of the Mormons and the Piedes generated ominous reports that the Saints were arming their Indian allies. In 1854 T. D. Brown had found the Santa Clara Indians "very industrious and simple as children—own but few guns and fewer horses, and many of them in trying to hold up a gun would put it to their left shoulder with the trigger upwards!"[64] Less than a year later, Lt. Sylvester Mowry claimed the Santa Clara band had "been supplied with arms and ammunition to a great extent." "More than seventy were counted in and around my camp," he reported, "all armed with good rifles. Two years ago they were armed with nothing but bows and arrows of the poorest description." Unless the government took precautions, Mowry believed, the Paiutes would become formidable allies of the Mormons.[65]

Mowry was practically alone in his evaluation of the Paiute's potential war-making prowess, and his charge that the Mormons were arming their Indian allies was only partly correct.[66] Brigham Young had decreed that no person could "give, sell, or in any way dispose of to any Indian man, woman, or child, any gun, powder, lead, caps, flints, or any other weapon or species of ammunition," but he found it good policy to arm some of them.[67] Young presented weapons to selected Indian leaders, informing Wakara in 1854, "I would rather give you a Gun for good feelings, than for [a] bad one."[68] He told Solomon Carvalho in 1854 that Utah's Indians had "possessed them-selves of arms in exchange and trade, from American travelers," and Young had him-self furnished them with the means of shooting their own game. Carvalho noted, "The Utah Indians possess rifles of the first quality. All the chiefs are provided with them, and many of the Indians are most expert in their use."[69] Self-interest suggests the Mormons did not arm Paiutes wholesale, but still the Indians managed to acquire firearms from a variety of sources.

The work of the Southern Indian Mission must have been frustrating, but its lim-ited success encouraged church leaders to expand their efforts among the Lamanites. Brigham Young called an additional one hundred sixty Indian missionaries in April 1855, enough to reach nearly every tribe in the United States. Individual accounts establish that the Mormons sent emissaries to the Crow, Cheyenne, Cherokee, Choctaw, Creek, Hopi, Shoshoni, Navajo, Bannock, and Nez Perce nations and all the Utah tribes.[70] The missionaries were called to prepare the Indians for their role in the impending apocalypse. Brigham Young said, "The day has come to turn the key of the gospel against the gentiles, and open it to the remnant of Israel." John C. L. Smith, who pre-ceded John D. Lee as Indian Farmer to the Paiutes, reported, "The people shouted, Amen, and the feeling was such that most present could realize, but few could describe." Joseph W. Young noted in May 1854, "A few suns and moons and all will be over with us here."[71]

Their expectation that the end of time was near fueled the Mormons' desire to be free of the American government. Aware that his contempt for federal power must eventually provoke a reaction, Brigham Young began casting about for a new refuge should it again become necessary to relocate Zion. He sent exploring parties south and west. In April 1855 the LDS church sent twenty-seven young missionar-ies to the East Fork of the Salmon River, a favorite fishing spot of the Nez Perces, Flatheads, Bannocks, and Shoshonis of Oregon Territory. Young ordered Thomas S. Smith to establish the Northern Indian Mission to proselytize all the tribes. Near today's Tendoy, Idaho, the missionaries founded Fort Limhi, naming it after a *Book of Mormon* king. Smith and his industrious followers built a fort, seven houses, and a blacksmith shop. Thomas Smith's success in the north contrasted sharply with failed explorations to the west and the discouraging conditions in southern Utah. The next spring Young sent more settlers to Limhi and grew increasingly interested in the prospects of the northern country.[72]

THE ANGEL OF VENGEANCE

The Mormons came to regard the Indians as a weapon God had placed in their hands. David Lewis addressed the Southern Indian Mission at Harmony on May 14, 1854. "My brother Benjamin was killed in Missouri," he said, recalling the massacre at Haun's Mill. "I am alive to avenge his blood when the Lord will." Lewis spoke of how the Saints would one day carry this work to the Indians: "We must treat them like children, by degrees, to quit their savage customs. Be diligent, faithful and patient, and the Lord will reward you when you have been proved. Ephraim is the battle ax of the Lord. May we not have been sent to learn to *use* this ax with skill?"[73] Wielding such a weapon would prove more dangerous than Lewis could have imagined.

Some Saints had personal assurances they would help to fulfill Joseph Smith's Lamanite prophesies. Their patriarchal blessings promised they would lead Indian armies in the Last Days and avenge the blood of the prophets. "Thou shalt be called to act at the head of a portion of thy brethren and of the Lamanites in the redemption of Zion and the avenging of the blood of the prophets upon them that dwell on the earth," Patriarch Elisha H. Groves prophesied as he blessed Col. William Dame in 1854. "The angel of vengeance shall be with thee. . . . [N]o miracle shall be too hard for thee to perform which shall be for the advancement of thy Redeemers Kingdom on earth. Thou shalt behold the winding up scene."[74]

"It is rather warm for the wicked!" Brigham Young wrote early in 1857. "We expect when spring comes there will be a scattering out of such as cannot abide righteousness and the purifying influences of the Spirit of God," he said. "Let them go, it is better for us to have them leave in times of peace," for in the coming troubles "their treachery might cost some of us our lives." He hoped "the fire will continue to burn and grow hotter until wickedness and iniquity shall be consumed and truth triumph over the whole earth."[75] For the Saints, the war at the end of time had already begun.

3

Political Hacks, Robbers, and Whoremongers

The settlement of Utah and the creation of a dynamic society in a hard country represented a triumph for the Mormon people, but throughout their first decade in the West it was clear that the pioneers of Utah maintained a perilous perch. During the 1850s, the Mormons endured a series of Mosaic signs and wonders—plagues of locusts, drought, massive fires, crop failures, famine, and Indian wars—as punishing as those the Lord had used to humble Pharaoh. These catastrophes hardened the settlers' resolve even as calamity after calamity brought Deseret's survival into question.

The troubled history of the Latter-day Saints had created a committed corps of believers whose bitter experience left them unalterably bonded, and their relentless hard work soon created settlements renowned for their beauty and order but also notable for their poverty. Without fail visitors commented on the transformation of Salt Lake Valley the Saints had accomplished in a remarkably short time. Outsiders also noted the bitterness they felt toward the U.S. government for its failure to protect them during their years of persecution. The rhetoric of the apostles and the devotion of their flock astonished strangers attending Mormon services. "They prophesied that the total overthrow of the United States was at hand," an emigrant wrote after hearing Pioneer Day speeches in 1850, "and that the whole nation would soon be at the feet of the Mormons, suing for mercy and protection."[1] After spending winter 1850 among them, Presbyterian minister Jotham Goodell concluded "that on the face of the whole earth there is not another people to be found, so completely under the control of one man, soul, body, and property, as are the Mormons to Brigham Young."[2] Sojourners who witnessed their fierce devotion left Utah convinced the Saints would do anything their leaders ordered.

The territory's political struggles with the federal government were as hard fought and bitter as the Mormons' battles with nature. The Saints regarded the "gentile" officials sent to govern them not only as carpetbaggers but also as yet another example of the persecution of their righteousness and a violation of their rights as Americans. The conflict generated a level of fanaticism in Utah that increased the government's suspicion. A series of federal officials either died mysteriously or fled to tell tales of rampant rebellion in the territory. Such stories offended politicians and inflamed the American public against this odd and unpopular minority.

PROPHET, SEER, AND REVELATOR

Brigham Young loved his office as governor of Utah and the salary and power that went with it, but he was never comfortable with his role as prophet. When he was sustained as Prophet, Seer, and Revelator in October 1857, Young said, "[The titles] always [make] me feel as though I am called more than I am deserving of. I am Brigham Young, an Apostle of Joseph Smith, and also of Jesus Christ."[3]

Young was caught in his role as a prophet whose religious insights lacked the certainty of Joseph Smith's personal conversations with the Lord. During the first years of his battle to succeed Smith, uncharacteristic hesitation marked Young's conduct. How would he lead the Saints if he could not speak with God face-to-face as Smith had done? The answer came on the morning of February 17, 1847, in a powerful personal epiphany. While planning the western migration, Young was suddenly taken sick, and his followers asked if he had had a vision. "No one can tell how I felt," Young said, "untill he dies and goes through the vail." Unable to get out of bed, the stricken apostle visited the world of spirits where "Joseph & Hyrum was." Even though "the vision went away . . . , as a dream you loose when you awake," a second dream answered his questions.[4]

Brigham Young found Joseph Smith sitting near a bright window. Taking Smith's hand and kissing him on both cheeks, Young asked "why we could not be together, as we once was." Smith told him "it was all right, that [they] should not be together yet." The dead seer addressed the question that most troubled his disciple: how to be a prophet and keep the spirit of the Lord. "[The] mind of man must be open to receive all spirits, in order to be prepared, to receive the spirit of the Lord," he advised. "When the still small voice speaks always receive it." Smith gave Young a sweeping vision of the plan of salvation. When it ended, "Joseph was in the edge of the light; but where I had to go was as midnight darkness," Young recalled, and he "went back in the darkness." Young told his fellow apostles to remember his dream, for it was "a vision of God and was revealed through the spirit of Joseph."[5]

This profound experience resolved Brigham Young's doubts about his role as Joseph Smith's heir. It gave him the confidence he needed to lead the Saints and inspired his belief that God had called him to implement Smith's vision. A new dynamism and conviction replaced Young's self-doubt and hesitation, for he believed God would inspire and direct his actions.

Young would discount his role as a visionary leader. "I don't profess to be such a Prophet as were Joseph Smith and Daniel," he confessed, "but I am a Yankee guesser." He never claimed to have spoken with God face-to-face. Smith "had the keys to get visions and revelations, dreams and manifestations, and the Holy Ghost for the people. Those keys were committed to him." Young had only "received the spirit of Christ Jesus, which is the spirit of prophecy."[6] Whereas Smith's revelations were prefaced with a simple "Thus saith the Lord," his successor had to guess the "Word and Will of the Lord."[7] Young's struggle to define his spiritual role as prophet encouraged his rhetoric and bluster, and his fiery sermons created innumerable problems for his church and for him as territorial governor. His folksy, direct, and crude style delighted his followers but left non-Mormon observers appalled. On his death, the *Salt Lake Tribune* denounced his public addresses as "the greatest farrago of nonsense that ever was put into print."[8]

Young passionately believed the Kingdom of God would triumph sooner than later, but the territory's dire economic conditions continually challenged his conviction. Instead of compromising, Young made greater spiritual and economic demands on his followers. He habitually blamed others for his own mistakes, from bad investments to disastrous emigration experiments. His insecurity about his role as prophet and his total devotion to the most radical doctrines of Joseph Smith also led to provocative acts that had fateful consequences for his people.

The public declaration of the doctrine of plural marriage in 1852 added to the Mormons' political problems. Unimpeachable accounts of polygamy in Utah, such as that in John Gunnison's *The Mormons*, forced church leaders to admit they were indeed practicing a marriage system most Americans considered barbaric. Ten years of passionate denials that they engaged in polygamy made the announcement a disaster for the public image of the LDS church in America. In England it substantially reduced the flood of converts and cash that fueled the growth of Utah Territory. The peculiar institution seldom promoted domestic tranquillity; the addition of a new wife into an established household often resulted in matrimonial warfare. Tired of the continual squabbles he was called on to resolve in polygamous families, Brigham Young vowed in 1856 to provide any unhappy wife with a divorce and free passage out of the territory within two weeks. The number of women who rushed to take advantage of his offer forced him to modify his promise.[9]

To Live above the Law

By the time the Mormons arrived in Utah, their experience with American justice had been long and unhappy. Their scriptures acknowledged that governments had the right to make laws to secure the public interest, but the Lord had announced, "Ye shall have no laws but my laws when I come."[10] Among the Saints natural law—God's law—had greater force than any man-made law, and they eventually challenged the very foundations of the legal system of the United States. In their isolated mountain sanctuary, the Saints codified their rejection of English common law, and besides Louisiana, Utah became the only American territory not to use some form of common law as the basis of its legal system.

This policy had a practical justification, for in its "labyrinth of abominations" English common law made polygamy a felony. The territorial legislature declared in 1854 that no law could be "read, argued, cited, or adopted in any court, during any trial," except those passed by the legislature or Congress, eliminating the precedence provided by common law.[11] This formalized the remarkable legal theory of "mountain common law" that George A. Smith presented in his first case as a lawyer, when he defended Howard Egan for killing a man who had seduced his wife. Smith argued that "If a law is to be in force upon us, it must be plain and simple to the understanding, and applicable to our situation." He reasoned that "in this territory it is a principle of mountain common law, that no man can seduce the wife of another without endangering his own life."[12]

Brigham Young believed that a better "common law which is written on the tablet of our hearts" should prevail in Utah. Its simple reliance on the maxim, "Do unto others as you would they should do unto you," superseded "the legal mists and fog" of English common law. (One historian attributed this to Young's delight in putting down lawyers and his "arrogant confidence in his own untutored common sense.") J. Ward Christian, who practiced law and medicine among the Mormons, recalled that the Saints maintained it was "in the power of man to live above the law by leading lives so perfect as not to be amenable to the law." The non-Mormon judges of the Utah territorial supreme court decreed in 1856 that common law "most positively extended over the territory," but their ruling failed to settle the matter. For all practical purposes, in Utah there was no law but God's law.[13]

Polygamy was a case in point: the Law of Abraham came from God, not Congress. Young received his wives from the Lord. He said, "[I did not] ask any lawyer, judge, or magistrate for them. I live above the law, and so do this people." Young noted that the census counted fifteen thousand prostitutes in New York City. "Is that law? Is that good order?" he asked. Only God's law offered salvation. "To talk about law and good order while such things exist, makes me righteously angry. Talk not to me about law."[14]

Even before they arrived in the Great Basin, the Mormons practiced what they came to call "lying for the Lord." Like other problematic practices, this policy had its roots in the early history of the church. Justus Morse recalled that the Danites in Missouri were directed to lie to protect each other "and to do it with such positiveness and assurance that no one would question [their] testimony."[15] The need to conceal the secret doctrine of plural marriage further justified lying. Joseph Smith publicly denied polygamy and denounced as liars those who accused him of taking multiple wives. Smith's moral relativism supported this contradictory policy of public denial and private action. "That which is wrong under one circumstance, may be, and often is, right under another," he wrote. "Whatever God requires is right, no matter what it is." It was appropriate to lie when necessary to protect the interests of the LDS church. This was perhaps what Brigham Young meant when he joked, "We have the greatest and smoothest liars in the world."[16]

The Saints came to regard the federal courts as obstacles to the rule of righteousness. To limit federal power after the departure of the first U.S. officials, the territorial legislature expanded the powers of the local probate courts, giving them original jurisdiction in both civil and criminal matters. The governor and legislature controlled the county probate courts, and they transferred legal authority from non-Mormon federal appointees to loyal Latter-day Saints. The typical Utah probate judge was also a Mormon bishop and assumed the powers of the federal district courts. "Thus the probate courts, whose proper jurisdiction concerned only the estates of the dead," observed a noted historan, "were made judges of the living."[17] From the pulpit in the tabernacle, LDS church authorities insisted on instructing juries on the verdicts they were expected to render, providing Mormon critics with plenty of ammunition to argue that Utah was not a federal territory but a theocratic dictatorship.[18] The power of the probate courts was a hotly debated issue for more than twenty years, and during all that time, the LDS church remained in effective control of Utah justice.

To Spring upon Me Like Hyenas

During the 1850s, the government in Washington and the frontier theocracy in Utah wrangled in a series of confrontations and blunders that further threatened the Mormons' fragile hold on the Great Basin. The struggle often resembled comic opera more than a political battle. As both sides talked past each other, hostile rhetoric fanned the Mormons' resentment of the government. From their viewpoint, they had patiently endured two decades of bitter persecution with great forbearance, but their patience with a long list of enemies had worn thin. Young's determination to complete the work of Joseph Smith at any cost and by any means created what historian D. Michael Quinn has called a culture of violence. The decision to do whatever was necessary to build the kingdom "encouraged Mormons to consider it their religious right to kill antagonistic outsiders, common criminals, LDS apostates, and even faithful Mormons who committed sins 'worthy of death.'"[19] What made Utah's violence unique in the West was that it occurred in a settled, well-organized community whose leaders publicly sanctioned doctrines of vengeance and ritual murder. What made it terrible were its grim consequences.

The Saints relished their isolation in the West and the independence it brought them. Among overland travelers who were simply passing through, they developed a reputation as hard but fair traders, but Mormon officials often ruthlessly exploited those who wintered in their settlements. Hundreds of them left the territory permanently embittered against Utah and its church.[20] Until the mid-1850s the Mormons encouraged emigrants to visit Great Salt Lake City, and Governor Young issued proclamations inviting travelers to rest and recuperate in Utah. But as conflict between the Mormons and the government increased, so did harassment of travelers.

This was especially true for those who ventured south on the long trail through the settlements strung along the territorial road to Los Angeles. Mormon leaders often picked their most devoted followers to pioneer the barren valleys and stark deserts of southern Utah. The red rock country was also a haven for Mormons from the American South who came from a more contentious and violent society than their Yankee brethren. These remote settlements concentrated old Mormon veterans with bitter memories of their sufferings in the United States. Men like John D. Lee openly boasted that their suffering justified stealing from any "gentile" within striking distance. This mix of extreme zealotry with the sparse grass and dismal poverty prevailing in the south provided a prescription for conflict and extortion.

Renowned as "the 'Botany Bay' of worn-out politicians," Utah drew an uneven collection of bureaucrats, but they were no worse than the general run of men appointed to govern the nation's territories.[21] Young's undisguised antagonism toward federal officials did not help matters. He despised the men sent to govern the territory and characterized them as "poor, miserable blacklegs, brokendown political hacks, robbers, and whoremongers—men that are not fit for civilized society."[22] The prophet believed greed and hatred of the Mormons were the only reasons anyone would serve in Utah. "It is obvious that no person comes here because he prefers this country. None but sinister or pecuniary motives can prompt those who are not of us to abide in our midst," Young orated one Fourth of July. "This country suits us merely because no other well informed people can covet its possession. If they do, it is because they grudge us an existence upon any part of God's footstool."[23]

Active hostilities began in June 1851 with the arrival of the first of President Fillmore's appointees, Judge Lemuel G. Brandenbury. After Young canceled several appointments, the judge learned the governor "did not wish an introduction, for none but Mormons should have been appointed to the offices of the Territory, and none other but d——d rascals" would accept them. Territorial secretary Broughton D. Harris arrived in July, in time to hear a round of speakers at the Pioneer Day celebration express their contempt for the U.S. government. Governor Young gave a rousing speech on the sins of a past president. "Zachary Taylor is dead," he thundered, "and in hell, and I am glad of it!" Young prophesied "that any President of the United States who lifts his finger against this people shall die an untimely death and go to hell!"[24]

Judge Perry Brocchus reached Great Salt Lake City on August 7. With the governor's permission, he tried to appeal to the better instincts of the local citizens to diffuse the conflict. Three thousand Saints heard the naive judge deliver a two-hour speech that Brigham Young found profoundly ignorant or willfully wicked. Brocchus gave what he thought was an innocuous oration on patriotism, but the Saints heard him attack polygamy and question the virtue of their women. The reaction, Brocchus recalled, convinced him the audience was "ready to spring upon [him] like hyenas and destroy [him]." When Young repeated his opinion of the fate of Zachary Taylor, a member of the audience asked, "How do you know it?" Young promptly replied, "Because God told me so." Heber Kimball put his hand on Brocchus's shoulder and added, "Yes, Judge, and you'll know it too; for you'll see him when *you* get there."[25]

Brocchus immediately began planning his escape from "the power of a desperate and murderous set." Much to Governor Young's aggravation, Secretary Harris, Justice Brandenbury, and Indian subagent Henry Day left with the nervous judge, carrying $24,000 in gold Harris had brought to pay government expenses. Indian agent Holeman became the only non-Mormon left to represent the federal government in Utah. The "runaway officials" broadcast reports throughout the East questioning the loyalty of the Mormon leaders, repeating Albert Carrington's comment "that the United States was going to hell as fast as it could, and the sooner the better," and Jedediah Grant's boast "that now the United States could not conquer them by arms."[26]

The Saints had in fact devoted considerable time and treasure to building their military forces. Holeman reported in 1852 that the territorial militia drilled once a week. An officer told him that in Nauvoo "they had but one state to oppose them, but now they have the whole United States." Holeman heard Mormons say "that 'God and the Governor Commands,' and they obey no one else."[27] Grant complained of "this eternal threatening of us with the armies of the United States!" and challenged federal domination of the territorial government: "We ask no odds of you, you rotten carcasses, and I am not agoing to bow one inch to your influence. I would rather be cut into inch pieces than to succumb one particle to such filthiness."[28]

LIKE A LUCIFER MATCH: THE GUNNISON MASSACRE

Territorial politics and Mormon Indian policy collided after disaster struck a federal railroad survey party on the Sevier River in central Utah. A southbound emigrant party killed three members of Kanosh's band, and when Pahvant hunters stumbled on the government expedition's vulnerable camp, the Indians could not resist the chance to take revenge. At dawn on October 26, 1853, they killed and mutilated Capt. John Gunnison and eight of his twelve men. Brigham Young did little to track down the killers, and the army instructed Lt. Col. Edward J. Steptoe, rumored to be President Franklin Pierce's choice to replace Young as governor, to investigate.[29]

Steptoe's two artillery companies and eighty-five dragoons spent the winter of 1854–55 in Great Salt Lake City, and the unruly soldiers raised hell. Gunnison had noted that the Saints dreaded "the contaminating influence of an idle soldiery among them," and the army proved their fears were justified. Mormons leaders "were afraid we were going to f——k our way through the town," Lt. Sylvester Mowry boasted.

"Perhaps we shall." Mowry worked hard to make good his threat, attempting to seduce Brigham Young's daughter-in-law and successfully bedding a "well developed" fourteen-year-old.[30]

Loyal Latter-day Saints regarded the army's presence as an insult. Attorney Seth Blair wrote in December 1854, "My feelings kindle and ignite like a Lucifer match when troops and coercive measures are spoken of concerning us. Have not people a right to self-government in a republican government?" Blair denounced the appointment of any alien as governor of Utah contrary to the will of her citizens and regarded Steptoe's selection as an indignity: "[I feel] malignant in the extreme. The very idea of a damned Gentile Governor & him a Military Character & backed by the United States troops to enforce his appointment on the citizens of Utah is so repugnant to my every feelings of the wright of American born citizens that I have no peace of mind." Blair condemned President Pierce and his cabinet as perjured traitors to the spirit of the Union.[31]

Mormon leaders had some justification for considering the soldiers a menace to public morality. The authorities banned the sale of alcohol, but this did not prevent a drunken riot between citizens and soldiers on Christmas Day 1854. A few days earlier Congress had approved Steptoe as territorial governor, and the press was full of speculation that Brigham Young would not permit the colonel to succeed him. Young announced he would be governor of Utah just as long as God wanted him to be. No one could prevent it. He conceded that "when the President appoints another man to be Governor of Utah Territory, you may acknowledge that the Lord has done it."[32] Steptoe declined the office as it would end his military career. Accompanied by a number of female refugees, the colonel left for California with his command in April 1855. Young remained territorial executive by default.[33]

Lieutenant Mowry prosecuted seven Pahvants who Chief Kanosh had decided to "throw away" for the Gunnison murders. Though justice was ill served in the comical trial, the army's investigation concluded that Mormons were not responsible for the killings. Brigham Young's contradictory accounts and his less than forthright handling of the matter—motivated by his desire to protect his Indian allies—created lingering suspicion about exactly what had happened that October morning on the Sevier River. Most historians reject the charge that the Mormons directed the Gunnison massacre. Young wrote Wakara "about the killing of Capt Gunnison and his party who were slain near Fillmore on the Sevier by the Pahvantes," and it is unlikely he would have lied to the Ute leader on a subject about which Wakara was well informed. The message explains Young's suspicious handling of the massacre. After spending an uncomfortable winter with Steptoe's detachment in Salt Lake, Young dreaded having more troops quartered in Utah. He assured Wakara he would try "to make them understand the truth about it so that they may not send their troops either against you nor the Pahvantes, altho' the Pahvants did not do right in killing them."[34]

However innocent Mormons may have been of involvement in the Gunnison affair, the fate of the murderers revealed how local religious authorities manipulated Utah's courts. Federal judge John Kinney directed the Mormon jury to acquit the defendants or find them guilty of murder. Instead the jury returned a verdict of manslaughter, following instructions from their religious leaders. The verdict demonstrated "that the *authority* of the *Priesthood* is paramount to the law of the land," Kinney complained to the attorney general. When the Pahvant convicts simply walked away from the territorial penitentiary and returned to Corn Creek, their escape did little to burnish the reputation of Utah's justice system.[35]

THE AMERICAN: GARLAND HURT

President Pierce appointed new territorial judges in 1855. Given the religious fervor gripping Utah, it is not surprising they did not fare much better than their "runaway" predecessors. The only LDS judge, George P. Stiles, who had advised Joseph Smith to destroy the press of the *Nauvoo Expositor*, was not Brigham Young's favorite Mormon. The morally impaired William W. Drummond of Illinois proved a disastrous choice. He had abandoned his family in Illinois and introduced the prostitute who accompanied him to Utah as his wife. He challenged local control of the courts and outraged the Mormons with his promise to disqualify all probate court cases except those that lay strictly within their jurisdiction. Drummond's dislike of the Saints was exacerbated when the probate court at Fillmore indicted him for striking a Mormon merchant of Jewish extraction.[36] When the Mormons learned of Drummond's unconventional domestic arrangements, he decided not to return to Salt Lake from Carson Valley, where he was holding court in the territory's western districts. Instead he started back to the states, cataloging the sins of the Saints as he went, while relations between Mormons and federal officials in Utah went from bad to worse.[37]

The character of some of the men appointed to judicial offices in Utah better suited them for a prisoner's stripes than a judge's robes, but the territory's Indian agents were superior to the general run of men in the Office of Indian Affairs. When Franklin Pierce named Garland Hurt to the Utah agency, he picked one of the most honorable men ever to serve the federal government. A self-taught physician and Kentucky state legislator, Hurt proved his mettle when he arrived in Great Salt Lake City on February 5, 1855, in the company of four mountaineers who had carried the mail over the winter trail. Hurt worked hard to establish good relations with the Saints, and his efforts to get along with Brigham Young, his immediate superior, marked his first year in the territory. C. L. Craig, Hurt's interpreter, said he never traveled "with a more perfect gentleman than Doctor Hurt whose energy and aim was always for the best." With the Utes still smarting from the Walker War and the death of Wakara, the new agent had his work cut out for him.[38]

Hurt's good relations with the Mormons did not last long. He found the Indian missionaries "a class of rude and lawless young men such as might be regarded as a curse to any civilized community." He warned, "There is perhaps not a tribe on the continent that will not be visited by one or more of them," and recommended that "the conduct of these Mormon missionaries be subjected to the strictest scrutiny."[39] To the non-Mormon federal agents charged with managing Utah's tribes, the call of the Indian missionaries was part of a scheme to forge strategic alliances with the Indians.

Many in the West believed hostile Indians and their renegade white allies acted under orders from LDS leaders. Brigham Young acknowledged that much of the trouble on the northern route to California had suspicious origins. He learned in July 1854 that a "numerous and well organized band of *white* highwaymen, painted and disguised as Indians, infest several points on the road, and drive off stock by wholesale, and recent murders are rumored from that quarter." This robber band, Young presumed, was made up of "the Arkansas murderer, and a large number of associated outlaws and fugitives."[40] Overlander D. A. Shaw recalled that not far from Salt Lake in 1853, a Wisconsin party "was attacked by the Indians, who were thought to have been instigated by some of the Mormon officials." The next summer an impromptu jury condemned a man to death for stealing a horse at Thousand Springs Valley. "During his trial he confessed that he was one of the many sent out by the Mormons, instructed to join with the Indians in the stealing of horses and stock."[41]

Such tales did not prove that Brigham Young sent agents to raid wagon trains, but a surprising number of travelers were convinced that he did. Freelancing mountain men probably inspired many tales of white Indians, for there were plenty of fur trade veterans closely allied with the tribes who did not hesitate to seize plunder when the opportunity arose. Desperadoes from the emigrants' own ranks compounded the danger. Government engineer Frederick W. Lander blamed trail depredations on whites who purchased stolen property and helped the Indians attack wagon trains. There were desperate men in the Rocky Mountains who were ready for any enormity. It would be "a hard thing to say that these are all Mormon outrages," Lander concluded, "but the property stolen certainly often finds its way into the upper Mormon settlements." He suggested stationing agents on the road to identify the murderers so that "whether Gentiles or Mormons, they could be brought to justice."[42]

Hurt did not comment on charges that the Saints were behind white Indian attacks, but he disagreed with almost every aspect of Mormon Indian policy. He found that feeding and clothing the Indians made them "clamorous and insolent, and ha[d] imposed upon the people of the Territory a most oppressive burden." Brigham Young would "endure all manner of insult rather than be at war with the Indians. . . . But the burden of this policy [fell] upon the poorer classes." To break the dependency, Hurt established large farms for the Utes at Sanpete, Spanish Fork, and Corn Creek. He achieved surprising success among the Utahs, who called him "the American."

They were sincerely fond of their protector. Even during the drought of 1856, Hurt claimed to have raised $20,000 worth of crops on the Indian farms, but he continually felt betrayed by Superintendent Young. In spring 1857 Hurt asked to be replaced immediately. He could no longer work "under the supervision of one who would decoy [him] into ruin, and who ha[d] so much disgraced the dignity of his position, and the name of an American Citizen."[43]

STATEHOOD OR EMPIRE

In addition to their political troubles, the Saints faced relentless pressure from the natural world. The Great Basin had never been an easy place to live, but in 1855 grasshoppers devastated Utah food supplies. "Nature was stingy with her rains but generous with her grasshoppers," and a two-year drought brought the Mormon kingdom to the brink of famine.[44] The 1855 harvest was only one-third to two-thirds that of previous years and was followed by the worst winter the Saints had experienced since they came to the mountains. The grasshoppers returned in summer 1856, and that year's crop was even worse than the terrible harvest of 1855. "Insects, countless and various, ravage our crops," complained the *Deseret News*. "Clouds fail to distill the timely showers; dews seldom, or never, moisten the parched herbage; streams and rivers shrink in their heated courses; treeless valleys, nude rocks, and desert plains meet the eye on every side." During the famine of 1855, Young considered abandoning the Great Basin altogether and moving the entire church to San Bernardino. "Perhaps we may have to take our line of march to your point," he wrote to Amasa Lyman, "to save ourselves from starvation."[45]

Desperate economic conditions contributed to the increasingly fervid religious and political convictions of the Mormons and fueled a new drive for statehood. Probate judge John D. Lee argued, "Our intercourse with the savages surrounding us [requires] the speedy and effective arm of a State government." Since the Saints had killed the snakes, made the roads, and built the bridges, they were entitled to make their own laws (especially those governing marriage), "the same as the people of other States."[46]

Apostate John Hyde wrote in 1857, "[Brigham Young] has one design, and one only. However wild in theory and improbable in execution, he entertains it seriously: and that is, to make the Mormon Church by-and-by control the whole continent."[47] Such allegations had no effect on Young. The enemies of the church, he preached in 1856,

> have succeeded in making us an organized territory, and they are determined to make us an independent State or Government, and as the Lord lives it will be so. (The congregation shouted amen.) I say, as the Lord lives, we are bound to become a sovereign State in the Union, or an independent nation by ourselves, and let them drive us from this place if they can; they cannot do it.[48]

Their prophet's exhortations did nothing to enhance the Saints' hopes of winning statehood for their beloved Deseret, as they insisted on calling their proposed state. Although Young talked often of independence, he would have settled for statehood, and in 1856 Mormon leaders decided to make one final attempt to have Utah admitted to the Union. If the appeal failed, as could be expected, Young was determined to shake off the dust of the U.S. government and set his eyes on a more ambitious goal: independence.[49]

Apostles John Taylor and George A. Smith took the statehood petition to Congress during the winter of 1856–57. As men of more than ordinary ability, they told the Mormon side of the stormy tale of Utah's relations with its federal officers. Their defense "formed a most spicy narrative in the annals of official scandal," one journalist noted, but it failed to explain "the utter subversion of Federal authority in the Territory." The apostles found Congress preoccupied with other matters, and the country was so hostile toward the Mormons that Taylor and Smith did not even bother to present the petition for statehood.[50]

Brigham's Sledge Hammer: The Reformation

By early 1856 Brigham Young felt the Saints had lost their commitment to righteousness and to the kingdom. Only this could explain the dismal conditions afflicting the territory. "Instead of the smooth, beautiful, sweet, still, silk-velvet-lipped preaching," he said, "you should have sermons like peals of thunder, and perhaps we can then get the scales from our eyes."[51]

"Do you know that I have my threads strung all through the Territory that I may know what individuals do?" Young asked, referring to his highly effective intelligence network. "If you do not pursue a righteous course, we will separate you from the Church."[52] Young encouraged bishops and home teachers to pry into the most intimate details of their flock's lives. "Do not let there be one place in your wards, about which you are uninformed," he directed.[53] The time was "fast approaching when words and *grass* will be laid aside, and sterner methods adopted to clear the moral atmosphere of Utah."[54] Young called for "a reformation in the midst of this people." "We need a thorough reform, for I know that very many are in a dozy condition with regard to their religion[,] . . . but now it is time to awake, before the time of burning."[55] The desperate poverty and great faith of the Mormon people, coupled with Young's rousing exhortations, created an orgy of religious extremism known as the Reformation.

Jedediah Grant, Brigham Young's cadaverous but charismatic second counselor, was the driving force behind the Reformation. Born in New York in 1816, Grant marched to Missouri with Zion's Camp. As leader of the last overland company in 1847, he had carried the body of his dead wife into the Salt Lake Valley. Grant was unanimously elected the first mayor of Salt Lake in April 1851 and later that year was sent east to counter the reports of the "runaway judges." With the help of Pennsylvanian

Thomas L. Kane, the key non-Mormon ally of the Saints, he convinced many east-ern papers that the officials had abandoned their duties and "ought to have stuck to their posts." A favorite of the Mormon people, he was affectionately known as "Jeddy, Brigham's Sledge Hammer."[56]

Grant created a catechism to quantify the sinfulness of the Saints. Distributed in spring 1856, it asked some eighteen questions, for example: "Have you ever commit-ted murder [or] shed innocent blood?" "Have you betrayed your brethren?" "Have you ever committed adultery?" It reflected Grant's obsessions, asking, "Do you wash your bodies once a week?" Even Brigham Young had trouble with the last require-ment. When asked if he washed once a week, Young said "that he did not [but] he had tried it. He was well aware that this was not for everybody."[57]

Grant toured Utah's northern settlements during September 1856. His impas-sioned sermons prayed that "all those who did not feel to do right might have their way opened to leave this people and Territory." He called for loyal Saints to renew their commitment to the church through rebaptism, and congregations unanimously rose to the challenge.[58] The apostle carried his revival to Farmington, where "the whole assembly rose with a sudden rush" to approve his measures. The next day 406 reformed sinners were baptized. Back in Salt Lake, Grant hurled the arrows of God almighty among Israel. The fiery apostle called for the Saints "to be baptized and washed clean from your sins, from your backslidings, from your apostacies, from your filthiness, from your lying, from your swearing, from your lusts, and from every thing that is evil."[59]

Utah church leaders carefully promoted the Reformation through the press and the hierarchy, but the call to "live your religion" struck a real response among rank-and-file members. "Every Bishop had the 'cue' given to him," Hannah King wrote, "and he rose up and lashed the people as with a cat-o-nine tails. The people shrunk, wept, groaned like whipped children. . . . The whole people seemed to mourn for all more or less came 'under the rod.'"[60]

Perhaps the most troubling aspect of the Reformation was the Mormon leader-ship's obsession with blood. Their rhetoric dripped with sanguine imagery, and their Old Testament theology incorporated this dark fascination in a perplexing doctrine known as blood atonement. Joseph Smith taught that certain grievous sins put sin-ners "beyond the reach of the atoning blood of Christ." Their "only hope [was] to have their own blood shed to atone." Strictly interpreted, the doctrine seems to have applied only to believing Mormons, but it led to the widespread belief that the LDS church shed the blood of apostates "as an atonement for their sins."[61] As the doctrine evolved under Brigham Young, it would have a powerful—and confusing—influence. Of all the beliefs that laid the foundation of Utah's culture of violence, none would have more devastating consequences.

Joseph Smith made apostasy and the shedding of innocent blood cardinal sins. Section 132 of the *Doctrine and Covenants,* which also authorized polygamy, assured Saints who were sealed by the Holy Spirit that they would "come forth in the first resurrection, and enter into their exaltation." But if the anointed should shed innocent blood, he would be damned. By definition, "innocent blood" included anyone under the age of eight years—for Mormons, the age of accountability—and those who had entered the new and everlasting covenant. If the faithful kept their covenants and did not shed innocent blood or betray their testimonies, the revelation promised they would "inherit thrones, kingdoms, principalities, and powers, dominions, all heights and depths." The only remedy for these unforgivable crimes was to shed one's own blood.[62]

Modern Mormon authorities insist blood atonement was a "rhetorical device" and "has never been practiced by the Church at any time," but historian Juanita Brooks concluded that blood atonement was "a literal and terrible reality. Brigham Young advocated and preached it without compromise."[63] If a Mormon committed an unpardonable sin, Young asked early in 1857, "will you love that man or woman well enough to shed their blood?" He knew hundreds of people who could have been saved "if their lives had been taken and their blood spilled on the ground as a smoking incense to the Almighty, but who are now angels to the devil." If a man wanted salvation and it was "necessary to spill his blood on the earth in order that he might be saved, spill it." That, said the prophet, was the way to love mankind. It was strong doctrine to cut "people off from the earth," he conceded, "but it is to save them, not to destroy them." Sinners should "beg of their brethren to shed their blood."[64]

Young's private statements exceeded even the violent language of his public sermons. "I want their cursed heads cut off that they may atone for their sins," he told the Council of Fifty in March 1849.[65] His interpretation of blood atonement evoked the Saints' vision of themselves as an Old Testament people, an identification so strong that the plans for the Salt Lake Temple included an altar "to Offer Sacrifices."[66] The gory details of blood atonement shock modern observers, but the common experience of butchering animals made them less repellent to a farming people.

The Saints had a "right to kill a sinner to save him, when he commits those crimes that can only be atoned for by shedding his blood," Jedediah Grant insisted. He claimed, "We would not kill a man, of course, unless we killed him to save him." At the beginning of the Reformation, Grant advised sinners to ask Brigham Young "to appoint a committee to attend to their case; and then let a place be selected, and let that committee shed their blood." "We have those amongst us," he said, "that are full of all manner of abominations, those who need to have their blood shed, for water will not do, their sins are of too deep a dye."[67]

John D. Lee's confessions reflect how the doctrine was interpreted—and practiced—in southern Utah in the 1850s. He linked blood atonement to obedience and wrote that during the Reformation everyone in Utah believed in it. "It was taught by leaders and believed by the people that the Priesthood were inspired and could not give a wrong order." If they did, the authorities were responsible for the consequences. Lee thought the doctrine was designed "to place the Priesthood in possession of every secret act and crime that had been committed by a man of the Church." The "right thing to do with a sinner who did not repent and obey the Council, was to take the life of the offending party, and thus save his everlasting soul. This is called 'Blood Atonement.'"[68] Eventually the American popular press would attribute almost every murder in Utah Territory to blood atonement. Whatever the doctrine's precise practice, the sermons of Brigham Young and Jedediah Grant helped to inspire their followers to acts of irrational violence.

The Reformation burned especially bright in zealous southern Utah. "Everyone was re-baptized," recalled Parowan schoolteacher Joseph Fish, "and all who wished to be Saints consecrated or deeded their property to the President of the Church."[69] The night of their return from conference in October 1856, William Dame and Isaac Haight "spoke by the Holy Spirit, and the congregation was cut to the heart. It was said the people were all on the road to hell, from the highest to the lowest." They called for the entire stake to be baptized for the last time with water. The southern Saints learned that "the dividing line between the righteous and the wicked was now drawn."[70]

Lee recalled hearing every Sunday "that the Mormons were to conquer the earth at once, and the people all thought the millennium had come, and that Christ's reign upon earth would soon begin, as an accomplished fact." Some Mormon leaders used the Reformation to settle old scores, and even an old warhorse like Lee did not escape. He claimed he was almost blood-atoned at Parowan when the secret tribunal of Utah brought him into a darkened room and tried him for violating his covenants with a Miss Alexander. "I expected to be assassinated in the dark," Lee wrote, "but for some reason it was not done." Lee was freed and never formally cleared of the charge but "for months . . . expected to be assassinated every day."[71]

Before launching the Reformation, Young devised a scheme to use carts instead of expensive teams and wagons to bring emigrants to Utah economically. If gold seekers with wheelbarrows could successfully cross the plains, he felt poor Saints could pull handcarts to Zion. The plan went awry when Apostle Franklin D. Richards dispatched the last of the 1856 outfits at a dangerously late date and blizzards caught the poorly equipped Willie and Martin handcart parties near Devils Gate. Hundreds of men, women, and children died of exposure, exhaustion, and starvation. When word of the disaster reached Utah, the church launched a heroic rescue effort that limited the casualties but further taxed the strained resources of the territory. Even with the massive rescue effort, more than two hundred Saints died, the worst disaster in the history of America's overland trails.

Even though Young had conceived the handcart venture, Mormon leaders refused to shoulder any blame for the catastrophe. From the tabernacle, Grant swore that "as planned and given by brother Brigham, our immigration will be free from the sad results of mismanagement." Typically, the fanatical preacher laid the blame on the victims. As Grant's biographer noted, he blamed the death and suffering of the handcart Saints on "the same disobedience and sinfulness that had induced spiritual sleepiness among the people already in Zion." With renewed vigor Brigham's Sledge Hammer laid the rod across the backs of the Saints until the middle of November. "We want the hay, the straw, the wood, the stubble, the dross, and every impure principle burnt up," railed the Mormon Savonarola, but he burned himself up with preaching and mass baptisms. By the first of December, Jedediah Grant was dead of typhoid.[72]

A deep gloom enveloped the City of the Saints. Brigham Young mourned the death of "a great man, a giant, a lion."[73] Though it had lost its most ardent proponent, the Reformation gained a martyr and its fires burned on. Young stopped the administration of the sacrament to Utah's Mormons, and in the last days of 1856 the apostles announced that the First Presidency had "retired from our midst because the people would not do what they are told." Church leaders threatened to take the Holy Priesthood "into the wilderness among the Lamanites, or to the Ten tribes."[74]

SURROUNDED BY DEVILS: JOHN D. LEE

Nowhere did the fires of the Reformation burn as brightly as in Iron County. Given the hardness of the country and the poverty of its inhabitants, it was not surprising that a host of problems troubled the southern settlements. The strong personalities assigned to this ragged edge of the Mormon frontier were bound to generate conflict.

After a court gave Robert Ritchie permission to build a sawmill in Pine Valley, Ritchie let Jacob Hamblin bring his stock into the fertile alpine grassland, provided he kept his cattle out of Ritchie's fields. Hamblin instead let his animals run free. To save his crop, Ritchie had to sleep in his fields. Hamblin falsely charged that Ritchie "had taken the name of God in vain" (a major transgression in Mormon Utah) and had "sworn by God that he would kill enough of [his] cattle to make a fence a round his wheat field." When the faithful were ordered to resolve their differences during the Reformation, Ritchie approached Hamblin. Hamblin agreed to make peace. The story about the cattle fence, Hamblin said, "was a lie when I told it."[75]

Hamblin was not the only southern Utah leader whose tactics aroused resentment. Blustering and dictatorial, John D. Lee could be a hard man to like. When the 1848 emigration had assembled on the Elkhorn River, Lee had "hard work to raise his 50," Hosea Stout noted. "The people do not like to go with him."[76] Lee was an aggressive, relentless personality and a mass of contradictions. His generosity was legendary, but he could be a ruthless businessman. "He was kind to his wives, a generous father, full of high spirits, and very fond of his numerous family," John Steele said. But Lee's reputation as a braggart and sexual predator dogged him. An apostate who knew him well characterized Lee as "a man who would divide his last biscuit with the traveler upon the desert, and cut that traveler's throat the next hour if Brigham Young said so."[77]

Lee's autocratic style did not win him friends in southern Utah. When Brigham Young organized a branch at Harmony, he nominated Lee to be presiding elder. "We would prefer another President," one missionary to the Indians objected, an almost unheard of action in the LDS church, where the unanimous confirmation of officials remains the rule. Rufus Allen backed the sentiment, for the community did not want Lee as their leader. But Young knew his adopted son was a reliable man who got results. "There was no duty assigned to him that he was not equal to," wrote missionary John Steele, and Lee could keep a secret. Mormon offices were not assigned based on popularity contests, so Young directed the people to "let John D. Lee preside."[78]

Young sent militia captain William Wall to survey conditions in "the extreme Southern Settlements" in 1853. Wall reported that "the regularity and good order of the Fort" at Parowan surpassed any he had seen and that the militia was well armed and drilled. Major Lee gave Wall a hearty welcome at Harmony. The captain found Lee's fort "situated on a commanding iminence" and strongly picketed. The Paiutes appeared to be "perfectly under the control of Major J D Lee, honest, industrious and obedient." Wall continued, "They excel all other Indians that I have met with in the Mountains for an anxiety to conform to the manner and customs of the Whites. They reverence Colonel J D Lee as the Mormon Chief & are willing to obey him."[79]

Lee pursued his assignment as Farmer to the Indians with characteristic single-mindedness. While the Paiutes worshiped him, Lee's relations with the missionaries were terrible. Clerk Thomas D. Brown complained that Lee had an abundance of dreams, visions, and revelations, "from which he instructs, reproves & governs," but his flock believed "his most important revelations are those he overhears listening as an eavesdropper." Brown told Brigham Young that Lee had appropriated the best land in Harmony, and he later charged him with cowardice, jealousy, and immeasurable selfishness. Lee publicly boasted he "would not hesitate to steal from the gentiles who had so often robbed the saints." Bitterly aware of his unpopularity, Lee complained, "I am always to be in hell & surrounded by Devils." People respected Lee's office, Brown wrote, but they abhorred his tyranny and oppression. Lee tied up "his own hands and [did] not know it."[80]

Utah pioneer George A. Hicks recalled it was in winter 1856 and 1857 when Mormons "first heard that there was hostile preparations being made by the government of the United States against the people of Utah and that an army was all ready to march in the Spring for Utah." The rumor about the army was premature, but Hicks captured the militant mood of the citizens of the territory. "We as a people were not frightened by the news, we put our trust in God and believed we were his people and He was able to take care of His Saints," Hicks wrote. "We believed the time was at hand that 'one man should, chase a thousand and two should put 10,000 to flight.' We believed it was our duty to do all we were able to do and God would do the rest and we were full of faith that the set time had come to favor Zion."[81] It was not a happy time for outsiders to visit the settlements of Utah Territory.

4

The Arkansas Travelers

In the first days of spring in 1857, wagons, tents, livestock, and families jammed the broad meadow at Beller's Stand in Carroll County, Arkansas. Hundreds of people camped in the wide fields stretching away from Crooked Creek, and hundreds more came to ask about the prospects of California or to bid farewell to kinfolk. The grass that powered wagon travel across the Great Plains was beginning to appear, so there would soon be enough forage to support draft animals. Blacksmiths made the air ring as they repaired wagon irons and forged ox shoes, chains, and ax heads. Wheelwrights set iron tires tightly onto wooden wheels—a job that would have to be done again once the wagons crossed the hundredth meridian into the arid West.

Women found camp life little different from the endless drudgery they knew everywhere else on the frontier. They tended lively tribes of offspring, milked cows, churned butter, baked bread and biscuits and cooked huge meals, darned and sewed, and even doctored the wounds their young sons received in battles with imaginary Indians. They hauled their laundry to two huge flat rocks on one side of the creek close by Caravan Spring, to do the family laundry beneath the shade of stately elms. The swarms of children who enlivened the camp could not escape the chores they did at home; they gathered firewood, carried water, and herded animals.[1]

Men worked on their wagons and assembled their outfits, trading guns, livestock, whiskey, and stories. They endlessly debated the merits of horses, mules, and oxen as draft animals for the long journey west and argued over the best way to get to the land of dreams, California. When they could, some of the men hunted, drank, swapped lies, and bet on horse races and shooting matches, but many of their number spent their free time in prayer and reflection. After dark the inhabitants of this movable village gathered in clusters of families and friends around large fires, where they made the air ring with fiddles and banjos sounding the high lonesome ballads their ancestors had carried across the sea.

The Fancher party provides a window into travel and travelers on overland trails in the 1850s. A close look at the train reveals that most emigrants went west in extended clans linked by complicated relations of blood and marriage. Though its wealth made it exceptional, the company's composition reveals distinct trends in overland emigration. The gold rush trains of 1849 and 1850 were almost exclusively male, but of its roughly 140 members, 70 women and children of the Fancher train can be identified by name, including some 50 children age sixteen or under. The 40 unidentified members were probably largely male, but easily two-thirds of the train was composed of women and children. Although long caricatured as a horde of faceless ruffians, the party's large number of women and children casts doubt on folklore that pictures its journey west as a drunken and murderous rampage.

As these Arkansas travelers demonstrate, the typical overlander was not a shiftless vagabond, for crossing half a continent by wagon was an expensive proposition. It cost a family about $2,000 to prepare for a journey to California, an amount worth more than $40,000 today. Many of the men had assembled cattle herds, intending to exploit the high price of beef in the gold mines, which drew livestock traders from as far away as Texas. The best chance a single man had to cross the plains was to work as a drover or teamster for these speculators. Dozens of boys appeared at Beller's Stand, hoping to hire on with one of the family outfits, preferably with a man who had the experience and reputation of Captain Fancher.

Alexander Fancher was a cattleman before there were cowboys. He purchased several hundred head of Texas cattle in Arkansas in spring 1857 and called the young men he hired to handle them drovers or simply hired hands.[2] Fancher had ranching in his blood, for his people had been in the cattle business even before they came to America as part of the Huguenot diaspora, and in 1850 his family still pronounced the name *Fan-sheer*, preserving its French origins. Thirteen Fanchers headed west in 1857. Alexander's wife, Eliza, watched over nine children, who ranged from nineteen-year-old Hampton to twenty-two-month-old Triphenia. In addition to Hampton and Triphenia, the children were William, Mary, Thomas, Martha, eight-year-old twins Sarah G. and Margaret A., and five-year-old Christopher Carson, named after the frontiersman. Alexander Fancher's kin included his cousins, Robert Fancher and James Mathew "Matt" Fancher.[3]

By 1857 Alexander Fancher had already crossed the plains two or three times. Born in Tennessee in 1812, he was three years old when his father, Isaac, was wounded at the Battle of New Orleans. Isaac Fancher moved to Illinois in about 1823, where he and his son served in the Black Hawk War during summer 1832. (Isaac's brother Gray Bynum Fancher was a friend of Abraham Lincoln and shared his horse with Lincoln on their return from the war.) Alexander married Eliza Ingram in east central Illinois in 1836. Isaac died in Coles County, Illinois, in 1840 but not before he had seen his grandson Hampton born in 1838 and perhaps another, William B., born the year Isaac died.[4]

Fancher Family trails west, 1850–57. Alexander Fancher made at least three trips to California in the 1850s. With his brother John Fancher, he drove cattle from Carroll County, Arkansas, to Salt Lake in 1850 and then went south to San Diego. The Fanchers and their families probably returned to Arkansas via the Isthmus of Panama. Alexander Fancher made a second trip west in about 1854, this time taking the "northern route" via Fort Hall and the Humboldt River. In 1857 Alexander, his wife, Eliza Ingram Fancher, and their nine children took the Cherokee Trail to Fort Bridger, perhaps cutting north to the main Oregon-California Trail to cross South Pass. On their way to southern California, all the family except two children were murdered at Mountain Meadows, Utah Territory, on September 11, 1857.

The Fanchers soon moved west, for their daughter Mary was born in Missouri in about 1841. The family had reached Osage Creek in the Ozark Mountains by 1846. Fancher settled near his uncle James and brother John and built one of the first mills in the country. Relatives recalled he was a fiddler, farmer, and stockman, "tall, slim, erect, of dark complexion, a singer, and a born leader and organizer of men"—a man of "great commonsense."[5]

Fancher served as a private with Capt. William C. Mitchell's Carroll County militia in an 1849 borderland vendetta known as the Tutt-Everett War. This "dark and bloody chapter of contention and crime" grew out of a feud between two powerful Ozark families. The militia marched from William Beller's farm on Crooked Creek to Yellville and saw "open war in all its pomp." After the defeat of the Everetts, the militia disbanded, but the feud dragged on for years.[6] Perhaps tired of fighting such pointless battles or merely intrigued by the golden prospects of California, Fancher caught a serious case of western fever. Sometime after April 19, 1850, brothers John and Alexander Fancher, with their large families and a drove of cattle, set out on their first trip over the arduous road to California.[7]

The Fancher brothers could choose from several roads to El Dorado. Local editors boasted "that the *shortest and best route* to the farthest West is through Arkansas." The Fort Smith Road ascended the Arkansas River until it met the well-established Santa Fe Trail to New Mexico. From there, emigrants could take "the southern route" to the Colorado River via the Gila River or Cooke's Wagon Road, blazed by the Mormon Battalion during the war with Mexico, and then make a torturous desert crossing to southern California. In 1849 a party from Indian Territory had opened a better route, the Cherokee Trail. It followed the Arkansas River to the trapper posts on the Front Range of the Rockies and reached Fort Bridger by a route to the south of the main Oregon-California Trail. Arkansans could also travel north on the Frontier Military Trail, which connected the forts along the border of Indian country, west of the Arkansas and Missouri state lines, and provided a convenient way for Southerners to reach the several branches of the Oregon Trail. So many citizens of the state were preparing to go to California in 1850 that it raised "the apprehensions of some . . . who say the country will be depopulated."[8]

Of all the American trails followed by men who rode in the dust of cattle, wrote historian J. Evetts Haley, no other is so little known as the trail to California. The great Texas drives to Kansas after the Civil War are part of the legend of the West, but the older cattle trails to California are all but forgotten. Texans had been driving cows to California since T. J. Trimmier of Washington County drove five hundred cattle to California in 1848 and allegedly sold them for $100 a head.[9] Several large herds left Texas in 1850 for El Dorado, and Walter Crow set out from Missouri that year with four sons, five hundred Durham cattle, and more than thirty cowhands and traveled a week ahead of the Fancher brothers, taking the same route across Kansas to Fort Kearny.[10]

The Fancher family's first trip west in 1850 at the height of the gold rush captured most of the adventures and trials of an early overland trek. They would be among the first to use one of the most challenging trails to California, the wagon road from Salt Lake to Los Angeles. From the very beginning of the journey their party took none of the roads promoted in the Arkansas press but crossed the Ozarks to Fort Scott, a military post some eighty miles south of the western trails' main jumping-off point at Independence, Missouri.

While a flooding stream detained the emigrants on the edge of Indian country, William Bedford Temple wrote home to Carroll County. Temple's vivid letter described a countryside depopulated by gold fever. "I am informed many farms are lying idle this season," he wrote. "One fourth of the men is said to bee gone or going to the diggins this spring. 60,000 men will leave Independence." His company of twelve wagons was a jolly one, but Temple complained, "I can not see how god will prosper men when his name is continuously blasphemed." Not all were so inclined, yet Temple found a large majority of the men desperate and profane. "Unless we get with a different crowd we will not go in peace," he predicted. Conflict was common among overland travelers, and Temple attributed the party's problems to the independence of its members—"the fruit of every man being Captain."[11]

Temple wrote a second letter from Pawnee country. "Now over 475 miles from home in the midst of the savage Indians," Temple admitted he had not seen one yet, for "they are afraid to come near the road." Approaching today's Kansas-Nebraska border, Temple saw increasingly grim evidence of the hardship of the route, passing four or five fresh graves every day. At the forks of the road from Independence, a seventeen-year-old named William Wilkerson was shot "for going in a tent to lay with a girl."[12] The boy's party denied killing him, but Temple reported that "a half breed Indian" had given him information on the subject. At Big Blue River, he described the often-fatal consequences of fording a river after a man and two mules drowned and several wagons sank. With three thousand cattle and "mules in great numbers" crowding the crossing, Temple had never seen "such a rush to cross, men on men, cattle on cattle." Here a man "died of diareer as many others [had] done," but none of the Arkansas folks were sick yet. Relations in the train had improved.

An incredible procession of humanity had joined the rush for gold. Temple estimated some seven thousand wagons were ahead of his party—"thick as pigeons." The fifty thousand emigrants of 1850, the largest number to head west by wagon during a single year, included "all kinds of people under the sun from the man of money down to the begger, from the man of honor down to the lowest thief on earth." They had chosen "all kinds of ways of going some in carts, some a foot." Temple saw "three large stout men with a wheel barrow, no joke."

Most Arkansas trains turned west when they met the Santa Fe Trail, but the Fancher brothers took their large cattle herd north to the heavily traveled but better-watered Oregon Trail. On the morning of June 1, five steers, including two belonging to Alexander Fancher, were missing. After the wagons rolled out, Fancher and Temple tracked the animals, searching a creek until they discovered their cattle "brushed in a thickett, herded by a Whiteman." "The fact is," Temple said, "more than one is ingaged in this way of doing—stealing and selling to the back trains." That is, these desperadoes rustled cattle from one wagon train and sold them to another. According to Temple, "Near all the stealing and killing is done by the Whites following the Trains. The number thus ingaged is very great—not a day [goes by] but Ponies or cattle is missing."

Such predators were infinitely more dangerous than most Indians, and Temple thought they would shoot a man for his provisions. He rallied his party to capture the rustler, but he escaped. "Had we found him poor fellow," Temple wrote, "he would have been no more but feede for Wolves." Alexander Fancher recovered his livestock, but this would not be his last encounter with white Indians.

Soon after meeting the rustler, the Fancher brothers and two other families left Temple behind with Captain Page's thirteen wagons. Despite his assurances that his health was "better than it was at home," William Bedford Temple died on June 24, 1850, and was buried near Chimney Rock.[13]

A SPRING ON THE RIM OF THE GREAT BASIN

At the Parting of the Ways, where the trails to Oregon and California separated, the Fanchers again chose an unorthodox route: they turned their wagons southwest toward Great Salt Lake City. After several weeks among the Saints, the Fanchers left Hobble Creek on October 9, 1850, in Washington Peck's company of "emigrants bound for the gold fields." The party consisted of twenty-nine wagons, two carts, ninety-two men, nine women, and twenty-eight children. Near Corn Creek, an emigrant traded a gun for a horse with a Pahvant, in violation of the company's rules. The next day the Indian stole the horse. When the party camped with Wakara, his band "gave [them] a war dance" and showed them two Shoshoni scalps. Peck's company reached "a spring on the rim of the Great Basin" on November 1 and camped at Mountain Meadows as the weather turned cold, dropping some seven inches of snow. They left the meadows on November 4, 1850, to find "roads bad, mud deep in places."[14]

On the Muddy River, the party met "a number of Indians of the Pautah tribe," whom they described as "a strong, robust set of men nearly naked, armed with bows and arrows." But the band of Moapits appeared friendly. Peck's wagons made the dry crossing of the Fifty Mile Desert in thirty-three hours without losing an animal. After camping at Las Vegas for five days, the party entered a country "without sufficient vegetation to feed a grasshopper." Weakened animals began to drop as the desert assumed a terrifying aspect for emigrants from the verdant woodlands of the East. "It appears as if the goddess of desolation and barrenness has erected her throne and reigns without a rival," Peck wrote. Some one hundred miles west of Las Vegas, "3 teams drove on—W. Mosley, Blodgett and Fancher," Peck reported after camping on Saleratus Creek to prospect for gold. "We are out of danger from the Indians." Peck found Blodgett camped near present-day San Bernardino on December 22, 1850, but the Fanchers had apparently moved on.[15]

Alexander and Eliza Fancher appear at San Diego early in 1851, along with seven children, including their eighteen-month-old twins, Sarah and Margaret. John Fancher was also in San Diego with his wife and four children.[16] The Fancher brothers moved to the Four Creek country of California by 1852, settling at Visalia in Tulare County.

Here the enterprising cattlemen registered the county's first brand in December. Visalia, located on the edge of the gold fields, was home to Arkansas cattlemen who Basil Parker recalled lived in a "very few log or board shanties." The Fancher brothers opened markets for their beef in Mariposa County, where John registered their brand in 1853.[17]

About that time Alexander Fancher returned to Arkansas, perhaps via Panama with his family, to purchase a cattle herd to drive to California in 1854 or 1855.[18] At a family reunion in 1955, Judge Frank T. Fancher said he traveled through southern Utah "both out and back, and was treated well by the Mormon settlers on both trips." An inscription on Register Rock at Massacre Rocks on the Oregon-California Trail (in present-day Idaho) suggests that on this trip the "Fanshiers of Ark" tested the Humboldt River road as a cattle trail. The enterprise was clearly successful, for Alexander returned to Arkansas in 1856 to buy more livestock. Judge Fancher claimed he carried a strong box containing $4,000 in gold coin to be used to buy land.[19] In addition to the gold, Alexander assembled a wealth of cattle to take west in 1857.

There were fortunes to be made driving cows to California. From the critical overland crossroads at Great Salt Lake City in 1854, Brigham Young commented on the high prices offered for wagons and stock in California, noting "that immense herds are annually driven to that market with great profit, when the stock and sales are managed with prudence."[20] Young seized this opportunity and sent missionaries to California in May 1857 driving six hundred or seven hundred head. The Mormons estimated seventy thousand loose cattle went to California that summer, but bad news awaited the cattlemen at the end of the trail.[21] Stockman Kirkbridge Potts of Arkansas wrote home in early 1857, "[I could not get] an offer for my stock that I thought would justify the time, trouble, and expense [of taking them across the plains]." Potts's letter was not published until June, too late to warn other emigrants of their economic peril. By then Alexander Fancher was again herding cattle west to the land of golden dreams.[22]

AMERICA IN 1857

Emigrants headed across the Great Plains in spring 1857 gave little thought to the wider world. Speculation in American railroad stocks created an economic crisis in Europe that eventually ignited a financial panic on both sides of the Atlantic, but this did not affect the price of wagons or cattle on the frontier. Edward Fitzgerald Beale left Camp Verde, Texas, in June to survey a wagon road and try out twenty-five camels as pack animals. The transatlantic cable had briefly opened instant communication between Europe and North America before it snapped, but overlanders were more interested in how long it would be before the telegraph reached California. In the wake of his nation's defeat in the Crimean War, Alexander II began the emancipation of Russian serfs, but in America debates over slavery grew more abrasive and exploded into a bitter border war between slavers and Free-Soilers that ravaged "Bleeding Kansas."

For the United States, the year dawned with bright prospects. The republic had survived a divisive presidential election in which the Republican platform of 1856 had promised "to prohibit in the Territories those twin relics of Barbarism—Polygamy and Slavery." John C. Frémont, explorer and national hero, was the first Republican presidential candidate, and his party's challenge to Southern slaveholders and Mormon polygamists fueled a vitriolic campaign. Hotheaded Southern politicians swore they would destroy the Union should Frémont be elected. The "know-nothing" candidacy of Millard Fillmore ultimately drained enough support from Frémont to give 45 percent of the popular vote to James Buchanan. Optimists hoped President Buchanan, who had magnificent credentials, could defuse the growing crisis over slavery. The Democrats now controlled the Supreme Court, Congress, and the presidency, but this concentration of power was deceiving. The Supreme Court's Dred Scott decision in March 1857 mocked the hope expressed in Buchanan's inaugural address that the court could settle the slavery issue speedily and finally. It was clear the president and his party had no plan of action, let alone a coherent vision of how to solve the problems that threatened to destroy the nation.[23]

To complicate matters in Washington, a defiant memorial from the Utah Territorial Legislature arrived in March 1857. It announced that its citizens would decide for themselves which federal laws to obey: they would observe acts of Congress only "so far as they are applicable to [their] condition in [their] territorial capacity." In addition, Mormons would reject any federal officers who failed to meet their moral standards. Buchanan's cabinet regarded this as treason and felt that such a serious challenge to the authority of the federal government could not go unchallenged.[24] Of all the complex difficulties facing the new administration, the Mormon problem offered the most tempting political opportunity and promised the most beguiling of solutions—military action, a course that might unify the nation in a popular crusade against the evils of Mormonism.

A BEVY OF FAMILIES: THE ARKANSAS EMIGRANTS

As Buchanan pondered his options, several wagon trains headed west from Arkansas. Kinship and geography determined their composition, for like most overland parties they were "a bevy of families related to each other by ties of consanguinity and marriage."[25] After reaching El Dorado, some of these travelers recalled there were three or four Arkansas companies on the northern roads to California that summer.[26] Family relationships suggest they crossed the plains in four close-knit groups. One consisted largely of Fanchers, Dunlaps, and Mitchells. One was made up mostly of Carroll County folk and dominated by the family of Capt. Jack Baker. A third company included the interrelated Cameron, Jones, Tackitt, and Miller clans; a fourth was led by trail veteran Basil Parker. All of the parties traveled in close association, exchanging members as personalities and trail conditions dictated.[27]

Alexander Fancher's party was said to consist of eleven families with twenty-nine children and sixty-five total members, traveling with eleven well-stocked wagons and large herds of cattle and horses.[28] Later that summer in Utah Territory, the Fanchers camped with the Camerons and the two Dunlap brothers, who had eighteen children between them, "some of them well grown."[29]

The sprawling Mitchell and Dunlap families came from present-day Marion County. Jesse Dunlap, thirty-nine, ran a general store, mill, and blacksmith shop with his partner, William C. Mitchell, then an Arkansas state senator. Dunlap's large family included his wife, Mary Wharton, and their ten children, who ranged in age from the eighteen-year-old Ellender to the infant Sarah Ann. In between were Nancy, James, twins Lucinda and Susannah, Margaret, Mary Ann, Rebecca, and Louisa. Their father left Arkansas with three wagons, nine yoke of oxen, thirty cattle, three guns (plus pistols and knives), provisions, "camp fixins, cooking articles &c," and some $320. Jesse's older brother, Lorenzo Dow Dunlap, was Senator Mitchell's son-in-law. Lorenzo Dunlap and his wife, Nancy, swelled the company with their eight children. Teenagers Thomas J. and John H. were old enough to do trail chores, while thirteen-year-old Mary Ann probably helped to manage her younger sisters, Talitha Emaline, Nancy, America Jane, Prudence Angeline, and infant Georgia Ann. The family left Arkansas with one wagon, four yoke of oxen, and twelve cattle. All told, at least twenty-two Dunlap family members traveled with the Fanchers.[30]

Senator Mitchell declined to go west with his daughter, but his sons Joel D. and Charles R. joined the expedition. Charles brought along his young wife, Sarah Baker Mitchell (Jack Baker's daughter), and their infant son John. William Mitchell recalled that his sons had $275 in cash. Before they left Arkansas with thirteen yoke of good oxen and sixty-two cattle, the Mitchells planned to purchase enough stock "so as to make one hundred head in all." They had guns, pistols, Bowie knives, camping gear, and other property worth some $2,513.[31]

Like Alexander Fancher, John T. Baker, one quarter Cherokee and fondly known as Captain Jack, was "always on the stretch for something new." Baker was born in North Carolina about 1805. His father moved to Alabama, built a plantation, bought slaves, and opened an inn. Baker married Mary Ashby, and by 1830 he owned one hundred acres. He "was quite a good fighter and not because he particularly enjoyed brawls but he frequently found himself in brawls, since he did regularly imbibe." A family tradition told how one fall day Baker went to town to buy supplies. He met three men "who to say the least, were not his best friends." They attacked Baker and "the ensuing fight lasted for over an hour and ended up in a woodyard where [he] dispatched the last of his three attackers." The details are dubious, but Baker apparently did kill a few of his neighbors. After the fight he recuperated at his father's plantation. On his return home, he found his barn burned and many of his cattle driven off. Baker stayed in Alabama until he moved his family to Arkansas in 1849, where they settled near present Harrison at Baker Prairie on Crooked Creek.[32] Baker owned eight slaves, and his neighbors considered him a very industrious man, a shrewd trader, and one of their "best citizens." Baker "was a warm friend and a bitter enemy; was possessed of good property, land, negroes, &c."[33]

Frontiersman Basil Parker had crossed New Mexico Territory to California in 1853 and returned in 1856 via Panama to collect his dead brother's wife and children in Carroll County. Parker was preparing to return west in spring 1857. "My doing so had a tendency to stimulate a man of the energy of Captain Baker," he recalled, "so he fitted out a splendid train and had about six hundred head of cattle, mules and horses."[34] Parker was flattering himself, for Baker's decision was a family matter. His two eldest sons had already traveled to El Dorado in 1852, and George W. "had spent some years in California, and had lived about Stockton, Sonora and Columbia." The Baker brothers returned from California in September 1854, and their father decided to join George on his next trip west to sell a large lot of cattle in California. But the clan's matriarch, Mary Baker, "wouldn't budge. She put her foot down and said: 'Arkansas is plenty good enough for me and Arkansas is where I'm going to stay.'"[35]

A neighbor recalled that Jack Baker started with a large drove of cattle. "The old man intended, as soon as he could settle, to return by water and bring out the remainder of his family." Baker collected 138 well-selected cattle "bought with the view to make quick sales on arriving at California." These "were Texas cattle, a good many of them Texas cattle with long broad horns"—the first longhorns to enter Utah Territory. Baker bought nine yoke of work oxen to haul his large wagon, two mules, and a mare to ride. Baker provided provisions, clothing, and camping gear for the five hands he hired to drive his stock. He had $98 in cash the morning he left home and was armed with a "fine rifle Gun" and a Colt repeater. His wife estimated the outfit was worth at least $4,148 and would bring $10,000 in the West. John H. did not accompany his father but traveled with him the first few days of the trip.[36] Captain Jack impressed the children in his party, for Rebecca Dunlap Evans recalled his long beard and Nancy Huff Cates remembered being held in his arms.[37]

Unlike his mother and brother, George W. Baker sold his Arkansas land and was moving to California with his wife, Manervia A. Beller, and their four children: Mary Lovina, Martha Elizabeth, Sarah Frances, and infant William Twitty. His nineteen-year-old brother, Abel Baker, traveled with him. George Baker had two wagons and some one hundred sixty cattle, including eight yoke of working oxen, two hired hands to drive his stock, and about $400 in cash. He also had charge of his wife's siblings, the orphans Melissa Ann and David W. Beller. As twelve-year-old Melissa Ann Beller's guardian, George Baker went west with $700 of her inheritance in cash or cattle.[38]

Allen P. Deshazo was related to the Bakers by marriage and contributed seventeen "likely heifers" to the train's herd. He carried a violin worth $10; perhaps he joined Alexander Fancher around evening campfires to play fiddle tunes. Twenty-eight-year-old Milum L. Rush added ten to twelve cattle to Jack Baker's trail herd.

Rush was a single man, traveling light, carrying only his clothes, three blankets, a rifle, knives, and about $25 in cash.[39]

The Baker party "was a credit to Carroll County for those times, and in addition to the fine outfit it [was] supposed the train had with them a considerable amount of cash" to buy land in the West.[40] Tradition tells that one of the wagons carried a chest filled with thousands of dollars in gold. The train was trailing as many cattle as they could reasonably manage, so the emigrants may have converted the rest of their assets into hard money. The Arkansas party may not have been "the richest and best equipped train that ever set out across the continent," yet the size and quality of its trail herd reflected its wealth. Some say the Fanchers and Bakers took slaves west in 1857, but California was a free state and no sources mention black members of the Fancher party. The Arkansans may have exchanged such valuable property for gold. At least seven hired hands, probably teenaged cowboys from Texas or Missouri, signed on to work for the Bakers.[41] Ironically, although it is now usually remembered as the Fancher party, most of the emigrants recalled traveling with the Baker party.[42]

The Cameron, Jones, Tackitt, and Miller families from Johnson County made up the third Arkansas company. P. K. Jacoby recalled in 1877 that "several families joined the train at a station in Indian Territory, which was the last point of departure from civilization."[43] Malinda Cameron Scott Thurston remembered leaving Clarksville with her son, Joel, and husband, H. D. Scott, on March 29, 1857, along with Scott's brothers, George and Richard, and his sister, Martha. They met Malinda's relatives in present-day Oklahoma. William and Martha Cameron, both fifty-one, left Arkansas with their sons Tillman, Isom, Henry, James, and Larkin, and their twelve-year-old niece, Nancy Cameron—and considerable wealth. Mrs. Thurston claimed her father hid $3,000 in "a place mortised under the wagon, in the hounds of it." The Camerons had two heavy wagons, a small traveling wagon, twenty-four oxen, some thirty cattle (mostly milk cows), and One-Eyed Blaze, a blooded racing mare valued at $3,000. Thurston's brother rode his fine racehorse "every single day that he lived." There "never was a morning that he did not get on that horse and ride all day, and come in at camp at evening."[44]

Twenty-six-year-old Matilda Cameron Miller was William Cameron's eldest daughter and the wife of Joseph (or Josiah) Miller. The Millers had four children, James William, John Calvin, Mary, and Joseph, who ranged in age from infancy to nine years. They joined the party in the Cherokee Nation to form a company of about four wagons. A young preacher, Pleasant Tackitt (or Tackett), traveled with his twenty-two-year-old wife, Armilda Miller Tackitt, and their two sons, four-year-old Emberson Milum and infant William Henry. Basil Parker recalled the wagon train "held Divine service in one of their large tents." Many witnesses commented on the piety of the emigrants.[45]

John Milum Jones, thirty-two, his wife, Eloah Angeline Tackitt, their son, Felix Marion, and a daughter, and John's brother, Newton, "constituted one company in family groups" that included Eloah's mother. The latter was forty-nine-year-old

Cynthia Tackitt, a widow, whose children, Marion, Sebron, Matilda, James M., and Jones M., ranged in age from twelve to twenty. Sebron Tackitt may have brought his own family along. Felix Jones recalled that his brother Newton had about $30 and a rifle and John was armed with a shotgun. Fielding Wilburn spent two or three days with them on the border of Indian Territory. Four yoke of first-rate work oxen pulled the Jones brothers' "large good ox waggon," which "was very heavily laden with clothing, beds and bedding, Provisions, &c." When the Joneses set out in April 1857, they had some sixty beef cattle. A man named Basham, perhaps George D. Basham, joined this company, which had "a general outfit to make the trip comfortable." Along with another family, probably the Poteets, George W. Baker camped near them.[46]

According to Arkansas's leading newspaper, the *Arkansas State Gazette*, the wagon train that assembled at Beller's Stand in April 1857 was composed of "neighbors, friends and acquaintances, and their families" and was known as Baker's company. It included

> John T. Baker and sons, George and Able, Charles and Joel Mitchell, sons of Col. Wm. C. Mitchell, of Marion county, Allen Derhazo, George Baker's wife and four children, Charles Mitchell's wife and child, Milam Jones and his brother, and his mother-in-law and family, Pleasant Tacket and family, Alexander Fancher and family, Wm. Cameron and family, widow Huff (whose husband, Peter Huff, died after they had started on the route) and some others.[47]

The newspaper boasted that troops could head west from Fort Smith "a month earlier than they can from the Missouri frontier" and on a better road than the one from Missouri.[48] In April 1857 some 250 emigrants broke camp, said their last good-byes, and headed west. Eighty years later one of them recalled, "Nearly a week was taken for the band to gather here. There were more than 200 in the train when it started out, but they split, part going a southern route [via New Mexico] and our division going on through the Utah way."[49]

As the Baker wagons crossed the Ozarks, Peter Huff from Benton County joined with his wife, Saladia Ann Brown, four sons, and four-year-old daughter, Nancy Saphrona. Two young brothers, William and John Prewitt, came from Marion County, as did Lawson A. McIntire. Tradition holds that the Alf Smith family of Newton County, the Lafoon, the Charles H. Morton, the James C. Haydon, and the Thomas Hamilton families made the journey west. John Beach, Tom Farmer, David Hudson, Charles Stallcup, Mordecai Stevenson, Richard Wilson, Solomon R. Wood, William Wood, and Silas Edwards may have been the otherwise forgotten drovers.[50]

THE CHEROKEE TRAIL

Basil Parker assembled his wagon company at Jasper, Arkansas, and fell in with the Carroll County outfits on the trail. His party started out in fine shape. But, he recalled,

"I had to manage everything. I tried to keep from swearing but it was no use as I soon found that those green Arkansas people had no idea of discipline or order." Parker did not mention the Fancher family, but he clearly recalled Jack Baker's company. He rendezvoused with them in the Cherokee Nation and "then travelled leisurely along. Frequently the two trains camped close together and the folks visited back and forth." Malinda Cameron remembered, "We would drive in with trains and stop over night and then in the morning we would separate." The emigrants "had many splendid rifles and guns, and plenty of them," Parker recalled, but he thought Baker's people were very wasteful of their ammunition and "could not resist the temptation of killing considerable" game.[51]

The Baker train followed the Cherokee Trail, a route named after the native gold seekers that opened it in 1849. It joined the Santa Fe Trail near present McPherson, Kansas, and followed its mountain branch up the Arkansas River to Bent's Fort and El Pueblo, where the trail turned north along the Front Range of the Rockies. The Cherokee route and its variants crossed the continental divide south of the main Oregon-California Trail, along the line of present-day Interstate 80, to join the main trail near Fort Bridger.[52]

Thomas J. Litton of Pope County was among the Arkansans driving cattle west. Just a few days behind the other herds, on June 18, 1857, Litton saw one hundred thousand buffalo in sight of the road. His cattle stampeded one night "in as hard a storm of rain as you ever saw." By morning his party had lost 150 of their 625 cows, but the drovers recovered all but two. Litton hoped to get through to California "with six hundred head and but little behind the rest."[53]

Basil Parker also recalled meeting "immense bands of buffalo." "Sometimes," he said, "the bands were so large that we had to let the train stand for hours while they passed." On the Arkansas River, "what looked to be fully five hundred indian men formed a line in front of [his] cattle." The warriors demanded cattle as payment for the grass they ate. Parker dashed up to an Indian who was preparing to shoot a calf. He recalled, "I leveled my pistol at him and yelled for him to 'vamos' or I would kill him." The Indians drew off, and he later boasted, "I never got away with a bluff so easy."[54]

Conditions on the trail were tough in spring 1857. For more than two years the Cheyenne Nation had waged war with the United States, posing a real threat to overlanders. Its warriors intercepted an army cattle herd in June, perhaps with the encouragement of eastbound Mormons who had met a party of some sixty Cheyennes on the trail.[55] The Baker party was warned that Indians were on the prowl. Not long before reaching Fort Bridger, the company was attacked at night and taken by surprise. Indian raiders stampeded "the 900 head of loose stock," and the emigrants drew straws to decide who would track down the lost animals. P. K. Jacoby joined the pursuit "under command of a noted plainsman and bullwhacker from Missouri." They tracked the cattle for three or four days, captured a lone Indian, and demanded he take them to the cattle or they would kill him. After some argument, the prisoner led the

men to the marauders' camp, which the emigrants attacked at nightfall, yelling and firing their guns. The Indians scattered and the emigrants recaptured all but sixteen of
their cattle. "To partially compensate for the trouble," they looted the Indian tents.
After his horses were run off, Parker recalled that he "took the indian chief a prisoner
and held him until the horses were brought back."[56]

Years later John S. Baker described his troubled trip across the plains in 1857.
Although not related to John T. Baker, his party started out on the same route as the
Fancher and Baker trains. They tried to overtake their fellow Arkansans. On the
Kansas River Cheyenne warriors killed four of their men, wounded a man and a
woman, and seized their property. Enduring "on the air and water," the survivors
walked to Fort Riley, near present Junction City, where they gave up and returned
to Arkansas.[57]

A scrap of news suggests how the emigrants crossed present-day Wyoming. In 1856
mountain man Tim Goodale told Texas Mormons under Preston Thomas "they would
not find grass or water on the old Arkansas trail from the [North] Platte to Green
River." Thomas headed north to join the main Oregon-California Trail on the Sweet-
water River. Similar conditions the next year may have turned some of the emigrants
away from the Cherokee Trail and over South Pass.[58]

The emigrants "travelled along in the most orderly fashion, without hurry or confusion. On Sunday they rested, and one of their number who had been a Methodist
preacher conducted divine services."[59] Near Fort Bridger, a "venomous creature," perhaps a tarantula or a black widow spider, bit Peter Huff on the hand as he slept. The
train halted, waiting for Huff to recover, but he died and was buried on the trail. His
widow, Saladia Ann, and her sons decided to press on to California.[60]

McLean and His Friends Will Kill Me

As the Fancher and Baker parties trekked west, they may have heard that an
aggrieved husband had killed Parley Pratt, one of the original apostles of the LDS
church, in western Arkansas some two weeks after they left the state. Hector McLean,
outraged at Pratt's appropriation of his wife, had tracked the apostle up and down the
Mississippi Valley and brutally murdered him on the Arkansas border near Fort Smith.
No one in the Fancher or Baker parties had anything to do with the affair, but it
would forever be linked to their fate.

At summer's end in 1856, Pratt had left Utah with his new wife, the former Eleanor
McLean, on a mission to the eastern states. Eleanor was determined to reclaim her
children, who were living in her parents' mansion in New Orleans. The Pratts crossed
the plains with a party of twenty elders and twelve women, traveling in a carriage
with another couple. When they reached Missouri, where Pratt was still under indictment for murder, Eleanor set off alone with $100 in borrowed church funds. Before
parting, Pratt made out his will and wrote instructions for his burial.[61]

In New Orleans Eleanor told her parents "she had been to Utah and had been a teacher there, had *boarded* at Gov. Brigham Young's, only *boarded*, had seen much suffering due to famine, and had seen also the error of her ways. Said she had been mad." She still believed the Mormons were good people and that Young and his associates were true prophets, but she won the confidence of her parents. One Saturday morning she spirited her children away and took them to Texas, hoping to rendezvous with Pratt. She worked in Houston as a seamstress and on March 4, 1857, left the city with Elder James Gemmel to join a Utah-bound wagon train assembling in Ellis County.[62]

Pratt headed east after spending a month incognito in St. Louis. He wrote to his brother Orson from New York that he intended to return to Utah in the spring, even if he had to go with a handcart: "This country is no place for me; the darkness is so thick I can literally feel it."[63]

Eleanor Pratt's brother had notified Hector McLean of her escape with their children. McLean pursued Pratt up the Mississippi and Ohio Rivers, but Pratt repeatedly escaped him. By early March Apostles George A. Smith, Erastus Snow, and Parley Pratt met in St. Louis as McLean closed in. A former Saint warned Smith that McLean "was in St Louis and seeking Elder Pratts life; that the city Police had orders for his arrest and a general search would be made for him the following night." She said many apostates were in league with McLean. Even Pratt had felt the approach of danger and kept himself hidden. Snow smuggled him in disguise to Bellefontaine Cemetery and at daybreak the next morning sent Andrew Sproul to him with a satchel of clothes and $100 in expense money. Pratt and Sproul left the city by a circuitous route westward, avoiding the roads. Pratt sent word to his friends not to worry if they did not hear from him for a year. In the meantime McLean, assisted by the police and former Mormons, "continued searching the Houses of the Saints and all places frequented by [them] in the city and adjacent country but without finding the object of their search."[64]

McLean learned his wife was in Houston using the name Lucy R. Parker and set off in pursuit. In Texas he intercepted a letter Pratt had sent to Eleanor, instructing her to "fly instantly" northward and rendezvous with him on the Arkansas River. "My carriage shall await you there if the Lord will," he promised.[65]

Armed with Pratt's instructions, McLean headed for Indian Territory. In April and May 1857 McLean said he scoured the country with "a dozen of my Masonic friends, who had gathered from all parts of the territory to aid me should the government not take any notice of my grievances."[66] After a long pursuit, McLean caught his wife in the Creek Nation and had her arrested. Eleanor said he threw her on the ground and seized the children. "After their shrieks had died away," a man claiming to be a marshal charged her, along with Pratt and Elias Gammell, with stealing clothing belonging to Albert and Annie McLean worth $10.[67]

Using the alias Parker, Parley Pratt was searching for his wife when he was captured by the federal marshal and troops pursuing him. After he was arrested and learned

Hector McLean had orchestrated his capture, Pratt "fairly wilted." He received "pretty sorrowful greetings" from Eleanor, who feared for his life.[68] U.S. Marshal Shivers had to stop McLean from killing Pratt immediately, and the officers told Pratt he was arrested for "fleeing justice and various other charges" that he would soon hear. As the apostle and his companion, George Higginson, marched in chains to Fort Smith, the prisoner's appearance impressed his captors. "Don't he look like a mighty man," observed one, and another said, "Come and see him, *he looks like a great lion.*" In Van Buren, Arkansas, Pratt was charged in U.S. circuit court with stealing the McLean children's clothes.[69]

The night before his hearing, Pratt told Higginson, "McLean and his friends will kill me." He made a sacred request to Higginson to let his family know he was perfectly reconciled to his fate. His way was hedged up on every hand, and he asked Higginson "to wait in Van Buren and see what became of him, and if he was murdered to make a full report to President Brigham Young of the true circumstances of his death and trial."[70]

The next morning before a packed courtroom, McLean related "the burden of [his] soul's anguish." Some five hundred spectators listened to him implicate the scoundrel apostle, producing intense excitement. Twice McLean thought the crowd would tear Pratt to pieces, but even he admitted he did not have sufficient evidence to convict his wife and her lover.[71]

Fearing the mob would lynch his prisoner, the magistrate postponed the case twice. The next morning he had Pratt's horse brought to the jail and quietly released him. McLean's friends reported Pratt's escape, and with two companions McLean tracked the unarmed man.[72] On the western border of Arkansas, McLean shot and stabbed his rival from horseback and left him for dead. During the two and a half hours it took Pratt to bleed to death, a farmer asked him why McLean had attacked him. "He accused me of taking his wife and children," said the dying man. "I did not do it. They were oppressed, and I did for them what I would do for the oppressed any where." Before help could arrive, Apostle Parley P. Pratt, a prophet, seer, and revelator of the Church of Jesus Christ of Latter-day Saints, was dead.[73]

McLean and his accomplices returned to Van Buren and "made the rounds of all the saloons, boasting of their brave deed." The killer stayed in town for several hours, Higginson reported, walking the streets with impunity. Citizens of Van Buren escorted McLean to the landing, and he "took his leave of the place." McLean was never arrested, let alone tried, for his crime. The Mormon press rebuked the *Fort Smith Herald* for rejoicing over the death of a human being, quoting the paper's boast that there was one Mormon less and its call "that the lives of *all* such men as Pratt should at *once* be put to an end."[74]

The next day Eleanor Pratt, now the widow of a martyr, relayed the painful news in a moving letter to Apostle Snow.

[I have been] to see the dead body of my beloved Parley. I saw his wounds—saw his blood dripping from his heart making a puddle on the floor and spattering a vessel put to catch it. Saw his coat full of holes where the balls passed through, and two rents made by the knife which gave him the death wound on his left breast.[75]

Eleanor visited the spot where Pratt died "and where he bore his dying testimony while his precious blood was dripping on the ground." Standing where her first husband had murdered her second, the widow Pratt prayed silently, "Oh! God of Israel let the blood of beloved Parley come up before thee. Let it plead the cause of the innocent, and condemn the guilty!!" She shrouded the dead apostle in "a very fine piece of linen beautifully white." When they got through, "he looked very well." The bereaved woman cried, "Parley thou are not dead but sleeping. And thy innocent blood and thy wounds are before the God of Israel, to plead for the innocent, and call forth vengeance on the guilty." Lost and penniless, the widow Pratt began her own troubled journey to Utah Territory.[76]

"I am now alone on my way and know not whither," Eleanor McLean Pratt wrote as she descended the Arkansas River. She visited New Orleans and made one last attempt to reclaim her children. Again disappointed, she headed to St. Louis. On June 16, 1857, she wrote to congratulate her mother for recapturing her children and "the shedding of innocent blood." Now "destitute and alone, and hunted down from place to place & from door to door by [her] bloodthirsty pursuers," she asked her mother to ship her trunk to Florence, Nebraska. "But if it adds to your happiness to think of me destitute," she wrote, "you can retain it."[77] The narrative of her ordeal ended abruptly, without a word of her swift and adventurous passage west across the plains to Utah.

THE ASSASSINATION OF OUR BELOVED P. P. PRATT

Word of Parley Pratt's death spread quickly. On July 1 the *Deseret News* reported his assassination. The news of the martyrdom of their most beloved apostle devastated the Saints and aroused sentiments of anger and grief. When Philip Margetts reached the Missouri River with a party of eastbound handcart missionaries in June 1857, his companions "felt like young lions and almost as savage in consequence of hearing of the assassination of our beloved P. P. Pratt."[78] The *Western Standard*, the Mormon voice in California, published the melancholy and heart-sickening news of Pratt's murder on July 3. The paper predicted that this diabolical transaction would "be the signal for a general jubilee throughout California" among all those who hated the servants of God, as it had been in the East. It mourned Pratt as a martyr for the cause of truth and predicted God would come out of his hiding place: "Upon this generation shall come all the righteous blood which has been shed from the time of Jesus to the present."[79]

Hector McLean wrote a boastful account of the murder, calling it "the best act of my life." "And the people of West Arkansas agree with me," he added. San Francisco's *Alta California* asked "whether the hot blood which must now be seething and boiling in the veins of Brigham Young and his satellites, at Salt Lake, is to be cooled by the murder of Gentiles who pass through their territory." In the wake of Pratt's murder the *Alta California* could not say "whether the 'destroying angels' of Mormondom, are to be brought into requisition to make reprisals upon travelers, or, whether, as has been done before, 'Saints' disguised as Indians are to constitute themselves the supposed ministers of God's vengeance in this case. . . . [N]o doubt that such thoughts, such intentions as these, are prevalent among those saintly villains, adulterers and seducers, of Salt Lake."[80] It was a lurid but remarkably accurate prophecy.

5

I Will Fight Them and
I Will Fight All Hell

The year 1857 opened with both auspicious and threatening omens for Mormon leaders in their Rocky Mountain stronghold. They felt the Latter-day Saints had patiently
endured the insults of the federal government, the abuses of its corrupt officials, and
the outrageous conduct of its troops under a territorial government that denied them
their constitutional right to govern themselves. If Congress again refused to make
Deseret a state, it was their duty as Americans to throw off the bonds of tyranny and
establish a government of their own. To Brigham Young this was inevitable, for Babylon, the America he had left behind, was doomed.

From his first days as president in March 1857, James Buchanan faced mounting
pressure to deal with the collapse of federal authority in Utah. As his few statements
on Utah made clear, the obligations of his office compelled him to send troops there.
None of the grandiose conspiracy theories devised to explain the Utah War provide
a credible explanation of the president's actions, but politics inevitably played a part.
The Republican Party's assault on polygamy had made the presidential election of 1856
a disaster for LDS interests. The Mormons had hitched their political fortunes to Sen.
Stephen A. Douglas's doctrine of popular sovereignty, a policy hated in the North for
its implicit endorsement of the extension of slavery. Buchanan, a Northerner with
Southern sympathies, hoped the Supreme Court would diffuse the rising crisis over
Kansas and slavery. The court's Dred Scott decision proved this was a vain hope, for
in ruling that slaves were property, the court opened the territories to slavery. As the
president cast about for "other questions of absorbing interest" to distract the country,
Utah caught his attention.[1]

The Mormons presented the president with a thorny problem, but at least one
of Buchanan's advisers felt the recalcitrant territory offered an opportunity to divert
public attention from the more troublesome dilemma of slavery. Robert Tyler, son of

U.S. Territories, 1857

a former president, believed there was a growing feeling that Mormonism "should be put down and utterly extirpated." He advised Buchanan to "*supersede the Negro-Mania with the almost universal excitements of an Anti-Mormon Crusade.*" "[The country will] rally to you with an earnest enthusiasm and the pipings of Abolitionism will hardly be heard amidst the thunders of the storm we shall raise," he said.[2]

Whatever appeal such calculations had for the crafty politician in the White House, when he explained his actions to Congress, he presented a simple but compelling case. Brigham Young had for years "been industriously employed in collecting and fabricating arms and munitions of war." Indians reported that Superintendent of Indian Affairs Young was tampering with the tribes "and exciting their hostile feelings against the United States." All the federal officers of the United States except two Indian agents had fled the territory. The president believed "there no longer remain[ed] any government in Utah but the despotism of Brigham Young." However deplorable the religious beliefs of the Mormons might be, Buchanan claimed no authority to interfere with them, but with the territory in open defiance of federal law and the constitution, he said he could "not mistake the path of duty." The Mormons had forced him to act. Tyler's suggestion that the "eyes and hearts of the nation must be made to find so much interest in Utah as to forget Kansas" offered an apparent escape from the new president's political maze. Yet Mormondom's brazen defiance of Washington meant that even Buchanan, a master of accommodation, was obliged to assert federal authority.[3]

Politics and duty characterized James Buchanan's Utah policy, but Brigham Young's defiance of the federal government appeared simply irrational. His conduct only makes sense, Mormon historian Richard D. Poll noted, "if one is willing to credit him with actually believing what he said many times during the long crisis." Young's much-heralded pragmatism was merely tactical, but his "religious convictions shaped his Utah War strategy as they shaped his life."[4]

A host of portents convinced the Mormon prophet and his apostles that the Second Coming was imminent. The "still small voice" of his vision of Joseph Smith assured Young that if the Latter-day Saints were righteous and brought about the conditions the martyred prophet had outlined for the Savior's return, God would usher in the millennium. The Indians were now prepared to play their crucial role in the Last Days. "The door has already been unlocked to the Lamanites in these mountains," Apostle Wilford Woodruff announced from the pulpit. "They will begin to embrace the gospel and the records of their fathers, and their chiefs will be filled with the spirit of God, and they will rise up in their strength and a nation will be born in a day."[5]

Brigham Young's pragmatism persuaded him to keep his options open, always maintaining a contingency plan in case his prophetic powers failed him. So it was that he punctuated his most violent rhetoric and bellicose threats with conditional *ifs*—at least when they appeared in print. As 1857 began he devoted scarce resources to gathering the Saints to Zion and redeeming the Lamanites while planning a trip to the north to find a possible escape route lest he should have misread the Lord's intentions. At the same time he reorganized and rearmed his military forces and pursued a provocative course apparently calculated to call down the wrath of the federal government on the Mormons. God, Brigham Young believed, would inspire the Saints to prevail over the most powerful military force the United States could send against them.

A CONTEST FOR THE SUPREMACY OF OUR LAWS: UTAH IN 1857

Amid the fires of the Reformation, mysterious crimes terrorized Utah Territory in what appeared to be a war against traitors and federal officers. In February 1857 apostate John Tobin, a would-be paramour of Brigham Young's daughter Alice, barely survived an ambush in Santa Clara Canyon. Garland Hurt implicated Brigham Young, Jr., in the attack, but Isaac Haight blamed it on "Mapaches," although Apaches were seldom seen north of the Colorado River.[6] The next month Gardner "Duff" Potter, brother of the Mormon guide killed in the Gunnison massacre, lured three apostates into a bloody ambush in Springville. Potter was caught in the crossfire that also killed William and Beeson Parrish. Orrin Parrish escaped to press charges later, but no indictments were filed in the Parrish-Potter murders.[7]

After he arrived in Utah in 1855, one of the critical conflicts between the Mormons and the federal government ensnared territorial surveyor general David H. Burr. Brigham Young had already appointed county surveyors to assign "inheritances" to loyal Saints, but these grants had no standing in American courts. "Not an individual in all Utah now holds a foot of land the title of which is derived from the United States," noted the *Washington Union* in June 1857, and "all parts of the Territory are at the present time open to pre-emption." LDS church leaders feared the government would evict them from their mountain Zion. Burr, a distinguished cartographer, attorney, and former Geographer to the United States, charged that local officials conducted a campaign of harassment against him and his men. Remembering the fate of another federal surveyor, John Gunnison, Burr and his employees began to fear for their lives, while the Mormons believed his surveys were insubstantial if not downright fraudulent. A mob stoned the house Burr had used at Fillmore in central Utah, and he complained that Danites had beaten his associate, Joseph Troskolawski, almost to death.[8]

Federal judge George P. Stiles was excommunicated for adultery on December 22, 1856. Mormon attorney James Ferguson threatened Stiles with violence in open court, and when he appealed to the governor for protection, Young advised him to close his court if he could not enforce the law. Events came to a head on December 29, 1856, when a mob seized the judge's law library and papers, dumped them into an outhouse, and set it on fire. Stiles believed that in its rage the mob had destroyed the court's official documents, which were federal property.[9]

The conflict between federal officers and Mormon power flared again in Judge Stiles's courtroom at a February 1857 hearing on the jurisdiction of the locally controlled probate courts. Mormon attorneys charged that Stiles was so biased that "the people were not willing to risk a case before him." They asked for a change of venue, claiming that only probate courts could try cases falling under the laws of the territory. Stiles agreed with them, but when David Burr challenged the ruling, havoc followed. Burr was "a cowardly cur who wished to attac[k] our laws clandestinely but had not courage to do it openly," charged James Ferguson, who wanted Burr's name struck from the bar "as a man too mean and inco[m]petent to plead law." Several Mormons took off their coats to do battle; two non-Mormons left the courtroom to avoid the impending fight. "This," wrote Hosea Stout, "was a contest for the supremacy of our laws."[10]

Mormon leaders laughed at the federal officials' fear for their safety, but by spring 1857 the officials were convinced their lives were in jeopardy. On April 15, 1857, before the snow had begun to melt on the mountains, Stiles, Burr, and U.S. Marshal Peter

K. Dotson—every remaining non-LDS federal officer in Utah except Garland Hurt—left the territory, "happy in having escaped with life."[11]

As his colleagues fled Utah, disgruntled judge William W. Drummond blasted off a bitter indictment of the LDS church, charging the "blind and treasonable" organization with disloyalty to the United States and violence against federal officials, including the murders of John Gunnison and Judge Leonidas Shaver. "It is noonday madness and folly to attempt to administer the law in that Territory," Drummond complained. In a provocative letter-writing campaign to the newspapers, he argued that only federal troops could restore order in the territory.[12]

If Brigham Young did not intentionally provoke a war with the United States, by early 1857 he was busily preparing for it. In September 1856 his Indian missionaries at Las Vegas began hauling sixty tons of lead ore north to Salt Lake. (The failure to separate silver from the lead fostered the legend that Mormons used silver bullets.)[13] In March 1857 the Saints began manufacturing pistols, and within a year they were producing twenty imitation Colt revolvers every week, along with gunpowder "in abundance."[14] In April Young called on the Saints to build storehouses to preserve enough grain to last seven years.[15] Apostle Charles C. Rich arrived in Salt Lake from San Bernardino on June 6, and Brigham Young's nephew told emigrant John Hillhouse that Rich had brought a wagonload of ammunition. Others said William Mathews had freighted the gunpowder to Salt Lake to carry on a "war with Uncle Sam."[16]

The Utah legislature voted on January 14, 1857, to reorganize the Nauvoo Legion, the territorial militia, as an independent military organization. At the church's April conference, Gen. Daniel H. Wells was made Young's second counselor and confirmed as a prophet, seer, and revelator. As the legion's commanding officer, Wells soon announced new regulations for the militia. "Our past experience with the natives of the soil has taught us the necessity of being always ready," he cautioned as he worked to perfect the reconstituted military force. Wells assigned Iron, Beaver, and Washington Counties to the Iron County Brigade, putting all the military forces in southern Utah "under the supervision of Wm. H. Dame."[17]

A Pleasure Ride: Brigham Young Visits Fort Limhi

As Wells prepared Utah for war, Brigham Young began to evaluate his options. In November 1856 he had sent Benjamin Cummings north from Fort Limhi into the Bitterroot Valley to deliver a bid to purchase Fort Hall from the Hudson's Bay Company.[18] Cummings carefully mapped the route and reported that the area held great promise. Mission president Thomas Smith carried Cummings's report of this "future abode of the saints" to Young. By February 22, 1857, Young had resolved to visit his northernmost outpost, the Limhi settlement on the Salmon River. He announced in April, "A few of us contemplate going north this spring [to] take a pleasure ride, see the country, enjoy ourselves and recruit our health." Young wanted to make contact with the northern tribes and investigate the possibilities of the Beaverhead country. He invited 114 powerful men, 22 women, and 5 boys to join him. Arapeen, now head chief of the Utes, accompanied the expedition, which left Great Salt Lake City on April 24. This was not a casual jaunt. For men like Col. William Dame and Lt. Col. Isaac Haight from southern Utah, the round trip was more than twelve hundred miles.[19]

This venture aroused the suspicions of Indian agent Hurt. Brigham Young, Hurt feared, intended to give most of the money appropriated for the Utah tribes to bands living outside the Utah Superintendency's jurisdiction and throw the financial burden on Hurt. He surmised that Young planned to use government funds to buy the allegiance of the Indians to the north. He notified his supervisors that Young was off on an "exploring expedition through the Territories of Oregon, Washington, and perhaps British America."[20]

Beyond building Indian alliances, Young evaluated the north country as a possible escape route should his looming confrontation with the United States fail to go as planned. What the Mormon leaders found when they finally reached Limhi and the Beaverhead Mountains must have exceeded their expectations. Samuel Pitchforth observed there was only room for one man to pass at a time through the narrow gateway to the trail Lewis and Clark had used to cross the continental divide. The route appeared to provide "a divinely planned corridor of escape from the U.S. Army, a covered route through the mountains to the fertile lands beyond." Should the Saints need to flee from Utah, this remote and rugged country offered a perfect refuge.[21]

The Mormon leaders organized the two dozen men at Fort Limhi into a militia company under Col. Thomas S. Smith. Young addressed the settlers and met with head chief Snagg and other Indians. In company with Arapeen, Young and the Bannocks had "a smoke and a long and very friendly talk." The next day the Mormons distributed presents among the bands camped around the fort.[22]

"Brother Brigham and the twelve Spoke to us and told us that We had to marry Squaws," wrote Limhi missionary Abraham Zundel. According to Lewis Shurtliff, Heber Kimball spoke to the group about Mormon doctrine concerning marriage to Indian women. The authorities encouraged the men to take Indian wives to enhance the Mormon alliance with the Lamanites and reduce the vulnerability of the remote outpost.[23] At least three of the missionaries obliged.

The visitors "seemed impressed with a sense of coming trouble," noted one missionary. Young warned the settlers they were too far from Salt Lake to expect aid in a sudden crisis and criticized the site of their stockade. The missionaries should have chosen "a broad open country, such as the Flathead country further north," instead of Limhi, which was situated in a mountain gorge. The existing fort "stood under the hills from which hostile Indians could easily fire on the inmates." Young advised the settlers to build a blockhouse on a knoll to the east of the fort and put up strong bastions.[24]

When Young returned to Salt Lake, he did not praise what he had seen, but Heber Kimball said, "Were we to go a great way beyond where we were, it would not be an easy job to touch us."[25] At the same meeting in the tabernacle, George A. Smith reported on his unsuccessful mission to Washington to win statehood for Deseret. The hefty apostle covered the implications of his failure with humor, joking that his travels had reduced him to a mere 237 pounds, "the poor, 'lean,' meagre man you see before you." He said, "[Washington believes] we are a very desperate set of fellows out here. Politicians are a little vexed, for they do not know what to do with us." Smith did not repeat the rumor he had reported to John W. Young twelve days earlier on the overland trail—"that a new Governor would be sent to the Territory accompanied by two or three thousand soldiers."[26]

This Kingdom Must Be Free and Independent

President Buchanan meanwhile had taken dramatic action to correct the state of affairs in Utah Territory. As early as May 8, 1857, the New York newspapers reported that the president had decided to send an army to Utah, and on May 24 the *Illinois State Journal* wrote that two thousand troops were on their way. These reports were premature, but Buchanan had made up his mind by May 20. He acted without making even a minimal inquiry and failed to notify anyone in Utah, including Brigham Young, that the army and a new governor were bound for the territory.[27]

Buchanan launched a search for a replacement for Young. After the leading candidates declined an office widely regarded as a political grave, Buchanan settled on Alfred Cumming, a Georgian who was said to be a gentleman of education, ambition, and executive ability. Cumming came with the endorsement of the Mormons' key ally, Thomas L. Kane, and was finally given the job on July 13, 1857.[28]

A rising outcry in the nation's newspapers supported Buchanan's move to put down the rebellious territory. Even such allies as Stephen Douglas turned against the Mormons. The senator reviewed charges that they were forming alliances with the western tribes and "stimulating the Indians to acts of hostility" while organizing "Destroying Angels" to "prosecute a system of robbery and murder upon American citizens." Should this be true, Douglas said, Congress must "apply the knife and cut out this loathsome, disgusting ulcer" by blotting the territorial government out of existence.[29]

"Orders having been dispatched in haste," Gen. Winfield Scott directed his officers on May 28 to collect "a body of troops at Fort Leavenworth, to march thence to Utah as soon as assembled." The army was to serve as a *posse comitatus* to "insure the establishment and maintenance of law and order." Despite the lateness of the season and his own reservations, Scott ordered Col. William S. Harney to assemble a force of twenty-five hundred men from army units scattered from Florida to Minnesota.[30]

The ragtag but determined Utah militia would soon face the most imposing force on the North American continent—the U.S. Army. Word of the government's determination to subdue Utah spread quickly across the frontier. On the present Wyoming-Idaho border, trader Frederick Burr heard by June 24, 1857, that troops were marching to Salt Lake. At the end of the month, Governor Young wrote to Thomas Kane about the prospects of armed intervention in Utah.[31] He made few public references to the rumors, perhaps waiting for the ideal time to announce the army's approach. He arranged a gala Pioneer Day "Pic-Nic Party" at the head of a rugged mountain canyon to celebrate the tenth anniversary of his arrival in Salt Lake Valley on July 24, 1847. Young could not have picked a more dramatic scene than the headwaters of Big Cottonwood Creek to reveal the news.

The Blood of Parley

As hundreds of wagons wound up the canyon road on the evening of July 23, a light buckboard thundered into Great Salt Lake City. It carried Bishop A. O. Smoot, Judson Stoddard, O. P. Rockwell, and Eleanor McLean Pratt. The men brought confirmation of momentous news: the government had canceled the territory's mail contract and a new governor, judges, and twenty-five hundred soldiers would soon start for Utah. Smoot and Stoddard had made the trip from Ft. Leavenworth in a mere twenty days. Rockwell's express had rushed the widow Pratt from Fort Laramie to Salt Lake in an incredible five days and three hours, perhaps passing the Fancher and Baker parties on the trail.[32]

The messengers left Salt Lake the next morning at 4:45 for Big Cottonwood Canyon. At noon they rode into the vast camp of twenty-five hundred selected Saints assembled to celebrate Pioneer Day. A bugle summoned the crowd at sunset, and their leaders addressed them from an eminence at the center of the campground. Their exact remarks do not survive, but according to the *Deseret News*, a "scene of the maddest confusion" followed. Young told the crowd "they constituted henceforth a free and independent state, to be known no longer as Utah, but by their own Mormon name of Deseret." Kimball "called on the people to adhere to Brigham, as their prophet, seer, and revelator, priest, governor, and king."[33]

Brigham Young often recalled that on reaching the Salt Lake Valley on July 24, 1847, he had said, "If the people of the United States will let us alone for ten years, we will ask no odds of them." He did not think about it again until ten years later, when he learned that Buchanan was sending troops to Utah. Now he predicted that the army would be followed by "priests, politicians, speculators, whoremongers, and every mean, filthy character that could be raked up [to] kill off the 'Mormons.'" The prophet's patience was at an end: "We have borne enough of their oppression and hellish abuse, and we will not bear any more of it. . . . In the name of Israel's God, we ask no odds of them."[34]

By Sunday, July 26, the Mormon leaders were preaching in Salt Lake. Kimball caught the defiant mood of the people: "Send 2,500 troops here, our brethren, to make a desolation of this people! God Almighty helping me, I will fight until there is not a drop of blood in my veins. Good God! I have wives enough to whip out the

United States; for they will whip themselves."[35] Along with his fellow apostles, Wilford Woodruff attended a prayer meeting in the evening at Young's "Upper Room": "Presidet Young expressed his feelings in plainness Concerning our Enemies." The meeting was apparently restricted to males, but they read Eleanor Pratt's impassioned letter describing her husband's murder and discussed their future plans. In his journal Brigham Young wrote, "*We prayed for our enemies.*"[36]

Woodruff "got an account of the death and burial of Elder P. P. Pratt" from Pratt's widow on August 1.[37] The long narrative expressed her bitterness against Arkansas and her certainty that Parley Pratt's innocent blood must be avenged. A lawyer in Van Buren had asked her "whether the Mormons would not avenge this man's blood, even if the Court did nothing." She assured him, "If the murderers can feel secure in any nation under heaven or upon any island of the sea they are welcome to feel so. One thing I know *McLean has to die and go to hell* for what he has done, and every man who assisted him in this deed."[38]

Decent men in Arkansas exceedingly regretted "the disgraceful affair that had transpired in their midst." The marshal in Van Buren told her that although many felt McLean had been deeply wronged, most were against those who "aided in bringing this man's blood upon our soil."

"Ah! yes Sir and it is innocent blood," answered the grieving woman. "You might have killed a million men in this state and perhaps not not [*sic*] have shed one drop of innocent blood. Tis the innocence of this man, that will give power to the cry of his blood, when it comes before the God of Israel. And t'was better for the state of Arkansas ~~and the United States~~ to have suffered seven years famine, than to have the blood of this man upon her soil!"[39]

Mormon leaders in Salt Lake barely mentioned Pratt's death over the next month, but Eleanor McLean had imagined the reaction of "Elohiem *Himself*" to her husband's murder:

> The blood of Parley shall not long before me plead,
> For wrath on him who did the fearful deed;
> And e'er it cease to cry, that nation *shall atone*
> For every widow's tear, and every orphan's moan.
> And every guiltless blood they ever shed
> Shall quickly come upon their own devoted head.[40]

THE LORD WILL FIGHT OUR BATTLES

As July passed into August, Brigham Young devised a defensive war strategy. He exploited the government's failure to notify him of his replacement or its reasons for sending an army to Utah by denouncing the approaching troops as a mob sent to "invade" the territory. The rush of events had convinced the Mormon prophet that the end of time was near: "The taking away of the Mail and sending forth of an

Army are strong evidence to us that the Lord is hastening His work, and that the redemption of Zion draweth nigh. May we be prepared when the time comes, and success crown all our efforts."[41] The cornerstone of his plan was to rally Utah's Indians to the Mormon cause. The orders, letters, and declarations of Brigham Young and officers of the Nauvoo Legion reveal how they sought to win the confidence of the Indians: "they must learn that they have either got to help us or the United States will kill us both." This message was repeated like a mantra by interpreter Dimick Huntington in his conversations with Goshutes and Shoshonis during August. Huntington's dramatic journal reveals how the Saints implemented their war policy in the north. In southern Utah, the zealous John M. Higbee later recalled, "every means in right and reason was used to secure the Friendship of the surrounding Tribes of Indians, so they could be used as allies should the Necessity come to do so."[42]

In a sermon on August 2, Brigham Young shared his belief that the Second Coming was fast approaching, if not already under way: "Sometimes my heart quakes a little, my nerves tremble in consequence of the great things that God is bringing forth. Do we realize that they are coming on us, I may say, faster than we are preparing ourselves to meet them? There is one sign after another, revelation after revelation. The Lord is hastening his work. He is bringing to pass the sayings of the Prophets faster than the people are prepared to receive them." Young warned, "The time must come when this kingdom must be free and independent from all other kingdoms," and asked, "Are you prepared to have the thread cut to-day?" A roar of support answered the question, but Young did not publicly cut the thread. He still made his rebellious declarations conditional when he spoke to audiences that included non-Mormons. "I shall take it as a witness that God designs to cut the thread between us and the world, when an army undertakes to make their appearance in this Territory to chastise me or to destroy my life," he said. Young counseled patience: "We will wait a little while to see; but I shall take a hostile movement by our enemies as an evidence that it is time for the thread to be cut." He promised, "I ask no odds of the wicked."[43]

Young's religious convictions left him little doubt the Saints would triumph if his followers met the challenge. "If the brethren will have faith, the Lord will fight our battles," he proclaimed. "Every man is like a troop; they are like lions." One righteous Mormon soldier would "chase a thousand, and two [would] put ten thousand to flight." The U.S. Army was as rotten as an old pumpkin and was marching to its own destruction. "We could go out and use them up, and it would not require fifty men to do it," the prophet boasted. "We have no desire to kill men, but we wish to keep the devils from killing us." He promised that if the Saints were faithful, "Our enemies could never cross the Rocky Mountains." Young challenged the government, "Come on with your thousands of illegally-ordered troops, and I will promise you, in the name of Israel's God, that you shall melt away as the snow before a July sun."[44]

Young began to consolidate the Saints' strategic position. On August 4 he directed George Q. Cannon in California to let as many Mormons as possible come through to the valley in the fall. He wrote to Nauvoo Legion colonel N. V. Jones, leader of the Mormon outpost at Deer Creek (present-day central Wyoming), asking, "Where is Col. Sumner, and where are the Cheyennes, and what success does he have against them? Have any of the boys learned their language? If not, lose no time but let some of them [set] about it immediately that we may have a free communication with them, also the Sioux and other nations." Young reported a bountiful harvest to his business agents in the East: "The Spirit of peace has never been more abundant in our midst, and we are determined to enjoy it if we have to fight for it." Asking if soldiers would be permitted to enter the Salt Lake Valley, the prophet gave an emphatic answer: *"No! they will not!!!"*[45]

In mid-August Young ordered Mormons in Carson Valley to sell their property and return home to Zion. "Secure as much ammunition as you can," he told them. "Be wise, and not let the right hand know what the left hand doeth." Even as Young sought to enlist the tribes in his cause, he distrusted them, warning the refugees to be "prepared to defend [themselves] against all . . . foes, both white and red."[46]

FULL OF HOSTILITY AND VIRULENCE: GEORGE A. SMITH TOURS THE SOUTH

To prepare for his mission to alert the settlements of southern Utah to the coming confrontation, Apostle George A. Smith was rebaptized on August 2, 1857. That Sunday afternoon he exhorted the faithful in the Bowery in a "rather strong" sermon. Twenty-five hundred men, he warned, were not enough to keep the peace in Indian country. The government's new officials came "to interfere with the rights of the people of this Territory, with fifteen hundred or two thousand bayonets to back them up." He protested, "Every man that had anything to do with such a filthy, unconstitutional affair was a damned scoundrel." There was not a man among them, "from the President of the United States to the Editors of their sanctorums, clear down to the low-bred letter-writers in this Territory, but would rob the coppers from a dead nigger's eyes." If he commanded thunder and lightning, Smith would not let one of the scoundrels reach Utah alive. The federal authorities intended to murder every man who stood up for Mormonism, but their evil plans, he said, "would fall upon their own heads, and . . . grind them to powder."[47]

At dawn Smith set out for southern Utah on the day a "company of emigrants arrived in G.S.L. City with a large herd of cattle."[48] Brigham Young later claimed Smith was hundreds of miles away when the Arkansas train reached Salt Lake and could have known nothing about it.[49] If this was so, it was a remarkable failure in the Mormon leaders' intelligence network, which one army officer considered a "damnable system of espionage," "better than that of the old Inquisition or Napoleon's police."[50]

Colonel Smith, who had founded the Iron County Battalion in 1850, took along Samuel Lewis, whose uncle had died in the Haun's Mill massacre. On his way south

Smith delivered Lt. Gen. Daniel H. Wells's August 1, 1857, orders to Nauvoo Legion officers reporting that "an army from the Eastern States is now en route to invade this Territory." Officers were to prepare their men "to march at the shortest possible notice to any part of the Territory" to defend against aggression. Wells rehearsed the outrages against the unoffending Saints who had seen "their leaders arrested, incarcerated, and slain; and themselves driven to cull life from the hospitality of the desert and the Savage." If an exterminating war was planned against them, "and blows alone can cleanse pollution from the nation's bulwarks, to the God of our fathers let the appeal be made." Militia officers were to enforce laws regulating arms and ammunition and "report without delay any person from [their] district[s] that disposes of a kernal of grain to any Gentile merchant or temporary sojourner or suffers it to go to waste."[51] Smith delivered these orders to Col. James Pace at Provo on August 3; to Gen. Aaron Johnson at Springville on August 4; to Major Bradley at Nephi on August 5; to Major McCullough at Fillmore on August 6; and to Col. William Dame at Parowan on August 8.[52] (Two years later U.S. Army captain Albert Tracy charged that "a formal meeting of the Mormons" had plotted the massacre of the Arkansas emigrants at Aaron Johnson's home.)[53]

Smith carried letters from Brigham Young to his bishops. "Save your ammunition, keep your Guns and Pistols in order, and prepare yourselves in all things—particularly by living your religion—for that which *may hereafter* come to pass," the prophet directed stake president Isaac Haight at Cedar City. "Save all . . . grain, nor let a kernal go to waste or be sold to our enemies. And those who persist in selling grain to the gentiles, or suffer their stock to trample it into the earth I wish you to *note* as such."[54] Despite the abundant harvest of 1857, Mormon leaders were determined to hoard food in preparation for a protracted war. Young restricted trade in grain even as he noted, "[There is] sufficient grain in the Territory for several years consumption, and all things are prospering with this people."[55]

On his way south, Apostle Smith fanned war hysteria and hostility toward outsiders in a series of militant sermons. After a late start from Provo on August 4, Smith and Lewis made good time, rising early and traveling until midnight. On reaching Parowan, they found the town's militia companies exercising on the square, ready to "strike in any direction" and march to wherever necessary to defend their homes. The people "were willing at any moment to touch fire to their homes, and hide themselves in the mountains, and to defend their country to the very last extremity."[56] Legend has it Smith advised the people to plant fruit trees on the public square and reminded them that bones made good fertilizer. "As for the cursed mobocrats," he added, "I can think of nothing better that they could do than to feed a tree in Zion."[57]

The Mormons feared the government would supplement the army marching up the Platte with troops from California or even Texas. Militia officer Elias Morris volunteered to go east and secure the passes on the trail Frémont had blazed on his disastrous fifth expedition. Morris recalled, "It was reported that a certain U.S. army captain had gone to Texas to beat-up volunteers to go against the 'Mormons,' and that they were to attack them from the South, while the regular army was approaching and attacking them from the East."[58] It was a testament to the paranoia in the settlements that they suspected the U.S. Army would attack them by a route Frémont himself probably could not have found again.

As he toured the scattered settlements where the fanaticism of the southern Saints seemed to burn like a fire, Smith poured fuel onto the flames, arousing both the Mormon settlers and their Paiute neighbors. On August 15 he started from Parowan on a military tour "to prepare for any eventuality." With Colonel Dame and several captains, including Smith's cousins, Jesse N. and Silas S. Smith, escorting him on "a mission of peace," he arrived in Cedar City to find the militia on parade. Dame drilled the troops of the Nauvoo Legion's Second Battalion of the Iron Regiment, and Smith addressed them. He reminded them they had been "long harassed and oppressed, driven, slain and plundered," but he at least was through with it. The Mormons would never trade with the army: "I say damn the man who feeds them; I say damn the man who sympathizes with them; I say curse the man who pours oil and water on their heads." Dame read the instructions from Salt Lake and expected the people would carry out their orders.[59]

The company arrived at Harmony at 10:30 P.M. and lodged with John D. Lee. The next morning Dame and Smith drilled and inspected the troops, after which the people assembled in church. Dame preached to the military and Smith to the civilians, but Smith "partook of the military more than the religious." The apostle admitted he "was perfectly running over with it." Rachel Lee found the sermon "full of hostility and virulence."[60]

Joined by Isaac Haight, John Higbee, and John Lee, the enthusiastic apostle followed Dame and his officers down Ash Creek through country of extreme beauty to the cotton farms on the Rio Virgin. The Ash Creek road was shorter than the route through Mountain Meadows, but it was awful, "passing in some places for miles over large rocks and in other places through very deep sand, rendering traveling very tedious." Three obstacles, Peter's Leap, Haight's Jump Up, and Jacob's Twist, made the road to the Santa Clara appear almost impassible. No one would attempt it, noted Adjutant James Martineau, "but the hardy sons of Utah, who have got used to it."[61]

Southern Utah was a miserable place in the summer, but Smith preached in Washington City and thanked the Lord "for the desert holes that we live in." The weather seemed hot to him, but the locals insisted it was a very cool spell even as the mercury rose to 136 degrees. The settlers could not say how the thermometer would read "in hot weather."[62] An express rider from Salt Lake overtook Smith's caravan on August 18 with an order from General Wells to William Dame outlining war measures. Wells ordered scouting parties into the mountains to prevent being taken by surprise. Officers were to find safe places in the mountains to hide women, children, and grain. And the Indians were to be reminded that the Mormons' enemies were theirs as well.

The government was continually fighting Indians somewhere, and in due time the army would attack Utah's tribes. The order concluded: "Be vigilant and active."[63]

To avoid the searing heat, Smith's entourage ascended the bed of the dried-up Santa Clara "in the dark of the night—a river upon whose banks many scenes of desperation [had] been enacted"—to the rough-stone Fort Clara some thirty-five miles west of Mountain Meadows. The Paiutes called it Jacob's Wikiup, and here the very friendly natives assembled to see the "Mormon Captain." The next evening the militia party struck the California Road and followed it another fifteen miles. Chief Jackson was anxious to have them stop overnight, but the Mormons forged ahead. On the dark river they were soon surrounded by hundreds of Paiutes. Smith recalled, "[They] took care of our horses, built us camp-fires, and roasted us corn, and made us as comfortable as they could." Kabbeet's band fed Smith corn and melons, and he never enjoyed a treat more.[64]

Smith claimed he enjoyed his "glorious interview" with the natives of the desert, but Lee found the large numbers of Paiutes that gathered around the Mormons impudent. As Lee translated, the apostle told them the Americans were their enemies and the enemies of the Mormons too. If the Indians helped to fight their mutual adversary, the Saints "would always keep them from want and sickness and give them guns and ammunition to hunt and kill game with, and would also help the Indians against their enemies when they went into war." This pleased them, Lee recalled, "and they agreed to all that [he] asked them to do."[65]

During their visit to the Tonaquints, Lee thought Smith was a little fearful of the Indians. Lee hitched up quickly and left. "Those are savage looking fellows," Smith said after a mile or so. "I think they would make it lively for an emigrant train if one should come this way." Lee said the Paiutes would attack *any* train. Smith went into a deep study and said, "Suppose an emigrant train should come along through this southern country, making threats against our people and bragging of the part they took in helping to kill our Prophets, what do you think the brethren would do with them? Would they be permitted to go their way, or would the brethren pitch into them and give them a good drubbing?" Lee said the brethren were under the influence of the Reformation and were still red-hot for the gospel. Any train would be attacked and probably destroyed. "I am sure they would be wiped out if they had been making threats against our people."[66]

Smith seemed delighted with Lee's answer and rephrased the question, "Do you really believe the brethren would make it lively for such a train?" Lee said they would, and he warned that unless Smith wanted the Saints to attack every train passing through the south, Brigham Young should send direct orders to Dame and Haight to let them pass. The people, Lee said, were bitter, full of zeal, and "anxious to avenge the blood of the Prophets." Smith said he had asked Haight the same question, and Haight gave the same answer. Smith thought the Paiutes, "with the advantage they had of the rocks, could use up a large company of emigrants, or make it very hot for them." Lee again warned that if Young wanted emigrant companies to pass unmolested, he must give Dame and Haight explicit instructions "for if they are not ordered otherwise, they will use them up by the help of the Indians." The conversation convinced Lee that Smith expected every emigrant passing through the territory to be killed. "I thought it was his *mission* to prepare the people for the bloody work," Lee wrote.[67]

Federal investigators were later convinced Brigham Young sent letters south "authorizing, if not commanding," the destruction of the Fancher train, but it is unlikely Young would commit such an order to writing.[68] Lee's tale of his ambiguous conversations with Smith on the Santa Clara may best reflect what actually happened. If Smith gave orders to kill the emigrants, they may have been no more explicit than to "use them up" or "give them a good drubbing." Mormon leaders often spoke in code words whose meaning was clear only to insiders. One of Young's favorite phrases, "A word to the wise is sufficient," meant, "Don't make me spell it out." This ambiguity had many advantages: it sheltered Mormon leaders from accountability and shifted responsibility from top leaders to local authorities. But orders couched in such enigmatic terms were easily misinterpreted, a serious problem given the volatile atmosphere and the slow pace of communications in Utah Territory.[69]

Lee arrived at his own conclusion: "I have always believed, since that day, that General George A. Smith was then visiting Southern Utah to prepare the people for the work of exterminating Captain Fancher's train of emigrants, and I now believe he was sent for that purpose by the direct command of Brigham Young."[70]

THE LORD WILL CUT SHORT HIS WORK

The Paiutes regarded Jacob Hamblin as a father, but on his tour of inspection Apostle Smith found the Southern Indian Mission in disarray. The evangelists were unhappy with their leader, Rufus C. Allen, who had reproved Hamblin "very roughly for some little thing that did not suit him," leaving Hamblin aggrieved. The missionaries prayed for the appointment of someone who had their confidence. Under the influence of the spirit, Hamblin prophesied that Allen would not preside very long.[71]

Brigham Young answered their prayers with a letter appointing Hamblin president of the Southern Indian Mission. Allen had lost Young's confidence, but he received comforting words from the prophet. Young gave him permission to return to northern Utah, for "the day is near at hand when the Lord will cut short his work." Privately, Young informed Isaac Haight that Allen was a good man. But he said, "I think it more to the interest of the 'Kingdom,' that his labors should be directed in another sphere." He referred Haight to Smith for general news, saying "Pay strict attention to the instructions which I forwarded to you by him."[72]

The prophet outlined his war strategy to Hamblin: "Continue the conciliatory policy towards the Indians, which I have ever recommended, and seek by works of righteousness to obtain their love and confidence, for they must learn that they have either got to help us or the United States will kill us both." Young described the appointment of the new territorial officials and their "body guard of 2500 of Uncle's Regulars," who could not decide if they would hang him with or without trial. Despite the threats against his life, Young felt confident and believed "every circumstance but proves the hastening of Zion's redemption."[73] The message to Jacob Hamblin was clear: secure the loyalty of the Indians and prepare for war.

Smith apparently directed Hamblin to take the Paiute leaders to Salt Lake, but Hamblin wrote that Tutsegabit had "felt anxious for a long time to visit Brigham Young."[74] Smith began his return to Salt Lake on August 24, and Hamblin and the Paiutes had joined him by the next day. Colonel Dame accompanied him to Paragonah, where the party took breakfast with Silas S. Smith. Orson B. Adams then drove them thirty miles to Beaver, and Silas Smith accompanied them on horseback. The apostle preached that evening in a crowded schoolhouse and married three couples.[75]

Smith told the congregation that a party of emigrants would reach Beaver in a few days, Robert Kershaw later recalled, and ordered the people not to trade produce with them under penalty of being cut off from the church.[76] In the morning Dame and Adams returned south, while Smith, Silas Smith, Elisha Hoops, Bishop Philo Farnsworth, Hamblin, and the Paiutes made a long day's drive of fifty-two miles. Apostle Smith recalled they arrived at Corn Creek Springs "some hours after dark and found encamped a company of emigrants, with about thirty wagons and a considerable herd of stock." Smith and his group drove across the creek and camped within forty yards of the emigrants. The Indians bedded down near their Mormon friends.[77] The party camped across the creek was the Fancher train.

I WILL FIGHT ALL HELL

In the midst of the crisis of 1857, Brigham Young told an audience that his printed remarks "often omit the sharp words, though they are perfectly understood and applicable here." Heber Kimball said Young's published sermons contained "buttermilk and catnip tea" in place of remarks that might offend "the weak-stomached world."[78] As provocative as the rhetoric in the *Deseret News* appears today, Young's speech was far more inflammatory than his printed sermons.

George D. Watt's manuscript minutes of Brigham Young's August 16, 1857, discourse reveal the contrast between his actual words and the later, sanitized versions—and how profoundly the powerful harangues moved his audience. This sermon was an impassioned statement of the Mormons' brief against the government and their plans to deal with the army. Young also announced a dramatic change in his policy toward outsiders. Since the gold rush of 1849 the Saints had welcomed emigrant trains, and usually the relationship had proved mutually beneficial. Emigrants brought much-needed goods and cash to the remote settlements, where travelers could resupply and trade worn-out stock for fresh animals. Governor Young issued proclamations to encourage emigrants to stop at Salt Lake, and the visitors often praised Mormon hospitality. With war clouds darkening the horizon, all that was about to end.[79]

"I hope that I may say to the people the things that the Lord would say," Young began that August morning. "I hope that what I do say will be in truth and in righteousness—dictated by the Holy Ghost." There was much excitement in the regions of darkness, the prophet told his congregation. Their ten years' peace in the mountains was the longest rest the Saints had ever enjoyed. The government had now "come out, not openly and boldly, but underhandedly, and sneekingly, raskaly—in the form of a mob—again to pour their intolerant persecution upon this people and break them up, and ruin them—to destroy and kill them." He held the United States responsible for the deaths of thousands of Saints. Joseph and Hyrum Smith had been murdered while under the protection of the state of Illinois, and the blood of the prophets continued to flow, for "they [had] killed Parley lately." The prophet vowed to lift his sword and slay those who wished to destroy his people, a promise the congregation greeted with "a unanimous shout, 'Amen.'"[80]

"I am at the defiance of all hell [and] Governments, but especially ours," Young said. Although the Mormon people loved the Constitution, the corrupt government dealt unfairly with them: "They turn good into evil, and they make light darkness. . . . Every Mobocratic spirit and institution, every violation of the Constitution, they pass over it as nothing, and raise a force to come and slay all the Latterdaysaints, men, women and children." The advancing army carried sealed orders to "decoy away every man and woman" and "use up the leaders, break up their organization, disperse the people, and call in [the] Gentile brethren and break up the Mormon kingdom."

The plains were alive with rumors that the army had vowed to hang Mormon leaders when it reached Utah, then declare martial law and massacre the people. Young swore he would not stand still while they took away his life. He would not trust government officers, he said, "any sooner than I would a wolf with my dinner."[81] He now joked, "As for their hanging Brigham, Heber, Daniel, or any of the rest of them, they have to catch them first, for they never can hang us until they have catched us. I am generally pretty wide awake." "I tell you, the Lord Almighty and the Elders of Israel being our helpers, they shall not come to this territory," roared the Lion of the Lord. "I will fight them and I will fight all hell."

Young feared that if the army came across a weak party of Mormon emigrants, it would seize their wagons and clothing and abuse the women and children. His concern was groundless, but he had already sent several hundred men to escort the emigration into Utah. He believed the army could not do anything during the fall. If the government sent troops to Utah in the spring, he said, "[I will] lay this building in ashes, I shall lay my dwelling house in ashes, I shall lay my mills in ashes, I shall cut every shrub and tree in the Valley, every pole, every inch of board, and put it all into ashes. I will burn the grass and the stubble and lay it waste, and make a Moscow of every settlement, and then I guess we will make a Potter's field of every Canyon they go into." The prophet's wealth meant nothing to him, for it was the Lord's: "I hope I may do with it as he wants me to. I do not care what it is."

Young denied objecting to the presence of a U.S. court in Utah or to "real gentlemen" serving as the territory's judges. "Who has ever mistreated them? No one," the prophet insisted. The government's policy was simply religious persecution. He invited every man and woman who did not want to follow him to leave now, for he would hew down and lay waste the heritage of any who refused "to come to the scratch" when the time came to destroy everything in the territory. "If any grunt about it, let me know," Young promised, "and I will carry you away in my best carriage. If you want to go to hell, I will carry you to the gate, but I do not want my horses to go any further."

"Can you flee to the mountains, men, women and children, and lay wast[e] and desolate every thing before them?" he asked. The congregation shouted back, "Yes." Young called for a show of hands, and every hand went up as the gathering of thousands broke into wild applause. The feeling that prevailed in the meeting, the clerk noted, could not be described.

The prophet advised the United States to solve its own problems: "Let the abolitionist lay down his weapons of war against the slave holder, and let the free-soilers cease their oppositions." If Americans failed to do so, the confusion would increase until they destroyed each other: "It would be one of the prettiest things in the world to make our enemies use themselves up, one of the easiest things in the world to make them do it."

Brigham Young had never felt better in his life, but he knew "it is a pretty bold step for a little handful of men . . . to think that they can cope with the extensive Government—the powerful Government of the United States." How would the poorly equipped Mormons fight the U.S. Army? The prophet and his top counselors had been wrestling with this question since they had learned troops were marching to Utah. Young realized his defiance of federal power presented a very real threat to the survival of the Mormon people in general and to him in particular. He would soon learn that the Nauvoo Legion's armory had only one hundred fifty pounds of gunpowder, and he now proposed to use the army as his supply depot: "I calculate they shall furnish us with Guns, powder, and lead, beef, pork, and all that is necessary."

Despite the bellicose tone of his sermon, one of the few options Brigham Young had to oppose federal power was his ability to close the overland road through the Great Basin. Given his limited alternatives, this was his trump card against the federal government's overwhelming strength. He now threatened to stop restraining the Indians and let them do as they pleased. The prophet outlined his new policy, telling his people to warn their American friends, "Don't pretend to cross this Contenant, for I will tell you honestly, and plainly, and in all good feeling, I will not hold the Indians while you shoot them." If not for the Mormons, he claimed, the Lamanites would have cut off nineteen out of twenty emigrants that season. The Mormons had done all in their power to save the lives of these men, women, and children, but this would stop if the government attacked.[82] "I have preached to the Indians, sent them presents, visited them and prayed for them, that they might become peac[e]able, and let the traveler alone." But now:

> If the United States send their army here and war commences, the travel must stop; your trains must not cross this continent back and forth. To accomplish this I need only say a word to the [tribes,] for the Indians will use them up unless I continually strive to restrain them. I will say no more to the Indians, let them alone, but do as you please. And what is that? It is to use them up; and they will do it.

The Saints would revolutionize the world "until we bring peace to mankind," Brigham Young promised as he ended his sermon, "and all hell cannot help it."[83]

Travel Must Stop: Closing the Overland Road

When services ended on August 16, Gov. Brigham Young turned his attention to implementing the policy he had described so forcefully that morning. He would not wait for the army to arrive in Utah to make good on his threats. With his interpreter, Dimick Huntington, Young met with about ten Yampa Utes. Huntington had spent two weeks explaining Mormon war policy to the Shoshoni and Goshute bands in northern Utah. He met with Little Soldier, who led a mixed body of outcasts and Northern Shoshonis known as the Weber Utes. (When the Mormons tried to persuade them to take up farming, Huntington complained "they set down on their buts & Howled like so many woolvs.") Little Soldier confessed he was afraid of the army and wanted to go "a way off in to the Mountains" to wait and see how the Mormons fared against it. Huntington said the troops would kill the Indian people as quickly as they would the Mormons and warned Little Soldier to prepare for a seven-year siege foreseen by Young.[84]

Huntington and his son then traveled north to meet with the leaders of some four hundred Shoshonis. He found them much excited and afraid of being poisoned. Huntington made a feast for them, killing six cows to accompany the three wagonloads of bread, potatoes, corn, and vegetables he delivered. Huntington knew the Shoshonis had stolen horses and mules from California-bound wagon trains, and he asked their leader, apparently Pocatello, about it. "The Chief looked much down [but admitted] he had heard a little that they had and asked me if I was mad." Huntington assured him neither he nor Brigham Young were unhappy with the raids. The chief brightened considerably and offered to show Huntington where the stolen horses were hidden. Huntington left feeling he had accomplished his mission and on August 12 went south to Ogden's Hole, where he made a feast for another one hundred Indians. "The Breathren," Huntington felt, "done first rate by the Indians."

Now Brigham Young met with Huntington and the Yampas, who also were reluctant to meet the army. Their leader, Antero, said he would think it over, but the resolute neutrality of Utah's tribes reflected their hard experience with their Mormon neighbors. The diligent work of Indian agent Garland Hurt had convinced many Utes that the U.S. government was a better friend to their people than the land-hungry Saints. Rather than take sides, the Utes would wait and see how the war turned out. When Huntington met with five Goshutes two days later, they expressed great sorrow over their lack of ammunition but "said they was afraid of the troops & would go home & wait and see how the troops came out." Huntington again warned that after the troops killed the Mormons they would then kill the Indians. The Goshutes and the Saints were one, Huntington said, but "the Lord had thrown the Gentiles a way."

The Indians' reluctance was based in part on their belief that the Mormons used poison and magic against them. On a later visit to Utah Valley, Huntington found a large band of Utes grazing their horses in local wheat fields and acting "verry saucy & ugly." Many of them were sick. One chief was very ill, and his whole village was angry. When Huntington offered the Utes a wagonload of bread, they jammed a piece in his mouth and said, "Eat it for it is poison & you want to kill us." Huntington responded to the affront by asking for more. Tabby, the only man who would speak with him, said Brigham Young must have "talked to the Great Spirit to make them all sick & die." Huntington denied that the Mormons caused the sickness, but Tabby refused to accept his assurances: "He sayed o shit you Lie."[85] Given such deep suspicions, convincing the Indians to ally themselves with the Saints seemed impossible.

Young had to choose between his fidelity to the U.S. government and what he saw as his duty as a prophet of God and his loyalty to the Mormon people. The superintendent of Indian affairs for Utah Territory was charged with protecting overland emigrants from Indian attacks, and on August 16 Superintendent Young had declared he would abandon that responsibility if the army came to Utah. Now Young explicitly violated his sworn duty and sent agents to encourage Indian attacks on wagon trains, dispatching Huntington north to the camp of some one thousand Shoshonis near Farmington. Huntington and a local bishop gave them four cows and four wagonloads of corn and melons. He told the Indians "the Lord had come out of his Hiding place & they had to commence their work." Huntington then "gave them all the Beef Cattle & horses that was on the Road to California [by] the North Rout," instructing the Shoshonis to hide the captured animals in the mountains. That the leading emissary of the Indian superintendent would encourage them to attack emigrant trains astonished the chiefs: this was something new. They "wanted to Council & think of it."[86]

At the Shoshoni camp Huntington spoke with Ben Simons, a mixed-blood Indian who had operated a ranch on the Weber River since 1854. As a leader in Little Soldier's band, like many Indians Simons played each end of the white world against the other.[87] After Huntington told him about *The Book of Mormon*, Simons "said his Father had told him about the same thing that they would have to rise up to fight but he did not think it was so near." He wanted Huntington to advise Brigham Young he could depend on his Indian allies. But Simons was nobody's fool. He immediately reported to Indian agent Hurt that Huntington had "told the Indians that Brigham wanted them to run off the emigrants' cattle, and if they would do so they might have them for their own." Simons assured Hurt he had advised the Snake chiefs to have nothing to do with the cattle. He implied the Mormons had hired Little Soldier to seize about four hundred animals from a Missouri emigrant named Squires.[88]

Huntington's mission to the Shoshonis exacerbated the violence that had already set the northern road to California ablaze from City of Rocks to the Humboldt River. By early September horrific accounts "of the almost total destruction of an immigrant train, by the Indians," filled California's newspapers. Indians had attacked a small train at Stony Point, a black man named Scott reported, and killed five men and a child. A woman "was shot in several places with arrows, scalped, and left for dead." Remarkably, she had survived, and her head had almost healed.[89]

Emigrants had no doubt who was behind these assaults. On reaching California, overlanders recounted "many sad evidences of outrage and murder" that they swore implicated the Saints. For three hundred miles emigrants had to run "the gauntlet of Indian attacks and Mormon treachery," Richeson Abbott complained. His party was ambushed at City of Rocks, and he was "satisfied the attack was led by Mormons, as they heard them cursing in regular Mormon slang, and calling out to them to get out of the country, as they had no business there." The Saints boasted they would kill them all.[90]

Panicked reports claimed hundreds of emigrants had been killed. For the press in California, it was "an undoubted fact that the Mormons were at the head of most of [the] outrages, and instigated the Indians to commit the murders." Louis Fine said white men supposed to be Mormons led an Indian attack on Samuel Beller and B. Redman of Arkansas near City of Rocks. For the next three hundred miles they were fired on or attacked almost every day. The emigrants "all appeared to have more fear of the Mormons than of the Indians." Their general feeling was that "the Mormons led the Indians in their attacks and murders."[91]

Angus McLeod of Arkansas left Salt Lake on September 4 with Louis Fine's train. He was attacked fifty miles from town by ten or twelve men mounted on newly shod horses. McLeod believed they were white men or Mormons. His party was assaulted again near City of Rocks, where forty or fifty Indians killed Oliver Bailey and drove off some seventy head of cattle.[92] At Salt Lake, a man named Pierce heard "vague declarations of a threatening character" that "next year 'the overland emigrants must look out'; and it was intimated that the last trains this year might be destroyed." A woman with the eastbound Mormon wagons evacuating Carson Valley warned, "The last trains of this year would not get through, for they were to be cut off."[93]

Even as he unleashed a new level of violence on the overland trail, Young understood the consequences of his new Indian policy. The United States was driving the
Mormons to war too quickly, he told Wilford Woodruff at the end of August. The
Saints had not had time to teach the Indians not to kill women and children and "those
who ought not to be killed." Responsibility for such innocent victims would fall to
American politicians, not on Mormon prophets. "The nation is determined to make
us free. They are determined to drive us to defend our selves & become independent," he said. "[The Lord] will fight our battles & we will become an independent
kingdom."[94] For Brigham Young, it was now the Kingdom of God or nothing.

6

We Are American Citizens and Shall Not Move

By 1857 the way west was no longer a mere trail. It was a national highway of commerce and communication, alive with freight wagons, mail couriers, and military units. Westbound travelers found the Oregon-California Trail crowded with faithful Latter-day converts headed west to Zion, but it also carried a stream of eastbound apostates fleeing the "theo-democracy" of Brigham Young. The poverty of the refugees was pathetic, for two years of grasshopper plagues and famine in Utah had pushed its people to the brink of starvation.

On the Blue River, Helen Carpenter met a large party of Mormons leaving Zion. "There seemed to be twice as many women as men and twice as many children as women," she wrote. "All were in rags and tatters and, must I say, scabs. . . . [They were the] very worst lot I ever saw. All who were large enough (except the drivers) were out of the wagons holding out rusty kettles and pans begging for milk." Another band of backouts (as loyal Mormons called them) said sardonically, "We have been in heaven long enough and are going to hell." Carpenter later encountered twenty wagons of disillusioned Saints who told her "there are plenty more that would be glad to leave Salt Lake if they could only get away."[1]

The seceding Mormons painted a lurid picture of life in Utah, providing firsthand accounts of the horrors of polygamy and of ritual assassinations executed under the strange doctrine of blood atonement. To escape from the territory, the bedraggled refugees complained, they had to abandon their possessions and depart in great secrecy.

Sober, Hard-Working, Plain Folks: The Fancher Party Assembles

By the end of May 1857 "all Western Missouri was in a ferment" with rumors of a war with the Mormons. By June word had reached Bear River that the United States government had sent an army to Utah to settle the Mormon problem once and for all.[2] If Arkansans on the overland road learned of the pending crisis between the Mormons and the government or of the murder of Parley Pratt, they probably did not attach much significance to the news. After all, they were merely passing through and carried no brief against the Mormons.

All the emigrant roads that led to Utah converged at Bridger's fort, which the Mormons had seized from Jim Bridger in 1853. After reaching the gold fields in October 1857, Arkansans who took the northern road to California recalled meeting the Bakers, the Mitchell brothers, Milum Jones, and the widow Tackitt at the fort near the end of July.[3] Here more than two hundred fifty Arkansans began to form the companies that would face the trail's most arduous challenge—crossing the last desert and mountain barriers on the long road to California. The emigration "was composed of antagonistic elements, which months of weary journeying and common peril did not seem to allay," P. K. Jacoby recalled. Debates over slavery divided the Southerners from the minority of Union men who had fallen in with the Arkansas travelers. Jacoby's small party from Ohio took their one hundred head of stock and set off down Bear River for California. Jacoby named the Bakers and the Huffs as the leading families in the train he left at the fort, in addition to the Reeds from Missouri—a father and son and their families—perhaps John Perkins Reed, the only known Missourian in the Fancher party. The company had sixteen wagons, one hundred oxen, and nine hundred cattle, making it "the richest and best-equipped train that ever set out across the plains." The Reeds and the Bakers were the principal owners of the stock and had a considerable amount of specie they planned to invest in California land. Jacoby said that a "large number of hired men accompanied the train as 'bull-whackers' and stockherders"—that is, cowboys.[4]

Frank Eaton King later claimed he and his wife joined the Fancher party at South Pass. King's middle name suggests that he might have traveled with emigrant William M. Eaton, a Hoosier farmer. Eaton had met some Arkansans visiting Illinois who persuaded him to join the Fancher party. He had a niece living in Salt Lake, and there he wrote his wife that all was well. The Fancher, Cameron, Dunlap, and Baker families left Bridger's fort separately, some days ahead of Basil Parker and the other Arkansas companies. (Parker stayed at the fort until at least July 28 to wait for Ellen Cecil to give birth.)[5]

Returning from a Mormon mission that summer, Eli B. Kelsey recalled trekking with the Fancher party from Fort Bridger to their camp east of Great Salt Lake City. He said he had never traveled with more pleasant companions. One young girl was "a lovely sweet creature, with dark flowing curls, who had been the life and joy of the camp" and the companion of the company's "venerable patriarch," perhaps Jack Baker. They "travelled leisurely, with the view of nursing the strength of their cattle, horses, and mules." They were "people from the country districts, sober, hard-working, plain folks, but well-to-do and, taken all in all, about as respectable a band of emigrants as ever passed through Salt Lake City."[6] The company had picked up a troublesome "Dutchman," perhaps a German doctor who by all accounts delighted in provoking the Mormons.[7]

Eyewitnesses described how the Fancher party took its final shape from the three or four companies from Arkansas consisting of "Fraziers [Fanchers], Camerons, and the two Dunlaps, and perhaps Bakers." The Bakers had not yet arrived, but eventually they joined the train. The families were camped six miles from Great Salt Lake City, perhaps at the mouth of Emigration Canyon or in the meadows at the head of Parley's Canyon. The emigrants had been there for some time and intended to stay until the weather cooled enough to ease the crossing of the Mojave Desert, which reflected the experience of their leaders. They expected "to make a stay of eight weeks all together."[8]

On reaching Salt Lake early in August 1857, the Arkansans must have felt like they had stepped into a hornet's nest. In the previous week Mormon leaders had worked their followers into a frenzy. Brigham Young announced, "God has commenced to set up his kingdom on the earth, and all hell and its devils are moving against it." This was the Kingdom of God that Daniel foresaw, "the kingdom that was to be set up in the last days."[9]

George Powers of Little Rock, Arkansas, passed three hundred armed men on the road to Salt Lake. The Mormons said they had sixty thousand pounds of flour stored at Fort Bridger and four hundred armed Indian allies awaiting orders nearby at Fort Supply. They were making determined preparations to fight the U.S. Army, and Powers found militia companies drilling every evening in Salt Lake. He reported, "The Mormons declared to us that no U.S. troops should ever cross the mountains; and they talked and acted as if they were willing to take a brush with Uncle Sam."[10]

Wagon trains had been entering Great Salt Lake City since July 20, sometimes with violent results.[11] Mormon thugs overheard apostate C. G. Landon, a clerk in the surveyor's office, telling emigrants the Mormons were damned rascals and "gave him a tremendous thrashing." They had questioned another clerk, William Wilson, with a gun to his head and a rope around his neck, and they beat Landon "with stones and clubs most unmercifully." Landon warned emigrants who witnessed the assault not to help him, for "it would only result in the destruction of them all." After the beating, Landon retreated to his home, insensible. He escaped another mob on July 27 to the shrieks and cries of his neighbor's wife and made his way north to the California Trail in disguise, where one "Indian Peter" told him "that Brigham Young had sent him out to get pungo (horses) and carabines (guns)." Landon straggled into Placerville on September 12, 1857, barefoot and nearly naked, to report, "Men, women, and children, have been slaughtered by wholesale [along the trail]."[12]

One emigrant dated the Fancher train's arrival in Salt Lake August 3, 1857, the day Mormon records noted the arrival of a company of emigrants with a large herd of

young cattle.[13] The authorities were determined to control the territory's food supply, and as the party passed through Salt Lake, Lorenzo Brown noted in his journal,
"The Bishop is requested to take charge of all property in the ward so that there be
no selling to Gentiles especially provisions."[14]

What happened to the Fancher party in Salt Lake is shrouded in conflicting tales
told years later. "Weary and footsore they encamped by the Jordan River," wrote
Fanny Stenhouse, "trusting there to recruit themselves and their teams, and to replen-
ish their stock of provisions."[15] Josiah Gibbs recalled they stopped at Emigration
Square, the block reserved for overlanders, while Mormon historian Orson Whitney
claimed the party camped on the Fifth Ward pasture near present 800 South and 600
West. Some deny the Arkansans had any problems in northern Utah, but other emigrants described the hostility that greeted outsiders the moment they entered the territory. Newspapers later charged that Brigham Young "issued a preemptory order" to
the Fancher party to leave the city immediately.[16] Even a historian sympathetic to the
Mormons reported the Arkansans found them "in no friendly mood, and at once concluded to break camp and move on."[17]

On August 1 Apostle Wilford Woodruff had called on "Eleanor Pratt & got an
account of the death & burial of Elder P. P. Pratt." Years later Charles Wandell, an
embittered Mormon apostate, reported that when the Fancher train passed though
Salt Lake, the widow Pratt "recognized one or more of the party as having been present at the death of Pratt."[18]

Wagon master Basil Parker recalled arriving in Salt Lake to find it filled with hostile Indians. Jack Baker's party reached town two days ahead of Parker and had already
left when he arrived. A Salt Lake man threatened Baker's train in Parker's tent, but
Parker could not warn his friends without risk to himself and his party. He heard that
the emigrants had insulted the local women and accused the Mormons of poisoning
the water that killed some of their cattle. Recognizing he was in "a very close place
just at that time," Parker behaved with extreme caution. The Mormons wanted "to
create a disturbance as an excuse to slaughter the entire train," Parker said. "I can now
see that the Mormons were cleverly planning a shield for themselves in allowing the
Indians to be the public aggressors, and on whom they could throw the blame of the
awful crime they intended to commit at Mountain Meadows a few days later." Parker
felt there was "every reason to believe that the Baker party was doomed to destruction before it left Salt Lake City."[19]

At Salt Lake emigrant trains had to choose between two hard roads across the
Great Basin, a northern route along the Humboldt River and a course through Utah's
southern settlements to the Mojave Desert. It was no secret in summer 1857 that the
northern road was particularly dangerous. Brigham Young himself warned, "The
Saints who come through the north route had better supply themselves with efficient
arms and keep strong guards, as the Indians on that route are said to be exceedingly
hostile."[20] Years later Young claimed Apostle Charles Rich had advised the Fancher

party to take the northern route to California, despite Rich's financial interests in San Bernardino and the known dangers of the route.[21]

Malinda Scott told a different story. She recalled that the Mormons persuaded her father, William Cameron, to take the southern route, saying it would offer better grass for their stock. Malinda's husband, H. D. Scott, decided he would rather take the northern route. The Mormons convinced him to camp outside the city, where his animals would have better feed. After traveling north for two days from Salt Lake, a member of their party killed Malinda's husband for unknown reasons. Within days the widow gave birth, "leaving her with four helpless children in the wilderness." Scott's party set off for California by the Humboldt River road.[22]

Jacob Hamblin said one of the men in the Fancher party told him the company "was made up near Salt Lake City of several trains that had crossed the plains separately." Being Southerners they preferred to take the southern route. By now aware of the bitter hostility of the Mormons, the emigrants began their journey south about August 5, 1857.[23]

Once the Fancher party left Salt Lake, it disappeared into a historical maze built of lies, folklore, popular myth, justifications, and few facts. After the reports of Malinda Cameron Scott and Basil Parker, all information about the emigrants' conduct came from men involved in their murder or its cover-up. Even the emigrant trains following the Arkansans relied on secondhand stories told by Mormons, who carefully controlled what they let outlanders see and hear. In light of their origins, all reports of the reckless behavior of a company composed mostly of women and children must be regarded with profound skepticism.

The skillfully crafted legends shrouding the fate of these murdered and maligned people make penetrating this mythology extremely difficult, but logic and common sense can test the evidence. The earliest sources tell a remarkable story, while the constants of time and distance provide a standard to sort fable from truth.[24] Yet from the morning the emigrants left Corn Creek, nothing is certain about the Fancher party except that in less than three weeks every member who could have given a reliable account of its fate would be dead.

The Hard Road South

After the Fancher family first traveled south from Salt Lake in 1850, the government had substantially improved the trail to southern California as a territorial road. The Mormons naturally ignored the five hundred miles of mountains and deserts separating the territory from the Pacific and used the federal largesse to improve the two hundred fifty miles of road passing through the broad open valleys that sheltered their southern settlements. For overland emigrants, the towns and farms crowding the first sixty miles of the journey south could be a blessing or a curse, depending on the availability of grass and the mood of the people along the way. South of Utah Lake, the empty valleys were drier and the passes dividing them steeper. Forty to sixty miles separated the handful of small towns—Nephi, Fillmore, Beaver, and Parowan—strategically scattered along the route, a distance a good carriage could cover in one long day but that took an ox team and wagon two to four days to traverse.

On leaving the Little Salt Lake Valley south of Cedar City, the road crossed the Harmony Mountains to the last resting place on the trail, Mountain Meadows, an oasis of lush grass and fine spring water wedged between the Pine Valley and Bull Valley ranges. A new route, Leach's Cutoff, shortened the Spanish Trail's passage to the meadows. Mail carrier and road contractor James B. Leach opened the $70,000 cutoff in 1855 with a Mormon road crew.[25] By Leach's new route, it was thirty-seven miles from Cedar City to the meadows, where sojourners had one last chance to prepare for the final four hundred arduous miles to the gardens and mines of California.

Leach had to hire Nephi Johnson, one of the original pioneers of Iron County, to direct his road crew, as devout men "could not stand [Leach's] rough language." Johnson was a strapping frontiersman with sharp black eyes who had won renown as the interpreter the Utes said "was the only man in the country that would talk straight." As his name indicates, Johnson had been born in the LDS church. He and his family had been intimate acquaintances of the Prophet Joseph, and Johnson had spent his youth sharing his religion's trials and adventures on the frontier. With the organization of the Iron County brigade, Johnson had joined the cavalry, or "Minute Man as we were called," and by 1857 he was a twenty-three-year-old lieutenant in Capt. Joel White's Company D.[26]

Dr. Thomas Flint's experience driving sheep through Utah in 1853 foreshadowed what the Arkansans would encounter four years later. After Indians robbed a Mormon train on the Platte River, his party provided the destitute Mormons with food. Coming into the Salt Lake Valley, two men met Flint and asked if they were "Saints or sinners." After learning his train's name, they wheeled around and rode toward the city. Two other men soon returned. "We know who you are," they said. "You are the ones that assisted our people on the plains." The Mormons invited the doctor to camp near the church gardens but told him to keep his stock off plowed lands. The warm welcome quickly vanished as Flint journeyed south and settlers ordered his party off unoccupied ground "on the pretext that it was neighborhood range."[27]

Local officials repeatedly subjected Flint's party to the harassment and extortion travelers typically endured in Utah. At Nephi the authorities charged G. W. Frazer's horses had strayed into their wheat stacks. They seized his stock and fined him $20, threatening to double the fine "*if he found fault or swore*." After leaving Mountain Meadows in late October, Flint was "right glad" that they had left Mormon territory. His people had not been "robbed or molested to an amount more than a set of horseshoes," but other trains, especially those from Illinois or Missouri, were harassed "in most every conceivable manner." Utah authorities imposed fines "for every infraction of their regulations, real or fictitious—enforced by men with rifles on their shoulders, making their demands very emphatic."[28]

Conditions deteriorated over the next four years. As the accounts of Flint and other non-Mormons demonstrate, harassment of travelers and conflicts over grass were a standard part of life on the road through southern Utah. The territory's 1851 law against profanity was only one example of the legal ploys local authorities used to extract fees and fines from passing travelers.[29] An even more profound cause of strife with the Fancher party was the need to feed their enormous cattle herd. The diary of Samuel Pitchforth, the only authentic surviving record of an encounter with the Arkansans, describes a confrontation over grass. A repeated theme of the later accounts that seem most authentic reports Mormon anger over the emigrants' use of their winter range, which was essential for their survival. In contrast, the emigrants allegedly asserted their right to "Uncle Sam's grass."[30]

Leading the first emigrant party to take the southern road in 1857, Jack Baker apparently managed the trail herd and the drovers while Alexander Fancher took charge of the family wagons.[31] Given Baker's known volatility, this may not have been an ideal arrangement, for immediately after leaving Salt Lake the Fancher party encountered the hostile reception George A. Smith had prepared for them. The emigrants were simply passing through Utah on their way to California, but the Mormons acted as if the Arkansans had made the journey solely to torment them. The people of American Fork would not sell them provisions, even though they had "an unusual abundance" of flour, bacon, vegetables, poultry, butter, cheese, and eggs.[32]

Such hostility would have continually reminded the party of their precarious situation, but the emigrants who followed them heard tales of their reckless conduct. The men were said to be very free in speaking and committed "little acts of annoyance for the purpose of provoking the saints." Perhaps the company's size gave it a false sense of security. As a fellow emigrant commented, "Feeling perfectly safe in their arms and numbers, they seemed to set at defiance all the powers that could be brought against them. And they were not permitted to feel the dangers that surrounded them, until they were cut off from all hope of relief."[33]

Yet these impressions of the Fancher party's behavior were based on hearsay. Reliable accounts consistently identified the company's large cattle herd, not intentional insults, as the main cause of friction. By the time it started south, contemporary reports claimed the party had between four hundred and nine hundred cattle. The emigrants grazed their animals on community fields set aside for winter, and when the Mormons confronted the Arkansans, they met the roughest elements of the party, the young cowboys.

Brigham Young's order not to sell grain to the emigrants increased the party's desperation. Even when famine haunted the northern settlements during 1855 and 1856, there was more than enough grain in the south to last until the next harvest, yet Apostle Erastus Snow reported that the inhabitants would sell none of it to travelers.

Anyone passing through southern Utah without proper supplies should "expect to grub their living across the desert."[34] George A. Smith later swore he told the people to furnish emigrants "with what they might actually need for breadstuff," but his actual instructions were no more ambiguous than Brigham Young's order not to let a kernel of grain go to waste or be sold to their enemies.[35] If the Arkansans had counted on supplementing their supplies in Utah, the ban on trade would have left them in bad straits. Their cattle herd provided a hedge against starvation, but Mormon hostility meant the company faced every prospect of having to grub their living across the desert.

Emigrant P. M. Warn believed the party's obvious wealth excited the greed of the poverty-stricken people of southern Utah. "An element of gain," Warn observed, "enters largely into all Mormon calculations." The Arkansas men were well armed and supplied with ammunition—exactly the items Utahns desperately needed in 1857 to oppose the U.S. Army—and their outfit indicated that they might have "considerable funds."[36]

Uncle Sam's Grass

The emigrants ran into trouble at Provo when they camped in a meadow west of the town commons. Local lawman Simon Wood rode down to make sure the settlement's winter pasture was not disturbed. The field of red top and timothy was marked off so "no one could mistake the purpose for which the plot was saved." Wood found the intruders and some four hundred cattle in the meadow. He calmly advised the party's captain that the Mormons needed the feed to survive the winter. Wood suggested the emigrants use a large valley of virgin grass a few miles to the west and offered to help move the camp. "This is Uncle Sam's grass," the cocky captain said with some feeling. "We are his boys. We have a better claim on it than a bunch of rebel Mormons which had to be kicked out of one state to another and finally out of the United States. We are staying right here."

"Your gauntlet is down," Wood said. He gave the party an hour to decide whether they wanted to fight or pull up stakes. The emigrants left.[37]

Nineteen-year-old William A. Aden of Tennessee had left St. Louis in spring 1857. His family last heard from him in July at South Pass, "saying that he expected to spend the winter in Provo, and proceed to California in the spring of '58." Aden's father proudly described him: "quite uprightly, a good sign painter, writes poetry and some prose pretty well, makes a good speech—picks the Banjoe tolerably well—pretty good looking and is regarded as one of the most ingenious men of his age." In addition, Aden was "a natural genius—particularly at PAINTING." Mormons recalled that he had sketched the overland trail and painted scenery for the Provo Dramatic Association. Aden decided not to winter in Utah, and he left Provo "aiming to overtake a party of emigrants, who were then some fifty miles ahead"—the Fancher train.[38]

Aden may have overtaken the Arkansans after they had crossed the low divide into Juab Valley in mid-August and camped in the shadow of Mount Nebo at Miller's Spring, present Mona, Utah. Bishop Jacob Bigler of Nephi sent a message asking the emigrants "to move for they were distroying [the] winter feed." Samuel Pitchforth reported, "They answered that they were American Citizens and should not move." Two days later, after spending Sunday at the spring, the company of gentiles passed through Nephi in the morning. They were probably unable to purchase the flour they wanted to buy. Pitchforth spent the next day "fixing" his gun.[39]

THE BACK OUT ORDER

In an effort to revive Joseph Smith's Law of Consecration, in 1854 Brigham Young ordered the Saints to make a general consecration of their property to the church. Members were expected to sign deeds of transfer of all they owned to the trustee-in-trust of the LDS church, Brigham Young. Loyal Saints executed at least 2,682 Deeds of Consecration, and on April 7, 1855, the prophet himself consecrated all he had, property worth $199,625. Typically the deeds conveyed a person's worldly wealth, down to their firearms, tools, livestock, farm implements, wagons, clothing, and bedding, but Swiss emigrant Frederick Rowlett consecrated his daughter. Even Indian converts were expected to join the movement, and Ute leader Arapeen deeded over Sanpete County.[40] It was an audacious demand, given Utah's grinding poverty and a gap between the wealth of the church hierarchy and ordinary citizens that one observer found to be as wide as that between Russian nobles and their serfs.[41]

Young used the Law of Consecration to battle the growing problem of apostasy. He saw consecration as a way to test those who were weak in the faith: "We will levy on your property and take every farthing you have on earth. I want to see if I can make some of you apostatize." He advised a potential defector in Parowan to consecrate all he had "that he might be kept with the Saints and saved, so that if you are tempted to go away, you may feel it best to stay where your treasure is." All were welcome to leave the territory, but those doing so could take nothing with them. During the Reformation, Charles Derry was told "no man would be permitted to leave the Territory, and if they attempted to leave, they must leave their property and their wives and children behind them."[42]

Mormon leaders had long hated and feared internal dissent. Traitors had caused all the great persecutions, Parley Pratt argued, and he blamed the troubles in Ohio, Missouri, and Illinois on such turncoats. "Sooner than be subjected to a repetition of these wrongs," he preached, "I, *for one*, would rather march out to-day and be shot down." Young recounted a dream in which he cut the throats of two apostates from ear to ear with a large bowie knife he wore "as a bosom pin in Nauvoo." He told them, "Go to hell across lots." Rather than let such traitors flourish in Utah, Young swore, "I will unsheath my bowie knife, and conquer or die."[43]

By fall 1857 many disillusioned Latter-day Saints were eager to leave the territory, and early reports suggest that apostates sought refuge with the Fancher party. For example, San Francisco editor John Nugent concluded a great proportion of the party "were 'Back Outs,' mormons disgusted with the rule of Brigham Young and his Danite crew, who had availed themselves of the fancied protection of a body of emigrants, to leave Salt Lake." And William Hyde, a Mormon mail courier who traveled a few days behind the train, wrote that many of its members "were of the 'back out order,' who had joined the California emigrant train for security in traveling." The Mormon recipient of Hyde's letter thought "the fate of the 'back outs' just and merited."[44]

One of the earliest Utah catalogs of the sins of the Arkansans claimed a few apostates joined their wagon train seeking protection. They came from Springville, notorious for the Parrish-Potter murders of the previous spring, and feared the Mormons planned to murder them. The apostate's leader gave a speech to the Fancher company "well calculated to inflame the minds of the Strangers and Confirm all their preconceived opinions and sentiments, against the Mormons." Local authorities soon arrived to enforce the Law of Consecration. They seized an apostate's team and wagon, which resulted in an acrimonious debate with the emigrants, especially when the Mormons forced the man to pay the alleged debt. "From this time on the travelers indulged more freely in their unjustifiable liberties and unmerited insults," claimed the likely author of this fable, John D. Lee, "and each day their Conduct became more reckless and reprehensible."[45]

They Appeared To Be Bitterly Hostile

The Fancher party was not the only wagon train to take the road south in 1857. Two companies under William C. Dukes and Nicholas Turner left Salt Lake with large cattle herds only a few days' march behind the Fanchers. Turner's party was five or six days behind the Dukes wagons and included ten men, five women, and fourteen children. S. B. Honea reported he had left Arkansas in early May with a third party he called the Crook and Collins company. As was typical of overland companies, these groups exchanged members as they traveled south and united at Beaver in central Utah. As they neared Las Vegas, the combined outfits consisted of 23 wagons, 125 persons (including 44 men who could bear arms), 440 cattle, 130 work oxen, and 45 mules and horses. The company divided again as it crossed the Mojave. The first train arrived in San Bernardino on October 31, "consisting of seventy-one souls altogether: twenty-two men, seventeen women, and thirty-two children; all enjoying good health." Turner's party arrived sometime in November.[46]

These parties occasionally camped with the Mormon freight train of William Mathews and Sidney Tanner that left Salt Lake shortly after August 25. A few emigrants joined the Mormon freighters in early September. Mathews, a religious leader in San Bernardino, had already delivered a wagonload of ammunition to Utah. Before he left for home Mathews discussed sending more guns and ammunition to Utah with Brigham Young, who predicted Californians would stop the mail and blockade Cajon Pass. Mathews promised to warn Young of any impending invasion from the south.[47]

This second division of emigrants on the road through southern Utah lost all their money and trail stock but escaped with their lives and some of their firearms. On reaching Los Angeles, its members gave the newspapers the earliest reports of the Fancher party's ordeal in Utah, providing some of the best accounts of events surrounding the massacre.

Arkansan George Powers left Great Salt Lake City ten days behind the Fancher train and traveled part of the way south with the Dukes company, hoping to overtake and join the lead company. At Buttermilk Fort (present Holden), Powers found the inhabitants enraged, declaring that the previous company had "abused the Mormon women, calling them w———s," and "letting on about the men." The people at the fort had refused to sell the Fancher party supplies and "were sorry they had not killed them there; but they knew it would be done before they got in." They were holding the Indians in check, but when their chief returned, he would follow the train and cut it to pieces. Powers bought butter from women at the fort, but as he was leaving, Powers reported, "the men came running and charging, and swore [the emigrants] should not have it, nor anything else, as [they] had misused them," even though Powers had apparently done nothing more than purchase the butter. The Mormon men "appeared to be bitterly hostile." "We were unable to get anything we stood in need of," Powers said. "We camped at this place but one night."[48]

An early but apocryphal Mormon account claimed the beleaguered Fancher party "brought destruction upon themselves by their own reckless conduct" as they pushed south to the territorial capital at Fillmore. The party stopped near the State House, the unfinished capitol building that dominated the hamlet, and some wit wondered "how far it was to any houses." According to this tale, the "crowing & insulting" emigrants—or trail hands—allegedly asked if there were any men in the place and challenged them to come out, for "they were ready to fight & able to kill them." In a blaze of profanity, these ruffians said the "Government had sent Troops to kill every G——— damed Mormon in Utah—they hoped they would do so & that they should like to help them do the job." A few miles farther south at Meadow Creek the emigrants allegedly acted even more aggressively than they had at Fillmore. When the citizens said they had no wheat to sell, the emigrants armed themselves and advanced, "cursing the Mormons & threatening them with the troops as at Fillmore."[49]

THE POISONED SPRING

A day's travel south of Fillmore, emigrants typically camped on a stream near the Indian Farm at Corn Creek. In 1855 Indian agent Garland Hurt appointed Dr. John A. Ray, a Mormon, to furnish the Pahvants tools and teach them how to farm at the reservation established for Kanosh's band, who were loyal clients of the LDS church. By 1857 the farm was implementing Hurt's plan to civilize Utah's native people by teaching them European agriculture.[50] After making camp there, the Fancher party bought thirty bushels of corn from the Pahvants, who "sent them away in peace."[51] Ray reported that the emigrants bought food, but he claimed they illegally purchased government grain and cattle at half its value, leaving the cheated Pahvants to starve.[52]

Late in the evening of August 25, George A. Smith and his mixed band of Mormons and Indians camped about forty yards from the campfires of the Fancher party. According to Smith's official journal, the alarmed emigrants immediately doubled their guard.[53] Three men soon visited the Mormon camp. One introduced himself as the captain of the company and asked if the Indians camped across the creek posed any danger. Smith said he told them that "if their party had not committed any outrage upon the Indians there would be no danger."[54]

Jacob Hamblin recalled his encounter with the Fancher party for U.S. Army officers in 1859. The emigrants were mostly from Arkansas and had "not over thirty wagons. There were several tents, and they had from 400 to 500 head of horned cattle, 25 head of horses, and some mules." Most of the men had families with them. "The people seemed to be ordinary frontier 'homespun' people as a general thing. Some of the outsiders were rude and rough and calculated to get the ill will of the inhabitants." The men asked him about the condition of the road and the disposition of the Indians. Hamblin asked how many men were in the camp, and the emigrants said they had between forty and fifty "that would do to tie to." Hamblin said that "if they would keep a good lookout that the Indians did not steal their animals, half that number would be safe." The men supposedly asked where they could find a good place to rest their stock, even though Fancher had already spent three days at Mountain Meadows in 1850. Hamblin recommended the spring four miles south of his ranch at Mountain Meadows as "the best point to recruit their animals before they entered upon the desert."[55]

The next morning, legend claimed, the emigrants "most likely did that which led to their destruction."[56] William Mathews's Mormon freight train carried the earliest version of the story to California, where it appeared in the *Los Angeles Star* in early October. He claimed the emigrants poisoned the meat of a dead ox and "water standing in pools, for the purpose of killing the Indians." In San Bernardino J. Ward Christian charged that the emigrants cheated the Indians—the first people to sell them food since their arrival in Utah—and *then* poisoned them. According to Christian, the emigrants used strychnine to poison the ox carcass and "also put poison of some description in the water." The poison killed several Indians, and the survivors set out in pursuit, selected an ambush site, "and arranged everything before the train arrived at the place where they were murdered."

California newspaper editor Henry Hamilton, long an ally of the Mormons, could scarcely believe that an emigrant party would commit such an act and endanger the lives of those following them. "Yet this is the story told by all who have spoken of the massacre," he wrote. Hamilton left it to readers to form their own conclusions.[57]

What happened at Corn Creek is a key to understanding what happened at Mountain Meadows. If the Arkansans poisoned ox meat, the Indians had a plausible motive to attack them. Indian agent Jacob Forney, the first man to seriously investigate this and other "equally unreasonable stories [that] were told . . . about these unfortunate people," asked a telling question. Why would a respectable emigrant party "carry along several pounds of arsenic and strichnine, apparently for no other reason than to poison cattle and Indians"? He found such charges "too improbable to be true."[58] Yet the story is not without supporting evidence: it appears, after all, in the first newspaper accounts of the event, and its persistence in Utah folklore is remarkable. Some 1857 emigrants actually tried to poison Indians. Elizabeth Brittain Knowlton recalled how men in her overland party put poison in a dead ox after a battle on the Humboldt River. "The object for poisening the meat was to kill the Indians," Knowlton recalled. She felt this was inhuman, for if the party had simply left the ox to the starving Indians, they might not have done any other harm, and "emigrants doing such things caused the Indians to commit more crimes."[59]

The poison tale had serious problems, however. As it evolved, it was never told the same way twice. Less than six months after the meeting, George A. Smith wrote that the emigrants gave a dead ox to a party of "Pah Utahs" and "Pah Edes" who were visiting the Pahvants. Ten of them died immediately after eating it. The survivors "saw the Captain of the company go to the carcass with a bottle after the main body of the camp had left the ground." Smith claimed the water was poisoned and several animals died after drinking it. "The news of this tragedy spread through the different bands of Indians for hundreds of miles," the apostle reported, "and caused the concentration of reckless warriors who consummated the Massacre."[60]

Twelve years later the apostle transformed himself into an eyewitness. While Smith's party was hitching up, the emigrant captain asked if the Indians would eat an ox that had died during the night. Smith told him they would. "As we were starting," Smith said, "Elisha Hoops asked me what the Captain was doing over at the dead ox with a bottle in his hand." Smith told Hoops he was probably taking a drink.[61] The story was embroidered in 1875 when Hoops testified he "saw a German doctor traveling with the Arkansas train stick a knife into the carcass of the dead ox in question in three places and pour something in the cuts out of a vial." Hoops even claimed the emigrants used several sacks of poison to taint a spring that emerged from small holes in the ground.[62]

John Ray and local herdsmen told Apostle Smith ten Indians died from eating the dead animal and others were very sick. Thirty animals also died, "apparently of poison from drinking the waters of Corn Creek, which the emigrants were accused of poisoning." In Ray's version of the story, an Indian watched an emigrant sprinkle something white on a dead ox. The unsuspecting Indians carried the meat to their encampment, and those who ate the meat got "very sick & one Squaw died from the poison thus taken." Mormon cattle began dying immediately. The animals "were observed to go to water drink & in a few moments fall dead," Ray claimed. Some twenty cattle died in less than a week, including two of his own oxen that died three or four days after the company left Corn Creek. While rendering the tallow of a cow, Ray's wife cut her hand and it immediately "swelled to the body." Flesh around the wound turned black, and he had to use caustic "to separate the decayed from the sound flesh."[63] Ray was actually in England in August 1857 and did not explain how he performed this operation at such a great distance or reveal how anyone could poison a flowing creek so that it could kill an animal as large as a cow in a few moments.

The legends attributed remarkable powers to the emigrant poison that match no substance known to modern pharmacology, but the tales never made clear who or what was poisoned. Jacob Hamblin said the Arkansans had poisoned a small spring. At Fillmore he heard that eighteen cattle had died from drinking the water and the dead cattle had sickened six Pahvants and one or two of them died. According to Smith, ten Indians and thirty animals died from drinking the waters of Corn Creek. Lee claimed in 1859 that the emigrants put arsenic in a spring and strychnine in a carcass, and "about twenty Indians and some cattle died from drinking of the poisoned water, and Indians from eating the poisoned meat." William Ashworth thought the Arkansans poisoned a spring and a mule. None of these tales explained how to poison a flowing creek or spring, an impossible feat. Such confusion led historian Josiah Gibbs to conclude that the poison stories were sheer nonsense.[64]

On his return south, Jacob Hamblin passed through Fillmore on the day the town buried young Proctor Robison. His father said the boy had been poisoned while "trying out" the tallow of dead cattle at Corn Creek. Two years later Ray described how Robison scratched a small sore on his nose while skinning an ox. The boy's head immediately swelled to an enormous size, and he died four days later from the effects of the poison. Ray had no doubt "but that the Emigrants poisoned the water & caused this death."[65] Robison's demise provides a way to gauge the accuracy of the poison stories. Proctor Hancock Robison died at Fillmore on September 21, 1857, almost a month after the Arkansans camped at Corn Creek, too long after their passing for the overlanders to have played any role in his illness.[66] Yet the man who orchestrated their murder immediately linked Robison's death to the Fancher party. John D. Lee learned of the boy's death on his way to Salt Lake and blamed it on the emigrants when he addressed a Provo congregation on September 27.[67]

Reports of witnesses who followed the Fancher party cast more doubt on the poison stories. When P. M. Warn camped at Corn Creek on September 5, a Mormon Indian agent (probably George Armstrong) told him six Indians had died of poison and others were sick and would die. When Warn asked the war chief Ammon how many of his people had died from eating poisoned meat, he said "Not any—but some were sick. He did not attribute the sickness to poison nor did he give any reason for it." Ammon and his people were "not only friendly, but cordial," and made no mention of the Fancher party. Immediately after the purported poisoning, there were about eighteen wagons camped with Warn at Corn Creek "with whom," he said, "the Indians were as friendly as with ourselves."[68]

Traveling a few days behind Warn, George Powers called Corn Creek the "place we found the Indians so friendly." All he heard about the Fancher party was that it had passed through several days before. On reaching Beaver, however, the residents told him the entire poison story—how a Mormon had seen an emigrant cut the carcass and "pour some liquid into the cut from a phial." They said the meat killed three Indians, and others were sick and would die. The local Saints were outraged at the train, but when Powers asked an Indian if there was any truth to the poisoned meat story, the man said in English he did not know. Some Indians had died and others were sick, but "their water melons made them all sick, and he believed that the Mormons had poisoned them." In her bizarre autobiography, John D. Lee's last wife also blamed Mormons for the deaths. The emigrants had an ox who "died on the Road," she recalled, and the Mormons immediately "filled the flesh of the Ox with poison." The Indians ate the ox, and "many of them died. This was done for the purpose of inciting and infur[i]ating the Indians against the Emigrants."[69]

Something was killing cattle at Corn Creek, and Indian agent Jacob Forney gave a likely explanation in 1859: "The ox unquestionably died from eating a poisonous weed that grows in most valleys in this Territory." Such cattle deaths were common. Forney believed one or two Indians died from eating the dead ox, but he had not heard that this "excited any of the Indians against the emigrants."[70] Noxious weeds at the Corn Creek campsite had given overland travelers trouble for years. Thomas Flint had lost fifteen sheep and had "a great many more on the ground in spasms" just north of Fillmore in 1853. Another party lost eighty-six head out of some four thousand animals at Corn Creek, and historian Charles Kelly wrote that nearly every train that camped there reported losing sheep and cattle.[71] Juanita Brooks concluded that the cattle poisonings were the result of a poisonous plant or polluted water and that Proctor Robison died of an infection. His symptoms suggest he died of anthrax. Such tales, Brooks concluded, "provided a fact upon which it was easy to hang a growing line of accusations."[72]

Emigrant George Davis gave the most telling assessment of the poison tale: everyone in the Dukes train regarded the story as "a fabrication, on the part of the Mormons to clear themselves of suspicion, and to justify the Indians in murdering that company of emigrants." Davis camped at Corn Creek just ten days after the Fancher party, and over four days he "never heard anything of the poisoning." "We used the same water," he reported, "and between five and six hundred head of our cattle and horses used the same water, yet we discovered no poison, nor heard anything of it, till we got to Parowan." Davis had no doubt about who started the story: William Mathews of San Bernardino.[73] Yet the poison story actually preceded the Fancher party on their trip south, so it appears Mathews merely repeated propaganda invented by someone else.

The use of poison against Indians by the Mormons themselves may explain why George A. Smith leveled the charge against the Fancher party. As early as 1845 their Illinois neighbors claimed the Mormons threatened to poison wells "to revenge the death of their pretended prophet."[74] Militia captain William McBride conducted a ruthless campaign in Tooele Valley in 1851 that killed eleven Goshutes. After the soldiers burned everything they could find in the Indian village, including their dried meat, McBride made a request: "We wish you without a moment's hesitation to send us about a pound of arsenic. We want to give the Indians' well a flavour. Also a spade to dig for water. A little strickenine would be of fine service, and serve instead of salt to their too-fresh meat." After signing the report, McBride added a postscript: "Don't forget the arsenic! Don't forget the spade and arsenic! Don't forget the spade, strickenine and arsenic!"[75] Native traditions support the belief that McBride received the poison he requested. One Ute tribal elder recalled, "Those poor Goshutes—you know the Mormons poisoned them."[76]

The poison story had too many problems to serve the Saints well. Indian agent Forney's strict inquiry into events at Corn Creek did not identify "any difficulty the company had with the Pah-vant Indians while camped near them." Forney thought the poisoning affair was "entitled to no consideration." "*In my opinion, bad men*," he said, "for a bad purpose, have magnified a natural circumstance for the perpetuation of a crime that has no parallel in American history for atrocity."[77]

Without the poison tales, there is no proof the Fancher party did *anything* to provoke Utah's Indians. Yet despite the lack of credible evidence, some historians continue to assert as fact that on the road south, members of the Fancher party provoked and "abused" the Paiutes.[78]

In his daybook Hamblin provided a chilling glimpse into what did happen that night at Corn Creek. While camped near the "company of emigrants from Arcan Saw on thare way to Calafornia," Smith spoke of the strange atmosphere surrounding the travelers. He believed some evil "would befall them before they got through."[79]

Apostle Smith's comment was a self-fulfilling prophecy. After he preached to a crowded house at Fillmore the next day, Smith and his entourage continued on to Holden, where Silas Smith and Bishop Seymour Brunson left to return south. Federal prosecutors later believed they carried what massacre veterans called "orders from headquarters." Silas Smith took supper with the Fancher party on Indian Creek, six miles north of Beaver. He later called the emigrants rough fellows because they used blasphemous language—specifically, they said, "By God." Silas Smith was the likely source of the poison story that preceded the Fancher party. Militia captain Joel White testified that a week before the emigrants arrived at Cedar City "runners came along the road to stir up bad feeling." They accused the emigrants of poisoning the spring at Corn Creek. The tale swept through the southern settlements, taking on a life of its own.[80]

In the Black Mountains

No matter what happened at Corn Creek, the Arkansans increased their speed dramatically after their encounter with Smith, Hamblin, and the Paiutes. From Salt Lake to Corn Creek, some 160 miles, the train had averaged a little more than eight and one half miles per day. For the 170 miles from Corn Creek to Mountain Meadows, the Fancher party averaged about twelve miles per day, about as fast as an ox train with a cattle herd could travel. In addition, the trail now entered rough mountain country that was substantially more difficult than the road from Salt Lake. On leaving Corn Creek, the train climbed 1,000 feet to cross the 6,000-foot pass of the Pahvant Range and then traversed a second pass at 6,785 feet to the broken country north of Beaver. Crossing the Black Mountains at the north end of the Parowan Valley took the party to 6,680 feet, and south of Cedar City they entered terrain more difficult than any they had met since leaving Salt Lake. Something about the encounter at Corn Creek caused the Fancher party to push hard to get out of Mormon country, indicating it was not the neighborly visit described in Utah sources.[81]

The emigrants' tormented journey continued through the last Mormon settlements on the southern road: Beaver, Red Creek (present Paragonah), Parowan, and Cedar City. Even before the party arrived at Beaver about noon on August 29, the town had heard the poison story. Despite George A. Smith's orders not to sell the emigrants anything, a Mrs. Morgan traded a cheese for a bed quilt with the Fancher party. She and her husband were later cut off from the church. Robert Kershaw testified the emigrants camped not far from town, where lawman Seth Dodge prevented people from trading with them. The company may have spent the next day, a Sunday, at this camp. Some say a Missourian who had been jailed at Beaver for some alleged offense joined the party and "urged them to hurry beyond the power of the Mormons."[82]

A tale told years later described how Rufus Allen met the Arkansans as they hauled their wagons over the Black Mountains. The former leader of the Southern Indian Mission was on his way to Beaver when "about half way up the grade of the ridge he met the lead wagon of this California-bound company." Allen pulled off the road and waited for the long caravan to pass. Soon the captain of the train rode up on a well-groomed, well-bred horse, trying to get to the head of the train. Allen saluted him in a friendly way and joked, "I see that you have not been killed yet by any of these Mormons." The captain answered, "No, the sons of bitches dare not tackle us or they would have done so before this."[83]

In contrast to the belligerent edge of the Rufus Allen story, John Hawley left a sympathetic eyewitness account of the troubles dogging the Fancher party. Hawley, a Mormon from Texas, met the emigrants about one hundred fifty miles south of Provo and traveled with them for three days. He found the train was made up of families with a large herd of cattle. Their captain told him they had some trouble at Provo and Nephi. "We have a Dutchman with us, a single man, and he has given us all the trouble we have had." He "would not obey orders but was sassy with officers in these places." Hawley recalled how the captain, perhaps Alexander Fancher, pinpointed the other main cause of trouble: "It all originated by our cattle being grazed on there herd ground, but we intend to observe the laws and rules of the territory." The party planned to camp at Mountain Meadows "till the other company came up and then would both travel together." Hawley left the Arkansans "satisfied the Saints gave them more trouble than they ought." By the time he arrived in Washington County several days ahead of the Fancher party, Hawley found John D. Lee and other officials were already "having their interpreters stirring up the Indians to commit hostilities on this Camp of emigrants."[84]

The conflicts the Arkansas train encountered on the trail mattered not at all in the final balance. As the Fancher party struggled southward, its fate was being sealed in a meeting in Great Salt Lake City between the leaders of the southern Paiute bands and the man they called "Big Um"—Brigham Young.

THE PAIUTES VISIT THE MORMON CHIEF

Whatever led to their massacre, one thing is certain: the attack was set in motion days before the Fancher party reached Cedar City. Someone had to gather the interpreters and rally the Indians (including the Moapits band, which lived some one hundred miles from Mountain Meadows on the Muddy River), and it could not be done overnight. Time and distance dictate that by September 1, as the Arkansas families drove their animals and wagons over mountain passes miles away, officers of the Iron County Brigade were organizing an attack on them.

After leaving Corn Creek, George A. Smith stopped to preach in Provo on Sunday, August 30. "I never was more gratified than to see the Indians on the Santa Clara & Rio Virgin," said the apostle. If Brother Hamblin continued his labors, "a great work [would] be done among the Lamanites." As for the territory's prospects: "The great hugh & cry in the States is to kill Brigham Young and the leading men of this Church." Smith spoke of resurrecting the Danites, the Mormon secret police. He said the Danites had only existed for some six weeks in Missouri but "their has been none for the last 19 years" (though the legend of this band of holy murderers lived on in the popular imagination). "You know that Dan was to be an adder in the path & I propose that we have some now to help to carry out the purposes of God," said the portly apostle. "Let Dan be on the alert & meet them on the way."[85]

Brigham Young had unleashed the battle-ax of the Lord against emigrants passing through Utah, Bishop Elias Hicks Blackburn explained to his congregation that afternoon. He quoted Brother Brigham: "[the] Enemy is in our hands if we will do right." Near Box Elder twenty-five Shoshonis had stampeded six hundred cattle and horses, leaving an emigrant company on foot. "[Brigham Young has] held the Indians back for 10 years past but shall do it no longer!" the bishop thundered. "As soon as this word went out they have commenced upon our enemies!"[86]

That evening, forty miles away in Salt Lake, as the U.S. Army marched on Utah, Brigham Young conducted a prayer circle. He addressed fears that the government was buying the loyalty of the Lamanites with presents. Even if the nation gave them a few million, Young said, it would not be all that was due the Indians, and they would "turn around & take the rest." The Saints should "have no fears but what the Lamanites will be prepared to fill their mission." The time had not come for a great deal of hard fighting, for the Lord would fight their battles. Young recalled Christ's warning that the time would come to sell your coat and buy a sword. "That time has come," said the prophet.[87]

George A. Smith arrived in Great Salt Lake City at 4:00 P.M. on August 31, "having traveled about seven hundred miles of rough roads and preached in all the Settlements of Iron, Washington, and Beaver Counties."[88] The next day Jacob Hamblin brought ten or twelve Indians "to See Brigham the great Morman chief." The Mormons treated their potential allies with respect and showed the Indian leaders workshops, gardens, and orchards to demonstrate the advantages of hard work. Over the next few weeks Hamblin met repeatedly with the First Presidency to answer questions about the Southern Indian Mission and discuss plans for the impending war.[89]

As the Fancher train made camp some seventy miles north of Mountain Meadows on the evening of September 1, 1857, Young met for about an hour with the southern chiefs to implement his plan to stop overland emigration on the southern road. The Indians included "the chief of the Piedes and of the Deserts and Santa Clara, and Rio Virgen, and of Harmony." Kanosh of Corn Creek was the dedicated collaborator who the Mormons rewarded with guns and wives. Ammon from Beaver Creek, the brother of the late Wakara, was now presumed leader of the Ute Nation. Youngwuds (also known as Yungweids or Youngquick) was chief of the Paiute band at Harmony, Lee's home. Also there was the Paiute "head chief" Tutsegabit, whose good relations with the Mormons empowered him to be "a Piede Chief over 6 Piedes Band[s]."[90]

Dimick Huntington had already given the Shoshonis all the cattle on the northern road to California, and only days before Little Soldier had seized some four hundred animals from a Missouri emigrant named Squires—the transaction Bishop Blackburn had reported in Provo. Describing his meeting with the Paiutes in his journal, Young claimed he could "hardly restrain them from exterminating the 'Americans.'" In truth, that Tuesday night Young encouraged the Indians to seize the stock of the wagon trains on the southern route. Juanita Brooks recognized the importance of this crucial meeting but could only speculate on its purpose. Historians have long assumed no detailed eyewitness account of the interview existed, but the diary of Young's brother-in-law and interpreter, Dimick Huntington, has survived in the LDS Archives since 1859. Describing the September 1 parlay, Huntington wrote:

I gave them all the cattle that had gone to Cal the south rout   it made them open their eyes they sayed that you have told us not to steal   so I have but now they have come to fight us & you for when they kill us they will kill you   they sayd the[y] was afraid to fight the Americans & so would raise [allies] and we might fight[91]

The language of Huntington's critical journal entry is archaic, but its meaning is clear. Even a devout Mormon historian has identified the "I" in this entry as Brigham Young.[92] The Paiute leaders had camped with the Fancher party only a week earlier at Corn Creek, so Young did not have to paint a picture for the chiefs to know whose cattle he was giving them. The donation of the cattle to the Paiutes was not a direct order to massacre every Mericat in southern Utah, but Indian Superintendent Young had told the apostles, "The "Gentile emigrants [will] shoot the indians wharever they meet with them & the Indians now retaliate & will kill innocent People." He understood it was likely that innocent women and children would die in the Indian attacks he tacitly authorized.[93]

Frontiersman James Gemmell had just returned from a mission to Texas and Indian Territory, where his name had appeared on the warrant used to arrest Parley Pratt. Gemmell claimed he was in Young's office when Hamblin arrived and reported that the Arkansas train was near Cedar City. If he were in command of the Nauvoo Legion, Governor Young said, he "would wipe them out."[94]

With the Shoshonis handling emigrants on the northern road, the Pahvants and Piedes now had their instructions. After their evening meeting with the Mormon prophet on September 1, the Paiute chiefs slept in Great Salt Lake City and left precipitously the next morning.[95]

THE DAY THE PICKET WAS BROKE ON MY HEAD

After crossing the Black Mountains, the Arkansans entered the broad valley of Little Salt Lake. Jesse N. Smith wrote that an emigrant train passed Paragonah on September 3, and claimed he "went home and sold them some flour and salt."[96] Silas Smith recalled trading with the Arkansans at the same camp on Red Creek.[97]

Longtime southern Utah resident Charles Wandell later charged that William Dame did not want the emigrants to see the town's military preparations and refused to let them enter Parowan's walls. The party camped on a nearby stream and tried again to trade for food. The local gristmill refused to grind the corn they had bought at Corn Creek. Occasionally "some Mormon more daring than his fellows would sack up a few pounds of provisions" and smuggle them into the emigrant camp, Wandell claimed, "taking his chances of a severed windpipe." An Englishman tried to sell the Arkansans provisions, but a bishop's son held a bowie knife to his throat to stop him.[98]

William Leany of Parowan recognized William Aden, the young artist who had recently joined the Fancher train, as the son of Dr. Samuel B. Aden, who had protected him from a mob while he was on a Mormon mission in Paris, Tennessee. Leany had Aden to supper and invited him back for breakfast. On leaving, Aden asked for a few of the onions growing by his host's door, and Leany said, "Well take all you want and welcome." To reward Leany's hospitality, Dame sent Barney Carter to reprimand him, and Dame's enforcer tore a picket out of Laney's fence and hit him on the side of his head. As one neighbor said, "The man has never been sound in his mind since."[99] Leany's mind was sound enough in 1883 to recall "the day the picket was broke on my head" and a number of deeds of blood and to denounce "mobing, robing, stealing, whoredom, murder, suicide, infanticide, lying, slander, and all wickedness and abominations" in Utah's high places.[100]

DAME'S WOODPILE

Militia colonel William H. Dame, born in New Hampshire, was only thirty-eight years old in 1857 but had already helped found Parowan and Paragoonah, had served in the territorial legislature, and was president of the Parowan Stake. Dame was fond of lengthy discourses. A neighbor recalled that he "occasionally would get more or less excited and overdo it." Unlike Lee, he did not readily accept responsibility for his acts: Dame was a man who pushed unpleasant tasks onto the shoulders of others. Many believed he was simply a coward who "would always have a loop hole for everything that was not agreeable for him." Dame's neighbors blamed him for the events of September 1857 more than the colonel or his friends would later admit.[101]

Persistent traditions tell that the fate of the emigrants was decided at a meeting at "Dame's wood pile." Colonel Dame's disposition of his forces in early September suggests the meeting planned not just the massacre of the Fancher train but also the destruction of every emigrant party on the southern road. As John Hawley observed, the general sentiment in the southern Mormon settlements that September was that "all that came in the Territory must be cut off."[102]

Haight, Dame, and another man met at the east gate of the Parowan fort wall, William Barton recalled, and because they sat on a pile of bark, the meeting was known "in certain circles as the 'Tan Bark Council.'" "Right there and then the whole program was changed and it was decided to destroy the whole company."[103] James H. Martineau, Dame's adjutant, later confirmed that the men got together on Dame's woodpile and planned the attack.[104] The militia leaders agreed to launch the assault where the wagon road made a steep descent to Santa Clara Canyon, near the river's confluence with Magotsu Creek near present Gunlock. They also dispatched orders to the outlying settlements to rally the Indians.[105]

Southern Utah historian Josiah Rogerson heard that Haight "had a long talk with Dame on the memorable pile of Cedar posts" in Dame's lane. Rogerson, offering what may be a window into Mormon thinking, noted that Haight left with Dame's tacit authorization to have the Indians dispose of the emigrant company with "the winked at assistance of Lee."[106] The officers knew the Paiutes lacked the motive or military ability to make such an attack alone, but they believed Lee could manage the fight and conceal white involvement, a dangerous assumption.

A Craze of Fanaticism: Cedar City

The Fancher train arrived at Cedar City on Friday, September 4, to find the fires of the Reformation burning brightly. John Higbee recalled in 1896 that the town was in the grip of "a craze of fanaticism, stronger than we would be willing now to admit." Church orators dwelled on the "wrongs of mobbings and rapine" in the Mormon past. The Nauvoo Legion was "fully organized and drilled, standing guard, building Forts and spying out passes in the mountains, discussing the best means for defending [themselves] and [their] families against the approaching army, [and] looking out places of security" should the Saints have to burn their towns and flee to the mountains.[107]

In the midst of this fervor, Mormons of conscience resisted the hysteria. Undisguised hostility usually greeted the Arkansans on their trek through Utah, but in Cedar City the emigrants found a friend in miller Joseph Walker, a "sturdy and bluff old Englishman," who milled the grain they had bought at Corn Creek. Bishop Philip Klingensmith sent an elder to order the miller not to grind the wheat, but the independent-minded Walker refused to be intimidated. "Tell the bishop," he said, "I have six grown sons, and that we will sell our lives at the price of death to others before I will obey his order."[108]

Folklore charges that the Fancher party provoked the town with what one Mormon scholar characterized as "violent attacks."[109] These tales describe a gang that swore like pirates and acted like a pack of drunken cowboys. One evil-emigrant story told how their teamsters popped the heads off chickens with their bullwhips, and one especially enthusiastic account even laid the crime to female drovers.[110] Years later, in the absence of contemporary reports of these events, local reminiscences summarized what had become the collective memory of the community.

For example, in 1882 Charles Willden provided a virtual catalog of the sins of the emigrants. He recalled seeing about twenty wagons drive into Lower Town and stop near the gristmill. Willden heard the men "talking in a loud excited and boisterous manner profaning and threatening to do bodily harm and kill some of the citizens." They boasted they had helped to kill Joseph Smith and other Mormons in Nauvoo and Missouri "and that By G—— they would kill some more yet." The men threatened to go on to Mountain Meadows and wait there until the U.S. Army arrived. They would then return to Cedar "and carry out their threats."[111]

Walter J. Winsor was about ten years old when he visited the emigrant camp with his father to trade poor horses for fat ones. Winsor recalled, "They were the wickedest, swearing people I ever listened to. They boldly asserted and stated that they helped to murder the Prophet."[112] Seventeen-year-old Ed Parry was working on an irrigation ditch when the Fancher wagons passed through Cedar. Parry told how two mounted men from the party approached a group of Mormons. "[The man] riding a large gray mare seemed to be spokesman. He tried to get some of the crowd to buy him a gallon of whiskey, but none would do it. . . . [He] became abusive, swore at us all, said that he had the gun that killed Old Joe Smith, and that his company would go on to California and get an army and come back and wipe out every —— —— Mormon."[113]

Bishopric counselor Elias Morris, a militia captain, recalled how the emigrants "acted very wickedly, and had threatened the people repeatedly with what they would do." Morris said they tormented several women, including his mother. While Barbara Morris crossed a street as the company passed through, a tall man on horseback "addressed her in a very insulting manner." He brandished a pistol in her face, using "the most insulting and abusive language, and with fearful oaths declared that he and his companions expected to return to use up the 'Mormons.'" Some claimed the Arkansans prevented the arrest of one of their men for swearing. Morris said that Higbee, "marshall of Cedar City, tried to arrest this man, but he refused to be taken, and his companions stood by him, and dared the 'Mormons' to arrest any of them." Lee said Higbee told them "it was a breach of the city ordinance to use profane language. The men were not impressed and told Higbee they 'did not care a d—— for Mormon laws, or the Mormons either; that they had fought their way through the Indians and would do it through the d—— Mormons.'"[114] Laban Morrill testified, "The emigrants swore that they had killed old Joseph Smith; there was quite a little excitement there." People believed, Morrill wrote, that some of the emigrants "had assisted in the crimes of murdering and driving from their homes [Mormons] in Missouri and that one of them had openly boasted that he had helped to kill [the] prophet."[115]

Given the mood of the Utahns, a confrontation in Cedar City seems possible. Yet would men with families act so recklessly and provoke people who were known to be intolerant of outsiders? The provocations and harassment the emigrants evidently endured were undoubtedly vexatious, but the tales of their supposed atrocities are suspect. None of these stories appeared until at least fifteen years after the events supposedly happened. No two witnesses told the same story, and no two tales described a specific incident. Many abuses attributed to the Fancher party were actually committed by other parties years before. The stories, usually based on hearsay, multiplied over the years. There is no evidence to determine whether they had a basis in fact or were popular myths created to justify murder. Southern Utahns certainly believed that the emigrants boasted of shedding the blood of the prophet, but we may never know whether that belief was based on actual statements or propaganda.[116]

"Every one of the many charges of bad conduct by the Fancher train," historian David A. White noted, "comes directly or indirectly from Mormon sources whose motives must be questioned." Many of these charges (like the poison tales) seem trumped up.[117] Some originated with murderers such as Lee and Higbee, who used them to justify their crimes. In fairness to the silent dead, such reports must be viewed with deep suspicion. Simple logic suggests the Arkansans tried to observe the laws of the territory and get out, as their leader had told John Hawley. The emigrants knew "they were in the enemies' country, and absolutely within the power of the Mormons," wrote Mormon gadfly Josiah Gibbs. "Those emigrants are entitled to the credit of having had at least common sense."[118] Moreover, even if some of the emigrants provoked the citizens of Cedar City, Nauvoo Legion officers were already organizing an attack on the train. Regardless of the Arkansans' conduct, Brooks noted, "when the facts are marshaled, there is not justification enough for the death of a single individual."[119]

INDIANS ENOUGH: LAMANITES AND LEGIONNAIRES

Soon after returning from a scouting trip to Panguitch Lake, Elias Morris recalled seeing Lee talking with Haight in Cedar City. "Lee seemed very determined that the company should be made to suffer severely for their impudence and lawlessness. . . . [He had] Indians enough around him to wipe the whole of them out of existence."[120]

Years later Lee claimed he received his marching orders from Haight at a meeting in Cedar City in early September. He said, "[We] took some blankets and went over to the old Iron Works, and lay there that night, so we could talk in private." Haight told Lee it was "the *will of all in authority*" to arm the Indians, "send them after the emigrants, and have the Indians give them a *brush*, and if they killed part or all of them, so much the better." Haight had sent Klingensmith and others to Pinto to force the Indians to attack the emigrants. Some of the Indians were on the warpath, and all of them had to be sent out "to make the thing a success." Haight was to order Indian interpreter Nephi Johnson "to *stir up*" all the Indians he could find "to give the emigrants a good *hush*." Lee told Haight the Paiutes would indiscriminately kill all the emigrants, including the children, who were by definition innocent blood. Haight swore and said, "There will not be one drop of *innocent* blood shed, if every one of the d——d pack are killed, for they are the worse lot of out-laws and ruffians that I ever saw in my life."[121]

More than fifty years later, Johnson recalled how a boy came to his ranch and told him Isaac Haight wanted him to talk to some Indian women in Cedar City who were stealing wheat from the fields. When Johnson arrived, Haight saddled his horse and the two men rode to the Paiute camp some four miles from town. Haight told him that Lee had come from Harmony the day before and wanted to gather up the Indians and destroy the emigrant train that had passed through Cedar City two days earlier. Haight had told Lee to go ahead but had sent a messenger to Brigham Young "to know what to do about it." He asked Johnson for his thoughts: "I said to him it would be a fearful responsibility for a man to take upon himself to distroy that train." Johnson advised waiting until word came back from Young. Haight said Lee had already gone to raise the Indians. Johnson would tell Lee to wait, but he also told Haight there was "a much better place on the Santa Clara to attack the train" than Mountain Meadows.[122]

Lee's son-in-law Levi Smithson remembered that Johnson led one band of Indians from Cedar City to Mountain Meadows. Smithson felt the military men in the Mormon militia were compelled to obey orders, and "John D. Lee received three notices from Col. Dame before he consented to go."[123] Mary Campbell saw Jesse Smith, Philip Klingensmith, John Higbee, and another man accompany Lee to an Indian camp near Cedar City. Afterward, "the Indian squaws came into the post and the bucks left for the Meadows: the squaws said the Indians were going to kill the 'Mericats.' The Indians started at once." At the same time, Haight sent Samuel Knight and Dudley Leavitt to collect the Santa Clara bands for an attack.[124]

Perhaps on Friday, September 4, Lee met a large band of Indians under Moquetus and Big Bill, two Cedar City chiefs on the road to Harmony. "They were in their war paint, and fully equipped for battle," Lee remembered. The Paiutes said "they had had a big talk with Haight, Higby and Klingensmith, and had got orders to follow up the emigrants and kill them all, and take their property as the spoil of their enemies." They wanted Lee to take command, but Lee "had orders from Haight, the big Captain, to send other Indians on the war-path to kill the emigrants." He told them to camp near the emigrants and wait for him. Lee sent Carl Shirts to "stir up the Indians of the South, and lead them against the emigrants," but Lee said Shirts, his son-in-law, was "naturally cowardly" and did not want to go. Lee gave him no choice.[125]

Lee sent runners and gathered Indians from the surrounding country and gave them a feast at Harmony.[126] He "fixed up as much like a military officer as he could with the clothes he had, a red sash around his waist and a sword in his right hand," one of Lee's neighbors recalled. He "marched around the inside of the fort, at the head of about 40 or 50 Indians," calling to his Lamanite cohort, "All that wish success to Israel say Amen." When only two or three answered back, Lee called for a better response. It was not much better.[127]

Many of the local Saints believed the dividing line had been drawn between Mormons and gentiles and that all the emigrants in the territory must be cut off. After leaving the Fancher party, John Hawley arrived at the village of Washington to find Lee and the other leaders had sent their interpreters to incite the Paiutes to attack the emigrant camp. The town's military and religious authorities sought to inflame the passions of their followers. The first counselor in the local bishopric, Nauvoo Legion captain Harrison Pearce impressed Hawley as the most militant authority. In a public meeting, Pearce said he wished to "see all the Gentyles strippt naked and lashed on their backs and have the Sun scorch them to death by inches."[128]

Yet the response of the militia companies to their call was not universally enthusiastic, as men of conscience resisted orders to assault civilian Americans. Two other men gave similar harangues, and then Hawley was called on to report as he had just come down from Salt Lake. He argued against Pearce's warlike position. Before he would take another's life, he would have to be convinced his own life was in danger. As for avenging the blood of the prophets, Hawley asked, who could say for certain these people had any hand in killing the prophets? The oath of vengeance required him to be certain he could justify killing a man, but the local Saints had no assurance that anyone in the Fancher party had participated in the murder of Joseph Smith. "You only suppose and that will not do for me," Hawley said.[129]

In retaliation, Captain Pearce called a secret council to debate Hawley's fate. Some thought Hawley ought to die, but others pleaded his case. The next day a friend warned him to be more guarded and not to oppose authority. Hawley responded, "[I am] as well prepared to die now as ever, and you may tell the council I will stand on the same ground I took yesterday."[130]

As the Fancher party sought refuge at Mountain Meadows, stake president Isaac Haight rose to address Sunday services in Cedar City. He recalled how Missourians had driven them out to starve; "When we pled for mercy, Haun's Mill was our answer, and when we asked for bread they gave us a stone. . . . [We went] far into the wilderness where we could worship God according to the dictates of our own conscience without annoyance to our neighbors. We resolved that if they would leave us alone we would never trouble them." But the gentiles would not leave them in peace. Although the Mormons had traded with and fed the gentiles, the nation had sent an army to exterminate the Mormons. "I have been driven from my home for the last time," Haight pledged. "I am prepared to feed to the Gentiles the same bread they fed to us. God being my helper I will give the last ounce of strength and if need be my last drop of blood in defense of Zion."[131]

At Harmony, Rachel Lee wrote on Saturday, September 5, "Bro: J. D. Lee went on an expedition South."[132] Lee probably used a pack trail from Ash Creek to reach Mountain Meadows. One of Lee's men gave the earliest account of the organization of the initial assault to government investigators in May 1859. Following a council at Cedar City, Haight, Higbee, and Lee appointed a large number of men to "perform the work of dispatching these emigrants." The men were ordered to report well armed at a set time in the hills near Hamblin's ranch. Here they "painted and otherwise disguised themselves so as to resemble Indians."[133] William Winsor recalled that these men included George Adair, Bill Stewart, Jim Pierce, and Carl Shirts.[134]

That night Lee camped with his Paiute war party. The Indians' leader dreamed that both his hands were filled with blood, a bad omen. In the morning he told Lee about the dream, but Lee reassured him, interpreting the double handful of blood as "a victory for the redmen, and that they would secure the blood of the emigrants."[135]

FAR INTO THE WILDERNESS: THE LAST MARCH

The emigrants left Cedar City late Friday afternoon and camped at the corner of the cooperative field some three miles from the town. Mormons later charged that they tore down the fence and used it for fuel and turned their animals onto the town's crops. Some said they spent another day near the city, but the party must have started for the meadows by Saturday morning, September 5, 1857.[136] One source claimed the Mormons sent three men to pose as apostates "to learn the strength of the party."[137]

In 1857 there were two roads between Cedar City and Mountain Meadows: the Spanish Trail by way of present Newcastle and Leach's Cutoff through Pinto.[138] By the latter route, it was thirty-seven miles from the town to the meadows. Today's roads follow the line of the cutoff west from Cedar City on Highway 54 to the junction of Dixie Forest 009, the Pinto Road. Passing to the south of Iron Mountain, this gravel road joins State Highway 18 at Mountain Meadows. To reach the meadows from Cedar City in two days, the Fancher party would have had to go at least as far as Iron Springs, some twenty miles, by the first night. From the wide fields at present Page's Ranch on Little Pinto Creek, the emigrants followed the wagon road across a low ridge to the Mormon village at Pinto. They then pressed on to pass Hamblin's summer ranch on Meadow Creek at the northern end of Mountain Meadows.[139]

By the mid-1850s the oasis at Mountain Meadows was notorious among the Saints. The apostates who joined Thomas Flint's train at Parowan in 1853 "were so much in fear of the 'Destroying Angels' that they did not dare to venture away from the camp fire at night."[140] Sending someone "over the rim of the basin," Lee recalled, was a "term used by the people when they killed a person." This early Mormon euphemism for murder evoked the isolation that made Mountain Meadows a preferred location for the quiet execution of unpleasant tasks.[141]

About noon one day in early September, Rachel Hamblin recalled that a large train passed her house at the upper end of the meadows. None of the people stopped, but there "may have been a man who came and inquired the way to the spring." The next morning a man made the four-mile trip from Cane Spring to buy butter and cheese. She had none, and the man stayed only a short time, saying his people would camp at the spring a while to recruit their stock. The Hamblins had an adopted son whose Shoshoni name meant "hungry," but they called him Albert. He saw a train come along the road near sundown, and Albert watched them make camp at the spring. "When the train passed me I saw a good many women and children," he told the army two years later.[142]

Strung out along the road and disorganized, the weary wagon party arrived in detachments at the meadows on Sunday evening. After crossing the imperceptible ridge that marked the rim of the Great Basin, the emigrants left the California Trail and headed to Cane Spring, a large fountain at the southern end of the meadows that lay at the bottom of a five-foot ravine filled with hardy grass. Below the spring, the arroyo deepened to ten feet, and about three hundred yards south of the campsite a shallow gorge cut into the creek from the west, forming a grass-filled bowl that was a natural cattle pen.[143]

The train's last wagons probably arrived after dark, their way lighted by an almost-full moon. Too exhausted to form an organized corral, the wagons scattered around the sheltered campsite beside Magotsu Creek, bordered by ravines on the east and south, low hills on the west, and volcanic ridges to the north.[144]

Lee led his men to the hills overlooking the wagons scattered on the plain at Mountain Meadows. Lee's profound belief in signs and portents led him to conclude that God had delivered the emigrants into his hands. The original battle plan called for the attack to take place a day's drive farther on as the party made the steep descent into Santa Clara Canyon, but there was no way to predict how long the emigrants intended to camp at the meadows. The Mormons and the Indians would have to wait too long for them to fall into the trap at Santa Clara. As the last wagons pulled into the campsite on Sunday night, Lee apparently saw his chance to attack the disorganized train when it was most vulnerable. In the moonlit darkness, the Mormon interpreters stripped for battle and donned war paint to disguise themselves as Indians. Jackson, a Paiute captain, later said all the Mormons were painted. Before daybreak on Monday morning, Lee deployed his men at the meadows, and at dawn they found a number of emigrants standing by the campfires.[145] As his men crept up to the wagons, John D. Lee prepared to avenge the blood of the prophets.

7

The Knife and Tomahawk

Even on hot days September mornings dawn cold in the mountains of southern Utah. In the dim gray light before sunrise on Monday, September 7, 1857, a few of the emigrants at Mountain Meadows rolled out of their blankets to rekindle campfires and begin brewing coffee. While it was still dark, raiders had crept down the ravine southwest of the camp and driven the emigrants' cattle up the draw. Undetected, the rest of the men descended the arroyo to Magotsu Creek and then slipped up its bed to within yards of the emigrant camp.[1]

At first light, gunfire ripped through the morning calm, raining fire on the camp. A child who survived the attack later wrote, "Our party was just sitting down to a breakfast of quail and cottontail rabbits when a shot rang out from a nearby gully, and one of the children toppled over, hit by the bullet."[2] The deadly barrage struck down between ten and fifteen victims, killing seven of them.[3] Three of the wounded men were taken out of the fight and died within days.[4] To avoid crossfire, coordinated attacks came from "the ravine near the spring close to the wagons and from a hill to the west."[5]

The emigrants grabbed their weapons. With a howl, painted men launched a frontal assault on the camp but quickly retreated in the face of withering fire from the emigrants. The attacking force was not large enough to overrun the camp or simply lacked the will to do the job. Arkansas marksmanship killed at least one Indian and shattered the knees of two Paiute war chiefs, Moquetus and Big Bill, and this tenacious resistance broke the back of the surprise attack.

In the predawn quiet of the upper meadows, Rachel Hamblin heard a great number of guns firing at Cane Spring. The "firing kept up until after daylight, all of half an hour, when it ceased."[6] The emigrants' quick response temporarily frightened away their foes. During the lull that followed, the Arkansans corralled all but

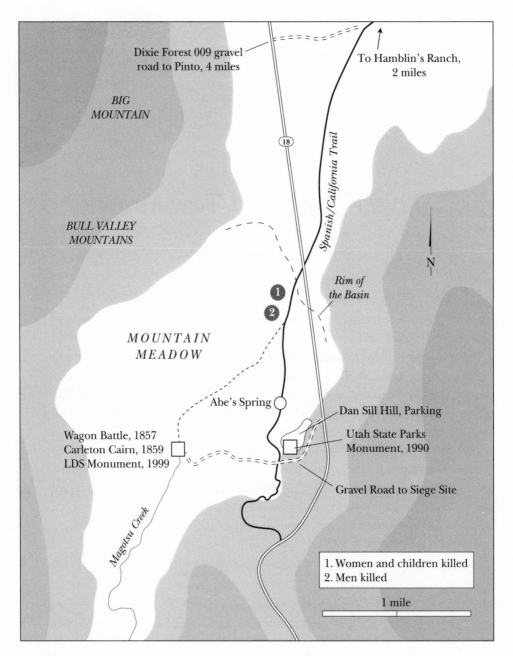

Dixie Forest 009 gravel
road to Pinto, 4 miles

To Hamblin's Ranch,
2 miles

*BIG
MOUNTAIN*

18

Spanish/California Trail

N

*BULL VALLEY
MOUNTAINS*

*Rim of
the Basin*

1

2

*MOUNTAIN
MEADOW*

Abe's Spring

Dan Sill Hill, Parking

Wagon Battle, 1857
Carleton Cairn, 1859
LDS Monument, 1999

Utah State Parks
Monument, 1990

Magotsu Creek

Gravel Road to Siege Site

1. Women and children killed
2. Men killed

1 mile

Mountain Meadows, Utah, today

one of their wagons about one hundred yards above the springs, away from the
sniper-infested ravines. They circled the wagons and shoveled dirt under them to
build a rough fortification.[7] Nancy Huff, four years old on that September morning,
remembered,

> We were in a small prairie. One morning before day I was woke up by the fir-
> ing of guns, and learned that our camp had been attacked, we suppose[d], by
> Indians. Some of the men folk were wounded. The men dug a ditch around
> our camp, and fortified the best they could. The women and children got in
> the ditches, and were comparitively out of danger.[8]

Rebecca Dunlap, six years old at the time, recalled,

> In the morning just before light about sixty Mormons, disguised as Indians, and
> a number of Indians attacked the train. The Indians were ordered to stampede
> the cattle and drive them away from the train. They then commenced firing
> on the emigrants. The fire was returned by the emigrants, who had corraled
> their wagons. The Mormons and Indians had the train completely surrounded
> and they were cut off from the spring.[9]

Four-year-old Emberson Milum Tackitt later told of the heroism of his aunt, Eloah
Angeline Tackitt Jones, as she fought alongside the men, using the gun of one of the
fallen emigrants.[10]

Family traditions claim both Alexander Fancher and John Baker were badly wounded
early in the fight. James Mathew Fancher took command and ordered the men to circle the wagons. Within minutes the emigrants had formed an effective defensive position—a wagon fort—and launched an aggressive counterattack. Several men left the
corral to investigate the cause of the firing and soon "were engaged in another battle
at close range" that cost several casualties but did little damage to the enemy, "who
took advantage of the boulders and underbrush for shelter."[11]

From the fading darkness, John Lee watched his ragged army crack in the face of
the emigrant's unexpectedly forceful resistance. "Now we knew the Indians could not
do the work," Lee recalled, "and we were in a sad fix."[12] The battle now locked into
a siege, a development the attackers apparently had not considered.

Someone had told the Paiutes, Lee recalled disingenuously, "that they could kill the
emigrants without danger to themselves." The dead warriors cast doubt on Lee's honesty and the power of Mormon magic in the minds of his allies. Nephi Johnson said
they were angry because Clem, Lee's interpreter and adopted Paiute son, "lied to them
so much," but it was the failure of the whites' magic that probably aggravated the Paiutes.
As the Mormons fell to bickering with their allies, Lee's hope for a quick victory evap-
orated with the dew on the meadow. The emigrants' prompt retaliation took the fire out
of Lee's hastily assembled force, and he could not immediately rally them for another
attack. The Paiutes later said "the emigrants had long guns, and were good shots."[13]

For the Mormons, the situation soon got worse. The Paiutes were in a frenzy,
Lee claimed, and his talk only increased their excitement. After persuading his allies
to let him go for reinforcements, Lee saddled his horse and headed down the California Trail. He went some fourteen miles to where the wagon road made a sharp descent
into Santa Clara Canyon, the place the Mormons originally planned to stage the

ambush. Here Lee found militiamen Samuel Knight, Dudley Leavitt, and "about one hundred Indians, and a number of Mormons from the southern settlements."[14]

After Lee left the meadows, his men rounded up the train's stock and drove the animals back to Iron Creek, leaving guards behind to prevent the emigrants from getting water. Thirst now compounded the emigrants' problems, for Cane Spring lay many yards outside their wagon fort. The Arkansans fired at their assailants "every time they showed themselves, and they returned the fire." The desperate emigrants improved their defenses, digging a pit to shelter the women, children, and wounded. Outside the circled wagons they dug a trench some twenty feet long and four or five feet wide and deep, with a bank two feet high.[15]

THE SUBSTANCE WAS FOR THEIR DESTRUCTION: CEDAR CITY

Figuring out what to do about the troublesome emigrants had obsessed the authorities in Cedar City since the wagon train left town on Friday evening. At their meeting around Dame's woodpile, the militia officers had decided to orchestrate an "Indian" attack on the Fancher train, but Isaac Haight needed public support for the plan. Haight raised the question on September 6, 1857 at "a prayer circle, composed of the members of the Cedar Stake Presidency, Bishop Klingensmith and Counselors, and the members of the High Council." Laban Morrill recalled the council generally met at about 4 o'clock, after Sunday services. Arriving late, he "saw there a little excitement in regard to something [he] did not understand." He "inquired in a friendly way, what was up." Morrill then heard many threats against the Fancher train. Haight and Klingensmith proposed killing the emigrants for boasting they had helped to murder Joseph Smith. John Higbee, perhaps humiliated by his failure to arrest the party's outriders, agreed.[16]

Haight introduced the subject of the Arkansas company. The radicals suggested harsh measures, but "others were in favor of letting the thing pass off and not bother the company."[17] Morrill recalled a hostile crowd; some were in favor of killing the emigrants, and some were not. Bishop Klingensmith argued forcefully for the emigrants' destruction, but Haight was taken aback by the opposition, which proposed "laying so important a matter before President Young." Morrill suggested, "We should still keep quiet, and a dispatch should be sent to Governor Young to know what would be the best course." After a unanimous vote in favor of sending a dispatch, the papers were allegedly drafted. No hostile action was to be taken until a messenger returned with Young's orders. Morrill returned to his home, "feeling that all was well." Yet his sensible proposal outraged his leaders. Morrill saw Daniel Macfarlane and Joseph Smith leave the meeting before it ended, and he later learned the two men had been sent to waylay him. Intuition saved his life, for after the council meeting Morrill "felt impressed to go a different way home—to Johnson's Fort. He did so, giving the horses the reins, and going in a hurry."[18]

Instead of receiving the approval he had sought, Haight now faced a dilemma. He had failed to get the community to endorse killing the emigrants, and he had no desire to send a message to Brigham Young that would make him appear indecisive—or to be questioning orders. Klingensmith recalled that "Haight jumped up and broke up the meeting and went out of doors," where he convened the men he could trust. "There a proposition was made," Klingensmith later testified evasively, "the substance [of which] was for their destruction," and the men discussed how to get the Indians to destroy the emigrant party.[19]

On Monday afternoon, as the emigrants tended their wounded and fortified their camp, Haight received word of the attack and finally acted on the High Council's decision to send a courier to the governor for instructions. Haight asked several men to volunteer before James Holt Haslam accepted the job. No copy of this critical message survived, but allegedly Haight's letter to Brigham Young said, "The Indians have gotten the emigrants coralled at Mountain Meadows and Lee wants to know what to do."[20] Haslam saddled a Spanish horse and left Cedar City shortly after four o'clock. At Parowan William Dame gave Haslam a note to carry ordering all bishops to furnish him horses. Haslam faced a tough job, but his ride was hardly the hell-bent-for-leather exploit often described. He picked up a fresh mount at Beaver and arrived in Fillmore before daylight, where he waited most of the day for the bishop (probably Seymour Brunson) to return from a hunt. Haslam then rode ten miles to Holden but was forced to wait until 3:00 A.M. to send back to Fillmore for a better horse. Early on September 9 Haslam reached Nephi, pausing only long enough to eat breakfast. He stopped again at Payson, Provo, and American Fork to change mounts.[21]

George Hancock of Payson told Indian agent Hurt, the sole non-Mormon government officer left in the territory, that "the California emigrants on the southern route had got themselves into a very serious difficulty with the Piedes" and were "compelled to seek shelter behind their wagons." Hancock was confident the expressman who told him this could make his six-hundred-mile round trip in the allotted one hundred hours. The next day a Ute from Sevier Lake told Hurt the Mormons had killed all the emigrants. If Lee hoped the remoteness of Mountain Meadows would keep his activities secret, his plan was already unraveling. On September 14 a Ute named Spoods gave Hurt more news of "the difficulty between the emigrants and the Piedes." Spoods thought the Paiutes "had been set upon the emigrants by the Mormons."[22]

To Attack This Train: Who Was There?

It is impossible to determine exactly how and when the attacking forces arrived at Mountain Meadows; to this day both the Paiutes and the Mormons blame each other for initiating the assault, and the tribe's traditions deny any involvement at all in the massacre.[23] Mormon witnesses reported that Lee, Higbee, and Haight "organized a party of fifty or sixty Mormons to attack [the] train," but Lee may have launched the initial assault with only a few whites.[24] After returning from the Santa Clara, Lee allegedly requested reinforcements from Haight at Cedar City under the pretext of rescuing the party. Lee claimed they did nothing, awaiting orders, but he probably launched more attacks.[25] Haight received Lee's call for help by Monday afternoon, and according to Higbee, a dozen or more "honorable good citizens" volunteered to go to the meadows. (The five trips Higbee recalled making between Mountain Meadows and Cedar City would have totaled 185 miles, suggesting he was present at the first attack and was the man sent to report its failure.)[26] A scouting party of six or eight men including Joel White, William C. Stewart, and Elliot C. Willden soon reached the meadows, "but they had no orders. They had come merely to see how things were."[27]

Lt. Carl Shirts and between ten and fifteen Nauvoo Legionnaires from Santa Clara reached the battlefield about one o'clock on Tuesday afternoon.[28] Lee said they included Capt. Harrison Pearce, Lt. Oscar Hamblin, Sgt. William Slade, Sr., Sgt. William Hawley, militia privates John W. Clark, Samuel Knight, Dudley Leavitt, James Mathews, William R. Slade, William Young, and two others, perhaps Pvt. George W. Adair and Sgt. George Hawley.[29] James Pearce and about six men arrived from Washington with "a little two horse wagon."[30]

Albert Hamblin, Jacob Hamblin's adopted Indian son, claimed a good many men came "over from Pinto Creek 'and about' and stayed around the house while the fight went on." Albert reported seeing Richard Robinson, Prime Coleman, Amos Thornton, and one Dickinson from the nearby village of Pinto at the meadows during the siege.[31] In addition, seventy-three volunteers from Cedar City arrived at the meadows over the next four days.[32] At least one hundred Mormon men, drawn from every settlement south of Parowan, eventually joined the fight.

The Santa Clara chiefs told Judge Cradlebaugh in 1859 that "a portion of their men were engaged in the massacre, but were not there when the attack commenced."[33] Years later Beaverite, said to be "Chief of the Beavers" and a brother of Kanosh, said not more than one hundred Indians were at the meadows. (Beaverite heard this from Moquepus, who died of his wounds a year after the fight.)[34] Even George A. Smith only "supposed that there were upwards of 200 Indian warriors engaged in this massacre." In 1875 Philip Klingensmith claimed about one hundred Indians joined in, but Joel White's recollection that there "might have been 40 or 50, somewheres along there—a good many Indians" was probably closer to the truth. John Higbee's report of three hundred to six hundred "wild Indians" on the field seems wildly exaggerated.[35]

The composition of the Indian forces at Mountain Meadows is hard to deduce. The force consisted largely of Paiute bands from Cedar City, Fort Harmony, Pinto, and the Virgin and Santa Clara Rivers. Tribal leaders said to have been at the massacre included Tutsegabit, Noucopin, Moquetus, Chickeroo, Youngwuds, and Jackson. (Tutsegabit, Youngwuds, and perhaps others had met with Brigham Young only a week before the attack.)[36] Feargus Willden recalled that several wounded Indians, Bill, Moquetus, Toanob, Buck, and others, "came to [his] house to be administered to."[37]

Lt. George M. Wheeler in 1869 characterized Toshob, chief of the Muddy River band, as "a wily, treacherous, cold-blooded old scamp, who was well known to have been the leader of the Indians" at Mountain Meadows.[38]

Mormon folklore tells that after the poisonings at Corn Creek, angry Pahvants followed the Fancher party south. Early reports often listed their leader, Kanosh, as a participant, but in 1859 Indian agent Jacob Forney concluded, "After strict inquiry I cannot learn that even one Pah-vant Indian was present at the massacre." Nephi Johnson swore in 1876 that he saw no Pahvants at the meadows.[39] Kanosh knew all the details of the massacre, but as a dedicated collaborator he stoutly followed the Mormon version of events, although he did not name any of his tribesmen as participants. Early in 1858 Kanosh told Thomas Kane the Paheats bands of Quanãras, Young-wuds, and Tutsegabit executed the massacre. Kanosh charged the Moapits band from the Muddy River pitched in: "Besides there were Indians from the Mõah pãh (Spirit Water) where the spirits of the dead go."[40]

A number of freebooters answered Lee's call for warriors. Men such as Enos, who had no strong tribal connection but lived alternately with the Utes, Pahvants, and Piedes, were ready to sell their services to the highest bidder. As the Mormons learned in their Indian wars of the 1860s, such men had fighting skills well adapted to a guerrilla campaign, but they were not soldiers who could mount a successful siege. Managing the Indians was a waking nightmare for Higbee and Lee. The Paiutes showed no interest in a long-running battle. They wanted the guns and beef they were promised, but they did not intend to die to get them.

White participants later claimed they only killed the emigrants to avoid an Indian war that would destroy their own families, but Mormon sources make it clear that they did not regard the Paiutes as a military threat. William Wall passed through Mountain Meadows in late 1857 and boasted that if he had commanded the emigrants, "he could have whipt one thousand Indians."[41] Judge Cradlebaugh concluded in 1859 that all the Indians in southern Utah would not, under any circumstances, "carry on a fight against ten white men."[42] LDS historians continue to claim the Paiutes greatly outnumbered Mormons in the southern settlements, but in 1858 Forney estimated the number of Paiutes in the area at only 2,200, roughly the same as the white population.[43] Higbee and Lee later tried to shift responsibility for their own crimes to the Indians by claiming they tried to save the emigrants from the "savages." If so, the fact that everyone in the party over six years of age ended up dead marks their effort as a distinct failure.

Despite the vivid pictures white participants later painted of crazed savages howling for blood, the few Indian accounts suggest the actions of their white allies shocked the Paiutes. By Indian standards, they made no sense. Why had the missionaries told them not to kill and steal yet now seemed bent on killing every last Mericat man, woman, and child? Why charge the emigrant fort again and again? Why not simply take the cattle and leave? Lee had promised the Indians "clothing, all the guns and horses, and some of the cattle to eat," Beaverite recalled. "So they went." Moquepus "always said Lee was the Chief over him in that fight. That was the bargain."[44] But the Paiutes had not bargained for their heavy casualties or the rage that possessed their white allies.

Returning from the Santa Clara, Lee met a small band of Indians deserting his force with about twenty cattle. By Tuesday, he claimed, only about two hundred Indians remained at the meadows, including the wounded chiefs, Moquetus and Bill, and other casualties. Although he claimed he participated in a second nighttime assault as a noncombatant, Lee described coming under fire in an attack on the north side of the wagon fort. "The bullets came around us like a shower of hail," he recalled. "One bullet passed through my hat and the hair of my head, and another through my shirt, grazing my arm near the shoulder." The Paiutes raised a "hideous yell," which the women and children in the emigrant camp answered with cries and shrieks.[45]

More Indians left on Wednesday, taking a few cattle with them. Lee kept his allies busy broiling beef and making their hides into lassoes, but his Paiute host was disintegrating before his eyes.[46]

Bedlam or Hell

A day or two after Isaac Haight told Nephi Johnson he had authorized Lee to destroy the emigrants, an Indian runner arrived at Johnson's ranch from Mountain Meadows. He said the Indians had attacked the emigrants the night before and had been repulsed. When he was an old man Johnson recalled, "I did not want anything to do with killing the emigrants for I was determined in my own mind that I would keep away from them." His reluctance was useless, for messengers came to his ranch and said Haight wanted him to go to Cedar City to talk with some Indian women who were stealing wheat. Haight had told them Johnson must come whether he wanted to or not.[47] In town Haight said "that Lee and the Indians had went to the Meadows to kill the emigrants, and had made three attacks upon them, but had found the emigrants better fighters than they had expected." Several Paiutes were dead and more wounded and they were getting tired of it. Lee wanted to let the emigrants go, but Haight sent Lee orders to finish what he had started.[48]

By Wednesday the Mormons had apparently displaced the Indians from their camp east of the emigrant fort. Maj. John Higbee admitted seeing two or three Mormons painted like Indians camped a mile to the east of the wagon fort at Abe's Spring, today headquarters of the Lytle Ranch. Some of the Paiutes camped on Magotsu Creek below the emigrant fort to cut off anyone trying to escape down its narrow canyon.[49]

The suffering of the doomed company defies imagining. The few details of the five-day seige recalled by the surviving children only begin to capture the horror of life inside the wagon fort. Huddled in the rifle pits, the terrorized women and children were relatively safe. The smell of dead animals—Lee counted sixty head—and unburied corpses corrupted the late summer air. Fear, hunger, and thirst stalked the camp as the Arkansans waited for the next attack, but they did not surrender to despair. Completely surrounded and cut off from the spring, the emigrants kept up their courage, recalled Rebecca Dunlap, "fighting like lions."[50]

As Tuesday dragged by under the September sun, the embattled families fended off another attack and worked on their defenses during breaks in the sniping. The Arkansans chained their wagon wheels together and deepened the rifle pit and the trench surrounding the wagon fort. The defenses had their limits, for as three-year-old Sarah Baker sat on the lap of her father, George W. Baker, a bullet tore through the lower part of her left ear, a mark she bore for life.[51]

Utah traditions suggest that the Arkansans hoped that a relief party from Cedar City would save them from the Indians, but it is unlikely the emigrants were so naive. Their bitter relations with the Saints during their ordeal on the California Road left them little hope they could expect help from local settlers. The sounds of the battle would have alerted the people at Hamblin's ranch to their predicament, and when no relief arrived, the emigrants could suspect Mormons were involved in the attack. Relief was coming from Cedar City, but it was in support of the attackers.

"When we got out there," Major Higbee remembered, "we found we were in bedlam or hell." A horrific scene greeted the militia. "The confusion and frenzy of these painted blood-thirsty Indians was terrible to behold," he said. The meadow was strewn with the carcasses of cattle and horses "the Indians had shot down through revenge," while the Paiutes "were painted like devils, as though they had just arrived from the infernal regions & howling with rage over some of their braves being wounded, all tending to make everything as hideous and demon like as could be imagined." Higbee claimed the Indians were determined "to accomplish the destruction of the company if they had to fight all the Mormons in the southern country."[52]

The Mormons had to explain the failure of their magic to protect their Indian allies. A witness who "stood by and watched [Higbee's] motions and listened to his prayers" told journalist C. F. McGlashan how Higbee tried to invoke a spiritual cure for two Indians whose bones were crushed to splinters in the initial assault. Higbee anointed their wounds with consecrated oil and "went through all the process of 'laying on of hands,' and fervently prayed that the Lord Jesus would heal them." Despite his efforts, both Indians died.[53]

Lee made one more attack on Tuesday night to try to end the fight without calling out more reinforcements. The assault was a disaster, creating more Indian casualties and making it abundantly clear that even with white support the Paiute warriors were no match for the desperate Arkansas farmers. Profoundly disturbed by their defeat, the Mormon officers held a council. After much deliberation they sent Higbee to inform Colonel Dame of conditions at the meadows. Higbee "proceeded at once to Cedar about thirty-five miles and reported to Major Haight." Higbee claimed he arrived at the meadows and returned the same night, making a seventy-four-mile round trip. He told Haight the emigrants "were fortified and were under a state of siege surrounded night and day by savages who were blood thirsty and crazy because some of their number had been wounded."[54] Communications between Dame and the meadows were better organized than Higbee admitted, for Bill Carter, Dame's son-in-law, carried messages informing Dame of "everything that went on [there]."[55]

Haight started for Parowan late in the evening in a light wagon with Capt. Elias Morris. Haight's "face and countenance indicated that something weighed heavily on his mind." They awakened Colonel Dame at 2:00 A.M., and he called in the leading men of the settlement to discuss the fate of the emigrants. Dame now learned that Lee and the Indians needed help to eliminate the Arkansans. Haight and Morris returned to Cedar City, arriving early Wednesday morning with orders Higbee carried to Lee that same day.[56] Late in life, Bishop Charles Adams of Parowan recalled that as a thirteen-year-old boy he prepared the officers' horses for their return to Cedar City. As the men left Dame's house, Higbee said, "You know what the council decided," referring to the stake High Council's decision to wait for word from Salt Lake.

"I don't care what the council decided," said Colonel Dame. "My orders are that the emigrants *must be* done away with."[57]

The exact nature of Dame's orders has been the subject of intense debate. Higbee claimed they directed Lee to compromise with the Indians "if possible by letting them take all the stock and go to their homes and let the company alone." Dame trusted that as Indian Farmer, Lee would "have influence enough to restrain Indians and save the company. If [that was] not possible, [he should] save women and children at all hazards." But even Higbee's version of the orders directed that under on no condition was Lee to start a war with the Paiutes "while there [was] an army marching against [the Mormons]." Another version, passed down by word of mouth, matched part of Higbee's story and, from the Mormon perspective, seems logical. Lee should "keep the friendship of the Indians at all costs, as in the case of war, they [would] be [the Mormons'] most valued allies or . . . most dangerous enemies." James Haslam recalled that Haight ordered Lee to keep the Indians in check until orders came back from Salt Lake, and he concluded Lee executed the massacre on his own responsibility.[58] Private Klingensmith later testified that Haight wanted to let the company pass in peace but later told him that "he had orders from headquarters" to kill everyone except the youngest children.[59] Various traditions claimed Lee received written orders to spare the emigrants, but no such document survived to exonerate his superiors.[60]

The substance of the orders Higbee delivered from Haight, Lee recalled, was "that the emigrants should be *decoyed* from their strong-hold, and all exterminated, so that no one would be left to tell the tale, and then the authorities could say it was done by Indians." Subsequent events indicate Dame and Haight sent direct orders to kill every person who could give an account of the ordeal. Emigrant George Powers met

Dame at Parowan on Wednesday, September 9, and asked him if he could not raise a company to relieve the besieged train. Although Dame was the senior Mormon militia officer in southern Utah, he replied "that he could go out and take them away in safety, but he dared not; he dared not disobey counsel."[61]

Lt. Col. Isaac Haight dispatched his forces from Cedar City in two groups. The first apparently left on Wednesday and included Capt. William Taite, Lt. Nephi Johnson, Sgt. Benjamin Arthur, and Pvt. Charles Hopkins. They began their march too late to reach the meadows and camped at Little Pinto Creek that night.[62] Early Thursday morning, September 10, the militia commanders rang the Cedar City town bell to call out the rest of the Nauvoo Legion. Haight ordered the regiment "to muster, armed and equipped as the law directs, and prepared for field operations." Klingensmith admitted "the militia was called out for the purpose of committing acts of hostility" against the emigrants, but he claimed it was "a regular military call from the superior officers to the subordinate officers and privates of the regiment at Cedar City and vicinity."[63] This was no general call-up of the militia as Klingensmith implied. The known participants indicate that only men chosen for their proven loyalty to the LDS church and drawn from the upper echelons of several companies were sent to Mountain Meadows. Each man had probably sworn the temple endowment oath to avenge the blood of the prophets.[64]

ADEN'S MURDER

Inside the embattled camp, the emigrants devised a plan to alert the outside world to their plight. On Wednesday night, they sent William Aden and perhaps another volunteer through the enemy lines under the rising half-moon to get help—not from the local settlers but from the wagon trains they knew were following them on the California Road. Lee said the notorious Dutchman was Aden's companion. Aden's story, derived exclusively from Utah sources, is hopelessly tangled, but all accounts agree Aden was shot down in cold blood when he approached a Mormon campsite. Lee claimed his guards saw "two men on horseback come out of the emigrants' camp under full speed, and that they went toward Cedar City." It is hard to believe the besieged men still had horses, but before the waning moon rose, messengers broke through the siege lines that surrounded the wagon fort.[65] They avoided Hamblin's ranch and the Mormon settlement at Pinto, only six miles from the meadows. They reached Iron Creek to find the flickering light of a campfire at about the point they could expect to meet the Dukes train. Aden approached the fire, and White, Stewart, and Arthur challenged him. As Aden explained his mission, Stewart shot and killed him. White allegedly wounded Aden's companion.[66] The second man was probably killed, but Lee claimed he was tracked back to the wagons. "White men have interposed and the emigrants know it," Higbee would allegedly tell Lee, "and there lies the danger in letting them go."[67]

Thursday's dawn saw another determined attack on the train. It was no more suc-cessful than the previous assaults, and the Santa Clara band had one man killed and three wounded. Many of the Tonaquints had had enough and were so enraged, Lee recalled, "that they left for home that day and drove off quite a lot of cattle with them."[68] The desertion deepened the crisis facing the militia officers. By Friday morn-ing there were no more than one hundred and probably as few as forty Indians left on the field. Without Paiutes to spearhead an attack—and absorb casualties—the chances that the Mormons could overrun the wagon fort without heavy losses vanished.

The stiff resistance of the Arkansans further demoralized their attackers. Late Thursday morning Lee watched two men run to the spring to fill buckets. "The bul-lets flew around them thick and fast, but they got into their corral in safety." Lee climbed the ridge to the west of the emigrant camp to survey the situation. While crossing the valley, the emigrants spotted him. Lee recalled, "As soon as they saw I was a white man they ran up a *white* flag in the middle of their corral." The Arkansans sent two little boys to talk to him, but he could not linger "for [he] did not know what orders Haight would send back." Lee saw two men leave the corral to cut wood. Despite taking steady fire, they "kept right along with their work until they had it done." The men acted so bravely it was impossible not to respect them, and Lee claimed the experience left him "nearly dead from grief." By noon militia reinforcements arrived at the meadows and some of the men began sniping at the emigrant camp "to keep in practice and to *help pass off the time.*"[69] Albert Hamblin said that three men pitched horseshoes at Hamblin's ranch to kill time as the siege dragged on.[70]

Lee watched his situation collapse. His men were now as undisciplined as their native allies, the Arkansans had seen him and knew there were white men on the field with the Indians, and the Paiutes and freebooters who had not abandoned the scene were, he claimed, howling for the emigrants' blood.

TO OVERCOME ALL OPPOSITION: STEWART VAN VLIET'S MISSION

As the crisis in southern Utah intensified and as summer faded on the high plains, advance units of the U.S. Army of Utah trudged over the Oregon Trail under no effective command. The government had dispatched the troops so late in the season that they risked being trapped by early snows, and none of the army's officers knew what to expect from the Mormons. To avoid a disaster that now seemed increasingly likely, General Harney ordered Capt. Stewart Van Vliet to go to the territory with the utmost dispatch. As quartermaster he was to arrange for the army to winter in Utah and assure the Mormons that the army's intentions were entirely peaceful. The army was confident it could easily beat the Mormons if it came to a fight, but like Capt. Jesse Gove most officers believed the Saints would be "very submissive." "It would be well for them if they are," Gove said. "They preach warlike sermons but that is all they can do."[71]

The army selected a model diplomat when it chose its envoy to the Saints, and even Brigham Young conceded Captain Van Vliet appeared to be very much a gentleman. As quartermaster at Fort Kearny, Van Vliet had employed Mormons and won their trust. As he approached Utah, mountaineers and refugee apostates warned that he would not be allowed to enter the territory, and if he did, he would run the risk of losing his life. The captain treated this as idle talk. Traveling as rapidly as possible using six-mule wagons, Van Vliet arrived in Great Salt Lake City on September 8.[72]

Young already knew the army was in trouble and believed the soldiers would not be able to reach Salt Lake by fall. He assured his followers, "If we live as we should live, they cannot come here," and pledged that if necessary he would "desolate this whole Territory before [he would] again submit to the hellish corruption and bondage the wicked are striving to thrust upon [the Mormons]."[73] Diarist Hosea Stout reported what the prophet's editors left out: Young said, "The Almighty recognised us as a free and independent people and that no officer apointed by goverment should come and rule over us from this time forth."[74]

Van Vliet's arrival forced Young to reconsider his declaration of independence. The captain's initial reception was pleasant, but the governor soon came to Van Vliet's quarters and told him in plain and unmistakable language that "*the troops now on the march for Utah shall not enter the Great Salt Lake valley.*" "[All] those present concurred most heartily in what he said," Van Vliet informed his superiors.[75]

Any remaining pretense of cordiality disappeared the next morning when the two men got down to business. Young warned, "If the government dare to force the issue, I shall not hold the Indians by the wrist any longer. . . . If the issue comes, you may tell the government to stop all emigration across the continent, for the Indians will kill all who attempt it."[76] In the face of this threat, Van Vliet remained calm. He told Young that the territory had been organized as a military department, as had Florida, Texas, and Kansas, and the troops were simply ordered to take a post in it. He had seen the expedition's orders, he said, and its troops would not molest the people of Utah, nor would the government interfere with the Mormons as a religious people.

Despite these assurances Young denied the quartermaster's request for supplies. The governor admitted there was an abundance of everything but declared that nothing would be sold to the army. Van Vliet warned Young that he might stop the small force now approaching Utah from getting through the rugged passes of the mountains that year, but the government would inevitably send enough troops to overcome all opposition. The Mormon leader acknowledged this but said that the army would "find Utah a desert. Every house will be burned to the ground, every tree cut down, and every field laid waste." The Saints had three years' provisions and were ready to "take to the mountains and bid defiance to all the powers of government." He promised, "There shall not be one building, nor one foot of lumber, nor a stick, nor a tree, nor a particle of grass and hay, that will burn, left in reach of our enemies." In the name of Israel's God, Brigham Young would lay waste utterly.[77]

RIDE FOR DEAR LIFE: HASLAM'S MESSAGE

In the midst of these discussions and as militia commanders in Cedar City mustered select elements of the Nauvoo Legion to march to Mountain Meadows, James Haslam tied his weary mount to the hitching post at Brigham Young's Lion House just after daybreak on September 10. Within fifteen minutes he was ushered into Young's office, where the Mormon leader was already meeting with half a dozen of his trusted counselors. Haslam handed the governor Isaac Haight's letter. Young read it and told the haggard rider "to go and take a little sleep." Asked if he could make the trip back to Iron County, Haslam said he could. The governor told him to come back at 1:00 P.M. for an answer. When Haslam returned, Young told the young rider "to start and not to spare horseflesh, but to go down there just as quick as possible."[78]

Fifty years later Hamilton G. Park, Brigham Young's steward, recalled finding a spirited horse saddled, bridled, and hitched to a post near the outer gate of the president's compound. The door opened and a man came out wearing leather leggings and large Spanish spurs and holding a small rawhide whip. A sorely troubled Young followed and told Haslam with great feeling, "I want you to ride for dear life; ride day and night." Haslam paused to adjust his saddle, and Young repeated the command. Haslam "sprang into the saddle and shot off like an arrow down Theatre Hill and was soon out of sight." Young went back into his office "with a troubled face and bowed head." Haslam "was on his way to Iron County with instruction that a company of emigrants then in Southern Utah and bound for California were to be protected and assisted on their way."[79]

This dramatic tale is enshrined in Mormon annals, but it does not tell the entire story. Isaac Haight's letter to Brigham Young does not survive. Young swore in 1875 that despite a diligent search his reply to Haight was lost, but Mormon officials located and published it in 1884. Although historians have debated the letter's authenticity, Garland Hurt's report confirms that the southern settlements sent a messenger north, and events indicate Haight received a message that at least resembled the draft found in Young's letterbooks. The letter began with a chatty report on the arrival of Captain Van Vliet and the happy news that Young expected the army not to "get here this season without we help them." He then turned to the critical issue:

> In regard to the emigration trains passing through our settlements, we must not interfere with them until they are first notified to keep away. You must not meddle with them. The Indians we expect will do as they please but you should try and preserve good feelings with them. There are no other trains going south that I know of. If those that are there will leave, let them go in peace.[80] ·

For the prophet's defenders, this letter is proof he did not order the massacre. Juanita Brooks concluded it cleared him of direct responsibility, yet she found the letter characteristic of Brigham Young's style. He often began a critical communication with generalities and inserted "the real message in a single terse sentence or two in the very heart of his letter." In this case the operative message was that the Indians would "do as they please." The order not to meddle with the emigrants was subordinate to the main message: let nothing interfere with the Mormon military alliance with the tribes. Brooks thought this strangely conditional letter suggested that Young might not condemn an Indian massacre.[81]

The letter begs several questions: Why did Superintendent of Indian Affairs Brigham Young have to send orders to the south *not* to "interfere" with the emigrants? Why did he later deny knowing anything about the massacre until weeks after it happened? As David White concluded, Young's shrewd reply seems calculated to correct a policy gone wrong if it arrived in time and to cover his tracks if received too late.[82] Whatever the letter's intent, it carried a hidden but clear message for Isaac Haight: make sure the Mormons could blame whatever happened on the Paiutes.

Cousin Lemuel Is out at Large

Brigham Young's attempt to intimidate Captain Van Vliet suggests he either failed to grasp the dangerous implications of events in the south or felt that an Indian incident would be a powerful demonstration of his power to stop travel on the California Trail. Within days of learning from Haslam about the situation in the south, Young used "rumors" of Indian raids on emigrants to punctuate a series of ill-considered threats in sermons and in a report to the government. He complained to the U.S. superintendent of Indian affairs that news that the Army was on its way to Utah had led to Indian raids on cattle herds. Young failed to mention his gift of cattle to the Shoshonis and Paiutes and pretended he had "the utmost difficulty to restrain them." "The sound of war," he wrote, "quickens the blood and nerves of an Indian."[83]

Although they gave Van Vliet no hint of it, his calm demeanor impressed Mormon leaders. His message forced Young to reconsider his defiance of federal authority, and typically the prophet left himself an avenue of retreat. On September 11 he wrote Van Vliet an ambiguous but vaguely conciliatory letter responding to the army's request for supplies. In barely penetrable bureaucratese, Young hinted that if the army stayed out of Utah and bought supplies in the open market, Van Vliet "might accomplish the object in view."[84] Given what Young knew of the crisis at Mountain Meadows, implementing such a moderate policy was well advised, but the governor could not restrain his violent threats. To impress the captain with the Saints' resolve, Young invited Van Vliet to Sunday services in the tabernacle. From the pulpit he reviewed Mormon grievances and war plans before an audience of four thousand whose devotion matched the fire of their leader's rhetoric. George A. Smith described his trip to the militant south, and then Van Vliet heard Brigham Young open his discourse by saying bluntly, "I am too angry this morning to preach."

Yet preach he did. Young said, "I do not often get angry; but when I do, I am righteously angry; and the bosom of the Almighty burns with anger towards those scoundrels; and they shall be consumed." His people had borne enough hellish abuse and would not bear any more of it. He had saved the government hundreds of thousands of dollars by keeping the peace, but now the Indians traveled hundreds of miles to see him. They asked "whether they might use up the emigrants, saying—'They have killed many of us; and they damn you and damn us, and shall we stand it?'" Although he had in fact encouraged the depredations he described, Young claimed he "always told them to hold on, to stop shedding blood, and to live in peace." Gentiles going east that season had shot at every Indian they saw between Carson Valley and Box Elder. The result? "Probably scores of persons have been killed," and animals had been stolen from nearly all the emigrants. The Indians now had more stock than they could take care of and came to the settlements with their pockets full of gold.[85]

Abusive white men had started the bloodshed. "And now," Young preached, "if they do not quit such conduct, they must stop travelling through this country; for it is more than I can do to keep the Indians still under such outrageous treatment." The Saints had been forced out of the states and into the savage wilderness, and Young savored the irony: "The people do not realize what they have done by driving us into the midst of the Lamanites." His prospective allies might consist of the most degraded classes of Indians, but now they understood their true standing before the Lord. Young warned, "[If the government persists in sending troops to Utah,] I want the people in the west and in the east to understand that it will not be safe for them to cross the Plains."[86]

In parting with Van Vliet that evening, the prophet expressed his hope that the captain would "report at Washington Just as things are here," but he was again unable to contain himself. "[If troops entered Utah,] I can see nothing but death & darkness before me and before this people." "[If volunteers came from California to fight in Utah,] they will find their own buildings in flames & so throughout the United States." Young swore that if war broke out he would not hold the Indians by the wrist any longer for white men to shoot: "I shall let them go ahead and do as they please and I shall carry the war into their own land and they will want to let out the Job before they get half through." Young issued a final warning: "[The government] must stop all emigration across this Continent for they Cannot travel in safety. The Indians will kill all that attempt it." Van Vliet agreed to deliver the message and promised he would leave the army if war broke out in Utah, for he would not shed the blood of fellow Americans. Young concluded his catalog of practical threats in terms that conveyed his messianic convictions, assuring the captain that God had set up his kingdom upon the Earth and "the Lord would sustain that kingdom & destroy all that fought against it."[87]

Captain Van Vliet left the territory convinced Brigham Young meant exactly what he said "in plain and unmistakable language." The people of Utah, the captain noted, were committed "to sustain Governor Young in any measures he might adopt."[88]

In a letter to his agent in Philadelphia, Young described his reaction to Van Vliet: "I think we may depend upon the Captain to use his best efforts in staving off the expedition this year." But he had no confidence in his assurances of peace: "My feelings are—to be ready for them." "The check rein has broken, and cousin Lemuel is out at large, in fact he has been already collecting some of his annuities. Day after day I am visited by their chiefs to know if they may strike while the iron is hot." If President Buchanan did not deal justly with the Mormons, "the war cry will resound from the Rio Colorado to the head waters of the Missouri—from the Black hills to the Sierra Nevada—travel will be stopped across the continent—the deserts of Utah become a battle ground for freedom. It is peace and [Mormons'] rights—or the knife and tomahawk—let Uncle Sam chose."[89]

8

The Work of Death

As dawn broke at Mountain Meadows on Friday, September 11, 1857, conditions in the embattled wagon fort could not have been worse. Fewer than two dozen men survived to defend the circled wagons. The women and children huddled in the rifle pit to escape sniper fire. Some of the wounded had died, and the survivors prepared to give them a hasty burial. The camp was cut off from water, and the defenders were almost out of ammunition. During the morning, the sniping that had kept the Arkansans trapped for five days suddenly stopped, and an eerie silence fell over the remote valley.

COUNSEL AND ORDERS: THE PLOT

Before dawn the Mormon leaders at Mountain Meadows had agreed on a plan to decoy the emigrants and kill them without having to storm their defenses. Supply wagons and Major Higbee's reinforcements had arrived in detachments during the night. Long after, William Edwards recalled reaching the meadows early Thursday evening. Edwards and others claimed that John D. Lee had tricked the militia by sending a message to Cedar City that Indians had massacred an emigrant train and he needed men to bury the dead.[1] Some believed the story was simply a ruse by the militia commanders in Cedar City. Haight "had sent out a company of men with shovels to bury the dead," said Nephi Johnson, "but they would find something else to do when they got there."[2] When Pvt. John Bradshaw answered the muster in Cedar City with a shovel, an angry Isaac Haight asked why he was unarmed. "I told him I didn't know we wanted a gun to bury the dead." Haight called him a fool. Bradshaw had no ammunition for his gun anyway, and Haight sent him home.[3]

Johnson recalled arriving at Hamblin's ranch on Thursday at about 10:00 P.M. with Higbee and "two or three wagons, and a number of men all well armed." He found

Lee conferring with the Paiute leaders. Lee told them the Mormons would try to "get the emigrants to leave their camp and give up their arms after which they would kill them."[4]

Lee described a priesthood council held Thursday evening. Higbee chaired the meeting near Abe's Spring, opening with a prayer that invoked the Holy Spirit. He handed Lee written instructions from Cedar City, which Lee later insisted he felt bound to obey as a direct military order. Haight had signed them, but he later told Lee the orders came from Colonel Dame. Higbee said the only safe course "was the utter destruction of the whole rascally lot." Higbee said everyone must be killed "except such as are too young to tell tales, and if the Indians cannot do it without help, [the Mormons] must help them." Lee claimed he objected to killing the women and children. "How can you do this without shedding innocent blood?"[5]

"Have not these people," Higbee replied "threatened to murder our leaders and Prophet, and have they not boasted of murdering our Patriarchs and Prophets, Joseph and Hyrum? Now talk about shedding innocent blood." He derided Lee's fear: "Why brethren, there is not a drop of innocent blood in that entire camp of Gentile out-laws; they are a set of cut-throats, robbers and assassins . . . who aided to shed the blood of our Prophets, Joseph and Hyrum, and it is our orders from all in authority, to get the emigrants from their stronghold, and help the Indians kill them." The coun-cil formed a prayer circle and invoked the spirit of God to direct them in the matter. Lee insisted that after the council meeting the Mormons on the field "all voted, every man of them, in the Council, on Friday morning, a little before daylight, to kill all the emigrants."[6]

Nephi Johnson recalled Lee wanted to let the emigrants go, but on Thursday evening Lee accepted Haight's orders "to clean up the dirty job he had started." In the darkness the militia leaders worked out the details of their plan to destroy the Arkansans. "It was the wish of all the Mormon priesthood to have the thing done," Lee con-cluded. They "believed all the Gentiles were to be killed as a war measure, and that the Mormons, as God's chosen people, were to hold and inhabit the earth and rule and govern the globe." After completing their plan, Lee and Higbee went to the Indian camp and explained the strategy to their allies. Johnson translated Lee's instructions, and this satisfied the Indians.[7]

FORLORN HOPE

While the Mormons plotted their fate on Thursday night, the emigrants made a sec-ond attempt to alert the world to their plight. They "drew up a paper addressed to the Masons, Odd Fellows, Baptists, and Methodists of the States, 'and to all good people every-where.'" The petition "implored assistance, if assistance could reach them, and, if not, that justice might be meted to their murderers." The message listed the emi-grants' names and ages, their birthplaces, last residences and occupations, and itemized their property. Because their assailants were well supplied with powder and guns, the emigrants suspected that white men were with the Indians. The survivors signed the letter, and then three of their best men slipped down the ravine of Masgotsu Creek and escaped, "starting afoot for California."[8]

The messengers were perhaps Abel Baker, Jesse or Lorenzo Dunlap, and John Milum Jones. Mormon interpreter Ira Hatch told a passing emigrant "that young Baker had an opportunity of escaping, went a short distance but returned; was afterwards wounded, in the arm; again escaped from the massacre, and had proceeded about ten miles this side [west of] the Muddy." This was probably Capt. Jack Baker's son, Abel Baker, nineteen.[9] Newspapers reported that a six-year-old girl had seen an arrow kill her mother, but her father had escaped to California.[10] The Dunlap brothers each had a daughter about six years old. Courier William Hyde later reported that the Paiute war chief, Jackson, had "a little book or journal of one of the emigrants in which was written the name, 'William B. Jones, Caldwell County, Missouri.'"[11] This would seem to identify a man who could have been one of the Mormons' Missouri persecutors, but more probably it was a garbled reference to Milum Jones of Carroll County.[12]

It was a sign of the emigrants' desperation that they would send three of their last able-bodied men on a mission that was at best a forlorn hope. But as one writer concluded after hearing their story from Jacob Hamblin, they were "three of the bravest men that ever lived."[13]

To Get Them in Our Power

As Friday dawned at the meadows, John D. Lee faced two daunting tasks. He had to convince the militia to murder defenseless men, women, and children who would place themselves in their trust. He then had to persuade the emigrants to surrender their arms and abandon their wagon fort.

Lee claimed his council broke up a little after daylight, and the officers turned all but three of the militia's horses loose. The outriders—Dudley Leavitt and William Stewart—took horses to run down any who tried to escape. The last mount was reserved for Adj. Daniel Macfarlane, to carry orders. Lee said the men ate breakfast and "the brethren prepared for the work at hand."[14]

The militia formed a hollow square in the upper meadow. Major Lee made a speech, saying that his orders from headquarters were to kill the entire company except the small children.[15] Lee explained "just how every person was expected to act during the whole performance." No one recorded the arguments he used to justify cold-blooded murder, but perhaps he roused fears that the emigrants would call down an army from California. Very probably he described the recent murder of their old friend Parley Pratt. He surely rehearsed the sufferings of the Saints and recalled their sacred vows to avenge the blood of the prophets. Lee recounted an address "by someone in authority" that stressed the old Mormon theme of giving unquestioned obedience to the priesthood, an address Lee probably delivered. "Brethren, we have been sent here to perform a duty," he said. "It is a duty we owe to God, and to our Church and people. The orders of those in authority are that all the emigrants *must* die." Their leaders spoke with inspired tongues, and their orders came from the God of Heaven. The men had no right to question, it was their duty to obey. The "thing has gone too far to allow us to stop now," Lee said. "We must kill them all, and our orders are to get them out by treachery if no other thing can be done to get them in our power."[16]

William Edwards recalled sixty-seven years later that as a fifteen-year-old youth he was summoned to the meadows to bury the dead emigrants. Instead he found the people were "alive and well fortified against the Indian siege," directed by Lee and other white men. Lee called his council and ordered the men to help the Indians kill the Arkansans. "Some of the council objected to the butchery but were silenced by said Lee and 2 or 3 others of our file leaders." Lee laid out the strategy: he would pledge safe conduct to Cedar City to trick the emigrants into surrendering their arms and fortifications.[17]

Most of the Paiutes had already left the scene. Just before daylight Lee ordered Nephi Johnson and the other interpreters to take the remaining warriors and set up an ambush in the oak brush and rocks, where they would "rally the Indians and rush upon and dispatch the women and larger children."[18] According to participants and survivors, most of these "Indians" were Mormons. Some fifteen whites, including Johnson, Carl Shirts, Oscar Hamblin, and William Young, donned war paint and hid in the grass and brush that lined the California Trail a mile and a half from the wagon fort. Here they would be invisible until what Lee called "the work of death" would commence.[19]

Despite the power of Mormon belief in obedience to authority, Jacob Hamblin testified that shortly after the massacre, Lee admitted that among the men "some would not act and some would." A powerful folk tradition tells that at least one man vociferously refused to obey orders. "Hot words ensued, and a heated scene followed" when William Hawley said he would rather "defend the emigrants than to kill them. Called them all bloody murderers. Said the curse of God would fall on them." The officers chained Hawley to a wagon wheel.[20]

Higbee and Lee devised a plan to let the militia kill the male emigrants easily and murder women and children separately. The scheme apparently had two goals: to prevent the Indian freebooters from killing their white allies in the heat of battle and to ensure that no Mormon shed the innocent blood of infants and children improperly. They intended to divide the emigrants into three groups. Lee would lead the first party in two wagons containing the wounded and the youngest children, with the women and older marching children behind them, thus isolating the innocent blood from the adult men. The men, who could be shot down in good conscience, would follow, marching in single file, each guarded by an armed escort.

DOUBT, DISTRUST AND TERROR: THE SURRENDER

Persuading the emigrants to go along with such an unreasonable proposal was a daunting task. Any plan so utterly mad should have aroused suspicion. Lee must have used all his powers of persuasion to convince the Arkansans to trust him, but the surrender was also a measure of their desperation. The party had lost more than a third of its men. Their nerves were shattered, and most of their ammunition was gone. Lee did "not think there were twenty loads left in the whole camp." If they had been well supplied with ammunition, he thought they would never have surrendered. "They were brave men and very resolute and determined."[21]

Although the Arkansans suspected white men were in league with the Indians, they probably had no certain knowledge. To the men, the brutal prospect of a last hand-to-hand fight to defend their women and children made any alternative attractive, and it was unimaginable that the Mormons planned treachery on such a scale. The emigrants simply could not believe that professed Christians could execute such a diabolical scheme.

Nancy Huff recalled the morning when "the attacking party went off": "Soon afterward a party that we thought to be friends came up with a white flag, and said that they could protect us. They said they were our friends, and if we would come out and leave what we had they would take us to Cedar City, where we would be safe, and that they would protect us, and see that none of us were hurt." Lee carried a flag of truce to the emigrant camp, promising protection if they surrendered.[22] The emigrants "laid down their arms, came out from their camp, and delivered themselves" to Lee.[23]

The actual story was more complicated. Under a flag of truce, the Mormon officers sent William Bateman, an English convert, to open negotiations. Bateman had been cut off from the church for "unchristian like conduct" in November 1856.[24] His conduct probably consisted of leaving the fold, but he returned to Utah in spring 1857. In late August Bateman confessed his sin of "going off to California" to the Cedar City congregation. He asked to be readmitted and promised to do better. The congregation voted to accept Bateman's penitence, and Bishop Klingensmith remarked "upon the course those take who go to California."[25] Since such reformed apostates "did not stand and be valiant for the truth," Heber Kimball said, "we are now going to place them in the front ranks, and put them to the test."[26] At Mountain Meadows Bateman's ecclesiastical and military leaders subjected him to an especially challenging test of faith.

Rebecca Dunlap recalled that when three wagons approached their camp, the emigrants dressed her eight-year-old sister Mary in white. The child "went out towards them and waved a white handkerchief in token of peace. The Mormons in the wagons waved one in reply and advanced to the corral." An emigrant delegation talked with the leading Mormons for about an hour and a half. Lee said if they gave up their arms "it would show the Indians that they did not want to fight." If the emigrants met these terms, "the Mormons promised to pilot them back to the settlements."[27]

According to Lee, a white flag met Bateman as he approached the camp and the two parties talked. Lee then entered the wagon fort at noon or a little after, while the troops stood down in formation within sight of the Arkansans. The "men, women and children gathered around me in wild consternation." Lee recalled. "Some felt that the time of their happy deliverance had come, [but others,] all in tears, looked upon me with doubt, distrust and terror."

Lee spent at least two hours hammering out an agreement. He watched some young men pay "the last respects to some person who had just died of a wound." Perhaps five other men had escaped to seek help, leaving behind only a handful of able-bodied defenders. Lee said a "large, fleshy old lady" told him that ten men had been killed during the siege, and the emigrants "wrapped the bodies up in buffalo robes, and buried them in a grave inside the corral." Lee opened negotiations with the emigrant leaders, probably using his government position and Masonic signs to win their trust. Lee told them "they must put their arms in the wagon, so as not to arouse the animosity of the Indians." The best the Mormons could do for them was to load a few belongings with the arms "and cover them up with bed clothes and start for the settlement as soon as possible." Lee later said he knew that he was doing a damnable deed, but his faith in the godliness of his leaders convinced him he was simply not worthy of the "important part [he] was commanded to perform." As the negotiations dragged on, Daniel Macfarlane rode into the camp to deliver Higbee's order to "hasten their departure," saying Higbee was afraid the Indians would renew the attack before he could get the emigrants to safety. The emigrants questioned Macfarlane to check Lee's veracity, and the men passed the test.[28]

Lee's proposal launched a debate among the emigrants. "If you give up your arms you are a fool," said one man. "Don't you be such god damn fools," said another. "If you do you are dead men." The emigrants finally surrendered on the promise of peace.[29] Rebecca Dunlap said the emigrants did not suspect treachery, but "if they did they were about famished from thirst, and were ready to accept almost any terms."[30]

A Fancher family tradition provides chilling details of the last hours in the emigrant camp, perhaps witnessed by five-year-old Christopher Carson Fancher. Burr Fancher "always heard in [his] family that Alexander was shot in the initial volley." Badly wounded, he turned over command to twenty-five-year-old James Mathew Fancher. Like his cousin, "Matt" was a natural leader and was cool under fire. When he described the surrender terms to his cousin, Alexander Fancher gasped, "Good God no, Matt." Believing Fancher was delirious from his wounds, the other men ignored him.[31]

To Slay Their Helpless Victims: Wholesale Murder

The emigrants finally accepted Lee's terms and let two wagons into their stronghold. Samuel Knight loaded their arms, piled bedding on top, and placed the wounded and some of the women and children in his wagon until it was loaded to capacity.[32] Although only three years old at the time, Sarah Baker later said, "It's funny how you will recall unimportant details, after so many years." She remembered the black borders on the bright red blankets in the wagon. "[The] wounded and the young children, including me, my two sisters and my baby brother were put in another wagon. My mother and father had been wounded during the fighting, so they were in the wagon with us children." Sarah's older sister, Martha Elizabeth, told a reporter in 1938 that "she heard her father tell her mother to get up and put the children in the wagon. That was the last time she saw her mother."[33]

Lee divided the emigrants into three groups and gave them their marching orders. He claimed seventeen children, clothing, and arms were loaded into Samuel McMurdy's lead wagon, but this wagon actually contained only the youngest children and some of the wounded. Samuel Knight's wagon followed with five wounded men and a teenage boy. The division of the emigrants into three groups was not nearly as precise as Lee remembered, for the older children who survived recalled marching with their mothers.

Late in the afternoon a strange procession began its march to the California Trail. Lee walked close behind McMurdy's wagon to set the course and avoid being caught "in the heat of the slaughter." He told the emigrant women to follow the road to the troops and then encouraged McMurdy to hurry up, to get out of sight before the firing began. Lee led the wagons east away from the camp, turning to the north as he passed the militia formation. Daniel Macfarlane led the second group consisting of the women and older children up to the troops, with the men following some fifty yards behind the last woman. The women and children were "hurried right on by the troops." The men marched until they were opposite Capt. Joel White's Company D and a Mormon soldier fell in by the side of each unarmed man. The Arkansans "cheered the soldiers as if they believed they were acting honestly." Lee, "anxious to be out of sight of the bloody deed," rushed the wagons ahead.[34] None of the men in the Mormon guard ever described their feelings as they received the cheers of the Arkansas men and escorted them up the field. None of them ever described what it was like to accept the trust of men they would soon murder in cold blood.

The march lasted perhaps half an hour. Lee claimed his wagon crossed over rising ground as it neared the rim of the Great Basin and he lost sight of the women and men. Perhaps a quarter mile behind the women, Maj. John Higbee marched the men to "a smooth open space on the west side of the road and a patch of oak brush" on the east.[35] Higbee fired a shot and gave the crucial order, "Halt! Do your duty!"[36] (Or perhaps, "Halt! Do your duty to Israel!") At the command, the guards turned and shot down the men. Just as he was coming onto the main road, Lee said, he heard "one gun, then a volley at once followed."[37]

Klingensmith, at the back of the ranks, did not hear who gave the order, but it "was passed down the column; the emigrants were then and there shot down." He was the only Mormon who ever admitted obeying orders and joining in the killing. "I discharged my piece," Klingensmith swore. "I did not fire afterward, though several subsequent volleys were fired."[38]

When asked if he tried to hit his man, Klingensmith said, "Of course I did." After the first volley, he saw only one man killed. The slightly wounded man begged for his life, saying, "'Higbee, I wouldn't do this to you.' He knew Higbee it appears." John Higbee replied, "You would have done the same to me or just as bad," and cut the man's throat.[39] This story indicates that apostates had joined the train and Higbee "blood-atoned" at least one of them. One descendant recalled that her grandfather's militia company was ordered to Mountain Meadows to help bury the dead. "To my grandfather's shock some of the people he helped bury were Mormons who were well known to him."[40] An early account reported it was necessary to blood atone several apostates. "When their dead bodies were found, after the massacre, it is said they were clothed in their endowment shirts."[41]

Each part of the field witnessed its special horrors. Nephi Johnson "gave the word to the Indians to fire at the last general killing" and saw it all.[42] The women and children "were overtaken by the Indians, among whom were Mormons in disguise." Painted Saints and Paiutes gave "hideous, demon-like yells" as they "rushed past to slay their helpless victims."[43] On reaching a spot where tall sagebrush covered both sides of the road, four-year-old Nancy Huff discovered they were trapped, for men had hidden in it and begun to shoot at her people. Then the men rushed from both sides, "killing everybody they came to." She recalled "[Capt. Jack Baker] had me in his arms when he was shot down, and fell dead. I saw my mother shot in the forehead and fall dead. The women and children screamed and clung together. Some of the young women begged the assassins after they had run out on us not to kill them, but they had no mercy on them, clubbing their guns and beating out their brains."[44]

Six-year-old John Calvin Miller was at his mother's side when she was killed and pulled arrows from her back until she died. He said he also lost two brothers and three sisters.[45] Emberson Milum Tackitt "thought he was to be killed and ran to a white man and begged for mercy." The terrified four-year-old offered to trade a new coat for his life.[46] Pvt. William Young saw the Paiutes kill as many as four women. Young later testified that an Indian killed an infant in a woman's arms with a knife, adding "And I saw them kill a boy with rocks. I saw an indian holding two girls one in each hand. He held them among the balance of the indians and I saw no more of the two little girls."[47]

Although he painted the massacre as strictly an Indian affair, Albert Hamblin captured the horror of the scene. The emigrants made up a big crowd. When they reached "the place where the Indians were hid in the bushes," the assailants "pitched right out onto them and commenced shooting them with guns and bows and arrows, and cut some of the men's throats with knives." The killers ran after them, "yelling and whooping. Soon as the women and children saw the Indians spring out of the bushes they all cried out." The women "scattered and tried to hide in the bushes, but the Indians shot them down." Albert saw two girls run a quarter mile to the east and said he tried to save them when they hid in some bushes. A tribal shaman "told the Indians not to kill them. The girls then came out and hung around him for protection." The shaman tried to save the girls, who "were crying out loud. The Indians came up and seized the girls by their hands and their dresses and pulled and pushed them away from the doctor and then shot them." It was now growing dark. "And the other Indians down by the road had got nearly through killing all the others. They were about half an hour killing the people from the time they first sprang out upon them from the bushes." The two murdered girls may have been the twelve-tear-old twins, Lucinda and Susannah Dunlap. Their surviving sisters, Rebecca and Louisa, recognized Albert as the man who killed them.[48]

Rebecca Dunlap "ran and hid behind a sage bush when the massacre began. Two of her older sisters were killed right near her, and were lying dead by her side." The six-year-old girl "heard her baby sister crying and ran to find her. She found her entwined in her mother's arms, but that mother was cold in death." Sarah Dunlap, an infant, was "shot through her right arm, below the elbow, by a large ball, breaking both bones and cutting her arm half off." Seizing her sister, Rebecca "rushed back to the sage bush where she had been hiding. She remained [there] until she saw a white man," who she took for Jacob Hamblin but who probably was one of his brothers. "She went up to him and begged him to save her and her little sisters."[49]

Legends told that the horrific work turned father against son. An unhappy wife of Brigham Young told the most plausible story, claiming Jim Pearce's father (Capt. Harrison Pearce) shot him as he tried to assist a girl.[50] Less likely tales told how a girl begged one of Lee's sons for her life, but Lee pushed his son aside and shot her through the head.[51] Klingensmith was said to have ordered his son to murder a young girl, threatening to kill him if he would not. When his son refused, "Bishop Klingensmith turned upon the poor girl himself and knocked her brains out with a club."[52]

Blood lust seized some of the killers. William Stewart "seemed filled with an insane desire to slaughter as many as possible, and he hewed them down without mercy."[53] Klingensmith swore that Stewart was among the mounted men stationed on the column's flanks to take anyone "on the wing that might run away" and thought he watched Stewart run down and shoot a man.[54] Legend claimed Stewart ordered a lad to kill a wounded woman who was recovering consciousness. "I've got none of this blood on my soul," the boy said, "and I don't intend to have any." The woman staggered to her feet, and Stewart "drove a bowie-knife to the hilt in her side." Stewart allegedly boasted that he "took the d——d Gentile babies by the heels and cracked their skulls over the wagon tires."[55] Others charged the crime to George Adair, who in "his drunken revels . . . would laugh and attempt to imitate the pitiful, crushing sound of the skull bones as they struck the iron bands of the wagon hubs."[56]

Twenty years later a newspaper asserted that Stewart and Joel White killed the older children. An Indian eyewitness told how the children begged for mercy. Many a little girl pleaded with Stewart "not to take her life. Catching them by the hair of the head, he would hurl them to the ground, place his foot upon their little bodies and cut their throats."[57] Lee claimed a six-month-old infant in his father's arms "was killed by the same bullet that entered his father's breast; it was shot through its head."[58] The father was perhaps Charles R. Mitchell, whose son John was the only infant among the victims.[59]

At the head of the column, Lee stopped the wagons when the firing began. The teamsters swore that Lee did the killing, while Lee blamed McMurdy and Knight. Samuel Knight reluctantly admitted he saw Lee "in the act of striking a person—I think it was a woman." He claimed he was too busy managing his fractious team to notice who killed the wounded, but McMurdy provided more detail. When the firing began, McMurdy said he turned to see Lee shoulder his weapon "and when the gun had exploded I saw, I think it was a woman, fall backwards." Like Knight, McMurdy said he was minding his horses but saw Lee draw his pistol and shoot two or three men and women in the head. When pressed, McMurdy refused to say whether he had killed anyone.[60]

If nothing else, Lee told a better story. He said McMurdy grabbed his rifle from the lead wagon and walked back to the wounded in Knight's wagon. McMurdy exclaimed, "O Lord, my God, receive their spirits, for it is for thy Kingdom that I do this." He then shot a man resting with his head on another man's breast, killing them both. Knight shot a man and struck a fourteen-year-old boy with the butt end of his gun, crushing his skull. Lee admitted he went to the wagons intending to do his part of the killing. He cocked his pistol, but it fired prematurely and grazed McMurdy, cutting his buckskin pants. Lee said this accident prevented him from killing anyone, for by the time he got over the excitement, the Paiutes had reached the wagons and killed the sick and wounded. Lee saw a Cedar City Paiute named Joe "catch a man by the hair, and raise his head up and look into his face; the man shut his eyes, and Joe shot him in the head." The Indians examined the bodies in the wagons and shot all that showed life.[61]

After nearly killing McMurdy, Lee claimed, he heard a child scream and saw an Indian drag a little boy by the hair from the back of a wagon, getting ready to cut his throat. Revolver in hand, Lee sprang at the Paiute. He shouted at the top of his voice, "Arick, ooma, cot too sooet (Stop, you fool)." After he saved the terror-stricken child, another Indian grabbed a young girl by the hair. "I rescued her as soon as I could speak," Lee said. He also claimed he told the Paiutes "they must not hurt the children—that [he] would die before they should be hurt." The Indians had already "rushed up around the wagon in quest of blood, and dispatched the two runaway wounded men."[62] Having snatched these children from the jaws of death, Lee picked up a child he believed was Charley Fancher, a bright boy whose father was captain of the train.[63]

There is no proof that Lee murdered the wounded at the wagons, but his heroic portrayal of his part in the massacre is hardly credible. He admitted, "If my shooter had not prematurely exploded I would have had a hand in dispatching the five wounded. I had lost control of myself, and scarce knew what I was about."[64] Some say Lee ultimately confessed to having killed five persons "and but for an accident to [his] gun would have killed more."[65] Newspapers charged that Lee and his aides dragged women and older children from the wagons "and cut their throats from ear to ear."[66]

"John Higbee gave the order to kill the women and children," recalled George Adair, who saw "the women's and children's throats cut."[67] One witness "saw children clinging around the knees of the murderers, begging for mercy and offering themselves as slaves for life could they be spared. But their throats were cut from ear to ear as an answer to their appeal."[68] Rebecca Dunlap recalled, "The Mormons and Indians shot down in cold blood the defenseless men, women and children, then pierced them with bows and arrows, then cut their throats with knives."[69] Mormons told Thomas Drewer that defenseless women and children "clung in numbers around the legs of the brutal savages in vain and offering themselves as slaves. They were not only scalped, but according to Mormon custom, their throats cut from ear to ear and heads severed from their bodies. The details of other private murders are equally as horrible."[70] Late in September 1857 Apostle Wilford Woodruff heard John D. Lee report that the Indians had "Cut the throats of their women & Children."[71]

Sarah Baker recalled that when the killing started she had her arms around her father's neck, while her sisters Betty and Mary Levina were sitting in the back of the wagon. Her mother held her baby brother, Billy. Sarah screamed in terror as she watched her father gasp for breath and grow limp. Although she was only three years old at the time, Baker insisted, "You don't forget the horror. You don't forget the blood-curdling war-whoops and the banging of guns all around you. You don't forget the screaming of the other children and the agonized shrieks of women being hacked to death with tomahawks. And you wouldn't forget it, either, if you saw your own mother topple over in the wagon beside you, with a big red splotch getting bigger and bigger on the front of her calico dress."[72] Elizabeth Baker never knew the fate of her older sister, Vina, the prettiest of the three Baker girls, who had "beautiful long black hair. She was eight years old." She remembered seeing Vina being led away as a captive. "I do not know whether she was killed or what ever happened to her."[73]

Lee claimed the last person he saw killed was a girl, about ten years old, who was covered with blood. "An Indian shot her before she got within sixty yards of us."[74] Lee told a different—and apparently more accurate—version of this story to his family. Lee's son claimed Harrison Pearce told Lee "to kill the last girl, but he refused so Harrison did it."[75] Mormon elder James Gemmell said "a few small children were not killed at once, but on consultation it was agreed they could tell too much after they grew up. They were then slain."[76]

Nancy Huff recalled that immediately after the massacre, the killers conducted a sadistic ritual, executing a young girl in view of the surviving children. "At the close of the massacre there was eighteen children still alive, one girl, some ten or twelve years old, they said was too big and could tell, so they killed her, leaving seventeen." Huff said she saw John Willis "shoot the girl after we were gathered up."[77] The child was too old to be spared, and this public execution demonstrated to the other children the consequences of knowing too much.

Massive bloodletting can trigger sexual violence, but most of the sexual atrocity stories told of Mountain Meadows are hard to credit.[78] Mormon theology condemned any type of sexual relations outside of marriage, and Juanita Brooks concluded that the tale of rape at Mountain Meadows "seems to be another example of how repeated suggestions and whisperings may grow into more and more impossible tales, which are then passed on as fact." Yet some of the earliest accounts of the massacre consistently implied that rape was part of the atrocity. An army report claimed Lee took "a beautiful young lady away to a secluded spot. There she implored him for more than life. She, too, was found dead. Her throat had been cut from ear to ear." Jacob Hamblin's testimony endorsed Albert's story of murder and hinted at rape. Gemmell heard that two pretty little girls survived the slaughter, "and the killers told them that if they would strip and dance nude upon the green sward they would spare their lives. The little Girls did so, but a little after were put to death." Gemmell saw "indignities that were perpetrated upon three persons after which they were shot. But they are too shocking to put on paper." As Brooks noted, such incidents seem fantastic, but the persistence of the tales suggests they cannot be discounted entirely.[79]

In the murderers' tales and children's memories that make up this catalog of horrors, it is impossible to tell truth from fiction or even identify patterns that might shed light on what actually happened. The killers had every reason to lie about their crimes, and they lied skillfully in church and state trials or when arguing their case in the court of public opinion. Investigations by Mormon authorities at the turn of the century provide some of the most honest accounts of the crime. Men like Nephi Johnson and Samuel McMurdy told whatever they believed was required to civil authorities, but they were reluctant to lie to apostles, although some men did not hesitate to do so. The standard accounts skillfully distorted the truth to shift blame to the Indians for the most horrible crimes, particularly the murder of the women and children. But as Nephi Johnson confessed, "white men did most of the killing."[80]

VOICES FROM THE DUST

All the accounts of Mountain Meadows can be challenged for a variety of good reasons, but a forensic analysis of the physical remains of more than two dozen victims provides scientific information about how the Arkansans lived and died. In summer 1999, work on a monument to the dead at Mountain Meadows accidentally unearthed a mass grave. It held the remains of at least twenty-eight men, women, and children that the U.S. Army buried in 1859 in the shelter the emigrants dug inside their wagon fort. Scientists at the University of Utah applied pathology and anthropology to "assess the skeletal trauma associated with cause and manner of death."[81]

The analysis generally corroborated historic accounts. The scientists partially reconstructed eighteen distinct skulls. Many of the 2,605 pieces of bone found at the site had been broken during the excavation of a foundation for the new monument. Almost all the cranial remains exhibited fatal wounds. Male and female skulls of adults and children showed evidence of both gunshot and blunt-force trauma. "The majority of gunshot wounds were located in the heads of young adult males, while the females and children exhibited primarily blunt-force trauma," which was "consistent with the types of force reportedly used in the massacre." Bullet trajectories indicated that "six individuals were shot from the rear, while five were shot from a face-to-face position. Blunt-force trauma was often directed from a position above the victims, as most of these individuals were children." At least five victims were executed at very close range by gunshots aimed straight at the back of the skull, while blunt-force trauma to the head killed two young adults and three children, who were roughly four, seven, and nine years of age.[82]

The forensic study included a few surprises, however. Noting that "emotion and propaganda surround this historic event," the report observed that "physical evidence can often provide a reality check, requiring all sides to reconsider what they have 'known to be true.'" A gunshot wound in the top of an older child's head, forensic anthropologist Shannon Novak wrote, "suggests that the killing of women and children may have been more complicated" than the story told in traditional massacre accounts. Despite the tradition that the women and children had their throats cut or were bludgeoned to death by Indians, physical evidence reveals that many of them were shot. A child believed to be between ten and fifteen years old exhibited a bullet wound in the top of its skull. The broken teeth of one female victim indicated possible gunshot trauma to the face.[83]

The report noted that forensics could not determine from the skeletal trauma whether Indians or whites did the shooting or the beating. There was no evidence knives were used as weapons, but such soft-tissue wounds seldom leave skeletal lesions, so the physical traces may "underestimate of the amount of trauma an individual experienced." The Salt Lake Tribune reported that the "study lends credence to Paiute Indian claims that the tribe did not participate in the infamous Mountain Meadows Massacre of 1857 to the extent history has recorded." Commenting on the evidence, Forrest Cuch, director of the Utah Division of Indian Affairs, said, "It is ludicrous to keep saying the Indians jumped out of the bushes and attacked these people."[84]

The lack of small bones and the damage pattern on the long bones indicated that animals such as wolves or coyotes heavily altered most of the remains. Splitting, flaking, and peeling suggest the bones "were exposed long-term to extremes in weather." After the 1859 burial, Maj. James Carleton wrote, "My opinion is that the remains were not buried at all until after they had been dismembered by the wolves and the flesh stripped from the bones, and then only such bones were buried as lay scattered along nearest the road." Carleton's conclusion "seems to be the most consistent" with the physical evidence.[85]

THROW OUT THE DEAD BODIES

By most accounts the massacre was over quickly. John Higbee said, "It did not seem five minutes from the time the Indians rushed past us until all was as still as death." Nephi Johnson thought the killing required no more than five minutes. Three or four survivors escaped "some distance, but the men on the horses overtook them and cut their throats," John D. Lee recalled. "Higbee said the Indians did their part of the work well, that it did not take over a minute to finish up once they got fairly started."[86]

When the work of death was finished, Lee ordered Samuel Knight to take his wagon off the road and throw out the dead bodies. Knight dumped them about one hundred yards from the road. As he walked from the wagons to the killing fields, Lee saw the corpses of six or seven women "stripped perfectly naked, . . . all of their clothing . . . torn from their bodies," the Indians having taken every remaining vestige of clothing from the dead.[87] When H. L. Halleck passed through southern Utah in December 1858, the Paiutes showed him the place where they lay in ambush to the east of the road. They "said some women came from a little settlement not far away and stripped the clothes" from the dead women. The Indians recalled "that John D. Lee was like a wild beast who had tasted of fresh blood. He was turned into a demon."[88]

Lee counted ten children from ten to sixteen years of age killed close to each other. The corpses of the women and children lay scattered along the road for quite some distance. Lee found Higbee, Klingensmith, Stewart, "and most of the brethren standing near by where the largest number of dead men lay." Higbee told him, "The boys have acted admirably, they took good aim, and all the d——d Gentiles but two or three fell at the *first fire*." Higbee directed his men to search the dead for valuables. Lee demurred but agreed to hold Higbee's hat while he looted corpses, dropping a little money and a few watches into the hat. "I soon got so sick," Lee claimed, "that I had to give it to some other person."[89]

The Mormon leaders devoted considerable energy to protecting the property of the dead emigrants from their Paiute allies, who later complained of being cheated out of their share of the spoils. Johnson took a posse to stop the Indians from looting the wagons. He let the Paiutes "take what they had and stopped them from doing any more."[90] When Lee surveyed the scene of the wagon fight the next day, the Indians had carried off the wagon covers, the clothing, and the provisions. Someone had ripped open the feather beds and emptied them on the ground, "looking for plunder." Lee said that the Paiutes even carried off all the ticks that cased the mattresses.[91]

SEVENTEEN LITTLE CHILDREN

Many of the killers later claimed they spent most of their time at Mountain Meadows trying to protect the surviving children. "I commenced to gather the children before the firing had ceased," Bishop Klingensmith swore. He drove the survivors in the regiment's baggage wagons to Hamblin's ranch, "and from there to Cedar City, and procured them homes among the people." Klingensmith said he gave no orders except to save the children, and he gave those as a bishop and "not in a military sense."[92] John Willis and Samuel McMurdy helped him. Lee claimed he ordered Knight and McMurdy to take the children to Hamblin's ranch.[93]

When the violence ended, Rebecca Dunlap recalled just seventeen children survived "this horrible massacre," none of whom were more than six years old. The Mormons may have had a horror of killing anyone under the age of eight, but they apparently were more concerned about disposing of any child old enough to be a credible witness. Dunlap said the terrified survivors "were placed in one wagon, several of them being wounded, while the clothing of nearly all of them was bloody with the gore of their kindred." Carl Shirts drove the wagon to Hamblin's house, where the children spent the night. Nancy Huff remembered that the children were divided. John Willis took charge of her and carried her to his house the next day. She saw Willis during the massacre. "I could not be mistaken," she said. Huff had a sister who was nearly grown and four brothers who were killed. "I was the youngest child of our family—the only one that was spared."[94]

Sometime in the night, Albert Hamblin recalled, David Tullis and the Indians "brought some of the children in a wagon up to the house" at Hamblin's ranch. "The children cried nearly all night. One little one, a baby, just commencing to walk around, was shot through the arm. One of the girls had been hit through the ear. Many of the children's clothes were bloody."[95]

Consistently, the children reported seeing the Mormons shed their war paint. Rebecca Dunlap recalled quite a number of white men washing the paint from their faces. Martha Elizabeth Baker could "distinctly remember the group disguised as Indians. There was not a real Indian in the group, for they went to the creek and washed the paint from their faces." While playing marbles with Josiah Gibbs in 1859, young Christopher Carson Fancher cocked his head and said, "My father was killed by Indians; when they washed their faces they were white men."[96]

A Secret from the *Entire* World

Back on the field, the Mormon commanders assembled and addressed their men. Lee recalled how he, Higbee, and Klingensmith "made speeches, and *ordered* the people to keep the matter a secret from the *entire* world. Not to tell their wives, or their most intimate friends." "We pledged ourselves to keep everything relating to the affair a secret during life." The men swore binding oaths to stand by each other "and to always insist that the massacre was committed by Indians alone." The officers ordered the men to spend the night on the field, and the soldiers retired to their camp at Abe's Spring. Lee, Higbee, and Klingensmith went to Hamblin's ranch, where they ate and slept. Lee calculated he had hardly slept for almost a week. After eating, "being heart-sick and worn out," he laid down on his saddle blanket. Using his saddle for a pillow, Lee "slept soundly until next morning."[97]

9

The Scene of Blood
and Carnage

As the massacre was taking place on Friday afternoon, Col. William Dame and Lt. Col. Isaac Haight, the senior Nauvoo Legion officers in Iron County, left Cedar City for Mountain Meadows. Haight and Dame stopped at the camp of the Mathews-Tanner freight wagons to get fresh animals before going on to the scene of the hostilities. The men rested an hour or two and took refreshments. "Be careful, and don't get shot, Mr. Haight," someone warned. Haight replied, "We shall have no shooting." He emphasized *we* and threw up his head, as if "to imply that the shooting would be all over before he arrived."[1] Haight and Dame left the wagon camp in good spirits and arrived at Hamblin's ranch by daylight on Saturday morning. The two men began arguing, and their loud voices awakened John D. Lee. Haight told Dame that if he planned to report the massacre, he should not have ordered it done. The two men "cooled down as soon as they saw that others were paying attention to them."[2]

The officers took their breakfast and went to the meadows to secure the property and supervise the burial of the dead. The ghastly sight of more than one hundred naked corpses confronted them. "Colonel Dame was silent for some time. He looked all over the field, and was quite pale, and looked uneasy and frightened," Lee recalled. He concluded the young colonel was "just finding out the difference between giving and executing orders for wholesale killing." Standing about two paces from Lee, "Dame seemed terror-stricken, and again said he would have to publish it." He "spoke low, as if careful to avoid being heard." Haight spoke boldly: "You know you counselled it, and ordered me to have them used up." As Lee watched, Haight pressed Dame, who claimed he had nothing to do with it. "You ordered it done," Haight pointedly reminded him. "Nothing has been done except by your orders, and it is too late in the day for you to order things done and then go back on it." Dame choked up. When he recovered, he said, "I did not think that there were so many women and children. I thought they were nearly all killed by the Indians." Confronted with the consequences of his order, Dame collapsed. "*I did not think there were so many of them, or I would not have had anything to do with it.*" This enraged Haight. "You throw the blame of this thing on me and I will be revenged on you," he swore, "if I have to meet you in hell to get it."[3]

THE BURIAL AND THE PLEDGE

Militia private George Adair helped to strip the bodies of their clothing and valuables. Playing on the superstitions of his men, John Higbee warned that if they took property belonging to the company it would burn them. Adair picked up a pouch filled with gold "but held it away from him as a thing accursed" until Higbee walked up, grabbed the purse, and shoved it in his pocket. "[After that,] I had no use for him," Adair recalled. "It was then that he caught me by the hair, pulled my head back, and drawing a big knife across my throat, said if you ever divulge what you have seen, I will cut your throat from ear to ear."[4]

Several weeks after the massacre, Rebecca Dunlap returned to the field with some Mormon girls. "None of the dead bodies had been buried, but wild animals and buzzards were eating the flesh from their bones," she recalled. She recognized the corpse of Jack Baker by his long beard.[5] Like Dunlap, most travelers charged that the killers did not bury the victims. George Powers passed through the meadows the night after the massacre with the Mathews-Tanner train and reported that "the bodies were left lying naked upon the ground, having been stripped of their clothing by the Indians."[6] A few days after the murders the American emigrants traveling in the Dukes party proposed to stop to inter their dead countrymen, but their Mormon interpreters warned that the Indians would kill them as well.[7]

John Aiken, the first non-Mormon to get a good look at the field, insisted the bodies were unburied. Aiken joined John Hunt's mail party at Pinto and accompanied it through the field of blood in late September. When Aiken told his story in California, he said he found the bodies naked and putrefying and "saw about twenty wolves feasting upon the carcases of the murdered." "Mr. Hunt shot at a wolf, they ran a few rods and halted," he said. "I noticed that the women and children were more generally eaten by the wild beasts than the men." Despite the killing field's proximity to the settlements, the Mormons seemed determined to leave the bones to bleach on the plains. Aiken knew Captain Baker and others among the dead but kept quiet while traveling with the Mormons, "knowing that [he] was traveling with enemies to [his] country and countrymen." "Mr. Hunt and his companions often laughed, and made remarks derogatory to decency, and contrary to humanity, upon the persons of those who were there rotting, or had become food to wild beasts."[8]

Despite their supposed mission as a burial detail, one of the first Mormon reports on the massacre claimed the militia had arrived at the meadows without picks and with very few shovels. George A. Smith told Brigham Young the men "obtained a few spades from Hamblin's Ranch and buried the dead as well as they could under the circumstances. The ground was hard and, being destitute of picks, and having a limited number of spades, the pits could not be dug to very great depth."[9]

The militia apparently made a halfhearted attempt to bury their victims, but wolves and water quickly obliterated all signs of their hasty work. Samuel Knight recalled digging a slight hole "and the slain were thrown into it, though the wolves subsequently uncovered the remains and picked the bones."[10] Samuel Pollock claimed the militia buried all the bodies they could find in "the most natural locality to get them in pretty deep." The ground was hard and impossible to dig, so the men threw the bodies in a wash and "put on dirt enough to keep them safe from the wolves."[11] The militia "piled the dead bodies up in heaps, in little gullies, and threw dirt over them," Lee wrote, and the men talked and laughed as they tossed the corpses into the ravine. Lee conceded it was "not much of a burial."[12]

After the burial detail completed its grisly chore, Nephi Johnson said the men formed a circle to hear "a great many speeches."[13] According to Lee, he, Dame, Haight, Klingensmith, Higbee, and Charles Hopkins spoke, praising God for delivering their enemies into their hands and "thanking the brethren for their zeal in God's cause." The officers stressed "the necessity of always saying that the Indians did it alone, and that the Mormons had nothing to do with it."[14]

At Dame's request Haight told the men "they had been privileged to keep a part of their covenant to avenge the blood of the prophets." The men closed the circle, each putting his left hand on the shoulder of the man next to him and raising his right arm to the square. Higbee, Haight, Lee, and Dame stood at the center, facing the four points of the compass. Stake president Haight led the men in a solemn oath never to discuss the matter, even among themselves, to keep the whole matter secret from every human being, and "to help kill all who proved to be traitors to the Church or people in this matter." Lee recalled the men voted unanimously to kill anyone who divulged the secret. It would be treason to the men who killed the emigrants and "*treason to the Church*." They were forbidden to tell their wives or even to talk of it among themselves. "The orders to lay it all to the Indians, were just as positive as they were to keep it all secret," Lee wrote. "This was the counsel from all in authority." Exhortations and commands directed the men "to keep the whole matter secret from every one but Brigham Young." The meeting ended after Colonel Dame blessed the men. In the afternoon, they broke camp and left for their homes.[15]

THESE HELPLESS ORPHANS

Rachel Hamblin later described how seventeen children had arrived at her home in "the darkness of night, two of the children cruelly mangled and the most of them with their parents' blood still wet upon their clothes, and all of them shrieking with terror and grief and anguish." The condition of the Dunlap sisters horrified her, and little Sarah, shot through the arm, could not be moved. Mrs. Hamblin nursed the wounded child until she recovered, but Sarah lost forever the use of her arm. Rebecca and Louisa Dunlap seemed to be greatly attached to their younger sister, and Rebecca recalled how they begged not to be separated from Sarah. Samuel Knight's wife Caroline lay in a wagon box in the Hamblins' yard, recovering from a difficult child-birth. She sobbed hysterically when she saw the blood on her husband's clothes and the wagonload of terrified children. She would not be consoled.[16]

Two years later Rachel Hamblin could talk about the killing of the emigrants without a shudder, but the plight of the children touched her heart. James Carleton, a hard-bitten army officer, praised her care of the sisters and especially her concern for Sarah Dunlap. When Lee distributed the children, Rachel tried to persuade him not to separate the sisters. Lee resisted but finally let the Dunlap girls remain at Hamblin's ranch. He dispersed the other children among the southern Utah settlements, with Bishop Klingensmith assigning most of them homes in Cedar City. As much as possible, the Mormons kept the children apart, taking special care to separate siblings. The isolation increased their control over the survivors and prevented the young witnesses from sharing information. On Saturday Lee and his men set off with the rest of the orphans in a wagon. The Paiutes scattered.[17]

In addition to the three Dunlap sisters who stayed at Hamblin's ranch, fourteen other children survived. The orphans included their cousins, Prudence Angeline, 5, and Georgia Ann, 18 months; three children of George and Minerva Baker, Martha Elizabeth, 5, Sarah Francis, 3, and William Twitty, 9 months; three children of Joseph and Matilda Miller, John Calvin, 6, Mary, 4, and Joseph, a toddler; two sons of Pleasant and Armilda Tackitt, Emberson Milum, 4, and William Henry, 19 months; a son of John Milum and Eloah Jones, Felix Marion, 18 months; and a daughter of Peter and Saladia Huff, Nancy Saphrona, 4.[18]

Lee took two children to Harmony, including five-year-old Christopher Carson Fancher, whom Lee called Charley. Initially, he also had a female child at his home, possibly Triphenia D. Fancher, 22 months. But Elizabeth Baker claimed she and her sister were kept with Lee's family until soldiers rescued them, and another Mormon family cared for her brother, William T. Baker. Richard Harrison kept a child at Pinto. In Cedar City, Klingensmith had two of the children, one of whom he was said to have given to a childless family named Birbeck. John Morris of Cedar City later turned over a girl who could "not recollect anything about herself" but who was perhaps Mary Miller. Elisha H. Groves had a boy, probably Joseph Miller.[19]

Nancy Huff recalled that the children were divided the day after the massacre. Huff spent the winter at John Willis's home in Cedar City, but in spring 1858 Willis moved to Toquerville. He had blankets, clothing, and other property Huff knew belonged to her mother. She recalled, "[When I claimed the items] they told me I was a liar, and tried to make me believe it was the Indians that killed and plundered our people, but I knew better, because I recollected seeing them kill our folks, and knew many things that they carried off that I saw in their possession."[20]

The surviving children proved to be the most moving evidence of the evil that had transpired at Mountain Meadows. For non-Mormons, they were living proof that the massacre was not simply an Indian affair, for as the California newspapers noted, sparing the children was "unprecedented in the barbarous acts of Indians."[21] Despite their youth, some of these last-living witnesses would not forget the murder of their mothers and fathers, brothers and sisters.

The Fate of the Forlorn Hope

Three men had escaped the fate of the rest of the Fancher party, Lee recalled, "but the Indians were put on their trail."[22] With no supplies and four hundred miles of deserts and mountains between them and California, Abel Baker, one of the Dunlap brothers, and John Milum Jones faced a daunting challenge. Even the earliest accounts tell contradictory tales, but it appears two of the men were soon tracked down and killed. The last survivor seems to have crossed almost one hundred miles to the Muddy River and perhaps another fifty to Las Vegas, only to be murdered by Mormon inter-preter Ira Hatch. Tracking the stories from the first reports to the final legend provides clues to the fate of the messengers.

Emigrant P. M. Warn heard the captains of the Mathews-Tanner freight wagons discuss the survivors. William Mathews said none of them would find refuge in his train. George Powers of Arkansas met Ira Hatch on about October 5 a day's drive east of the Muddy River with brothers Henry T. and Cau Young, horse thieves fleeing from justice in San Bernardino. Hatch told Powers a wildly contradictory story, claiming he had met the Youngs at the Muddy River with one of the surviving Arkansans. Hatch said there were no Indians in sight when he arrived, and he "had to give the whoop to call them from concealment." Hatch then claimed he found the Indians in hot pursuit of the three men. Before he could stop them, the Paiutes "jumped upon the emigrant and killed him before his eyes." Hatch said he only saved the Young boys with great difficulty.[23] More likely, as S. B. Honea reported, Captain Baker's son met the Young brothers about ten miles west of the Muddy River. Baker returned with the horse thieves to the river, where Hatch and the Indians murdered him.[24]

Jacob Hamblin told the army a similar collection of odd tales in 1859. The three men who escaped were herding stock when the attack was made or crept out of the corral at night. One man disappeared but must have been murdered on the road or perished of hunger and thirst in the mountains. One man made it to the Muddy River where the Indians cut his throat, while another reached Las Vegas totally naked, only to meet the same fate. One of the Youngs told Major Carleton he had met a wounded man on foot, unarmed, without provisions or water, and terror-stricken as

he approached the Muddy River at daybreak. The man was deranged and talked inco-
herently about the massacre and his mission. The brothers persuaded him to return
to the Muddy, where they stopped to make breakfast. They began frying pancakes,
which attracted a large crowd of hungry Paiutes whose chief would grab them "as fast
as they were done, and eat them. At last one of the Youngs struck the chief with a
knife, whereupon all the Indians rose to kill the three men." The Youngs drew their
revolvers and held the Paiutes off until they got to their horses. When they looked
back, their companion sat staring at the fire, not comprehending what was going on.
"He had not left the spot where he sat. Three or four Indians had him down and were
cutting his throat!" Abandoning their camp and provisions, the Young brothers
escaped.[25]

James Lynch reported in July 1859 that Ira Hatch told him the last man escaped
to Las Vegas, followed by five Mormons who persuaded him to return to Mountain Meadows with them. Hatch admitted that contrary to their promises, the
Mormons "butchered him, laughing at and disregarding his loud and repeated cries
for mercy."[26]

Jacob Hamblin was the source of most of the later stories of the fate of the messengers. The "honest old Mormon" said the Indians tracked the men some forty miles
and ambushed them while they slept. Two men died in the gunfire; the third was
wounded in the wrist. Some say he made his way to Las Vegas, but Chief Jackson
boasted of burning a man alive after finding him asleep between the Santa Clara and
Virgin Rivers. Jackson later took Hamblin to see the remains and gave him the papers
he found on the man's body, apparently the document drawn up before the messengers left the wagon fort, or perhaps the little book or journal of Milum Jones. Hamblin became "perfectly acquainted with its contents," which included the names of all
the emigrants and an itemized list of their property. "If the Masons and Odd-fellows
knew how many of their brethren were in the train," he said, "they wouldn't let the
accursed murderers go unpunished." Hamblin claimed he kept the record safe for
months, but when he showed it to Lee, Lee promptly destroyed it.[27]

More than fifty years after the event, Mormon chronicler Josiah Rogerson used
local folklore to provide interesting details on the fate of the papers of the messenger killed with the Young brothers. Before being murdered, the man allegedly
"unfastened a broad belt which he had round his body" and threw it in the bushes,
where San Bernardino refugees found it that fall. The belt contained papers naming the emigrants and the number of animals they owned. The refugees gave the
belt to Hamblin on the promise he would take it to Brigham Young. On his way
to Salt Lake, Hamblin inadvertently let Lee see the belt and examine the contents.
After Hamblin returned from checking his horses, he found the belt in flames.
When he rebuked Lee for his breach of trust, Rogerson said Lee replied "that was
his business, that the record was gone to hell where all the emigrants had gone in
the massacre."[28]

After hearing these contradictory accounts, James Carleton concluded the Young brothers and Ira Hatch had brought the last survivor back to the Muddy River and set the Indians on him. Whatever the fate of the messengers, within five days of their escape they were all dead. The last credible witnesses to the events at Mountain Meadows had all been eliminated. "The fate of these three men," Carleton noted, "seems to close the scenes of this terrible tragedy."[29]

THE MOST TERRIFIC NIGHT OF MY LIFE

The Fancher train was destroyed, but the other overland parties still in southern Utah posed a serious problem for the officials of Iron County. Mormon freighters Tanner and Mathews had taken George Powers and P. M. Warn into their company, and the two non-Mormons had to be carefully supervised as they passed the scene of the crime. The Mathews-Tanner train left Cedar City at noon on September 12. A few hours later they met four men returning from the meadows in a wagon. "Mathews and Tanner held a council with them apart, and when they left, Mathews told me the entire train had been cut off," Powers reported. Mathews said that because the road was still dangerous, it would be better for them to pass the spot in the night.[30]

At about dusk the train met William Dame, Isaac Haight, and two other Mormons returning from the scene of the slaughter with a band of some twenty Indian warriors and a two-horse wagon carrying two or three Indians and driven by a white man. Blankets hid its contents. Many of the Paiutes "had shawls, and bundles of women's clothes were tied to their saddles," Powers said. "They were also all supplied with guns or pistols, besides bows and arrows. The hindmost Indians were driving several head of the emigrants' cattle." Dame and Haight "seemed to be on the best of terms with the Indians, and they were all in high spirits, as if they were mutually pleased with the accomplishment of some desired object." The men greeted them with noisy cordiality, but Powers did not learn much. Dame warned the non-Mormons to hide under blankets while passing through the mountains, as the Indians were deadly hostile to all Americans. If the Paiutes saw them, he said, the whole train would be in danger. After leaving Dame, the freight wagons drove all night in silence and camped at daylight "three miles beyond the scene of the slaughter."[31]

Francis M. Lyman, an apostle's son, was traveling with the Mathews train. Lyman recalled how they followed orders from a local committee to cross the meadows at night. Cattle from the Fancher train rushed around the wagons, "making the night hideous with their bawling." The unearthly stench of the decaying bodies made it the most horrific night of Lyman's life.[32] The experience would haunt the future apostle all his days.

It is easy to presume that the men responsible for the massacre at Mountain Meadows immediately regretted their terrible deed, but this is not necessarily how men act in the wake of an atrocity. Many of the rank and file who did the actual killing may have soon regretted their actions, but at least some of the men experienced the exhilaration that can follow brutal violence. By all reports the leaders were pleased with their work and considered it a victory for the Lord. Just two days after the massacre, the Sunday services in Cedar City had the tone of a victory celebration as the sermons praised the work of "Cousin Lemuel." Patriarch Elisha H. Groves "spoke upon the principles of the gospel, and of the Lamanites [being] the battle axe of the Lord." Elias Morris remarked on "living our religion." President Haight opened the afternoon meeting with a singing prayer and "spoke upon the spirit of the times, and of cousin Lemuel being fired up with the spirit of their fathers." Bishop Klingensmith closed the meeting with a benediction in song.[33]

Some said James Haslam arrived in Cedar City from Salt Lake while the church service was in progress. Haslam later testified he met Isaac Haight coming to see if he had returned. Haslam handed him the letter from Brigham Young. Haight read it and said, "Too late, too late," and "he cried like a child." When Haight recovered he handed the message to Haslam to read. Haslam returned it, and Haight put the letter in his pocket.[34]

At Fort Harmony on the Sunday morning following the massacre, Rachel Lee watched as "a great number of Indians returned from an expedition South west" with her husband.[35] John D. Lee claimed he crossed the mountains on Saturday with his Indian son. About two miles from Harmony, he overtook some forty Indians returning from the massacre, driving several head of cattle and carrying bloody clothing. They were glad to see Lee, who led them to his fort, where they "marched around inside, after which they halted and gave their whoop of victory." Lee ordered his family to feed the Paiutes, and they gave them some bread and melons.[36]

One of Lee's workers, Benjamin Platt, remembered that the major returned on Sunday morning "with a company of Indians loaded with plunder such as beds and tinware." Lee and his Paiute escort rode into the stockade and around it to the well on the south side of the fort. "Thanks to the Lord God of Israel that has delivered our enemies into our hands!" Lee shouted. One Harmony resident recalled he gave them "a treat with mellons, squash, punkins and pies." At afternoon services that Sunday, Lee gave a lurid description of the massacre. Platt recalled that Lee "seemed to glory in the deed which he said was the 'will of the Lord'" and did not exhibit any signs of remorse: "Lee was the same jovial, companionable man that he was prior to the massacre."[37] Mormon frontiersman Peter Shirts wrote that Lee gave the history of the massacre at the meeting and "told the number killed, which was *96*." Apparently to keep his vow of secrecy, Lee pretended he had seen the massacre in a vision some six months earlier.[38]

Despite their pledges, the killers could not keep the massacre a secret. The Indian telegraph was alive with news of the fight. At the Indian farm at Spanish Fork, word spread that someone had murdered all the emigrants on the southern road. Other visitors confirmed the report for Garland Hurt. The Indians insisted that Mormons, not

Indians, had killed the Americans. By September 17 the news "had become so much the subject of conversation" that Hurt sent a young Indian named Pete to Iron County by a secret route. Six days later Pete returned from Ammon's village near Beaver to report that the Piedes had joined in the massacre, but Lee and "the Mormons had persuaded them into it." After three failed attacks, the Mormons "with lying, seductive overtures, succeeded in inducing the emigrants to lay down their weapons of defense and admit them and their savage allies inside of their breastworks." Pete said that "*they cut all of their throats but a few that started to run off, and the Piedes shot them!*" Fifteen or sixteen children had survived and were in a bishop's care.[39]

TO STOP FURTHER MISCHIEF: THE DUKES TRAIN

After two or three hours' rest a few miles beyond Mountain Meadows, the Mormon teamsters in the Mathews-Tanner freight train drove all day to camp near Jackson's village on the Santa Clara River. The Paiute warriors, who had been taught by their white allies to distinguish between Mormons and Mericats, angrily "pointed out Mr. Warn as an American." Powers watched nervously as his Mormon companions denied it, but Jackson "appeared mad; stepped round; shook his head, and pulled his bowstring. He then sent several men on [the] road ahead. Mr. Mathews advised [the train] to leave there as quick as possible, as it was getting dangerous." At Jackson's camp, the train hired Ira Hatch as an interpreter. Mathews told Powers that if Hatch could not get him over the road, nobody could. Hatch left the next morning, apparently to scout the road, and the freight train met him returning with the Young brothers. Hatch told his conflicting stories of how Indians had killed the last survivor of the Fancher party.[40]

The reports of emigrants such as Powers, Warn, and Honea appeared in California newspapers within weeks of the event. Powers reached San Bernardino on October 1, where William Mathews told him not to associate with the damned apostates, for "they were cut throats of the worst character." Mathews offered Powers a job in the mountains and warned him not to talk too much about what he had seen. Many people expressed to him their satisfaction with the news of the massacre. The Mormon state legislator, Jefferson Hunt, said from the pulpit "that the hand of the Lord was in it; whether it was done by white or red skins, it was right! The prophesies concerning Missouri were being fulfilled, and they would all be accomplished." Quoting Brigham Young, Mathews said the work would continue until Uncle Sam and all his boys "should come to Zion and beg for bread." Powers quickly left San Bernardino. "It did not appear to be a free country," he said, "for I am an American, and like freedom of thought and speech."[41]

After his harrowing adventures with the Saints, Powers felt they "would not have hesitated to kill him for any unguarded words." When the Indians passed wearing the women's clothes and exulting in their crimes, his blood boiled, but Powers dared not speak. As one of the leading Mormon officials in California, William Mathews began the systematic defamation of the murdered emigrants that presaged the large body of folklore that would vilify the victims to justify the crime. Mathews told Powers not to grieve, for Dame had examined their bodies and found that the women were all prostitutes. Mathews "rejoiced greatly at the massacre, and considered it the beginning of long delayed vengeance."[42]

The southern route was still crowded with wagons bound for California, and handling them proved to be much more difficult than simply diverting the few non-Mormons in the Mathews-Tanner train had been. Until Brigham Young's message reached Haight, southern Utahns were primed to obliterate all the remaining trains on the road and had even gone so far as to send sentinels down the trail to cut off any survivors. It seems that only Young's directive that his people "must not meddle with them" spared the Dukes and Turner parties from meeting the same fate as the Fancher train. But Mormon leaders William Dame and Jacob Hamblin made sure the emigrants left Deseret with nothing but their lives, wagons, and teams.[43]

William Dukes's train camped at Beaver on about September 9, planning to stay for some time to take advantage of the good grass and to have smith work done, but wild rumors and an Indian battle in the middle of town disrupted their plans. Honea heard that the Fancher party had been murdered and it would not be safe for the emigrants to proceed any farther. A man told Honea he was glad the train had been killed, for they carried poison with them, and they "had only got their just reward."[44]

Bishop Farnsworth warned the emigrants that Indians planned to attack Nicholas Turner's wagons some six miles behind them on Indian Creek. They sent five men back to assist Turner's train, and five Mormons joined them. Before the relief party could reach the train, warriors began to shoot at Turner's camp, and the emigrants wounded one Indian. While under attack, the wagons harnessed up and moved to join Dukes's camp, and the Indians succeeded only in wounding some of the cattle. The Mormons stopped the emigrants from firing, warning that if they injured an Indian the party would all be killed. "From this we became more apprehensive of the interpreters than of the Indians," Honea wrote, "feeling that we were completely in the power of an unscrupulous enemy."[45]

The next morning the Indians demanded five cows from the emigrants, who waited for Bishop Farnsworth to handle the matter. Turner's wagons joined the Dukes party and the two captains went into town. Indians opened fire on Turner and Dukes as they stood in the street in the middle of Beaver, shooting Turner through the hip and grazing Dukes with two or three bullets. An emigrant named Collins begged for protection at a blacksmith shop but "was pushed out of the house and the Indians shot him, breaking his arm, shattering the bone very badly." A Mormon galloped into the emigrant camp and told them to stay with their wagons. When Turner, Dukes, and Collins returned, badly wounded, the emigrants circled their wagons and prepared for a fight.[46]

That evening Ammon visited the camp with Bishop Farnsworth. The Ute leader had returned from his meeting with Brigham Young at Salt Lake, and with the bishop's support he demanded cattle. The emigrants gave him six animals, and Peyton Welch paid the Pahvants $150 for the grass his cattle had eaten. Honea had to surrender a horse he had bought from an Indian, since the Pahvants recognized it and were angered at seeing the horse in the possession of an American.[47] Although Ammon did not hesitate to practice such extortion, he appeared reluctant to support the Mormon war plans. He had gone to Iron County before the attack on the Fancher party "to persuade the Piedes to leave the road." A bishop told him he had no business interfering with the Paiutes and warned him to leave, which led to an altercation between the two men.[48]

Pvt. David Carter of the Nauvoo Legion had accompanied the emigrants from Provo. He rode a mule almost forty miles to Parowan in three hours on September 10 with word of the Indian attack at Beaver. William Dame sent Capt. Silas Smith and nine men to handle the problem, but on reaching Beaver, they found the emigrants had made peace with the Indians and all was quiet.[49] The morning after Ammon's visit, the emigrants headed south.

At Parowan Dame authorized trading with the Dukes train. Still fearing the Indians, the emigrants spent a day at the town and "placed themselves almost entirely under the counsel and direction of Pres. Dame, seeking his counsel in everything." By Sunday Dame had received Haslam's message from Brigham Young to let the emigrants go in peace. The next day, September 14, as commander of the Iron County Military District, Dame ordered his officers to calm the Indians and to "assist in passing through the trains now upon the road." In a classic understatement, Dame said the Paiutes "manifested many signs of hostility towards the whites and passers-by." His officers were to send out the best interpreters to clear the road of Indians, provide guards for the trains, and return any stolen property.[50] Having limbered up the battle-ax of the Lord, Dame now had to check it—while at the same time using the Indian threat to strip the last emigrant trains of their cattle, firearms, and cash.

The Dukes train paid Dame in advance for the services of David Carter, Nephi Johnson, and Carl Shirts, who agreed to guide the party to the divide between the Santa Clara and Virgin Rivers. To prevent the emigrants from seeing the field at Mountain Meadows, Dame ordered them "not to pass where the other train had been massacred, but to take a left-hand trail." No wagon road actually existed on the left-hand trail down Ash Creek, now the route of Interstate 15. Only the month before, James Martineau had said the road from Harmony to Washington was "about as bad as can well be imagined." At the fork of the trails to Harmony and Pinto, the emigrants met the Young brothers, who warned them about the Indians on the Muddy River and advised them to hire more interpreters. The emigrants agreed to pay Ira Hatch and three other guides $500 each, in advance, to take their wagons to Cottonwood Springs west of Las Vegas. On being hired, Oscar Hamblin warned that the interpreters would not do any fighting, "for they were friendly with the Indians who were Mormons."[51]

According to Johnson, as the train passed Harmony, Lee proposed using the Indians to ambush and destroy the emigrants. "There has been too much blood shed by you already," Johnson claimed he replied. "I have been instructed to see them safely through, and I will do so or die with them." Lee threatened him and called him ugly names.[52] Lee later charged that Johnson tried to persuade *him* to attack the party.

The guides warned the emigrants not to swear in front of the Indians, "as they would know [them] to be Americans and probably kill [them]." The interpreters persuaded their clients to give cattle to the Santa Clara and Virgin bands, but the party continued to lose animals to marauders. Samuel Weeks had $302.50 disappear from his wagon, and the emigrants were certain their Mormon guides had stolen it. Dudley Leavitt joined the party on the Virgin for no obvious reason. The company later concluded "that the plan was concocted here, between Hamblin and Hatch, for [their] robbery." On the advice of their interpreters, the Dukes train sent tents, blankets, and some clothing to the Moapits band on the Muddy. On reaching the river, they saw no sign of the gifts and decided the Mormons had appropriated them. The interpreters then said that the Indians wanted ten cows. The emigrants gave them six, and the Paiutes appeared to be satisfied. Although spared the fate of the Fancher party, the fearful emigrants realized the Mormons were systematically defrauding them.[53]

Dame warned Jacob Hamblin that Indians were gathering on the Muddy to wipe out another company of emigrants using arms and ammunition taken from the train destroyed at the meadows. At Pinto Creek Leavitt told Hamblin the rumors were true, and "all the Indians in the southern country were greatly excited and 'all hell' could not stop them from killing or from at least robbing the other train of its stock." Leavitt reported that several interpreters from Santa Clara were with this train. Hamblin maintained he sent Leavitt south with orders for the interpreters "to stop further mischief," to recover any stock the Indians ran off, and prevent further depredations.[54] What Hamblin actually did was make sure the emigrants left Utah Territory with nothing of value. "This policy of robbing the passing emigrants," observed Leavitt's granddaughter, "was clearly a part of the general war tactics."[55]

After extorting or stealing almost all the party's cash, in early October the Mormons and their allies stripped the emigrants of their remaining cattle.[56] The train reached the Muddy about 10:00 A.M., "and being surrounded by about 200 Indians," prepared to leave that afternoon. They kept the Paiutes out of their camp but not without considerable difficulty. The wagons moved on and were soon "scattered along on the road, as large trains commonly are." Seven miles down the canyon, hundreds of Indians began yelling in the surrounding hills. Nephi Johnson advised the captains to leave the cattle and guard the wagons with the women and children. The Indians "made a descent on the cattle and run them off—to the number of 326 head and five horses." When the travelers prepared to fire on the Paiutes, the interpreter warned they would all be killed if they resisted. The Indians "sent word, if we wanted to fight to come on." Johnson insisted an emigrant trade the scout's gun for a valuable revolver needed to fire a warning shot. When Johnson fired the pistol, all the interpreters deserted the train, and Nephi Johnson and the Navy Colt "were not again seen."[57]

The emigrants noted a striking peculiarity in the Paiutes surrounding their wagons on the Muddy River. Some of the "painted Indians had blue, gray, and different colored eyes; they had straight, curly, and fine hair, differing materially from the other Indians in this respect," George Davis wrote. He noticed many of them had streaks and spots of white in the creases round their eyes. Around their ears "the skin of the white man was quite apparent. The painted *whites* were shy; they did not act with the same freedom and boldness as the aborigines did." Davis and the other emigrants were convinced the whites were the leaders of the robbers.[58] But if there were white men among the Indians, Peyton Welch recalled, "they could holler just as loud as the Indians." When the emigrants left Utah Territory, "all they had left was what they had hitched to the wagons."[59]

Once the Mormons deserted the emigrants, their relations with the Paiutes improved dramatically, and the train reached Las Vegas without further molestation. "The Indians were peaceable, and the interpreters not being with us, we had to give them only one animal."[60] Two years later Maj. James Carleton concluded that without a doubt the interpreters "*were sent forward to run off the stock themselves.*" Carleton said the Mormons "*stampeded* the loose stock, consisting of over three hundred head of cattle and nine mules, and left the emigrants to pursue their way over the desert with only the cattle then attached to the wagons."[61]

The emigrants struggled on to Cottonwood Springs, some 275 miles from the first California settlement, where they sent nine men ahead on foot. After "almost incredible sufferings from the want of food and water," the exhausted men reached San Bernardino. When the rest of the Dukes train finally arrived, its members complained bitterly that the interpreters had robbed them. Denouncing Mormon fraud and extortion, Honea said the company had paid the six interpreters the enormous sum of $1,815. The guides had agreed to take the company the three hundred miles from Cedar City to Cottonwood Springs, "yet this contract was not fulfilled, although payment was made in advance."[62]

To Repel Any and All Such Invasion: Martial Law

On September 15, two days after Captain Van Vliet left Salt Lake, Brigham Young issued a proclamation of martial law implementing radical war measures. Its three directives were clearly beyond the powers of a territorial governor. The first forbade "all armed forces, of every description, from entering this Territory under any pretence whatever." The Nauvoo Legion was to be ready to march at a moment's notice to repel an "invasion" of U.S. territory by American troops. Young ordered that "No person shall be allowed to pass or repass into, or through, or from this Territory, without a permit from the proper officer."[63]

It might "seem strange to Americans, that they are not permitted to travel on their own soil, in Utah, without first obtaining passports," emigrant John Aiken thought on learning he needed "a passport from the War Department of Young's army, to secure [his] safety through the settlements." Aiken had met Nauvoo Legion surgeon general John L. Dunyon east of Salt Lake. If the army entered the Mormon settlements, Dunyon told him, "*every city, town and village in the States of California, Missouri and Iowa should be burned immediately—that they had men to do this who were not known to be Mormons!*" The Saints "would cut off all the emigrant trains, army stores, stock." No man, woman, or child would cross the plains without being scalped, and the Mormons "expected the Indians to perform this infernal and cowardly part of their designs." After speaking with the surgeon, Aiken applied for and received a pass from Daniel H. Wells on September 21, 1857.[64]

The pass served Aiken well. William Dame endorsed it at Parowan on September 28, and the lone traveler journeyed south without too much trouble. Mormon officers and Indian chiefs stopped him along the way, "declaring that no American could leave the Territory without showing his authority and paying the Indians for the privilege." On the southern trail, he confirmed that the Mormons had stolen the Dukes train's cattle. Ira Hatch told him the company had lost more than two hundred head to the Indians, but on October 15, a few days after the robbery, Aiken heard Jacob Hamblin tell Hatch "to go and brand *his own cattle*, before he turned them out with his." The comment excited Aiken's curiosity, and he heard Hamblin attribute the poor condition of a steer to its having been driven to the Muddy River and back. Two days later Aiken saw the tracks of a large herd of cattle going up the Santa Clara toward the Mormon settlements with "the tracks of several shod horses and mules following behind." Aiken accurately estimated from the appearance of the trail that the drove consisted of at least three hundred head.[65]

John D. Lee described this rustling operation, alleging that the interpreters were all tools for Jacob Hamblin, who told them "how and where to relieve this company of the large herd of stock." Nephi Johnson ordered the Indians to drive the stock to the Clara, and Hamblin gave the Paiutes a few of the cattle for helping him to steal the drove. The rest of the animals went to the man Lee bitterly called "the *secret keeper,*" Jacob Hamblin.[66]

The stolen cattle were called the public herd at Santa Clara, where almost everyone was acquainted with the affair. Hamblin made great efforts to keep the episode from destroying his reputation. Apparently believing no Californian would cross four hundred miles of desert to collect a few cows, Hamblin had replied to a query from Joseph Lane that he did not want the animals and did not know of anyone who did. To his surprise the emigrants sent Lane as their agent to retrieve their stock. Instead of surrendering the stolen cattle, Hamblin hid them in the mountains, for as Bishop

Crosby observed, "it would break Brother Hamblin up if all these cattle should be taken away." (Crosby himself had nine of Lane's cows.) The Santa Clarans spent three weeks leading Lane on a wild goose chase before surrendering a few animals.[67]

Brigham Young made his own inquiry about what had happened to the emigrants' property, and in June 1860 he probably learned more than he wanted to know when George F. Hendrix sent him a confidential report. Massacre veteran Samuel Knight "must know the history of this cattle affair from beginning to end," but Hendrix believed Knight's loyalty to Jacob Hamblin would prevent him from giving an honest account. The "taking and having the cattle was no secret," and Hendrix was sure "almost any one out of the Hamblin connection would or could give a history of this matter."[68] No historian succeeded in giving an accurate account of this matter for one hundred forty years, but Hamblin's reputation for honesty has been an enduring and beloved Mormon legend.

Josephs Blood Had Got to be Avenged

The militia leaders who had seen the results of their destruction of the Fancher party bitterly debated how to report the event to Brigham Young—and who would handle the delicate task. Haslam's message revealed a major policy change, and reports of the militia's recent triumph might not be as well received in Salt Lake as its officers had expected. Unbeknown to Lee and Haight, the Mormon prophet learned of the massacre less than a week after it happened. Tutsegabit and Youngwuds "came from the Santa Clarra" and reported the news from the south. Dimick Huntington did not record what the Paiutes told him, but the prophet ordained Tutsegabit an elder "to let him to go & preach the Gospel & Baptise among the House of Israel."[69] Perhaps he was simply recruiting a new missionary, but Young's ordination of Tutsegabit to Mormonism's higher priesthood appeared to be the Paiutes' reward for their part in the massacre.

Arapeen, "head chief of the Utahs," brought Young definitive word of the massacre on September 20, 1857. He told the prophet how "the Piedes had killed the whole of an Emigrant Company & took all of their stock." Young encouraged Arapeen to help "himself to what he wanted," but Arapeen's hesitation led the governor to call the Ute leader a squaw. Arapeen countered that the Americans had not hurt him, but if they hurt one of his men "then he would wake up." He would maintain his neutrality and "go off & stand still & see how the Battle went." Huntington warned "he might go as far as he could get but the Lord would fetch him out & he must doo the work that God & the prophets had said they must," Brigham Young's interpreter wrote. "Josephs Blood had got to be Avenged & they had got to help to do it."[70] For Brigham Young and his followers, the massacre at Mountain Meadows was a battle won, but the war went on.

10

Plunder

Shortly after the massacre, Lt. Col. Isaac Haight went to the wagon fort, where Nephi Johnson and two men were guarding the dead emigrants' possessions from the Indians. Haight asked the interpreter what he would do with the property. Johnson inquired if he wanted to know his real feelings, and Haight said yes. "You have made a sacrifice of the people," Johnson told him. "I would burn the property, and let the cattle roam over the country for the Indians to kill, and go home like men."[1] But Haight could not bring himself to destroy the goods. His avarice set in motion events that left little doubt that the Mormons were deeply involved in the murders at Mountain Meadows. Travelers identified stolen animals in the possession of prominent Mormons. In Cedar City S. B. Honea saw President Haight himself "riding a large bay horse" that he recognized as the property of a murdered emigrant, Silas Edwards.[2]

On reaching California, emigrant P. M. Warn charged that the Fancher party "was known to be in possession of considerable valuable property, and this fact excited the cupidity of the Mormons." The emigrants had more than four hundred head of stock besides mules, they were well supplied with arms and ammunition, and "their outfit indicated that they might be in possession of considerable funds."[3]

The Paiutes left the scene with a few animals and whatever trinkets, tinware, and clothing they could carry, but the whites took control of the livestock and the wagons. According to most accounts, Klingensmith, Haight, and Lee distributed the loot from the massacre. Most of the surviving stock was driven to Iron Springs, where Klingensmith, John Ure, George Hunter, and Ira Allen spent a day marking about fifty cows with a cross, the church brand. Others say Haight told Klingensmith to take the wagons and goods to the tithing office in Cedar City.[4]

Jacob Hamblin had a white ox at his ranch in 1859, which he said was the only property left at the meadows after the massacre. Albert Hamblin said the Mormons left the flour to the Indians but hauled the wagons and all the goods to Cedar City. The Paiutes only got about twenty horses and mules while the Mormon officers claimed the best animals for themselves, a measure of their contempt for their allies. Albert saw two yoke of cattle hitched to each wagon, but the "rest of the stock had been killed, to be eaten by the Indians, while the fight was going on, except some which were driven over the mountains this way and that." Lee estimated the train had a little more than five hundred animals, but complained, "I never got the half of them." Some of the Arkansans' cattle were probably killed during the wagon fight, but despite contrary claims, most survived. Some say Haight traded forty or fifty of the animals to William Hooper, the territorial secretary of state, for boots and shoes. Maj. James Carleton believed the Mormons sold 248 of the cattle to army supply officers. The animals "were without doubt the cattle taken from the emigrants."[5]

In March 1858 Brigham Young directed John D. Lee and Jacob Hamblin to use the stolen cattle for the best interests of the missionaries and their clients. He instructed Lee to take charge of the remaining cattle and property from the Fancher train "and take care of it for the Indians." Lee later claimed he collected about two hundred head at Harmony and put his brand on them, distributing the animals as the Indians needed them, "or rather when they demanded them," he said. "I did that until all of the emigrant cattle were gone." Lee claimed managing the cattle cost him money, because the Paiutes felt they owned everything with his brand on it.[6]

In contrast to his recollection, Lee's journals suggest he disposed of the cattle in a variety of ways. He complained early in February 1858, "J. M. Higbee Sold 2 yoke of oxen & put the money in his Pocket, that had been turned over to me by Pres. B. Young for the benefit of the Indians." Lee sent seventy cows to pay his debts to Levi Stewart and W. H. Hooper in April 1858. He may have donated Fancher party teams to the Perpetual Emigration Fund to finance Mormon wagon trains, for Lee gave the fund two wagons and eighteen yoke of oxen.[7] The cattle also served as breeding stock. Fifteen years later at Pipe Spring, Arizona, Bishop Winsor showed journalist J. H. Beadle cattle descended from animals taken at Mountain Meadows.[8]

Lee recalled that Haight, Higbee, and Allen each took one of the eighteen wagons in the Fancher train, including one with an iron axle. A persistent folk tradition tells that massacre veteran Samuel McMurdy led a train of eighteen wagons said to be from the Fancher party to Cache Valley. A former shipwright, McMurdy burned the wagons and used the iron to build an enormous barn that still stands in Paradise, Utah.[9]

In the desperately poor country of southern Utah, the spoils of the slaughtered emigrants became a source of envy and conflict. Some of his neighbors felt that Lee had swindled them out of their share. Lee, they told government investigators, distributed the wagons and guns among the Mormons and kept a carriage for himself. According to army reports, the Indians seem to have gotten only a few firearms, while many of the weapons captured in the massacre were seen in the hands of the Mormons. The loot included "the clothing stripped from the corpses, bloody and with bits of flesh in it, shredded by the bullets from the persons of the poor creatures who wore it." The property was taken to Cedar City and the bloodstained clothing lay "in the cellar of the tithing office (an official building)" for about three weeks, and its smell still lingered in 1859. Eventually the property was sold at public auction.[10] James Lynch learned in 1859 that the "ill-fated train consisted of eighteen wagons, eight hundred and twenty head of cattle, household goods to a large amount, besides money, estimated at eighty or ninety thousand dollars." Most of the loot, Lynch believed, "now makes rich the harems of this John D. Lee."[11]

Jacob Hamblin had learned of the massacre from Indian reports while in Salt Lake, and on the trail south he received an eyewitness account from Lee. Arriving at his ranch with a new wife on about September 26, Hamblin found his wife Rachel, who had a young child of her own, caring for the three orphaned Dunlap girls, including the horribly wounded Sarah. The "home appeared to be anything but cheerful." What Hamblin saw when he visited the killing fields shocked even this hardened frontiersman: "Language fails to picture the scene of blood and carnage. [Wolves had disinterred] the babies and stripped the bones of their flesh, [and] had left them strewn in every direction. At one place I noticed nineteen wolves pulling out the bodies and eating the flesh. . . . [The scene] was dismal in the extreme. This was one of the gloomiest times I ever passed through."[12] Rumor said that Hamblin had orders to deal with Paiute complaints that they had been cheated of their share of the loot. George Hendrix's report to Brigham Young charged that Hamblin distributed the cattle stolen from the Dukes party to reward the Indians "that assisted at the mountain meadows."[13]

Hamblin was deeply involved in covering up the crime, but he later claimed that had he been at home at the time the massacre would not have occurred. Lee was skeptical of Hamblin's claim of "great sympathy with and sorrow for" the fate of the emigrants. He could only judge what Hamblin would have done by the fact that Hamblin arranged the theft of the Dukes train's cattle.[14] Hamblin's advice to the Fancher party at Corn Creek to camp at Mountain Meadows seems suspect, and like Lee he probably would have done whatever Brigham Young wanted.

The massacre wrecked the hopes of Mormons such as Hamblin that the Paiutes could be transformed into civilized farmers. Lee complained the Indians did not plant any grain in the spring "with a view to living on the spoil of their Stolen Booty taken from us." Twenty years later a newspaper reported that the Indians who participated in the fight still declared that "the Mormons cheated them egregiously in dividing the spoils." The Muddy River band complained to the army in 1859 that they had been charged with the massacre of the emigrants, but, they said, "where are the wagons, the cattle, the clothing, the rifles, and other property belonging to the train? We have not got them or had them. No; you find all these things in the hands of the Mormons."[15]

LAY THE WHOLE MATTER BEFORE BRIGHAM YOUNG

According to Lee, three or four days after the massacre Isaac Haight came to Harmony with Brigham Young's letter. "We are all in a muddle," he said. Haight claimed he had sent Higbee an order to save the emigrants, but the messenger failed to go to the meadows. Lee realized they were all in a bad fix and asked what to do. Haight said the High Council wanted Lee to "lay the whole matter before Brigham Young." Lee resisted, arguing that as responsibility belonged to the military, Haight, a senior militia officer, was the right man to report to the governor. Haight countered to Lee, "You are like a member of Brigham's family, and you can talk to him privately and confidentially." He told Lee to assume responsibility "and not expose any more of the brethren than you find absolutely necessary." Haight promised Lee a celestial reward and a share in the spoils when the sword of vengeance shed the blood of the wicked. Lee claimed he believed everything Haight said.[16]

A reluctant John D. Lee set out for Great Salt Lake City on September 20.[17] When he arrived in Fillmore he learned Proctor Robison had died on September 21, 1857, and within a week he would blame the boy's death on the Fancher party. Near Fillmore Lee met Thales Haskell and Jacob Hamblin, who were both returning south with new wives; Hamblin had married Priscilla Leavitt on the very day of the massacre. Haskell recalled meeting a rider "coming post haste to deliver a message to Brigham Young that the Indians and some white men had massacred a company of immigrants at Mountain Meadows." Despite the supposed vow of silence, Lee told Hamblin what had happened, admitting that he and other white men had perpetrated the deed.[18]

James Gordon, Lee's former neighbor, saw some of the plunder from the massacre when Lee stopped at his home on his way to Salt Lake. Lee had a high-topped black silk hat filled with loot he said he had recovered from the Paiutes. He "poured it out onto the table for all to see: watches, jewels, and silver items." Lee apparently turned over the booty to the General Tithing Office, for its receipt book for December 1857 listed many of the trinkets Gordon described: a gold chain, a gold watch, a gold ring, a silver watch, silver tongs, a looking glass, and other items valued at $150.[19]

Other tales described what happened to the money and jewels stolen from the dead emigrants. Within days of the massacre, Garland Hurt heard that Lee's spoils included a large amount of money. Judge Frank T. Fancher said in 1955 that his kin had carried $4,000 in a strong box to purchase a ranch. Juanita Brooks connected this tradition with $4,000 in gold coin that traveling Bishop Amos Musser received at Holden, Utah, from William Stevens on January 17, 1876, as an offering for temple building. Stevens had long been anxious to make the donation, Musser noted, and "felt much relieved after placing it in [his] possession." James Lynch swore in 1859 that after the children were rescued, they "pointed out . . . the dresses and jewelry of their mothers and sisters that now grace the *angelic* forms of these murderers' women and children."

Journalist J. H. Beadle claimed jewelry from Mountain Meadows "was worn in Salt Lake City, and the source it came from not denied."[20]

Perhaps bearing this booty on his trip north, Lee stopped in Provo and addressed a Sunday morning congregation on September 27. Stake president J. C. Snow introduced "Judge Lee from Washington Co" who spoke regarding "Lemuel," a favored Mormon term for Indians. Lee could not resist celebrating his recent exploits and embroidering his tale with details picked up on his trip north:

> There was some Emigrants passd through & boasted verry much & they killd an ox & poisened it for the Indians. Four or five of them Died [and] one Mormon boy died & the marshall arrested one of them & they said where is your Damd Bishop & such like conduct. They then went out, & Cousin Lemuel told them that they was friends too the cause of Isreal but they were enemies too the gentiles & they killd all but three that got away in the night. One was overtaken the next day & they was on the track of the other two. That this was the condition of the Lamonites out where he was living & many other things. He said of them seventeen Children was saved & brought intoo the settlements & that he was trying too live near untoo the lord that we all might have an interest in the Kingdom that we might be permitted too return too our father & mother in peace for which may the Lord Bless you all. Amen.

President Snow "then aroze & said how do you like it?" He said he talked plain and would talk plain all the time. He said he hoped "that Every Damd shit ass had left the territory that there was. . . . I have no sympathy for such people."[21]

Mormon Indian agent George W. Armstrong delayed reporting the massacre until he could discuss the matter with the federal official responsible for the Paiutes, Indian Farmer John D. Lee. Armstrong's report to Superintendent Brigham Young followed the authorized fiction. The "poisoning [of] a part of the band of Parvantes" by a company of emigrants killed four natives and made many of them dangerously sick. In Armstrong's version, the poison was put in a cow, not a spring. The Indians "held a council and determined to be revenged upon the camp," and they followed the emigrants to "a place known as Mountain Meadows where they attacked the camp and after a desperate fight they killed fifty-seven men and nine women." Thus the first official comment on the subject in federal records blandly passed off the largest act of violence ever to take place on the overland trails—an event that would have triggered immediate retaliation anyplace else in the West—as the fault of the victims. "Until emigrants will learn to use wisdom and prudence in their treatment of the untutored savage," Armstrong warned, "they may expect to be severely handled by them."[22]

Brigham Young already had mixed feelings about the massacre. It was a righteous and necessary act of vengeance that confirmed his hope the Lamanites were ready to take up their role as the battle-ax of the Lord and help usher in the millennium. But he recognized the peril to him and the Latter-day Saints' cause if word leaked out that

Mormons had joined Indians in the slaughter of an entire wagon train. By the time he talked with Lee, he was well aware of the need to put as much distance as possible between himself and the atrocity.

Young had made a remarkable confession in July 1857. "I do not profess to be very good," the prophet admitted. "I will try to take care of number one, and if it is wicked for me to try to preserve myself, I shall persist in it; for I am intending to take care of myself."[23] To Lee's misfortune, he lacked this insight into the Mormon leader's character when Young arranged a series of meetings in late September designed to protect himself and to handle all contingencies that might arise from the massacre. Exactly what Lee told Young is a key piece to the puzzle of Mountain Meadows. Lee and Wilford Woodruff provided the two best accounts, but their stories directly contradicted each other.

Lee claimed he went directly "to the President's house and gave to Brigham Young a full, detailed statement of the whole affair, from first to last." Young was recovering from one of his frequent bouts of illness, this one so severe that it had kept him from preaching the previous Sunday.[24] Lee insisted he told Young everything, including "the names of every man who had been present at the massacre." "I told him who killed the various ones," Lee said. "In fact I gave him *all the information there was to give.*" Young replied that Haight had already sent him word "that if they had killed every man, woman and child in the outfit, there would not have been a drop of innocent blood shed by the brethren; for they were a set of murderers, robbers, and thieves."[25] Yet Young felt this was the most unfortunate affair that ever befell the church and expressed his fear of treachery among the participants, which would "work us great injury." He instructed Lee "*never* to tell this again, not even to Heber C. Kimball," and ordered him to write "an account of the affair, charging it to the Indians."[26]

The killing of the women and children for the sins of the men troubled Young. "This whole thing stands before me like a horrid vision," Young told Lee. Lee insisted his men were following orders, "and acting for the good of the Church, and in strict conformity with the oaths that [they had] all taken to avenge the blood of the Prophets." Referring to the temple vows of vengeance and obedience, Lee said Young must "sustain the people" for what they had done or release them from their oaths. Young wanted to consider the problem overnight. The prophet "went right to God with it," and the next morning he told Lee, "John I feel first rate. I asked the Lord if it was all right for the deed to be done, to take away the vision of the deed from my mind, and the Lord did so, and I feel first rate. It is all right. The only fear I have is from traitors." Lee claimed he started for home soon after the meeting, but he actually remained in the city for the October conference.[27]

Woodruff's diary told a different story of how Lee brought an express from Harmony and told his "awful tale of Blood" to the Mormon prophet. He heard Lee say that many of the one hundred fifty men, women, and children had belonged to the mob in

Missouri and Illinois. As they traveled south the emigrants "went damning Brigham Young Heber C. Kimball & the Heads of the Church saying that Joseph Smith ought to have been shot a long time before he was." To do all the evil they could, the emigrants "poisoned Beef & gave it to the Indians & several of them died. They poisoned the springs of water. Several of the saints died." The outraged Indians surrounded the emigrants on a prairie and "fought them 5 days untill they killed all their men about 60 in Number. They then rushed into their Carrall & Cut the throats of their women & Children except some 8 or 10 Children which they brought & sold to the whites." When Lee found out, he organized a burial party, "a horrid awful Job." Apparently to support Dame's slander that all the women were prostitutes, Lee added a strange detail, claiming, "Many of the men & women was ro[tten] with the pox before they were hurt by the Indians."[28]

If Woodruff had stopped there, historian David L. Bigler observed, "he may have provided evidence that Lee withheld from Young the truth." Instead, Woodruff recounted a discussion of innocent blood—an irrelevant detail if the killers were Indians. Young spoke "of the cutting of the throats of women & children as the Indians done" and said it was heartrending, but the emigration "must stop as he had before said." Lee argued there was not a drop of innocent blood in their camp. He had two of the children in his house, and they swore like pirates. The discussion of innocent blood indicates Lee's account was more forthright than Woodruff admitted. The contradictions in Woodruff's account suggest it described an event staged to provide Young with what later politicians called "plausible deniability." Whatever its origin and purpose, Woodruff's diary viewed the massacre in prophetic context: "The scene of Blood has Commenced & Joseph said we should see so much of it that it would make our hearts sick."[29]

Lee's presence at Provo on Sunday, September 27, supports his version of what happened. By the next day Lee's story had reached the office of the church historian, whose official journal noted, "Reports reached town that the companies of Cala. Emigrants going south were all used up by the Indians—100 men & 1000 head of cattle,—at Mountain Meadows." This suggests a scenario: Lee met with Brigham Young on Monday evening, as he claimed. After praying about the matter, Young ordered Lee "to keep the whole thing as a sacred secret" and lay the blame to the Indians. Lee then told his story before witnesses on Tuesday morning, including Woodruff. Afterward Lee crossed the street to the historian's office, whose journal entry for September 29, 1857, noted, "A bro from Iron Co. came into the office & confirmed the report of yesterday."[30]

Generations of Mormon historians have worked hard to prove that Lee lied to Brigham Young about Mountain Meadows, which assumes that Lee believed he could conceal the facts from Young. As well as anyone in Utah, Lee knew the futility of trying to hide a crime as enormous as Mountain Meadows from a man who had eyes and ears in every corner of Mormondom. Indian agent Hurt had already learned that Mormons were involved in the murders, and it is absurd to claim Brigham Young was oblivious to this fact for a dozen years. After all, Young had learned that much from James Haslam's report more than two weeks before.

Other witnesses supported Lee's version of events. Philip Klingensmith swore that Lee told him he had made a full report "to the President, meaning the commander in chief," Brigham Young.[31] Klingensmith said he visited the prophet with Lee and Charles Hopkins. The prophet took them on a tour of his barnyard "and showed [them] his fine things." In the Beehive House, he turned to Klingensmith and said, "Dispose of that property, let John D. Lee take charge of it." Young warned the men, "What you know about this, say nothing about it."[32]

Lee said Young told him to write a report as Indian Farmer, "laying the blame on the Indians." Lee's November 20 letter to Superintendent Young attributed the massacre to "the southern tribes." He claimed "Capt. Fancher's company of emigrants" had poisoned four Pahvants at Corn Creek. This "raised the *ire* of the Indians[,] . . . firing them up with revenge till blood was in their path." Lee dated the massacre to about September 23, apparently to provide himself with an alibi. "Just to show off," Lee later claimed, "and help Brigham Young to get something from the Government," he attached charges of $2,200 from W. H. Dame for cattle and wagons. "I never gave the Indians one of the articles named in the letter," Lee recalled.[33] The wagons, ox teams, cows, and chains that Lee listed in his accounts as gifts to the Indians and that Brigham Young subsequently charged to the federal government suspiciously resembled loot from the murdered emigrants.

In December Lee's old companion, Levi Stewart, submitted a voucher for "articles furnished sundry bands of Indians near Mountain Meadows . . . on superintendent's orders" on September 30, 1857, the day following Lee's public interview with Young. The articles included 171 pairs of pants, 135 shirts, 39$^{1}/_{2}$ pounds of gunpowder, 109 pounds of lead, and 14,000 firing caps, plus other items with a total value of $3,527.43. Stewart swore the articles "were furnished for an expedition to the southern Indians." Dimick Huntington and Lee certified they were present and saw the articles distributed to the Paiute chiefs and their bands. Superintendent Young signed the voucher despite his interview with Lee in Salt Lake on the day before the affidavit claimed Lee was at Mountain Meadows distributing the goods.[34]

In an 1875 deposition Young was asked what Lee reported to him. Young swore that Lee called at his office some two or three months after the massacre and had a great deal to say about the Indians and their "being stirred up to anger and threatening the settlements of the whites." He claimed he refused to listen when Lee began giving an account of the massacre: "I told him to stop as from what I had already heard by rumor, I did not wish my feelings harrowed up with a recital of detail."[35] However much the Mormon leader may have wished he had never learned the awful details, for the next two decades the massacre at Mountain Meadows would continually harrow up his feelings.

THE MORMONS WILL KILL YOU! THE ESCAPE OF DR. HURT

Indian agent Garland Hurt had been a constant irritant to LDS authorities, and by late September 1857 the brave doctor knew too much about events at Mountain Meadows. As Lee spoke to the congregation in Provo, members of the Nauvoo Legion moved to capture Hurt. His even-handed policy toward the Utes had won him the respect of the tribe's leaders. While meeting with chiefs from Uinta Valley on Sunday, September 27, 1857, to discuss establishing a new Indian farm, six Utes suddenly rushed into Hurt's office. "Friend! friend!" they called, pointing out the window. "The Mormons will kill you!" Hurt saw some one hundred mounted troops on the road a mile from his office. As he collected his papers, the Utes reported that the militia had blocked Spanish Fork Canyon and were marching to the Indian farm from Springville.[36]

The excited Indians hastily packed Hurt's bedding and clothes until his interpreter burst in and exclaimed, "Doctor, you're done in!" He handed Hurt a note from Bishop John Butler stating that the Mormons would not allow Hurt to leave the territory. Hurt determined "to extricate [himself] from the dilemma, or die in the attempt." He evaded the patrols and escaped with one white and three Ute companions, including Pete, who had brought the first report of Mountain Meadows. Reduced to surviving on roots and tallow, some twenty Utes escorted Hurt to Uinta Valley and north to safety. The "American," as his devoted clients called him, spent twenty-seven days crossing mountains and deserts to reach the westbound Army of Utah on October 23. "The sufferings of his naked escort on the journey were severe," noted a journalist who watched the Utes and their agent ride into the army camp. "It was an act of devotion which has rarely been excelled in Indian history."[37]

The day after Hurt's escape, Nauvoo Legion general Aaron Johnson received orders from Brigham Young to bring Hurt to Salt Lake, but Johnson had to report "the bush had been shook and the bird flown." Young later said he simply wanted to provide Hurt with a comfortable carriage for his "speedy and safe transportation" to the American forces, but Bishop Butler's note and Young's own orders indicate that the prophet's claim was dubious at best. George Hicks, one of the men called out to capture the agent, wrote, "I am glad we did not get him for more than likely he would have been killed if we had."[38]

As Garland Hurt searched for the U.S. Army, some two thousand soldiers struggled to reach a safe haven before winter shut off travel across the Rockies. The Tenth Infantry Regiment had left Fort Leavenworth on July 18, but it would take almost two more months to assemble and dispatch the rest of the units assigned to the Utah Expedition.[39]

Politics complicated the army's problems. In late August the War Department ordered General Harney to remain in Kansas and assigned Col. Albert Sidney Johnston to lead the Army of Utah. A consummate professional soldier, Johnston assumed command on September 11, warning his men to expect the "toil, privation, and hardships incident to frontier service." While Johnston hurried west, command of the advanced units fell to Col. Edmund B. Alexander, whose chronic indecision led his impatient officers to call him "old granny."[40] Alexander boasted early in September that he would reach Utah "in a condition of perfect efficiency and discipline." Less than three weeks later he admitted it was "almost certain that nothing but self-protection can be attempted this season."[41] Alexander had met Captain Van Vliet at South Pass and learned that he could expect no supplies from the Mormons, who were determined to resist the army's entry into Utah.

When Johnston took command, his army faced a host of problems, ranging from the poor quality of its green troops to a chaotic supply system. The Utah Expedition was scattered along the Oregon Trail from the Missouri to South Pass—Johnston himself left Leavenworth only in mid-September with six companies of the Second Dragoons—and, even worse, the advance elements lacked any cavalry to deal with the "well-mounted and tolerably well armed" Mormon militia.[42] Alexander concentrated the army's lead elements near Hams Fork, thirty miles east of the Mormon troops holding Fort Bridger, where by late September his forces had only two weeks' forage. Alexander let a fortnight of beautiful weather slip by before he moved west to try to find a better location for winter quarters.

Meanwhile, the Mormons walked a dangerous tightrope. They worked desperately to stop the army before it could enter the territory even as they tried to avoid igniting a bloody confrontation that would lead to war. They implemented a defensive strategy based on local geography. There were two practical ways to get the army into Utah, the first following the main road west through Echo Canyon along the line of present Interstate 80 and the second and longer route going north to the Oregon Trail and Soda Springs and then south along the Bear River. On both fronts, the Mormons strengthened their defenses. They fortified Echo Canyon, forty-five miles east of Salt Lake, building crude rock breastworks on top of its steep walls. They dammed the gorge and dug ditches; these improvements might not permit the Saints to drown Johnston's men like Pharaoh's army, but they would let the defenders flood the road for several miles. Their efforts impressed Stewart Van Vliet as he viewed them on his return to the army in mid-September. Though the fortifications were of dubious military value, they convinced Alexander the canyon would be a death trap. To the north, the Mormons sent out parties to secure the approaches down the Bear River and deliver appeals and instructions to Shoshoni bands living along the Oregon Trail.[43]

Alexander called a council of war on October 6 to devise a strategy to get into the Utah settlements before winter caught the army on the high plains. Fearful of the Echo Canyon fortifications, he decided to try the Bear River route. He believed the Mormons would make a stand at a fortified place near Soda Springs, where he would force a general engagement. With victory certain, Alexander could either obtain quarters and provisions or "force [his] way into the valley of Bear river and occupy some of the Mormon villages."[44]

Set Fire to Their Trains: The Nauvoo Legion Strikes

Utah's militia was a ragtag, poorly armed band of amateur volunteers commanded by officers with no formal military training and little grasp of strategy and tactics. "A singular idea seemed to possess these people," noted U.S. Army captain Albert Tracy. They believed their enemies would "move in solid and compact bodies to whatever point was convenient for them to resist."[45] Despite the illusions that guided its military strategy, what the Nauvoo Legion general staff lacked in professionalism or experience, it made up for in determination and enthusiasm, and its men possessed a detailed knowledge of local terrain and geography. The legion had an experienced core of Mexican War veterans and years of practical training fighting Utah's Indians, and the Saints brought a fanatical devotion to their cause missing in the desertion-depleted ranks of the U.S. Army.

Nauvoo Legion commander Daniel Wells and his staff left Salt Lake for the front on September 27. Wells decided to burn Fort Bridger and send raiding parties against the advancing army, which learned of the Mormon plans when they captured Wells's orders. The Mormons were to annoy troops "in every way possible," the orders directed. "Use every exertion to stampede their animals and set fire to their trains. Burn the whole country before them, and on their flanks." The Legionnaires should ruin the army's sleep by night surprises, block the road with trees, destroy the fords, and set fire to the grass to envelope the supply trains. "Take no life," Wells ordered, "but destroy the trains, and stampede or drive away their animals, at every opportunity."[46] He sent cavalry units under Robert T. Burton, John McAllister, Porter Rockwell, and Lot Smith to harass the army's supply wagons and cattle herds, which were strung out for hundreds of miles. When Wells retreated to Cache Cave, he left Fort Bridger and the Mormon settlement at Fort Supply in smoking ruins.

Rockwell, operating independently as a ranger answerable only to Wells, already had experience raiding the army. At 2:00 A.M. on September 25, Rockwell and five men stormed through Alexander's camp near the continental divide at South Pass and stampeded the army's mule herd. Unfortunately for the Mormons, the herd's bell mule caught his picket rope in the sagebrush. Rockwell's men had dismounted, and when the army bugler sounded stable call, the mule herd reversed course and returned to the army camp, taking the raider's horses with them. Rockwell and his men followed the army on foot. The next night they captured fifteen horses and rode back to the Mormon lines.[47]

The most famous incident in the Utah War took place when Lot Smith's raiders burned three supply trains. According to legend, when the Mormons seized the first two trains in the predawn darkness on October 5, 1857, a wagon master cried, "For God's sake don't burn the wagons!" "It's for his sake," Smith allegedly replied, "that we are burning them!" One of Smith's men recalled a more ominous encounter. The wagon master told Smith, "I guess you will have to burn them," but the red-bearded Mormon pointed at the teamsters' stacked arms at the head of the corral. "There is your guns," he said. "You can take them and we will try for it." The wagon boss declined to confront the maniacal guerrilla and said he would rather see the wagons burn than fight it out with the Mormons.[48] The raiders burned seventy-two wagons hauling provisions, mostly flour and bacon. Smith compounded the army's problems when he joined forces with Rockwell a few days later and ran off fourteen hundred head of government cattle. Smith's adventures ended quickly after mounted federal troops arrived, and Capt. Randolph B. Marcy nearly captured him.[49]

By mid-October the Nauvoo Legion had eleven hundred men under arms in the mountains and seven hundred men in reserve in Salt Lake. Three thousand more troops could be called up to defend the canyon on fifteen hours' notice. The Saints remained fearful, however, that the army would ignore their trap and attack Utah by way of the Bear River, the territory's vulnerable back door. Wells ordered Lot Smith to stop raiding the supply trains and join other forces near present Cokeville, Wyoming. If the soldiers stayed on the road to Fort Hall, the troops should not be molested, but if the army turned to enter Utah, Smith was to "pitch into their picket guards and sentinels, and among them all." If it threatened the northern settlements, Young ordered the legion to harass the army "both by night and by day, until they take their final sleep." "Pick off their guards and sentries & fire into their camps by night," he said, "and pick off officers and as many men as possible by day." A month after the holocaust at Mountain Meadows, Young told his commanders in Echo Canyon, "Wisdom now seems to dictate a cessation of the destruction of trains, both individual and Government." Young referred to freight trains rather than emigrant parties, but his reason for sparing the private trains was instructive: "We may need the articles they contain." If the troops attempted to enter Utah, the Mormons would "fall heir to the property in their possession."[50]

The road up Hams Fork proved impassable, and a snowstorm stopped the lethargic Colonel Alexander's advance, forcing him "to give up . . . designs of penetrating Salt Lake City." He decided to plod back to the overland trail, where he remained paralyzed by indecision.[51] The tired army wasted eight valuable days and balmy Indian summer weather at its untenable camp. Once again, fortune had narrowly defused an explosive confrontation between the army and the Mormons.

Johnston arrived with the winter weather to replace Alexander's dithering with his own decisive style. He ordered a march to Fort Bridger, the only logical place east of the Utah settlements for winter quarters. He personally directed the advance through blizzards and intense cold, sometimes marching on foot with his men. After fifteen arduous days, the army staggered into Fort Bridger, having lost more than three thousand animals in the preceding month.[52] The Mormons remained uncertain of the army's intentions, and Brigham Young directed that if Johnston should move toward the settlements, "policy dictated that the Officers and mountaineers with them be as rapidly disposed of as possible." If the army moved west from Fort Bridger, Wells ordered his commanders to "pitch into them in every possible way."[53]

The celebrated exploits of the Mormon guerrillas were mere irritants to the advancing army. The Saints had destroyed three hundred thousand pounds of supplies, but the expedition had ten times that amount of materiel moving west. In addition to food, the burned wagons contained mechanics' implements, stationery, and horse medicines that were hardly vital to the army's survival. Had Lot Smith burned the next three wagons in the train, he would have destroyed the expedition's essential winter clothing. "The loss, although great," Johnston wrote, "is less than I apprehended." His men would survive until more supplies arrived in the spring.[54] Food was rationed during the long winter on Blacks Fork, but the starvation imagined in Mormon folklore is wildly exaggerated.

The American army hunkered down for winter on the high plains. Johnston selected a spot sheltered by high bluffs about two miles above Fort Bridger to build Camp Scott, while the civil officers "fixed their quarters in a little nook in the wood above the military camp." To ensure that he had transportation for the spring, Johnston dispatched Captain Marcy and thirty-five volunteers and two guides to New Mexico, seven hundred mountainous miles away. Finally, Johnston sent men north to the Flathead country to get horses to remount his dragoons and to persuade the mountaineers to drive their cattle to Fort Bridger.[55]

NOT ALTOGETHER INDIANS: THE SOUTHERN TRAIL

Brigham Young had been ordering non-Mormon merchants to leave the territory since August. William Bell, partner in the firm of Livingston & Bell, left Salt Lake on November 8, 1857, after selling out to the LDS church. His train included adventurer John I. Ginn, who forty years later wrote a colorful if not particularly reliable account of the trip. According to Jacob Hamblin, Young sent orders instructing him to use his best endeavors to get the company through safely. At Santa Clara, Hamblin hired Tutsegabit to help guide the train to the Muddy River, hoping he could manage the Paiutes who were still "much excited and eager for spoil." Hamblin led the train through some one hundred Indians gathered on the Santa Clara and another large crowd of Paiutes at the Muddy. They met two missionaries Colonel Haight had sent to work with the Indians to carry out Mormon war policies. "For some cause" the men had a plan to kill the emigrants. Hamblin explained he had written orders from Brigham Young "to take this company through safe," but the missionaries "held out the idea . . . that there was secret instructions that [he] knew nothing of."[56]

A vexed Hamblin and the non-Mormons quickly crossed fifty miles of waterless desert to the springs at Las Vegas, where massacre veteran Dudley Leavitt and suspected murderer Ira Hatch joined the party. The Mormons accompanied the train as far as the Mojave River, where refugees from San Bernardino warned Hamblin that if he went to the town he would not return. On reaching California, the Dukes company had blamed Hamblin for the theft of their cattle, but he ignored the warning and continued up the Mojave. Near the head of the river Hamblin met some old friends who again warned that there were men at San Bernardino who would hang him on sight without benefit of judge or jury. This warning, a dream, and other spiritual manifestations persuaded Hamblin to return to Utah with the $300 he was paid for taking the party through safely.[57]

William Clark, a teamster discharged from the Utah Expedition, traveled through southern Utah in December 1857. He stopped overnight in Springville with Bishop Redfield, who took a liking to the young man. The bishop warned, "The Indians are mighty bad [on the Southern road], and *not altogether Indians.*" As he said this, recalled Clark, "tears rolled down his cheeks." Clark joined the last Mormon wagon party to take the southern road from Salt Lake in 1857. Amasa Lyman met the train at Cedar City and sent for Ira Hatch, "their best Indian interpreter." Escorted by Joel White, captain of one of the militia companies at the massacre, the party proceeded to Mountain Meadows. The guides ordered Clark and the other non-Mormons "to stay close to [their] wagons, and not be looking around, as it would not be safe [if they] did." Clark nonetheless counted eighteen skeletons "mostly of women and children with hair still on their skulls." "It was enough," he said, "to make a man's blood run cold, and to know that some of the perpetrators of that deed were in our train!"[58]

God Will Fight Our Battles

Semiannual LDS church conferences were always major social events in Utah Territory, but the threat of war gave added significance to the gathering in October 1857. The army was still marching on Salt Lake when Brigham Young addressed the assembled Saints. Many of them wanted a revelation on how the contest with the government would turn out. Young avoided specifics but assured his followers that at the end of the conflict Mormonism would be "higher and greater in power and influence than ever it was before." The Saints would "enjoy an influence that we never enjoyed before; and the Lord will have his own way in bringing about these things." Young promised his people would "sustain themselves against all that can come to annoy, destroy, desolate, and drive the Saints of God." He remained supremely confident. "God will fight our battles," he said, "and he will do it just as he pleases."[59]

Years later an anti-Mormon pamphlet charged that a few weeks after the massacre, Young spoke in the old tabernacle before thousands of people, some of whom were still living in Salt Lake in 1884. These witnesses claimed Young said, "The blood of those emigrants and of the whole of the people of Arkansas would not atone for the blood of Apostle P. P. Pratt." Allegedly, the prophet repeated the statement the next spring in the Seventies Hall.[60]

The territorial legislature met in an oddly festive atmosphere in December 1857, with George A. Smith, Isaac Haight, and John D. Lee representing the southern settlements. Haight proudly exhibited a canister of rifle powder manufactured in Cedar City, and Lee may have given Brigham Young the "little book or journal" describing the Fancher party that Chief Jackson had taken from Milum Jones.[61]

That month Young first told the story of those "killed by Indians at the mountains meadows" in a letter to San Bernardino Stake president William Cox. Citing the most reliable sources, Young claimed the emigrants "tarried some weeks on Meadow Creek, a little south of Fillmore." As they were about to resume their journey, they poisoned a spring and the carcass of an ox or cow. "Several Indians were killed by drinking the poisoned water and eating the poisoned meat, and some of the settlers were injured by the water, and one boy nearly if not killed." Such "nefarious conduct so exasperated the Indians that they pursued the emigrants." Confusing the Fancher party with the Dukes party that actually suffered the attack, Young said the Indians would have killed the emigrants at Beaver, save for the interposition of the Mormons and Ammon. Such a "narrow escape did not learn the emigrants ordinary prudence and good conduct." After reaching Mountain Meadows, "they still breathed out strong threats against all the Indians, and expressed a strong wish for the arrival of U.S. troops that they might join with them to exterminate the Indians." This outrageous treatment was more than the Indians could bear. "If white men in their boasted enlightenment suffer themselves to act thus unwisely and fiendishly towards the red men, what can they expect," the prophet asked, "and who do they expect will be able to control for their benefit the ruthless outbursts of the untutored and much abused savages?" Young told Cox to warn the editor of the *Los Angeles Star* that "unless he ceases publishing such infernal lies about Utah and her people, his lies may to his utter astonishment, become truths."[62]

In the governor's message to the legislature, Young made his first public comments on the massacre with a veiled reference to the murdered Arkansans. He denounced "passers-through" that had "cheated, and then poisoned and wantonly slain untutored savages." Aware of the bitter reaction to the massacre in California, Young complained that "lying and corrupt" newspapers charged every murder and massacre on the trail to the Saints. This "prolonged howl of base slander" was simply "to excite to a frenzy a spirit for [their] extermination."[63]

Despite such rhetoric, a subtle change was overtaking Young's war policy. He remained confident his cause would triumph, but he no longer spoke with certainty of Mormon independence or victory in an armed confrontation. Instead he discussed the issue from the perspective of a federal official. Young continued to claim he was governor, and the legislature charged the president of the United States with "forcing profane, drunken, and otherwise corrupt officials upon Utah at the point of the bayonet." To justify the rejection of the new federal officers, the legislature asserted that the appointments were unconstitutional, as the people had no voice or vote in electing them. The lawmakers again petitioned Congress for the Mormons' right "to choose [their] own rulers and make [their] own laws without let or hindrance."[64]

As the Mormons prepared for an aggressive spring campaign, a strange euphoria intoxicated the territorial capital. Snow had sealed off Echo Canyon, and Daniel Wells reduced the guard watching the federal troops on Blacks Fork to only twenty men. The Saints "enjoyed a pleasant, social winter," historian Norman Furniss noted, "the weather providing more protection than 10,000 rangers." Salt Lake saw a dizzying round of parties, concerts, and sleigh rides. Haight and Lee attended opening night at the theater on January 2, 1858, as guests of Brigham Young.[65] The festivities diverted the citizens and masked whatever anxiety the people felt about the looming confrontation with the army.

On the day after Christmas, Lee and Haight went "to get [their] likenesses taken."[66] The two images form an interesting contrast: Haight appeared confident and self-assured, but Lee looked haunted. Lee's portrait suggests a profoundly troubled man, and it is easy to assume that his thoughts had turned to the previous September, but perhaps the press of public and private business left him distracted. An attractive young English survivor of the handcart ordeal, Emma Batchelor, had caught Lee's eye. By his account, the young woman told him "that I on first site was the object of her Choice" as a husband. Two days later Young counseled Lee to bring Emma to him, and he would seal her to Lee. Lee noted that on January 6, 1858, Young signed a number of his vouchers "as claims against government for Servises amoung the Indians."[67]

As Indian superintendent, Brigham Young submitted his report to Indian Commissioner James Denver the same day. "Capt. Fancher & Co. fell victim to the Indians' wrath near Mountain Meadows," Young wrote, quoting Lee's November 1858 report of the massacre. "Lamentable as this case truly is," commented the governor, "it is only the natural consequences of that fatal policy which treats the Indians like the wolves, or other ferocious beasts." Young said he had tried for years to persuade emigrants not to follow such a suicidal policy and his people had frequently risked their own safety to help travelers. He noted that his expenses had increased considerably as a result of "the disturbed state of . . . Indian affairs."[68]

Along with his formal report, Young submitted his financial accounts. These claims are among the most puzzling aspects of his management of the Mountain Meadows problem. In an audacious fraud, Young billed the government $2,220 for charges from Indian Farmer Lee that included items obviously looted from the Fancher party, a bold if ill-considered expression of his contempt for the government. Young's accounts for the last quarter of 1857 listed payments of $463 to P. K. Smith for food and $3,527.43 to Levi Stewart for goods distributed at Mountain Meadows on September 28, 1857. Stewart gave the items to the Paiutes under the watchful eyes of Lee and Dimick Huntington, at least according to statements both men certified "on honor."[69]

In his private sealing room, Brigham Young married Emma Batchelor to John D. Lee on January 7, 1858. To celebrate, Lee provided a treat of cherry brandy, sugar, and liquors, while Mrs. Ezra Taft Benson "Made the Bride a cake & a good Dinner." Lee's guests, including Isaac Haight, ate, "drank & made merry & had a firstrate good time." The prophet married Isaac Haight to Elizabeth Summers on January 24, the day before Lee, Haight, and their new wives left Salt Lake. Lee gave Haight a brace of Colt revolvers, perhaps as a wedding gift. Lee had taken the initiative in contracting his marriage to Emma, but the timing of the two weddings inevitably led to charges that the new brides were the men's reward for their work at Mountain Meadows.[70]

Following the ceremony, Young spoke with Lee for more than an hour about the political situation. No matter how cautious his public statements might have been, Young remained convinced his confrontation with the government would end in violence. He told Lee to encourage the manufacturing of gunpowder and "the getting out of Lead, & wake up the Saints in all the Southern settlements to do their duty."[71] The crisis would come as soon as spring melted the snow that barred the army from the valleys of Utah.

11

All Hell Is in Commotion

On the day the Mormon militia buried the dead at Mountain Meadows, the palatial steamship *Central America*, bound for New York with a shipment of twenty-one tons of California gold, foundered in a hurricane off North Carolina with the loss of 425 lives. Speculation in railroad stock had left the American economy in a similar sinking condition. As bank failures spread across the country like falling dominoes, land values collapsed, railroads went bankrupt, factories shut their doors, and the stock market plunged. By autumn the United States was in the grip of a full-blown financial panic. A resulting religious revival filled churches in the East, and before it was over the Methodists had baptized 180,000 new members. The crash "swept over the United States like a tornado, and down went banks, brokers, traders, companies, manufacturers, and even politics," the *Deseret News* reported, "and up went a joint and loud wail from the worshippers of Mammon." Amid the economic wreckage, President Buchanan realized that the Utah Expedition was losing public support. It was clear "the sooner it was quieted, the better for the welfare of the Democratic party."[1]

Reports of the disaster at Mountain Meadows reached the Mormon colony at San Bernardino within three weeks of the crime and spread through California like a contagion. On the last day of September 1857, Addison Pratt wrote that William Mathews "had reached home, and brought the melancholy intelligence of a large party of emigrants from Missouri, to Cal—being killed by indians." The Indians "pursued the party & killed all, save a few children, and they were taken to Filmore city, and left with the saints." At a church meeting Caroline Crosby heard Mathews, Sidney Tanner, and William Hyde describe the massacre of a large number of emigrants, "quite an exciting affair."[2] A week later William Warren complained to Apostle Amasa Lyman that the Mathews train had brought in two gentiles, George Powers and P. M. Warn, who "told all they knew & probably a great deal more." San Bernardino's numerous apostates "one and all pronounced it a Mormon act and no Indian affair at all." They planned to raise five hundred men to escort the Dukes train into the settlements, but Warren suspected they would also try to "raise a sufficient force to just rout us out of here, and if they can prevent us from joining you in the vallies of the Mountains."[3]

As the last emigrant parties crossed Cajon Pass, a mail carrier told San Bernardino judge John Brown of the massacre of a whole train of emigrants. Judge Brown, a mystic who had parted ways with the Saints after he claimed they tried to ambush him, carried the news to Los Angeles. He reported "that a whole train of emigrants from Salt Lake city, for San Bernardino, composed of twenty-five families, comprising ninety-five persons, men and women, had been cruelly massacred on the road." Brown said the surviving children were being brought to California. On October 3, 1857, less than three weeks after the event, the *Los Angeles Star* reported the chilling outlines of the disaster. "No further particulars are known, nor any names given nor any account of the finding and disposition of the bodies," it said. "We give the rumor for what it is worth." The news was too shocking to be believed: the rumor was generally accepted in San Bernardino, wrote editor Henry Hamilton of the *Los Angeles Star*, but "we confess our unwillingness to credit such a wholesale massacre."[4]

The next week's *Star* confirmed "the foulest massacre which has ever been perpetrated on this route," with details carefully orchestrated by the San Bernardino Saints. J. Ward Christian, the son-in-law of wagon master William Mathews, carefully reported "the murder of an entire train of emigrants, on their way from Missouri and Arkansas to this State." It was, he wrote, one of the most horrible massacres he had ever had to report, and it would inevitably be attributed to the Mormon people. Christian charged that the emigrants had cheated the Indians who sold them wheat at Corn Creek and had put strychnine in water holes and poisoned a dead ox to kill the Indians. The *Star* printed Christian's report but accepted the general belief that "Destroying Angels" were behind the attack. The truth "will not be known until the Government make[s] an investigation of the affair."[5]

Messengers from the Dukes train reached San Bernardino in mid-October. Christian claimed "they neither saw nor heard anything that would lead a rational or unprejudiced mind to believe, or even suspect, that any of the Utah inhabitants" instigated the massacre.[6]

William Webb, one of the messengers who had "traveled on foot to that city" to seek help, disagreed. Before he left the Dukes party, the emigrants warned him to say nothing against the Mormons that might excite them and lead the Mormons to "cut them all off before they could get in" or fail to send the supplies needed "to keep the company alive." Mormons immediately surrounded Webb and his party when they reached San Bernardino and took them to a corral where Ellis Eames questioned them and Christian "done the writing." Eames and Christian separately interrogated the emigrants for several hours without offering them food, even though the men had eaten "but one scanty meal for four days." Christian read the statement back to

Webb and Irah Baise, and they signed it, but Webb insisted he had been egregiously misquoted and denounced the published statement as a lie. He was convinced "the late horrible massacre and robberies, perpetrated upon emigrant trains in Utah Territory, were committed by the Mormons and Indians under Mormon influence."[7]

A CRUSADE WILL START AGAINST UTAH

For all practical purposes, the attempt of the San Bernardino Mormons to manage the story of the massacre failed. Less than a month after the murders, the *Los Angeles Star* reported the public's pervasive belief that "the blow fell on these emigrants from Arkansas, in retribution of the death of Parley Pratt."[8] Christian's fear that the Mormons would be blamed for the affair was fully justified, for no one believed the clumsy tale of the poisoned ox or that the killing was exclusively the work of Indians. The *Southern Vineyard* later charged that no sane man who knew the Indians would believe they had perpetrated this act of barbarity. It was "beyond the power of credulity" to believe natives had acted as the Mormons claimed, since the "extermination of so large a number of men, without the escape of a solitary individual, is unheard of in Indian warfare." The paper quoted Christian's own account to prove that "this unparalleled crime of fratricide" was not the work of Indians, who would have taken the women captive rather than kill them. The statements of other travelers through Utah, the paper concluded, "fix, in the most positive manner, the complicity of the Mormons in that tragedy."[9]

Reacting to the initial reports of the massacre, George Q. Cannon, editor of the *Western Standard*, defended the Mormons from San Francisco and denounced the venal and incendiary press for failing to credit the poison story. It was common practice, he said, for border ruffians to "shoot down every Indian they can get sight at," and leaving poisoned carcasses was a common "means of entrapping the unsuspecting savage." If the story had come from anywhere but Utah, it would have been believed without question.[10]

On arriving in Los Angeles with seventy Australian converts, missionary William Wall found "great excitement in the town against Mormons on account of a company being massacred by the Indians, which they laid to the Mormons." Wall barely escaped lynching by a mob of angry citizens that included three apostates, one of whom swore "he would sooner see Gov. Young's hearts' blood run, than to see cold spring water when he was dry."[11]

Californians expressed their outrage at a public mass meeting on October 12 in Los Angeles. They charged the Saints with systematic "thefts, robberies, and murders, promoted and sanctioned by their leader, and head prophet, Brigham Young." Resolutions blamed the Mormons and their Indian allies for the atrocious act at Mountain Meadows and called on the president to take prompt measures to punish "the authors of the recent appalling and wholesale butchery of innocent men, women and children."[12]

If Brigham Young planned to provide a dramatic demonstration of his power to close the overland road, the message rang out clearly in California. The *Los Angeles Star* wrote that unless the government took speedy measures, "the tide of emigration by this route will be entirely stopped." Emigrants going west could not rely on the government for protection. They were doomed if they could not defend themselves "against the unknown and unforeseen dangers of the route." Geography worked in Young's favor: "There are passes, and cañons, and gorges on the way, where a small force could defeat the whole army now on its march." The Mormon leader had "wisely chosen his ground. In a country difficult of access, surrounded by hordes of Indians with whom he is in league, it will be a long and tedious warfare to reduce him." A costly and sanguinary war appeared imminent. According to the *Star,* a call for volunteers would meet such an enthusiastic response in California that the government could "exterminate the rebels, root and branch, and throw open the great highway to our State to the unmolested travel of the citizens of the Union."[13]

News of the massacre triggered anger and panic in the California press. The *San Francisco Herald* wildly overstated Mormon military power, estimating some ten thousand fighting men were in "close alliance with at least fifty thousand hostile Indians."[14] Such fears generated a call for revenge. "The blood of American citizens cries out for vengeance from the barren sands of the Great Basin," thundered the *San Francisco Bulletin*. "A crusade will start against Utah which will crush out this beast of heresy forever." Thousands of volunteers could ask for no better job "than the extermination of the Mormons."[15]

Even the Spanish newspaper in Los Angeles denounced the massacre and the lawlessness of "quel gefe de la prostitucion [that boss of prostitution] Brigham Young." *El Clamor Público* regarded the event as yet another example of American jingoism and regretted that enterprises born in the United States "to liberate and civilize poor, misfortunate Latin-American countries, do not direct their attention toward Salt Lake!" The editor feared "the thieving leaders of the Filibuster Party," specifically, adventurer William Walker and the Mormons, "might make an alliance, because a certain likeness exists in their prophecies." Brigham Young "prophesied that in ten years he would be president of the United States," while Walker "announced that in less time he will be president of all the republics from Mexico to Cape Horn!" The editor concluded, "We shall see."[16]

TROUBLE ON THE FRONTIER

Among the options Brigham Young considered if the army forced him to evacuate Utah Territory was a retreat to the north along the line of his spring reconnaissance to Fort Limhi. To support this escape route, in early September 1857 Young suggested making a settlement between Salt Lake and Fort Limhi, perhaps near Fort Hall. Wilford Woodruff noted, "It was thought best to do so." Young said, "The North is the place for us not the South. No one but the Saints would want the cold North country. This is the key of this continent—and I think we had better keep nearer the lock and have the key in our own hands." He wanted a company to leave immediately so they could plant grain.[17] George A. Smith informed William Dame that fifty men had been selected "to make a look out station 200 miles north of the city at the Black foot fork of the Snake river."[18] The settlement, near present Blackfoot, Idaho, was "to watch any movement that might be made by Johnston's army or other hostile forces in that direction."[19]

Young sent Samuel Richards east in early August with orders to recall all the elders from the eastern states and Europe to Utah. From now on the Children of Israel would "take care of themselves, while the World goes to the Devil." It was unsafe for the Saints to remain in the States, so everything would be done "as far as possible towards clearing the country." Richards was to go to Liverpool and divert European emigrants to Canada, so that the next summer they could "meet the Saints in the mountains by a *new* northern Route through the British Possessions." Richards expected an outcry in the states. "[The gentiles will] never again put their yoke upon Israel, and some funny times will be Seen before they will acknowledge us or our Independence."[20]

Young tried to keep his plans secret, but the *Alta California* reported on October 8 that Saints from Carson Valley were bound for the Salmon River to found a settlement "extending north into the Russian possessions."[21] Word spread north to the Bitterroot Valley, where Indian agent John Owen charged that Mormons were meddling with the Indians. The people at Limhi thought they would "have to flee to the Mts to carry out the prophecy of Joe Smith." They had seven years' provisions cached in the mountains, but the "deluded beings," as Owens referred to them, believed "Brigham Young is going to save the republic & that he will be president of the U.S." He warned the Indian superintendent in January 1858 that the Mormons might soon attack. Brigham Young's declaration of martial law had thrown the whole country into a state of alarm. Owen took the reports so seriously that he spent "a week of unceasing labor" inventorying his trading properties.[22]

Never one to limit his options, in late January 1858 the Mormon prophet sent word to Lee to locate a resting place for his family and the First Presidency near present St. George. Three weeks later Young ordered Haight to prepare "to send out some old men and boys to the white and last mountains west of the settlements and find places where we can raise grain and hide up our families and stock in case of necessity."[23] Despite his interest in the southern country, the unsettled northern territories offered Young the best refuge if he had to abandon Utah.[24]

Young's activities did not go unnoticed in Washington Territory. George Gibbs reported in late 1857 that the Klickitats claimed "Choosuklee (Jesus Christ), had recently appeared on the other side of the mountains," signaling that "the whites would be sent out of the country, and all would be well." The authorities connected this with Brigham Young's visit to the Flathead country the previous spring. Col. N. S. Clark feared that successful Mormon military operations could provoke "an Indian war extending along [the] whole frontier." Maj. W. W. Mackall warned Colonel Steptoe that "it is not improbable that the Mormons may move north." A conflict in Utah, he warned, "may be a signal for trouble on the frontier." Steptoe, no stranger to the Mormons, questioned whether they were serious about leaving the country, but he concluded it was probable they had taken steps to arm "against us all the Indians living on the principal routes to Utah."[25]

EVACUATION OF SAN BERNARDINO

Brigham Young's conflicting orders to the colonies at Carson Valley and San Bernardino illustrate his uncertainty in fall 1857. In August missionaries in Carson Valley received a letter from Young written in early June stating they "were not and are not recalled from [their] mission," but on August 15 he ordered Peter Conover to evacuate the settlement and "bring in all the ammunition you can get." Young directed San Bernardino's leaders in early August to "make arrangements as fast as possible to gather up," and on October 1 he instructed that "all in your place and region who desire to live as becometh saints should use all diligence to make their way into Utah." These orders reached San Bernardino on October 30, and the news spread quickly. Stake president William Cox told his flock to leave for Utah as soon and with as little noise as possible, but in Salt Lake Brigham Young was second-guessing himself.[26] He told Woodruff on October 26, "I want Sanbernardino & Carson valley to remain & not be disturbed for I want the people there to raise stock to supply us from time to time as we need."[27]

It was already too late to rescind the prophet's marching orders. Loyal Saints in southern California sold their holdings at tremendous losses, and some two-thirds of San Bernardino's three thousand inhabitants packed up, sold out, and moved to Utah.[28] The refugees were horrified when they crossed Mountain Meadows and saw the physical evidence that littered the site. Justus Wellington Seeley recalled finding bones, and he may have been the boy who "took a skeleton and thrust it into the wagon opening, and terrified the girls."[29] Sarah Dunn Thornton remembered the terrible night her family spent at Mountain Meadows. Some of the apostles returning from missions "washed their hands in a stream of water, said they were innocent of such a deed and knew the Church had sanctioned no such thing." At Hamblin's ranch she "saw a little girl five years old who had been saved from the massacre. She seemed to be filled with fear and cried most of the time. Those people told them that John D. Lee and his men disguised as Indians had come upon the train of emigrants and mercilessly murdered them."[30]

The faith of many of the refugees never recovered from the experience. James Skinner recalled "living in San Bernardino Cal in peace with all nations minding our own business and treating everyone right and just" and believing he would be able to live there for many years in comfort and peace. Skinner did "not like to talk, much less write about such a dastardly" act, but "it was the cause of [their] leaving home, and moving to Utah." He camped not far from "where their Bodies were left." Many in his party found skulls, bones, and long tresses of silky hair scattered and unburied. It was a ghastly sight, "once seen, never to be forgotten." The massacre caused "a terrible amount of Prejudice, not without just cause. For it was a dastardly outrage commited by People who had been taught and knew better, than to kill their fellow man. It has left a stain on the Church they will never out live."[31]

The evacuation of San Bernardino brought a host of unhappy Saints to Utah who deeply resented losing their homes in California largely as a result of the massacre and who asked probing questions. In mid-December Apostle Lyman arrived in Cedar City to manage the evacuation and assume command of the southern military district. He quickly called a special meeting. Aware of the grisly evidence left on the field at Mountain Meadows, Lyman spoke at some length on not encouraging the Indians "to shed the blood of strangers and passers by."[32]

While camped at Cajon Pass with the refugees at the end of November, a returning missionary (probably William Wall) paused. He laid a curse on California: "We seal the fate of this wicked State, and it shall be subject to the curse of Almighty God,— to famine, drought, war and earthquakes. . . . Farewell!"[33]

THE STANDING ARMY OF ISRAEL

The California mail arrived in Great Salt Lake City on January 3, 1858, bringing bad news for the Saints, including reports that the government planned to reinforce the army via the southern road. "All hell is in commotion," Lee wrote. The "government intends Sending ten thousand troops by the South rout & as many by the North Rout."[34]

The flood of Mormon refugees reported the vehemence with which California newspapers rejected stories that blamed the massacre on Indians. This apparently prompted George A. Smith to search for a more credible story to replace the unlikely poison tale. The emigrants had "made a business of shooting down the Indians of the Desert for many years," he wrote. "The same game was carried on this season by a Company from Arkansas." The "Santa Clara Indians gathered and surrounded the Company and fought them for several days." It was rumored that one hundred emigrants were killed, and the loss among the Indians was unknown but must have been considerable as the company had fortified themselves in their wagons and made a spirited defense. Smith repeated the fiction that "the Indians spared the lives of the children, which have since been ransomed, and cared for by some of the Southern settlers." This was the first time the Paiutes had ever taken such a step. "It has rendered the greatest caution necessary even for our people to pass through their country, notwithstanding we have always treated them with the greatest kindness."[35]

In mid-October 1857 Brigham Young was inspired to create a private professional army to supplement the territorial militia. He proposed forming a mounted force to guard the approaches to Utah.[36] Mormon legislators approved Young's plan early in 1858 and established a full-time army variously called the Standing Army of the Kingdom of God, the Standing Army of Deseret, the Army of Israel, or simply the standing army. Modeled on the Continental Army, the force was "to be raised of 1000 or 1100 men from levies from the different Wards and Counties." The levy was imposed by decree, and local wards were ordered to sustain the army with donations of horses, firearms, and food enough to support a soldier (or one-half or one quarter of a soldier). Military districts would maintain the existing efficiency of the Nauvoo Legion and were obliged to raise specific numbers of additional troops. The financially exhausted population found their property taxed to equip the army, which was organized into two regiments, ten battalions, and twenty companies of mounted riflemen. Gen. William Kimball was assigned operational command.[37]

In the first Mormon account of the Utah War, French convert Louis Bertrand described the plan to use the new army "to take the offensive in the spring. Twelve squadrons of mounted riflemen of one hundred each were recruited and equipped in a few days." At least in theory, each soldier received two horses, a revolver and carbine, and food for six months. These cavalrymen would seize South Pass, intercept supplies and reinforcements, and blockade the overland road while two squadrons attacked Captain Marcy's relief column from New Mexico. "General Johnston with his sixteen field guns and three thousand heroes at Fort Bridger," Bertrand wrote, would be forced to surrender "without even the satisfaction of having fired a single cap."[38]

The Army of Israel played no role in the outcome of the Utah conflict, but its existence revealed the determination of Mormon leaders to resist the federal forces waiting on their doorstep. Though he moderated his rhetoric to cover any outcome, during winter 1858 Young focused on how to fight a war, not how to avoid one. The standing army, historian David Bigler observed, "existed for only about three months, but in that time it became one of a kind in American military history."[39] Charles Derry, a beleaguered English convert, recalled how "the Lord accepted the sacrifice and the standing army was disbanded. But Brigham's lord forgot to return the poor man's cow, or horse" when the army quietly disappeared. "Perhaps Brigham needed them."[40]

At his winter quarters at Camp Scott near the ruins of Fort Bridger, Albert Sidney Johnston, now promoted to brevet brigadier general, faced a different set of problems. The Army of Utah hunkered down to wait for spring. Perched atop windy buttes to the west, a handful of Nauvoo Legion sentries kept a cold eye on federal activities. Both commands had orders to avoid violence, but the dangerous standoff between the army and the territorial militia continued through the long winter.

Encamped with the army were Utah Territory's new federal officials. The new governor, Alfred Cumming, was a portly bureaucrat who was regarded as "a worthy and conscientious public officer." He had served on Winfield Scott's staff during the war with Mexico and in the difficult position of superintendent of Indian affairs at St. Louis. Unfortunately, the vain but overweight Cumming was obsessed with his public image, jealous of his powers, and suspicious of the army, and his unfortunate appearance made him look "more like a waddling clown than a territorial executive."[41]

Arriving at Camp Scott after a march "attended with the severest hardships," the new governor assumed office on November 21, 1857, and issued a proclamation to the people of Utah directing all armed parties in the territory to disband. Defiance, he warned, was treason, but the Saints were not impressed. Cumming complained privately of the puerile reasoning they used to justify treasonable acts and rebellion, but the army already felt he was too lenient with the Mormons. Delana R. Eckles, Marshal Peter K. Dotson, Garland Hurt, and other federal officials cooled their heels and vented their rage against the Mormons at Ecklesville, the civilian encampment built next to the army's winter quarters. Chief Justice Eckles convened his court in December and organized a motley grand jury that indicted a long list of Mormons for treason.[42]

Despite the Utah Expedition's shaky start, the government refused to abandon its resolve "to chastise insubordination and quell rebellion." And although the campaign's political support was collapsing in the East, the secretary of war was determined to do whatever was necessary "for crushing treason at a single blow." As the Army of Utah endured the long and dreary winter, surprisingly morale improved. Journalist Albert Browne, who wintered with the army, wrote, "Confidence and even gaiety were restored to the camp, by the consciousness that it was commanded by an officer whose intelligence was adequate to the difficulties of his position."[43]

Brigham Young's habit of taunting his enemies led to a serious blunder involving poison. In early December sentries at the army camp detained a party of Mormons and a number of mules loaded with salt, an item in scarce supply on Blacks Fork. The men had a letter for the commander they insisted on delivering in person. In Johnston's reception tent, the two messengers "presented the letter of Brigham Young of Nov. 26th."[44] The letter was a wonderful piece of sarcasm but a diplomatic disaster. Young informed Colonel Alexander that his favorite mule was now "in [Young's] stables, where it is well fed and cared for." Alexander should leave the mule in his care, so it would be in good shape when he returned east in the spring. Before baiting Alexander, Young outraged Johnston with veiled threats against prisoners held by the Mormons. Even more provocative was a gift of eight hundred pounds of salt, which the army desperately needed. It was not the salt that offended Johnston but the prophet's assurances that it had not been poisoned. If anyone suspected that the salt contained "any deleterious ingredients," Young suggested having his messengers "partake of it to dispel any groundless suspicions." Should this fail, "your doctors may be able to test it to your satisfaction."[45]

Johnston carefully read and reread the letters. In his impressive manner the general said, "I will not accept of this salt sent by Brigham Young—not for the reason hinted in his letter—but I can accept nothing from him so long as he and his people maintain a hostile position to my government." The suggestion that he test the salt for poison particularly offended Johnston: "There is no portion of the American people who would be guilty of so base an act, and none to suspect it." Johnston told the messengers he had no reply, and he ordered them to direct future letters to Governor Cumming. "I have been sent here by my government," Johnston concluded, "and I shall advance."[46]

AID AND COMFORT: THOMAS L. KANE'S MISSION

By fall 1857 the question of what Congress would do about Bleeding Kansas had mesmerized the nation. As for Rebellious Utah, Americans were no more interested "in news from that remote region than in tidings from the rebellion in India or of the wars in China." Despite the economic crash and growing criticism of his Utah policy, James Buchanan remained determined to force the Mormons to accept federal authority. Secretary of War John B. Floyd called for new regiments and prepared to reinforce Johnston with almost four thousand men. In his annual message, Buchanan rebuked Brigham Young for tampering with the Indians and for his attempts to preserve his despotic power. This was the first rebellion in a U.S. territory, the president said, and "humanity itself requires that we should put it down in a manner that it shall be the last."[47]

A peaceful resolution of the Utah problem appeared unlikely, but one hopeful prospect appeared at the White House in late December in the diminutive form of Thomas L. Kane, son of a prominent Pennsylvania judge, an honorary colonel, and a trusted agent of the Mormons. A disciple of French socialist Auguste Comte and brother of a famous and recently deceased arctic explorer, Kane saw himself as a defender of the oppressed in general and the persecuted Saints in particular. Kane proposed to go to Utah and arrange a settlement, and on the last day of 1857 the president wrote two letters commending his efforts without offering official sanction for the mission. The letters withheld the promise of executive clemency Kane had hoped to take to the Saints, but their message was clear enough to express the president's desire for peace and his unofficial support of Kane. Given the explosive situation in Utah, this was a fortunate decision of national importance. Conflicts as dangerous as the crisis of 1857 almost inevitably lead to combat, and the consequences of a religious civil war on the American frontier were so grim as to defy imagining. Though eccentric and self-absorbed, Kane has been widely praised for his accomplishments as a peacemaker, and he deserves it.[48]

Kane left New York on January 5, 1858. He traveled by ship from Panama to San Francisco, then went south to San Bernardino. Disguised as "Dr. Osborne," he traveled up the central southern route to Utah. He met Amasa Lyman on the road. Wearied by supervising the evacuation of San Bernardino, Lyman escorted Kane north on a route that bypassed Mountain Meadows. Kane probably had heard many contradictory stories in California that raised questions about the Mormons' role in the massacre. Kanosh put to rest whatever doubts Kane might have had about the Mormon cover story when the two met, probably at Corn Creek. The Pahvant chief dutifully repeated the poison story, properly seasoned with colorful new details that made it even more believable. According to Kane's diary, Kanosh told him the Pahvants visited the campground shortly after the Fancher party left.

> [The Indians] noticed a white like flour upon the grass and the Mormon cattle & the Indian cattle was running around and they noticed one critter went off a little and died right off. The Indians went to work & skinned this critter. One load[ed] it on his shoulder & took it up to Camp and it nearly killed him. One or two of the Indians got thirsty and stooped down to drink at this Spr[in]g where the Emigrants got their water and drank and one died and a number more came very near dying. The friends of the man who died set up a howl and followed them that night. Kenosh tried not to have them follow them but he [cou]ld not prevent them. They followed them that night shot at their camp wounded one man & stole four head of cattle. One of the Emigrants on guard Supposing he shot an Indian killed his own mate. The Parvans Indians passed this word on to the Pah éats [Paiutes] in whose country is where the Mountain Meadows are. It is about a hundred miles to the Mountain Meadows from Corn Creek and there the Paheats boxed them again.
>
> By law the Indians wanted pay for their travelling through the country burning their wood wasting their grass &c. They killed a beef for them but must have poisoned it. For four men and a number of women & children (the number I don't remember) died of eating that beef. That is all I got from Kenosh. Then they got so mad! They passed the word around & gathered all together and used them up.[49]

Kanosh even named the Paiutes who participated in the killings, including the bands of Quanãra, Youngwuds, Tatsegabit, and "Indians from the Mõah pãh." Kanosh's dutiful lies in behalf of his patrons played an essential role in maintaining the loyalty of Kane, the Saints' most powerful non-Mormon friend.

After a journey that left Kane, a hypochondriac, physically exhausted, he arrived in Great Salt Lake City on February 25, 1858, with Lyman, who brought disturbing rumors of an invasion from the Colorado River. At eight o'clock that evening, Joseph A. Young introduced a worn Kane to a council of LDS leaders in Brigham Young's Beehive House. Kane addressed them, speaking with great difficulty. Exaggerating his role, he claimed he came as an ambassador of the president and asked the Mormons to send aid and comfort to the soldiers "now suffering in the cold & snows of the mountains." Kane spent thirty minutes alone with Brigham Young. What the two men discussed is not known, but as Mormon chronicler B. H. Roberts noted, "whatever recommendations the colonel made, they evidently were not acceptable to President Young."[50]

The euphoria of the previous months in Great Salt Lake City had vanished before Kane arrived, and the settlement was on edge. In early February the California mail brought news of Buchanan's call for four new regiments to march against Utah. On the Saturday night following Kane's arrival, "several persons disguised as Indians entered the house of Henry Jones, and dragged him out of bed with a whore and castrated him by a square & close amputation."[51]

Kane spent two weeks trying to persuade Brigham Young to make peace with the government. George A. Smith informed Dame, "[Kane] wants us to spare the lives of the poor soldiers camping about Bridger." Smith wrote, "Mr. Buchanan would like us to feed them, and not destroy them until he can get sufficient reinforcements to them to destroy us—this is as near I can learn the design of the President of the United States." He summarized the Mormon response to Kane's conciliatory proposals with one word: "Bah!"[52]

Young spoke to Kane with typical bluntness: "I would take no man's counsel upon the face of the earth, but I would follow the counsels of God. You may think it strange of me, but you will see that I am right." He said he would act only "as God directed [him]." Young was waiting for a sign from the Lord, and in the waning days of winter he anticipated that sign would be an assault on Utah by the U.S. Army, an event that would unambiguously signal the beginning of the last days. Young later told the Saints that Kane had pleaded with him to "stay the hand of the brethren against the army, for they were in our power," but Young insisted that only the spirit of the Lord would guide him. Unable to sway the Mormon leader by reason, Kane finally agreed that Brigham Young "would dictate and he would execute."[53]

A discouraged Thomas Kane left Great Salt Lake City for the army camp on Blacks Fork on Monday afternoon, March 8, 1858, with an escort of "b'hoys" commanded by Porter Rockwell.[54] Despite two weeks of pleading, Kane could not persuade Brigham Young to give an inch. The prophet refused to offer the army food or make any other conciliatory gesture, which Kane had hoped to use to diffuse the confrontation. The best Kane could do was to get Young to agree to let federal civil officials into the territory. But Young stubbornly refused to let the army enter the Great Basin without bloody opposition.[55]

Early on the very day Kane left Salt Lake, an express had arrived from the north with grim news for the Mormons.[56] The remote Indian mission at Fort Limhi now assumed a key role in the confrontation between the army and the Mormons. At Oregon City, Indian agent R. H. Lansdale had heard in January 1858 that the Mormons "on Salmon River [had] invited all Indians willing to fight [the] U.S. to take powder and lead for that purpose." Mormon missionary Lewis Shurtliff told a different tale. On December 8, 1857, "the Indians came up to us and demanded our powder riding in their war Circles," he said. "But they were plainly told that they would get no powder only through our rifles. This they did not like and very sullenly left us." The settlers gave the Indians a feast at the end of the year, but relations between the northern tribes and the Mormons continued to deteriorate.[57]

Plans to forge the Lamanites into the battle-ax of the Lord had gone awry on the Salmon River. In an ill-considered effort to win the affection of all the tribes, the missionaries had extended their hospitality to a Nez Perce war party, angering the Bannocks, who complained that the Saints had fed the intruders with crops grown on Bannock land. Despite their initial promises, the settlers had never paid the Indians anything for their land, and the Bannocks were already outraged. They claimed the Mormons had furnished firearms and ammunition to their enemies, and when the Nez Perces stole all of their horses using these arms, "they were on this account outraged at the Mormons."[58]

On the morning of February 25, 1858, some two hundred fifty Shoshoni and Bannock warriors surprised the settlers, killing two men and wounding five others, including Col. Thomas S. Smith, who they caught far from the fort chopping wood.[59] Smith finally stumbled into the fort covered in his horse's blood and with his hat shot off and suspenders cut. The Indians blackened the hills on both sides of the river and headed for the cattle herd. Under fire, George McBride dashed down among the Indians and turned two or three droves until he fell from his horse and was scalped. The Indians drove off all the stock and left the settlers in what Israel Clark termed a deplorable condition. "Our feelings cannot be described," Clark wrote, "[with] most of our cattle gone and over three hundred miles from friends."[60]

To add to the despair of the missionaries, most of their attackers were baptized Mormons. Only some two dozen men remained alive to defend the sixteen women and children at the fort, leaving them outnumbered ten to one. Colonel Smith ordered Baldwin Watts and Ezra Barnard, an experienced mountaineer and guide, to reshoe the best mounts to prepare for a rescue mission.[61] As their comrades hammered scythes into spears, the two men left on the night of February 28 with dispatches sewn into the lining of Watts's coat. The messengers slipped through the Indian lines to begin a desperate race to Salt Lake for help.

Averaging fifty miles a day in brutal weather, the pair took only six days to reach the present Utah border. On fresh mounts they rode to Salt Lake, arriving at the Beehive House on the morning of March 8, 1858. Within hours, orders went out to Col. Andrew Cunningham to take command of a relief expedition to Fort Limhi. The one hundred forty men who made up Cunningham's Salmon River Expedition included units from the Nauvoo Legion and a company from the standing army. An advance party of ten men received orders on March 9 to carry word to Fort Limhi that help was on its way. After a series of storms and bold gambles, the relief party arrived at Limhi on March 21, and the settlers began packing for their return to Utah.[62]

The news from the north had a profound impact in Great Salt Lake City. Since the New Year, the millennial bubble that inspired the Saints had stretched thin in the face of bad news from all points of the compass. Bold measures saved Fort Limhi, but the Shoshoni and Bannock bands that raided the Saints' northernmost outpost burst Brigham Young's visionary hopes and abruptly shut the door on his most promising escape route from the U.S. Army.[63] The unexpected Indian attack was not the sign from the Lord the prophet had anticipated, and it was now clear the Lamanites were not yet ready to play their prophesied role in ushering in the Second Coming. Once again, God unexpectedly tarried.

Ironically, it was the guerrilla warfare of the rough-and-ready mountaineers and their Indian allies that stopped Brigham Young's dream of independence as deftly as David's stone felled Goliath. Mormons and mountaineers had been sparring to control the resources of the Rocky Mountain West since Jim Bridger rode away from Brigham Young's camp on the Little Sandy on the morning of June 29, 1847. When the army marched to Utah, the mountaineers rallied to the cause. One of their Mormon neighbors reported "most of the Mountain Men are after money and are not for us but against us and will be on hand to render the soldiers all the aid they can."[64] It is impossible to determine how involved the mountaineers were in the attack on Fort Limhi, but the Mormons held their old rivals and a federal agent responsible.

General Johnston had sent a civilian, B. F. Ficklin, to the headwaters of the Missouri in December 1857 to buy five hundred cows and to persuade the mountaineers and Indians "to bring in any horses they might wish to sell." Recruited from a government survey party, Ficklin was well on his way to becoming a western legend. He was a distinguished veteran of the Mexican War and had warned army officers of Mormon plans to burn their supply wagons before Lot Smith's raids. His ten men were equipped with thirty days' rations, twelve horses, six mules, and four gallons of whiskey. Ficklin had written orders not to incite the Indians against the Mormons and to avoid a confrontation. "I took every opportunity to tell all Indians and whites whom I met with on my trip," Ficklin swore, "that Colonel Johnston did not desire, and would not permit, any interference from Indians." At the popular wintering ground on Beaverhead River, Ficklin found that Mormon threats and their raids on the army had inspired the mountaineers to hastily decamp for the Flathead Valley, "a more distant and secure spot." At Deer Lodge he arranged to purchase three hundred cattle and about one hundred horses from Indian traders like John Grant, but "no price" would induce many mountaineers to deliver stock for fear of the Mormons.[65]

A hardboiled frontiersman named John W. Powell played a key role in driving the Mormons from Fort Limhi. Said to be an educated gentleman, he "chose the wild life to civilization at his old home in Virginia."[66] Powell admitted he was at Fort Limhi when the Indians attacked but claimed he warned the Mormons and insisted "he was not engaged in the affair in any manner." Mormon records confirm that Powell tried to warn the settlers the day before the assault that the Indians were talking of burning their haystacks and stealing their livestock. Only dimly aware of the Indians' rage, Thomas Smith thought they might try to run off a few cattle, but the settlement was completely unprepared for a violent attack.[67]

Powell's role in this affair would seem impossible to sort out, but a statement by John Healy, an early Montana pioneer, suggests that after Powell reported the impending attack, the Mormons may have refused to let him leave and imprisoned him in the Limhi stockade. A light and active young man, Powell scaled the stockade's walls by climbing a travois. "After that Powell and the Bannocks made war upon the Mormons and actually forced them to leave," Healy recalled. "The Mormons offered $1000 for Powell's head but they were never able to get him."[68]

None of the Mormon journals mentioned the presence of whites at the "Limhi Massacre," but Watts and Barnard linked Powell to the attack when they reported to Brigham Young. The *Deseret News* claimed Powell was with the Indians "and assisted them in the plundering, wounding and killing peaceful and unoffending American citizens."[69] Mormon histories blamed the mountaineers for ruining the relationship between the missionaries and the Indians, charging that Powell was closely associated with the unfriendly Indians and "dressed and painted himself as they did, and was one of them in all their deviltry." Since he had warned the settlers, the mission history concluded that Powell was not wholly bad, but they charged that Ficklin "was seeking recruits among the mountaineers for an onslaught on the fort to carry off the cattle and sell them to the army."[70]

HE HAD CAUGHT THE FISH: THE UNEASY PEACE

Immediately after receiving the bad news from Fort Limhi, Brigham Young reversed course and accepted Thomas Kane's peace proposals. Young wrote a short note to Kane on March 9, 1858, claiming he had just learned that the troops were in dire need of provisions. He offered the army beef and tons of flour, revealing that the previously inflexible prophet had abruptly changed his mind. He sent his son, Joseph A. Young, to carry the message to Kane.[71] It must have been surprising but welcome news to the hopeful peacemaker. Brigham Young desperately wanted to stop troops from entering Salt Lake Valley. "You might as well tell me that you can make hell into a powder-house," he had said, "as to tell me that you could let an army in here and have peace."[72] But the attack on Fort Limhi and his growing awareness of the military power threatening the Saints compelled him to make peace. Given the circumstances, it seems miraculous that the Utah Expedition did not end in a bloodbath. The mountaineers and their Indian allies at Fort Limhi played an unexpected but pivotal role in the peaceful resolution of the crisis.

General Johnston rejected Young's offer of beef and flour as resolutely as he had returned the salt to the "enemies of the Government." Kane told the army an improbable tale, claiming that the Saints were divided into two camps with Brigham Young at the head of the peace party, but the military officers believed none of it.[73] Comedy quickly replaced drama at the army camp when Johnston sent an orderly to invite Kane to dinner, but the orderly instead arrested the Pennsylvanian. Insulted, Kane challenged the general to a duel and wrote his will. Johnston never received the challenge, and Judge Eckles ordered Kane to cease and desist.[74] Further bumbling ensued when a sentry almost shot Kane as he returned from a meeting with Mormon couriers.

Kane's peace overture did not impress the army officers at Camp Scott. Fitz-John Porter found Kane's proposals insulting and considered the self-constituted ambassador to be "like an ass—because an ass." The theatrical Kane's conceit, coupled with his small stature and feminine appearance, alienated the military men but may have endeared him to the ungainly Governor Cumming.[75] Sensing the hostility between Johnston and Cumming, Kane proceeded to drive a wedge between the military and civil authorities, creating an opening that Brigham Young exploited brilliantly. Kane wrote Cumming that his mission appeared hopeless, but he persuaded the governor to take a bold gamble that would end the war and circumvent the army.

Cumming informed Johnston on April 3 that he would go to Great Salt Lake City to assert the authority of the government without so much as a platoon for an escort.[76] After surviving a journey through country "infested by hostile renegades and outlaws from various tribes," Cumming picked up an escort headed by Porter Rockwell and was treated to an "illumination" in his honor that poured fire from the rim of Echo Canyon as he passed by in the dark. Mormon soldiers paraded in circles to give the new governor an inflated impression of the size of Brigham Young's army. Traversing the settlements, Cumming found that far from being met by insults or indignities, he was "universally greeted with such respectful attentions" as were due a representative of the American government. In Salt Lake, Brigham Young called on Cumming and offered his successor every facility he required.[77]

On delivering his gullible charge, Kane told Young "he had caught the fish, now you can cook it as you have a mind to." George A. Smith at first considered the governor a toper, but on closer examination he concluded that Cumming "was a moderate drinker and a hearty eater." No lightweight himself, Smith guessed the governor weighed about two hundred forty pounds and "thought he had more chops than brains." The new governor, however, was completely charmed by his genial hosts. Cumming said the illumination of Echo Canyon "outstripped anything he had ever expected to see," and he complimented the superb cook who prepared his first meal among the Mormons at Yellow Creek.[78]

Governor Cumming informed Johnston that the court records and missing government property, a prime cause of the conflict with the Mormons, were intact. He offered assistance to all persons who wanted to return to the states, but only fifty-six men and thirty-three women accepted his proposal. Most of them, the governor thought, were simply seeking to improve their circumstances. Cumming's appearance in the tabernacle was of intense interest to the Saints and profoundly educational for Cumming. When a speaker charged that the government was determined to force troops into Utah, a wild uproar ensued, convincing Cumming that the Mormons would gladly encounter certain death rather than submit to military power. He promised "the military posse would not be resorted to until other means of arrest had been tried and failed." Brigham Young calmed the congregation, and several speakers apologized for their intemperate language.[79] By the time Cumming realized "it was all a humbug," the fish had been cooked exactly to the prophet's liking.[80]

Having the ear of the governor, the Mormons immediately condemned the army for provoking Indian depredations and charged Garland Hurt with inciting the Utes in Uinta Valley "to acts of hostility."[81] With the collapse of their war plans, Mormon leaders sought to deflect public attention from their own attempts to forge an alliance with Utah's tribes. The *Deseret News* blamed federal agents for the attack on Fort Limhi and reported the rumor that the army had offered the Indians $150 for every Mormon they brought to the army. The paper claimed the government was paying "thousands upon thousands of dollars for presents to the wild men of the mountains" to incite Indian depredations against American citizens.[82]

Federal officials denounced the charges as slanderous. Utah's new Indian superintendent, Jacob Forney, denied assertions that the officials had incited the Indians against the Mormons, for bribes were not necessary to secure their loyalty to the government. James Bridger swore that Johnston had told Washakie to take his people buffalo hunting and not to become involved in the hostilities. Yet the powerful Shoshoni chief complained bitterly of the wrongs perpetrated against his people by the Mormons, who were "constantly attempting to prejudice him and his people against the government and all persons who were not Mormons."[83]

The army had in fact used the Indians to spy and contemplated using the Utes as allies if the Nauvoo Legion threatened Randolph Marcy's relief column. When he learned the Mormons were organizing some two hundred men to capture or stampede Marcy's animals, Johnston decided "to rely upon the Indians," but nothing supported charges that the army offered a bounty for captured Mormons.[84] Apparently concerned about his role in the atrocities he had recently incited in southern Utah, Apostle George A. Smith later unloaded a barely rational tirade on the army's alleged use of Indian allies. He charged President Buchanan with "savage barbarity in employing the Indians to murder, butcher, roast and eat his countrymen." Could the president "atone for the innocent blood which his Indian allies have shed, or even wipe away the tears of widows and orphans" resulting from his fear and enthusiasm to destroy Mormonism? The president's offer of a "pardon to the guiltless, while his own hands are dripping with the blood of the innocent, comes with an ill grace."[85]

The Mormon effort to shift attention from their own use of Indians in the Utah War was not entirely successful. Governor Cumming returned to Salt Lake on April 23 with plans to head south almost immediately. The next day Daniel Wells informed Brigham Young that the governor intended "to investigate the Mountain Meadows affair and [would] go as far as Harmony." Cumming wanted Brigham Young, Jr., to accompany him as a guard, but as Wells noted, "the boys dont any of them feel much like going but he must be cared for while he remains in our midst." General Wells felt it was "rather risky to let him stay so long, and hope[d] that his life is insured long enough to last him back to camp."[86] Cumming later told an intimate friend he began inquiring into "that damned atrocity soon after [he] entered Salt Lake City." "Brigham Young, by some means, getting wind of what I was doing, came to my office and informed me that he was about to sift the affair to the bottom" and bring the guilty parties, "whoever they might be," to justice. Young's assurances convinced him to "trust the whole matter in his hands," since Cumming was convinced Young could "put his finger upon the miscreants" whenever he wanted.[87]

Buchanan dispatched two commissioners in early April to explain his Utah policy to the Mormons. Lazarus W. Powell, a former governor of Kentucky, and Ben McCulloch, a hero of the Texas revolution, were men of national reputation. They had no authority to negotiate, but they carried a blanket presidential pardon for sedition and treason to take effect if the Mormons accepted the territorial officials and the government's promise not to interfere with their religion. On June 2 the commissioners left Blacks Fork for Salt Lake, where they spent two weeks living in a wagon while Brigham Young decided what to do.[88]

THE MOVE SOUTH

After the debacle at Fort Limhi, Brigham Young realized armed resistance was futile. He adopted a new plan aimed at "baffelling the oppressive purposes of Prest Buckhannan" and winning public sympathy in the states. "If we whip out and use up the few troops at Bridger," Young asked, "will not the excitement and sympathy which is now raising in our favor in the states, be turned against us?" If the Saints simply burned their homes and fled from federal forces, the "folly and meanness" of the president would be more apparent and Buchanan and his measures more unpopular.[89]

Casting about for a credible response to the likely triumph of federal authority, Young still sought an alternative to capitulation. On March 10 he sent an expedition to explore Ibapah Valley on the western edge of the Salt Desert. At the same time Young ordered William Dame to seek a refuge for the Saints in central Nevada. From the pulpit, Young announced there was probably room in that region for half a million people. Dame organized sixty men, including massacre veterans Nephi Johnson, William Stewart, Jabez Nowland, and James Pearce, into the Southern Exploring Company, but Young recognized the futility of his hopes long before Dame reported the failure of the expedition.[90]

Instead the prophet decreed the Move South, a petulant exercise that demonstrated his power at no small cost to his people. Beginning with five hundred of the poorest and most helpless Salt Lake families "who had never been driven from their homes," Young directed all thirty thousand residents of northern Utah to abandon spring planting, pack up their belongings, and decamp to Utah Valley and points south. The move puzzled some of the most devout Saints. Returning from the relief of Fort

Limhi to find the northern settlements deserted, Abraham Zundel hardly knew what to think. "[I was] most bewilderd," he said, "for we had made up our Mind to fight it out on the line but the Lord knows best about these things."[91]

The stated purpose of the Move South was to protest the stationing of troops in the territory, but it was also an object lesson for the new governor. Rumors spread that the Mormons would abandon the Great Basin and move to Sonora. As late as May 24, Brigham Young was still threatening to burn Great Salt Lake City and all the northern settlements. "Our necks," said Young, "shall not be given to the halter." As usual, the prophet blamed the failure of his millennial hopes on the Mormon people. "Some may marvel," he preached on March 28, "why the Lord says 'rather than fight your enemies, go away.'" It was "because many of the people are so grossly wicked, that were we to go out to fight, thousands of the Elders would go into eternity, and women and children would perish." He likened the Saints' predicament to the Crucifixion: it was a necessary evil. God had selected corrupt leaders to rule them because the people were wicked and would not hearken to the Lord.[92]

Commissioners McCulloch and Powell made clear they had come to report the president's policy to the people of Utah, not to negotiate. The Mormons could accept federal authority and the president's pardon or face the consequences. In public meetings with the commissioners in June 1858, Mormon leaders hid their capitulation behind a flood of face-saving rhetoric, arguing that the Saints had committed no crimes. But Young grudgingly accepted the pardon, swallowed the president's terms, and agreed to let the army enter the territory.[93] The soldiers marched through the deserted Mormon capital on June 26, 1858, with the strictest order and discipline, after which the displaced population returned to their homes. Johnston established his headquarters at Camp Floyd in the desolation west of Utah Lake, some forty miles from Great Salt Lake City. The two hostile camps settled into an uneasy peace.[94]

The Saints would claim they had achieved all their objectives in their confrontation with the government, but Brigham Young hardly savored his victory. He retreated to seclusion in the Beehive House, bolting the doors and surrounding the walled mansion with guards. He held few public meetings and never left his compound without bodyguards. Young's strange silence was one of many signs he had entered a period of profound depression. During his term as governor, "a throng of clients beseeching indulgences and instruction" had continually besieged Young's office, but now he hid from the public, "never appearing in the streets, nor on the balconies of his mansion-house." Even Pioneer Day passed uncelebrated. After June 1858 Young did not appear in public until December, when he was compelled to testify in Judge Charles C. Sinclair's court. Then the prophet "rested his head upon his hand, and his countenance wore a careworn, melancholy expression."[95]

Capt. Jesse Gove succinctly summarized the outcome of the Utah War: "Wounded, none; killed, none; fooled, everybody." Governor Cumming had learned its lessons well. "I can do nothing here without your influence," he admitted to Brigham Young.

Cumming believed the army could have overwhelmed Utah's militia, but this would have subjected the country to an expensive and protracted guerrilla war. The governor was eager "to announce that the road between California and Missouri may be travelled in perfect security by teams and emigrants of every description." He proudly informed the secretary of state on May 11, 1858, "that the Road is now open" and emigrants could "pass through Utah territory without hindrance or molestation."[96]

The overland road was open again, but the story of the dead at Mountain Meadows remained to be told.

12

They Have Slain My Children

Federal authorities and Mormon leaders had arranged an uneasy peace in Utah by mid-1858, but the unsettled details of their confrontation threatened to rekindle the fires of war as long as the army stayed in the territory. The many unanswered questions about the murders at Mountain Meadows were among the most troublesome of these conflicts. Nothing revealed the flaws and inherent contradictions in the cover story Utah authorities used to explain and justify the crime more clearly than the surviving children. The pleas of their relatives and the story of their suffering led to national outrage against Mormon theocracy and the exposure of the truth about the murders by federal investigators.

As reports of the massacre spread through the West, volunteer militia companies spontaneously sprang up across northern California to conduct a crusade against the Mormons.[1] The *Alta California* calculated that the state's population would respond to a formal call for troops, "so bitter [was] their experience" on the Salt Lake road.[2] Units such as the Plumas Rangers, the San Francisco Lancers, the Sierra Rangers, the Mariposa Mounted Riflemen, and the Soquel Crusade Rangers were eager to serve in a Mormon war. The Nevada Rifles, all excellent "food for powder," were ready to make their reputation "at the cannon's mouth before the gates of Brigham's residence."[3]

News of the massacre reached the eastern United States with the California newspapers. From these reports, William C. Mitchell hoped his grandson might be among the children allegedly taken to San Bernardino. Sadly, Charles Mitchell's infant son, John, was among the dead, and all the surviving children were still in southern Utah. Mitchell asked Arkansas senator W. K. Sebastian to use his power as chairman of the Indian Affairs Committee to have the matter investigated. He was "anxious to be in the crowd" sent to put down the Utah rebellion, Mitchell wrote. "I must have satisfaction for the inhuman manner in which they have slain my children, together with two brothers-in-law and seventeen of their children."[4]

During January 1858, news of the deaths of "some of our best citizens" swept through the Ozarks. "What will the Government do with these Mormons and Indians?" a letter from Carroll County asked. "Will it not send out enough men to hang all the scoundrels and thieves at once, and give them the same play they give our women and children?"[5] By late February a public meeting in Carroll County protested the massacre, charging "an emigrant train with 130 persons from Arkansas was attacked by the Mormons and Santa Clara tribe of Indians near the rim of the Great Basin" and was "then and there massacred and murdered." The citizens called on the government to investigate the "dreadful tragedy, and deal out retributive justice to the parties guilty of the monstrous deed." They called for the rescue of the surviving children and offered to raise four military companies to put down "the spirit of insubordination and treason, that is now rife amongst the Mormons."[6] By spring 1859 fears of vengeance troubled Utah Territory, where a rumor circulated that Arkansas and Missouri volunteers "were coming over the mountains to Iron County to use up the folks there."[7]

The massacre at Mountain Meadows became a subject of debate in Congress on March 18, 1858. California senator William Gwin asked the secretary of war to report "what steps have been taken, if any, to punish the parties implicated in the massacre of one hundred and eighteen emigrants to California, at the Mountain Meadows." Gwin had assumed troops would be sent from California to support Johnston, but Congress failed to fund the force. "Since the Americans commenced to travel over the plains," Gwin said, "no such reverse, no such loss, has been inflicted on us as the destruction of these one hundred and eighteen emigrants." The details of "this horrid massacre" remained shrouded in mystery, but women and children had been slaughtered without cause and their blood was unavenged. Many well-advised parties identified the Mormons as the instigators, and Gwin had no positive evidence to prove the Indians were guilty of so horrible a crime. He denounced the utterly unreliable poison story as simply "a calumny on the unburied dead. Yes, sir, on the unburied dead!" An expedition from southern California should "inflict upon the guilty parties a vengeance so summary as to be talked of with terror in every wigwam in the great Salt Lake basin."

Sen. Sam Houston, who had lived among the Cherokees and was renowned for his Indian sympathies, suggested the government should identify the guilty parties before punishing anyone. Gwin countered, "[There is] nothing like this atrocious deed in the history of our country. Not one of the whole party of one hundred and eighteen was left. They only spared a few children under five years of age, in order to make slaves of them; all the adults were murdered so that they should not have an opportunity to divulge who committed this terrible crime. I want a force to be sent there to make the inquiry, and then to inflict punishment. That is all I ask." The next day Houston withdrew his objection and the Senate passed Gwin's motion.[8]

OUR WARM FRIEND

Using a combination of flattery and browbeating, religious leaders in Utah bent the pliable Alfred Cumming to their will. In late May 1858 a Mormon missionary met Thomas Kane returning east, having accomplished his mission to Utah. Kane told him, "[Cumming] appears to be our warm friend and has pledged himself in writing to sustain the Saints and will call them out to oppose Johnson [*sic*] and says his Wife shall go where our Saints go and bro Brigham and he can whip all the troops." Cumming and his allies pursued a policy his supporters called "conciliatory adjustment," which hoped to pacify the Mormons through judicious compromise.[9]

An illusion of peace returned to the territory. The Saints appeared to have yielded to the rule of law and to the power of the federal government, but in an otherwise fawning letter to Cumming, Young wrote, "I cannot be responsible for the safety of certain Governmental appointees," especially Garland Hurt, if they ventured into the Mormon settlements. Rulers, lectured the former governor, must realize that their real security was "based upon their own correct official and private conduct," which alone assured the protection and respect of good men.[10] Implicit in his reference to the safety of federal officials was a threat of violence. His assertion of popular sovereignty over the rule of law was precisely what the Utah War had been about, yet Young insisted the Saints retained the right to reject officials who did not meet their standards of morality—or pliability.

Theologically the prophet refused to give an inch. His profound belief in the millennium remained unshaken, even if its imminence required recalculation. The return of Christ, the Mormon conquest of Babylon, and the triumph of the Kingdom of God were merely postponed until the Saints and the Lamanites were worthy to usher in the end of time. Ironically, the Utah War proved a mixed blessing for the Mormon prophet, for as he had predicted in October 1857, the conflict dramatically improved his national image. "Brigham Young no longer seems to the American public a religious mountebank," commented the *Atlantic Monthly*. "On the contrary, he begins to appear as a man of great native strength and scope of mind, who understands the phases of human character and knows how to avail himself of that knowledge."[11]

Governor Cumming's recognition of the realities of governing Utah Territory served his primary task of making and keeping peace with the Mormons. He found the Saints generally ignorant, fanatical, and superstitious, but he felt the government had to accept the power of the LDS church in Utah. It was his duty to protect the civil rights of Mormons if they renounced violence and obeyed the laws of the United States.[12]

Indian Superintendent Jacob Forney and U.S. Attorney Alexander Wilson, allies of Thomas Kane, shared Cumming's sympathies. Other federal officials and General Johnston were not nearly so conciliatory and regarded their new neighbors as fanatics whose treachery was only temporarily forestalled. Johnston considered Cumming completely under the control of Brigham Young, and conflicts over the use of troops to protect the federal courts quickly destroyed his relationship with the governor. To Cumming's aggravation, the secretary of war had ordered Johnston to protect the courts without requiring authorization from the governor. The ensuing battle over jurisdiction provided an opening that the Mormons exploited brilliantly.

Alfred Cumming was simply not up to the task of investigating a mass murder with the devastating implications of Mountain Meadows. He feared the consequences that would inevitably follow an aggressive inquiry into such a crime and saw no political advantage in scrutinizing an explosive subject that could destroy the fragile peace. Like many outsiders, Cumming found the horrific story so outrageous that he was reluctant to believe his attentive hosts could perpetrate an atrocity on the scale of the massacre. He was naive enough to accept Brigham Young's "solemn promise that he would have the principals speedily delivered to the proper officers." Yet the hapless Georgian's character left him singularly unqualified to stand up to the Mormon leaders. In Young's hands, one observer noted, "Cumming is mere putty."[13] Emigrant Hannah Clapp described the governor in 1859 as a "superannuated, brandy-soaked, Buchanan Democrat" who believed the territories should control their own peculiar institutions in their own peculiar ways. He assured travelers they had nothing to fear from the Mormons "while passing their *their* [sic] territory, if we would not talk their religion with them; pass through quietly, not argue with them at all, or meddle with their religious views." Clapp realized she was not on American soil in Utah: "This is 'the Independent State of Deseret.'"[14]

WHETHER OR NOT WHITE MEN WERE CONCERNED:
FIRST INVESTIGATIONS

Mormon leaders recognized that the massacre had sown the wind, and they would have to deal with the consequences. The California newspapers reflected the rage the event provoked outside Utah, and as the story of the crime spread through Utah it left loyal church members profoundly shaken. Refugees from San Bernardino were especially bitter, for many of them felt the massacre was the direct cause of the loss of their homes. Brigham Young also had to contend with the aggravating presence of federal authority. More than a quarter of the U.S. Army was soon stationed only forty miles from his headquarters, and Young feared that if the federal authorities could get him to Camp Floyd "he would not last five minutes." He "did not believe they wanted anything of him only to lynch him."[15] Providing a credible explanation of the events at Mountain Meadows became a question of life and death for the Mormon leader.

Jacob Hamblin later testified he reported the part white men had played at Mountain Meadows to Brigham Young and George A. Smith soon after the massacre took place, apparently when the men met on June 18, 1858. Young allegedly said "that as soon as a Court of Justice could be held, so that men could be heard without the influence of the military he should advise men accused to come forward and demand trial on the charges preferred against them for the Mountain Meadow Massacre." Hamblin testified that Young told him, "As soon as we can get a court of justice we will ferret this thing out, but till then, don't say anything about it."[16]

Mormon accounts claimed Young sent Smith and Hamblin to interview Cumming and assure him the Saints would provide all possible assistance to investigate the massacre. Smith allegedly urged the governor to investigate the "horrid affair" so that any white men who had participated "might be justly punished for their crimes." Cumming, the Mormons claimed, "did not wish to go behind" President Buchanan's amnesty to search out crime. In an explanation composed years after the interview, Smith said, "[If] the business had not been taken out of our hands by a change of officers in the territory, the Mountain Meadows affair is one of the first things we should have attended to when a United States court sat in southern Utah. We would see whether or not white men were concerned in the affair with the Indians."[17] He apparently had forgotten that Hamblin had just told him of the part John D. Lee "and some other white men" had played in the murders.

Events indicate Smith actually promised Cumming the Mormons would handle the matter themselves, for shortly after their conversation, Smith visited southern Utah. Had Colonel Smith wanted to learn the truth about the massacre, as a senior officer in the Nauvoo Legion he could have convened a military court of inquiry. Since Hamblin's report in June 1858, the facts were already well known to Mormon leaders. Smith was sent south not to learn the truth but to devise an explanation church leaders could provide to external enemies, non-Mormon allies, and the increasing number of loyal members who had questions about the affair. Smith visited Mountain Meadows on July 29, 1858, with eyewitness Nephi Johnson as his guide.[18] The physical evidence of the separate piles of male and female remains told a curious story. "From appearances," Smith explained "the men had run away and left the women."[19] Even while viewing their bones, Smith could not resist defaming the victims.

Reversing the course of his tour of August 1857, Smith left the meadows for the Mormon settlements along the lower Santa Clara. All was not well at Fort Clara, where Jacob Hamblin ruled with an iron hand. A year later at Brigham Young's request, George Hendrix reported on conditions in the settlement, where the clandestine marriage of a sixteen-year-old girl had "produced a great excitement amongst the people." A hearing on the matter before Hamblin created even more bad feeling, and Apostles Amasa Lyman and Smith came down to settle matters. They ordered Hamblin to lay out the town properly, for "the place was built up with no regularity or order, for there was a house and a hog pen, a hog pen and a house." Hendrix charged that Hamblin used the opportunity to run a political enemy out of town and give the man's property to his brother. "From all I have been able to learn," Hendrix told Young, Oscar Hamblin, Dudley Leavitt, Samuel Knight, and Albert Hamblin "participated in the mountain meadow affair." There "is no law nor order at Fort Clara," Hendrix concluded, "and every thing is not told yet."[20]

After trying to make peace at Santa Clara, Smith arrived at Harmony on August 3 with his fellow apostles Amasa Lyman, Erastus Snow, and Charles Rich. The whole company stayed with John Lee, "the Master Spirit of this Place." When they left, Lee presented each apostle with a small gift of gold. (They did not question Lee too closely about where he got the money.) The apostles asked Lee to accompany them to Cedar City to attend "an investigation of some things that was between Bro. Haight and Bro. J. Hamilton." The inquiry began on the afternoon of August 5, 1858, to consider complaints against President Haight and Bishop Klingensmith, while Lee stood accused of using his influence against Haight. The apostles exonerated Lee, concluding the charge was founded on "blind Prejudice only," but the investigation continued through the next day. At its conclusion the apostles reproved the local authorities for unwise policies but took no other action. Obviously pleased with the results, Lee returned home, where he recorded a vision. While praying that he would not fall into the hands of his enemies, Lee was caught up in the air and carried to the top of Brigham Young's mansion where he "was out of the reach of [his] Enimies."[21]

Reports of this meeting did not mention a murder investigation, but the next day Smith and his clerk drafted their first report on the massacre from "the most authentic sources." It resolutely blamed the Indians and the victims. After poisoned springs killed several of their people, two hundred exasperated Indians attacked the emigrants. The citizens of Cedar City heard of the assault and sent out a party to investigate, but when Nephi Johnson arrived at the scene and sought to conciliate them, the Indians threatened "instant death if they did not either leave immediately or turn in and help them." The scouts found they could do nothing for the emigrants, so they returned to Cedar City and reported the situation. Dame and Haight finally arrived on Saturday to stop the fighting, only to find the Indians had killed everyone but a few small children who the Mormons saved but not without difficulty.[22]

Unbeknown to Lee, the apostolic investigation was not over. William Dame demanded a hearing to clear him of thirteen complaints filed by fourteen individuals. On four successive days, Lyman and Smith "carefully and patiently investigated the complaints" against Dame at Parowan. The hearing involved senior militia officers directly implicated in the massacre, including Isaac Haight, Nephi Johnson, and John Higbee. The complaints "were the result of evil backbiting and talking. It was one of the most laborious and intricate cases that [apostles] had sat on since the days of Joseph." Dame's accusers were ashamed of bringing charges and "said the rumors and statements made out of doors would not bear investigation when they came into council."[23]

This "laborious and intricate case" could not have excluded a discussion of the dark secrets that were tearing apart southern Utah. A high-strung man, given to long, impassioned tirades, Dame was not popular among those who had to suffer under his leadership. The charges in the official minutes were vague but generally complained of Dame's autocratic style and abuses of power, such as attempting to swindle a man out of fifteen bushels of wheat. None of the recorded accusations specifically referred to Mountain Meadows, but several were clearly linked to the crime. One charged that Dame had ordered Barney Carter to inflict a brutal beating on William Leany for giving onions to William Aden of the Fancher party. Tradition claimed the hearing tried to determine who would accept responsibility for the atrocity at Mountain Meadows. "You can not lay this onto me! I will not take it!" Dame allegedly declared. "If you dare try, I'll just put the saddle onto the right horse, and you all know who that is!" No one in the room needed to ask what Dame meant. The right horse, Juanita Brooks concluded, could only be George A. Smith.[24]

Isaac Haight recorded the verdict: "After a patient but painful investigation for three and a half days, most of the charges proved not true. Much good council and instructions were given, and some severe chastisement by Elders Smith and Lyman."[25] On August 12, 1858, twenty-three men signed a document summarizing the court's conclusions.[26] The verdict exonerated Dame. The court was "fully satisfied that his activities as a Saint, and administration as a President, has been characterized by the right spirit." In short, they found the complaints were without foundation.[27]

Perhaps Dame's hearing did not discuss his disastrous conduct of military affairs, but Smith continued to investigate the massacre and composed a longer report for Brigham Young. It provided details not in the letter written eleven days earlier but again failed to address critical questions. Smith rehearsed the tale that the Arkansans had poisoned and killed ten Indians. He blamed the death of Proctor Robison on the poison and claimed the emigrants had boasted of driving the Mormons from Missouri. The emigrants threatened "to kill every 'God damned Mormon' that there was in the mountains." They spread the rumor "that some four or five hundred dragoons were expected through on the Fremont trail," a "rumor" that Smith himself had carried south. If the Mormons had killed any Indians while defending the emigrants, Smith argued, it would have been little else than suicide because of the vulnerability of the southern settlers. The Arkansans' provocations inspired an indifference about what the Indians might do, but "nobody dreamed of nor anticipated so dreadful a result."[28]

Juanita Brooks called Smith's reports "a deliberate attempt to befog the affair and direct attention away from any possibility of Mormon implication." B. H. Roberts, Mormonism's most valiant defender, conceded that Smith had learned of Lee's involvement in the massacre from Hamblin, a fact that "seems to have been forgotten" when the apostle filed his report. Rather than search for the truth, Smith wanted to determine who could be blamed for the massacre, and his several hearings demonstrated that no one in southern Utah wanted to shoulder the responsibility. But Smith's report ended with a mysterious sentence: "John D. Lee and a few other white men were on the ground during a portion of the combat, but for what purpose or how they conducted [themselves] or whether indeed they were there at all, I have not learned."[29] The apostle had already identified the most promising scapegoat for the crime.

Such Crimes Ought to Be Punished

For more than a decade the LDS church would cling to the explanation of the massacre George A. Smith drafted in 1858. It was not a singular success, as nothing could stop reports of what had actually happened at Mountain Meadows from permeating the territory. Some told of a reign of terror aimed at suppressing news of the massacre. Zephaniah J. Warren wrote Governor Cumming in November 1858 that he had learned of the horrible massacre at Mountain Meadows in fall 1857 "and told many persons that such crimes ought to be punished." Eight of Springville's lawmen pulled him from a sickbed, dragged him down the road, and threw him into a ditch. Warren wrote "[The police said] that if I would swear never to tell of them, nor write against them, and would go to their bishop and pay tithing, they would let me live." When Warren's son approached, the gang compelled him "to swear to be still and join their church, or they would kill [them] both as traitors."[30] At Spanish Fork, Scots farmer Peter McAuslan learned that Mormons and not Indians "were responsible for that horrible crime." His faith in the LDS church, which had never been strong, was shaken. McAuslan and other apostate families left Utah with an army escort in June 1859.[31]

The specter of Mountain Meadows shadowed the uneasy peace between the government and the Mormons. Indian Superintendent Jacob Forney received orders in 1858 "to use every effort to get possession" of the surviving children, who Jacob Hamblin reported were in the care of his white neighbors. Forney hoped to go south in fall 1858 to retrieve the children, but because of the chaotic state of the territory's Indian affairs it would take almost a year to redeem his promise. Blaming his duties and bad weather for the delay, he ordered Hamblin to collect the survivors. With considerable effort, Forney said, the children were "recovered, bought and otherwise," from the Indians.[32]

Brigham Young had already directed Dame and Haight "to have Brother Jacob Hamblin make arrangements to gather up those children that were saved from the Indian Massacre at Mountain Meadows last fall."[33] Hamblin had found fifteen of the orphans by December 1858, but he was "satisfied that there were seventeen of them saved from the massacre." He claimed two children had been taken east by the Paiutes, a fiction that may have been an attempt to extort government money to pay nonexistent ransoms. In February 1859 Governor Cumming requisitioned "a suitable military force to be *stationed* at such points" between Mountain Meadows and Santa Clara to "secure the emigration and other travelers from Indian hostilities." Forney planned to visit the tribes in advance of the troops that would move out soon after March 1.[34]

Hamblin took "Chas. Fancher" from Lee on March 2, 1859. With typical audacity but claiming the government ordered it, Lee wrote out a bill for the boy's "Boarding, clothing & schooling," and a ransom he claimed to have paid to the Indians. Two days after he learned of Forney's arrival at Cedar City, Lee got word that Enos, a Pahvant freebooter, was asking about him, claiming General Johnston had offered $500 for Lee's scalp. Hamblin ordered the authorities in Washington County to take twenty men and shoot Enos, but the freebooter got word of what was afoot and fled.³⁵

Troubling questions continued to land on Brigham Young's desk. The father of William Aden, the young artist murdered while seeking help for the Fancher party, asked for aid in locating his son. Young replied in April 1859, "I regret having to inform you that I have at no time known either your son or his whereabout[s]." He inserted a request for information about Aden in the *Deseret News* and promised to report any results at the earliest opportunity. In July he wrote that Aden's son had "joined the Emigrant company that was massacred at the Mountain Meadows." Young could not offer "the least hope that he is now alive."³⁶

THE FEARLESS CRADLEBAUGH

On his arrival at Ephraim Hanks's way station at Mountain Dell in November 1858, associate justice John Cradlebaugh of Utah's Second Judicial District impressed his host with his sympathy for the Saints. Hanks, a notorious hard case but no mean judge of character, reported that "the judge possessed but one eye and that is a very good one." George A. Smith found the jurist refreshing and full of pluck, but life in the territory quickly changed Cradlebaugh's outlook. By spring 1859 "the fearless Cradlebaugh" was Brigham Young's most dangerous enemy, and his relentless investigations nearly ignited a war between the army and the Mormons.³⁷

Two of Utah's federal judges, Chief Justice Delana R. Eckles and Charles C. Sinclair, had arrived in the territory with the army. Both men proved to be fierce opponents of the LDS church. At Camp Scott, Eckles had indicted many of the LDS leaders for treason, and in spring 1858 he charged a grand jury to investigate polygamy. Later that year Sinclair moved to disbar James Ferguson for abusing Judge Stiles, and he hauled Brigham Young into court as a witness.

No one caused the Mormons more trouble, however, than John Cradlebaugh, a tall, lean, middle-aged lawyer from Ohio. Early in 1859 the judge learned much about the massacre at Mountain Meadows from Henry Higgins and Richard "Cat Fish" Cook, apostates from the south. Higgins told U.S. Attorney Alexander Wilson "there were other persons engaged in the massacre besides Indians, and that these other persons, it is alleged, were Mormons." Wilson conducted a secret inquiry in the hope of securing reliable information to support a public investigation. "A mystery seems to shroud this wholesale butchery," he wrote, "but I entertain the hope that an avenging God will speedily bring to light the perpetrators."³⁸ Yet Wilson's "masterly inactivity" indicated he was not in a great hurry to prosecute the murderers.³⁹ Young believed Wilson would follow Governor Cumming's lead, but he feared that Cradlebaugh would join what Young characterized as the "junto" opposing Mormon theocracy.⁴⁰

Cradlebaugh left Camp Floyd with a military escort on March 7, 1859, for Provo, where he convened a grand jury in the local seminary. He charged the jury to diligently prosecute all persons who had violated the law and called their attention to the great number of long-ignored crimes in his district, which reached to the territory's southern border. Failure to prosecute the March 1857 Parrish-Potter murders at Springville, the murder of California emigrant Henry Forbes, and the castration and murder of Henry Jones revealed "an effort to cover up instead of bring to light and punish" crime, he said. Cradlebaugh spoke passionately of the "horrible crime" at Mountain Meadows, which had been ignored for so long that the failure to act indicated "there is some person, high in the estimation of the people, by whose authority it was committed."[41]

To limit the power of the federal courts, the 1859 territorial legislature assigned jury selection to Mormon county officials, most of whom had been appointed by Brigham Young. They "placed upon the juries the very criminals themselves, together with their relatives, friends and accomplices." Cradlebaugh dismissed juror Wilbur Earl after an affidavit implicated him in the Parrish murder. Six witnesses swore they had certain knowledge of various crimes emanating from the authorities of the LDS church. They considered their "lives and property in imminent peril from the Mormon communists."[42] One of them was the mysterious James Gemmell, who later claimed to have witnessed Brigham Young's September 1857 meeting with the Paiute chiefs.[43]

Despite Judge Cradlebaugh's determination to punish crime, the grand jury hearing degenerated into a political brawl between the judge and the Mormons. The territory's Mormon attorney general, Seth Blair, claimed sole authority to prosecute cases under local laws. Cradlebaugh rejected this as an attempt to create confusion and transfer jurisdiction over these explosive cases to the Mormon probate courts. The actions of the government's own prosecutor proved even more damaging to Cradlebaugh's hopes for swift justice. U.S. Attorney Wilson seemed "closely allied to the Mormons by some mysterious tie." He conferred constantly with his adversaries, and rather than address the crimes before the court, he called up old complaints against Indians for petty crimes, leaving a non-Mormon reporter to wonder if Wilson "was counsel for the prosecution or for the defense."[44] Wilson vigorously countered these charges after he left Utah, claiming it would be "altogether foolish and useless to institute any investigation" unless it had reasonable prospects of success. This required ample funds and holding court "as near the scene of the massacre as possible." William Rogers told Wilson he had no money to raise the "stong force" necessary to collect evidence or summon witnesses in southern Utah, and U.S. Marshal Peter Dotson declined to deputize John Kay, the Mormon territorial marshal, to do the job.[45]

The Saints raised a firestorm of protest over Cradlebaugh's use of federal troops to protect his court. Probate judge Silas Smith charged that Cradlebaugh used soldiers he could not keep away from liquor to intimidate jurors and witnesses. Apostle George A. Smith arrived to counter Cradlebaugh's investigation, but feelings already ran high in the

Mormon settlements. Smith helped to draft petitions and directed a coordinated response to the judge's inquiries, but he rejected a Provo City Council report that even he considered too rabid.[46] When the judge ordered the arrest of Provo mayor Isaac Bullock and Bishop Aaron Johnson for complicity in the Parrish-Potter murders, outraged citizens took to the streets and the local hierarchy disappeared into the mountains to avoid arrest. As rumors spread of an impending guerrilla war, Sheriff William Wall enlisted two hundred Mormons as special deputies. The situation was so volatile that General Johnston sent eight hundred more troops from Camp Floyd to preserve order and guard Cradlebaugh's prisoners. Governor Cumming concluded that the military presence was unnecessary and asked Johnston to remove the court's guard. The general declined.[47]

Disgusted with battling for two weeks with a prosecuting attorney who was "not on the same side of the fence" and a grand jury that "utterly refused to do anything," Cradlebaugh dismissed the jurors with a stern rebuke. He denounced them for refusing to indict fellow Mormons for the massacre at Mountain Meadows and for a string of local homicides. In frustration, he released Indians the grand jury had indicted for rape and freed two non-Mormons charged with theft. If the community refused to punish its murderers, Cradlebaugh would not protect it from "the peccadilloes of Gentiles and Indians." Aware that freeing the accused rapists would outrage the Saints, the judge warned, "If this court cannot bring you to proper sense of your duty, it can at least turn the savages in custody loose on you."[48]

As the grand jury ground to a halt, Smith provided rambling answers to English convert T. B. H. Stenhouse's questions about the massacre. To address a critical problem with the cover story—why the Paiutes would spare the children—Smith argued that their "mode of warfare was extermination of adults and slavery of children." He said Mormons always pursued a peaceful policy to protect their families "from the poisoned arrows and tomahawk of these savages," but emigrants customarily shot down Indians at every opportunity. Smith told the story of the poisoned ox, now claiming that survivors of the incident "saw the Captain of the Company go to the carcass with a bottle." Ten Indians died immediately from eating the ox and several Indians drank poisoned water. The news spread through the different bands and "caused the concentration of reckless warriors who consummated the massacre." Smith assured Stenhouse that a fair and impartial investigation would establish these facts beyond doubt.[49]

In the meantime, Cradlebaugh gathered evidence and witnesses. He issued bench warrants on April 2, 1859, that set off a general stampede for the mountains, "more especially among the church officials and civil officers." Cradlebaugh resolved to visit Mountain Meadows and expose the persons engaged in the massacre if he could. The judge said he "embraced an opportunity of accompanying a small detachment of soldiers" sent south by General Johnston.[50]

A Just but Offended God: Discursive Remarks

While Cradlebaugh wrestled with his grand jury, the ponderous machinery of the federal government began to move. Indian Superintendent Forney at last set out to retrieve massacre survivors in March 1859, guided by no less an expert on recent events than Ira Hatch. Forney spent seven days at Cradlebaugh's court at Provo, met federal deputy marshal William Rogers at Nephi, and proceeded to Corn Creek, where he distributed goods at the Pahvant Indian farm and picked up Chief Kanosh.[51]

James Lynch, a seasoned frontiersman who would have a long and intriguing relationship with the events at Mountain Meadows, left Camp Floyd in spring 1859 with thirty-nine men bound for Arizona. Lynch found Forney at Beaver City, deserted by Hatch and his Mormon guides. The agent was "without a man, . . . guarding his mules and wagons." Forney's guides had warned that if he went south, the people would "make an eunuch of him." Lynch cheerfully placed his party at the agent's command, though he was suspicious that Forney had employed "the very confederates of these monsters, who had so wantonly murdered unoffending emigrants, to ferret out the guilty parties." At Parowan, the people showed great hostility and would not communicate with the gentiles. Risking their own lives, Lynch and two companions drove Forney's teams to Mountain Meadows.[52]

Deputy marshal Rogers found the "scene was one too horrible and sickening for language to describe," but Lynch left a vivid record of what he saw: "Human skeletons, disjointed bones, ghastly skulls and the hair of women were scattered in frightful profusion over a distance of two miles." Water, he said, had washed these relics into little mounds that stood as monuments to the cruelty of man. Lynch "found the remains of an innocent infant beside those of some fond, devoted mother, ruthlessly slain by men worse than demons." He had witnessed many harrowing sights on fields of battle, but never had he experienced the horrible emotions evoked as he contemplated "the remains of the innocent victims of Mormon avarice, fanaticism, and cruelty." The holes dug to sink the wheels of the wagons still marked the campsite at Cane Spring, and the ridges west and north of the camp had breastworks with "bullet marks upon them on the side towards the corral." Imperfect skeletons revealed where the work of slaughter began. The bones bleaching in the sun bore "a mute but an eloquent appeal to a just but offended God for vengeance."[53]

After visiting the meadows, Forney and Lynch found Jacob Hamblin at Santa Clara. Lynch recalled that Hamblin "repeated the story of the children being held captive by the Indians." Angered at the deception, the federal officers pointed their pistols and rifles at Hamblin's head and said, "Produce them or we will kill you." Hamblin quickly delivered the orphans.[54] Lynch claimed the young survivors were "in a most wretched condition, half starved, half naked, filthy, infested with vermin, and their eyes diseased from the cruel neglect to which they had been exposed." Forney's party spent three days at Fort Clara while clothing was made for his charges.[55]

With thirteen of the survivors in tow, Forney visited Lee on April 22, 1859, to demand the surrender of the property belonging to the murdered emigrants. Having been warned of Forney's approach by Kanosh, Lee was "absent till a late hour of the Night," but Forney and Hamblin took supper with his family. The next morning Lee went to Forney's tent and invited him to breakfast, which the agent declined. Lee said it was a free country and he could suit himself. Forney and Hamblin followed Lee to his sitting room, where Lee said he would cheerfully give all the information he had about the massacre and the emigrants' property. Despite assurances that Forney had no warrant and "did not wish to take the advantage of [him]," a suspicious Lee launched into a long tirade about the constitutional rights of American citizens. The president's pardon, he insisted, covered crimes of any nature, which should be forgiven and "buried in an oblivion." Anything done before to the pardon was none of his damn business. Brigham Young had more patience than Lee, and but for Young the "army would have been used up & not a gre[a]se spot of them would have been found now." Here Lee's journal broke off in mid-rampage, just as he appeared about "to give all the information" he had on the massacre. The sixteen pages, now missing, apparently contained Lee's story of the murders.[56]

A long-ignored manuscript called Discursive Remarks suggests what those missing pages contained. Written in about 1859 by a purported non-Mormon who would render his views "strictly impartial, having an eye to truth, justice and equity," the essay was clearly the work of an old-line Latter-day Saint. If not actually composed by John D. Lee—as it apparently was—Discursive Remarks is one of the earliest insider accounts of the atrocity at Mountain Meadows. His subsequent career demonstrated that Lee had excellent reasons to re-create his past, and with its compelling detail, vivid prose, and high drama, Discursive Remarks is a virtual case study of how to bring a total falsehood to life.[57]

According to the manuscript, nothing remarkable happened early in the emigrants' trek "except the unlicensed shooting of Chickens, purloining of hay, and frequent uncomplimentary remarks bestowed upon the Mormons generally." At Springville a few apostates joined the party, who "apprehended an attempt on the part of the Mormons, to murder them." The local authorities seized the team and wagon of an apostate to pay an alleged debt. After this the "travelers indulged more freely in their unjustifiable liberties and unmerited insults, and each day their Conduct became more reckless and reprehensible." The emigrants would "break down fences and turn their cattle into fields and private pastures, ridiculing expostulation, and defying law."

At Cedar City, their evil genius led them into fatal error. One of the company "cooly leveled his rifle and Killed a very fine specimen of the Shanghai Rooster." Accosted by the owner, the emigrant blasphemed and denounced the Mormons as "a pack of d——d thieving Scoundrels." "If half of you had your due," the emigrant continued, "you would be hanged on trees, for the Crows to pick. . . . [T]he Army will be in here one of these days, and wipe every d——d one of you out. . . . That old humbug, Jo Smith paid for his imposture and the whole d——d pack of you ought to follow him; with old Brigham at the head, who is the biggest damned Scoundrl, and murd——." The insulted Mormon "with a single stroke felled the insulter, stunned and bleeding to the earth." As the emigrants went for their guns, "a tall powerful built man suddenly leaped in their midst; holding in each hand a revolver, and in a voice of thunder cried Hold! Let the first man but dare lay a hand upon a gun, and he instantly dies."

This heroic figure, the Mediator, asked, "Would you shed innocent blood?" and defused the crisis. But the humiliated emigrant swore, "I will yet be revenged, d——n you." The next morning some half-dozen Piede Indians approached the emigrant camp. The strangers gave them a "goodly portion of fresh beef, and a small quantity of flour." With "that imperturbable stoicism so peculiar to the race," the satisfied Indians left. Then the "company raised Camp and proceeded on their journey; little dreaming of the dreadful fate that awaited them."

They merited their fate, for the Mormons found their deserted campground "covered with dead cattle, in the vicinity of the springs, their bodies greatly swollen and bloated. The truth was too apparent—the springs were poisoned." With insatiate animosity, the emigrants "attempted to consummate their evil designs, and schemes of groundless vengeance." Some Mormons favored summary chastisement of the evil-doers, but the Mediator called for a legal investigation as "the only proper and legitimate plan of action." Aware of the possible serious results of trying to arrest the emigrants, the Mediator approached a young man to carry an express to Salt Lake City. In "less than thirty minutes, the Courier was en route."

Toward the close of the day, Indians "from an encampment some two miles distant, came rushing into the settlement, whooping and screaming like mad men, apparently in a state of deepest excitement." The Mediator went to investigate, and a "heart rending scene" met him at the Paiute camp. "Some dozen or more Indians and Squaws lay here and there about the Camp, uttering alternate screams and groans, betokening the presence of extreme suffering. . . . To all inquiries as to the cause of the sudden ailment, the Indians made no reply, but pointed to some beef hung up before one of the Lodges, and continued their wild manifestations of mingled rage and sorrow." The meat had "assumed a greenish hue, and emitted a nauseous odor, extremely unpleasant and sickening. The truth quickly flashed upon their minds—the meat was poisoned."

"It is but true," said the Mediator, "those inhuman wretches have certainly poisoned the beef, & given it to these poor Indians. God help them should any of these unfortunate creatures die. Blood alone can appease their anger, or satiate their thirst for vengeance." Despite every effort, three Indians died during the night in terrible convulsions. Comprehending the fatal trick played on them, the tribe's warriors "gathered up their ponies, mounted and struck out in a southerly direction."

"Professed Christians," the citizens of Cedar City could not stand idly by. "A party of some fifteen men, headed fortunately by the Mediator," set out in pursuit of the strangers. At the emigrant camp the Mediator warned, "we came not to argue the matter, but demand the guilty parties; and if you are wise, you will at once accede to the demand." A "somewhat rough looking personage now stepped forth, apparently the leader or captain." He denied poisoning the springs and said, "You shall not detain the whole or any part of the Company."

"Gentlemen," said the Mediator, in a tone more of sorrow than anger, "you will certainly seal your own doom and I fear, a dreadful one it will be if you thus persist in screening the murderers of those Indians. Look around you—do you wish to see your wives and helpless children butchered in cold blood before your very eyes? I tell you, those Indians will assuredly avenge the death of those who have perished."

"We are sufficiently able," said the captain, "to protect ourselves against any onslaught of the Indians, and shall be prepared to give them a warm reception if they make any attempt of the kind. . . . We can take care of ourselves."

"Then God help you," said the Mediator. His "heart revolted at the probability of innocent women and helpless children being sacrificed to Indian vengeance."

Two days later "the deep stillness of the midnight hour" at the emigrant camp was suddenly broken "by the shrill whistling of the messengers of death, and the savage yells of a stealthy foe." The Indians poured three or four volleys "with deadly effect, upon the terrified emigrants." The men "rushed half awake, and wholly bewildered for their arms, and fired a random volley regardless of aim or object." During the night, they "formed their waggons into a compact circle, and sinking the wheels into the earth, succeeded in producing a comparative shelter against the bullets of the enemy."

The people of Cedar City were not inclined to interfere in the matter. Late in the evening of the second day after the attack, "a messenger arrived from the city, bringing a letter from President Young. The laconic epistle, directed to the people, was in substance, the following: Suffer the strangers to proceed, and on your lives commit no acts of violence." That night "the Mediator succeeded in obtaining a few volunteers, and early the following morning set out . . . with the hope and determination of saving if possible, those suffering people, notwithstanding their evil deeds."

It was too late. The volunteers "arrived only in time to witness the closing scene of the bloody tragedy. . . . The camp now presented a spectacle of revolting horror, far beyond the possibility of an adequate description. Men, women, children and suckling babes, indiscriminately covered the gory earth, weltering in warm pools of blood, dreadfully disfigured and mutilated by the merciless tomahawke or scalping knife. The Mediator and his party, with painful reflections, and heavy hearts returned to their homes."

Three nights later, alone in his room, Brigham Young "paced the floor the live long night, while at intervals tears of anguish trickled and fell at his feet. 'My God! Tis horrible, horrible!'" he said, "indicating the nature of the painful reflections that oppressed and weighed heavy upon his heart:—He had learned the fate of the Emigrants."

The author—could it have been anyone other than the heroic Mediator him-self?—concluded, "If White men were participants in the murder of those unfor-tunate emigrants, I have been unable to glean any evidence of the fact. . . . But of one thing I am certainly convinced, that the 'Leaders' of the Mormon people were nei-ther directly nor indirectly in any way whatever concerned in the affair; nor had they the slightest cognition of the matter til after the consummation of the deed. This con-viction is based upon evidence too strong and palpable to admit of a doubt."

"With these few brief comments," wrote the inventor of this remarkable fiction, "I have done."[58]

Discursive Remarks probably closely resembled the tale Lee told Jacob Forney, for the agent returned to Salt Lake "somewhat impressed with J. D. Lee's statement of the massacre."[59] James Lynch recalled that Lee conceded he was present at the massacre but only to prevent bloodshed. Lee told Forney "he was present three successive days during the fight, and was present during the fatal day," but he also claimed he reached the site just after the massacre ended and that Isaac Haight and another prominent dig-nitary arrived soon after him. Lee's confused alibi convinced Forney that white men were present and directed the Indians. He knew too much of the truth to accept Lee's account of "the most extensive and atrocious massacre in American history."[60]

Yet Forney's conduct astonished his escort. Perhaps the influence of Thomas Kane, Forney's political patron, made him overly sympathetic to the Mormons, and like Governor Cumming he felt they had treated him well. He considered Garland Hurt's refusal to return to the territory without the army unjustified. "These fears are imaginary," Forney wrote. "I have never been treated kinder than by these people." He had hoped his investigation would vindicate all white men from any involvement and "saddle the guilt exclusively upon the Indians," but the evidence he saw and the stories he heard in the south convinced him the Indians "acted only a secondary part." The massacre "was concocted by white men and consummated by whites and Indi-ans." He intended to recover some of the property, rumored to amount to some $30,000, from the leading church dignitaries.[61]

Forney's delicate handling of Lee did not sit well with the men who had risked their lives to protect him on his trip to Mountain Meadows. In Lee's hearing, Lynch and his men refused "to share the hospitality of this *notorious murderer*—THIS SCOURGE OF THE DESERT." They were outraged that Lee could entertain government officials like Forney at his table while the surviving children pointed to Lee as "one of them that did the bloody work." Lynch charged that despite all he had seen, Forney supported Lee's claim that the president's pardon included murderers and that the Mormons would not be tried or punished for any of their crimes. In disgust Lynch denounced Forney as a "veritable old granny."[62]

Marshal William Rogers was more sympathetic to the agent's actions. Forney believed Lee had some of the emigrants' property and planned to demand its surren-der. Lee claimed he knew nothing about the murders and only arrived at Mountain

Meadows after the killing ended. Lee "applied some foul and indecent epithets to the emigrants" and in general terms justified their deaths. After this stormy meeting, Lee agreed to accompany Forney to Cedar City to discuss the matter with Haight and Higbee in the superintendent's presence. Lee had second thoughts, for on the way he rode ahead and vanished. The federal officers did not see him again. Forney met with Higbee and Haight "and received about the same replies from them that Lee gave."[63] His main mission of recovering the children accomplished, Jacob Forney picked up three more children at Cedar City and set out with the orphans for Great Salt Lake City, where his reports would very nearly ignite a war.

Parley Parker Pratt, circa 1857. As one of the original and most beloved apostles of the LDS church, Pratt was known by the cognomen "the Archer of Paradise." Hector McLean, the husband of Pratt's twelfth wife, murdered Pratt in May 1857 in Arkansas. Courtesy Utah State Historical Society.

Eleanor McComb McLean Pratt. As the first wife of Hector McLean and the last wife of Parley P. Pratt, Eleanor played the role of Helen in the story of Mountain Meadows. From the *American Weekly*, September 1940.

Lt. Gen. Daniel Hamner Wells. Commander of the Nauvoo Legion, counselor to Brigham Young, and mayor of Salt Lake City, Wells coordinated Mormon efforts to convict John D. Lee at his second trial in 1879. His "disagreeable cock-eye" inspired the *Salt Lake Tribune* to characterize him as "the One-Eyed Pirate of the Wasatch." Courtesy Utah State Historical Society.

Bvt. Brig. Gen. Albert Sidney Johnston. One of the most respected officers in the U.S. Army, Johnston assumed command of the Army of Utah in September 1857. Even Brigham Young acknowledged the discipline his troops displayed when they marched through the empty streets of Great Salt Lake City on June 26, 1858, but the two men almost went to war when Johnston's officers investigated Mountain Meadows in 1859. From *Harper's Weekly*, June 12, 1858.

George A. Smith, circa 1856. A cousin of the Mormon prophet Joseph Smith, Apostle Smith directed the founding of Parowan in 1851 and became known as "the father of southern Utah." His wig, false teeth, and eyeglasses led Indians to call him Man Who Comes Apart. Smith's inflammatory speeches during an August 1857 tour of Utah's southern settlements set the stage for the Mountain Meadows massacre. Courtesy Utah State Historical Society.

Col. William H. Dame and wives, circa 1880. LDS genealogical records list six marriages for Dame: Lovina Andrews, September 15, 1851 (or October 2, 1857); Sally Ann Carter, February 10, 1856; Virginia Lovina Newman, October 9, 1856; Sarah Ann Carter, October 9, 1856; Lydia Ann Killian, December 1, 1868; and Mary Pearson, July 6, 1869. Note the black servants in the background. Courtesy Special Collections, Sherratt Library, Southern Utah University.

Philip Klingensmith. Bishop of Cedar City and a Nauvoo Legion private in 1857, Klingensmith's 1871 affidavit describing the massacre was the first participant confession of the atrocities committed at Mountain Meadows. Courtesy Special Collections, Sherratt Library, Southern Utah University.

Maj. John M. Higbee as mayor of Cedar City, 1867–71. Higbee gave the order to begin the slaughter at Mountain Meadows. His 1894 "Bull Short" mea culpa codified Mormon justification of the murders by blaming the victims and the Southern Paiutes. Courtesy Special Collections, Sherratt Library, Southern Utah University.

Eliza Ann Snyder Haight, Mary Ann Haight, and Isaac C. Haight, circa 1857, when Lieutenant Colonel Haight served as stake president, the senior Mormon ecclesiastical authority in southern Utah, and second in command of the Iron County Brigade of the Nauvoo Legion. Courtesy Special Collections, Southern Utah University.

Jacob Hamblin. As president of the Southern Indian Mission, Hamblin escorted Paiute leaders to meet with Brigham Young in early September 1857, and his testimony helped to convict John D. Lee of murder. This hardy explorer and frontiersman became a Mormon folk hero as their Apostle in Buckskin, but to John D. Lee he was Dirty Fingered Jake.

Mary, Daniel, Dudley, Ira, and Mariah Huntsman Leavitt. Few Latter-day Saints practiced "the principle" as devotedly as Dudley Leavitt, who had forty-eight children by his five wives. Courtesy Utah State Historical Society.

Nephi Johnson. As Nauvoo Legion lieutenant, Johnson led the killing of the women and children at Mountain Meadows, an act that tormented him to his deathbed.

George Armstrong Hicks. Renowned as a singer and writer of several enduring folk songs, Hicks was an 1861 pioneer of southern Utah who opposed John D. Lee. Confused by the contradiction between public statements and his own experience with the perpetrators, Hicks wrote to Brigham Young, "If you are in favor of the Mountain meadows massacre I would like to know it." Courtesy Dawn Nodzu.

Christopher Carson Fancher. In 1873 Fancher died in Arkansas at age twenty-one at the home of his great-uncle, Hampton Bynum Fancher. During the second trial of John D. Lee, stagecoach robber Richard Sloan convinced Lee that he was "William Fancher," the survivor Lee called Charley who lived with the Lee family after the massacre. Courtesy Utah State Historical Society.

Mary Elizabeth Baker Terry, one of the two Baker sisters to survive and leave an account of the 1857 massacre. Courtesy Charles Kelly and Utah State Historical Society.

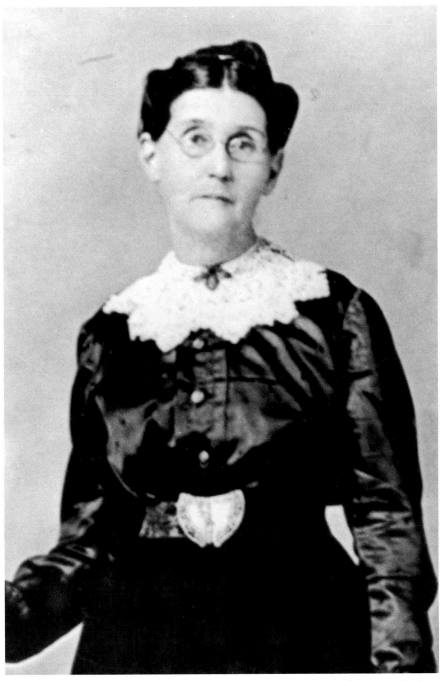

Sarah Frances Baker Mitchell, the second of the two Baker sisters to survive Mountain Meadows and leave a powerful account of the experience in later years. She insisted, "You don't forget the horror." Courtesy Charles Kelly and Utah State Historical Society.

James Lynch. "Captain" Lynch helped to rescue the orphaned survivors of the Mountain Meadows massacre in 1859 and described his experience in telling detail. At age seventy-four, Lynch married survivor Sarah Dunlap, thirty-eight, on December 30, 1893. Courtesy Utah State Historical Society.

Dr. Garland Hurt. The Utes at the Spanish Fork Indian farm called Indian agent Hurt "the American" and helped him to escape from the Nauvoo Legion, the Mormon militia, in September 1857. He carried word of the Mountain Meadows massacre to the U.S. Army that November. Courtesy Utah State Historical Society.

Maj. John D. Lee. Marsena Cannon probably took this portrait of a troubled man at Salt Lake on December 26, 1857. Lee was serving in the Utah Territorial Legislature, only three months after the Mountain Meadows massacre. Courtesy Utah State Historical Society.

John D. Lee and the law, 1876. Lee is seated at the center. Left to right: William W. Bishop, lead attorney at Lee's second trial and editor of his client's *Confessions*; Justice Jacob S. Boreman, presiding judge at the two Lee trials; Enos D. Hoge and Wells Spicer, Lee's legal counsel. Extreme right: unidentified. Courtesy Utah State Historical Society.

John D. Lee "writing his autobiography" in the Beaver City penitentiary, while under sentence of death for complicity in the Mountain Meadows massacre. There was no "Beaver City penitentiary." The picture shows Lee writing his memoirs while in detention at Fort Cameron shortly before his execution. From the cover of *Frank Leslie's Illustrated Newspaper*, April 7, 1877.

Wilford Woodruff. Apostle Woodruff's lengthy journal provided key insights into early Mormonism, especially during the 1850s, and contains evidence long used to prove that John D. Lee lied to Brigham Young when he reported the massacre. As president of the LDS church in 1890, Woodruff renounced the practice of polygamy. Courtesy David L. Bigler.

George Q. Cannon. Nephew of the Mormon prophet John Taylor, the dynamic Cannon served as a newspaper editor, business manager, spokesman, and apostle for the LDS church. Although he learned the facts about Mountain Meadows while passing through southern Utah in 1858, Cannon wrote the last church editorial blaming the massacre on the Indians in 1869. As Utah's territorial delegate, Cannon represented Mormon political interests in Congress. Courtesy David L. Bigler.

Judge John Cradlebaugh. As a federal judge, Cradlebaugh visited southern Utah and Mountain Meadows in 1859. His investigation revealed the basic facts of the atrocity. Cradlebaugh issued warrants for the arrest of almost one hundred murderers, including some thirty-eight participants in the Mountain Meadows massacre, but not one of them was arrested by local or federal officials until 1874. Courtesy Utah State Historical Society.

Charles Wandell. After viewing the massacre site with George Q. Cannon in 1857, Wandell spent fifteen years investigating the crime. He engineered Philip Klingensmith's confession, and his "Argus" letters challenged Brigham Young to explain his role in the massacre at Mountain Meadows. Courtesy Community of Christ Archives, Independence, Missouri.

Robert N. Baskin. As federal prosecutor at the first John D. Lee trial and author of sweeping federal antipolygamy laws, Baskin made good on his pledge to destroy the power of Mormon theocracy and avenge the murder of his friend Dr. J. King Robinson. Courtesy Utah State Historical Society.

Curmudgeon-historian Charles Kelly "cocking a snook" at the 1932 Mountain Meadows marker. Kelly's gesture evokes his general contempt for the Mormon accounts of the Mountain Meadows massacre and his particular aggravation with the marker. Courtesy Michael Harrison, copy at Department of Special Collections, University of California Library, Davis.

Juanita Leavitt Pulsipher Brooks, the "minstrel of Mountain Meadows," whose belief that "nothing but the truth can be good enough for the church to which I belong" drove her lifelong pursuit of the story of Mormonism's darkest secret. Courtesy Utah State Historical Society.

Rachel Lee's shanty at Jacobs Pools. No image better captures the raw nature of life on the ragged edge of the Mormon frontier than this Powell Expedition photograph. It appears that the woman on the right is Rachel Lee, the man with the dog is John D. Lee, and the men at either side are members of the expedition. Courtesy Ken Sanders Rare Books.

y-buts, Williams, Joe
Brother

Southern Paiutes, circa 1880. This image from the William R. Palmer Collection identifies these Southern Paiutes as Y-buts, Williams Brother, and Joe. Such photographs reveal that the Paiutes were not the degraded subhumans often described in overland trail accounts. Courtesy Special Collections, Sherratt Library, Southern Utah Univesity.

President Gordon B. Hinckley of The Church of Jesus Christ of Latter-day Saints speaking at the dedication of the Mountain Meadows Monument, September 11, 1999. Photograph by Al Hartmann. Courtesy *Salt Lake Tribune*.

View from the 1990 monument. The 1990 monument on Dan Sill Hill offers a sweeping view of the land-scape and lists victims and survivors of the 1857 Mountain Meadows massacre. The massacre took place on the open ground in the upper right of the image. Photo by Chris Smith. Courtesy *Salt Lake Tribune*.

Brigham Young's compound, circa 1858. The Beehive House (center) and the Lion House (left) still stand on today's South Temple Street.

The Mountain Meadows massacre. Perhaps the most famous image of the event, like other nineteenth-century pictures, this anonymous engraving is not historically accurate but captures the horror of the atrocity. From T. B. H. Stenhouse, *The Rocky Mountain Saints*, facing page 426.

The scene of the Mountain Meadows massacre, Utah Territory (from a recent sketch). This horrific image appeared on the cover of *Harper's Weekly*, August 13, 1859, to illustrate Capt. Charles Brewer's eyewitness report, which brought the story to national attention.

13

Vengeance Is Mine

As Jacob Forney headed north from Cedar City with his sad collection of orphans, U.S. Army units from Camp Floyd and southern California converged on southern Utah. On April 17, 1859, General Johnston ordered Capt. R. P. Campbell to take two companies of infantry and his Second Dragoons to "Santa Clara and remain in that portion of the country as long as the interests of the Government and the objects of the expedition require." The Santa Clara Expedition was sent to protect travelers on the road to California and investigate reported Indian depredations. Johnston offered Campbell additional forces if necessary but warned him not to use force to chastise Indians "except for depredations and murders committed while you are in the vicinity and which need prompt punishment." Two days later Johnston directed Campbell to escort Judge Cradlebaugh to the Santa Clara as there was "no way to hold or secure offenders against the law, except through the aid of the army." Campbell was to detain any prisoners the federal marshal might turn over to him. He would rendezvous with Bvt. Maj. James H. Carleton and the First Dragoons from Fort Tejon in California and escort paymaster Henry Prince to Camp Floyd with the post's payroll, $150,000 in gold. Carleton was also sent "to bury the bones of the victims of that terrible massacre."[1]

The army and judicial reports of 1859 would confirm that the worst rumors about the massacre at Mountain Meadows were true. The federal officers saw the grim evidence firsthand, and it stiffened their resolve to bring the perpetrators to justice—a task that proved impossible in the strange conditions prevailing in the territory. Mormons panicked when they learned of the investigations and prepared to take desperate military and legal measures to protect Brigham Young from arrest and, they believed, lynching at the hands of the army. Mormon leaders intimidated Utah's weak and gullible governor into inaction, and once the crisis passed they fell back on stalling, dividing the opposition, and complaining about violations of their rights until political decisions in Washington, D.C., hamstrung their enemies.

Campbell's command met Jacob Forney with sixteen orphans at Corn Creek. Kanosh had told Forney two more children were still in Cedar City. Marshal Rogers agreed to return south with the soldiers to find them, and Judge Cradlebaugh gave Rogers warrants for the arrest of John D. Lee, Isaac Haight, and John Higbee. A messenger warned Haight that two hundred troops were at Beaver, "coming south," Haight said, "with the sworn intention of taking me and some other of the Brethren and hang us without trial." Haight and Higbee fled north, picking up William Stewart at Beaver. The fugitives arrived at Nephi on May 7, 1859, and slept in the tithing office. The next evening they "went up in the mountains to a camp called Ballegard, where quite a number of Brethren who were proscribed by our enemies had fled for safety."[2]

Since Haight and Higbee had vanished, Marshal Rogers proceeded to Harmony, only to discover that Lee had "played the same dodge" and disappeared. Alerted by Forney's investigation, Lee closely monitored the movements of the federal agents. He retreated to the mountains around Kolob Canyon with Philip Klingensmith. His companion soon left him, but Lee remained in hiding, haunted by dreams of a river of blood and fearful that half his neighbors "would turn traitors and go over to the soldiers."[3] Lee returned home when the soldiers left, but he was extremely nervous and would remain so for the next fifteen years.

As Rogers searched for Lee, a man told him one of the missing orphans was at Pocketville (present Virgin) with his wife, who "was very much attached to it." Rogers hired Jacob Hamblin to retrieve the child. Rachel Hamblin delivered Joseph Miller, "a bright eyed and rosy cheeked boy, about two years old," supposedly ransomed from Indians, to Major Carleton's camp. Rogers never found the second child Kanosh reported, though he diligently looked for it. Hamblin told Rogers he had learned much more about the massacre while recovering the boy but had promised to name the whites involved only to the governor. Alfred Cumming later told the marshal that Hamblin had "revealed nothing to him in regard to the massacre or those concerned in it."[4]

Campbell's command consisted of two infantry companies, one hundred dragoons, and one hundred discharged teamsters "amounting to 300 men." Three miles south of Cedar City, soldiers looking for wood discovered human bones scattered in the bushes and later found an entire skeleton. After a march of two hundred sixty miles, the army and Judge Cradlebaugh arrived at Mountain Meadows on May 5. The next day Captain Campbell buried the bones of twenty-six victims in two separate graves some fifty yards from the California Trail.[5]

Campbell reported "human skulls, bones, and hair, scattered about, and scraps of clothing of men women and children. [He] saw one girl's dress, apparently that of a child ten or twelve years of age."[6] Surgeon Charles Brewer "found masses of women's hair, children's bonnets, such as are generally used upon the plains, and pieces of lace, muslin, calicoes, and other material, part of women's and children's apparel." Many of the skulls "bore marks of violence, being pierced with bullet holes, or shattered by heavy blows, or cleft with some sharp-edged instrument." Long exposure to the elements had bleached the bones, which revealed that the men and women were killed in separate locations. Some of the bodies appeared to be "lightly buried, but the majority were scattered about upon the plain." The men, Brewer concluded, were taken by surprise and massacred. Their skulls "showed that fire-arms had been discharged close to the head." At the site of the wagon fort, the doctor supervised the burial of the remains "at the base of the hill, upon the hill-side of the valley."[7]

Campbell's men marched to the Santa Clara on May 8, where they waited for Major Carleton. Local Indian leaders visited Judge Cradlebaugh and gave him their version of the massacre through interpreter James Gemmell. The Paiutes admitted participating but claimed they were not there when the attack commenced. After the initial assault, Chief Jackson said, a white man came to his camp with a piece of paper from Brigham Young directing him "to go and help to whip the emigrants." Jackson claimed an Indian interpreter named "Huntingdon" had brought Young's orders "authorizing, if not commanding, that the train should be destroyed." Jackson said his band went to the meadows, where his brother was shot and killed, but they did not assist in the fight. Lee, he charged, led a force of sixty men, and all the Mormons were painted.[8] According to William Dame, the army literally dragged the information out of the Paiute leader at Jacob's Twist on the Santa Clara. Mail carriers had reported that the soldiers caught Chief Jackson, put a rope on his neck, dragged him about, and threatened to hang him. Jackson "got away swearing veangeance."[9]

Carleton's dragoons rendezvoused with Campbell's party at Santa Clara on May 15, 1859, and the next day both detachments camped at Mountain Meadows. "Even at this late day," Carleton found the site "horrible to look upon. Women's hair, in detached locks and in masses, hung to the sage bushes and was strewn over the ground in many places. Parts of little children's dresses and of female costume dangled from the shrubbery or lay scattered about." Skulls and bones bleached white by the weather lined the California Trail. Nearly every skull "had been shot through with rifle or revolver bullets." "I did not see one that had been 'broken in with stones,'" he said. He reported seeing several bones of what must have been very small children.[10]

The army officers quickly concluded the Paiutes were entirely incapable of executing the massacre. Campbell thought they were "a miserable set of root-diggers, and nothing is to be apprehended from them but by the smallest and most careless party." The emigrants "could have whipped ten times their number of Pah-Ute Indians." Major Carleton argued that the "whole plan and operations, from beginning to end, display skill, patience, pertinacity, and forecast," which only the Mormon settlers possessed.[11]

Surgeon Brewer described "the most brutal butchery ever perpetrated on this continent." He denounced the Mormons for treacherously massacring the brave band of emigrants in cold blood. Some of the children told him of pulling arrows from the bleeding wounds of their parents. Brewer believed infants had been butchered in their mothers' arms and accused Mormon leaders of violating some of the women before "they wreaked their hoarded vengeance" on the helpless children. He charged that Mormons led the attack and were the most active participants in the crime, while the Indians "but obeyed the command of Brigham Young." Their victims' bones "bleached in the elements of the mountain wilds, gnawed by the hungry wolf." Brewer asked "one calm, quiet question": "Are these facts known in the land where I was born and bred?" They would be when his story—illustrated with a lurid engraving of wolves gnawing on skeletons—exploded on the front page of *Harper's Weekly* three months later, forcing the grisly details of the atrocity to the attention of the American public.[12]

Maj. Henry Prince mapped and measured the whole landscape from the center of the emigrant camp. He sketched their defenses near the spring on Magotsu Creek, showing the ravine where the attack began and the bullet-pocked heights on the west that sheltered snipers. Prince even specified the site where he said "the Mormons painted & disguised themselves as Indians."[13] Carleton ordered distances measured "from point to point on the scene of this massacre." From the wagon fort "to the point upon the road where the men were attacked and destroyed" was 2,325 yards, while the spot "where the women and children were butchered" was 2,895 yards from the spring. Here Campbell's men had buried some of the remains. One of them, Pvt. Tommy Gordon, noted on May 6, 1859, that he "helped to bury the bones that was laying overground in two graves, the first one 2,500 yards north of the Spring and 45 yards from left hand side of road (Mens grave). Second grave 150 yards north of first one (Womens grave) 50 yards from road on Same Side as the other."[14]

Jacob and Rachel Hamblin spent the night of May 19 at the army camp. The next morning the major took statements from their adopted Shoshoni son, Albert, and Mrs. Hamblin. Jacob impressed Carleton as "a shrewd, intelligent, thinking man." (Major Carleton felt that among the local Mormons Lee "was the smartest man of the lot," but his neighbors believed he had swindled them out of their share of the loot.) During the interview, Hamblin concealed the facts Lee had revealed to him in Fillmore in 1857. He watched carefully as his wife described the massacre and, Carleton noted, "also took very good care to give her occasional promptings."[15] Major Carleton initially thought Hamblin was "acting in good faith, and gave what he really believed was a true account of the massacre and of the Mormon part taken in it," but he felt John Cradlebaugh had discovered Hamblin's motive. While pretending to expose the Mormon role in the massacre, Hamblin had "learned many of the Judge's purposes" and warned one of the Cedar City suspects to keep out of the way.[16]

Guided by the Hamblins, Carleton "took a wagon and a party of men and made a thorough search for others amongst the sage bushes for at least a mile back." Hamblin pointed out a spot on the right side of the road where he had partially buried a great many bones. The soldiers gathered the skeletons of thirty-four persons and interred them on the north side of the emigrant's rifle pit. Company K of the First Dragoons hauled stones from the neighboring hills and raised "a rude monument, conical in form 50 feet in circumference at the base and 12 feet in height." They topped the cairn with a cross hewn from red cedar bearing an inscription "carved deeply in the wood: 'Vengeance is mine: I will repay, saith the Lord.'" The soldiers erected a slab of granite and inscribed it, "Here 120 men, women and children were massacred in cold blood early in September, 1857. They were from Arkansas."[17]

This Nest of Thugs

Leaving Campbell's military escort at Mountain Meadows, Judge Cradlebaugh went to Cedar City with Marshal William Rogers. He contemplated holding court in the town if General Johnston provided protection for his witnesses and a posse to aid in making arrests. Cradlebaugh believed he had divined the secret of this "catalogue of blood, the cowardly, cold-blooded butchery and robbery at the Mountain Meadows." Participants visited the judge under cover of darkness and gave him a full account of the massacre, claiming their bishops had forced them to participate. Cradlebaugh took statements from apostate Mormons who promised to "furnish an abundance of evidence in regard to the matter," if he could offer them military protection. The investigation produced warrants for thirty-eight men, including virtually all the principal leaders of southern Utah, but just as Campbell and his troops returned to Cedar City, they received orders to return to Camp Floyd. General Johnston had learned the Mormons were assembling in armed bodies in the mountains for unknown purposes.[18] Without an escort, Cradlebaugh concluded it was too dangerous to stay in southern Utah, and he accompanied Campbell back to Camp Floyd.[19]

On their march north Captain Campbell's men detained a suspicious band of horsemen at 2:00 A.M. on Chicken Creek to inspect the party's mounts for stolen horses. At daylight the soldiers let the men go. The riders included Isaac Haight, John Higbee, and William Stewart. Haight wrote, "Right glad we were to get away from them, as some of our bitterest enemies were in camp," including Judge Cradlebaugh. "[Our enemies'] eyes were blinded so they did not know us, although some of them had seen us at Cedar City. We felt that the Lord had delivered us from their grasp."[20]

In a letter to President Buchanan, Cradlebaugh described his visit to "the place where the 119 emigrants were massacred at the Mountain Meadows, on the 10th of September, 1857." "Eighty or more white men were engaged in that affair." The entire population "within 150 miles of the Meadows does not exceed 1,100—with not more than 200 of an adult male population." The evidence showed that the crimes were committed by "order of council." Cradlebaugh noted that temple oaths bound the perpetrators, who were often men holding high civil and church offices. He complained that the immunity criminals enjoyed in Utah made it impossible for the marshal to serve writs without military support.[21]

Marshal Rogers and Surgeon Brewer reached Camp Floyd on June 1 with macabre evidence of the murders. Capt. John Phelps saw two skulls from Mountain Meadows, while another officer "had held in his hands long tresses of dark and blonde hair of some of the tender victims of this massacre." The orphans told Capt. John Robinson "they had seen these white men take off disguises and wash the war paint from their faces." From the children's accounts, Phelps concluded it was probable Mormons were engaged in the murder. Yet the government found "some strange political value to this Utah Affair which renders these skulls perfectly unimpressive," Phelps wrote. "Instead of breaking up this nest of thugs our government seems to be cherishing them." To divert "the country from slavery, the horrid monstrosity of Mormonism is fostered and cherished, and to such an extent that the murder of upwards of a hundred persons is overlooked."[22]

While biased, the report James Carleton wrote at Mountain Meadows remains one of the earliest and most accurate sources of information on the massacre. In July 1861 the major outlined the difficulty of bringing the participants to justice: "Who compose the jury to find the indictment? The brethren. Who are generally the witnesses before that jury? The brethren. Who are the officers and jailers who have custody of the prisoner before and after the trial? The brethren. Who are the members of the jury before whom the trial takes place? Still the brethren. Who are the witnesses for the prosecution, and, more particularly, who are those for the defense? The brethren." The major complained, "Suppose the criminal should, after all this, be convicted and sentenced, there is still a pardoning power. Thus running a gauntlet all the way between the brethren (if they do not want him out of the way), what are not his chances for his life?"[23]

Carleton asked, "What can you expect if the wholesome operation of our laws interferes with the absolute sway of the leaders, or with the interests or purposes or safety of the church, or with the liberty or life of a single member of the fraternity?" Malignant hatred, crime, open sedition, and treason among the whole people was Carleton's answer. Attempt to administer the law as applied in the rest of the nation, he wrote, "and they laugh at you to your face."[24]

On returning to California, Carleton expressed his fury at the Mormons even more bluntly to a fellow soldier. "All fine spun nonsense about their Rights as citizens, and all Knotty questions about Constitutional Rights, should be solved with the sword," he wrote. "We might as well look this devil right in the face at once." Their lawlessness demanded that "this set of ruffians go out from amongst us as people." The Mormons should be banished from the United States immediately: "Give them one year, no more; and if after that they pollute our soil by their presence, make literally Children of the Mist of them."[25]

Accessory Before the Fact: The Arrest of Brigham Young

Jacob Forney's recovery of the massacre orphans and the army's Santa Clara Expedition provoked an immediate and intense reaction in Salt Lake. As Cradlebaugh investigated the scene of the crime, Mormon authorities in Salt Lake cataloged complaints against him, charging that the one-eyed judge was running roughshod over their constitutional rights. Aurelius Miner swore Cradlebaugh had said "he would hang Kanosh if he could, without Judge or Jury, and that he would hang him whether he was guilty as one of the perpetrators of the Mountain Meadows massacre or not." Miner claimed that in speaking of Mormons charged with capital offenses, Cradlebaugh said if "he could get anyone of them convicted he would hang them so quick that he could not possibly have time to procure a pardon from the Governor." C. V. Spencer and Brigham H. Young, who were monitoring troop movements at Camp Floyd, described the army's investigative techniques. Mormon prisoners "were taken out of jail, ropes put around their necks, strung up to a beam and threatened to be hung until they were dead, unless they confessed to what they knew of the Mountain Meadows affair." Two companies had left Camp Floyd with a load of ammunition for Mountain Meadows to capture four bishops and sixteen other Mormons. The army was "feeding some 20 Indians to have them pick out men connected with the Mountain Meadows affair, which men, they swear they will hang as soon as they get them."[26]

In their catalog of government abuses, the Saints repeated their claim that federal officers were manipulating the Indians. U.S. authorities had offered Enos, the Indian freebooter, money, blankets, shirts, drawers, and other goods worth about $1,000 for the head of John D. Lee.[27] Jacob Hamblin appeared before Mormon judge Elias Smith and described a conversation in Judge Cradlebaugh's tent at Santa Clara. The judge and Deputy Marshal William Rogers asked Hamblin "to employ the Piute Indians to go into the Mountains and hunt up John D. Lee" and to bring Lee into camp dead or alive. According to Hamblin's statement, the Indians told him where Lee had "camped two nights before, but on going to the place, [he] found that [Lee] had left." Cradlebaugh informed Hamblin "he had employed an Indian to testify in relation to the massacre at the Mountain Meadows, and that he had paid him in blankets." The judge had more blankets, and he asked Hamblin to hire a large number of Indians to search the country and bring in Lee. Hamblin thought the Paiutes would help the marshal if they were well paid, but he warned that Lee "was armed with three revolvers and a six-shooter rifle, and it would cost life to take him." The officials "did not care what it cost, if the Indians would hunt him up." Hamblin declined their offer as being contrary to his instructions from Forney not "to encourage the Indians, in any way, to interfere with the Whites."[28]

Two weeks later, Hamblin swore before Judge Smith that on June 15 in Jacob Forney's office he heard an army major say he believed Brigham Young had ordered every one of the murders committed in the territory, "God damn him." The major wanted to have the first shot at Young and "would like damned well to have the Mormons fire just one shot at their men . . . so that they could have had an excuse for wiping out the Mormons."[29]

Rumors swept Utah that the army was preparing to march on Salt Lake to batter down the walls of the Beehive House and arrest Brigham Young. On March 21, 1859, Daniel Wells ordered the Nauvoo Legion to prepare immediately but quietly to repulse the army. Mormon congregations notified their men to have their arms and ammunition ready. General Johnston heard that four hundred Mormons had mysteriously assembled in the mountains above Utah Valley. U.S. Army captain Albert Tracy believed something like a thousand men were "organized and under arms for a purpose not explained."[30] One Mormon historian claimed five thousand men "flew to arms" in response to Wells's orders. Wilford Woodruff wrote, "Unless the Lord wards off the blow it looks as though we were to have war & Bloodshed." Governor Cumming told Hosea Stout on April 8 there would be a warrant issued for Young and "it will be necessary for him to give himself up & that he will not be harmed." Stout noted the Mormon reaction: "this will not do."[31]

In the wake of Cradlebaugh's hearings, the rumors intensified. Woodruff heard that a company of volunteers from Arkansas was on its way to Iron County "to punish those who had a hand in the Mountain meadow massacree & that a thousand men are on the way to guard the Governmet money in route for the armey." Salt Lake was filled with rumors that General Johnston was marching on the city with two regiments and had told Governor Cummings "if he did not straighten out Brigham Young & the mormons he should take the matter into his own hands." Judge Cradlebaugh was on his way south with several hundred men to make arrests. The next day Woodruff packed all the records in the church historian's office "to save them from being burned in case the City should be burned."[32]

As tension mounted, Brigham Young, Daniel Wells, and George A. Smith paid a surprise late-night visit to the governor. Young asserted that troops were preparing to attack Great Salt Lake City and complained that the army had been sent "all the way here purposely to destroy the leaders of this people." The army was driving hundreds of men into the mountains, which would result in famine as the Mormons had raised next to nothing the previous year. The church's enemies were "at war with God & his kingdom & the Holy Priesthood." Young was not guilty of any crime, nor had he sanctioned any criminal act, but he refused to face a military court at Camp Floyd "for he should not live 5 minutes when he got there." The army's only desire was to lynch him, he said. "I will not be nosed about by the military and I will not go into their camp alive. It is in your power to put a stop to this difficulty, and if you do not do it, an action of the people will have to do it." The governor would lose all influence if he let the army trample civil authority and walk over him.[33]

The Mormon leaders cleverly manipulated Cumming's dislike of the military, but they underestimated his bureaucratic instincts, for he had already decided to do nothing until he received instructions from Washington. Cumming told Young he did not know what to do and complained about the troublesome ambiguity of his instructions. Young claimed the Mormons "could have cut the [army] in pieces, if we had chosen, and all they could have sent." Once more he threatened to burn "all the property that he had and give them the Territory as bare and desolate as [they] found it." If necessary he would lead his people to the mountains and "waste away those that oppress [them]."[34]

"With all due respect to your Excellency," Young said, "I do not calculate to take the advice of any man that lives, in relation to my affairs, I shall follow the counsels of my heavenly father, and I have the faith to follow it, and risk the consequences."[35] Typically, Cumming did nothing.

Jacob Forney arrived in Great Salt Lake City from Cedar City on May 4, 1859, with sixteen of the massacre orphans. Jacob Hamblin soon delivered the seventeenth child he had found at Pocketville. None of the children had lived among the Indians. Forney found them intelligent and good looking with "not one mean-looking child among them." Only a few of them remembered their actual names. Forney wrote a carefully worded account of his investigation that concluded "the Indians had material assistance from the whites" but that did not name any suspects.[36] Kirk Anderson, who had launched Utah Territory's second newspaper, the *Valley Tan*, in November 1858, printed Forney's report six days later.

Forney's cautious summary—the first mention of the massacre published in Utah—set off a firestorm as panicked Mormon leaders responded with drastic countermeasures. Fearful that federal authorities would arrest him for the murders, Brigham Young decided to have a Mormon probate court order the Mormon sheriff to arrest him, exonerate him before a Mormon jury, and shield him from federal justice.

In early May probate court judge Elias Smith of Great Salt Lake County drafted a warrant. A cousin of Joseph Smith, Jr., and a reliable member of the Mormon hierarchy who had helped Brigham Young plot strategy during the Utah War, Judge Smith could be trusted to oppose any legal threat against his church or its leaders. His warrant noted that an unspecified complaint had charged that certain parties, "at present unknown, did attack with malice . . . a Company of Emigrants on their route to California . . . and did murder the emigrants." Smith's draft warrant charged that Brigham Young, acting as governor of the territory of Utah, "did by letters written in his office in the County of Great Salt Lake, signed by him, and by verbal messages sent therefrom, aid and abet in the said murder as accessory before the fact." He directed the county sheriff to locate the accused "if he be found in this County, or if he have fled to any other County within this Territory to pursue him thither, and take and safely keep him, so that you have his body before me forthwith, to answer the said complaint and may be further dealt with according to Law."[37]

This warrant was not executed, but on May 12, 1859, Young appeared voluntarily before Judge Smith to make a remarkable statement.

Brigham Young Sen., who being duly sworn according to law, says that on or about the time between the ninth and thirtieth day of September A.D. one thousand eight hundred and fifty Seven, a company of Emigrants to the number of one hundred persons, more or less, comprising men, women and children, names to the deponent unknown, while passing through the Territory aforesaid, on their way, as he supposes, to California, were, as he was informed, attacked by a party of armed men, and by them murdered in the region of Country known as the "Mountain Meadows."[38]

Young blamed his failure to take any action on the massacre on "the disturbed state of affairs in this Territory during the fall and winter subsequent to the aforesaid murder"; thus no court was held in the district in which the murders allegedly were committed. Young complained that Judge Cradlebaugh had charged him with "interfering with the courts of justice, and preventing the punishment of offenders, thereby charging him as being accessory after the fact" to the murders. Even worse, Cradlebaugh had blamed him for "instigating the committal of the murder," making Young an "accessory before the fact to the murder." These claims had been published to the world and had acquired more or less credence. The indignant prophet was not willing "to rest under the Stigma of such infamous charges and accusations." Young claimed "the privilege of a fair and impartial investigation and trial and the rendition of a just verdict on the Judgment of his peers," all of whom would, of course, be Mormons.[39]

That evening Young met with Daniel Wells, George A. Smith, Ezra T. Benson, Hosea Stout, and Territorial Attorney Seth Blair in the Beehive House to discuss "a question of accessory." Judge Smith ordered Salt Lake County sheriff Robert T. Burton to arrest Young and hold him until an investigation could be mounted and the case could be "dealt with according to laws." Burton signed the warrant on May 13, after serving the writ "by arresting Brigham Young Sen and having him now in [his] Custody Subject to the Court."[40]

No further record of Young's case or its disposition survives. Perhaps it was simply dismissed for a lack of evidence. The surviving records of the probate court contain no mention of the incident. No known federal justice department or court records refer to the arrest, and there is nothing to suggest that it ever came to the attention of the federal authorities.[41]

The purpose of this exercise is mysterious, but the heated atmosphere of May 1859 and the timing of Elias Smith's warrant point to a likely explanation. The prophet and his advisers feared Judge Cradlebaugh would order Young's arrest as an accessory to the Mountain Meadows murders. Young's attorneys probably hoped to secure his acquittal in the carefully controlled confines of a Mormon probate court where they could produce a "just verdict on the Judgment of his peers." If federal officers later arrested him for the crime, a not-guilty verdict would provide the prophet protection under the constitutional ban on double jeopardy. Something apparently convinced Mormon authorities that this was a dangerous strategy, for the matter was dropped, leaving no trace of Young's arrest but the warrants and affidavits buried in the files of the LDS Church Historian's Office.[42]

Young found an unlikely ally in his successor as superintendent of Indian affairs. Dr. Jacob Forney had sent the names of the "hell-deserving scoundrels" who executed the murders to U.S. Attorney Alexander Wilson, who was still preparing to investigate the massacre. Ultimately, Wilson's investigation went nowhere, and Forney complained that the *Valley Tan* had published the suspects' names before they could be captured. Forney and Wilson insisted Cedar City was the proper place to prosecute the crime, but Judge Eckles refused to do so. Forney feared certain parties had "a greater anxiety to connect B. Young and other church dignitaries with every criminal offense, than diligently to endeavor to punish the actual perpetrators of the crime."[43]

One night in May as he worked late, Brigham Young visited George A. Smith in the historian's office. Young allegedly said that when the present excitement subsided and the army could be kept from interfering with the judiciary, he intended to investigate all the charges Judge Cradlebaugh had "made such a stink about." Young would try to persuade the governor and the federal district attorney to go to Washington County "and manage the investigation of the Mountain Meadow Massacre, themselves."[44] Young repeated this claim for decades, using it as a mantra to answer any and all questions about the massacre, but his actions belied his words. As late as October 1859 Forney wanted the Washington County probate court to take up the massacre, and Young thought Governor Cumming wanted to do the same. But the pliant U.S. Attorney Wilson abandoned his post, and even Forney concluded there was only "a slender prospect" of the case coming to trial.[45] The Mormon-controlled probate court took no action in the matter, and although Brigham Young was acknowledged as the most powerful man in Utah, he did nothing to secure justice for the dead and orphaned of Mountain Meadows.

In requesting his own arrest, Brigham Young overreacted. Word reached the territory in late June 1859 that U.S. Attorney General Jeremiah Black had disarmed the federal justice system in Utah when he directed that only Governor Cumming could requisition troops to protect the courts. In a territory the person with power to call out the army "can make war and peace when he pleases, and holds in his hands the issues of life and death for thousands," Black warned. He insisted no one intended to give judges, marshals, or deputies such tremendous authority.

After rendering his judges powerless, Black noted "it is very probable that the Mormon inhabitants of Utah have been guilty of crimes for which they deserve the most severe punishment." The government did not intend "to let anyone escape against whom the proper proofs can be produced," but even in the face of extensive conspiracies, citizens must be prosecuted in a "regular, legal, and constitutional way." Black informed U.S. Attorney Wilson that his reports had come to the attention of the president and urged him to get to the bottom of one of the most atrocious crimes that had "ever blackened the character of the human race." "All the circumstances seem, from the correspondence, to be enveloped in mystery," he noted, but he expected Wilson to learn "all that can be known upon this subject."[46] The curiously ambivalent Wilson did nothing but write letters to justify his inaction.

General Johnston complied with Black's decision and notified the territorial marshal that the army could not assist the civil authorities until the governor determined "that the services of a civil posse are insufficient." The general regretted turning loose men charged with atrocious crimes, but he had no other alternative.[47] If John Cradlebaugh wanted to prosecute the Mountain Meadows massacre in Utah, he must do so without military protection.

The Mormons' political victory halted efforts to prosecute thirty-eight men for the murders at Mountain Meadows. U.S. Marshal Peter Dotson reported on June 3, 1859, that he had no power to execute the judge's warrants. Since he could not rely on local citizens to help him, Dotson had asked the governor to requisition a small number of troops as a posse to arrest the persons involved in the crime, but Cumming declined.[48] Cradlebaugh later charged that the government's "weak, timid, temporizing, cowardly" Utah policy led to "anarchy and to the open violation of the most sacred rights." Dotson had arrest warrants he could not serve for almost one hundred murderers, the judge noted, "including the participators in the horrible butcheries at the Mountain Meadows."[49]

How Those Little Fellows Have Suffered: The Survivors

In the military budget for 1859, Congress appropriated $10,000 to transport the survivors of Mountain Meadows back to Arkansas.[50] The action aggravated Brigham Young, who was tracking the progress of the federal investigation closely. He complained that the appointment of two commissioners to return the survivors to their relatives and "the large incident expenditure of public money are very farcical, to all who know." He insisted "those children could at any time have been forwarded, at a trifling expense, with any company going to the States."[51] The army felt differently: General Johnston ordered two companies of dragoons to escort the children to Fort Leavenworth.

In late June 1859 the Salt Lake probate court appointed Jacob Forney guardian of the orphaned children with the power "to collect and receive all property belonging to the murdered Emigrants." Forney still hoped that with proper diligence some of the property looted from the Fancher party could be recovered.[52] His efforts to secure common justice for the orphans failed. By fall he reported that not one particle of the property had been satisfactorily accounted for, but he said he had no doubt it was in the possession of "the *white* inhabitants who participated in this affair."[53] In the end the government never recovered a single item looted from the Fancher party.

The children left Camp Floyd on June 27, 1859, escorted by Companies A and C of the Second Dragoons. General Johnston "ordered spring wagons to be furnished for the conveyance to Fort Leavenworth." Maj. Daniel P. Whiting was "instructed to see that good care [was] taken of these children, and that they [were] provided with everything needful on the route."[54] Forney arranged for three men to do camp chores and five women to accompany the "unfortunate, fatherless, motherless, and penny-less children" and directed they should feed their charges "properly arranged and well-cooked food." He reported that the children were given at least three changes of clothes, plenty of blankets, and "every appliance" to make them comfortable and happy.[55] The Mormon authorities detained several of the women Forney hired, claim-ing they still owed money to the church's Perpetual Emigration Fund.[56]

Ten days after the children departed, Maj. Fitz-John Porter answered a June 12, 1859, letter from John Fancher of Visalia, California, inquiring after his missing niece and nephew. Porter informed him that Charles and Annie Fancher would "be taken to Fort Smith, Arkansas, and delivered to their relations, if any there be." Porter stated, "The children are represented as very interesting and intelligent, the first named about 7, and the last about $3^{1}/_{2}$ years old."[57]

Reports on the condition of the rescued children contrast sharply. James Lynch charged the children "were in a most wretched and deplorable condition." "*With lit-tle or no clothing, covered with filth and dirt*, they presented a sight heart-rending and mis-erable in the extreme." James Carleton railed against the fiends who "dared even to come forward and claim payment for having kept these little ones barely alive." Sur-vivor Sarah Francis Baker said thirty-six years later, "[The Mormons] did not violently abuse me, but we were poorly fed and clothed. They sold us from one family to another. They did not allow the children to stay together, but kept us mostly in sep-arate families." Age changed her opinion, for in 1940 she recalled, "We had good food, and plenty of it. We had lots of rice and also honey right out of the comb." Her only unpleasant memory was that one of the older Mormon children had pushed her down a set of stairs.[58]

Marshal William Rogers reported that the children were well, with the exception of infected eyes apparently resulting from a local epidemic.[59] Jacob Forney said, "I feel confident that the children were well cared for whilst in the hands of these people. I found them happy and contented, except those who were sick." He insisted the orphans were in better condition than most of the children in the settlements in which they lived. Forney rejected a number of claims for ransom of the children as it was well known they "did not live among the Indians one hour," but he subsequently authorized payment of $2,961.77 of the more than $7,000 in claims for the children's care.[60]

In their hunt for the survivors, Forney and his agents—particularly the well-paid Jacob Hamblin—left no stone unturned in southern Utah. The earliest and most reli-able reports indicate only seventeen children were rescued from the massacre, but folktales claimed one or two of the children remained in Utah to be absorbed into the local culture.[61] Many of the victims' families clung to these stories in the hope that a loved one survived the atrocity. According to Sarah Baker, her sister "Vina," seven-year-old Mary Levina Baker, was never heard of after the massacre. Her sister Martha, Sarah recalled, "saw the men leading her away about the time the murder-ing stopped. She thinks Vina was spared."[62] Malinda Cameron also hoped one of her relatives had survived the massacre, but at age thirteen Nancy Cameron was too old to have been spared; even William Cameron's youngest child, eight-year-old Larkin, was killed.[63]

Hamblin had tracked one infant to Pocketville and took him to Salt Lake, despite the foster mother's deep attachment to the child. There is every reason to believe Hamblin returned every surviving child and then charged the federal government for their upkeep. Traditions that a Mormon mother refused to give up a beloved adopted child are touching, but the reality of pioneer life in poverty-stricken southern Utah was that children (including illegitimate children of mysterious origin) were plenti-ful. Federal gold, in contrast, was as scarce as it was valuable.

The myth that the federal authorities overlooked one child survivor had a pow-erful appeal to both the families of the victims and the people of southern Utah. For relatives of the dead, it kept hope alive. For relatives of the perpetrators, the idea that one of the massacre's victims had remained in Utah and adopted their beliefs mitigated guilt for the atrocity. However comforting these tales might be, they remain impos-sible to verify. The first published report of a Utah survivor did not appear until 1950 when Juanita Brooks described how a childless couple in Cedar City raised a baby girl saved from the massacre who became a Mormon and was married in the temple. Brooks later believed the survivor was thirteen-year-old Nancy Cameron, a known victim, suggesting Brooks had fallen victim to local mythology.[64] A recent claim that descendants of Alexander Fancher survive in Utah is emotionally powerful, but nei-ther the scientific evidence nor the historical record support it.

Emigrant Hannah Clapp saw the "very bright, nice looking" children camped with their army escort thirteen miles from Great Salt Lake City. "Not one," she wrote, was "able to tell us his or her surname," except for the two oldest boys, who were recalled to the city from this camp. The soldiers did not have a good word to say about the Mormons, and Clapp herself concluded the Saints were "a lot of miserable, wicked land pirates."[65]

After the orphans left Utah Territory, George A. Smith ridiculed the army escort. He claimed several of the children bitterly resisted efforts to get them into the carriages. They did not want to go with those men, because they "got drunk and swore so much." One girl lay down on the pavement and screamed, but "two negros" seized her. With the "persuasion of a citizen who was acquainted with her, she was finally put into the carriage." A child "supposed to be old enough to testify to the massacre, was sent off, it is said because she was such a liar, but probably because she would not swear and stick to just the things desired." Smith charged that two older boys had remained behind for undefined "ulterior purposes."[66]

Superintendent Forney reported from Fort Laramie in early November. He had the two oldest survivors, John Calvin Miller and Emberson Milum Tackitt, with him and proposed taking them to Washington, D.C., to testify against the murderers of their parents. Both boys were remarkably intelligent and gave him "a very interesting account of the massacre." The agent believed they would make competent witnesses. As Emberson Tackitt had no near relations, Forney said he was anxious to adopt him.[67]

Forney arrived in the capital with the boys on December 12, 1859. "He has had an interview with Judge Black and others," Brigham Young's Washington agent, George Q. Cannon, reported the next day. Cannon believed Forney had "told his version and with some effect. . . . He will be of service." As Forney apparently supported the Mormon position, their critics would "not have it all their own way," Cannon concluded. "At any rate, this is the way he talks." Perhaps Arapeen had taught Forney the advantages of telling the Saints one thing and the government another. Young initially informed William H. Hooper, Utah's congressional delegate, "I was really pleased to learn that Dr. Forney had acted as your friend and the friend of Utah, he will in no wise loose his reward." But Young learned of Forney's duplicity when he read the agent's Mountain Meadows report in an executive document, and presumably the double-dealing agent lost his "reward."[68]

Much worse from the Mormon perspective was news that Attorney General Black had received Carleton's report—"a malignant document, full of base slanders and reckless, unwarranted charges," Cannon wrote. "Our enemies" among the former territorial officials were "determined to make all the capital out of it they can," Cannon said. He feared Carleton's powerful narration had impressed some government officers, but he was confident the poor wretches who wanted the case prosecuted would "run themselves out."[69]

With the Union on the verge of disintegration, the national will to prosecute the murderers of Mountain Meadows was indeed "running out," as was the government's ability to manage an investigation riddled with corruption and incompetence. Curiously, the two young survivors spent only one day in the capital before an army major escorted them to Fayetteville, Arkansas.[70] No official record of the boys' testimony survived. Milum Tackitt and his large family were living near Berryville, Arkansas, in 1895, and he was said to have been the only survivor who revisited Mountain Meadows. His brother William Tackitt died in Taney County, Missouri, in 1893, leaving a wife and five children.[71]

Only fragments of what the orphans told their rescuers survive. James Lynch reported that several children retained "a very vivid impression of much connected with the massacre," especially the very intelligent Becky Dunlap. She saw David Tullis murder her father and reported that Hamblin's Indian son, Albert, killed her two sisters. Both Dunlap and Milum Tackitt *recognized dresses and a part of the jewelry belonging to their mothers, worn by the wives of John D. Lee.* Tackitt also identified his father's oxen, which were in Lee's possession.[72] Some said the children "frequently pointed out carriages and stock that belonged to the train, stating to whom it belonged." One of the most compelling stories was attributed to the boy identified as "John Calvin Sorrow," actually John Calvin Miller, the eldest son of Joseph and Matilda Miller, who had "picked arrows from his mother's body." The boy saw his grandfather, grandmother, aunt, father, and mother murdered. "Clenching his little fists," one of the orphan's nurses recalled, "he would burst into a little passionate speech like this: 'When I get to be a man I'll go to the President of the United States and ask for a regiment of soldiers to go and find John D. Lee. But I don't want to have anybody kill him; I want to shoot him myself, for he killed my father. He shot my father in the back, but I would shoot him in the face.'"73

The children were in Missouri and Arkansas in 1863 when John Cradlebaugh told Congress "their testimony could soon be taken if desired." He recalled, "No one can depict the glee of these infants when they realized that they were in the custody of what they called 'the Americans,' for such is the designation of those not Mormons." On the way to Salt Lake John Calvin Miller sat "in a contemplative mood, no doubt thinking of the extermination of his family." He said, "Oh, I wish I was a man, I know what I would do; I would shoot John D. Lee; I saw him shoot my mother." Said Cradlebaugh, "I shall never forget how he looked."74

THOSE UNFORTUNATE CHILDREN: THE RETURN OF THE ORPHANS

The government appointed Arkansas state senator W. C. Mitchell as an agent for the survivors and authorized him to pick up his grandchildren and the other orphans. He was to pursue the strictest economy but not at the expense of the health and comfort of the children. Mitchell set out for Fort Leavenworth on August 10, 1859, and reached the post on August 22. Three days later the children arrived from Utah in fine health. The friends and relations of the five boys and ten girls took charge of the unfortunates on September 15 at Carrollton, Arkansas.75

The children's reception at the Carroll County Courthouse remained alive in the minds of participants for more than half a century. Arkansas senator James H. Berry recalled witnessing the return as a youth of seventeen. He saw the children lined up on benches at the village courthouse, while Mitchell "told the people whose children they were, at least, whose he thought they were." Berry noted Sarah Dunlap's broken arm, which had not healed properly and dangled at her side. Berry later saw war in the border states in all its horrors, but nothing ever impressed him as much as the sight of the orphans. Their fathers, mothers, brothers, and sisters were "dead on the far-off plains of Utah, and they [were] absolutely without means, with no human being to look to." The rescued children could not remember much, Berry recalled,

> but they could tell that white men and not all Indians assisted in the massacre. They could tell it was a white man who came into their corral and induced the emigrants to give up their guns; that it was white men that drove the

wagons in which they rode; that it was white men who shot the wounded men who had been placed in one of the wagons.[76]

Mitchell provided a home for his grandchildren, Prudence Angeline and Georgia Ann, the daughters of Lorenzo Dow and Nancy Dunlap. Rebecca, Louisa, and the wounded Sarah, the daughters of Jesse and Mary Dunlap, went to their uncle, James Douglas Dunlap. Christopher Carson and Triphenia Fancher found a home with their cousin, Hampton Bynum Fancher; "Kit" died single in 1873, while Triphenia married, had nine children, and in 1897 died at age forty-four.[77] Relatives and friends in Arkansas made homes for the other survivors, except for Saphrona Huff, who settled with her grandfather Brown in Tennessee. The Miller children returned to Johnson County and lived with their aunt, Nancy Cameron Littleton. "They always acted so strange and bewildered," she said, "and the youngest child was like a wild goose."[78]

John T. Baker's widow, Mary, took charge of her three grandchildren. Elizabeth Baker recalled that her grandmother identified William Twitty by his disfigured index finger and the girls by "clothing, and the sunbonnets which were quilted in a certain design still in [their] possession." Her younger sister, Sarah Francis, remembered they were treated as heroes and were given a buggy parade through Harrison. Her grandmother, "a stout woman and mighty dignified, too," waited for the children on her porch. "When we came along the road leading up to the house she was pacing back and forth but when she caught sight of us she ran down the path and grabbed hold of us, one after the other and gave us a powerful hug." Sarah's old mammy, Leah, caught her up in her arms and would not let her go. She carried the child around all the rest of the day and even cooked supper with her in her arms. Leah baked a special apple turnover for each of the children. "We had creamed potatoes for supper that night, too, and they sure tasted good. I've been specially fond of creamed potatoes ever since," Sarah said. She remembered, "I called all of the women I saw 'mother.' I guess I was still hoping to find my own mother, and every time I called a woman 'mother,' she would break out crying."[79]

"I was intimately acquainted with the most of the persons killed in that train," a witness wrote on the orphans' return to Carroll County. "It almost chills the blood in my veins to think of the horrible affair, and how those little fellows have suffered. It does seem to me that our government at least ought to make ample provision for the education and raising of those children."[80] In the chaos of the Civil War, the call went unheeded. Various schemes to get compensation for the orphans from the government or the LDS church persisted well into the twentieth century, but they grew up during the war and came of age in the grinding poverty of Reconstruction. Few of them received much education; some of them prospered, but most became, like their dead parents, simple, hardworking country-folk. None of the survivors, even those with no living memory of the massacre, ever forgot the horror that had overtaken them on the road to California. One of the girls would wake up screaming because of her memories of Mountain Meadows. For generations, "emigrant families remembered what happened." It was a memory that refused to die.[81]

To Refute the Lies: Brigham Young's Defense

In the wake of the massacre, fear, disgust, and a general economic collapse resulted in a general depopulation of the southern Utah settlements. While staying with John D. Lee in August 1858, George A. Smith revoked the orders requiring Mormons to get permission from their local leaders before they could move. This merely acknowledged that a majority of the settlers of the Iron Mission had already abandoned their homes. Smith claimed the failure of the iron company caused the desertions, but the demoralizing impact of the massacre also had its effect. Brooks reported that 857 families had lived at Cedar City in 1857, but two years later only 386 were left. Official church records indicate the depopulation was even more dramatic, that only about twenty families remained in Cedar City in April 1859.[82]

Smith "disorganized the Stake" at Cedar City on July 31, 1859, releasing Bishop Klingensmith, stake president Haight, and counselor Higbee from their religious callings. The virtual collapse of the population in the south undoubtedly contributed to the reorganization of the stake, but Isaac Haight asked for his release, claiming persecution by enemies who, he said, "swore they would destroy me if they could get me, and there was little prospect of my being home much." The murderers at Mountain Meadows were now known outlaws, although they long retained their standing in their communities. John Higbee served as mayor of Cedar City from 1867 to 1871.[83]

After Cradlebaugh's inquiry, keeping notorious murderers in high LDS church positions was no longer tenable. Protecting them, however, became a priority. The involvement of high church leaders in preventing prosecution of the crime reveals the level of support the killers received. Lee had engaged two attorneys to defend him should he be "arrested & brought before the District court upon the charge of aiding in the Massacre at the Meadows." He wrote in August 1859, "Although I am innocent of the crime, yet I am compelld to employ council to direct the case in the prope[r] channel." One of Lee's lawyers, Apostle Smith, had personally investigated the crime for Brigham Young and was well qualified to direct Lee's case through the proper channels. A month later an express warned Lee that a company of federal marshals was on its way south to shoot him down, along with Klingensmith, Haight, Higbee, and Stewart, each of whom had a bounty of $5,000 on his head. More ominously, the message warned Lee not to "expect Justice from the court, neither Sucour, Simpathy, or Pity from our Brethren."[84]

When Marion Shelton, a Mormon schoolteacher, tried to locate the suspect on September 11, one of Lee's wives said he had gone to the mountains with seven hundred Paiute warriors. Meeting the fugitive that evening, Shelton learned that Lee "had heard that the Soldiers had a writ for him and he was determined not to be taken. He had three Colts buckled on him." Lee apparently had agreed to give Jacob Forney a statement describing his role in the massacre, for Shelton "had some business with him in relation to the statement he was going to make." Lee refused to tell Shelton anything and "would make no statement or have any business with any one but those whom he chose."[85]

Throughout summer 1859 Mormon leaders resisted growing pressure from the federal authorities to bring the perpetrators of the massacre to justice. Governor Cumming had proposed "a surrender by the church of the fugitives, upon condition that the judges shall have a certain understanding with them as to the constitution of their juries," Justices Cradlebaugh and Sinclair charged. The federal judges "indignantly spurned" such an arrangement.[86]

Brigham Young held a series of meetings in Salt Lake with Apostles Lyman and Smith in August 1859, where they apparently discussed the recent inquiry into the massacre. Young met with U.S. Attorney Alexander Wilson on August 22, 1859. He knew that Wilson had spent $4,000 on his recent wedding and was unable to pay his bills, and he told Thomas Kane he was "sorry to say that District Attorney Wilson makes much use of liquor altogether too freely for his own good." Wilson had asked Young why he had not brought the guilty parties to justice. The prophet replied that "if law and justice could take place, no one would be more willing than he." When Wilson reached Washington, D.C., in November 1859, Mormon officials wanted the U.S. Attorney "to refute the lies being told about Utah." For unknown reasons, Wilson seemed ready to argue the Mormon case in the nation's capital.[87]

But Washington could not ignore the obvious lack of progress in prosecuting the men involved in the massacre. In fall 1859 the Utah correspondent for the *San Francisco Bulletin* reported the arrival of Col. Samuel C. Stambaugh with instructions to Governor Cumming from the president to investigate the massacre at Mountain Meadows. Buchanan had reportedly "rapped Cumming over the knuckles" for his failure to execute the law. The governor assigned William Rogers to act as U.S. marshal for Stambaugh's inquiry. When Rogers learned that Cumming had named Bill Hickman, Porter Rockwell, and other "notorious 'Destroying Angels'" to the civil posse assigned to help him arrest the suspects, Rogers "indignantly spurned the proposition." The *Bulletin*'s correspondent complained Cumming was inclined to whitewash everything and "would shield the devil himself" rather than support the army against the Mormons.[88]

For his part, Brigham Young did nothing to further the prosecution of the crime. As a federal officer in 1857, Indian Superintendent Young could have tried to stop the robbery of the surviving children. After all, as attorney Robert Baskin caustically noted, most citizens of the territory regarded an order from Young "as a divine command." Had the Mormon leader actually wanted the Mountain Meadows murderers brought to justice, Baskin said, the guilty parties certainly would have been indicted and punished "long before the lapse of seventeen years."[89]

Thomas Kane pleaded with Brigham Young to provide him with "affidavits and evidence concerning the Mountain Meadow massacre." The president had interrogated Kane about the murders, and Attorney General Black repeatedly contacted him about the matter.[90] The request set off another flurry of activity in Salt Lake as Smith and the clerks in the church historian's office spent the evening of December 8 "copying correspondence from G.A.S. to Prest. B. Young in regard to the Mountain Meadow Massacre, till 9 P.M."[91] Young responded to Kane in mid-December:

> I occasionally perceive, from papers East and West, that the massacre at the Mountain Meadows still elicits more or less notice and comment, a great share of which is not very creditable either to candor or veracity. And some of the efforts made to arrive at the facts in that case have not been characterized by that good policy, impartiality, and observance of the people's rights which should accompany legal proceedings in a Republican Government, else I presume the affair, long ere this date, would have been thoroughly understood and correctly adjudicated.
>
> Neither yourself, nor any one acquainted with me, will require my assurance that, had I been appraised of the intended onslaught at the Meadows, I should have used such efforts for its prevention as the time, distance, and my influence and facilities, should have permitted. The horrifying event transpired without my knowledge, except from after report, and the recurring thought of it ever caused a shudder in my feelings. It is a subject exclusively within the province of judicial proceedings, and I have known and still prefer to know nothing touching the affair, until I in common with the people, learn the facts as they may be developed before those whose right it is to investigate and adjudicate thereupon. Colonel, you may think this a singular statement, but the facts of the massacre of men, women, and children are so shocking and crucifying to my feelings, that I have not suffered myself to hear any more about them than the circumstances of conversation compelled.[92]

Despite his delicacy and general ignorance about a matter that threatened to destroy him, Young artfully shifted the discussion from murder to civil rights. He sent Kane one of Smith's 1858 reports, which he assured his ally was "the most reliable that can be obtained, until such time as the matter can receive an impartial judicial investigation." The matter could long since have been resolved if the federal judges would only leave it to the probate courts. "Bayonet courts" like John Cradlebaugh's were "not likely to make much progress towards bringing persons, whether guilty or not guilty, before them." Although every federal court had ruled that Utah's probate courts had no criminal jurisdiction, Young asked for another written opinion on the matter from "the learned Attorney General of the U.S."[93]

Remarkably, this cumbersome strategy paid off. At a critical moment, Brigham Young diverted the attention of the beleaguered Buchanan administration from a question of mass murder to one of legal technicalities. His obstruction of justice in Utah delayed the prosecution of the Mountain Meadows criminals until the outbreak of the Civil War absorbed the nation. The public lost interest in the affairs of a remote and inconsequential territory, and for fourteen years Young's power stopped any federal prosecution of the crime.

When it came time to account for Governor Brigham Young's failure to investigate Mountain Meadows or to help his successor prosecute the case, his defenders assigned blame to the federal officer who had been the most consistent champion of Mormon rights, Alfred Cumming. The governor had used his office to protect the Saints, going beyond moderation to leniency "to assuage the bitterness rankling in their minds." He considered indicting the Mormon leaders as accessories to the murders at Mountain Meadows, but he accepted their control of the territory and sought to avoid adding to their claims of persecution.[94] Cumming feared that the Mormons would go to war rather than submit to a vigorous prosecution of the crime, and he had no stomach for the prospect of such a bloodbath. His hard work to implement his moderate policies won the governor the contempt of non-Mormons.

In return, once Cumming was dead and unable to defend his record, Brigham Young blamed him for the long delay in justice. And subsequent generations of Mormon historians also shifted the onus for the embarrassing failure to prosecute the crime to the hapless Georgian.[95] Cumming's critics blamed him for trusting Young's promises. Years later, when one man was prosecuted for the murders, an old friend recalled a conversation he had with Cumming in about 1862. The former governor complained that despite his promise to "get out the whole truth," Young never made an effort to track down the murderers, and "God Almighty couldn't convict the butchers unless Brigham Young was willing." The Mormon leader was "one of the damndest rascals that ever went unhung" and "the prime mover in the conspiracy that consummated that massacre" who should have been indicted as an accessory before the fact for the murders. "Brigham Young deceived me, Cumming said."[96]

Apostate Charles Wandell claimed Cumming told him how keenly he felt his failure to investigate the murders at Mountain Meadows, and he upbraided Brigham Young for lying to him. The political situation left him tied hand and foot, however, and he "could only move as Brigham moved him." No man saw this more clearly than Cumming himself.[97] Despite his many good intentions, in the face of intimidation Governor Cumming repeatedly surrendered his authority and dignity to Brigham Young. In the end, this decent but inept man lacked the courage to pursue the case.

With the onset of the Civil War, Gov. Alfred Cumming, the last non-Mormon federal official still in the territory, left Utah on May 17, 1861. T. B. H. Stenhouse asked the departing governor how his successor would fare. "Well enough, if he will do nothing. There is nothing to do. Alfred Cumming is Governor of the Territory, but Brigham Young is Governor *of the people*." He mused, "This is a curious place!"[98]

There is No More a United States

The national crisis of 1861 revived Brigham Young's spirits and renewed his millennial expectations. Once again the signs of the times appeared to indicate the approach of the Second Coming. The Saints recalled Joseph Smith's 1832 war prophecy, which had predicted that a civil war would begin in South Carolina and eventually consume the entire world. Young was unusually cheerful as he contemplated the disintegration of the Union following its "wicked attempts to root up the Kingdom of God, and afflict his saints." Speaking in the tabernacle in March, Young said, "There is no Union to leave; it is all disunion. Our Government is shivered to pieces, but the Kingdom of God will increase."[99]

When war erupted in April, the Mormon prophet confidently believed it would continue until both sides had destroyed each other and prepared the way for the inevitable triumph of the Saints. An especially welcome sign was the removal of troops from Utah. Philip St. George Cooke struck the army's colors at Camp Floyd (now renamed Fort Crittenden because of Secretary of War John B. Floyd's treachery), but most federal soldiers had long since left the territory when Cooke and his men abandoned the post on July 27, 1861.[100]

The collapse of the Union and the removal of federal forces from Utah encouraged Young to continue his support of religious violence. On May 12, 1861, he gave a strange blessing to Howard O. Spencer, a fugitive for the murder of an army sergeant on a Salt Lake street in August 1859. "President Young set him apart to kill every poor devil that should seek to take his life and gave him permission when he came across a poor mobocrat to use him up."[101]

Perhaps the guns of Fort Sumter prompted Brigham Young to make his first visit to the southern settlements since the end of the Utah War. Such excursions were elaborate processions. Young's daughter Clarissa recalled her father was "very particular and careful of the smallest detail, and when he traveled he took with him everything that anyone could possibly want." As Young's caravan passed through the rural villages, his followers greeted the great man with military escorts and brass bands, and even the poorest hamlets tried to provide an elaborate feast. "Armful after armful of the choicest fruits, meats, and vegetables of every variety were placed upon the tables," was how one of Heber Kimball's sons remembered such meals. "Waiters actually groaned and tables tottered under the heavy weight of custard pies, frosted cakes, preserved fruits, and scores of other delicacies awaiting the hungry Salt Lakers."[102]

A key purpose of the May 1861 excursion was to ensure that southern Utahns understood the need for silence on the subject of Mountain Meadows. John D. Lee met his adoptive father near his mansion in Washington County. Brigham Young greeted him with a hearty welcome and took him into his buggy. The entourage of twenty-three carriages followed them to Lee's mansion house, where the "whole company seemed to Enjoy themselves well." While Young's party visited Toquerville,

Lee butchered a steer and two sheep and prepared a second feast at Harmony, this time for some 125 people. Lee had never seen Brigham Young feel better. The prophet spoke for two hours in Lee's Family Hall. He praised Harmony as "the best Fort that had ever been built in this Territory."[103]

After this meeting, Lee recorded the private conversation in which the prophet revealed his feelings about the massacre. He said the "company that was used up at the Mountain Meadowes" were the fathers, mothers, brothers, sisters, and relatives of those who had murdered the prophets and merited their fate. The killing of the women and children was "only thing that ever troubled him," but under the circumstances it could not be avoided. Young feared those who wanted to betray the brethren, but he told Lee those who revealed the secret would be damned and go down to Hell—and for now, such traitors had run away. He then told Lee what had happened six days earlier as he pondered the fate of the Arkansans at "the monument that contained their Bones."[104]

On a cold May morning in 1861, the Mormon prophet and his entourage of some sixty men, women, and children stopped at Mountain Meadows. They viewed Carleton's monument at the site of the wagon battle, "put up at the burial place of 120 persons killed by Indians in 1857." The monument was beginning to tumble down, but the wooden cross and its inscription, "Vengeance is mine; I will repay, saith the Lord," still stood above the rock cairn.[105]

Brigham Young read the verse aloud, altering the text to fit his mood: "Vengeance is mine saith the Lord; I *have* repaid." Dudley Leavitt recalled how Young directed the destruction of the monument so that all present could deny that he had ordered it. "He didn't say another word. He didn't give an order. He just lifted his right arm to the square, and in five minutes there wasn't one stone left upon another. He didn't have to tell us what he wanted done. We understood."[106]

14

A Hideous Lethargic Dream

On his way to California in 1865, attorney Robert N. Baskin met Thomas Hearst, a mining agent, in Salt Lake. Hearst persuaded him to visit the mines at Alta and assured him that its vast mineral wealth and the soon-to-be-completed transcontinental railroad made Utah Territory an excellent place to practice law. What Baskin saw in the steep-walled canyon convinced him Hearst was right, and the short, cool, red-headed lawyer abandoned his plans to go to California, rented an office, and began to study the territorial statutes. Two odd provisions caught his attention: the first directed that no Utahn could be compelled to pay an attorney, and the second dictated that English common law, which banned polygamy, had no force in the territory.[1]

Like most outsiders, the order and neatness of the city impressed the young man. At first Baskin found it hard to credit stories about the evils of Mormonism, especially the frequent assertions he heard that the massacre at Mountain Meadows was ordered by Mormon officials and was carried out by the militia. The atrocity "was so revolting and showed such depravity and utter disregard for all religious restraint" that he was loath to believe it. Stephen DeWolfe, former editor of the *Valley Tan*, assured Baskin the stories were true. After DeWolfe published William Rogers's first detailed report of the massacre in 1860, police magistrate Jeter Clinton had demanded a retraction or he would not be responsible for DeWolfe's safety. The editor not only refused to print a retraction, he drafted a defiant editorial charging the murder had been sanctioned from the pulpit of the Mormon tabernacle. The next day Brigham Young's bookkeeper cursed DeWolfe "from head to toe, and wound up by cursing [his] powers and parts of procreation." DeWolfe told Baskin he threw the man out of his office.[2]

Kindred spirits, Baskin and DeWolfe became law partners. Rumors later said Baskin had shot someone in Ohio and married a woman he had represented in a divorce case. Newspaperman George Alfred Townsend, probably a hired Mormon sympathizer, vilified Baskin as "lean, lank, rather dirty and frowsy," but even Townsend had to concede he was "a lawyer of shrewdness and coolness."[3] Baskin went on to a remarkable career as mayor of Salt Lake and chief justice of Utah's supreme court. He would also prosecute John D. Lee for murder and spend the next fifty years fiercely battling the political power of Mormonism.

As Baskin's initial reaction indicated, the very enormity of the massacre provided its perpetrators with one of their best defenses. Sir Richard Burton, a perceptive observer of nineteenth-century cultures who visited the Utah capital in 1860, dismissed the crime with a footnote in his book about the City of the Saints. He reported the LDS defense: if the massacre took place, why had the murderers not been brought to justice? The Mormons could not be held "responsible for the misfortunes which men who insult and ill-treat the natives bring upon themselves."[4]

There was no reliable account of the atrocity, and exactly what had happened was hotly debated. During his 1861 visit to what he called "the only absolute monarchy in America," Samuel Clemens heard that the dreadful massacre "was the work of the Indians entirely, and that the Gentiles had meanly tried to fasten it upon the Mormons." Some said both Indians and Mormons were to blame, while others insisted the Mormons "were almost if not wholly and completely responsible for that most treacherous and pitiless butchery." Having "got the story in all these different shapes," Clemens gave up trying to settle the question after two days. He wryly noted, "I have seen newspaper correspondents do it in one."[5]

Maintaining the mystery that surrounded the event, however, required the continued silence of southern Utah. Lee claimed Brigham Young told a Cedar City congregation that members of the Fancher party had persecuted the Saints and "killed our Prophets in Carthage Jail." Their relatives had rejected the survivors as the children of thieves, outlaws, and murderers. Young had learned there were persons ready to identify the killers, but anyone who did not keep the secret would "die a *dog's* death, and be *damned*, and go to *hell.*" "I do not want to hear of any more *treachery among my people.*" Young's words, said Lee, "gave great comfort to all of us who were out in the woods keeping out of the way of the officers."[6]

Lee's story was clearly incorrect in some particulars, but there is no question the prophet's public statements masked an official policy of secrecy. No reliable accounts of Young's southern Utah sermons after the massacre have survived, but the silence adopted in the region for generations was a fact. The need to maintain different public and private policies made managing the Mountain Meadows problem a never-ending headache for Brigham Young. In public he mourned that justice was delayed, but in private he made sure nothing was done to bring the killers to trial. The complications of such tactics hounded the Mormon prophet for the rest of his life.

THE EARTH A SEA OF WATER:
THE FLOOD OF 1862

A remarkable prosperity blessed John D. Lee in the years immediately following the massacre. He acquired wives, children, land, wealth, and power at an astonishing rate. At Washington he built a stone mansion and molasses mill that netted him $40 a day during the harvest. At the 1860 Washington County fair, the Lee family took first place awards for best mare, colt, heifer, cotton, and man's straw hat. He claimed property worth $49,500 in the 1860 census, indicating he was by far the richest man in southern Utah. To celebrate his prosperity, Lee planned to abandon the crumbling adobe fort at Harmony and build another mansion, along with cottages for each of his wives. Called to be presiding elder of the branch at Harmony on December 22, 1861, he was sustained with the typical unanimous vote and invited everyone in the settlement to a great Christmas feast. Before the celebration ended, it began to rain. It would not stop for forty days.[7]

The great storm transformed the face of southern Utah and wreaked havoc with its people. Brigham Young had sent three hundred families to revive the southern settlements, and the rain caught the new settlers camped in their wagons on the town site at St. George. Years of overgrazing took their toll as the rains washed out fertile bottomlands, leaving gorges and gravel where lush grasses had grown. Great torrents ripped through the fields of Mountain Meadows and cut the trace of Magotsu Creek into a deep arroyo. The resulting disruption of the water table changed the valley from a luxuriant oasis into a sagebrush plain, a transformation that helped to inspire the local belief that God had cursed the place.

Dudley Leavitt and William Hamblin abandoned their homes at Gunlock for tents and watched their belongings float off down the Santa Clara. The flood swept away all but one corner of the stone citadel at Fort Clara. The deluge destroyed all the hamlets on the upper Virgin—Rockville, Grafton, and Pocketville—along with Philip Klingensmith's house, cane mill, and blacksmith shop at Adventure. Nathan Tenney lost his home and part of his family.[8]

At Harmony, Lee closed his 1861 journal by noting "prospects dark and gloomy; the Earth a sea of water"—and the worst was yet to come. Lee's barn and part of the old fort collapsed on January 15, 1862. The sun appeared briefly on January 31 but soon vanished, and a new storm dumped ten inches of snow. Lee had moved all of his families to higher ground except for Sarah Caroline's, and now the upper story of her house collapsed and crushed two of their sleeping children, killing them. Lee, who saw the hand of God in everything, blamed himself for the catastrophe.[9]

We Ploughed Around It: Lincoln and the Mormons

During the sixteen months between the closing of Fort Crittenden in July 1861 and the arrival of the California Volunteers in October 1862, there was no American military presence in the Mormon kingdom. The resurgence of militant theocracy and a series of violent episodes made this period one of the most significant and revealing in the history of the territory.[10] The outbreak of civil war helped to trigger this revival. "This Nation is guilty of sheding the Blood of the Lords anointed, of his Prophets & Saints and the Lord Almighty has decreed their destruction," Apostle Wilford Woodruff wrote as 1860 drew to a close. "The Lord has Commenced a Controversy with the American Government and Nation in 1860 and he will never cease untill they are destroyed from under heaven."[11]

One of the first victims of this new militant millennialism was Alfred Cumming's replacement as governor, John W. Dawson, who endured the rigors of federal service in Utah for a mere three weeks. In December 1861 he proposed that the territory meet its federal tax obligations to demonstrate its loyalty to the Union, open public schools, and survey the public lands. The local response was not favorable. Within days an unknown assailant fired five shots at a new federal judge on East Temple Street. After being accused of making sexual advances to a widow, Dawson left the territory on the eastbound stage. At Mountain Dell on New Year's Eve, local thugs robbed Dawson, beat him senseless, and may have castrated him. Two federal judges and the territory's Indian superintendent soon followed the governor east, for reasons, wrote the *Deseret News*, "best known to themselves."[12]

Yet as the Civil War weakened federal power in the West, Brigham Young faced growing resistance from inside the LDS church. English convert Joseph Morris had received revelations on the reform of the Mormon religion since 1857. He led a band of dissidents near Ogden and named the date—repeatedly—of Christ's return. Justice John F. Kinney, who "did nothing without first checking with Brigham Young," issued a warrant on May 10, 1862, to Col. Robert T. Burton of the Nauvoo Legion for the arrest of Morris and his counselors. The Morrisites were justifiably paranoid, and when a band of Indians passed through their fort, they concluded these were the Indians responsible for the Mountain Meadows massacre and "that they had again allied themselves with the Mormons to repeat the bloody deed." With tales of the massacre fresh in their minds, the Morrisites were reluctant to surrender. If they did, they feared they might "be letting themselves and their families in for a similar fate."[13]

After an artillery bombardment that killed two women and horribly wounded a fourteen-year-old girl, Burton led an assault on Kingston Fort that killed Morris, a second dissident leader, and two more women. One of the women had cried that this was "another Mountain Meadow Massacre" before Burton shot her. Witnesses charged that coroner Jeter Clinton cut the spinal cord of one of the victims. Burton was eventually found innocent of willfully killing Morris and the women, but suspicion remained that the Morrisites were murdered on the direct orders of Brigham Young.[14]

The Saints hoped to use the Civil War to consummate their dream of statehood for Deseret. The legislature drafted a constitution, elected William Hooper and George Q. Cannon provisional senators, and in April 1862 petitioned Congress for admission to the Union. Territorial delegate John Bernhisel had warned, "There is not the least prospect of our being admitted for a few years yet," and a week later the committee on territories unanimously denied Deseret statehood. "I do not know," Bernhisel wrote, "a single member of either the Senate or the House who will vote for the admission of our Territory."[15]

That summer Bernhisel reported his conversation with John S. Phelps of Missouri, who "brought up that horrid Mountain Meadow Massacre." "This atrocious affair has done us," Bernhisel said, "and still continues to do us as a people, incalculable injury, and will prove a serious obstacle to our admission into the Union as a sovereign and independent State." He told Brigham Young he was sure "the miscreants who were engaged in this cold blooded and diabolical deed, will have a fearful account to render in the judgment of the first day."[16] In Utah, however, they had nothing to fear.

Mormon historians have generally glossed over Utah's Civil War history with an anecdote describing how Abraham Lincoln explained his Mormon policy to businessman Stenhouse. When clearing land, the Lincolns occasionally encountered a log that "was too hard to split, too wet to burn and too heavy to move, so [they] ploughed around it." The president had resolved to treat the Mormons like the stump and to let them alone. But Lincoln's Utah policy was not simply to plow around the Mormons; he was determined to fence them in. To do this, he sent enough military power to Utah Territory to enforce federal authority. Despite efforts to have Brigham Young reappointed governor, none of the officers Lincoln named to positions in Utah were Mormons. He carefully managed the political situation while challenging the Mormons' most treasured doctrine. Lincoln had observed during a speech in 1857 there was nothing in the U.S. Constitution or law that banned polygamy, and he corrected the situation in 1862 when he signed Justin Morrill's bill to ban polygamy in the territories. The Mormons simply ignored the law, and in the tumult of the Civil War it became a dead letter.[17]

Beyond calling up a single company of Lot Smith's cavalry for ninety days, Lincoln did not mobilize Utah's Nauvoo Legion. Instead he sent Col. Patrick Edward Connor and the Third California Infantry, troops desperately needed elsewhere, to guard the overland trails and ensure the loyalty of the Saints. Unfettered by the politics that had shackled his predecessors, Connor marched his troops into Utah in October 1862 and occupied the heights east of Great Salt Lake City, where he built Camp Douglas.[18]

Despite their mutual hostility, the Mormons and the military collaborated in the largest massacre of American Indians in the history of the West. Perhaps hoping for a

Shoshoni victory, Porter Rockwell guided Connor's men to Bear River where the soldiers attacked Bear Hunter's entrenched band at dawn on January 29, 1863, killing at least two hundred fifty men, women, and children. Slaughtering Indians was about as much common ground as existed between the two groups, and the army and the church settled into a standoff. Although the two rivals never met, Connor and Young eventually developed a grudging respect for each other. Connor believed he could use the territory's mineral wealth to bring in non-Mormon settlers and break the hold of the LDS church on Utah politics, a strategy that ultimately greatly diminished Brigham Young's political power.[19]

So it was no wonder Brigham Young expressed his contempt for "such Cursed scoundrels as Abe Lincoln and his Minions." Wilford Woodruff predicted the nation was doomed to destruction and no power could save it. The American people had lost "all right and title to Redemption or Salvation at the Hand of the Lord or his Saints." Let judgment be pored out upon the land, Woodruff prayed, "untill the Blood of the Prophets & Saints is avenged before the Lord."[20]

Such Precision and Exactitude:
The Brigham Young Indian Accounts

Carleton's report had linked Lee, Dame, Huntington, and Klingensmith to the massacre, and the appearance of their names in the bills Young submitted to the federal government apparently finally stirred curiosity in Washington. Former federal officials such as Garland Hurt and John Cradlebaugh, now territorial delegate from Nevada, complained bitterly of Young's abuse of office as territorial Indian superintendent.

In August 1860 William P. Dole, U.S. commissioner of Indian affairs, ordered Utah Indian Superintendent Benjamin Davis to examine former superintendent Brigham Young's accounts for illegal charges. Davis was directed to conduct "a rigid scrutiny of all the claims and accounts in question." He met with Dimick Huntington, Levi Stewart, and other witnesses on February 7, 1861, to review the accounts from the last quarter of 1856 to the first quarter of 1858. The testimony impressed Davis, for in all his many years at the bar he could not recall a single instance in which so many witnesses "concurred with such precision and exactitude." Their perfect recollection, he wrote, "could not have failed to convince the most skeptical of the truthfulness of their statements."[21]

Superintendent Davis completed his report early in 1862. He also determined that the government owed Brigham Young $346.46 for his service as territorial governor from July 1 to November 20, 1857, when Alfred Cumming arrived in the territory. The government agreed to pay the salary, but Bernhisel regretted that the money had been credited to Young's Indian accounts, which despite Davis's glowing endorsement remained unpaid. The agent's report led Commissioner Dole to conclude the claims had been satisfactorily proven, except for one "peculiar transaction." Blacksmith

B. F. Pendleton admitted he substituted other goods for the coats, vests, and shirts he had billed to the government. Huntington had sworn the charges were correct, but Dole considered "his 'certificates' as more a matter of form than fact."[22]

The accounts were more fiction than fact, for Brooks believed Brigham Young charged the government for property stolen from the murdered emigrants.[23] Most surprising was Levi Stewart's claim to have distributed more than $3,500 worth of goods to "sundry bands of Indians near Mountain Meadow" on September 30, 1857, nineteen days after the massacre. Both Huntington and Lee certified "on honor, that [they] were present, and saw the articles mentioned distributed to Tat-se-gobbits, Non-cap-in, Mo-quee-tus, Chick-eroo, Quo-na-rah, Young-quick, Jackson, and Agra-pootes and their bands."[24] Lee was in Salt Lake on that date, and it appears Huntington was too, but his sworn statement lent credence to Carleton's charge that Huntington had carried Young's orders south and was present at the massacre.

Despite these problems and a host of internal contradictions, the report exonerated Brigham Young and recommended that Congress pay his claims. Congress hesitated, and Bernhisel feared he could not get money in the current session and perhaps not until the Civil War ended, "if it ever comes to an end." He suggested "employing the machinery (the men & means) frequently resorted to here in prosecuting private claims." Bernhisel knew a man who could solve the problem for 22.5 percent of the final settlement. "It is a very difficult thing to get a money claim through congress now from what it was before the bombardment of Fort Sumpter, and it may be more difficult hereafter."[25] Later that year prospects were much brighter, and Bernhisel expected to get the accounts approved during the next session.[26] The "fixer" was Simpson P. Moses, for in 1863 Young asked Judge John Fitch Kinney to report "what and how much" Moses was doing to settle the claims.[27]

Cradlebaugh denounced Young's "claim for thirty or forty thousand dollars, which includes about four thousand dollars for goods distributed by John D. Lee to the Indians about the Mountain Meadows, within twenty days after the massacre." In 1861 Congress had appropriated some $52,000 to compensate Utah Territory for suppressing Indian hostilities during 1852 and 1853, a claim Cradlebaugh insisted was fraudulent. Young's 1857 accounts included "pay to Lee while he was engaged in the commission of the massacre." "Whether Brigham will get it or not," the judge wondered, "I do not know." According to Young's biographer, "payment of these accounts, totaling $34,145, was finally made in 1866."[28]

Even as the nation was embroiled in civil war, investigations into affairs in Utah continued. Brigham Young learned in March 1863 that one J. M. Rossé had been solicited "to represent to the President of the U.S. the causes of complaints which have been made against [him] and the people of Utah" by federal officers. Young wrote Rossé to deny disloyalty, lawlessness, and the allegation "that influential Mormons encourage the robbery and massacre of emigrants by Indians." Young unequivocally announced, "I have the means of knowing that it is absolutely false."[29] The

Mormon leader seldom spoke about the massacre in public, but the next Sunday he addressed the subject in the Old Tabernacle.

"Who wanted the army of 1857 here? Who sent for them?" Brigham Young asked. "Liars, thieves, murderers, gamblers, whoremasters, and speculators in the rights and blood of the Mormon people." The government wanted to destroy the Mormons, in violation of every principle of law and justice. The army assigned to "use up the Mormons" arrived just as "a company of emigrants were traveling on the south route to California."

> Nearly all of that company were destroyed by the Indians. That unfortunate affair has been laid to the charge of the whites. A certain judge that was then in this Territory wanted the whole army to accompany him to Iron county to try the whites for the murder of that company of emigrants. I told Governor Cumming that if he would take an unprejudiced judge into the district where that horrid affair occurred, I would pledge myself that every man in the regions round about should be forthcoming when called for, to be condemned or acquitted as an impartial, unprejudiced judge and jury should decide; and I pledged him that the court should be protected from any violence or hindrance in the prosecution of the laws; and if any were guilty of the blood of those who suffered in the Mountain Meadow massacre, let them suffer the penalty of the law; but to this day they have not touched the matter, for fear the Mormons would be acquitted from the charge of having any hand in it, and our enemies would thus be deprived of a favorite topic to talk about, when urging hostility against us. "The Mountain Meadow massacre! Only think of the Mountain Meadow massacre!!" is their cry from one end of the land to the other.[30]

Brigham Young failed to explain why he did not now use his considerable power to resolve the issue. "[He] did not mean a word of it—not a word," Lee wrote in 1877, recalling Young's pledge. "It was one of Brigham Young's cunning dodges to blind the government." Much about how the legal system operated in Utah is revealed by the name of the probate judge in Washington County before and after the massacre: John D. Lee.[31]

Lee's neighbors knew that asking too many questions about what had happened at Mountain Meadows could have fatal consequences. Three horsemen confronted massacre veteran Dudley Leavitt on his way to a gristmill. Someone had been talking, they said, telling stories and using men's names. "I looked them straight in the eyes," said Leavitt. "I don't know what you're talking about," he said. "You are the first to ever mention any massacre to me. This is the first time I ever heard tell of such a thing." The men let Leavitt go.[32]

Olive Coombs was not so fortunate. A San Bernardino refugee, the widow shared her fellow exiles' interest in the murders. Mormon adventurer Walter Gibson told Brigham Young the massacre was the chief grounds for apostasy in San Bernardino.

After her husband died on the road to Utah, Coombs settled in Cedar City with two daughters to teach school. She "acted too interested in this incident, asked too many questions about it. Word went out that she was collecting evidence and planned to publish her findings." A barroom debate accused her of "being a wolf in sheep's clothing, pretending to teach their children while she tried to fasten crimes on their parents." George Wood, who had been a militia officer in Cedar City in 1857, went to her house and shot Coombs twice, killing her. The Parowan probate court convicted him of murder and sentenced him to life in prison, but Gov. James Doty pardoned Woods in 1865.[33]

To Murder Dr. Robinson

The triumph of the Union cause in 1865 postponed the millennial hopes of the Mormons and once again forced their leaders to deal with Babylon. The LDS church had long discouraged the settlement of non-Mormons in Utah Territory. "I would make a wall so thick and so high around the Territory," Brigham Young declared, "that it would be impossible for the Gentiles to get over or through it." Yet the legal basis of the Mormons' own Utah land claims remained ambiguous. In 1866 entrepreneur and physician J. King Robinson began building a workshop for a hospital he hoped to erect at Warm Springs in Salt Lake. Robinson challenged the territory's land laws in court, seriously threatening existing titles. The police tore down his workshop and warned him "it would not be healthy for him to renew his operations there." When another attorney declined to represent Robinson for fear it would subject him to personal violence, Robert Baskin instituted the doctor's lawsuit against the police.[34]

Robinson's claims not only challenged LDS land titles but also threatened to open the floodgates of non-Mormon emigration. In fall 1866 a mob armed with axes vandalized one of Robinson's buildings and demolished his bowling alley. The doctor had the chief of police and members of his force arrested for destroying his property. Robinson called on Daniel Wells, then mayor of Great Salt Lake City, and asked him to restrain the police. Wells insulted the doctor and ordered him out of his house. At midnight two days later, a stranger called at Robinson's home and said that a friend of the doctor had been badly injured. Despite his wife's pleadings, the doctor accompanied the man to the city, where Robinson was brutally murdered at the corner of Main and Third South Streets. Witnesses saw seven persons flee the scene of the crime, but no one would identify the killers.[35]

Gen. Edward Connor had no doubt it was "Brighams destroying angels" who assassinated Dr. Robinson. "Great God how long is this state of things to last?" he asked the day after the murder. A loyal American citizen had been "shot down like a dog, for appealing to the Courts, for his rights. The Gentiles are Panic Stricken and dare not express opinions of the foul deed." The general believed he might be the next target but vowed, "As long as I have breath I shall denounce and cry aloud for vengeance on the foul assassins."[36]

Robert Baskin went to view the body of his dead friend, which bore graphic evidence of the brutality of the fatal attack with a knife or a hatchet and a pistol shot to the head. Baskin said, "I mentally resolved while looking upon the mutilated body of my murdered client, Doctor Robinson, to do all that I possibly could do to place in the hands of the federal authorities the power to punish the perpetrators of such heinous crimes."[37] The Mormon theocracy had acquired an implacable enemy, and the fearless Baskin would be as good as his word.

Brigham Young blamed the murder on non-Mormons who hoped to incriminate the church; "he had no doubt that some wretch had been hired for about $10.00 to murder Dr. Robinson." Young allegedly said the doctor was one of the worst men he had ever met: "He was saucy and impudent, and pushed himself right up against us." He regretted that Robinson's bowling alley had been vandalized under cover of darkness: "I'd have gutted it at noon, torn it down and destroyed it in the light of day, so that every man might see me." Young said he "was sorry that the doctor had been killed, for he wanted him to live and die in the ditch like a dog."[38]

Dr. Robinson's murder became a national scandal. Baskin recalled that Gen. William Tecumseh Sherman (whose military department included Utah) telegraphed Brigham Young. The general "hoped to hear of no more murders; that he was bound to give protection to all citizens and that murderers must be punished; that the country was full of tried and experienced soldiers who would be pleased to avenge any wrong committed against any American citizen." Baskin's memory was faulty, for Sherman actually sent his telegram six months before Robinson's death, in response to the murder of a non-Mormon who had married the polygamous wife of an absent missionary. Newton Brassfield was killed on a Salt Lake street thronged with people, and the assassin escaped and was never arrested.[39]

Responsible officers, General Sherman informed Young, had told him of the murder in Salt Lake of four men "styled Gentiles." The next day Young made a characteristic reply, assuring Sherman his information was unreliable. He asked for "the names of [his] informants, that the report may be corrected here." He conceded, "Mr. Brassfield came here and seduced a Mormon's wife, and was shot in the street by an unknown person; but neither I, nor the community at large, know any more about it than an inhabitant of St. Louis." Young said such outrageous slanders would have led to an outbreak of vigilantism in any other western community, and he blamed the excitement on a few speculators who hoped to profit from having troops sent to Utah. He assured the general that gentiles were as safe in Utah as Mormons, "and acts of violence occur more rarely in this City than in any other of its size in any of the new States or Territories."[40]

Young's policy of publicly denouncing the murders while privately shielding its perpetrators inevitably led to confusion. He said in a December 1866 sermon that a detective was coming to Utah to search for Dr. Robinson's murderers. Such crimes were "too horrible for me to contemplate," the prophet said. "The massacre at Haun's mill, and that of Joseph and Hyrum Smith, and the Mountain Meadow's massacre and the murder of Dr. Robinson are of this character." It was hard to believe even savages could perform such inhuman acts. "If any man, woman or child that ever lived has said that Brigham Young ever counseled them to commit crime of any description, they are liars in the face of heaven. If I am guilty of any such thing, let it be proved on me, and not go sneaking around insinuating that Brigham knows all about it."[41]

BETTER TRY THE REMEDY: GEORGE A. HICKS

George Hicks of Harmony took Brigham Young at his word. His song "Once I Lived in Cottonwood" gave eloquent voice to the challenges of pioneering in southern Utah. An independent soul, Hicks was "sometimes disposed to treat with levity the solemn sermonizing of the brethren."[42] When local authorities told him to stop singing the ballad U.S. soldiers had composed after visiting Mountain Meadows in 1859, he quoted Young's denunciation of the murderers in the January 1867 *Deseret News* and continued to sing the song. Hicks found Young's sermon so comforting that he carried the article in his pocket and read it to a great many people. "At length I was gently warned that my course of conduct would be punished if I continued," he said. Lee's adopted son, James Pace, said he "ought to be stopped from singing the song if it took [his] life," Hicks recalled in 1877. "[At a dance] Lee, Pace, and some of Lee's boys were to take me out 'and lay me aside' [if I sang the song]." Hicks learned of the plan and took his Navy Colt to the dance.[43]

For years his church's protection of the Mountain Meadows murderers had troubled Hicks. Young's sermon had generated considerable comment in southern Utah, but Lee stood up in a public meeting and claimed Brother Brigham uttered such sentiments "to *blind* the eyes of the gentiles" and satisfy a few disgruntled individuals like Hicks. A confused Hicks thought Lee's claim "was a base slander against a true servant of God" and finally wrote to Young in October 1867, asking what had prompted him to denounce the murderers. "If you are in favor of the Mountain meadows massacre I would like to know it," he said. Hicks believed Young was opposed to shedding blood but pointed out, "John D. Lee is in full fellow ship and is frequently called upon to preach much to [the] annoyance of Good men. Last Sunday he asked the Bishop for and obtained a recommend to Get another wife and will." Hicks hoped the perpetrators "of that bloody deed would soon be punished for their Crimes or [if] they were not punished, their names would be stricken from the Church books." This injustice caused Hicks "some trouble of mind." "A few words from you will dispose of all my dark fears," he wrote.[44]

Hicks mailed his humble letter from Kannarah, but postmaster John Willis intercepted the letter, put it on public exhibition at the post office, and then, incredibly, gave it to Lee. "I went to get it and *got nothing but insults for my trouble*," Hicks complained. Despite more than twenty-five years of loyal service to the LDS church, he had "been insulted in the public streets by some of John D. Lee's family only for encourageing the people to believe that the sixth commandment should be obeyed." Lee's boast that Brigham Young did not mean what he said about the massacre was not generally believed, Hicks said. "I scorned the idea at first but now I hardly know what to think, doubts and fears beginning to rise in my mind in relation to the matter, in short, my peace of mind is almost gone." Was it "possible that the Church whose destiny [he had] so long followed through sufering privation and sorrow" would protect "a Company of men whose hands have been stained with the blood of innocent women and children?" If Lee could not be punished for murder, Hicks asked that he be deprived of his standing in the church. Lee could then "say what he pleases at his own option and not at the expense of the Church." Hicks pleaded for "such words of Consideration as will be for my best good."[45]

An aggravated Brigham Young blasted off a harsh but typical reply. Although Hicks's letter simply asked him to explain where he stood on the matter and clearly expressed Hicks's hope that the perpetrators would soon be punished, Young pretended otherwise.

> What would be the judgment of any reasonable being after reading your letter, since you say, "The bloody scene passes before you day and night," and "it rests with such weight upon your mind" &c, why, that you yourself must have been a participator in the horrible deed. If this is correct, one can readily imagine why "it rests with such weight upon your mind," and "why you cannot sleep at nights"; the surprise would be that you could. In such a case, if you want a remedy—rope round the neck taken with a jerk would be very salutary.[46]

If the rope did not appeal to Hicks, continued the prophet, there were courts of law in the territory and he could appeal to them. "If you are innocent you give yourself a great deal of foolish trouble," Young advised. The massacre did not concern the Latter-day Saints. "As to your faith being shaken, if the Gospel was true before the 'Mountain Meadow Massacre,' neither that nor any other event that may transpire can make it false." Young again blamed Governor Cumming for the failure to investigate the crime. He had pledged to lend "every assistance in [his] power." "This offer I have made time and again, but it has never been accepted. [I have had] neither doubt nor fear on my mind but the perpetrators of that tragedy will meet their reward. God will judge this matter and on that assurance I rest perfectly satisfied." "If you are innocent," advised the prophet, "you may safely do the same; if you are guilty, better try the remedy"—the rope around the neck.[47]

"Of course I did not take his prescription," Hicks recalled, "for I had not taken 'any part.'"[48]

Brigham Young's clever reply—which did not answer Hicks' central question, "What is your true policy on Mountain Meadows?" allowed him to denounce the massacre without condemning anyone who was actually involved. Hicks received a clear message: mind your own business and ask no more questions. Young apparently became quite fond of the story, for George W. Gibbs believed he directed a similar response to Isaac Haight. One of Brigham Young's clerks told Gibbs that late one night in winter 1869 he replied to a letter in which Haight described his terrible state of mind, hoping to get an expression of sympathy from the prophet. Young's curt response was: "A rope fastened around your neck, attached to a tree, and you strung up two or three feet above the ground would provide salutary medicine for you." Brigham Young supposedly signed the letter and sent it to Haight.[49]

The prophet told a variant of this story to distance himself from Lee. When Lee made his initial report and denied that white men had been involved, Young told William Ashworth he had said, "You are not telling the truth." Lee returned the next day and asked for advice. Young claimed he hesitated a moment and then said, "John D. Lee, my advice to you would be to take a rope and go to some remote part of the country where you will never be found, and there hang yourself to a tree, near enough to the ground so the coyotes can eat the flesh from your bones." According to Ashworth, these were Young's exact words.[50]

Young's pastoral advice to Hicks did nothing to quiet the conflict that had been raging over the massacre in the southern settlements—especially those where Lee made his several homes. In April 1868 "a Ficticious Letter was found at the office," purportedly written at Camp Douglas by a Major Burt, "commander of 2000 guerrilers," which gave Lee ten days to escape before he would be hunted down and hanged for his role at Mountain Meadows. Emma Lee blamed "Georgee" Hicks and John Larson for the letter and called Hicks "a poor sneaking, pusylanimous Pup & always Medling with other men's Matter & that he had better sing low & keep out of her Path or she would put a load of salt in his Backside." Lee knew this was the third letter making such charges. He denounced Hicks as a traitor who pointed out "all the Brethrn who he thought had been at Mountain Meadow when Indians killed" the emigrants.[51]

Hicks charged Emma Lee with un-Christian conduct before Bishop Wilson Pace, who concluded Hicks had "provoked Emma by a Train of abuse" and ordered both parties to be rebaptized. Lee was angered that his wife was punished for defending him against the insults of a traitor, but he advised his wife to submit. Emma Lee, however, got even. She asked for the right to choose the man who would rebaptize her and then selected Bishop Pace, who had been "so inconsiderate as to require a woman to be immersed when the water is full of snow & Ice." Although Hicks "stood out to the last & defyed all the authority," Lee decided to leave the event in the hands of God. Hicks was picked to speak at the 1869 Fourth of July celebration, which an offended Lee found rather dull. He denounced "this Hick" as an apostate who said Brigham

Young "was led by Green backs & not by the Spirit of the Lord." Lee refused to join in the evening's dance, for he "did not Strike hands with the Enemies of this Kingdom," and he would not make merry with those who defamed the character of the prophet Brigham.[52]

"On the seventh day of April 1874, I saw John D. Lee ride into Kanarrah on horse back by the side of Brigham Young's carriage, and reported the same to THE TRIBUNE," Hicks wrote in August 1874. LDS church officials suspected Hicks was the source of the story, and Bishop Henry Lunt of Cedar City questioned him about the matter. "I did not deny the fact," Hicks wrote, "and was immediately cut off without even a hearing of any kind." "If I had only been A PIOUS MURDERER," he complained, "I might have rode 'cheek by jowl' with the Prophet as Lee has done, and been in good standing in the Church."[53]

George A. Hicks continued his contrary ways until his death in 1926. In September 1877, eleven days after the demise of Brigham Young, he made a "Public Confession" of "my errors and acknowledge my follies, and ask forgiveness of all Saints who have been offended by my writings and sayings, for I desire to be restored to the fellowship of Saints, and to be forgiven of my heavenly Father."[54] Hicks moved north to Spanish Fork and took up sugar beet farming as a devout Republican. His descendants recalled that Brigham Young's response to Hicks's letter was, "Go and drink soup with a needle." Hicks could not keep out of trouble and was apparently excommunicated again in 1886 for publishing a five-act drama on celestial marriage. As time healed old wounds, Hicks was forgiven, and Apostle Reed Smoot informed him in 1923 that he had been reinstated in the LDS church with all his former blessings.[55]

When he recalled Brigham Young's advice about Mountain Meadows in his 1877 life history, George Hicks wrote, "That letter settled my mind." He now believed that Lee was correct when he claimed Young's denunciation of the massacre was a ruse. "I think that Brigham Young gave the counsel that caused that slaughter," Hicks concluded.

Hicks was not the only southern Utahn troubled by the massacre to plead for spiritual advice. George Spencer had been Harrison Pearce's adjutant in the Iron County Brigade of the Nauvoo Legion in 1857.[56] He wrote to Erastus Snow ten years later because his heart was "too full for utterance." "I feel that I shall break down if I should not undertake to *talk*. I feel like I was slowly waking from a hideous lethargic dream." Spencer had spent nearly fifteen years in the LDS church, but he mourned, "Oh! what a life I have led. I was in that horrid 'Mountain Meadow affair.'" Spencer apparently had recently lost a child and blamed himself for it, as he said his son's life had been "crushed out (last summer) through my lack of watchfulness! through my not being humble and full of the Holy Spirit!!" "What can I *now* do?" he pleaded. "I feel like a little child lost in the woods that needs a father to show me the path that leads to open ground. May God give you his spirit to direct me."[57]

With a Mad Spirit in Him: John D. Lee

Bishop John Hawley of Pine Valley also refused to join the conspiracy of silence that protected Lee and his fellow murderers. Like massacre participants John Ure and William Slade, Hawley came to Utah from Lyman Wight's failed Zodiac colony in Texas, but he took a bold stand against the massacre. Hawley asked Lee how he "could face the Judge at the last day with a clear conscience before God if half that is reported that he did were true." Lee complained he had been more persecuted by Hawley "about that mountain affair than all the rest." "He wished me to understand that he would look for a reward in heaven for my persecuting him," Hawley recalled. Lee ended the conversation "with a mad spirit in him."[58]

Many decent Mormons, including prominent church leaders, were appalled at the continued protection of criminals such as Lee. Even Joseph A. Young, the prophet's son, allegedly refused to accompany his father to Lee's home, saying, "I'll be damned if I'll eat dinner with a murderer and butcher of women and children!" When Lee was first brought to trial in 1875, the *Salt Lake Tribune* reported that one of the apostles, probably Albert Carrington, said in 1866, "Lee should have been hanged years ago." When asked why, the apostle said for shedding innocent blood. "Such has been the feeling of thousands of the Mormon people for years," the *Tribune* reported.[59]

Apostle Amasa Lyman's obituary said that having lived "right among those who had murdered immigrants," he "learned the whole of the facts attending that wholesale and inhuman butchery." Although he dared not speak publicly, Lyman advised massacre participants to tell what they knew. According to his friend John Isaac, Lyman encouraged these men "to make a full confession and take the consequences." Isaacs credited Lyman's "quiet influence" with helping to bring forth the facts of the massacre.[60]

As the years passed, Lee became famous both for his hospitality and for his lack of remorse for his part in a mass murder. The vow of silence he had taken after the massacre may have barred him from telling the truth about what had happened, but Lee was willing to spin any number of self-serving tales about it to anyone who would listen. "Like the Ancient Mariner," wrote Ann Eliza Young, Lee "went up and down compelling every person whom he met to listen to his story of an emigrant train that had been murdered by the Indians."[61] George Cannon Lambert visited Lee at Harmony, where after a delicious supper Lee volunteered "to tell [him] all about" the massacre. Lambert knew nothing about it and did not want to know anything. He threatened to leave if Lee talked about it. Lee agreed not to force the story on him. He assured Lambert, "I never did anything in that connection but what I felt bound by my covenants to do," referring to his oath to avenge the blood of the prophets. Lambert knew his covenants did not require him to take part in a massacre and felt Lee wanted to make his religion the scapegoat for his conduct.[62]

Even in the midst of the Mormon community that shielded Lee from the law, bitter legends surrounded him. Perhaps the darkest was the persistent story that he murdered one of the surviving children. "Lee said the children must not be asked questions, as he wished them to forget the occurrence," Harmony resident Ann Eliza Hoge testified, and she swore that a boy disappeared after he blamed a man for killing his father.[63] It was whispered that at Lee's home in Washington County, "figs ripened black over the grave of a refugee child from the Mountain Meadow massacre killed and buried by Lee when she talked too much."[64] Lee's last wife, Ann Gordge, recalled decades later that he visited Washington County with a girl who had survived the massacre. One Sunday morning Emma Lee appeared "dressed in a Rich Moreantic Silk Dress, Leghorn hat trimmed with Black and Pink Ribbon & heavy gold buckles, Gold Watch and Chain, & heavy Gold Ear Rings." Lee was sitting close by and heard the girl say that Emma was wearing her mother's dress. Lee walked over, "reached down took the Child by the head and bent her head back and cut her throat from ear to ear then threw her body in a well close by." Ann Lee wrote solemnly, "This I saw with my own eyes."[65]

As Lee approached sixty, a neighbor described him as "a stout, heavy set man of fair complexion, rather corpulent," with "a low forehead and short thick neck." Although a powerful and experienced orator, he was not known for the accuracy of his scriptural quotations, and he was given to creating inspiring if exaggerated fables about the Mormon past. Rumor said he had seen angels and conversed with them. In addition to local folklore that reflected the fear he generated among his neighbors, Lee's domineering personality spawned speculation about his business dealings and sexual habits. "Lee was a swindler in dealing; a liar in conversation and a low sensual brute of a man," who had eight wives living with him in a home "that was but little better than a house of ill fame," wrote the embittered George Hicks.[66]

The charge that Lee's sensuality "exceeded the limits of reason and belief," wrote Josiah Rogerson, "was common talk and proverbial."[67] While opening a road down Ash Creek, Isaac Duffin found a red-headed skeleton many thought was a hired hand Lee had killed for his stock. One of his Harmony neighbors referred to "many things concerning Lee's brutal and immoral conduct of his home life, which are unprintable."[68]

Lee flaunted his intimacy with LDS church leaders, and for years the hierarchy did nothing to distance itself from the man most of the nation reviled as a monster. Lee handled his position as presiding elder of the Harmony branch with typical arrogance until he was relieved in March 1864.[69] On Salt Lake's Main Street in 1867, handcart veteran John Chislet directed Robert Baskin's attention to a carriage escorted by a mounted guard. "That man in the carriage with Brigham Young is John D. Lee, the leader of the Mountain Meadows massacre," said Chislet, "and the carriage in which they are riding is one which the emigrants had owned."[70]

Threats Half Expressed and Half Implied: The Godbeites

Shortly after the completion of the transcontinental railroad at Promontory Summit in 1869, powerful members of the Mormon financial and intellectual elite mounted the most formidable challenge ever posed to Brigham Young's religious authority. Resenting his regressive economic and social policies, a number of prominent and wealthy Saints under the informal leadership of businessman William Godbe organized the "Church of Zion" to save what was true about Mormonism and reform the rest.[71]

Many of the Godbeites, as they came to be known, had long-standing grievances against the Mormon leader, but the death of John V. Long on April 13, 1869, inspired personal reasons for many of them to fear Brigham Young. Last seen with Bill Hickman, Long "was found dead in a ditch, *'drowned' in three inches of water.*" Rumors circulated that as Brigham Young's clerk, Long "was the only person who heard the conversation between Brigham and the messenger sent from George A. Smith, just before the Mountain Meadow massacre, and who *wrote out the instructions* for the man to carry back."[72]

Prominent Godbeites had asked questions about Mountain Meadows since George A. Smith first told the cover story to T. B. H. Stenhouse in April 1859. Ironically, an investigation of justice of the peace Jeter Clinton prompted William Godbe to challenge the LDS church. Clinton, the recipient of the vitriolic "knife and tomahawk" letter Brigham Young had written the day after the massacre, had been accused of murder in the Morrisite affair and probably knew the details of Dr. Robinson's killing. As a city councilman, Godbe was assigned to investigate whether Clinton merited a pay raise. He discovered Clinton had been pocketing fines and collecting bribes worth thousands of dollars, including $150 to dismiss charges against a rapist. Godbe took his concerns to Brigham Young, who admitted he had long known of Clinton's graft. Mayor Daniel Wells told Godbe to drop the matter. Clinton allegedly sent Young letters filled with "threats half expressed and half implied" that indicate why the prophet protected such a sordid character. Ronald Walker, a prominent Mormon historian, has suggested Clinton's blackmail was related to Mountain Meadows. Whatever the cause, Godbe's inquiry convinced him the Mormon theocracy was both dishonest and corrupt.[73]

Loyalty or fear made many of the Godbeite dissenters reluctant to break with the powerful prophet, but entrenched corruption, religious violence, and the murder of their friend Long strengthened their resolve. They considered Young a hopeless case and found him "destitute of the magnanimity of a great soul and intensely selfish." They charged Young was determined to build a dynasty and resented his attempts to cut wages and restrict mining. The aging leader donned his mantle as prophet of the Lord on October 16, 1869, to denounce the "great and secret rebellion" that was shaking his church. Nine days later George Q. Cannon prosecuted a public religious trial before the Salt Lake Stake High Council in city hall. The men had refused to acknowledge that "President Young has the right to dictate . . . in all things, temporal and spiritual," and the religious tribunal handed Godbe and his friends over to the buffetings of Satan.[74]

The challenge to his power could not have come at a worse time for Brigham Young, whose grip on the territory was already under siege. The railroad ended Deseret's economic isolation and brought in a host of non-Mormons with no sympathy for Utah's dominant religion. At the same time Young attempted to fight the Ute Nation in a secret church operation. Utah's Black Hawk War dragged on from 1865 to 1872 and at times appeared endless. Using the Nauvoo Legion as a private army, Young concealed the conflict from the press and the U.S. military. This decision cost the LDS church millions, and Young's policies helped to protract the violence of a hopeless guerrilla war. This brutal Indian conflict—which had a much greater impact on the lives of ordinary Utahns than the Mountain Meadows massacre—disillusioned many Mormons who had not questioned their prophet's infallibility. The failure of Young's martial leadership allowed the federal government to disband the Nauvoo Legion and destroy Mormon military power, further crippling Young's theocratic rule.[75]

The Godbeite movement provided a standard around which Young's Mormon opponents could rally. The "New Movement" wielded considerable influence in Washington, D.C., and joined the Liberal Party to oppose the church-controlled People's Party. The reformers actually aspired to take over the leadership of the LDS church. Godbe and his partners transformed their *Utah Magazine* into a weekly newspaper, and on January 1, 1870 the first issue of the *Mormon Tribune* appeared in Salt Lake. A year later the Godbeite publication dropped "Mormon" from its name "and became a secular newspaper with strong anti-'Mormon' proclivities." The *Salt Lake Daily Tribune and Mining Gazette* soon became a powerful forum that continually raised disturbing questions about the massacre at Mountain Meadows.[76]

HIS DEATH HAS BEEN FEARFULLY AVENGED

The woman who many felt had played the role of Helen in the massacre at Mountain Meadows ended her days as a lonely and impoverished widow still obsessed with bitterness and vengeance. On November 9, 1869, "H," the western correspondent for the *New York World*, visited Eleanor McLean Pratt. Her home was "a low, one-story concern, built of adobes," whose one room served as both school and bedroom, with a kitchen at the back.

The wife of the martyr had once been vibrant and attractive, but the trials of her past had "greatly interfered with her good looks," and the reporter now found her cold and distant. She was "of medium height, thin faced, plainly and even slovenly dressed, with a certain wildness of manner and of the eye at times which denoted a mind diseased." The widow was "crazy upon two subjects: Mormonism and the killing of

Pratt by her husband." The reporter's tale of Pratt's murder was incorrect in almost all its sensational detail, but he apparently captured Eleanor Pratt's feelings accurately.

"I firmly believe that Joseph Smith was a prophet, as much as any of those in the Old Testament," said Mrs. Pratt. "I have never had a doubt concerning the truth of Mormonism." She recalled how "all was excitement in the streets" of Van Buren, Arkansas, when her first husband hunted down her second: "People ran out to the edge of town to see him killed; but when Parley's body was brought in, a solemn stillness succeeded the hubbub of the hour previous. The people spoke with hushed voices and affrighted looks, as though they began to realize that a servant of God had been slain, and to feel that the judgments of the Almighty would fall upon them for the deed."

The reporter asked if Hector McLean was ever punished for killing Pratt. "No," she replied. "But his death has been fearfully avenged upon the nation that has permitted the blood of the Prophets to be spilt without punishing the murderers."[77] The reporter did not ask what she meant.

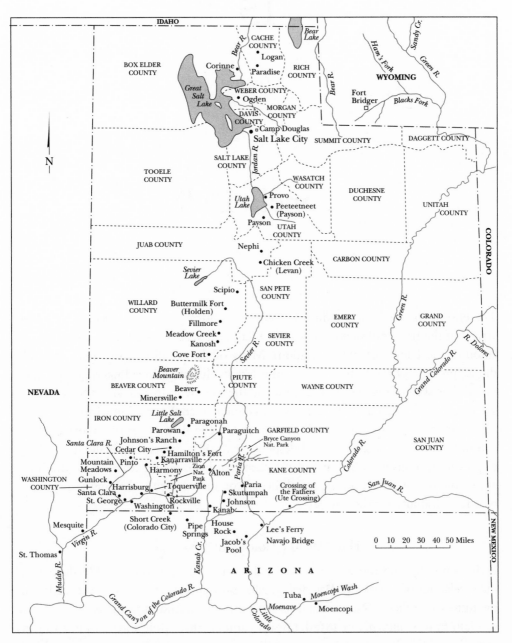

The Utah of John D. Lee. From Juanita Brooks, *John Doyle Lee: Zealot, Pioneer Builder, Scapegoat*. Based on map courtesy Arthur H. Clark Company.

15

Lonely Dell

The end of the civil war produced profound political changes in America, and the arrival of the transcontinental railroad in Utah four years later ended forever the isolation of the Latter-day Saint kingdom. Many of the conditions that made possible the suppression of the facts about the murders at Mountain Meadows no longer prevailed. The web of deception spun to shield the men who had executed the massacre grew ever more tangled as new explanations contradicted the old. Time had eaten away the foundations of the stone wall that protected the dark secret of southern Utah, and though Mormon leaders tried desperately to shore it up, they could do nothing to prevent its collapse. Once it became clear that blaming the murders on the Indians would no longer work, the search began for a new story and a new scapegoat to bear responsibility for the atrocity.

BARBAROUS TRAGEDIES: ARGUS

Perhaps nothing did more to expose the lies surrounding Mountain Meadows than the revelations of Charles W. Wandell. A Mormon since 1837, Wandell had worked in the historian's office in Nauvoo and served a mission to Australia in 1851.[1] On his way to Utah from California in 1857 he heard rumors "that white men and not Indians were the principals in the massacre, and that they were men in authority in the Mormon Church." He saw the scattered bones of the victims at the meadows.[2] And he and George Q. Cannon soon learned from "statements of the brethren in Southern Utah that it was Governor Young's militia that did the job!"[3] Beginning in summer 1870 and with mounting outrage during 1871, the *Utah Reporter*, voice of the rollicking "Gentile capital" of Utah since the arrival of the railroad, published a series of open letters to Brigham Young asking him hard questions about the massacre. Wandell wrote the articles using the pen name "Argus."

Argus painted a dramatic picture of the condition of the Fancher train as it passed through Utah. He claimed Eleanor Pratt identified one or more members of the party in Salt Lake and charged they had been present at Parley Pratt's murder. Even while camped in the city, the company was weary and footsore and "their work cattle nearly 'used up' by the labors of the long and toilsome journey." Brigham Young ordered the emigrants "to leave their camp at the Jordan with almost empty wagons," and by the time they reached Mountain Meadows their supplies were nearly exhausted. Argus blamed the hostility the outsiders encountered on the territorial governor, whose duty it was to protect them. Far from being protected, the Arkansans "were ordered to break up their camp and move on; and it is said that written instructions were sent on before them, directing the people in the settlements to have nothing to do with them." The emigrants would not have faced certain death by starvation as Argus claimed, but at Mountain Meadows they had only forty days' rations for the seventy-day journey to San Bernardino.[4]

The *Reporter's* letters directly challenged Brigham Young. Wandell had been disfellowshipped from the LDS church in 1864 for prospecting. When he moved to Nevada in July 1866, Young's "creatures" circulated reports at Pioche that Wandell was a veteran of Mountain Meadows, and they later charged that he wrote the Argus articles to exonerate himself. Although he realized the Mormons would never forgive him, Wandell hoped his friends would "not suffer Brigham Young to altogether overwhelm [him] with calumnies and to destroy [him] simply because he thinks he can."[5] In addition to writing articles, Wandell gave a series of lectures, including a January 1873 speech to some three hundred people in Salt Lake. Faithful Mormons in the audience could not believe Brigham Young was responsible for the massacre. But Wandell did and continued to challenge Young to answer his charges in public. His letters contained a strange mix of truth and fiction, and some of his stories appear to be based on intentional falsehoods fed to him by Mormon authorities. Even western newspapermen found that Wandell's bitterness often led to "exaggerations not exactly truthful, and thr[e]w suspicion on [his] reliability."[6]

While flawed and sometimes suspect, Wandell's research was often surprisingly accurate, even though many Americans simply could not believe the bizarre story and disturbing details of the massacre. Yet Wandell's relentless pursuit of the truth eventually produced the first confession by a participant, and the interrogation he conducted as Argus put before the public a host of questions Brigham Young would never answer.

As Suddenly as a Well-Drilled Regiment: The New Story

As public attention again focused on Mountain Meadows, the subject hounded the LDS church, from its general authorities to its rank-and-file missionaries. In the public mind Mormon participation in mass murder was a stubborn fact. The tales added credibility to anti-Mormon claims that the church engaged in the systematic assassination of its enemies. As one Montanan asked, if the Saints "would murder people by the hundred and more, might we not very reasonably believe they would murder a single individual?"[7]

It is impossible to determine exactly what drove the LDS church to change its policy, but as the 1860s drew to a close there was no doubt church leaders faced mounting pressure to account for the murders at Mountain Meadows. Territorial delegate William Hooper allegedly swore to several senators that no Mormon had anything to do with the massacre, and he employed journalists to write the Latter-day Saint version of the story. Journalist J. H. Beadle, sometime editor of the Corrine *Reporter*, wrote that in about 1865 the Saints grudgingly began to admit that "a few reprobate whites were engaged—men of no standing in the community."[8] As late as November 1869, Brigham Young, Jr., publicly defended the story that the massacre was simply an Indian affair. He retold the poison story and added new details to the evil emigrant tales for a Philadelphia newspaper. "That is the history of the 'Mountain Meadow Massacre,'" Brigham Young, Jr., insisted, "for which we have always received the blame."[9]

An entertainer named Sinclair commented on Mountain Meadows at the Salt Lake Theatre in November 1869. Nothing in her lecture offended the audience, the *Deseret News* commented, but simple justice demanded the facts be stated correctly. *News* editor and Apostle George Q. Cannon repeated the old story that the Arkansas company was hostile to the Indians and poisoned an ox at Corn Creek and probably poisoned the spring. Ten Paiutes died, and the survivors rallied their neighbors to attack the emigrants at Cane Spring. Cannon had known the truth for more than a decade, but he claimed the citizens from Cedar City heard rumors of a battle but arrived too late to help. Brigham Young later offered to use every effort "to sift the matter to the uttermost, and discover the guilty ones," but the story justified keeping troops in Utah. Cannon claimed Young and the people had always "been ready to give every aid in their power to have this occurrence rigidly examined."[10]

Cannon's December 1869 article was the last official LDS attempt to deny Mormon involvement in the massacre. Such crude dismissals failed to persuade even the LDS people, for most of them had long known the truth. Convert John MacNeil warned his parents in Scotland early in 1874 not to believe stories in the church newspaper, for "there has been & is Lies told in the Millenniel Star." He complained, "We was told in the Millennial Star that the Mountain Meadow Massacre was Committed by Indians but It is known by Everybody here to have been done by Mormons." Brigham Young called it "a heartless butchery but harbers the very Men that did it and there is One if Not More of them Bishops."[11] Pressure from outside Utah probably had little effect on Mormon leaders, but questions from loyal church members and the probing revelations of internal dissenters like the Godbeites convinced Brigham Young the official lie could stand no longer.

The *Salt Lake Tribune* later noted the policy change. "For twelve years their voice was one of indignant denial that any Mormons were engaged in the affair. [After a few hesitating admissions, in 1871] the whole Mormon people changed front as suddenly as a well-drilled regiment," the paper noted caustically. LDS newspapers had furiously denounced the *Tribune* for accusing Mormons, but the denunciations were now aimed at Haight, Higbee, and Lee. "The defense they then had for *all* the Mormons they now reserve for Brigham Young and the heads of the Church," the *Tribune* noted. "If they were so badly mistaken in the former case, is it not just possible that they are mistaken as to Brigham's innocence?"[12]

THE ONLY MAN WHO WOULD STAND IN THE GAP: THE SCAPEGOAT

Erastus Snow, southern Utah's senior church official, had long been forced to deal with the consequences of Mountain Meadows. In 1870 he reported the massacre had created a new crisis, but the cause of this crisis is not known. A Snow family tradition told that when the apostle gave him the bad news, Brigham Young said, "Oh God! Now it will start again."[13]

As Brigham Young realized he could no longer defend Lee, he began to cut his ties to his adopted son. During one of Young's 1870 trips to southern Utah, he apparently convened a summit meeting to discuss what to do about the massacre problem. Thomas Judd witnessed a meeting in 1870 with Haight, Dame, Nephi Johnson, George A. Smith, Daniel Wells, Jacob Hamblin, Brigham Young, and John D. Lee. Judd did not recall what took place, except "the whole matter was heard in toto."[14] Mormon chronicler Josiah Rogerson reported that Young called Haight, Lee, and Dame to St. George "for a full hearing and investigation of the whole matter and to find out who was the person that led and brought about the fearful tragedy." Rogerson claimed Lee "was heard in his own behalf to the fullest extent, and was then and there found to be the one most guilty." There is, however, no documentary evidence to indicate that such a church trial ever took place. Rogerson was soft on specific details, dating the hearing to both 1868 and 1870, and he represented the vague memories of his informants as fact.[15]

At this time a mysterious rumor claimed that an 1857 letter containing Brigham Young's orders for the massacre had surfaced. The tale appears connected to the church's renewed attention to Lee. Charles Wandell charged that Lee could produce written proof that he had simply executed orders at Mountain Meadows, acting as a subordinate officer under Young's command. Argus claimed Lee was heard to say in January 1871 that Young "offered him $5,000 for that fatal order."[16] Other anti-Mormon sources said Young offered Lee $4,000 for the letter, while the faithful insisted it was a forgery created by Lee to blackmail the Mormon president.[17]

The story told in Lee's journals is certainly incomplete. According to the journals, Lee met Brigham Young at Beaver in February 1870 and sat with him during church services. The prophet privately advised Lee to sell his Utah holdings and move south. With his farms and families prospering, Lee failed to heed the advice. Young returned south in September, and Lee joined his entourage as a commissioner to locate a road to the Colorado River with explorer John Wesley Powell, Dimick Huntington, and William Dame. If a hearing was held to assign blame for the massacre, it probably took place at about this time, but Lee wrote nothing about it in his diary. While the party camped on the Kanab River, Young gave Lee "some kind Fatherly council." He advised Lee to move his family across the Colorado, where he could "EnJoy Peace the balance of [his] days." Young repeated his advice that Lee move south. Lee said, "By the help of the Lord I will try & Make a Move in that direction." A guard interrupted the conversation at that moment, and Lee was sent with messages to Kanab.[18] If Lee's account is accurate, Young apparently could not bring himself to tell Lee of his pending excommunication—or perhaps the guard's interruption prevented him from doing so. Thus when Lee learned two months later he had been cut off from the religion to which he had devoted his life, it came as a complete surprise, at least according to the story he told in his journals.

Much more may have transpired in this or later conversations. Events suggest Young was trying to tell Lee he had been selected to take responsibility for the massacre, a tradition repeated by Lee's sons. Christopher Layton told John Amasa Lee that he attended a council of prominent men to decide what to do about the problem. Layton said Young selected Lee to stand trial "because he knew Lee would do whatever he told him to do." Others were asked to stand trial but refused. "If we live to meet your father hereafter in the same glory he is in," Layton told Lee, "we will be satisfied." High councilman Rhile Merrill told Frank Lee he also was present at the meeting. "He knew that John D. Lee was a good man. That there had to be a sacrifice and he was called on to make it. This is what was decided in the council." Frank Lee believed "the massacre was all planned beforehand by the Church leaders." John D. Lee "did not need to die for it, but he was the only man who would stand in the gap. Dame was President of the Stake, but he would not stand trial."[19]

Whatever the truth, by mid-November 1870 Lee was struggling to move his families from their established homes to the desolate Paria River country. On a trip to Kanab, Lee learned that along with Isaac Haight and George Wood, he "had been expelled from the Church, but for what cause it [was] not stated." Lee was remarkably unmoved by the news. His conscience was clear, and he "borrowed no trouble about the Matter." Near Pipe Spring the next day, a messenger brought Lee a letter from Apostle Albert Carrington officially notifying him "of the action of the 12."[20]

Wilford Woodruff's journal confirms that Lee was excommunicated on October 8, 1870. The twelve apostles unanimously "Cut off Isaac Haight, John D. Lee & [George] Wood for Committing a great Sin & they were not to have the Privilege of Returning again to the Church again in this life." Lee's writings contain more details about his painful separation from the LDS church, such as a dream he had on the day he was excommunicated. In it he faced a charge that "was false & groundless." "I declared My innocence & asked [for] an investigation. [The dream] rested heavily on My Mind. I was aware that Satan was working through certain Persons to inJure Me." A second dream, in which he "was caught up & wafted over" the heads of his enemies, reassured him: "I hope to raise above the presant opposition through the help & Mercy of God." He recalled an old vision in which Brigham Young took his armor and laid it aside but protected him from "the Lion & Tiger who arose to devour [him]." Lee felt that the apostates and the Godbeites were trying to implicate Brigham Young in the Mountain Meadows affair and it was "needful to stop their mouths." Lee was confident Young had allowed him to be cut off "for a wise purpose & not for any Malicious intent."[21]

Lee apparently was on the list of the excommunicated read to the LDS church conference in April 1871. His name did not appear in clerk James G. Bleak's minutes, which named the other excommunicants. Brooks concluded there was an agreement not to mention the massacre in any official church records. At the time Lee's family had questions about his religious status, for in December 1870, Lee's wife Lavina went "to see Prest. B. Young for council & to know whether [he] was in reality cut off from the church or not." Young bluntly told her he was and he had ordered that Lee was never to be rebaptized. He advised her to leave Lee, for the Lord had commenced to "work out righteousness." This set the pattern for Young's public treatment of his old ally. James Andrus claimed he saw the two men meet at Shirt's Creek. The prophet's "arraignment and censure of John D. Lee was so direct and pertinent" he could not forget it. Lee begged for forgiveness, but Young said, as far as he knew, there was none for him in this life. He castigated Lee for "the extent of the odium and ban that he had put upon the Church."[22]

Lee drove to St. George in December 1870 and sought out Young, who greeted him quite warmly at first but "afterwards appeared a litle cool." Lee asked how thirteen years after the massacre "all of a sudden [he] Must be cut off from this church. If it was wrong now, it certainly was wrong then." Young told Lee the new story of what had happened following the massacre and claimed he had only recently learned the particulars. Lee countered that he had told "the Truth & the whole Truth" when he originally reported the event in September 1857. "What we done was by the mutual consent & council of the high counsellors, Presidents, Bishops & leading Men, who Prayed over the Matter & diligently Sought the Mind & will of the Spirit of Truth to direct the affair. Our covenants & the love of Righteousness alone prompted the act," Lee said pointedly. He asked for a rehearing and said, "If I am denied I will appeal to My Father in Heaven."[23]

"You can have a rehearing," Young told Lee, "[but] I want you to be a Man & not a Baby." Young called in Erastus Snow, the apostle in charge of the southern colonies, and left the two men to set a date for the church court. Snow seemed astonished when Lee presented the facts in the case. He agreed to hold a trial the following

Wednesday, but the next day Snow told Lee the council had decided not to investigate since "it would result in no benefit as the least Said at presant, the better."[24]

Lee visited Isaac Haight at Toquerville and found him disheartened. Haight "feared that he would never get a hearing until there would be a change of Dynasty." Lee assured him "there was Justice in the rulers of Israel yet." The next day Lee learned just how blind Mormon justice could be. On returning to Harmony, his son David handed him a message. "If you will consult your own safety & that [of] others," the unsigned letter in Apostle Snow's handwriting warned, "you will not press your self nor an investigation on others at this time least you cause others to become accessory with you & thereby force them to inform upon you or suffer. Our advice is, Trust no one. Make yourself scarce & keep out of the way."[25]

Strangely, this brusque advice seemed to give new life to Lee. As 1870 drew to a close, the old pioneer again prepared to abandon his home and move far from the settlements. Despite his unceremonious expulsion from the LDS church, Lee continued to seek justice for economic claims—successfully—in Mormon religious courts. He began a vigorous defense of Brigham Young that contradicted the traditional understanding of the massacre in southern Utah. Young had no foreknowledge of the event, Lee told Daniel Page, the postmaster at Parowan, and tales claiming he did were "false as hell." The surprised postmaster looked at Lee and said, "I always understood that B. Young counselled that Matter to be done." Lee said Young "was innocent of the charge & knew nothing of the unfortunant affair until it was all over" and always spoke of it with regret.[26]

Many Lee family members refused to believe that the family patriarch had been excommunicated. Lee's daughter Amorah told Edna Lee Brimhall that Lee was not disfellowshipped. President David A. Cannon of the St. George Temple had told Amorah it was done to mold public opinion against him. The Lees were convinced Brigham Young "selected John D. Lee as 'the goat' because he was well aware that Lee would never refuse to do anything he was called on to do by the authorities." Lee willingly accepted the role of scapegoat for the Mountain Meadows massacre "and gave his life for the church." John D. Young recalled, "At the time of the execution all of us felt that [Lee] was no more to blame than any other man in it, but they decided to saddle it all off onto one man and John D. Lee was willing to take the blame." In return Brigham Young and his emissaries repeatedly promised Lee that "if he would stay quiet he would come out unharmed."[27]

A curious tale apparently was crafted to help Lee disappear. In February 1871 Argus announced, "John D. Lee is dead!" The story claimed Lee's body had been found at Grapevine Springs. Argus denounced the murder as another vile assassination of a man of rare courage by Brigham Young, adding more evidence of his complicity at Mountain Meadows.[28] This odd story suggests that Charles Wandell, whose articles were a mix of fact, folklore, and propaganda, was occasionally a conduit for misinformation from well-placed Mormons.

ACTS OF HOSTILITY: KLINGENSMITH CONFESSES

The gaunt figure of "Philip Klingon Smith" appeared before the clerk of the Seventh Judicial District Court of the State of Nevada on April 10, 1871. He swore out an account of the massacre at Mountain Meadows in which a participant finally described what had happened to the Fancher party in 1857 with reasonable honesty.

Of all the officials involved in the affair, only Klingensmith had voluntarily left the LDS church. A horse kicked him and fractured his skull in 1858, and the next year George A. Smith released him as bishop. He began wandering the remote settlements, helping to establish Toquerville and Adventure, living in Pocketville and Rockville, and hiding in the mountains with Lee. Klingensmith joined Jacob Hamblin's 1863 expedition to open a wagon road to the Little Colorado and gather the Hopi Indians under what Brigham Young called "the wings of Israel's Eagles." He answered a call to settle the desolate country of the Muddy River, but by 1870 Klingensmith had abandoned Mormonism and settled near Bullionville, Nevada.[29]

The *Salt Lake Tribune* later claimed Klingensmith exposed "the butchery at Mountain Meadows more for self-protection than anything else." He allegedly quarreled with his son, "Bud," who pointed him out to the people of Hiko, Nevada, during winter 1867. Wandell, serving as a local judge, warned him that his son had implicated him and helped to hurry him out of town. Klingensmith said he had told his story to Wandell but no one else before making his statement. For years he carried an 1871 letter from U.S. Attorney George Caesar Bates offering him a presidential pardon if he would testify against his fellow murderers.[30]

Klingensmith's confession portrayed the massacre as a military operation. The local militia received "a regular military call" for "the purpose of committing acts of hostility against" a party of emigrants. Haight, Higbee, Dame, and Lee ordered the regiment to prepare for field operations. Haight initially hoped to let the company go in peace, "but afterward he told me that he had orders from headquarters to kill all of said company of emigrants except the little children." Klingensmith was only a private and did not know "whether said headquarters meant the Regimental Headquarters at Parowan, or the Headquarters of the Commander-in-chief at Salt Lake City."[31]

Klingensmith claimed he went to Pinto to persuade the people to let the emigrants "pass on their way in peace," but on returning to Cedar City he met Ira Allen, who told him "that the decree had passed, devoting said company to destruction." He participated only as "a matter of life or death to me." He said Dame, Haight, and Lee had attended a military council at Parowan, where they decided to kill the entire company except the small children. Lee persuaded the men to carry out their orders and then negotiated the surrender of the emigrants. Klingensmith confessed to firing his gun in the first volley, but he did not fire again and set about saving the children. He heard Haight tell Colonel Dame if he was going to report the killing of the emigrants, he should not have ordered it. Lee told him he had related the facts to the commander-in-chief of the territorial militia, Brigham Young. Klingensmith made his statement to a Nevada court because, he said, "I would be assassinated should I attempt to make the same before any court in the Territory of Utah." "And further," the deposition ended, "deponent saith not."[32]

Wandell's charges had been explosive, but Klingensmith's confession cracked the case. One Mormon historian characterized the apostate bishop as a latter-day Barabas and a "self-confessed assassin, one of the chief promoters and participators in the terrible tragedy" who confessed only to "exculpate himself and gratify a feeling of hatred and revenge."[33] His detailed and passionless account of treachery and bloodshed was appalling, but it carefully omitted the damning fact that the Mormons had led the Paiutes. As it was, the former bishop presented the massacre as simply a militia operation and omitted any mention of Indians. Yet his statement was the most honest and comprehensive account of the murders ever made by a participant.

Klingensmith failed to answer the central question about the massacre—who was ultimately responsible for the crime?—but most Americans had little doubt. The newly founded *Mormon Tribune* quoted John D. Lee as saying that news reports accusing Brigham Young of masterminding the murders had the saddle on the right horse. Outraged, Lee denounced the story in his journal. A Reverend Braun had warned Lee "that 9 Tenths of the People believe that Brigham has Treacherously through fear Made [him] a scape Goat." Braun suggested Lee would be all right if he would "tell us that Brigham Young counceled it, which almost every body believd." But Lee insisted Young "knew nothing of the Mountain Massacre until it was all over; & verry Much regretted it when he heard of it, & I am satisfied that he never would have suffered it, could [he] have prevented it." Lee added, "I would never betrey an innocent Man to Save my own Neck, no, I would hang a thousand times first."[34] He trusted, too, that Brigham Young would never betray him.

HE CANNOT BE CUT OFF

Despite the official actions of the LDS church, in 1872 Lee claimed he was still a staunch Mormon and believed "that if a man is guilty of nothing which would separate him from the Church he cannot be cut off."[35] Lee was sure Brigham Young shared his feelings, and Young's actions indicate he did. Despite his status, on November 11, 1871, Lee received a timely warning from Daniel Wells of the First Presidency, who telegraphed that writs were out for Lee and others. Three days later Lee and Haight met Jacob Hamblin, who had encouraging reports from "headquarters" in the form of "Big News & not Bad." Lee was not to let "the left hand know what the right hand did"; otherwise, he gave no indication of what the messages said, but he found Hamblin's news "Much to [his] satisfaction." Later that month Lee met with fellow fugitives Haight, Higbee, and Daniel Macfarlane "who had come hither for the same purpose"—though the purpose remains a mystery.[36]

Lee followed the LDS church's directive that polygamous husbands should deed their property to their wives. After he completed the deeds on November 16, 1871, Lee received orders to "make a Road to the crossing of the Colorado River." Hamblin had first explored this route in 1858 and had visited the confluence of the Paria River with the Colorado some half dozen times since. John Wesley Powell's first expedition reached the site in 1869. That winter Hamblin supervised the building of Fort Meeks at the crossing and in the spring cleared a farm along the riverbanks "with a gun strapped on [his] back in case of a sudden attack by Navajos." The venture failed, but church leaders concluded it was a good place to make a settlement and invited Lee to occupy it. Two wives set out with him to find refuge at the place Emma Lee named Lonely Dell. Lee considered it a church mission, as indeed it was, for Lee's Ferry became the Mormon gateway to Arizona Territory for colonists and polygamist refugees. It also placed Lee at a western crossroads where he met prospectors, Navajos, explorers, and journalists.[37]

On Powell's second expedition in 1872 he visited the miserable ranch at Lonely Dell, and artist F. S. Dellenbaugh described his encounter with "the notorious John D. Lee." He had been cut off, the artist wrote, "nominally at least, from the Mormon Church, and had lived in the most out-of-the-way places, constantly on his guard." The men found Lee plowing a field. "When he first sighted us he seemed a little startled, doubtless thinking we might be officers to arrest him." Rachel Lee—a fine shot, Dellenbaugh learned afterward—retreated to the cabin and kept watch, but Lee greeted them pleasantly and invited them to take their meals at his house. Emma Lee, a stout, comely young woman with two small children, appeared entirely happy. Dellenbaugh found Lee genial, courteous, and generous. The explorers had no plans to capture their host, but a rambunctious companion loved to get behind Lee and cock a rifle. "At the sound of the ominous click, Lee would wheel like a flash to see what was up." On Sunday Lee favored his guests "with a lengthy dissertation on the faith of the Latter-Day Saints." He gave his own version of the massacre, claiming he had tried to stop it, "and when he could not do so he went to his house and cried."[38]

Francis Marion Bishop met "the celebrated John D. Lee" at Jacobs Pools, eight miles from the ferry. Bishop and Lee had a long talk about the causes of the "unfortunate affair." Lee "seemed to talk very freely and said he could prove he was not on the ground at the time and that he opposed the whole affair in the council." He admitted members of the council authorized the killing and "were actually present and stained their hands with the blood of men, women, and children." Bishop thought "parts of his statement don't sound right in connection with the statements of other parties."[39] Photographer E. O. Beaman also saw "the veritable John D. Lee himself" at Jacobs Pools. "Although a fugitive from justice, with a price set on his head, meeting him here in his stronghold we found him hospitable, while his manner was marked by that eternal vigilance which is the price of safety," Beaman wrote. Lee told him those who "abetted the outrage for which he [was] outlawed" were God-fearing men who "knelt and prayed to be guided in council!" Beaman was sure Lee had given a full report to Brigham Young, but Lee maintained that the governor "did not uphold the 'enthusiasts,' though he has failed to punish them, except in Lee's person."[40]

"Lee protested to me that he really did not injure anyone and tried to prevent the slaughter," Dellenbaugh said, "but of course that was not true." Lee had a hard time convincing anyone of his innocence, but he persuaded John Wesley Powell and his men that Brigham Young had nothing to do with the massacre. Dellenbaugh said he believed Young shielded Lee because of his long years of service to the church but concluded "Brigham Young would not have entertained such an act for a moment on purely political grounds if no other." "The murder of the people of that caravan," he noted, "was a frightful thing, but Haight, Lee & K[lingensmith] had the murder of Joseph Smith and his brother as an example. That affair was still fresh in mind."[41]

Lee received "a confidential Letter of More importance than all" in June 1872. It said if he "continued faithful & true to that Mission, that I never should be captured by My Enemies" and promised "timely warning of the approach of Danger." He would be remembered for his "integrity & interest in the welfare of this People & Kingdom." Brooks concluded that the letter unquestionably came from Brigham Young.[42]

Lee technically had been an outlaw since 1859, and strangers at Lonely Dell met Major Doyle, the name Lee used when he ferried journalist John H. Beadle's horses across the Colorado early in July 1872. It must have been a strange moment for Beadle, who had already written of Lee's life "of misery": "He is shunned and hated even by his Mormon neighbors, he seldom ventures beyond the square where he lives, his mind is distracted by an unceasing dread of vengeance, and his intellect disordered."[43] Beadle was a fierce anti-Mormon, but his pleasant meeting with Lee extended over the Fourth of July. When Beadle asked about Mountain Meadows, Lee said he spoke freely and treated Beadle to two of his favorite tales of the moment. "Told him that I did not consent to it & was not presant when it was done, although I am accused of it. Neither had Brigham Young any knowledge of it until it was all over," Lee wrote. He gave the journalist an account of the massacre "exactly as it stood." "[I could have cleared my name] at any time by just saying who was who. I could have proved that I was not in it, but not without bringing in other men to criminate them," Lee told Beadle. "But I wouldn't do it." Beadle advised Lee to make a plain statement and have it published to the world.[44]

The nature of Brigham Young's punishment of the men cut off from Mormonism continued his former policy of denouncing the murderers in public while privately protecting them. Despite statements to the contrary, the excommunications apparently included assurances that those cast out in 1870 would ultimately have their blessings restored if they remained loyal. Ultimately came sooner for some than for others. Isaac

Haight regained his LDS church membership in March 1874 and was rebaptized at Toquerville. His descendants believed all Haight's "former Blessings, priesthood Washings, anointings and endowments were restored in full by the instructions of Brigham Young." Haight's favorite daughter, Caroline Eliza, died in childbirth as her father was being rebaptized.[45] Caroline Parry, an obsessive family historian whose life's mission was to restore her grandfather's reputation, told an even more dramatic story. She claimed Haight met Brigham Young on March 3, 1874, and the two "talked for hours and then they went to the creek east of St. George and Isaac C. Haight was baptized and President Young blessed him and restored him to full fellowship."[46]

There would be no forgiveness for John D. Lee, at least in public, but for a man expelled from the church, Lee maintained surprisingly intimate ties to Mormondom. He still commanded the respect of his LDS neighbors and was even invited to preach to their congregations. He remained especially close to Brigham Young, who sent a number of messages to him via Jacob Hamblin. In January 1874 Young and George A. Smith sent detailed instructions about managing the ferry at Lonely Dell and promised, "When we come along with our company, we shall expect to pay you liberally for your servises."[47]

Lee returned to the settlements and visited Brigham Young at St. George on April 5, 1874. The prophet "received [him] with the kindness of a Father" and invited him to dinner where the "table was furnished with every thing that the country would afford," from oyster soup to Mormon rice. Lee told of a dream that ended when "the spirit said, Keep in the track of the church, for in it there is safety!" Young was impressed and shared with his old companion his great fear that the Saints were drifting down to hell. He invited Lee to accompany him to Kanarah to hear him preach and "to prepare [Lee] for the Future, using his own words." As Young's entourage passed Lee's mansion at Washington, Young stopped and bowed to Emma. When they parted ways on April 8, the prophet warned Lee that he was consorting too closely with the gentiles, playing cards and swearing like them. Young said he knew he could trust Lee to do anything he wanted to be done, and he hoped recent bad reports about him were false. He warned, "John, you Must be careful & stand to your integrity." Young blessed Lee and drove on.[48] The two men would never meet again.

THE SWORD OF JUSTICE

Brigham Young sent his nephew, James A. Little, to upstate New York in 1872 "to do some good in the papers." Little asked for advice on how to handle the most difficult questions—particularly those about Mountain Meadows. He had met intelligent men who believed LDS church authorities must have been aware of the massacre. Should he "touch the subject at all? Will it do to give a fair history of the affair," especially of the extenuating circumstances? Little asked for "the documents pertaining to it," he thought as "any fair paper" would publish the account they contained.[49] Despite Little's request, the LDS church made no official statement about the massacre until years after the death of Brigham Young.

In contrast, the church's enemies had many stories to tell, and no one told them with such devastating impact as a Godbeite couple, Fanny and T. B. H. Stenhouse. They published two books in 1873 and 1874: *The Rocky Mountain Saints: A Full and Complete History of the Mormons, from the First Vision of Joseph Smith to the Last Courtship of Brigham Young*, by Stenhouse; and *"Tell It All": The Story of a Life's Experience in Mormonism*, by Fanny. Both contained extensive sections on the Mountain Meadows massacre based largely on the experiences of their friends and the investigations of Charles Wandell. *Rocky Mountain Saints* reprinted long sections of Wandell's Argus letters, bringing both his insights and his errors to a national audience. The story told in the Stenhouses' books profoundly influenced every subsequent history of the massacre, extending even to the recollections of survivors and the prosecution of the crime.[50]

Much of the Stenhouse story relied on Utah mythology. It mixed impossible claims with likely possibilities, such as the report that a woman in the last stage of pregnancy was among the murdered. Like Wandell's account, the couple's tales confused fact and propaganda. They were the first to claim that the Fancher party included a band of young ruffians who "named themselves 'Missouri Wild-cats.'" *Rocky Mountain Saints* assumed these were the only two wagon trains on the road to southern California in 1857, simplifying the complex reality. The supposed camp of the reckless Wild-cats "resounded with vulgar song, boisterous roaring, and 'tall swearing,'" while "the peace of domestic bliss and conscious rectitude" prevailed in the wagon train. After "hearing the nightly yells of the 'Wild-cats,'" Eli Kelsey advised the families to separate from them as much as possible while passing through the settlements and Indian country. Kelsey knew how easy it was to provoke trouble in the war hysteria of 1857 Utah. He tried to impress on the leaders the urgency of not associating with the Missourians. The emigrants said they would follow Kelsey's advice, and it appears they did, leaving the "venturesome spirits seeking fortune" behind.[51]

The "Missouri Wild-cats" may well have been the Dukes party that followed the Fancher train. Its leader, William Dukes, and at least eight other men were Missourians; virtually everyone in the Fancher train came from Arkansas. (Interestingly, three Dukes party members were apparently apostates from Utah.)[52] The Nicholas Turner company occasionally joined the Dukes party, and the *Los Angeles Star* called it "Capt. Turner's train, of Missouri."[53] Although the "Wild-cat" story was an anachronism, historians made much of it. And one went far beyond the evidence to speculate that the Missouri contingent quietly slipped out of the meadows and escaped the fate of the rest of the party.[54]

The Stenhouses' books may have been a stew of fact and fable, but they captured the horror of the massacre. Thousands of readers drawn to their titillating exposé of polygamy were horrified at this awful tale of betrayal and blood. National outrage built with every copy sold, and public demand for the punishment of those responsible would soon be politically irresistible.

After the election of U. S. Grant in 1868, the Mormon political situation deteriorated dramatically when Grant appointed J. Wilson Schaffer territorial governor and James B. McKean chief justice. Schaffer abolished the Nauvoo Legion, and McKean, a former Methodist preacher, launched a legal assault on Mormon theocracy and polygamy that quickly became a crusade. At the request of acting U.S. Attorney Robert Baskin, a non-Mormon grand jury indicted Brigham Young under an 1852 territorial law prohibiting lewd and lascivious cohabitation. The U.S. marshal detained the prophet on October 2, 1871, and subsequently arrested former Nauvoo Legion generals Daniel Wells, William Kimball, and Robert Burton on various murder charges. Judge McKean forced Brigham Young to return from St. George in January 1872 to face indictment for his alleged role in the November 1857 execution-style murder of a rich group of Californians known as the Aiken party.[55] As Lee commented, "All hell seemed to boil over about Salt Lake City." George A. Smith believed President Grant "was determined to hang President Young whether or no." In retaliation, the territorial legislature refused to fund McKean's court, paralyzing federal justice in Utah. Ultimately the U.S. Supreme Court's *Englebrecht* decision invalidated one hundred thirty Utah grand jury indictments, including the murder charges against Young.[56]

As investigations of Mountain Meadows intensified in October 1872, the LDS church sent George A. Smith on a mission to Palestine to dedicate the Holy Land for the return of the Jews. Many suspected Mormon leaders were more concerned about putting distance between Smith and the investigation of Mountain Meadows than they were about the restoration of Judea. If anyone could testify to Brigham Young's complicity in the massacre, Argus wrote, "Geo. A. Smith is that man." His enemies charged that Apostle Smith probably would not survive the trip, but even at the risk of his life he had to avoid the pending investigation "of the Mountain Meadow horror."[57]

Territorial associate justice Cyrus Hawley lobbied Congress and President Grant to establish a military post at Beaver, Utah, to support "the largest number of dissenting Mormons south of Salt Lake" and serve as a base for the prosecution of the Mountain Meadows murders. Most of the principal men engaged in the massacre lived in the district, Hawley wrote, "and their influence is a controlling one." He warned that the new settlement at Kanab, established under Lee's old missionary companion, Levi Stewart, was "now the Gibralter for such persons whom the Church Authorities imagine will be liable to be proceeded against as criminals."[58]

Brigham Young quickly informed the secretary of war that only a few farmers and stock raisers lived at Kanab, "and at no time, were there more than thirty white men there. A peaceful, rural district, as unlike, in every respect, to a 'Gibraltar' as can well be imagined." The prophet repeated his claim that John Cradlebaugh's posse of gamblers, thieves, and camp followers actually "took a course to screen offenders, who could easily hide from such a posse under the justification of avoiding a trial by court martial." The prophet blamed officers like Judge Hawley for using "every opportunity to charge the crime upon prominent men in Utah, and inflame public opinion against our community." The malicious misrepresentations of characters such as Judges Brocchus, Drummond, Cradlebaugh, and Hawley created disturbances. "And it is not improbable the same efforts may be made with these troops at Beaver," Young said. "That is what I am opposed to and wish to prevent."[59] Despite Young's protests, the government established Camp Cameron at Beaver in May 1873.

U.S. Attorney George Caesar Bates had been wrangling with Mormons since 1851, when he prosecuted James Strang, the king of Beaver Island, Michigan. Bates asked the attorney general to appoint a special attorney for "the celebrated '*Mountain Meadow Massacre*'" case and to let him impanel a grand jury. Judge Hawley objected, pointing out that under the current rules for selecting Utah juries, any attempt "to prosecute the leading perpetrators of that atrocity *would be but a farce and a mockery.*" Hawley had quietly made himself "somewhat familiar with the facts of the massacre," and at the proper time, he thought, they could be made available to the government. But he felt "it would be far better to allow the Sword of Justice to remain pointing at that atrocious crime, its perpetrators and to the penalty of the law" than to prosecute the criminals unsuccessfully. It is impossible to sort out the politics behind this exchange, but Bates's subsequent behavior suggests he was hoping to have the case heard before a Mormon probate court. As one veteran of the Utah War complained in 1868, it was a fact that a Mormon jury would not convict a Mormon prisoner.[60]

After Mormon hard case Bill Hickman implicated Mormon officials in a variety of crimes, Robert Baskin gave notes of his 1872 interviews with the gunman to George Bates, who hired Baskin to help prosecute cases based on Hickman's confessions. Baskin and Bates "went along harmoniously for several weeks," but Bates declined to try the cases and ordered Baskin to turn in his commission as a federal prosecutor. Baskin implied that Bates had been bribed, for soon after his removal, Bates became an attorney for the LDS church and was hired by Brigham Young to defend John D. Lee.[61] When Stenhouse visited Washington in winter 1871, he was surprised to find congressmen who boldly declared their opposition to any investigation of Mountain Meadows. Meeting with several senators, the apostate learned something of the ways of politics in the Gilded Age. "It is very evident, Mr. Stenhouse," one solon told him, "that Brigham Young has a financial agent in Washington."[62]

President Grant replaced Bates with William Carey, who was reputed to be incorruptible. Utah territorial delegate George Q. Cannon found Carey was "not as radical as the successor of Mr. B. might be expected to be." Cannon told Young it was unlikely the government would select Carey "to carry out a vindictive policy; besides, he is not a vindictive looking or acting man."[63]

Robert Baskin was another case entirely. He said he fought to create a system in Utah that would give every man an equal chance "to attain the highest social, political and business advancement without having to lay his manhood down at the foot of the priesthood, or kiss the great toe of some pretended prophet." Baskin believed congressional legislation was the key to overthrowing Utah's theocracy. He launched a frontal assault on Mormon power with the Cullom Bill in 1869, whose draconian measures reformed Utah's courts and elections, revoked its land laws, outlawed cohabitation, and authorized the president to send forty thousand troops to the territory to enforce its provisions. The bill passed in the House but was bottled up in committee by James Nye of Nevada, a notoriously corrupt senator who had publicly offered to sell his vote during the impeachment of President Andrew Johnson. Undeterred, Baskin worked tirelessly to see that the provisions of the Cullom Bill were enacted in other legislation, convinced that "the evils it sought to eradicate were so radical, deep seated, and strongly protected" in Utah that nothing less would have much effect.[64]

In *Ferris v. Higley*, the relentless Baskin challenged the territorial legislation that gave probate courts jurisdiction in civil and criminal cases. He wrested control of Utah's courts from the LDS church when the U.S. Supreme Court voided the legislature's 1852 attempt to limit the power of the federal courts.[65] When the Poland Bill redefined the jurisdiction of the Utah courts in 1874, the wheels of justice began to turn. The bill eliminated the territorial attorney and marshal and assigned their duties to the U.S. attorney and the U.S. marshal, restricted the authority of local probate courts to their traditional functions, and opened Utah juries to non-Mormons. In September 1874 the first grand jury called under the law indicted Lee, Dame, Haight, Higbee, Klingensmith, Stewart, and three others for the murders at Mountain Meadows.[66]

Contrary to Brigham Young's repeated protests that the local courts could have settled the matter long ago if the government had simply let them, Utah's probate courts had taken no action on the territory's most notorious crime during the seventeen years they claimed the authority to do so. The Nauvoo Legion never held a court of inquiry, let alone a court-martial, into the conduct of its officers at the scene. Apostle-historian Orson Whitney argued that the crusades of anti-Mormon federal authorities forced loyal Saints "to stand aloof and refrain from extending the aid which otherwise would have been willingly given." If the federal judges and marshals had only sought to ferret out "the actual criminals, the people would have rendered them greater assistance, and their efforts would have been attended with earlier and probably better success," Whitney wrote.[67] Yet the apostle did not attempt to explain why officers of the probate courts such as Judge John D. Lee and Sheriff John Higbee failed to take any action whatsoever against the perpetrators of a mass murder.

To the End of the Earth, or Texas: James Gemmell

Perhaps it was inevitable someone would attempt to use Mountain Meadows to blackmail Brigham Young. A. L. Tomblin wrote from Iowa in July 1871, "I am requested to say to you that a person requires of you 1000$ one thousand dollars. [If the money was sent immediately] & no questions asked there will be no further demands—for he says that he was at the *Mountain Meadow Massacre*. I write this at his request & sign my own name." In a postscript Tomblin said he did not know on what grounds his accomplice claimed the money, "only that he was at the Massacre" and "*you* know him *very* well." His friend could not write and understandably did not want his name known. Tomblin advised Brigham Young to send the money directly to him.[68]

Young undoubtedly ignored such crude attempts at extortion, but he learned of a much more threatening development in October 1872 when adventurer James Gemmell wrote to Young's nephew and business partner, Feramorz Little, from Montana Territory. A quiet, unassuming man, Gemmell had lived an astonishing life even by frontier standards. Born in Scotland in 1814, he immigrated to America and subsequently "lived a checkered life, being at times a sailor, soldier and farmer, an exile and prisoner." An English court condemned him to death for his role in the Canadian rebellion of 1837, but Daniel Webster intervened and had his sentence reduced to transportation to Australia. Gemmell seized a musket from a prison guard in Van Dieman's Land and escaped to New York, where in June 1842 Horace Greeley and James Gordon Bennett lionized him in their newspapers. Gemmell married but soon headed west, hoping to join in the anticipated war with England over Oregon. He accompanied Jim Bridger on a trading expedition to Yellowstone in 1846, but the next year he drifted into the new settlement at Salt Lake "worn and tired out." Gemmell cast his lot with the Mormons.[69]

Gemmell was sealed to Elizabeth Mahala Hendricks on November 27, 1850, but within a year Orson Pratt preached her funeral sermon. Gemmell must have embraced Mormon doctrine with some enthusiasm, for his gravestone described him as polygamist with four wives and twenty-two children. In part because of his "improved ditching machine," the Utah legislature appointed Gemmell supervisor of territorial roads in 1850. He opened City Creek Canyon using "one hundred men throughout the season making roads, and as fast as he had the road made up one of these canyons, Brigham would be locating saw mills on the stream."[70]

As Montanan Joseph C. Walker later told his story, Gemmell received a mission call to Texas in February 1854, with orders not to return until he got all the Mormons in Texas to Utah.[71] Friends assured him this meant he "had a five years work on his hands." Confronted with a hard proposition, Gemmell "left Salt Lake City scratching his head and kept scratching it" all the way to Texas, but on the way he got "his thinker to working nicely." A quintessential frontier entrepreneur, he knew the Mormon farmers in Texas had a wealth of young cattle, but they could not afford to sell their farms in a state where land cost a dollar per acre. Gemmell advised his congregation to keep their land titles but to sell their slaves and goods and invest in more young cattle, which they could sell in the West and "make more for them than they could make in Texas in three years." Within two years he had them all on the road to Utah, where the price they got for their stock "made their eyes fairly bulge." Brigham Young hated defections, but Gemmell told the prophet it was up to him to keep the Texans in Utah. The men went home; Young "evidently thought best to let this Texas outfit go." Gemmell returned with them, for in May 1857 his name appeared on the warrant used to arrest Parley Pratt in Indian Territory, apparently for aiding Eleanor Pratt's flight through Texas.[72]

On July 21, 1857, Gemmell passed a Mormon freighting station on Horse Creek, near Fort Laramie, with Apostles Snow and Taylor, and he arrived in Utah with them on August 7, 1857. He claimed he was "in Brigham's office when Bishop Hamlin came in and reported the Arkansas train near Cedar City" on September 1 and "heard Brigham tell Hamlin that if he (Brigham) were in command of the Legion he would wipe them out." Gemmell told Walker he was with Young "when a courier came to the office with the horrible news of the Mountain Meadow massacre." By October Gemmell was campaigning with the Nauvoo Legion in Echo Canyon.[73]

Gemmell was one of the six government witnesses at Provo in 1859 who considered their "lives and property in imminent peril from the Mormon communists," and he served as Judge Cradlebaugh's Indian interpreter on the expedition to Mountain Meadows in May 1859. He helped to bury the dead and recalled the killing ground as "the most gruesome, pitiful, heart rending and sickening sight he had ever beheld."[74]

All this would be easy to dismiss as more fantastic lore but for Gemmell's letter to Feramorz Little now in the Brigham Young papers. It suggests that the adventurer was still on intimate terms with his old Mormon friends and knew enough about what had happened in Governor Young's office on September 1, 1857 to make him a very dangerous threat to the interests of the Mormon kingdom.

> I have been very much annoyed lately by the officials of Montana, as they say through the request of their Friends in Utah, to accertain of me what took place, and what was said in President Youngs office, on my arrival from Texas, between Jacob Hamblin President Young and others, in regard to the Arkansas Train then passing through the southern settlements of the trouble they had with the Inhabitants, and of their boasting, of Parley been killed in their neighborhood before they left. And of them threatening to Poison the springs and what Conversation took place between the President Hamlin and others at that time in the Presidents Office. And if I knew what was the purpose of the Instructions sent South, and if I thought the massacre was in retaliation for the killing of Parley, and of what I remembered of the evidence gleaned from the Indians and others from Judge Cradlebaugh when I was his Interpreter.[75]

How the investigators acquired this information was a mystery to him, Gemmell wrote, but perhaps Bill Hickman had picked it up during one of their whiskey sprees in Echo Canyon. Gemmell expected to be put in restraints and forced to go to Utah to give evidence. "I would much rather go to the end of the Earth, or Texas, than be compelled to go down there," he wrote. "Go I must as that would be the only way I have of avoiding them, but I am dead broke as usual [and] have not the means of leaving a large family."[76]

Gemmell's headstone reported he "fled for his life with one wife" to Montana and was "Excommunicated by Brigham Young because of what he found out about Mountain Meadow Massacre."[77] His friendly if vaguely threatening 1872 letter hints that he may have acted as a double agent in 1859, and there is little to suggest that the government investigation had penetrated so deeply into the secrets of Mountain Meadows as his letter indicates. Yet Gemmell's message carried a grim warning: the relentless inquisition into Mountain Meadows was dangerously close to implicating Brigham Young, and neither the public nor the government would be satisfied until blood had answered for blood. "Please write as soon as you receive this," Gemmell's letter ended. "And give me Council for the best."[78]

16

As False as the Hinges of Hell

THE TRIALS OF JOHN D. LEE

By 1874 John D. Lee had been a fugitive from justice for fifteen years, since Judge Cradlebaugh had issued a warrant for his arrest. In southern Utah Lee had long since become a legend, despised by many of his Mormon neighbors but a folk hero to a sizable portion of the population. Their lore told how Marshal William Stokes once stopped Lee near Panguitch as the old frontiersman led twenty-one of his sons hauling lumber out of the hills with twenty-one teams. Lee was driving the lead wagon when Stokes gave the order to halt.

"Is this John D. Lee's wagon train?" the federal officer demanded. The answer came back yes, and Stokes asked, "Is old John D. Lee in this train?"

Lee himself replied, "Do you think John D. Lee is fool enough to be here in broad daylight when he knows that Marshall Stokes is after him?"

Stokes agreed. "I understand he is a damned sly old fox. I'll arrest him later." The marshal let the wagons drive on.[1]

Besides his notoriety as an outlaw, Lee was renowned in the isolated Mormon settlements as a healer. He had cured people as early as 1843 and was temporarily healed himself in 1846 when Brigham Young laid a cane on his breast made from a branch of the Nauvoo Temple's Tree of Life. Lee's wives had great faith in his powers and often asked him to bless them during childbirth. In an argument with his wife Aggatha, he appeared to call down the chastening hand of the Lord. He once rebuked a scolding wife who fell violently ill and suffered great pain until Lee "laid his hands on her head and blessed her, at which she was relieved." His healing powers were tested in 1860 when massacre veteran William Slade blasted away the skull of William Woods's daughter while shooting at a crow. Lee calmed the neighbors who flocked to the scene and "rebuked the Powers of Death, & asked the Lord to raise it, & the child immediately came to." (The fate of the poor girl is not clear, but Lee hoped the incident would be a warning to all about careless shooting.)[2]

After his excommunication, Lee blessed Samuel B. Tenney's niece, who suffered from rheumatism. "Brother Joseph, the Priesthood of God has seen fit to divest me of my Priesthood and I haven't the right to lay hands upon your daughter," Tenney recalled Lee telling the girl's father, but he did have the right to kneel down and pour out his soul to the powers that be. During the blessing, those present "could see his lips moving and the tears running from his eyes like rain." When finished, Lee promised the child would get well and become a mother in Israel.[3]

To some, Lee's tortured life had conferred on him apparent spiritual powers. After listening to Lee offer family prayers at Lonely Dell, missionary William Solomon noted, "A more pathetic and fervant prayer I have not heard in a long time." Solomon overestimated his host's "great litary Atainment," but he found Lee "full of energy and determination in the building up of the Kingdom of God upon the earth." He concluded Lee had been the subject of much misrepresentation.[4]

Yet the abrasive Lee was a man who made bitter enemies as often as he made devoted friends. Repeating a charge that had followed Lee since missionary Thomas Brown made it in March 1855, George Hicks attributed Lee's powers not to his spiritual nature but to trickery: "Lee would go to where men were assembled and play the eavesdropper and in a day or two would make known what he had heard and say the Lord had revealed it to him."[5] Despite the authorities who protected him, Lee lived in constant fear that someone would betray him to the federal marshals who dogged his trail.

The pursuit of Lee was but one campaign in the war against Mormon theocracy, a war that had one overriding objective: the destruction of Brigham Young. Former intimates became defectors who undercut the prophet's power and left him wary of traitors. Governor Young had once recommended attorney William Hickman for a federal judicial post, but as a turncoat, "Wild Bill" wrote *Brigham's Destroying Angel* with the help of J. H. Beadle in 1872. He described his murderous career as a Danite in lurid detail and implicated the Mormon prophet in his crimes. The prophet's last wife, Ann Eliza Webb, sued for divorce and demanded $1,000 a month in alimony, launching a complex series of legal maneuvers by polygamy's friends and foes.[6] Her lectures and best-selling memoir, *Wife No. 19, or the Story of a Life in Bondage*, ridiculed and denounced her former husband.

Lee's repeated assertions that Young had nothing to do with the Mountain Meadows massacre reflected a lifetime of dedicated loyalty, but if he failed to keep his promise to accept responsibility for the murders, no one posed a more dangerous threat to the aging prophet.

Thunder-struck with Astonishment: The Arrest of John D. Lee

Newly empowered by the Poland Bill, U.S. marshal for Utah Territory, George R. Maxwell, a disabled Civil War hero, sent warrants for the arrest of nine Mountain

Meadows participants to his deputy, William Stokes. Maxwell wanted Lee, the most important of the fugitives, arrested first. He warned Stokes that capturing the outlaw would be a dangerous undertaking, for Lee had vowed he would never be taken alive.

Marshall Stokes learned his quarry was at Harmony. Before Stokes could act, Lee set out for his stronghold on the Colorado River. Stokes sent Thomas Winn to Panguitch to see if Lee had stopped at the settlement. Stokes left Beaver on November 7, 1874, passing Brigham Young near Buck Horn Springs. "I have no doubt but that he thought I was there to assassinate him," Stokes said of the Mormon prophet, "for he had four of the best fighting men of Beaver City with him as a guard." Stokes met Winn at Red Creek and learned Lee was at Panguitch. The marshal sent five agents to the town and under cover of night approached the settlement himself. When two of his Mormon deputies failed to make a rendezvous shortly before dawn, Stokes feared they "were captured, and more than likely *blood atoned*," so he dashed into town hoping to spring the trap on the fugitive.[7]

Brigham Young had been warned of Lee's peril. Collins R. Hakes was visiting relatives at Parowan when the prophet and his retinue stopped overnight. That evening Marshal Stokes arrived and began organizing his posse to arrest Lee. About nine o'clock, D. P. Clark, Hakes's apostate brother-in-law, asked if Hakes wanted to warn Young. If Young felt Lee's arrest would be against the interests of the people of Utah, Clark said, "I will have two good horses all ready and you and I can beat the Marshall to Lee."[8]

Hakes relayed the offer to Young, who called his advisers together and had Hakes explain the situation. "Brethren, now what shall we do? Be free but quick. Have any of you any suggestions?" The prophet "dropped his chin into his hand and all was still as death." The silence continued for several minutes. "If you will not talk, I will," Young said finally, "but it is all right. The time has come when they will try John D. Lee and not the Mormon Church, and that is all we have ever wanted. Go to bed and sleep, for it is all right." He thanked Hakes for the information.[9]

As dawn broke at Panguitch, Stokes located all his men, but the locals refused to provide any information about Lee or his families. The posse seized a small boy who proved to be Lee's son, Beadle wrote, "and threatened him with death unless he directed them to the house." The little Mormon refused to cooperate: "Shoot away, d———n ye; I don't know nothin' about it."[10]

At the home of Lee's wife Caroline, Stokes saw a woman peering into a log chicken coop, apparently talking to someone. Stokes dragooned two of Lee's sons to help him search for their father, and their misdirection led him to Lee's hiding place in the hay-covered pen. The lawman noticed two rifles aimed at him from the main house. Stokes drew his pistol and pointed it through a crack in the roof of the chicken coop, placing the muzzle a mere eighteen inches from Lee's head. He ordered Winn to disarm the outlaw. "I promise you," Stokes said, "if a single straw moves, I will blow his head off."[11]

"Hold on boys, don't shoot, I will come out," said Lee. His son-in-law pleaded with Stokes not to kill an old man. The marshal said Lee was not going to die like a dog, nor would he let Lee escape. When he read the murder warrant, Lee asked why he wasn't charged with wholesale murder: "They meant it." The officers went to the house, where Lee quieted the women, who were "wild with excitement, some of them crying and all unreasonable in their language." He ordered breakfast for the officers and directed his sons not to interfere with the arrest. He told Stokes the time had come for him to have a fair trial. Rachel Lee accompanied her husband to jail in Beaver, where "the people were almost thunder-struck with astonishment to know that John D. Lee had been arrested."[12]

Federal authorities soon arrested William Dame and committed him to the territorial penitentiary. Not long after his father's arrest, Rachel's son William Franklin Lee recalled that two men arrived at the ferry to search for books or records. "They said the church wanted them, and we always thought it was to keep the truth hidden." The men "sat up all night looking through books. They both took records of some kind."[13]

DANCE ON NOTHING: LEE'S FIRST TRIAL

The national press followed the sensational revelations of Lee's trial in detail, creating a public fascination unequaled until the Lindbergh kidnapping case and exceeded only by the O. J. Simpson trial of the 1990s. Newspapers from across the country sent representatives to Utah Territory, and the vivid reporting of Frederick Lockley in the *Salt Lake Tribune* revived the anti-Mormon paper's sagging fortunes.[14]

Convinced Brigham Young had ordered the 1857 massacre, Utah's federal officials were determined to bring him to justice, but they faced a determined opposition that had successfully obstructed justice for fifteen years. To defend William Dame and protect its interests, the First Presidency of the LDS church employed George Caesar Bates, the former U.S. Attorney once charged with prosecuting the criminals of Mountain Meadows, and his partner, Jabez G. Sutherland, who had served as Brigham Young's divorce attorney. Bates tried to negotiate the surrender of the other men under indictment, including William Stewart, Isaac Haight, and John Higbee, on the condition they would be granted bail while awaiting trial. He claimed to have visited the fugitives in their stronghold and told a dramatic story of "going in at night and returning the next day, by a way so devious that none but Indians or the most accomplished scouts could find it."[15]

Mormon historian Orson Whitney claimed Judge Jacob Boreman's hostility led the fugitives to refuse to surrender. Boreman regarded Bates as a traitor and was outraged at his proposal that the court negotiate with fugitives. The judge suspended Bates from practicing law and ordered him to show cause why he should not be disbarred. "For downright effrontery and cool impudence," Boreman told Bates, "your proposition is unsurpassed even in Utah."[16]

Preliminary hearings began before Judge Boreman in July 1875 amid rumors that Lee would turn state's evidence. Concerned Lee would betray them, Mormon leaders closely monitored events. George A. Smith warned on July 14, 1875, that Lee had arranged "to turn States' evidence against Dame and eighteen others. It is believed he is promised a reward in money if certain persons are convicted."[17]

Dame's attorneys sought to have their client tried first, apparently fearing Lee would implicate him. Smith was said to have told a church meeting in Beaver in February 1875 that if Lee were guilty, "it was only right that he should be punished. In the next breath he asked the prayers of the congregation for the safe deliverance of brother Dame." This news apparently shook Lee's confidence that he "would never stretch hemp," and Lockley reported that Lee resented this "sanctimonious treachery." When visitors warned that his former friends had decided to give him up, Lee vowed to make "a clean breast of it."[18] He dictated a statement, but his effort "to submit the facts as far as I know them" did not impress the prosecutors. The confession blamed Haight and Higbee and failed to acknowledge the complicity of Dame or any higher authority in the crime.[19] Beadle and many non-Mormons considered the confession "a tissue of lies from beginning to end" and regarded it as "a Church trick from the start." The prosecutors refused to accept any statement that exonerated Brigham Young, believing witnesses such as Philip Klingensmith and Joel White would prove more useful than Lee's confession, which shielded "the real instigators of the butchery."[20]

Lee's defense of Brigham Young made him a hero to the Saints, and he was even serenaded by the Mormon band at Beaver. Reassured of Lee's loyalty, the First Presidency directed Sutherland & Bates to assume his defense from Wells Spicer, joining with Judge E. D. Hoge, W. W. Bishop, and John Macfarlane of St. George.[21] Young's decision to bankroll the defense reflected his confidence that he could control the outcome of the trial. It was a disastrous miscalculation with enduring consequences for the prophet and his church. While he could profoundly influence the verdict, Young's strategy allowed his enemies to launch a political trial that told the story of the massacre and all its horrors to a national audience.

The resolutely honest U.S. Attorney, William C. Carey, led the prosecution, assisted by the fire-eating Robert Baskin. In a last attempt to use the Mormon-controlled probate courts to limit hostile testimony, Lee's lawyers persuaded a justice of the peace to issue warrants charging Klingensmith and other witnesses with complicity in the massacre. Even Mormon historians found the attempt to arrest federal witnesses "somewhat out of the usual order," and Frederick Lockley denounced it as sharp practice. In response, Marshal Maxwell swore he would arrest any constable who tried to interfere with federal witnesses. Maxwell moved Klingensmith ("the most obnoxious of all apostates to the Church party") into his own quarters for protection.[22]

Lee was arraigned and pled not guilty. The jury selected the next day was composed of three non-Mormons, one former Mormon, and eight Latter-day Saints. The trial began on the upper floor of the Beaver City Cooperative, but the spectacle attracted such a crowd it was moved next door to a saloon. Proceedings opened on July 23, 1875, with U.S. Attorney Carey's impassioned description of the crime.

Like much American justice, Lee's first trial was a disordered affair. None of the attorneys had looked at an 1857 calendar to determine when the massacre actually happened. The legal process was chaotic. In their eagerness to answer the larger questions about the massacre, the prosecutors apparently forgot they needed witnesses and evidence to convict Lee of murder. As Lockley observed, they "were less desirous to convict and punish the prisoner than to get at the long concealed facts of the case." Baskin's purpose was more specific: rather than prosecute an unwinnable case, he launched a no-holds-barred attack on Brigham Young's national reputation. Lee's defense team was more confused than the prosecution, for his attorneys had two loyalties: one to their client and one to Brigham Young. To save Lee, Wells Spicer and William Bishop were willing to blame the Mormon leader for issuing orders Lee was obliged to obey, but George Bates and Jabez Sutherland wanted the inquiry to stop with Lee.[23]

Philip Klingensmith was the prosecution's star witness. To derail his testimony, the defense pointed out that he was under indictment for murder. Carey entered a nolle prosequi, and the "heavy, rather solid looking Dutchman, six feet high, well muscled, slow, heavy," and "phlegmatic as an oyster," proceeded to testify. He began slowly, but "gradually grew more animated; his dull eye lit up, the blue veins stood out on his forehead, and his every feature and muscle seemed to work in sympathy with the horrors he was reciting."[24] He had first learned of the emigrants when he heard they had been ordered away from Salt Lake and were on their way south. He had not mentioned Indians in his affidavit, but under cross-examination he testified that "the hills were pretty full of them," and he later estimated there were 100 to 150 Indians present. Klingensmith described the disposition of the loot, his October meeting with Brigham Young, and Young's orders: "What you know about this affair do not tell to anybody; do not even talk about it among yourselves." He admitted shooting at one of the Arkansans—"obeying orders to the fullest capacity"—but failed to testify that Lee had killed anybody. He also did not know if the order for the massacre came from George A. Smith. Klingensmith's testimony simply confirmed his previous account, but his detailed story of treachery and murder horrified the country. After hearing these tales, Lockley predicted Lee would hang: "he will soon dance on nothing."[25]

The prosecution elicited startling testimony from other witnesses but to little avail. John Bradshaw claimed that at a Sunday meeting before the massacre, Isaac Haight said "if it hadn't been for some old fools tampering with the indians they would be dead and in their graves by this time. Never mind he said they have only got further into the net."[26] The prosecution called William Young, John H. Willis, Samuel Pollock, and James Pearce and got them to admit to being present at Mountain Meadows, but none of the men would testify they had seen Lee commit any crime.[27]

At the end of July 1875, Lee's jailers engaged in a nasty fight with Emma Lee. Brooks reported a Utah tradition that Emma Lee heard one of the guards ask, "Who is that handsome woman?" and the answer: "Oh that is one of John D. Lee's whores." Emma struck the man across the face with a buggy whip and then fled Beaver, fearing arrest. Others claimed the federal marshals had found "the necessary implements" for an escape in Lee's cell and put him in chains. Emma Lee "struck the jailer with a rock because she was not permitted to enter Lee's cell. She was locked up." The *Tribune* reported she pelted Lee's jailer with stones, raised her fists, and challenged the deputy "to come on."[28]

The streets of Beaver were packed with people drawn to see John D. Lee before the bar of justice. During a recess, Marshal Maxwell warned Judge Boreman of ugly threats and advised him to request troops from Camp Cameron to guard the court. Boreman felt the mob's leaders were too cowardly to do open violence, but he told Maxwell to speak to the crowd and "hint to them that they might find every body about the court ready to meet them." Maxwell replied, "I'll do it." In the street the old veteran roared, "We are ready to meet you—come on & do your best— & we will hang any G——d——d Bishop to a telegraph pole & turn their houses over their heads—We'll show them who is going to run things down here." After a string of profane and blunt oaths, the "whole crowd knew that Maxwell was utterly fearless & brave as a lion." When Maxwell finished, the bailiff reported that the storm was over.[29]

Jabez Sutherland rocked the courtroom on July 28 when he announced he had just received an affidavit by telegram from the doctor of two defense witnesses too feeble to come to Beaver: George A. Smith and Brigham Young. (The caustic John Beadle claimed it was dread of Mr. Baskin's cross-examination, not age or ill health, that kept them out of the courtroom.)[30] Baskin thought it was a novel affair to make an affidavit by telegram. Boreman ruled the statements were irrelevant and refused to admit them.[31] The newspapers, however, soon published both and had a field day pointing out their contradictions.

Before the defense began its case, Baskin and Sutherland sparred for two hours over whether Sutherland could present evidence that "the red men were masters on the field, and compelled the whites to take part in the butchery." This strategy was an ingenious revision of the original cover story blaming the Indians. Lee now claimed, "The Indians made us do it." His appeal for sympathy stood no chance if Americans believed he had organized and led an Indian attack against his countrymen. Baskin argued there was no legal justification for unlawful killing, but Sutherland countered that "the Indians of all Southern Utah were collected on the ground to lord it over the sparse settlers." Having failed to overrun the emigrant defenses, the Indians "compelled the peaceful inhabitants to go out and take part in the assassination." Baskin won the argument by pointing out that duress could not justify such killing, since social duty and the law required a man to die before killing an innocent person, but even Baskin accepted Lee's story that the Paiutes made the first attack.[32]

It is not clear why the prosecution did not locate any of the survivors or use their 1859 statements in the trial, but prejudice kept them from calling Indians as witnesses. The non-Mormon citizens of Beaver expressed fear of a Mormon revolt in a petition to Governor Emery. The many Indians camped around the town during the trial "on several occasions inquired when the Mormons and the 'Mericats' were going to war." The petition revived the old stories that the Saints told the Indians they were the battle-ax of the Lord.[33]

One correspondent spent several days in search of the "chief of the Beavers." He located Beaverite, who provided an interesting account of the massacre from the Indian point of view. His nephew Kanosh had told him that "the story of the poisoned ox is not true, nor of the poisoned springs." The water at Corn Creek was running water, not a spring. "No persons ever poisoned it as the Mormons say," Beaverite insisted. "No Corn Creeks, Pahvants nor Beavers ever went to Mountain Meadows." Lee had recruited his old friend, Moquetus, to help kill the emigrants. Lee "led the Indians at the massacre, and Moquetus always said Lee was the Chief over him in that fight. That was the bargain." Now Lee had "got scared and says the Indians did it." Beaverite denounced the cowards who "tried to throw all the blame on the Indians."[34]

"John D. Lee is feeling very downcast," observed Frederick Lockley, who sat next to the defendant in the crowded courtroom throughout the trial. "I suppose he steeped his soul in the blood of women and children slain from a mistaken sense of religious duty, and the terrible rehearsal of his treac[h]ery must certainly appall him." The impact of the gruesome testimony on the accused moved even Lockley. "Sitting at his elbow day after day, and seeing his deep affliction, I cannot help but be a little moved at it; but when I think of his life of crime, I recognize the justice of his punishment."[35]

Wells Spicer opened Lee's defense. He blamed the Arkansans' own wicked acts for inciting the savages. Lee "tried to protect the emigrants, and wept when the massacre was proposed." Haight, Klingensmith, and Higbee plotted and carried out the massacre using their military authority and "from fear of death at the hands of the Indians."[36] The emigrants were treated kindly in Utah and furnished supplies but acted badly and caused "great trouble, so much so that the train divided and had two captains." Lee was the only man at the massacre who spoke on the emigrants' behalf, the "one man who wept for them; [the] one man who begged for reinforcements to save the emigrants." Lee alone, he claimed, stood up and said "if any five men would go with him, he would go into the corral of the emigrants, and with them, fight it out with the Indians." The hundreds of Indians at the battle compelled the twenty or thirty white men present to help in the killing, "because if they didn't the Indians would kill them and sweep off their homes, and families and settlements." Spicer divided the killers into two classes: those "prompted solely by the dictates of their own wicked hearts" and those who merely obeyed orders. John Higbee pointed a loaded rifle at Lee's head to silence his objection to "the slaughter of the innocents." Spicer told stories so incredible that even Lee did not try to pass them off when he wrote his autobiography.[37]

Spicer's associates quickly concluded his line of argument was damaging their case, which the press derided as "Spicer's boomerang," for the "more they used it against the enemy, the more it would rebound and hurt his friends." Specifically, Sutherland thought the claim that Lee acted under orders would raise the inevitable question, "Whose orders?" When Spicer returned from the noon recess, Lockley reported he read a prepared statement "in which he adroitly took back all he had said in the morning, and left the gentlemen of the jury in a hapless state of mystification." But Spicer made one very telling point: the prosecution had not presented a scintilla of evidence to prove Lee had "raised his hand to slaughter a single individual."[38]

The defense called witnesses to support its theory that the emigrants had provoked the Indians. Elisha Hoops told the poison story, claiming he saw a German doctor at Corn Creek pour the contents of a vial into a dead ox. The emigrants left bags of poison in the spring and a "boy named Robinson drank the water from one spring, and died from the effects," Hoops testified. Indians told him some of them had died the same way. Hoops faced hard questions from the prosecutors, and Robert Baskin recalled that his clumsy defense of the poison tale made him a laughingstock. Lee's attorneys called on Philo T. Farnsworth to support Hoops's testimony, but again Baskin's cross-examination demolished the story. The defense had built no solid theory of the crime before it rested on August 2.[39] As Lee noted, his lawyers were defending "some person not in court," and the divided nature of his defense caused a host of problems. Unable to agree with his co-counsels, Wells Spicer failed to appear in court for two days. "I guess they have got enough of me," he said.[40]

Closing for the defense, Sutherland claimed the Mormons had no desire to kill the emigrants, but with "one humane impulse, rushed to their aid." The Mormons had been lured to the meadows for the best of humanitarian reasons, but the Paiutes "were implacable in their wrath, and threatened even the Mormons for their efforts to pacify them." Lee negotiated the surrender in good faith, but the Indians fell on the defenseless emigrants "with the fury of demons and spared neither age nor sex." With unintended irony, Sutherland charged, "This is the way Indians generally fulfil their agreements." His co-counsels followed with attacks on Klingensmith. William Bishop spoke for five hours, Frederick Lockley wrote, "at a loss to conceive why the Almighty should have made such a man as Klingensmith."[41]

Prosecutor Baskin gave a blistering closing argument, charging that Mormon leaders had failed to investigate the crime and had thrown every impediment in the way of the law. He pointed out that Lee's counsel, George Bates, had refused to bring a single suspect to justice during his tenure as the territory's federal attorney. Most of the emigrants' property was "appropriated by the men who murdered the parents of those little orphan children." He arraigned Brigham Young as an accessory, since under Young, in Utah "no man, bishop, or any other subordinate officer, would have dared to take such an important step, or engage in such heinous scheme, if he hadn't the direct or implied sanction of the head of the church." Governor Young had violated his oath of office, failing even to prevent the robbery of the surviving children. Having abandoned any hope that the Mormon jury would convict Lee, Baskin said that no juror who had been through the temple rites at "that iniquitous grease-vat, the endowment house," could find a verdict of guilty, and he did not expect it.[42]

Judge Boreman charged the jury to determine the innocence or guilt of the defendant. Even if the Arkansans had provoked the Indians, it did not justify the murders, and there was no evidence any white man had been compelled to participate in the slaughter. If Lee had conspired in the killings, he was guilty, even if he had not slain anyone with his own hands. "Be careful to do right. Your duty is not only to the prisoner at the bar, but also to the people and your own consciences," the judge concluded. "Your action will be looked to with great interest far and near, and it behooves you to act candidly, carefully and conscientiously."[43]

The case went to the jury on August 5, 1875. "All Utah," John Beadle wrote, "waited in deep suspense for the verdict." Prevailing wisdom had it that the LDS church would dictate the outcome and Lee would be acquitted. "Agreeable to Western instincts, there was much betting on the result," Beadle said. He claimed the Mormon jurors had been instructed to find Lee not guilty, but when a "far worse case was proved than even the bitterest anti-Mormon had looked for," the church decided Lee had to be convicted. George Bates telegraphed John W. Young that a conviction was certain, and Brigham Young's son took all bets offered at the Chicago Board of Trade. The church's reversal came too late: the jurors failed to understand signals made in open court and the insiders lost their bets, for as Baskin had predicted, the hopelessly deadlocked jury did not convict. All the Mormons and the backslider J. C. Heister voted to acquit Lee; the three non-Mormons voted to convict him.[44]

The deadlock ignited a firestorm of protest across America. Longtime resident John Beadle wrote, "Utah was excited as I never saw it before." One newspaper demanded the arrest of Brigham Young before he could flee the country; another wanted the streets of Salt Lake to be ornamented with the heads of Mormon leaders. The *Chicago Tribune* wished "the fate of the slaughtered women and children might be visited upon such of the Mormon fiends as are still on the hither side of hell." Idaho's *Owyhee Avalanche* expressed the nation's general opinion of justice in Utah: "it would be as unreasonable to expect a jury of highwaymen to convict a stage robber, as it would be to get Mormons to find one of their own peculiar faith guilty of a crime." The *Sacramento Record* denounced the crimes of the "priestly demons" as "unparalleled in the long annals of human perfidy and crime." The *Leavenworth Commercial* observed that the desperate effort to exonerate Brigham Young would never convince "the world that the old sinner was not guilty of participation in the preliminaries to the inhuman outrage." Virginia City's *Enterprise* concluded the Lee trial and a thousand other atrocities meant Mormonism would be regarded "as a felony, and not a religion." *Zion's Herald* rejoiced, "It can only be a question of a limited time, and this impure and murderous abomination will be swept from the face of the earth."[45]

Robert Baskin lost an unwinnable trial, but in the process he destroyed Mormonism's public image in the court of American opinion. "There can be little doubt that Brigham Young is the arch-fiend who planned and directed the atrocity," wrote the *Indianapolis Herald*. Its call to hang "every Mormon concerned in the massacre, from the highest to the lowest," reflected a national consensus.[46] Baskin had fulfilled the vow he had made at the side of his murdered friend Dr. Robinson, for he had inflicted wounds on the Mormon theocracy that would never heal.

No Regrets for the Past: The Death of George A. Smith

On his return from Palestine in 1873, Apostle George A. Smith, the "father of southern Utah" whose vitriolic sermons inflamed the region in 1857, resumed his duties as first counselor to Brigham Young. He promoted the United Order, the prophet's last attempt to bring communalism to the Mormon people, and served as the first president of Zion's Savings Bank. While returning from St. George to Salt Lake, he visited John D. Lee at Fort Cameron on a Sunday afternoon in February 1875. The guard ignored the men as Lee spoke with his old friends during an emotional visit. The apostle shook hands with the prisoner and recalled Lee's days as Joseph Smith's bodyguard and his help for the people in their troubles. Smith asked, "John, you never turned a hungry person from your door, did you?" As Lee nodded, William Ashworth "noticed tears as large as peas running down his cheeks." Ashworth visited Lee two or three times with other leading Mormon authorities and heard similar conversations.[47]

In addition to poignant recollections, the talk turned to Lee's impending trial. A few days after his arrest, Lee recalled a visit by Apostles Smith, Orson Hyde, and Erastus Snow and other church leaders. "They each and all told me to stand to my integrity, and all would come out all right in the end," Lee wrote. On one of his annual visits to the south, Brigham Young met with Rachel Lee one night and received her with the utmost kindness. The prophet promised, "Tell Brother John to stand to his integrity to the end, and not a hair of his head shall be harmed."[48]

Following his visit with Lee in Beaver, Smith fell ill with lung trouble. Suffering intensely and unable to sleep, he never recovered. On the morning of September 1, 1875, Smith sat down in his parlor fighting for breath, and in a few minutes he was dead at age fifty-eight. The dying apostle had told Brigham Young, "I have no regrets for the past or dread of the future," but Charles Kelly claimed Smith's doctor said his patient died of fright. Lee recalled Smith as "a Man Much beloved" and a "true friend to the Truth."[49]

Federal investigators suspected that in August 1857 Smith carried Brigham Young's orders to massacre the Fancher train to southern Utah. Charles Wandell charged that

Smith (who he called Brigham Young's "fat Aide-de-Camp") issued the "orders from headquarters" to kill all the emigrants except the little children at a military council in Parowan attended by Haight, Dame, and Lee. Yet Robert Baskin, Smith's bitter enemy, said there was "very strong circumstantial evidence" the apostle gave Haight the orders at Cedar City but conceded there was no direct evidence he ordered the murders. There is no doubt, however, that Smith inflamed the hysteria that made the massacre possible.[50]

IF WE HAD PLENTY OF MONEY: THE DEAL

After his first trial, federal officers moved Lee to the territorial penitentiary in Salt Lake and offered to free him if he would testify against fellow participants and implicate Brigham Young. Deputy Marshal Stokes visited Lee in September 1875 and pressured him to strike a deal with the prosecution. Lee advised Stokes to tell his fellow federal officers "that if the Truth will Satisfy them they can have it," but he would remain in prison "till I rot & be Eat up with the Bedbugs before I will dishonor myself by bearing fals[e] witness against any Man, Much less an innocent Man." Marshal George Maxwell had befriended Lee and tried to persuade him to turn state's evidence, but he gave up when it became clear Lee would be loyal to the Mormons until it was too late. Lee told him, "I chose to die like a man then to live like a villian." Bill Hickman received a similar answer when he urged Lee "to Make a clean sweep of all & be free." Lee stuck to his resolve as he entertained a constant stream of visitors and journalists, all eager to meet the Great Terror of the West.[51]

William Dame joined Lee at the prison on September 25, 1875. The two men reconciled, and Dame told Lee "in a low voice for us to be patient & keep quiet, that Higbee and Stewart would Soon be out of the country where they could not be found." Dame borrowed Lee's razor and gave his fellow prisoner peaches, apples, "a paper of Tea," and Dr. Ingram's Macadona Magic Oil.[52] The two consoled each other until Dame was transferred to Beaver in mid-January 1876.

As Lee and Dame languished in jail, the marshals intensified their hunt for the other suspects. In September 1875 they searched the houses of W. H. Branch and John Macfarlane—Dame's attorney and an eyewitness to the massacre—for Haight and Higbee, who again escaped. The deputies captured George Adair, Jr., in November 1875 and jailed him at Beaver. The failure of the national and territorial legislatures to fund the federal courts delayed the Dame and Lee trials, originally scheduled for September 1875, and a scandal led to the replacement of Marshal Maxwell. His critics charged Maxwell had been intoxicated most of the time he was in Beaver and let Lee and Dame "have their women or *concubines* to cohabit with in their place of confinement."[53] One of Lee's guards complained that Lee did in fact have "connection with Rachael" every night and, falling back on his old habits, "used to boast about it."[54]

Lee's motives for protecting Young were complex, but they were not selfless. His daughter claimed that after the first trial, Daniel Wells came to Beaver to find a scapegoat. "Wells went to Dame and told him it was better for one man to suffer than the whole Church." Dame would have none of it and told Wells, "My life is as sweet to me as yours is to you; you get me out of here or I'll put the saddle on the right horse!" Wells took his problem to Lee "about staying low and letting the bed-bugs pack him out." Lee replied, "I always said I would stand between the cannon and Brigham Young before I will turn traitor to my people."[55] Lee's daughter Miriam Lee Cornelius recalled, "He promised that if any one had to be tried for the Mountain Meadow trouble he would do it."[56] Lee could not believe that the church would desert him. "I had every confidence that Brigham Young would save me at last," he said. "I had his solemn word that I would not suffer."[57]

As his financial situation deteriorated, Lee struggled to raise money to pay his attorneys. A warden suggested Lee could make $2,000 lecturing at the Centennial Exposition. Lee considered "getting up a brief sketch of [his] life with Photograph &c" for his contemplated lecture tour. He discussed it with William Bishop, but the attorney was too busy to help his client get started in show business. Bishop had strongly advised avoiding a second trial before Judge Boreman and proposed to "exhaust all we know of law, Management, trickery and curuption before we permit the case to be tried again before one who is so thoroughly opposed to the defendant."[58]

Sumner Howard of Michigan replaced William Carey as U.S. Attorney for Utah Territory on April 25, 1876.[59] Through George Q. Cannon, his man in Congress, Brigham Young had closely monitored the appointment. Fearing that the new U.S. Attorney would not be sympathetic to the Mormons, Cannon gathered information on Howard's character, learning that he was forty to forty-five years old, was in comfortable circumstances, had been a temperance lecturer, and was a recent convert to Methodism and a licensed preacher. All admitted he had ability, was a fine speaker, and was considered "one of the best criminal lawyers," Apostle Cannon reported.[60]

One of Cannon's sources thought Howard was fair and would not conduct a crusade. If Howard were "inclined to take a wrong course," Judge Philip Emerson and Jabez Sutherland, the First Presidency's attorney who knew Howard well, could influence him. Howard was popular, but many people questioned his integrity and thought he "was on the make." He lacked good judgment but would be a good choice to get "a case put through." Cannon's informant asked if the Mormons had plenty of money and "plainly intimated that [they] could 'fix' him." "In reply to which I said that was not our style, and that if an officer thought he could be blackmailed, he had better not go there," Cannon said. Nonetheless, Howard "could be managed if taken in hand before he took the wrong *chute*." The U.S. Attorney General wanted to avoid further legal controversies in Utah and "hoped [the Mormons] would find him a good man." Still skeptical, Cannon concluded that if he did not learn something more favorable, he would work to defeat the nomination. He tried to delay Howard's confirmation, but in late April the nomination was "pressed through by the influence of his friends." "I trust it will be overruled for good," Cannon wrote.[61]

The "embarrassments to the situation" Sumner Howard found in Utah surprised him. His office was "in a *most wretched condition*—no files, no history of any of the many important cases to be attended to and every one of these old matters to be looked up and put in shape for trial." There was no proper office or library. But Howard promised, "I want to succeed and *will if it takes a leg*." Judge Emerson endorsed all that Howard said but noted, "He has not and can not as yet fully comprehend the magnitude and extent of the work before him."[62]

Howard would have done well to listen to veterans of the government's war with the Mormon theocracy. Robert Baskin believed that as a lion, Brigham Young was not of much consequence, but when he failed "to accomplish his purpose in [that] role . . . he will assume that of the fox, in which he is very formidable."[63] Young had ceased to roar about Mountain Meadows, and he now proceeded to match wits with the ambitious prosecutor, whose political survival required him to convict *someone* for the massacre. Only a conviction would appease his superiors in Washington, who in turn felt immense pressure from a public outraged at the perversion of justice embodied in the deadlock of the first Lee trial. Given conditions, Howard seemed to face certain defeat, for in early 1876 it appeared extremely unlikely that any Utah jury would convict Lee. In a case that threatened to shake the LDS church to its foundations, the prosecutor found he could only secure a guilty verdict with the cooperation of Mormon authorities. As attorneys do, Howard made a deal.

Neither side revealed the specific terms of the arrangement, and it is unlikely they were written down. Characteristically, Brigham Young conducted the negotiations himself. Marshal William Nelson told a Mormon friend he and Howard had been appointed specifically to prosecute Lee. On reaching Utah "they went to Pres. Young and asked him for his aid in the matter, that is to put them on the line where they could get the witnesses." Young said they were the first U.S. officials to ask for his aid in the matter and they would have it. Nelson said he tracked down the witnesses and now "knew more about this tragedy than Brigham Young ever did."[64]

The marshal did not specify the exact terms of the agreement, but Baskin had no doubt that U.S. Attorney Howard agreed to impanel a Mormon jury, place the letters and affidavits of Brigham Young and George A. Smith in evidence, and exonerate Mormon authorities of complicity in the massacre. In exchange, Young would deliver witnesses and documents—and guarantee the conviction of John D. Lee.[65] Most important, Howard would drop indictments against the prisoners in government custody, notably William Dame.

With Howard's appointment, Lee's second trial was delayed to September 1876, and Lee, Dame, and Adair were released on bail. Lee toured southern Utah, visiting his families, who were scattered across the Mormon frontier. As his children recalled, he acted as if his death was a forgone conclusion. Lee counseled them to cling to the

LDS church but predicted the church would not survive very long under Brigham Young's leadership. As he prepared to leave Lee's Ferry for the last time, the doting father said farewell to each of his children, "embracing and bidding [them] good-bye." One daughter, seven-year-old Mereb Emma Lee, was missing. She recalled, "They found me with my small roll of worn quilts and clothes which I had gathered together, huddling in the corner of the wagon, ready to go along, and Oh! how my heart was broken when father told me I could not go." Lee kissed his daughter. "[He] put me and my belongings out. I cried until I cried myself to sleep and when I awoke, I was still crying." Emma Lee said that word from Mormon authorities arrived at Lonely Dell in late August telling Lee to jump bond and go into Mexico. But Lee had already left, and he seemed to prefer to face death rather than break his bond.[66]

After Young withdrew his support, the firm of Sutherland & Bates abandoned Lee's defense in the second trial. Wells Spicer and William Bishop, "a little man with a Big Heart," remained in Lee's corner, with the addition of J. C. Foster. On being released on bail in May 1876, Lee learned Daniel Wells had been "tampering" with his wife Emma to gain control of the ferry, which Lee claimed began to "shake [his] faith in the anointed of the Lord." When he entered the court at Beaver, he wrote, "I was met with the same hypocritical smile and whisper, as on other occasions, and told to 'Stand to your integrity. Let the will of the Lord's anointed be your pleasure. My mouth is sealed, but I know you will come out all right.'"[67]

To Fasten the Rope around My Neck: Lee's Second Trial

On the nineteenth anniversary of the massacre, September 11, 1876, Lee returned to Beaver for his second trial, again before Judge Jacob Boreman. Perhaps fearing Lee "meant to take leg bail," businessman William Hooper withdrew his $15,000 bond, a "strange and mysterious" move that landed an astonished Lee in jail.[68] If his friends betrayed him, he would not betray them. "I ain't going on the witness stand to save my scalp," he said. "Cowards and traitors only do that." He constantly talked about being true to his friends, even if he hanged for it. Lee professed to be confident, but it was "plainly discernable" that he was extremely uneasy.[69]

On the day the trial began, prosecutor Sumner Howard quashed the indictment against William Dame, claiming he lacked enough evidence to prosecute him. The deal he had struck with Brigham Young troubled even Howard. On the first day of the trial, the prosecutor stopped Judge Boreman as he was going to court. "Judge, I have eaten dirt & I have gone down out of sight in dirt & expect to eat more dirt," Howard said. He assured Boreman he had done nothing wrong and asked for "a chance to show to the world that what [he has] done or may do is right." He pledged "to leave no stone unturned to show who the instigators & promoters of this massacre were." "Give me time & I will show that my course has been proper."[70] Howard's faith in his ability to outsmart Young was matched only by Lee's long-held faith that his adoptive father would not betray him. Neither man appreciated the ability of Mormon leaders to manufacture evidence and manipulate justice.[71]

Brigham Young's second counselor, Daniel Wells, arrived in Beaver to oversee the interests of the LDS church during the second Lee trial. In many ways it would be the last battle of the Utah War for the former commander of the Nauvoo Legion. Wells immediately preached a "red-hot sermon" on duty and then directed the selection of jurors. Amorah Lee Smithson learned of the plan to sacrifice her father when she crawled up to a bonfire out in the brush where Wells was meeting with local authorities. Frank Lee recalled that each designated juror had "a star pinned under his arm so it would be known whom to chose." Lee's attorney, William Bishop, showed a list of prospective jurors to a group of Mormons and had them select those who were certain to acquit Lee under any circumstances, and Lee claimed church leaders promised Bishop these men would acquit his client.[72] Robert Baskin was not involved in prosecuting the second Lee trial, but when he learned "that all the Gentiles had been challenged off the jury, and that Daniel H. Wells was present at the trial, [he] stated then that John D. Lee was doomed." Although personally convinced of Lee's guilt, Baskin felt that even Lee "was entitled to a trial by a jury which was not subject to any outside influence, and had not been packed for the purpose of securing his conviction by a Mormon jury."[73]

"The One-Eyed Pirate of the Wasatch," as the *Tribune* called Wells, was the prosecution's first witness. Wells took the stand "batting his swivel eye like a toad in an ash heap" to testify that in 1857 Lee was Farmer to the Indians, was popular with them, and had been a major in the militia, although Wells thought Lee had been replaced earlier in 1857.[74] Judge Boreman excluded Wells's irrelevant testimony but recognized that his mere presence let the jury know that the LDS church supported the prosecution. As the judge watched the trial progress, "it slowly began to dawn upon the minds of the people that Howard had made some kind of a deal with the heads of the church, whereby witnesses who had been in hiding were brought forth and their tongues loosened."[75] Lee charged Wells was sent to Beaver "to have the thing cut & dried which he did to perfection."[76]

President Wells kept Brigham Young informed of the trial by telegraph. As the trial began on September 14, 1876, his message appeared to report that the prosecutor was fulfilling his part of the bargain with the LDS church. "Dame was discharged," Wells wired. "Howard made no effort to get Gentiles on the Jury—In fact the word Mormon was scarcely mentioned in Court at all today—There is no excitement but the people were completely taken by surprise at the change from what things were here-to-fore—all well."[77] Mormon authorities had assured William Bishop that his client would not be convicted, so he "was completely taken by surprise when he saw that the Church was actually aiding the prosecution." Bishop concluded Howard had a secret understanding with Brigham Young that if Lee were convicted and executed, the matter would stop there. Bishop finally realized what he was up against in "Brother"

Howard. "We now know we are fighting the indictment," he told the court, "and also the secret forces and power of the Mormon church."[78]

In his opening statement, Howard made it clear he had not come to try Brigham Young and the LDS church but to prosecute John D. Lee for his crimes. He claimed Lee had induced the Indians to attack the emigrants in direct opposition to the desires of Mormon leaders. Lee had drawn other men into the fight under false pretenses; he had devised the scheme to kill the emigrants; he had killed at least four of them himself; and he had plundered their property for his own use. Despite mounting evidence to the contrary, Lee still believed church leaders and prominent Mormons would save him. He only slowly realized that "those low, deceitful, treacherous, cowardly, dastardly sycophants and serfs had combined to fasten the rope around [his] neck."[79]

I Did Not Wish My Feelings Harrowed Up:
Brigham Young's Affidavit

One of Howard's first moves was to enter into evidence the July 1875 affidavits of George A. Smith and Brigham Young. Although his lawyer told him the statements were not "legal evidence," Lee insisted the affidavits be admitted.[80] Given the problems with the sworn statements, Howard appeared to be suborning perjury, but the affidavits convinced the jury that Lee and not the LDS church was on trial. Brigham Young's statements attempted to soften the hard edges of his policy during the Utah War. His August 1857 orders not to "let a kernal go to waste or be sold to our enemies" were not ambiguous, but Young now swore he had advised citizens not to sell grain as livestock feed but to let emigrants "have sufficient for themselves if they were out." Asked if he had the letter from Isaac Haight inquiring what to do about the emigrants, Young said, "I have not. I have made diligent search for it, but can not find it." He apparently could not find the September 10, 1857, letter that was later produced from the church's files which directed Haight not to meddle with the emigrants but to "preserve good feelings" with the Indians.[81]

The manuscript copies of the affidavits now in the LDS Archives not only reveal that Young had the luxury of revising his written answers but also that he reworded the questions. Question 9 asked whether Lee reported the massacre, "and if so, what did you reply to him?" Young initially wrote, "He did.—I think he called within three months after the massacre—he had much to say with regard to the Indians, their being stirred up to anger threatening the settlements of the whites—and after considerable conversation from Lee he commenced to give me a detail[ed account] of the massacre—I ~~requested~~ told him to stop ~~I did not wish to hear anything about it   as I had heard from various others enough to sicken the heart of any man, and so I utterly refused to hear any of his details~~." In the final draft Young conceded, "[Lee started to give me] an account of the massacre—I told him to stop, as from what I had already learned by rumor, I did not wish my feelings harrowed up with a recital of the details." As one historian noted, Brigham Young's "singular delicacy" has never seemed wholly convincing.[82]

The press had already demolished Young's "very thin" statement. Many noted the contradiction between his claim that Isaac Haight had alerted him "concerning a company of emigrants called the Arkansas company" and his assertion that despite his position as Indian superintendent, he learned nothing of the attack "until some time after it occurred—then only by floating rumor." The *Sacramento Record* observed, "It is adding insult to injury for a man in Young's position to affront the intelligence of the nation with so bald, so puerile a tissue of flummery as this." Robert Baskin concluded the affidavits were designed to break the force of the testimony at the first trial that implicated Young and Smith as accomplices in the crime.[83] In addition to the sworn statements, Howard submitted Young's proclamation of martial law, his January 1858 report to the Office of Indian Affairs, and Lee's November 20, 1857, report of the massacre.

Howard now presented his witnesses. While not a single faithful Mormon appeared for the prosecution at the first trial, enough testified at the second to make up a respectable congregation. The jury heard from Laban Morrill, James Haslam, and Joel White. Wagon driver Samuel Knight charged that Lee clubbed a woman to death, and Samuel McMurdy claimed he saw Lee shoot a woman and two or three of the wounded.[84] During their testimony, Lee broke down and had to be removed from the courtroom. The outraged Lee paced the floor of his cell, Beadle reported, "cursing the Mormon leaders who, he said, had betrayed him." Lee claimed Knight and McMurdy "swore that [he] committed the awful deeds, that they did with their own wicked hands."[85]

According to the family traditions of Howard's two star witnesses, Nephi Johnson and Jacob Hamblin received letters from Brigham Young ordering them to testify and telling them what to say. Like Lee, Johnson had been a fugitive for years. After he dismounted his mule in Beaver, the local bishop introduced him to the sheriff, who said he did not recall seeing him before. "No," said Johnson, "you've never seen me, but I've seen you many, many times."[86]

Johnson testified he had watched the massacre from a nearby hill and swore that "Klingensmith and John D. Lee seemed to be engineering the whole thing." Johnson, a Nauvoo Legion lieutenant, had in fact ordered the assault on the women and children. He claimed he saw Lee shoot a woman and help the Indians pull the wounded from the wagons.[87] An embittered Lee soon wrote, "Nephi Johnson was the last man that I could have believed that would have sealed his damnation by bearing false testimony against me, his neighbor, to take away my life."[88]

Jacob Hamblin, who Judge Boreman considered an uncouth backwoodsman who was "ready to do anything that the church desired him to do," volunteered a bizarre story. He claimed Lee had told him in September 1857 that a Paiute chief had captured two girls the Indian thought "*didn't ought* to be killed" since they were pretty, but Lee insisted they were too old to let live. The Indian shot one of the girls and Lee killed the other. "He threw her down and cut her throat," Hamblin testified. His testimony "convinced some who heard it that another crime was committed before the girls were killed," as Beadle described Hamblin's implication that Lee had raped the girls.[89] By charging Lee with crimes probably committed by his adopted son, Albert, Hamblin may have been settling old scores.

Lee's attorney asked Hamblin why he had not told his story before. "Because I did not feel like it," he answered. "It is the first time I ever felt that any good would come of it. I kept it to myself until it was called for in the proper place." Hamblin admitted that "pretty soon after it happened," he had told Brigham Young and George A. Smith everything he knew about the massacre, including apparently the horrific details, for then he "recollected more of it." Young informed him that "as soon as we can get a court of justice, we will ferret this thing out, but till then don't say anything about it." Bishop asked if Hamblin felt the proper time had now come. "I do indeed," said the old missionary, but he conceded he had not told all.[90]

As Brooks noted, Hamblin "could not remember what he did not want to tell; like others, his whole purpose was to convict Lee without involving anyone else." Non-Mormons were convinced this most excellent citizen told lie on top of lie at Brigham Young's request "and covered himself fathoms deep with perjury" to protect his fellow Mormons. "The cross-examination though severe especially on Johnson elicited nothing to help the defense except to furnish some buncombe," Daniel Wells telegraphed Salt Lake. "Lee's counsel find their hands full at present."[91]

Lee complained that none of these witnesses testified to the whole truth. "Some have told part truth, while others lied clear through, but all of the witnesses who were at the massacre have tried to throw all the blame on me, and to protect the other men who took part in it." Lee reserved his bitterist invective for the man he called "Dirty Fingered Jake," Jacob Hamblin. "The old hypocrite," Lee wrote to his wife Emma, "thought that now was his chance to reek his vengeance on me by swearing away my life." He called Hamblin "the fiend of Hell" and bitterly resented his perjury, but he now realized the lengths to which LDS authorities would go to convict him.[92]

By the time the prosecution rested, Lee knew he had been betrayed. In despair he ordered his attorneys to present no defense. Rachel Lee told her son, "Lawyer Bishop cried like a baby when Father turned him off just before the last trial, and said it would be the end of him." Rachel pleaded with her husband to "tell what he knew. He always said to her, 'Get behind me, Satan.'" In his summation, Bishop argued that Lee simply followed orders. Now "the Mormon Church had resolved to sacrifice Lee, discarding him as of no further use." Sumner Howard used his closing statement to defend the authorities of the LDS church. He "had unanswerable evidence that the authorities of the Mormon Church knew nothing of the butchery till after it was committed" and that Lee had "misrepresented the facts to President Young." Howard had received all the assistance any U.S. official could ask for from the church. "Nothing had been kept back." He demanded Lee's conviction, neatly offering the all-Mormon jury the choice of assigning blame for the massacre to Lee or to their church.[93]

The case went to the jury at 11:45 A.M. on September 20. By 3:30 P.M. the jurors had convicted John D. Lee of murder in the first degree. "Mormonism prevented conviction at the first trial," William Bishop concluded, "and at the second trial Mormonism insured conviction."[94] The jurors themselves knew that Brigham Young had furnished the witnesses and evidence to convict Lee. Andrew Corry was the last to vote to find Lee guilty. Juror Walter Granger "talked and reasoned with me," he said, "but I felt miserable, just as though the devil had some power over me." Finally, juror Stephen S. Barton related a dream that the jury was in the harvest field with their rifles. A flock of blackbirds flew by, followed by a flock of white geese. The mob and the apostate blackbirds wanted Brigham Young, and Lee knew it. The jurors shot a white goose and "the great flock of blackbirds rose. Lee was the white goose." Correy concluded, "Some one had to be sacrificed, so at last I gave in." He recalled how the hero Nephi had killed Laban in *The Book of Mormon*: "Better for one man to die than for a whole nation to dwindle in unbelief."[95]

The verdict surprised no one, except perhaps John D. Lee, who found himself "perfectly whiped out." He could justly complain that the evidence used to convict him was "as false as the hinges of hell, and this evidence was wanted to sacrifice [him]." His conviction convinced him that some men would "swear that black is white if the good Brethren only say so." Since his return to Beaver he had suspected "there was treachery and conspiracy on foot," but even after the verdict he refused to believe he was doomed. "I have many a warm hearted noble minded friend whom I believe will never see me sacrificed at the shrine of imposition bigotry & falsehood & ignorance," he wrote. "My firm conviction is that all will come out right in the end."[96]

Lee was in more trouble than he knew, but trouble entangled almost everyone involved in his case. Like many of the federal officers who cooperated with the Saints, George Bates found himself not only scorned but also unpaid. Brigham Young had hired Bates & Sutherland to defend Lee, but in 1877 Bates asked Baskin to sue the LDS church "to recover for the services so performed, as payment of a large portion thereof had been refused by Brigham." Baskin filed a complaint, but Bates married and left the territory without collecting the debt.[97]

17

He Died Game

THE EXECUTION OF JOHN D. LEE

As Rachel Lee passed through Johnsonville on her return to Arizona after her husband's trial, her son John Amasa Lee recalled, "Nephi Johnson approached her wagon and spoke to her and offered to shake her hand." Rachel considered the offer of the man whose perjured testimony had helped to condemn her husband. She said bitterly, "Let every dog shake his own paw." Johnson drew back and replied, "Sister Lee, I am not to blame for the way you feel about me, for I said only what I was told to say."[1] Lee's daughter Amorah said Johnson later told her that if he had it to do over again, "he would rather die himself than to swear that man's life away."[2] Johnson could never bring himself to admit publicly that he had led the killing of the women and children at Mountain Meadows, but years later when others lied about the massacre even to Mormon apostles, Johnson told the truth: "White men did most of the killing."[3]

THE CORE OF THE ROTTENNESS

Judge Boreman sentenced Lee to die on October 10, 1876. Territorial law gave Lee the choice of being hanged, shot, or beheaded, the preferred method of blood atonement. By choosing to be shot rather than beheaded, Lee seemed to indicate he had no need of blood atonement. At the sentencing Boreman charged that Lee's trials revealed high LDS church authorities had "inaugurated and decided upon the wholesale slaughter of the emigrants." From the time the crime took place there had been "a persistent and determined opposition to an investigation of the massacre" throughout the territory. The pro-Mormon *Ogden Junction* called Boreman's outburst a disgraceful act for a public officer and an attack on District Attorney Howard's veracity.[4]

Judge Boreman was not the only person in the territory who questioned the federal prosecutor's honesty and tactics. The *Salt Lake Tribune* charged that Sumner Howard's deal with Brigham Young had cost him "the confidence of every honest man in Utah in his integrity."[5] The virulent reaction to his victory threatened to end Howard's private ambition to succeed Judge Boreman on the Utah bench. His conduct of the Lee trial won him Mormon support, but to be credible to the Republican administration in Washington, Howard had to demonstrate that he was as well equipped to deal with Utah's impossible legal problems as anyone. Howard had to discredit his political enemies among the territory's small but vocal non-Mormon community and vindicate his actions and legal strategy to the U.S. Attorney General, Alphonso Taft.

District Attorney Howard and Marshal William Nelson signed a letter claiming their predecessors had boasted they would fix the odium of the "butchering upon the Mormon Church." Howard had won a conviction, but his critics had only succeeded in wasting a large amount of public money to no purpose except the advancement of their own political ambitions. Howard and Nelson said it "became apparent early in the investigation, that there is no evidence whatever to connect the chief authorities of the Mormon Church with the Massacre." They praised LDS church leaders for "their assistance in unravelling the mystery of this foul crime" and for producing proof it was the work of an individual.[6] Howard did not attempt to explain how an individual could murder one hundred twenty people or why his innocent Mormon allies had obstructed justice during the first trial by withholding evidence.

Two weeks later Howard reversed course in a letter to Taft. He claimed he had provoked Utah's non-Mormons to lull the suspicions of the Mormons. Now Howard hoped to arrest Haight, Higbee, and Stewart, but he apparently still believed he did not have enough evidence to convict their commanding officer, William Dame. Lee's conviction was "working its *intended* results," and he would "arrest the others, who are nearer to the 'seat of power' than Lee ever was, thus gradually work our way to the core of the rottenness."[7]

Having already publicly exonerated Brigham Young, it is not clear where Sumner Howard expected to find the core of the rottenness. He again claimed Lee's conviction had stolen the thunder of those who had been unable to win a guilty verdict themselves: "It seems marvelous that any set of men should regret the conviction of the chief butcher of Mountain Meadows, but disappointment and envy together with the loss of political capital will drive men into strange positions." Howard accused his enemies of making malicious misrepresentations to the public, and he was sure their complaints had reached Washington. His fears were confirmed when former deputy marshal Edwin Gilman charged that Howard had suppressed the portions of Lee's confession that implicated Young.[8]

George Q. Cannon reported to Young in January 1877 that Howard was in Washington. "So far as I could learn he spoke fairly about us," Cannon wrote, "and has endeavored to give a correct idea of the situation of affairs in the Territory." Howard appeared to be sympathetic to the LDS church's stand in the Ann Eliza Young divorce case and was exceedingly anxious to replace Judge Boreman as a territorial justice. "He has urged me to use my influence for him," Cannon noted, "and has promised that he will deal fairly with us, and says we will never have reason to regret securing him the appointment." Cannon concluded that getting the office for Howard "would be as good a move as could be made under the circumstances." "If Boreman were to get reappointed, we have nothing to hope from him except persecution and ignorant proceedings. If anybody else were to be appointed, we might get somebody as bad or worse."[9]

The Justice Department again recalled Sumner Howard to Washington in summer 1877 to answer accusations he had formed an unholy alliance with Brigham Young. Howard easily refuted the charges and began an alternative assault on Mormon power so inept as to raise questions about its sincerity. He bungled an attempt in July 1877 to challenge the naturalization papers of Utah congressional delegate George Q. Cannon, which led Cannon's Liberal Party opponent, Robert Baskin, to break off relations with the prosecutor. Howard hoped to use the testimony of apostate S. D. Sirrine to reopen the Morrisite case but warned his superiors there would be resistance, riot, and perhaps bloodshed if he arrested his suspects.[10]

Circumstances suggest that the Mormons had corrupted Howard, but he may simply have been an honest public servant trying to make the best of an impossible situation. In this case "the best" was perhaps the conviction of a single man. Howard continued to support legislation to limit the power of Mormon theocracy and stressed "the great importance of following the conviction of Lee with that of others equally guilty." He asked for funds to hire a special detective to track down the fugitives, complaining that every move the federal marshals made was watched and noted. Taft appointed William Stokes to investigate, but these efforts came to naught. In late April 1877 Howard proposed examining Brigham Young's 1857 Indian accounts. Howard wrote that he had very good evidence "Young had the benefit of the property of the murdered Emigrants and defrauded the United States." He received copies of the financial records, but having already exhausted the territorial court's annual budget, his investigation produced nothing.[11]

Defense attorney William Bishop believed Howard had successfully convicted Lee by "beating the Mormons at their own game of trickery," but it is not apparent who had been tricked. The prosecutor's ambition to replace Judge Boreman proved futile. His single accomplishment as federal prosecutor in Utah Territory was the conviction Brigham Young had arranged for him in the Lee trial. The Justice Department replaced Howard in February 1878, warning his successor to pursue only worthwhile cases.[12] Perhaps by then Howard appreciated the insight of Robert Baskin: the Lion of the Lord was in truth a very formidable fox.

Less than two weeks before Lee was scheduled to die, William Stewart, the Mountain Meadows veteran who had murdered artist William Aden in 1857, wrote to Brigham Young from Cedar City. "For the last three years I have been an outcast," he reported. Since his indictment in September 1874, the press had denounced Stewart as one of the most bloodthirsty villains of the massacre, but as a fugitive he had done the church's work, serving missions to the Orabis and Navajos and exploring two roads to the Colorado. "I am getting tired of being hunted by Government Officials," he said. Because of his situation, he was "not so well off in this worlds goods as many who could stay at home." Stewart asked the church president to find someone to buy his share of the Cedar City gristmill for $600. "I would like with your consent and approbation to go to Scotland and gather a geneaology of my friends," he asked, "and perhaps do a little good there and also be out of the way untill this trouble is over. . . . A word from you without signature will be sufficient."[13]

The federal government would not bring another prosecution for the murders at Mountain Meadows.

COME UP AND FACE THE MUSIC

The LDS church got the verdict it wanted at Lee's second trial, but it did so at considerable cost to the consciences of jurors and witnesses. Walter Granger told John Amasa Lee "if he had to do it over he would die before he would sign another man's life away." Lee "paid the penalty, but just the same he was a good man," Andrew Correy claimed. "Lee was as much a sacrifice for the Church as any man had ever been."[14] Lee had no unkind feelings toward the jury that convicted him. "The evidence was strong against me," he said. And with the court's instructions, Lee felt, the jury could do nothing but convict.[15]

Of his many wives, only Caroline, Emma, and Rachel remained loyal to Lee. Their devotion was astonishing. "I have not sold out yet," Emma Lee wrote. "I will stand by you in all your travails till the last let what may come [and] all Hell may boil over for all I care." She believed her husband's protests that he was innocent. "Put the saddle on the right horse & then all will be right," she urged. "You should have done it before now." She wished Daniel Wells had drowned in the Colorado and that the Navajos had burned "that old black devil of a Jacob Hamblin" when they had him, but they would "catch him yet."[16]

In the wake of his conviction, Lee lost all sympathy for his fellow murderers and felt they too "should come up and face the music." He devised a scheme to deliver Haight, Higbee, and Stewart to the authorities in exchange for his freedom. He directed Rachel to ask three or four of his sons to collect some twenty Indians, "say Buck & Steetum to find out the retreat of the 3 men." The boys and the Indians would then "slip up on their camp at Night—get good positions & lay there till light" and "get the drop on them." They "all could be covered with guns at once & be compelled to surrender." Lee warned his boys to "disarm them at once [and] let there be no fooling in the matter." They should deliver the prisoners to Judge Boreman at Beaver. "Remember," he warned, "my liberty will depend on the capture of these men."[17]

Richard Sloan, a "highwayman" who had shared the Beaver jail with Lee during the second trial, played a part in this bizarre scheme. Using the nom de guerre Idaho

Bill, Sloan passed himself off as one of the massacre orphans and convinced Lee and his wife Rachel he was "the identical Chas. Fancher; the little boy that [Lee] saved from the Indians at Mountain Meadows."¹⁸ Sloan claimed his father, Allen Fancher, had been captain of the murdered emigrants and that his sister Mary had married a fellow survivor, J. W. Baxter, and was living in Wyoming.¹⁹ No stranger to deception himself, Lee was taken in by this clever charlatan. Idaho Bill and Nate Hanson of Pioche joined the plot to capture Haight, Higbee, and Stewart. Lee wrote to his son Harvey Parley Lee recommending Idaho Bill, but the highwayman was unexpectedly "lodged in the Pen" in Salt Lake. The scheme had the support of Marshal Nelson, and on his advice Lee asked Hanson to capture the three fugitives. Lee hoped Hanson would carry out the plan as "understood by you & me—use dilligence & caution— Keep matters close & if you succeed you will be liberally rewarded."²⁰

There would be no romantic escape from justice for Lee. The leaders of his church had deserted him, but "if there is a god in heaven," he wrote, "they will surely have to atone for their damnable treachery & hypocrisy." Lee would write his memoirs and try to "remove that foul odium & dark cloud of collumny that has so long clouded the atmosphere of myself & Family & let the blame rest where it belong[s]."²¹ Until the end he could not accept personal responsibility for his crimes. "If I have sinned and violated the laws of my country, I have done so because I have blindly followed and obeyed the order of the Church leaders," he wrote. "I was guided in all that I did which is called criminal, by the orders of the leaders in the Church of Jesus Christ of Latter-Day Saints."²²

THE SINS OF MY BRETHREN: LEE'S CONFESSIONS

Several unsuccessful appeals delayed Lee's execution until March 1877. Lee asked Rachel to bring his journals to his cell in Beaver to take to the territorial penitentiary. "I will have the privilige there of writing a sketch of my life & by doing so I hope to let the world learn the true facts in the mater," he noted dryly, "cut who it may." Lee urgently asked his family to send all his personal records—journals, letters, and account books. He needed them for references as well for facts that might be helpful to him. His situation brought home to him "the absolute necessity of having all [his] Journals carefully looked up & carefully packed together and brought to [him]." He requested "all of [his] Diaries from the time that [he] came into Iron county with G. A. Smith in 1850 down to the present date." He wanted his letters and communications with Brigham Young, particularly the "letter of instruction about the General move and mode of warfare" and one "about the indians preparing for war." Lee specifically asked for his Indian Farmer account book, which he had buried. He was sure Rachel and Emma would leave no "stone unturned" until they found them.²³

Some say an 1857 journal containing Lee's own story of the Mountain Meadows massacre survived until after his capture. Historian Charles Kelly claimed that in 1875

Lee's son-in-law, Henry Darrow, and a stranger went to Lee's Ferry and "took certain papers from his desk and ordered the rest destroyed, which was done by Emma Lee." Emma allegedly said three men came to Lonely Dell looking for Lee's 1857 diary. "It had the three orders from Dame and Haight to go and take part in the massacre, pinned in the book." Emma said the men burned it.[24] Lee himself believed most of his private writings and journals had been destroyed or at least kept from him. He could have told more about "the doings of the Church" if he had them, but he had delivered several journals to Brigham Young "and never could get them again."[25]

When his records failed to appear, Lee asked his daughter Amorah and her husband, Lehi Smithson, to collect them. Smithson went to Arizona and retrieved the 1859 journal, which Lee described as having a "yellow back sheepskin cover made in the pocket book style tolerably large." Smithson tore out the pages that contained writing and discarded the rest "because he could not pack it a horse back." Emma insisted that the journal was incomplete and that Lee would be vexed when he saw it, but Smithson said "he took all the writing there was in the book," though he agreed "there was some gone."[26] Lee gave the journals in his possession to William Bishop with the right to use them as he thought best.[27]

Mormon authorities pressured Emma Lee at Lonely Dell to surrender control of the ferry, her only source of income. Lee vehemently denied that the ferryboat was church property. He complained of Brigham Young's avarice and his desire to "control everything where there is a dollar to be made." Referring to himself in the third person, Lee caustically noted that when "John gets tired of giving all he has & is not willing to continue to be a serf any longer, John all at once is considered to be an Enemy to the Church." In the same letter to Emma, he denounced his former mentor with a vehemence he would soon pour into his confessions:

> you Know the policy of Brigham is to get into possession & control everything where there is a dollar to be made. . . . If he considered [himself] no accessory to the deed why would he bring men whose hands have been died in human Blood to swear away my life & make an offering of me to save his guilty Petts. . . . He thinks it a friendly act, to sacrifice me, to make me attone for the sins of his Pets as well as my own by shedding my blood. You know that is one of his peculiar ways of showing his Kindness to some men by killing them to save them but that Kind of Friendship is getting too thin, it is too much like the love that a Hungry wolf has for an innocent lamb.[28]

An observer claimed in March 1877 that the only relic of the past Lee clung to was his temple garments. "These he still wears, but it seems to be more from habit, or superstition, than from any fealty or allegiance which he owes to the Mormon Church."[29] Closer to the scene, the non-Mormon *Beaver Square Dealer* noted that until his conviction, Lee had always declared that Brigham Young had nothing to do with the massacre. His boast that "he would place the saddle on the right horse, was found to refer solely to John M. Higbee." Most of Lee's statements exonerated church leaders, and his silent execution would "be a receipt for Brigham Young for all time to come" against charges the prophet engineered the massacre of the Arkansas emigrants.[30]

So it was that as his end approached, the national press asked hundreds of times, "Will Lee make a confession?" The answer came when the *San Francisco Call* trumpeted that Lee had at last confessed—and it was "no partial, white-washing, made-up confession, but a full, clear, comprehensive confession of all the preparations, details and incidents of the great Mountain Meadows massacre." He was now ready to name names, and even Brigham Young would not be spared. Lee had been at work writing a history of the massacre since his conviction, which came upon him "like a thunderbolt" after Young had assured his wife not a hair of his head would be harmed.[31]

The statement Lee delivered to Howard in February 1877 was only one in a series of Lee confessions: one journalist counted four. The confession he drafted before his first trial was rejected by the prosecution but served its purpose, because it won the support of the church attorneys in Lee's defense. Only portions of this confession seem to have survived. William Bishop sold a statement "made by Lee some months ago" to the *New York Herald* "for a high price."[32] The federal prosecutors received several confessions from Lee, but "the last one alone contained the truth." Howard kept the last confession secret until after Lee's execution.[33]

Historians have ignored these earlier confessions and their many revealing contradictions in favor of the better-known version Bishop completed in May 1877 as *Mormonism Unveiled; or the Life and Confessions of the Late Mormon Bishop, John D. Lee.* The book was so personally incriminating, so full of believable detail, and expressed so much unvarnished rage against Brigham Young that its true purpose deceived not only contemporary journalists but also generations of historians who relied on it to reconstruct the story of the massacre. Lee's various tales carefully masked his role and that of the Mormons in recruiting the Paiutes and blamed them for attacking the emigrants. By claiming that Indians initiated the assault, Lee was able to shift primary responsibility away from both the LDS church and himself. His painfully detailed story of how the Mormons agreed to slaughter the Arkansans to prevent an Indian war that threatened their own families was developed during Lee's trial. It subtly revised the original cover story—"The Indians did it"—to one much more acceptable to Lee's fellow white Americans: "The Indians made us do it." Virtually every subsequent participant account of the massacre followed Lee's example and laid the blame on the hapless Paiutes—and, of course, on John D. Lee. Less justifiably, generations of historians generally accepted Lee's tale, disregarding the Paiutes' total dependence on their Mormon sponsors and the many contradictions in Lee's various accounts.

All of Lee's confessions were a tangled mix of truth and fiction. His reasons for lying were many and complex. His chief motive was to protect himself, but he also sought to shield the Mormon people. In his eyes, at Mountain Meadows he simply executed the orders of his ecclesiastical superiors and fulfilled his sacred oath to avenge the blood of the prophets. This made him innocent of the crime of murder, no matter how much blood he had actually shed. Lee felt his blamelessness and the precarious political situation of the Mormon people justified "lying for the Lord." His exaltation, sealed as it was with his Second Anointing and his acceptance of his role as scapegoat for the massacre, was now doubly assured.

Hundreds of southern Utahns petitioned Governor George Emery to grant Lee clemency. Emery considered the petitions and sought advice from Col. Henry Douglass, commander of Fort Cameron at Beaver. He recommended that if Lee would make a full and explicit statement of all the facts, name his accomplices, and provide proof to back up his charges, his life should be spared. "This I have been informed the prisoner can do," Douglass wrote, but Lee declined to make the confession that would save his life.[34]

Following the denial of his appeals, the government again tried to persuade Lee to implicate Brigham Young. Lee's position in the chain of command apparently left him without hard evidence to incriminate Young, and despite the bitter denunciation of his old friend in *Mormonism Unveiled*, Lee had often insisted he could not "bring in Brigham Young and the Heads of the Church." Lee had told J. H. Beadle years before, "If I was to make forty confessions, I could not bring in Brigham Young. His counsel was: 'Spare them, by all means.' But I am made to bear the blame. Here I am, old, poor, and lonely, away down in this place—carrying the sins of my brethren. But if I endure, great is my reward." Lee was lying, but he stuck to his guns, always refusing to bring trouble on his people. "I won't consent to give 'em up," he swore. Some said Marshal Nelson selected Carleton's cairn at Mountain Meadows as the site of the execution in the hope that Lee would make a complete confession when brought face-to-face with death. It was a miscalculation: John D. Lee was embittered by Brigham Young's betrayal, but he was resigned to his fate as scapegoat and martyr.[35]

Marshal Nelson and Sumner Howard arrived in Beaver on about March 20 to prepare for the execution. They had good reason to believe Rachel Lee and two of her sons had tried to enlist Indian warriors to help in a rescue attempt, but they felt these efforts did not amount to much and had "no fears on that score." More disappointing to the authorities was Lee's silence. Howard was "now satisfied that it is useless to expect any information from the prisoner as was expected and as he indirectly promised."[36]

In his last message to his children, Lee wrote, "I have done nothing designedly wrong in that unfortunate and lamentable affair with which I have been implicated." He said he had "been treacherously betrayed and sacrificed in the most cowardly manner by those who should have been [his] friends." "[Brigham Young] has sacrificed me in a most shameful and cruel way," Lee wrote. The night before he left Fort Cameron, Lee told his son John David he was not afraid to face death. He hoped his execution would divert attention to him and stop the enemies of Mormonism from "trying to involve the church" in the massacre. Always remember that this is the church of Jesus Christ, John D. Lee told his son, and that he was "willing to give his life if it might safeguard Christ's Church upon this earth."[37]

CENTER MY HEART, BOYS!

On the afternoon of March 21, 1877, Marshal William Nelson and U.S. Attorney Sumner Howard loaded John D. Lee into a closed carriage and drove south. The pending execution was supposed to be secret, but Howard had alerted the press and some twenty citizens, and the parties traveled separately to avoid attracting attention.[38] The night before, a detachment of twenty soldiers under Lt. George Patterson had left Fort Cameron. Patterson's orders directed him to observe "the utmost secrecy," and his men left the fort hidden in their wagons. The soldiers reached Leach's Spring shortly before dawn, where Marshal Nelson and his prisoner met their escort. Following the emigrant trail, they arrived at Mountain Meadows at 9:30 P.M. Despite the secrecy, the next morning Nelson had to ask Patterson to protect him from the groups of observers that arrived shortly before Lee was to be shot.[39]

Decades of overgrazing and erosion had transformed the once-verdant meadows into a scene of desolation. "Over that spot the curse of the almighty seemed to have fallen," historian Hubert Howe Bancroft wrote. "The luxuriant herbage that had clothed it twenty years before had disappeared; the springs were dry and wasted, and now there was neither grass nor any green thing, save here and there a copse of sagebrush or of scrub-oak, that served only to make the desolation still more desolate."[40] On the morning of March 23, 1877, the officers deployed pickets on the surrounding hills and drew three wagons into a semicircle some one hundred yards east of the ruin of Carleton's cairn, destroyed and rebuilt so many times that it was now but a mass of rocks. The special correspondent for the *San Francisco Bulletin* found the scene "weird and strange beyond description" as officials assembled a coffin of rough pine boards and raised a screen of blankets to conceal the firing squad.[41]

Lee slept soundly in a carriage, but his snoring disturbed the more nervous sleepers in the camp. Dressed in a red flannel shirt and a sack coat, Lee had a hearty breakfast and drank a cup of coffee. He told reporters he had not been on the ground since 1857, and recalled visiting the meadows ten days before the massacre with George Smith as he toured the settlements, preaching against the emigrants. "I don't know that he meant those particular emigrants," said Lee. "I did all in my power to save those people. . . . I consider myself sacrificed."[42]

Despite the efforts of the federal officers, a crowd of about seventy-five Utahns gathered to watch the execution. Contrary to legend, none of Lee's relatives were there. News of the event spread quickly, and Mormons such as Collins Hakes hurried to the scene, where Josiah Rogerson helped him get "up close" to watch Lee die. Methodist minister George Stokes of Beaver had accompanied the sullen and silent

Lee from Beaver, but Lee began to talk with his spiritual adviser on Friday morning. Stokes claimed Lee admitted to killing five people. Following their conversation, Lee stoutly denied it, but Hakes reported Lee admitted the killings and said he would have killed more "but for an accident to [his] gun."[43] Lee's face betrayed no emotion. He conducted himself with perfect coolness.

The makeup of Lee's firing squad has been an enduring mystery. Attorney General Alphonso Taft refused to allow soldiers to participate in the execution, as traditionally the military did not take part in American civil executions. Apparently the firing squad was recruited locally and armed with nonmilitary Springfield "needle guns."[44] John Amasa Lee claimed the federal officers believed his father was innocent and had the Mormons shoot him. The executioners were hidden to protect their identities.[45]

The soldiers arranged three wagons to conceal the firing squad. Lee made out his will, dividing his property between his three remaining wives. He sent $9.50 to Rachel to defray his funeral expenses. Lee passed around a bottle of "bitters" and took a last drink with a few of the men around him. When all was ready, Reverend Stokes helped Lee to his coffin, where he threw off his overcoat and sat down "as naturally as though it was an every day business." Marshal Nelson read the death warrant and asked if Lee had any last words. He wanted the privilege of keeping his hat on, at which all present uncovered their heads. Lee requested photographer James Fennemore to provide each of his three faithful wives with a copy of his portrait. Howard responded, "He says he will do it, Mr. Lee." Lee stood, looked around calmly, and began speaking.[46]

"I feel resigned to my fate," he told the crowd. "I feel as calm as a summer morn, and I have done nothing intentionally wrong. My conscience is clear before God and man. I am ready to meet my Redeemer." He faltered briefly when he spoke of parting with his family. "Many of them are unprotected and they will be left fatherless." He again claimed he had tried to save the Arkansans. "I would have given worlds, were they at my command, if I could have averted that calamity, but I could not do it. It went on." Death held no terror to him: "I shall never go to a worse place than I am now in." Lee bitterly denounced Brigham Young's betrayal: "I studied to make this man's will my pleasure for thirty years. See, now, what I have come to this day! I have been sacrificed in a cowardly, dastardly manner." Young was leading his people astray, Lee said, but he remained a true believer in "the gospel that was taught in its purity by Joseph Smith, in former days. I have my reasons for it."[47]

When Lee finished, Reverend Stokes knelt with him and offered a fervent prayer. Marshal Nelson blindfolded Lee but at the prisoner's request left his arms untied. Lee sat bolt upright on the end of his open coffin and raised his hands over his head. To avoid mangling his body, Lee called to the firing squad, "Center my heart, boys!" and the newspapers said he murmured one last complaint against Brigham Young. At exactly 11:00 A.M. Nelson gave the order, "Ready, aim, fire!" and a "line of flame shot out from the wagons." John D. Lee fell quietly into his coffin, his feet still resting on the ground, and died without a struggle. "The old man never flinched," reported the *Salt Lake Tribune*. "It made death seem easy, the way he went off."[48]

The hostile national press agreed that Lee "displayed the most extraordinary courage, and met his fate either in the belief that he was a martyr or a hero."[49] While this troubled, deeply flawed fanatic is a hard man to admire, it is impossible not to recognize his contrary integrity and his unshakable commitment to his beliefs. He neither apologized for his part at Mountain Meadows nor begged for forgiveness. To the bitter end he remained convinced he had done nothing wrong. He denounced the man who had sacrificed him, but he was certain he was bound for the mansions of bliss God had prepared for his faithful servants.[50] As historian Peter DeLafosse observed, if only one man could die for Mountain Meadows, Lee was an excellent choice. In the final analysis, any reasonable accounting must reckon Lee as a profoundly tormented and evil man, but at the end he faced the consequences of his acts with simple courage while others buried their guilt under an avalanche of perjury and evasion.

The way Lee met death impressed even the *Salt Lake Tribune*. At the end of this "extraordinary spectacle," its correspondent concluded that whether Lee was a martyr or simply a callused, obtuse old man, "I know not, but he died game."[51]

Brigham Young sent three representatives to observe Lee's death.[52] "I stood near John D. Lee at the time he was executed," Apostle Anthony Ivins said. "I heard the last words he ever uttered, and saw the men who fired the rifle shots that ended his life." Lee, recalled Ivins, did not incriminate the leaders of the LDS church. He "said simply that he had been misled; that he had done what he thought was a justifiable thing, but which he now fully realized was an error, and met his death without fear and without asking favor."[53] President David Cannon of the St. George temple told Amorah Lee late in 1877 that he had been sent to watch the execution. When Cannon reported to Brigham Young that Lee had remained true to the church, the prophet "fell on his knees and cried like a baby. Then Brigham said, 'John always told me he would stand between me and the mouth of the cannon, but I was afraid he would falter when it came to the test.'"[54]

THE BURIAL, RESURRECTION, AND LEGACY OF JOHN D. LEE

William Prince and Harvey Lee met the wagon carrying Lee's body at Paragonah and escorted it to Caroline Lee's home.[55] After the two-day trip to Panguitch, the body was so decomposed the family simply laid his temple clothes over his corpse and buried it. Local tradition tells that the family feared someone would steal the body from its often-desecrated grave, so they quietly reburied Lee in the basement of Caroline's home. The house is now a bed-and-breakfast known as the William Prince Inn.

Despite his public execution, Lee refused to die. A legend still circulates in southern Utah that Lee faced a firing squad whose guns were loaded with blanks and afterward escaped to Mexico. What is surprising is one source of the legend: Lee's former attorney, George Bates. Bates wrote a long letter to the *Denver Republican* in 1882 claiming that Marshal Nelson staged Lee's death in exchange for a confession that implicated LDS leaders. Mormon historian Brigham Roberts blamed these "slander-ous inventions" on Bates's fall into intemperate habits. Nelson subsequently denounced the *Republican* for printing "such scandalous and baseless charges against anybody on such worthless authority."[56] The denials did little to slow the growth of the myth.

Lee's posthumous autobiography was his most puzzling legacy. His attorney, lit-erary executor, editor, and friend, William Bishop, sent the manuscript to his publisher in St. Louis on May 17, 1877. Having been unable to pay for his services, Lee had assigned publication rights for "the *true history* of my life" to Bishop. As a sacred trust, he directed Bishop to divide the book's profits with his family. A flood of pretended Lee confessions had already hit the market, "collected from fragmentary newspaper reports, and advertised by certain unscrupulous publishers as genuine," Bishop com-plained. Except for the short statements Sumner Howard gave to the newspapers, his book could legitimately claim to be "the true and only LIFE AND CONFESSION OF JOHN D. LEE." *Mormonism Unveiled* became an immediate national best-seller.[57]

For a book assembled so quickly, it was quite a production. It began with pref-aces by both the publisher and Bishop, including endorsements for its authenticity from marshals Nelson and Stokes and prosecutor Sumner Howard. Bishop ably sum-marized Lee's life and trials. A rambling 176-page autobiography took the story to 1848. Lee complained he was not allowed any reference books in prison: "I am forced to rely on my memory for names and dates, and if I make mistakes in either, this must be my excuse." Despite a few failures of memory, the account was astonishingly accu-rate. Beyond its sensational elements, Lee's life story painted a vivid history of early Mormonism.[58]

More problematic than the autobiography was Lee's "last" confession, which he dictated to Bishop and finished on March 16, 1877, one week before his death. It covered some eighty printed pages and substantially revised many of the details about the massacre provided in the earlier—and perhaps more honest—confession delivered to Howard. In *Mormonism Unveiled*, Lee reconstructed his chronology of the mas-sacre to distance himself from the initial attack, and he denounced the men who had testified against him, blaming them for stirring up the Paiutes. Lee claimed he had "no enemies to punish by this statement; and no friends to shield," but he relentlessly set-tled old scores. Apostates such as Philip Klingensmith and Joel White received no mercy. The fifty-four "names of assassins" Bishop listed consisted exclusively of admit-ted participants, Lee's enemies, and the dead.[59]

Without the manuscript of *Mormonism Unveiled*, there is no way to resolve the question of its authorship, but internal evidence reveals that no one but Lee could have composed it. The Lee family generally denounced the book as a total fabrication, while many scholars have assumed that William Bishop liberally enhanced his dead client's work. Bishop denied this. He helped Lee write his story and corrected his client's spelling and punctuation but said he used "the writings and confessions in the exact language of John D. Lee." Roberts charged that Lee could not be accepted as a reliable witness, but Brooks concluded his testimony was as reliable as anyone's and explicitly accepted Lee's authorship.[60]

Lee's postconviction letters in The Huntington Library are as bitter as his memoir and validate this conclusion. The book's quick publication also supports Bishop's claim, but Bishop simplified the details of its creation, saying that Lee composed it after his conviction.[61] Court stenographer Josiah Rogerson gave a more accurate account of how the book was compiled. At Bishop's request, Rogerson wrote, in July 1875 Lee began dictating his autobiography to Adam Patterson, an official court reporter. Rogerson saw Patterson's daily shorthand notes taken in the Rock Jail at Beaver. Patterson would go to the jail in the evening and "note down Lee's dictation." The dictation lasted for seven weeks, until the end of the first trial. Rogerson recalled that this covered most of the book and that Lee wrote the rest of it in February and March 1877.[62] This account of the book's composition explains the dramatic shift in viewpoint from that of a true believer evident in its early sections to its disillusioned conclusion.

Mormonism Unveiled made Lee the sphinx that guarded the secrets of the massacre for generations. Its damning personal indictment of Brigham Young obscured the subtlety of Lee's story. Lee denounced Brigham but protected President Young the prophet, much as a Catholic historian might attack the Borgias but defend the papacy. For all its tales of murderous blood atonements and shameless financial frauds, Lee's book ultimately—and carefully—exonerated Brigham Young from ordering the massacre. It clearly made Young an accessory after the fact, but it shifted immediate responsibility for the crime to lesser LDS church leaders: George A. Smith and local militia officers. Lee remained true to the LDS church and defended it until the end. He told his children shortly before his execution "to always remain true to the Gospel no matter what happened to him; that he was doing something for the Church that it could not do for itself." Lee said misfortune, not guilt, had brought this trouble upon him. His family recalled Lee's last prophecy: "If I am guilty of the crime for which I am convicted, I will go down and out and never be heard of again. If I am not guilty, Brigham Young will die within one year! Yes, within six months."[63]

OLD, CRAFTY, EXPERIENCED AND SYMPATHETIC: BRIGHAM YOUNG SPEAKS

"The only thing that will satisfy the country and the Press," *Deseret News* editor David O. Calder telegraphed John W. Young in St. George at the end of March 1877, "is a statement over the signature of your father giving the truth of his subsequent knowledge of the Mountain Meadow matter." Brigham Young must establish his innocence, and Calder believed a statement to the Mormon-friendly *New York Herald* would "quiet things down." The prophet should quickly explain "his share in this massacre." The editor then asked a wonderfully ironic question: "What is the story of this tragedy?" He urged, "Talk to your father about the matter."[64]

That same day Brigham Young telegraphed President Rutherford B. Hayes. He had read Lee's statement in the *New York Herald*, "which if true," he wrote, "directly implicates me as accessory after the fact & by implication makes me liable as an accessory before the fact." Young repeated his claim that he offered Governor Cumming his help "in obtaining the evidence necessary to furnish the guilty ones," but "whatever they may have been worth," his services had never been accepted. Young asked Hayes to appoint a commission with authority to try and punish the offenders of "that inhuman slaughter."[65]

In the wake of Lee's execution, Brigham Young dedicated the St. George Temple, the first temple to be opened since the Latter-day Saints arrived in Utah. The event should have been an occasion of great celebration, but his sermon on April 8, 1877, captured the seventy-five-year-old prophet's dark mood. He castigated the Quorum of the Twelve for resisting his economic program and called men such as Apostle Erastus Snow a curse to the community. With increasing heat, "Br Brigham whipped and scolded the tradesmen and almost every body and every thing." In his rage Young pounded the podium with his cane. Still in use, the podium bears the marks he made that day. A freak storm obscured the angry prophet's concluding remarks as the wind rose to a fearful tempest. Young had to order the congregation, fearful that Satan himself was on the rampage, to "sit down and calm yourselves and let the devil roar!" Indeed, "the devil did roar for perhaps two hours," wreaking much destruction in his fury.[66]

More ominous signs dogged the prophet. The day after the dedication, bouts of violent "purging" struck the Mormon leaders. According to his grandson, Apostle John Taylor "wondered if it was the alkaline water or an attempt at retaliation by poison"— vengeance for the execution of John D. Lee. Some claimed Young had planned to abdicate at St. George in favor of his son, Brigham Young, Jr., but the Mountain Meadows affair caused him to postpone the announcement until the October conference.[67]

Even before Lee was dead, James Gordon Bennett, Jr., had telegraphed Brigham Young that Lee's confession in his *New York Herald* accused him of being "directly responsible for the massacre at Mountain Meadows." The *Herald* would gladly pay to telegraph Young's answers immediately.[68] If Lee made such a statement, the prophet responded, it was utterly false. "My course of life is too well known by thousands of honorable men for them to believe for one moment such accusations."[69] In May 1877 a *Herald* correspondent caught up with Young and Daniel Wells in Cedar City to give the Mormon leaders a chance to present their side of the Mountain Meadows story to the nation. It remains Brigham Young's only detailed interview concerning the massacre.

As could be expected, Wells and Young spent much time damning Lee, but surprisingly they spent more time providing an alibi for the recently deceased George A. Smith. The two men repeated most of the traditional story. "Some of the Arkansas party boasted that they had the promise from the United States that the Mormons were to be used up by the troops," Young said, and they "had boasted, too, of having helped to kill Hyrum and Joseph Smith and the Mormons in Missouri." This "may have embittered the feelings of those who took part in the massacre." The prophet suggested Lee "and his *confreres* took advantage of these facts and the disturbed state of the country to accomplish their desires for plunder." Young still believed in blood atonement, but he stoutly rejected Lee's claim that he murdered the emigrants "to shed their blood for the remission of their sins" as the same old folly of his enemies. He claimed "they said it themselves, that they were waiting for the arrival of the army. It was very noticeable that they did not hurry along like other emigrants."[70]

Some of the First Presidency's new stories were contradictory or highly unlikely. Brigham Young revealed a surprisingly detailed knowledge of the company's supposed travels in Utah. He recalled that Apostle Charles Rich "advised them to go north, and he believed they went as far north as Bear River. They returned, saying they would take the southern road." Given the distance and their rate of travel, it would be geographically impossible for the Fancher party to have made a one-hundred-fifty-mile detour to Bear River. Young said the emigrants "lay idle for six weeks, when they should have been travelling, and when they moved they moved slowly."[71]

Daniel Wells laid out the logic of this argument. "That company, remember," Wells said, "was not in the Territory when George A. Smith left Salt Lake to make his southern tour. How, then, could he, as has been said, kill the people by arousing malicious feeling against the emigrants—saying they poisoned springs, &c.—at a time when the emigrants were hundreds of miles away, when he had not seen any of them, and no one knew any of their names, and when the emigrants themselves had not determined upon their route through Utah?" Wells insisted the emigrants' maltreatment of the Indians doomed them. He knew "that one Indian had died from the effects of eating poisoned meat, and that they had tied one Indian to a wagon, kept him there some time and whipped him, which made them mad." "If this be true," asked the former commander of the Nauvoo Legion, "and I have no reason to doubt it, what could we do about it? We had all we could do ourselves to keep peace with the Indians at that time." Wells contended the blasphemous braggadocio and the profanity of the men in the company aroused the hostility of the southern settlements. But: "I don't believe that even a man like Lee—old, crafty, experienced and sympathetic as he was—could have got together a force of Mormons in all of Utah 'to do' the massacre." Wells blamed the deed on "John D. Lee, perhaps a crony or two and a lot of dupes and thieves and savages under his command."[72]

Having cleared the air, Brigham Young and his entourage headed north. Despite Lee's counsel to his family not to seek vengeance, his memory haunted the prophet's final visit to southern Utah, and the Mormons took no chances. Young's usual party constituted no small caravan, but Christopher Layton recalled that a special escort of some twenty-five young men accompanied their leader through Beaver. They "deemed this precaution necessary because of threats said to have been made against the President's life by some of the relatives or sympathizers of John D. Lee."[73]

As the prophet's procession passed through the village of Ephraim, Ole Peterson waited angrily for his carriage. Peterson believed Young had sent him on a mission so that he could steal the Scandinavian convert's land. As Young's carriage drove past him, Peterson shook his fist and shouted, "Oh you cheat! Oh, Church Fraud! You coward to forsake your tools! You are the man they should have hung instead of Lee!" Brigham Young grimaced and clenched the seat of his coach as the cavalcade rolled on.[74]

Amen: The Death of Brigham Young

For decades Brigham Young had survived the most determined assaults on his power. Even Judge McKean's militant crusade against the Saints and their prophet ultimately backfired. When Young refused to pay fees arising from his divorce case with Ann Eliza Young, McKean held the prophet in contempt and sent him to spend a night in the territorial penitentiary during a March 1875 snowstorm. The spectacle of the aging and ailing Mormon lion dragged to prison generated a wave of public sympathy, and his old enemy Patrick Edward Connor even offered to pay Young's fine. Within days, President U. S. Grant removed McKean from the bench.[75]

Oscar Young had told Lee in April 1876 that his father "was broke down & would never be a well man again." By the time Brigham Young dedicated the lower story of the St. George Temple on New Year's Day 1877, his health was so poor he had to be carried from room to room in a sedan chair. Yet the Lion of the Lord seemed to rally on his return north, and he felt well enough the next summer to swim in the Great Salt Lake. On August 23, 1877, however, Young fell ill with cramps, purging, and vomiting said to be brought on by eating green corn and peaches. Despite the services of four physicians, he was dead within a week. Most medical experts now agree Brigham Young died of appendicitis.[76]

His biographer, M. R. Werner, an irreverent gentile, suggested that the prophet's last words were "I feel better," but eyewitnesses such as Richard Young and Dr. Seymour Young said nothing about the subject. A week after the event, the *Deseret News* wrote that Brigham Young's last words were "Joseph! Joseph! Joseph!" The powerful symbolism of the story has beguiled historians, and Young's daughter recalled "the divine look in his face seemed to indicate he was communicating with his beloved friend, Joseph Smith."[77] More probably, the prophet's last word was what the *Deseret News* reported immediately after his death: "Amen."[78]

Shortly after Young's return to Salt Lake from St. George in spring 1877, two of John D. Lee's sons were allegedly caught in the prophet's bedroom in the Beehive House, and after his death a rumor spread that the prophet had been poisoned.[79] But most members of the Lee family took the advice of their patriarch. They remained loyal to the LDS church and quietly noted that Lee's prophecy of Brigham Young's death had been fulfilled, almost to the day.

18

The Mountain Meadow Dogs

The death of Brigham Young removed the driving force behind the federal prosecution of the crimes of Mountain Meadows. The territory's budget had barely been able to pay for Lee's trials, and there was little money and less will among federal authorities to prosecute his accomplices. The surviving perpetrators, notably Haight, Higbee, and Stewart, remained fugitives, but now their haunting memories pursued them more aggressively than federal marshals.

Brigham Young had not defined a policy to assure an orderly succession to the presidency of the church. On his death the Quorum of the Twelve asserted the governing authority of the apostles, and their president, John Taylor, became the religion's leader almost by default. Like Young it would take him three years to reconstitute the First Presidency. What had been a serious legal threat to the church was now a never-ending public relations problem. As John Taylor complained, "That bloody tragedy has been the chief stock-in-trade for penny-a-liners, and press and pulpit, who have gloated in turns by chorus over the sickening details." He felt it was not fair to accuse the Mormon people of the crime, but the story remained a millstone around the neck of the church.[1] As the participants grew old and died, LDS leaders labored to explain the massacre to the world while the surviving fugitives struggled to come to terms with their past.

The massacre never ceased to torment the men who lived with its memory. Many of the participants were decent men who could not rest in peace after the "dreadful deed." The memory "withered and blasted their happiness, and some of them suffered agonizing tortures of conscience," wrote Mormon dissenter T. B. H. Stenhouse. Two men were "said to have lost their reason entirely, and others have gone to early graves with a full realization of the terrible crime upon their souls."[2] Repeating gossip current in Utah in 1875, Brigham Young's apostate wife, Ann Eliza, claimed one veteran "always imagined he was followed by spectres, and he grew haggard and worn from constant terror. 'Brigham Young,' he used to say, 'will answer for the murder of one hundred and twenty innocent souls sent to their graves at his command.' On his death-bed he besought those watching by him to protect him from the spirits that were hovering near him, waiting to avenge themselves, and he died in the fearful ravings of a horrible terror." Ann Eliza wrote that a second man said, "'the terrible scenes at Mountain Meadows haunt me night and day. I cannot drive them away.'" Returning in terror from his hayfield, "the cold, calm faces of the dead women and children were never out of his sight."[3]

Even in Cedar City, Charles Wandell wrote, the men who had carried out the massacre were known as "Mountain Meadow Dogs." By the early 1870s there was increasing resentment in southern Utah against Lee and his "confederates, apologists, and protectors." Isaac Haight was the most notorious of the fugitives. From 1874 until his death in exile in 1886, Haight wandered between the LDS settlements in Arizona, Colorado, and Mexico using the alias Horton. One of John Wesley Powell's men found Haight "an agreeable man in camp. It is hard to believe him guilty of the crimes laid to his charge. Can it be that he would sanction and assist in the murder of women and children?" John R. Bringhurst recalled meeting Haight during winter 1873 at Toquerville. "He looked to be the most miserable and unhappy man I ever saw," he said. In about February 1874 Brigham Young told the bishop of Toquerville, "Isaac Haight will be damned in this world and will be damned throughout eternity." Haight told Frank Lee many times that he was tired of living. Despite his pleasant personality, Haight's reputation dogged him. "I have never a peaceful moment," he lamented. "I am ever on the dodge and am always fearful."[4]

The story of "Parson" Williams shows how Haight's past followed him. George Calvin Williams was born in Tennessee in 1836 and settled in Texas. A Union man, he fought Indians on the Texas frontier during the Civil War. After the war his neighbors ostracized Williams, and he moved to northwestern Arkansas and became a Baptist circuit rider. In the Ozarks he officiated at the marriage of massacre survivor Eliza-beth Baker Terry. He set out for Washington Territory in 1875, but a friend diverted him to Arizona, where he converted to Mormonism and took a fifteen-year-old girl as his second wife. Parson Williams (as his Mormon neighbors called him) moved to Mexico in 1885, leading the initial polygamist colonization of Sonora. He purchased the twenty-by-fifteen-mile Horcones grant on the Bavispe River in 1892 from the local warlord, but the vast area contained only 1,800 scattered acres that could be farmed. Over the next five years the colony endured the privations of hardscrabble farming and ranching in an unforgiving country remarkable even in the annals of Mormon pioneering.[5]

In Mexico he formed many new acquaintances, Williams recalled, "and among others . . . got acquainted with a man who went by the name of Horten." Williams had brought horses to Turley's Camp, later Colonia Dublan, to help Apostle George

Teasdale explore the country. In a priesthood meeting the apostle asked all the High Priests to raise their hands, and one of Williams's companions "happened to notice Brother Horten's hand stuck up." "He asked me if I knew that man. I whispered, 'yes, that is Brother Horten.'"

No, said his friend. "It is Isaac C. Haight, the man that give the orders to kill all the women and children at the Mountain Meadows Massacre." The news, Williams said, "made my blood boil for I had 13 blood relations murdered there at the orders of this man, now a High Priest in the same church with me." He told Apostle Teasdale, "Mexico wasn't big enough to hold Horten and I both, and . . . one of us better get out of Mexico and do it quick." Williams never saw Haight again, but he wrote to President John Taylor to ask "if the Church was held as a cloak to cover and conceal cold, blackhearted murderers." "He never answered my question but wrote me a very sympathetic letter, advising me not to let the misdeeds of others cause me to make a shipwreck of my faith."[6]

Ironically, less prominent massacre participants were among Williams's acquaintances in Pacheco and Oaxaca, including perhaps William Bateman and William Stewart. The difficulty of paying for his Mexican grant plagued Williams, and Joseph Fish considered him "the bluest man that I ever saw. He would lie down and groan like a horse with a bellyache." After Williams asked LDS authorities to terminate his membership, Anthony Ivins excommunicated Williams for apostasy in December 1895. Apostle Abraham Cannon considered him a very good man, but because of Haight's status Williams asked "to be dropped from the Church."[7] George Williams never reconciled with Mormonism, but Isaac Haight died alone at Thatcher, Arizona, on September 8, 1886, a member in good standing of the Church of Jesus Christ of Latter-day Saints.[8]

THE CHURCH WILL KILL ME, SOONER OR LATER:
PHILIP KLINGENSMITH

Like Haight, many massacre veterans found sanctuary in Mexico. In 1881 a story spread that vengeful Mormons had murdered Philip Klingensmith in Sonora. Speaking at a secluded spot in Beaver after the Lee trial, the disillusioned bishop told the *Salt Lake Tribune*, "I know that the Church will kill me, sooner or later, and I am as confident of that fact as I am that I am sitting on this rock. It is only a question of time; but I am going to live as long as I can." The body of the man who exposed the Mountain Meadows massacre allegedly was found in a prospect hole in Sonora, and a letter from Mexico indicated he had been murdered. He had died "just as he expected."[9] The *Deseret News* denounced the *Philadelphia News* for accusing Mormon authorities of inspiring the murder, but it attacked the character of the "confessed villain and murderer." Klingensmith's "oath was not worth anymore than his reckless, unsworn word." He was such an arrant liar, the *News* charged, that he might have started the story of his death himself. If the Mormons were a killing people there were "infamous scoundrels right close to home who would be made to bite the dust."[10]

Klingensmith may well have survived his alleged death in Mexico. Family tradition insisted he died among the Indians in Arizona, but one of his sons believed he was killed by the Mormons and buried in a dry wash south of Caliente near his Nevada ranch.[11] Josiah Gibbs heard that Klingensmith hid among the Indians on the Colorado River in Arizona, opposite Colorado Canyon, where he died in about 1902, "as filthy and degraded as any of the 'Lamanites.'"[12]

WITHOUT A NAME OR A HOME: JOHN M. HIGBEE

John M. Higbee's career prospered in the immediate aftermath of the massacre. He served as mayor of Cedar City from 1867 to 1871, and Brigham Young appointed him president of the town's United Order in 1874, but the organization dissolved after only one year.[13] During Utah's Black Hawk War, Captain Higbee and a fellow veteran of Mountain Meadows, James Pearce, led a militia party to Long Valley to protect settlers from marauding Navajo bands. The Navajo leader agreed "to let the settlers go in peace if they would give their loose stock to the Indians," but his men were not happy with the agreement. With unintended irony, one historian wrote that by "whooping, jeering and throwing sand into the oxen's eyes," the Navajos "endeavored to provoke the settlers to some rash act so that they would have an excuse to massacre the whites and take their stock."[14]

After Lee's arrest Higbee fled deeper into exile. The field commander at Mountain Meadows devised a number of self-serving explanations for his conduct that proved as dramatic and compelling as they were dishonest. Lee told equally elaborate lies, but Lee at least accepted some responsibility and died with dignity. In contrast, Higbee was ready to blame anyone or tell any tale that would distance him from his crimes. There are simply too many reports of Major Higbee's bloodthirsty conduct at Mountain Meadows to accept his claims of innocence.

At first Higbee apparently tried to explain the massacre as larceny run amok. In the early 1870s Samuel Gould heard Higbee tell his story to Jesse N. Smith and ask that no one repeat it "until you are sure we have all been dead at least two years." Early one morning in 1857, Higbee said, Philip Klingensmith came to him. "I've got a scheme that we can make some money easily and quickly," Klingensmith allegedly said. Higbee was interested, "of course," and learned that "the Indians are going to massacre that train of emigrants" and that they were "gathering by hundreds from all over the country for that purpose." Somehow, Higbee "knew that to be a fact." Klingensmith suggested they go and ask the Indians for "the property they don't want, such as wagons, harnesses, tools, etc." This struck Higbee as "just the thing." "So I suggested that we go see brother Isaac Haight and see what he thinks about it," he said. Haight "fell right in with us. So we started right in to get ready to go. We never told a soul, not even our wives." They said they were going north on very important business.[15]

The men spent four days among the Paiutes at Mountain Meadows trying to make them understand that once they had disposed of the emigrants, "[they] wanted the property that [the Indians] did not want." Since the men "could not talk Indian very well," they sent for Lee to act as interpreter. When Lee arrived, Higbee said, "instead of him interpreting for us he took the management of the whole thing." Lee "helped the Indians plan an attack and two of the Indians were killed. Then the Indians told us we'd have to help them. They held two of us as hostages and sent the other two for help, telling them if they weren't back by a certain time, they would kill the other two and declare war on the Mormons."[16]

When the militia reached Leach's Spring, Higbee and his companion told the men that if they would obey orders, their officers would be responsible for every act. They went on and "helped the Indians do the awful work." When "everything was over and quiet again, eight men from Parowan rode up, [and] Bro. Dame commenced wringing his hands and saying, Too bad, too bad." Lee "spoke up in the presence of all the boys and said, It is too bad to see all these people lying dead around here, but wasn't it too bad for you to order it done." This was Lee's way of throwing the responsibility on someone else. The statement claimed Dame knew nothing about the massacre, even though the seven men who accompanied him to the meadows believed Dame had ordered it—"even Jesse N. Smith did not know but what he had."[17]

This tale of greed and conniving was ghastly enough, but like many similar southern Utah folktales it served to obscure the darker truth of what actually had happened at Mountain Meadows. Using the alias "Bull Valley Snort," Higbee described the massacre for his family in a document written in February 1894. Discovered by Juanita Brooks, "Snort's" account stressed his own pitiful story and denied any personal responsibility. "If the publick ever get a true account of the tragedy," Higbee initially wrote, "it will read almost as I have written it here." He then crossed out "almost." His tale contained some remarkable admissions, such as acknowledging that two or three of Lee's men were painted like Indians. Higbee claimed he made two round trips to the meadows before finally marching out with the militia on Thursday, suggesting he was present at the initial attack.[18]

Building on Lee's tales, Higbee claimed the entire plan had been devised to save the women and children. The Paiutes agreed to let the women and children go to Cedar City unmolested if the Mormons "would get the men of the company out where they could get at them." Lee told his men that if they were too cowardly to "help the Indians," they could shoot in the air and let the Paiutes finish "their savage work." After firing the initial volley, the Mormons "squatted down and the Indians seemed to be there the same moment as they jumped out of the brush and rushed like a howling tornado apast us." Some of the doomed men fled into the midst of the women and children, and the Indians forgot their promise. The chiefs "could not keep their young warriors from killing all but a few little children that some of the old Indians saved and they wanted pay for saving them."[19]

Higbee described the Indians' "treachery" and the terror they generated in the Mormons in colorful terms: "And the hideous, demon-like yells of the savages as they thirsting for blood rushed past [us] to slay their helpless victims. It seemed to chill the blood in our veins." Higbee did not express a word of regret for the fate of the emigrants, except for the suffering their murder brought on the murderers. "There was a great many blood kirdling stories told about some of those that had been out to help burry those that had been killed," he wrote. "These men generally, seeing the growing prejudice and feeling bad and ashamed of the cowardly part they were compelled to take in that tragedy realizing they could not prove a negative, they kept very still over the matter. Their reticence was taken for guilt by their neighbors." Higbee ended his confession with another complaint. He had "been driven from the face of man and called a fellon for a third of a sentuary." The massacre left him "damned, his family scattered, some dead, others grown up and strangers to him. The heritage left them & their children is Grandfather & Father was a fellon and a fugitive from justice." "It seems Somebody," Higbee concluded, "has contracted a *Great* debt."[20]

Who was accountable? Higbee said "the marching of Buchannen's army against Utah was the cause of the excitement and this was the soul cause of all this trouble and the cause of this tragedy." People said Lee had reported "all this matter to Governor Young," who took steps to have it investigated, but he was replaced as governor of Utah before it could be done. "That," said Higbee, "ended his responsibility."[21]

Decades after it was issued, prosecutor David H. Morris of Washington County moved to dismiss Higbee's federal indictment, arguing that statehood made the territorial charges invalid and there was not enough evidence to warrant a trial. Judge Higgins dismissed the charges in Beaver on February 27, 1896, disposing of "the last indictment pending found against those implicated in the Mountain Meadow massacre, except that against William C. Stewart, who is dead."[22]

Higbee made a less known second statement in 1896 for his "Family, Friends Of My Youth And Exile, or Any Whom It May Concern." He expressed his gratitude to God and all those who had befriended him during his thirty-eight-year exile. He called the massacre revolting but again claimed the Mormons "used all the influence we could to save the Company." He declared, "Our efforts saved the children that were spared, yet I have been accused and represented as one of the worst." Higbee blamed all his afflictions on John D. Lee, but he admitted using every means to secure the Indians as allies. Word arrived from the far north that the U.S. Army and the Nauvoo Legion had fought a battle, "so the word spread like 'Wild Fire' that hostilities had begun."[23]

Ambitious for glory and without consulting Colonel Dame, Higbee said Lee "sent runners and gathered Indians from the surrounding country, and made a feast for them." He trained the Paiutes "on his own volition, disciplining them for service to be used as he affirmed against the approaching Army." As tension mounted, the Arkansas company came along and "boasted of mobbing and made threats of what they would yet do, bringing on themselves some trouble with the Indians at Corn Creek." Higbee repeated the old tale of the poisoned ox, but swore, "Now whether Lee's Indians of their own accord got up the fight, or were otherwise prompted for revenge may never be known, but the fight was gotten up all the same, and this news spread over the Southern country." Once the Indians had assembled, "all the men of Southern Utah could not control them, not even Lee himself, they were like a lot of infuriated wolves." The "confusion and frenzy of these painted blood-thirsty Indians was terrible to behold."[24]

Without mentioning his own role as field commander, Higbee tried to exonerate all his fellow officers—except, of course, Lee. Dame "sent an Express to Lee to do all he could to pacify the Indians, to let the Company go" and make the Indians return home. Higbee claimed Lee had called for volunteers to help bury the dead emigrants. He did not devote a word to the emigrants' ordeal or murder, but Higbee gave chapter and verse on his own pain. "To say that some of us have suffered and been obliged to leave our families and all that was near and dear or was worth living for, as wandering refugees to live an underground life, is putting it very lightly," he wrote. He mourned the status of "my own family, who have suffered great indignities by being called the children of a man roaming over the earth without a name or a home." Beyond blaming President Buchanan and the Paiutes, Higbee assigned total responsibility to Lee, "an aspiring Glory Seeking man, who ran before he was sent." Klingensmith and Lee "sought to implicate all the leading men of Iron County, and the Leaders of the 'Mormon Church' who did not know anything about the matter in time to save the Emigrant Company." After so many years in exile, which he blamed on "these peculiar conditions over which I had no control, in the proper discharge of my duty," Higbee welcomed the dropping of his indictment. Even Mormon sources cast doubt on Higbee's credibility. In his last conversation with Josiah Rogerson, Higbee "charged the weight of the mistake on Dame, yet laid a goodly portion of blame on Lee's assumption of authority."[25]

Higbee's contradictory and self-serving tales had little concern for the truth. He enhanced Lee's claim that "the Indians made us do it" with the fable that the Paiutes betrayed their agreement and killed the women and children. Higbee never explained what he planned to do with all those widows who would have witnessed the murders of their husbands.

John Higbee would tell his tale of woe until his death in Cedar City in December 1904. His lies unfairly damned the Paiutes, but generations of southern Utahns happily embraced his justifications, since they explained how their ancestors could execute such a horrible crime. The promotion of this mythology by powerful local figures such as stake president William Palmer ensured its survival, but the story's lack of credibility made it impossible to pass off to even the most gullible outsiders.[26]

In Vindication of Prest. B. Young: The New History

Long after Brigham Young's death, Mountain Meadows remained a festering sore in the LDS church. The church maintained Young's long-standing policy of silence for years, but by the early 1880s it was clear that ignoring the problem would not make it go away. Missionary elders were met "with the statement that the 'Mormon' Church, with Brigham Young at its head, is a bloody church," wrote *Deseret News* editor Charles Penrose in 1884. "Wherever the servants of God have gone to preach the gospel, the Mountain Meadow massacre has been thrown in their teeth."[27]

Penrose, an English convert and future apostle, became spokesman for the church on the massacre. He set out to determine whether "the charge that has been made against the 'Mormon' people has any foundation in fact." Penrose was actually only part of a large and coordinated public relations effort to search the church's vast records for evidence that would provide a credible defense of Brigham Young. The Lee trial and the commercial success of Lee's *Mormonism Unveiled* had left little doubt among the American public about who was responsible for the massacre. As the bitter war over polygamy escalated during the 1880s, the story was used as a cudgel to batter Mormonism. The First Presidency asked Charles Penrose to answer charges that the church practiced blood atonement and that Brigham Young had ordered the Mountain Meadows massacre.[28] They authorized him to call on the resources of the Church Historian's Office and the *Deseret News*.[29]

Apostle and assistant church historian Franklin D. Richards was already hard at work on the problem in February 1882 as part of the effort to help Bancroft write his *History of Utah*. Richards met with his fellow apostles to discuss the Mountain Meadows problem. The quorum directed him to "get together material in vindication of Prest. B. Young & the Church against the perpetrating the *Mountain Meadow Massacre*." Richards spent the next day gathering material and searching records. Erastus Snow and Wilford Woodruff agreed "to make affidavits of what they know of *Prest. B. Young's ignorance* of the affair until after its accomplishment." Richards recorded that on February 25 he took Aaron F. Farr's "deposition of Lee's misrepresentation of *M. M. Massacre* to him in 1857." Farr's affidavit "not being what it should be at first writing," Richards noted it "was corrected and completed" the next day.[30]

As Richards's diary indicates, LDS historians were not overly concerned with the facts of the case. By doctoring problematic evidence and ignoring records from the Utah War that contradicted Young's later sworn statements, they violated even the primitive historical standards of their time, but their success in assembling a credible defense of the dead prophet was a tribute to their skill. As deeply religious men, they felt they were doing the Lord's work. A simple syllogism dominated the labor of these devout Mormon historians: Brigham Young was a prophet; prophets do not commit mass murder; therefore, Brigham Young was not responsible for the Mountain Meadows massacre. Their beliefs justified defending the great man's beleaguered reputation by any means necessary. Whatever their sins as historians, these men were devoted to defending the LDS church and resolving its most vexing historical problem, the grim legacy of Mountain Meadows.

No one had ever successfully tackled the difficult task of telling a coherent version of the Mormon side of the murders. During the Lee trial, Brigham Young had collected the records that shielded him from the charge that he was an accessory to the crime, and he had presented evidence that established his own innocence to the satisfaction of the prosecutor. Having sat through both trials as court stenographer, Josiah Rogerson knew the second trial transcript provided a wealth of material that could be used to exonerate Young.

Born in England in 1841, Josiah Rogerson, Jr., survived the ordeal of the 1856 Edward Martin handcart company. He settled at Parowan in June 1858. "During the summer and fall," he recalled of his first year in southern Utah, "we heard of The Massacre at The Mountain Meadows, blended with whispered hints that some white men besides Indians had taken part in the tragedy." As residents abandoned the region, Rogerson became satisfied whites had taken part in the sad affair, and he publicly denounced the massacre as an unjustifiable crime. Dame, Haight, and Higbee knew of his opinion, but Rogerson claimed he was never censured or disciplined for his opinion, "which I repeated as often as I chose till the blame was fastened where it belonged and the guilty one was punished." Rogerson said Brigham Young told him that Americans could not "charge or accuse this people of anything that we preach teach or profess excepting the case of the Mountain Meadow massacre." In a painful confession, Rogerson said Young denounced it as "A WANTON, UNCALLED FOR AFFAIR, ONE THAT I NEVER AUTHORIZED OR ENDORSED. COULD WE HAVE HAD A TELEGRAPH LINE IN OUR TERRITORY AT THAT TIME THAT THING WOULD NEVER HAVE HAPPENED.'"[31]

In 1876 Rogerson showed the shorthand notes he made as court stenographer at the Lee trials to Brigham Young at John Murdock's home in Beaver. The prophet charged him to take good care of the records and asked him to visit Salt Lake as soon as possible. "We want every word of these notes transcribed," Young said, "for which we will pay you." He ordered Daniel Wells to see that Rogerson was paid. Wells did not immediately follow up Young's request, but in about 1883 President Taylor ordered him to make the transcriptions. "We made three Copies of all the notes," Rogerson recalled, and in 1911 he described the records he had compiled some thirty years earlier. The church historian had the notes and the elders could "get any point in question out of this massive document." The notes contained all the testimony, motions argued, and opening and closing statements from both Lee trials, comprising more than 1,250,000 words, all of which Rogerson had typed. Charles Penrose and Franklin Richards relied on these transcriptions in their work on the massacre. Rogerson's task was completed by March 5, 1885, when the Church Historian's Office noted that it had received from Taylor the "report of John D. Lee's trials, type written, two copies of each; first trial, five books; second trial, one book."[32]

WHEN I GET ACROSS THE RIVER: WILLIAM DAME

Over time, Mormon historians collected dozens of statements from residents of southern Utah affirming the innocence of Brigham Young in regard to Mountain Meadows. One chink remained in the armor LDS historians had forged to protect Young's reputation: the persistent silence of William Dame.

Sumner Howard dropped charges against Dame in September 1876 as part of the deal to convict Lee. A hearing in October 1879 ended Dame's legal concerns about the massacre, and he was subsequently elected Iron County recorder.[33] Dame's official biography reveals his continuing status in the LDS church, for he served as president of Parowan Stake from 1856 until 1880. He was agent for the presiding bishop from 1866 to his death, and Dame helped to launch one of Brigham Young's pet economic projects, establishing the first cooperative store in Utah.[34]

Rogerson had long known the enigmatic Dame. He had managed the stake president's farm while Dame was on a mission to Europe. As a manual laborer, Rogerson conceded, "Dame was a worker, from the rise to the setting of the Sun," but otherwise there was no love lost between the two men. He attributed Dame's fondness for church meetings to "his love to preside and dictate." Rogerson's personal contempt for the man reflected the widespread belief in southern Utah that Dame was much more responsible for the massacre than anyone dared to admit. Dame could have stopped the massacre at "any hour of the day or night, from the hour of the first attack, to the morning of the slaughter," Rogerson insisted. He undercut the excuse that the Indians forced the Mormons into murder, stating that Dame could have stopped the Paiutes instantly, "for the moment an Indian sees a well armed and determined white man, he knows that two or three of his race is going to bite the dust for every white man in the fight."[35]

Rogerson explicitly blamed Dame for covering up the murders, charging that he "kept his mouth shut like a coward and poltroon" and sat by when letters were written to Brigham Young misrepresenting the whole matter. While his troops marched to Little Creek to fight the Utes during Utah's Black Hawk War, Dame "stayed at home collecting bread and quilts." "Quite a number of the male citizens of Parowan and Red Creek learned from that evening the true character of the warrior Dame," Rogerson wrote. He concluded that at "a military parade with his tin cased sword he was a swelled chested brave General," but when push came to shove, Dame was a coward.[36]

Much of Rogerson's bitterness stemmed from Dame's refusal to exonerate Brigham Young. In spring 1884, when he had nearly finished his trial transcriptions, Rogerson stopped at Dame's home in Paragonah and pleaded with him to make a statement about the massacre. A paralytic stroke had left Dame enfeebled, and he could only get around with a crutch. He invited his guest into a room on the east side of the house and closed the door. Taking a seat, Dame asked, "How are you getting along with the transcript?" Rogerson responded, hoping to get another statement that Lee was solely to blame for the massacre. He asked Dame to tell the truth under oath before a justice of the peace. "Lee has paid what penalty he could and Haight and Higbee are gone," he said. "You that were their Superior in military and Church matters, are the greatest to blame unless you can clear yourself by your deposition."[37]

President Dame, Rogerson said, "sat confused and somewhat thoughtful for a few moments." The reserved Dame then made a characteristic reply. "My days are numbered," he said, "and I do not care to say anything more about this matter, than I have said on one or two occasions—that Bro. Haight mis-understood me, and that John D. Lee was advised and requested to do all that he could to keep the Indians off till the answer came back from Governor Young." Unlike his comrades, he refused to vindicate Young and gave no reason for his silence. Dame simply concluded, "I am willing to be tried when I get across the River, and am willing that Our Father be the Judge."[38]

Discouraged, Rogerson said he "could not get another word of admission" from Dame. "A month or so after our interview, another and the second paralytic stroke took him across the River." Dame died at his home at Paragonah on August 16, 1884, "of Paralysis of the Brain."[39] Whatever secrets Dame knew about Mountain Meadows the former militia colonel carried to his grave.

All the Light That Can Be Obtained

Rogerson's investigative efforts bore fruit when Charles Penrose presented what became the standard Mormon interpretation of the massacre to a standing-room-only audience at the Twelfth Ward Assembly Hall in Salt Lake in October 1884. "No one can palliate the crime," he admitted. To think any white person would be involved in such a terrible outrage was "most horrible to my mind, most repugnant to my feelings." He quoted extensively from anti-Mormon sources such as Stenhouse and Beadle to show that the Mormon people could not be indicted for the massacre. He repeated the stories that maligned the emigrants and added one from the 1877 Young-Wells interview: "They caught an Indian, tied him to a wagon wheel and whipped him severely." Penrose admitted he was unable to say if the stories of the emigrants' outrageous behavior were true or false, but they were told and people believed them. It was also stated, he said, "that John D. Lee led the first attack of the Indians against those emigrants." He reprinted George A. Smith's affidavit from the Lee trial and argued that LDS authorities had simply prohibited trading grain to feed stock, not to feed people. "We all know," Penrose assured his audience, "that George A. Smith was not a man of vengeance or a man of blood."[40]

Lee, Penrose told the audience, "made a great many so-called 'confessions' which are rather contradictory." He argued that Lee provided "particulars and data to Mr. Bishop, who worked them up with some of his own notions and fabrications into this book." Despite denouncing *Mormonism Unveiled*, Penrose used Lee's work to prove

Brigham Young's innocence. If he had ordered the murders, why did Dame and Haight argue over how to report it? The dramatic story of Haslam's ride was the centerpiece of Penrose's analysis, and he used it to show that Young could not have been an accessory before the fact. Penrose reproduced for the first time the complete text of Young's September 10, 1857, letter to Isaac Haight, which was filed in the president's office in the same letterbook containing Brigham Young's order to list the names of those who sold "one kernal" of grain to the emigrants.[41]

Penrose turned to the more difficult question of "President Young being an accessory after the fact." He called on Apostle Wilford Woodruff, "an honest, upright, truthful man, whose word can be relied upon implicitly," to refute Lee's claim that he told Young all about the massacre. Woodruff swore in an October 24, 1884, affidavit, "Lee did not intimate by a single word that any white man had anything to do with the massacre." Woodruff claimed Young remained ignorant of the truth until fall 1870, when Erastus Snow presented evidence that convinced the apostles, who unanimously voted to excommunicate Lee and Haight. From the apostle's "large trunk full of books comprising my journal," Woodruff produced his 1857 diary, from which Penrose copied the entry of September 29, 1857.[42]

Woodruff recalled this critical interview in several affidavits made in the 1880s, adding details about "innocent blood" not present in his journal account. He recollected that Brigham Young had expressed much regret, "especially that any innocent Blood should be shed in this Country." Lee, Woodruff said, "remarked there was not a drop of innocent Blood in that Camp."[43]

"What do you call the Blood of women & Children if not innocent Blood?" Young allegedly shot back, a detail missing from the journal, which continued, "The scene of Blood has Commenced." Woodruff swore that Lee did not reply. He did not explain why the issue of innocent blood should be of concern to Lee and Young in the context of an Indian massacre.[44]

To explain why the apostles waited until October 1870 to excommunicate Lee, Snow described how he had engaged in "ferreting out the facts" about the massacre. When he told Young about Lee's involvement, Snow said Young expressed great astonishment. Apparently forgetting that Jacob Hamblin had told him of Lee's crimes in June 1858, Young "wondered how and why these facts had so long been concealed from him." Penrose reviewed the Lee trial materials and sorted through the confusing facts to prove that they, too, exonerated the church. "Brigham Young's name stands to-day clear from the guilt which malignant people have tried to fasten upon it," Penrose announced. "Truth is mighty and will prevail."[45]

Within a month, the LDS church's critics responded to "Penrose's harangue." A broadside by "Vindex," perhaps William Nelson, charged that at Mountain Meadows "Brigham lighted the torch and others applied it as a duty." Vindex said that Haight's wife threatened to produce evidence that "would implicate some very high in authority" if her husband was given "the same traitorous treatment" as Lee.[46]

Vindex's rebuttal was soon forgotten, but Mormon historians would return to Penrose's arguments again and again to explain the darkest episode in their history. Even investigators with little sympathy for the LDS church found his arguments compelling. Popular writer Hoffman Birney examined selected church records in the early 1930s. They convinced him the massacre did indeed take place but church leaders "did not order it, had no advance knowledge of it, and the most gross distortion of the evidence cannot implicate them as accessories before the fact."[47] While Penrose's account came to be the accepted story of the church, historians recognized his whole purpose was "to clear the name of Brigham Young from any implications of guilt."[48] If one accepted the limits of evidence and analysis Penrose imposed, he produced a believable explanation, but the questions he did not ask and the records he did not produce told quite a different story from the one he presented that October evening at the Twelfth Ward.

Perhaps the greatest measure of the success of Penrose's story of the massacre was its acceptance by Bancroft in his *History of Utah*. Bancroft worked in cooperation with official Mormon historians for almost a decade before publishing this volume of his massive history of the West in 1889. Church historian Orson Pratt offered to write the history if Bancroft would print it "without mutilation," but Bancroft would only agree to treat the subject fairly. "Every truthful writer of history," he explained, "must hold himself absolutely free to be led wherever the facts carry him." John Taylor discussed Bancroft's proposals with the apostles on January 26, 1880, and they agreed to furnish the historian with all the information he needed. Pratt assigned Franklin Richards to help Bancroft, and in July 1880 Richards visited with the historian for two weeks in San Francisco. The two men and their wives began an enduring friendship. The Bancrofts spent six weeks in Salt Lake in 1884, meeting with Mormon leaders and gathering materials for the history. Bancroft acknowledged his deep obligations to Richards, and Richards called Bancroft "the greatest historian of our age." The help the Saints gave Bancroft influenced his sympathetic portrait of their history, but in *History of Utah* he stuck to his principles and created the best account of the massacre that had yet appeared. Bancroft balanced the Mormon story told in the text with a critical rebuttal in the footnotes.[49]

Bancroft gave little credence to the tales of Missouri wildcats and poisoned springs but generally endorsed the key elements of the LDS interpretation. Although he used many of its details, Bancroft placed little reliance on Lee's account, and he accurately determined that the attack began on Monday, September 7, rejecting Lee's claim that the fight started the next day. Apparently the first investigator to look at an 1857 calendar, Bancroft established September 11, 1857, as the most reasonable date for the massacre. He concluded that the story of Haslam's ride, so essential in vindicating Brigham Young, was not "a mere trick of the first presidency." The selected evidence he saw in the church's records convinced Bancroft "this horrible crime, so persistently charged upon the Mormon church and its leaders, was the crime of an individual, the crime of a fanatic of the worst stamp." He believed the hierarchy knew nothing of Lee's intentions, and church members high and low abhorred his bloody acts. Just as a century later pundits did not believe a politician as skillful as Richard Nixon could be involved in a bungled burglary, Bancroft simply could not credit that "the shrewd and far-sighted" Brigham Young would have endorsed the massacre.[50]

Bancroft's influence was apparent in Bishop Orson Whitney's massive apologetic history of Utah, which appeared in four volumes between 1892 and 1904 and gave a faithful Mormon rebuttal of some of Bancroft's less flattering conclusions. In 1892 the First Presidency called Danish convert and self-taught historian Andrew Jenson to go on a "special mission" to gather information about the Mountain Meadows massacre for Whitney's history. Whitney would use little of Jenson's material, but Wilford Woodruff, now president of the LDS church, and his counselors gave Jenson a letter of introduction. It explained that although many facts had already been published about the massacre, "there is an opinion prevailing that all the light that can be obtained has not been thrown upon it." Many of the participants were dead, and "ere long there will be no person alive who will know anything about it only as they learn it from what has been written." The First Presidency is "anxious to learn all that we can upon this subject, not necessarily for publication, but that the Church may have the details in its possession for the vindication of innocent parties, and that the world may know, when the time comes, the true facts connected with it." The letter advised that it might be prudent not to mention names. Jenson could be trusted, "and any communication that you wish to make to him will be confidential, unless you wish them published."[51]

Jenson spent a week in southern Utah interviewing "a number of the old veterans who freely gave [him] the desired information." He admitted that "some white people were implicated in the Mountain Meadows Massacre, besides the Indians," but he had "learned nothing that in any shape or form could connect the general authorities of the Church with the affair." The job was not as easy as Jenson's published comments indicated, for the stories he heard kept him awake at night. "I felt tired and fatigued, both mentally and physically when I returned home," he wrote in his journal. The notes of Jenson's interviews "cannot be located in the LDS Church Archives," two official LDS church historians noted. "One supposes that they were placed in the vault of the First Presidency of the Church and still remain there."[52]

The final formulation of the LDS version of the Mountain Meadows story came in the early twentieth century with Brigham Roberts's *Comprehensive History of The Church of Jesus Christ of Latter-day Saints*. Originally published serially between 1909 and 1915 in the *Americana*, a non-Mormon historical journal, this official history was finally released in six volumes on the church's centennial in 1930. A dedicated defender of the faith, Roberts was arguably the greatest intellect the LDS church ever produced, and by the standards of his time he was an excellent historian. He admitted his bias but sought to portray the church's history honestly, and he "steadfastly insisted upon recognizing the faults and foibles of the Saints."[53]

Roberts's better qualities failed him when he addressed what he termed "the most lamentable episode in Utah history, and in the history of the church." The Mountain Meadows massacre was "the most difficult of all the many subjects" he had to deal with in his massive study. Roberts probably addressed this challenge as well as he could in his role as official historian, but his cursory treatment put the interests of his church before his duty as a historian. His work was perfunctory, containing little original material. Roberts knew much more about the massacre than his history revealed, but he simply repeated the Bancroft version with only a few additional comments on idiosyncratic details.[54]

Roberts claimed he had not written an argumentative history, but his account argued many debatable points, such as whether Brigham Young had forbidden the Saints to trade with emigrants. He gave preference to Young's later statements denying he had restricted such sales while ignoring the evidence in Young's 1857 letters showing that he did. He passed over the glaring inconsistencies in George A. Smith's 1858 report and echoed some of the weakest claims of the Penrose defense. He noted Jacob Hamblin's story of how he gave Young the facts about the massacre in 1858, but he claimed LDS officials remained ignorant of the details of the event until 1870. His chapter on responsibility for the massacre evaded the question. Roberts did not vilify Lee, but by exonerating the LDS church of any responsibility for the crime, he begged the question, if not John D. Lee, who?[55]

BURNED INTO MY MEMORY: THE TWO JOSIAHS

Ironically, two old Utah pioneers, not professional historians, would write the next chapter in the history of Mountain Meadows. Composed not long after the beginning of the twentieth century, their narratives captured some of the last participant and eyewitness accounts of the event and created historical records not easily ignored.

Josiah Gibbs and Josiah Rogerson both spent long and honorable lives in the service of Mormonism, and both were profoundly troubled by the 1857 atrocity. Of the two Josiahs, Rogerson would remain faithful to his religion, but Gibbs would not. Gibbs's "real trouble with the prophets" began in 1891 when as a country editor for papers such as the *Deseret Blade* and the *Marysvale Free Lance* he began writing articles condemning the church's role in politics.[56] It culminated with a 1910 pamphlet on the Mountain Meadows massacre that remains one of the best sources on the subject. Gibbs's work would achieve some degree of notoriety and enduring repute, but the rebuttal Rogerson composed for the LDS church would remain a secret for almost a century.

Josiah Francis Gibbs was born in Nauvoo in August 1845. His family crossed the plains to Utah in 1857, and his father worked as a carpenter for Brigham Young, standing guard at the Beehive House once a week with his son. Gibbs claimed to have played marbles with "Charley" Fancher, who told him in Salt Lake in 1859 that the Indians had not acted alone at Mountain Meadows. The Gibbs family moved to Beaver County in 1864, where their employer, a Mr. Stewart, had a brindle cow he said was one of the four hundred cattle taken from the emigrants. One of Stewart's hands, Nate Dodge, delighted "in pouring the horrid story into my ears, and in singing a lot of doggerel composed on the massacre" until the tale was "burned into my memory." Gibbs served in the Black Hawk War and went on a mission to England in 1867. He later claimed his faith in Mormonism had failed by 1871, but after that date he became a polygamist. His disillusionment with Mormonism was more civil than religious. His fight against what he called "the political encroachments of the prophets on the civil rights of the people" and a general neglect of duty resulted in his excommunication in 1908. He began writing a book on the LDS church and launched an intensive investigation into the Mountain Meadows massacre, although a prominent Salt Lake editor advised him it was best forgotten. He was motivated by a sincere friendship for the Mormon people, Gibbs said, but he held "inexpressible contempt for their 'prophets.'"[57]

Gibbs's two studies of the massacre were quite balanced. His years as a newspaperman served him well as he traveled through southern Utah interviewing survivors and collecting evidence. Gibbs found the non-Mormon accounts distorted and faulted them for holding an entire people responsible for the crime. He believed Mormon advocates equally untruthful and unfair for first placing the entire responsibility on the Indians and then transferring all blame to Lee and a few rogue Mormons. Gibbs accepted most of Lee's story of the massacre, but he concluded that Brigham Young "was guiltless, before the fact, of any part in the Mountain Meadows massacre," beyond preaching the doctrine of unquestioned obedience and its "twin sister, the doctrine of blood atonement." Gibbs rejected Young's claim that he knew nothing about the massacre for years after the event, however, citing Jacob Hamblin's testimony that Young knew it all. The "Mormon people, as a people, were—are—blameless," Gibbs concluded. It was pointless to prosecute the last unatoned participants; "let Justice slumber," he advised. Gibbs blamed "the accursed doctrine of unquestioning obedience that impelled those mistaken men to stain their souls with murder"—a doctrine he found alive and well in the LDS church.[58]

When Josiah Gibbs's conclusions appeared in print, Mormon leaders felt obliged to respond. Perhaps his persistent practice of quoting Joseph F. Smith, the current prophet, compelled them to reply. To do so, the First Presidency recalled Josiah Rogerson, who had now lived in southern Utah for more than fifty years. Rogerson's extensive experience with the case recommended him for the job—he had, after all, witnessed Lee's trials and execution—but his lack of professional writing experience and fading memory made him a poor choice for such a delicate task. He also had something of a reputation as a crackpot. Still, Rogerson worked for expenses and a promised share of the royalties, and he had a wealth of personal stories about the massacre and its aftermath that he hoped to publish in a two-hundred-page book.[59] Apostle John Henry Smith supervised his work for the First Presidency and spent most of the morning of March 29, 1911, "reading some documents on John D. Lee by Josiah Rogerson."[60]

Rogerson faithfully delivered the answers his employers sought. After three days and nights conversing with the brethren of southern Utah, he reported to the First Presidency in April 1911, "The guilt of Lee stands out like a monolith, and not a particle of any blame or censure reaching Prest. Young or Geo. A Smith."[61] Rogerson toiled on his book from about February 1911 until he delivered a draft in June. Two months later he learned it had "been deemed inexpedient to publish my true history of the Mountain Meadows Massacre at present" and that its release had been indefinitely postponed. Apostles Charles Penrose and John H. Smith had found no good reason to publish Rogerson's study, for as Brigham Young had learned, the more the church stirred this particular manure pile, the worse it stank.[62]

The affronted writer complained that his work had been rejected "before it has been read, criticised and toned to meet the requirements of all our missionaries" for whom it had been written. The $235 he had been paid did not compensate him for his hard labor "writing and compiling that valuable manuscript." He had worked night and day, and the money was simply to cover rent and household expenses and tide him over until he received royalties. The First Presidency's decision prevented him from deriving any benefit from "the immense sale that it would receive, as I know that the demand would be great even in Utah alone." Rogerson complained that he would have been better paid if he had stayed at the telegraph office in Beaver, warning, "I cannot and do not, my brethren, relinquish all my rights, title, and interest in and to that valuable document." But the frustrated historian's final request was humble; he asked only for an additional $165, or about $100 per month for the time he spent on the project.[63]

Receipts in Rogerson's file indicate that the authorities came to an accommodation with the old pioneer, who died on March 15, 1926, never having pursued his threat to publish his book on the massacre. His transcripts and opus came to rest in one of the First Presidency's vaults and might have vanished without a trace had not historian Dale Morgan alerted Juanita Brooks to its existence in 1949. In the catalog of the LDS church library, Morgan found a reference to the "Trial of John D. Lee. Josiah Rogerson, Reporter. July 1875 to January 1885." Morgan wrote to Brooks, "The location number of this is '1621 (Big Safe).'" Both the First Presidency and LDS church historian Joseph Fielding Smith maintained safes where they stored an odd mix of rare but well-known books and sensitive documents. These highly secret records include reports from investigations of Mountain Meadows, variant accounts of Joseph Smith's first vision, and, some say, a dictated autobiography of Porter Rockwell. The "Big Safe" was probably the large green vault in Smith's office. Morgan surmised that Rogerson had attended the Lee trials in the interest of the church. "Why the 'January, 1885,'" he wrote, "I wouldn't even guess."[64]

Brooks never saw the records of Josiah Rogerson's investigations, but scraps of it are available in a miscellaneous collection of Mountain Meadows documents at the LDS Archives.[65] It is not clear how much of Rogerson's work remains locked away in the vaults of the First Presidency.

ANCIENT BITTERNESS: BASKIN BATTLES WHITNEY

It is hard to recall the bitter political struggles of territorial Utah without at times wishing both sides could lose. Ironically, at the end of this conflict both Robert Baskin and the people of Utah were the winners. Over five decades, relentless opposition forced the LDS church to abandon its political agenda and modify its most troublesome doctrines. The Saints made a noble resistance, but ultimately the battle produced a more democratic society and a more viable religion. Deseret died hard, but all Utahns benefited from its passing.

Orson Whitney's four-volume *History of Utah* codified Charles Penrose's conclusions as the definitive Mormon account of Mountain Meadows. Not surprisingly, Whitney's work paid homage to objectivity, but such recent church historians as Davis Bitton and Leonard Arrington acknowledged that he consistently offered "a pro-Mormon interpretation, one consonant with the official church position." Whitney's inflated style and overblown literary ambitions (he hoped to be Mormonism's great epic poet) marred his work, as did his deification of Brigham Young, who he compared to Julius Caesar and Bismarck.[66]

Whitney's abridged *Popular History of Utah*, published as a text for Utah's schools in 1916, evoked a passionate rebuttal from Brigham Young's old nemesis, Baskin. Referring to Baskin as "this Bourbon of the dead past," Whitney charged that his recently published *Reminiscences of Early Utah* revived the ancient bitterness between Utah Mormons and gentiles. Baskin was delighted to respond to Whitney's charges and was especially passionate in his telling of the Mountain Meadows story. He branded Whitney's account of the murdered emigrants' behavior an infamous libel and his work as a historian reckless and unscrupulous. Losing none of his old fire, Baskin blamed the "cut throat sermons of Brigham Young" and "the covenants of unquestioned obedience to the priesthood, and the avengement of the blood of the prophets" for causing the crime.[67] Today even official Mormon historians concede that Baskin won the contest. Some of Baskin's points "are well taken," Bitton and Arrington concluded. "Current scholarship on almost all if not all of the topics he mentions would come closer to his interpretation than to Whitney's."[68]

As he looked back at his long career, Mayor Baskin quoted Apostle Whitney's charge that he had been "the human mainspring of nearly every anti-Mormon movement that Utah has known." Baskin gloried in the accusation. "I am very proud of the fact," he wrote, "[that I] honestly and untiringly strove to Americanize theocratic Utah." His work helped to end the bitter conflict that had torn the territory apart. The great irony of Baskin's life—and of nineteenth-century Utah history—was that the efforts of anti-Mormons to strip the LDS church of polygamy and its radical theocratic practices laid the foundation for the faith's great success in the twentieth century. Robert Baskin himself appreciated the irony. "Though not a prophet," he concluded in his reply to Whitney, "I have been profitable to the masses of the Mormon people."[69]

THE FATE OF THE PAIUTES

Though the record of their passing is sketchy at best, most of the Paiutes who had been at Mountain Meadows did not long survive the Arkansans who died there. After their war chief, Jackson, spoke to James Carleton in 1859, he disappeared from Utah records. Tutsegabit served as a Mormon missionary to the Apaches and was displaced in 1858, but he signed a treaty at Pinto in 1865 surrendering his people's lands. In return he was to receive a house and five acres of plowed and fenced land on the Ute reservation in the Uintah Basin, plus $100 a year for twenty years. The Senate never ratified any of the 1865 treaties with Utah Indians, and the attempt to move the Paiutes to live in a cold mountain valley with their old enemies the Utahs was a complete failure. As the tribe's history noted, they became "a nuisance that the Mormon people felt compelled occasionally to feed."[70]

An epidemic of what the Mormons called the bloody flux struck the Muddy Valley bands about 1860 and was so devastating the bodies of the dead were simply dumped in a gully. The renewal of the southern Utah colonies in 1861 increased pressure on the native population as the Saints built their Cotton Mission settlements directly on the sites of Paiute farms. The settlers arrived so rapidly that they overwhelmed the natives without generating any memorable Indian wars. Paiute scouts were instrumental in helping the Mormon militia defeat Navajo raiders during the 1860s, but as scholar Ronald Holt noted, this "was the last major need of the colonists served by the Paiutes." After 1870 all references to Paiute irrigation disappear, and there was a dramatic but ignored decline in the Indian population. The bands surrounding Mountain Meadows were particularly devastated. In 1944 local historian Angus M. Woodbury recorded that of the thousand Paiutes living on the Virgin River during the 1850s and 1860s, there was only one survivor.[71]

After 1869 the Paiutes faced two choices: either settle in ghettos, the Indian villages found on the fringes of many southern Utah settlements, to live off begging and provide cheap seasonal labor; or move farther back into the most marginal desert lands. Those who stayed near the settlements had to endure well-meaning paternalism, as when Bishop Robert Gardner of Price advised Moqueak not to "trouble me any more, for more land. I know better what is good for you, than you do yourself." The Paiutes failed to conform to white expectations. "Many a priesthood meeting was spent discussing what to do with the Indians" and the Relief Society, a Mormon women's auxiliary, discussed how to teach "their Indian girls white ways." But the

Paiutes "had become paupers to be fed, a sort of nuisance to be put up with." The Mormons found the Indians who lived among them a decided liability.[72]

By the 1890s it was difficult to find any survivors of the Paiute bands who had close contact with whites. Mineral discoveries led to the founding of the first Southern Paiute Agency at St. Thomas, Arizona, and to the creation of the Moapa Indian Reservation on the Muddy River in Nevada in 1873, but many Paiutes found refuge with bands far removed from the settlements.[73] Some joined the Shivwits in northern Arizona and some went south to the Moapits. Recording a visit to their reservation in 1876–77, frontier trader Don Maguire found about 375 natives living at St. Thomas. "They are really a group of renegades, even though credited with being Paiutes, from the Digger Indians of California, the Hualapais and Mojaves of Arizona, Utes and Paiutes from Utah, and a few of the Shoshone from southern Idaho and Wyoming, all of which make up these Muddy River rascals," Maguire wrote. "They are a poor, degenerate lot of people who are rapidly becoming extinct."[74]

The Paiutes refused to recognize that they were part of a vanishing race or that their extinction was inevitable, but they faced a hard road. Even those who found refuge in the remotest corners of the Southwest could not escape the settlers' insatiable appetite for land, as the Shivwits band learned in 1891. Anthony Ivins acquired the interests of the Mojave Land and Cattle Company, which had purchased water rights from Paiutes living near Mount Trumbull in northern Arizona. Ivins knew that ranching would not succeed as long as the Shivwits occupied the land. He complained that insolent Paiutes often killed cattle for food and, when reproached, replied "that the country was theirs, and that the white man, with his flocks and herds, should move away, and leave them in peaceful possession." Ivins enlisted the federal bureaucracy to remove one of the last bands of free Paiutes from their homeland for "their own good." The government obliged, appropriating $40,000 to establish a reservation in the desert west of St. George "where they would be among civilized people, and subject to proper government supervision."[75]

The Paiute reservation was located in the home of the Tonaquint band, but by the time the Shivwits arrived, "there were not enough living members of the other bands to even perpetuate their names."[76] Ivins was appointed Indian agent and gloried in his reputation as a friend of the Indian, while the cattle that had replaced the Paiutes in northern Arizona added to his growing fortune. Today it is hard to view Ivins's cynical manipulations in quite the paternalistic light in which he saw them.

The surviving traditions of the Paiutes claim their people had nothing to do with the massacre at Mountain Meadows. Like the Mormon lore of southern Utah, they lay the blame on someone else, but these tales have a striking consistency of detail. For example, almost all the Paiute stories describe warnings from the whites not to touch gold or silver coins on the field, much as John Higbee told George Adair the emigrants' gold was poison.[77] These traditions preserve a telling truth. According to tribal elder Clifford Jake, two hunters saw the massacre take place from afar. They warned their people that they "had seen something really bad happen. So they said I want you people to get prepared, for we're going to get blamed for it."[78]

Minnie Jake of the Eagle Valley band also recalled that two Indians saw the Mormons kill the white people at Mountain Meadows. One said they killed everyone, even women and children. "The Mormons asked these two Indians to help them pack up all the booty. The Mormons kept the horses and milk cows, and they told the two Indians that if they saw any round gold pieces (coins) lying on the ground the Indians were not to pick them up because they were poison and would kill them." But the Mormons picked up all the coins and put them in a sack and kept them. "They hid everything else in a tunnel in a round red place down there someplace. The two Indians didn't help the Mormons in the killing."[79]

Hans Peter Freece told Charles Kelly that the last Indian participant in the massacre died at Panguitch Lake in 1906.[80] The last known Yannawant, Peter Harrison, died in St. George in 1945. "With his death," commented one local historian, "ended that particular band."[81] Mormon descendants of participants number in the hundreds of thousands if not millions, and even the children who survived the massacre often left large families, but the Paiute bands that were lured into the killings have vanished.

This Affair Should Never Be Mentioned

In about 1927 a small group of John D. Lee descendants met with President Heber J. Grant while the Mormon prophet was visiting Arizona. They complained about the treatment of Lee in Apostle Joseph Fielding Smith's *Essentials in Church History*, a textbook used in LDS church schools. One of Lee's granddaughters had been ostracized because of Smith's vilification of her ancestor. The family discussed Lee's "relation to the Mountain Meadow Massacre and the present and future attitude to be cultivated toward the affair" with the church president. Grant acknowledged he had authorized Smith's book but admitted he had never read it and promised it would no longer be used as a text in church schools. He then told a chilling story about the massacre. Grant said President Joseph F. Smith told him had he not been in Hawaii at the time of the massacre but in southern Utah, Smith "would no doubt have been in the midst of the fray." Grant added, "I would have been in it too, or I hope I would." He advised, "This affair should never be mentioned."[82]

In other forums Grant worked hard to obliterate the memory of John D. Lee. Early in 1929 historian James McClintock warned that the Arizona legislature was considering naming the new span that crossed the Colorado River at Marble Canyon "Lee's Ferry Bridge." This would be an outrage to the Mormon people, Grant wrote, and he "would drop everything and go to Arizona at once and make a personal appeal to the legislature that this be not done." Apostle Ivins agreed. He said, "We can see no reason why the name and memory of Lee should be perpetuated." As good as his word, Grant made a special trip to Phoenix to talk to Arizona lawmakers. Accompanied by the governor, Grant addressed a joint session of the legislature. Using Lee's name would "reflect on all the Mormon people, in every land and every clime," and Grant suggested naming the bridge after Jacob Hamblin, since Lee had been at the ferry only briefly. Eventually lawmakers dubbed the structure the Navajo Bridge.[83] Grant won his point, but Juanita Brooks believed his visit broke the subject of Mountain Meadows "wide open" both within the LDS church and among the many friends and descendants of Lee.[84]

Like his predecessors, Heber J. Grant tried to suppress the story of the massacre. Apostle and senator Reed Smoot noted in his diary that he met with the First Presidency to discuss an article written for the *Saturday Evening Post* that "recited all the details" of the massacre. The feature was generally complimentary to modern Mormonism, but Grant and Smoot asked the writer not to publish it. The author tore up the review copy and said it would not be used, "a great relief to us all."[85] But the dark story refused to die.

John D. Lee's grandson, Rex E. Lee, traveled from St. Johns to Vernon with church historian Andrew Jenson in November 1931. "John D. Lee was not guilty of the crime which the world charges against him," Jenson said. "The truth of that affair has never been printed." Lee, he said, was a victim of circumstances, and William Dame, Isaac Haight, and John Higbee participated to a much greater extent than Lee. Based on the stories he had heard in southern Utah in 1891, Jenson claimed the plan had been to disarm the emigrants and escort them to Cedar City, but "the situation got beyond control, and then the thing that had been started had to be finished." Jenson thought Lee was a man of God, not a man of blood, and that his autobiography was "the attempt of cheap writers to gain from a spectacular lie." This was the same story Rex Lee had heard from his father, and he asked Jenson to provide a written statement for the Lee family. Jenson backed down and asked Lee never to repeat what he had heard outside his family. Jenson's reluctance to take a public stand was due to his fear of Grant, whom he called an extremist. Rex Lee asked Jenson "if the truth had to be suppressed and many made to suffer out of fear for the power and position of one man."

"I don't like the way you put that, Brother Lee," Jenson replied, "but it may be too near the truth."[86]

TURNED THE VERY DEVIL LOOSE

As participants died and the zealotry of frontier Zion became a distant memory, southern Utahns struggled to explain the deed that stained their history. Coming to terms with this collective guilt required vindicating saintly ancestors, and the community found that the simplest rationalization was to vilify the victims. In the process, the historic Alexander Fancher, a law-abiding man who only wanted to get his family and friends to California safely, was transformed into "Charles" Fancher, a perverted monster. The fabricated evil acts of the murdered emigrants grew and the threat posed by the vicious Paiutes became more intimidating with each telling. The stories might appear increasingly incredible to outsiders, but they filled a desperate need.

One elusive tradition was that the persecutors of the Mormons "ravished" LDS women. Not a single documented case of such a sexual assault can be found in Missouri or Illinois, but some suggest that social attitudes hushed up such atrocities to protect the victims. Whatever the truth, Mormons in Utah heard from the pulpit that such charges were true. Joseph Fish would not vouch for the truth of the story, but he reported that about forty members of a Missouri mob had lashed two LDS girls to benches and raped them. One girl died, but the other was living in southern Utah in 1857. Fish recalled that members of the Fancher party bought "Sage Brush Whiskey" at Klingensmith's mill. "Getting a little more of this than they should they talked very freely and boasted of what they had done to the Mormons and what they would do." From the boasts of emigrants at the mill, it was understood that some of them were part of the mob "that so inhumanely treated these girls."[87]

Alva Matheson was born near the ruins of Cedar City's old Chaffin-Walker mill in 1902. He recalled John Higbee coming to visit his family when he was ten or twelve. Matheson is convinced he met the major of Mountain Meadows fame, but he may have met the officer's son, John Mount Clark Higbee, as Major Higbee died the year after Matheson was born.

Matheson's tale reveals much about how southern Utahns wrestled with the secret that haunted their past. His Higbee described "Charles" Fancher as "a domineering, ill principled man who took what he wanted and gave nothing in return," a bitter anti-Mormon who had helped to drive the Saints from their homes in Nauvoo. The emigrants poisoned water holes and oxen and shot six Indians outright. Fancher himself shot down chickens, pigs, and dogs in the streets of Fillmore and Beaver. Local Indians heard of these outrages and were on the warpath—only the strong hand of John D. Lee persuaded Captain John, the local chief, to let them pass in peace. On the streets of Cedar City, Fancher boasted he would wipe out "every G. D. Mormon S.O.B in the territory." Going to Lee's mill, Fancher took what he wanted and "spit in Lee's face and told him that he was one of the mob who had killed old Joe Smith." Fancher boasted he still had the pistol the prophet had used at Carthage Jail to kill one of his attackers, a friend of Fancher. He told Lee that he and seventeen of his men had raped Lee's sixteen-year-old daughter: "I think we all took a whack at her." She fought like hell the first few times, the villain boasted, "just like a wild cat but we soon took the fight out of her. She wasn't no match for us. After the first few times she just laid there and bawled like a branded calf." Higbee cried as he repeated the story he claimed he heard directly from Lee. The rape "turned the very devil loose inside of brother John D."[88] In truth, Lee had no connection with the mill and no daughter living at Cedar City.

Descendants of Joseph Walker, the miller said to have ground grain for the Fancher party at Cedar City, preserve a similar tradition. In their story the victim was an Adams girl whose father and brother followed the train and killed the man who did it, drawing "first blood" of the confrontation.[89] While interesting as cultural artifacts, these stories are clearly modern inventions, as there was no mention of sexual aggression by the Fancher party until the twentieth century. Like similar southern Utah legends, these awkward efforts of loyal descendants used questionable legends to explain and justify the actions of their ancestors.

A Voice We Loved Is Stilled: Survivors

Bishop William Edwards of Beaver County, Utah, appeared before a notary public on May 14, 1924, at age eighty-two to make a sworn statement about what he had seen as a fifteen-year-old boy at Mountain Meadows. Edwards went to the meadows with some thirty men and older boys, allegedly to bury the dead.

> We arrived at said Mountain Meadows early in the evening only to find John D. Lee and several other white men already present, and the said emigrants alive and well fortified against the Indian siege. After surveying the situation for some time we were called to a council of white men by said John D. Lee and by him ordered to assist the Indians in their purposes. Some of the council objected to the butchery but were silenced by said Lee and 2 or 3 others of our file leaders. The strategy, as laid out by said Lee, was that said Lee would trick the said emigrants into giving up their arms and fortifications by pledging them safe conduct to Cedar City. After the said emigrants were a safe distance from their defences, a gunshot would signal us to keep our weapons conspicuous for the benefit of the Indians who would at that moment rush upon us, and that the best way to display them would be to join in the slaughter. The next day the said plan was carried out under the supervision of said Lee except that your affiant together with many of the other white men refused to discharge his weapon.[90]

William Edwards died on April 24, 1925, less than a year after making his statement.[91] Sixty-eight years had passed since the massacre, and with Edwards's death the last known Mormon participant was gone, but John T. Baker's granddaughters would survive for almost two more decades. All three of George and Manerva Baker's children lived well into the twentieth century. In summer 1938 Mary Elizabeth, then Mrs. Betty Terry of Harrison, Arkansas, vividly recalled "the massacre of the westbound Arkansas caravan in Utah more than 80 years ago" for readers of the *Arkansas Gazette*. Her family Bible recorded that she had been married in 1874 by the Rev. Calvin Williams, the same parson who later denounced Isaac Haight. Her brother, William T. Baker, lived near Harrison for many years, worked as a teamster, and recalled being robbed by Jesse James. He allegedly divorced his first wife when she converted to Mormonism. He remarried in his fifties and died at Marshall, Arkansas, in 1937. Remarkably, three of his daughters, Betty Baker Thomas, Pauline Baker Bratton, and

Bonnie Baker, were alive and well in 1991, in Porterville, California, not far from the destination their Arkansas ancestors never reached in 1857.[92]

Of all the survivors of Mountain Meadows, none had bleaker prospects or a happier story than Sarah Dunlap. Her arm was crippled during the massacre, and the eye disease she acquired in southern Utah left her blind. She attended school in Little Rock, Arkansas, and eventually settled with her sister Rebecca and her husband, John W. Evans (or Evins), in Calhoun County. James Lynch, the adventurer who had helped rescue the children in 1859, never lost touch with the orphans. After retiring to Texas, Lynch visited the survivors. He called at the Evans home, "and almost before anyone knew what happened, he had wooed and won Miss Sarah." When the couple married on December 30, 1893, the groom was 74 "and his blind bride was 38." The Lynches ran a store for a time in Woodberry, where Sarah taught Sunday school. They eventually moved to Hampton, where Sarah died on November 13, 1901. Her ornate gravestone and vault were "proof of the tenderness that James felt for Sarah." For decades the community recalled how Captain Lynch "never tired of telling how he rescued her from the Mormons." James Lynch died in about 1910 and was buried next to his bride in an unmarked grave. His fellow Masons conducted his funeral, "the likes of which have never again been seen in these parts."[93]

By 1940 eighty-five-year-old Sarah Frances Baker Gladden Mitchell, of Checotah, Oklahoma, was "the only person still living who was in that massacre." Her sister Betty had died only a few months before. In 1940 "Sallie" Mitchell told her story of the massacre in vivid detail to the *American Weekly*. She recalled John Steward, who as a sixteen-year-old in 1857 hauled Parley Pratt's coffin "out to the burial grounds in his daddy's ox-cart. They didn't have any preacher. Mrs. McLean did the only talking that was done and among other things she said Pratt had been crucified." Just before the Baker family set out for California, two Mormons showed up and asked a lot of questions. "Then they turned back north, along the same route our party followed a few weeks later," she said. "It certainly looks like those two Mormons found out that we were figuring on passing through Utah on our way to California and told the Danites, or Destroying Angels of the Mormons, to be on the lookout for us, because we were from the same district where Pratt was murdered."[94]

When Sallie Baker Mitchell died, all living memory of the Mountain Meadows massacre died with her. But the story's bitter legacy had taken on a life of its own.

19

Nothing but the Truth
Is Good Enough

As Mormonism shed the controversial practices of its youth, it lost much of the reputation for holy murder and spiritual wifery that had so troubled it during the nineteenth century. The church will always be associated with Brigham Young and polygamy, but in the twentieth century it gained a reputation as a solidly conservative if slightly odd religious movement. Incidents like the Mountain Meadows massacre faded from national memory. Except in the hill country of Arkansas and in the southern Great Basin, it was essentially forgotten. As the most interested parties, Mormons fought and won the battle to define the history of the event and vindicate Brigham Young of any connection with the crime. The memory of the atrocity endured in southern Utah as a forbidden legend told in whispers if told at all, and residents were reluctant to go too near a story that almost everyone agreed was best left alone. The massacre would remain shrouded in silence until the mid-twentieth century, when a devout and courageous Mormon historian began to tell its secrets.

THE LITTLE SCHOOLTEACHER

Juanita Leavitt returned to Bunkerville, Nevada, in August 1918 to teach school in the neighboring town of Mesquite. At church on her first Sunday home, she sat next to Nephi Johnson and was "greatly attracted to this patriarchal old man, with his sharp black eyes and long beard." One afternoon she found Brother Johnson standing at her gate. "I want to give you a patriarchal blessing," he said. The old man led her across the street to the home of his scribe, who was not available. The young teacher recorded her own blessing, which she recalled "was a good blessing, not so wordy and elaborate as some I have read."[1]

One afternoon Johnson came to the schoolhouse and waited behind the teacher's desk for the final bell. When the children left, she pulled up a chair. The old pioneer leaned forward on his cane and said, "I want you to do some writing for me. My eyes have witnessed things that my tongue has never uttered, and before I die, I want them written down. And I want you to do the writing." Miss Leavitt had a church meeting that evening, but she told him, "I do want to do it, and I will do it. We can make a start on Saturday, and go on into Sunday if we need to." Johnson agreed, "We'll do it another time. Maybe if you could come down to the ranch after school has closed."

"The Little Schoolteacher," as Johnson called his friend, never found time to make the trip. One evening in late spring she learned that Johnson was very sick. His kin said it "looks like he might not get up again." The next morning before sunrise, the young woman rode to Johnson's ranch. His daughter Maggie greeted her. "I'm so glad you came," she said. "He's been so restless about what he must tell you." Maggie led her to a long lean-to with a blue ceiling where Johnson lay semiconscious. The teacher took Johnson's hand, and his daughter told him, "She has come to do your writing for you." Johnson mumbled, "Good, good," but he was too weak to say anything else. "Rest awhile," said the teacher, "and then we can talk. I'm going to stay right here and not go away." Johnson looked greatly relieved.

During the morning, the teacher thought Johnson had died and called in his daughter, who revived him. Shaken, Leavitt went into the yard. "Why couldn't you let the old man die?" asked Uncle List, one of Johnson's relatives. "He's been ready for two or three days, but was waitin' for you to come. Then he relaxed and could have gone." The next time death approached, he said, "hang on to your shoelaces, and wait."

Troubled and delirious, Johnson lived for two nights. "He prayed, he yelled, he preached, and once his eyes opened wide to the ceiling and he yelled, 'Blood! BLOOD! BLOOD!'" Outside, the teacher asked Uncle List, "What's the matter with him? He acts like he is haunted."

"Maybe he is," said List. "He was at the Mountain Meadows Massacre, you know." The schoolteacher did not know. The shadow of that grim event had fallen across her own family—she was a granddaughter of Dudley Leavitt, a veteran of the massacre—and she had heard the official explanation blaming the murders on the Indians. Still, her sharp intelligence and intuitive understanding of her culture led her to suspect much of the story remained untold.

Nephi Johnson never became lucid. He did not "rally enough to say anything positive or coherent about the massacre, but it was on his mind right to the end." He died on June 6, 1919, at the age of eighty-six; despite his attempt to tell his story, many of his secrets died with him. The Little Schoolteacher became known to the world as the historian Juanita Brooks. She never forgot the old patriarch and his compelling desire to tell the story he had never uttered. Brooks always regretted she had not written Johnson's story "when he was eager to talk, all ready to tell it all!"[2] She would spend the next five decades piecing together the dark puzzle of Mountain Meadows.

Brooks was not the only Latter-day Saint touched by the massacre. The event haunted southern Utah, and a subtle sense that its brutal details threatened "the entire promise of the restored gospel and even the promise of life implicit in Christ's atonement."[3] For generations local residents had erected a wall of silence against the challenge that Mountain Meadows posed to their belief in Mormonism and to the memory of their ancestors—and Brooks's curiosity and candor ran directly into that wall.

Something of a Troublemaker

Tragedy marked Juanita Leavitt's early life. Her husband, Ernest Pulsipher, died of cancer in January 1921 only a year after their marriage. He left his widow to raise a three-month-old son in a desperately poor community. She worked her way through Dixie Normal College and graduated from Brigham Young University in 1925, after which she resumed her career as a teacher. She began a difficult year in New York in September 1928, taking a master's degree in English from Columbia University. When she returned to Dixie College, she was appointed dean of women.[4]

Although Brooks remained loyal to the LDS church all her life, as a Democrat and an intellectual she was always an outsider in St. George, where she developed a reputation as something of a troublemaker and an agitator. She was also much more skeptical than most of her neighbors. Brooks found the temple endowment that preceded her marriage deeply disturbing, and her irreverent remarks about the rites offended even her mother. There was nothing in Mormon culture to prepare her for the pageant of the temple ceremony, and she later wrote of her "desire to giggle, a wish that I could nudge somebody and talk about it, a nervousness, a consciousness of my clothes." The washings and anointings seemed indecent, and she found the explicit references to blood and violence shocking, especially when her arm was anointed to "be strong in the defense of Zion and in avenging the blood of the prophet." She was surprised when an officiator brandished "an actual long, shining, sharp sword" to represent the flaming blade at the gates of Eden. As her biographer, Levi Peterson, noted, these rituals eventually gave Brooks "a window upon the past. She would come to think of it as a vestige of the pioneer era and could therefore understand more readily the vengeful anger" that led to the Mountain Meadows massacre.[5]

On August 20, 1932, seventy-three men built a four-foot-high and thirty-foot-square stone wall around the burials at Monument Point, site of the wagon fight at Mountain Meadows. After Brigham Young directed the destruction of Carleton's cairn, it had been rebuilt but lay in ruins by the time of John D. Lee's execution. A pile of stones marked the site when Josiah Gibbs photographed it in 1909, but even the remnant was largely gone by 1917. After years of neglect, a pile of rocks was all that was left of the cairn Carleton's men had built in 1859, and it was in danger of toppling into Magotsu Creek. Erosion had eaten away half of the old emigrant campground, and human remains were scattered across what remained. Stake president William R. Palmer, who probably had as complete an understanding of the massacre as anyone alive in 1932, directed the volunteers. Church leaders had told him "to stay away from there and leave things alone," but he raised the money for the monument and against considerable opposition convinced doubtful LDS officials not to oppose the venture. Palmer's work party gathered native stone and reinforced the side of the wash to slow erosion.[6]

On September 10, 1932, a hot, sunny day, a crowd of some four hundred people gathered at Mountain Meadows, including state and church officials and a host of descendants of massacre participants. They dedicated the stone enclosure and a bronze tablet that commemorated the massacre, the "splendid gift" of the Utah Pioneer Trails and Landmarks Association and the people of southern Utah. In a brief address, Palmer assured his audience the monument was not "prompted by any unholy desire to advertise or to commercialize in any way the great tragedy of Mountain Meadows." It was simply "to place with humility and becoming reverence this added protection around the graves of those who perished here." Palmer did not offer excuses or apologies. Unaware of the survivors in Arkansas, he claimed no one who was on the ground seventy-five years before was still alive. "No living person is responsible in any way for what happened here," he said, and the controversial aspects of Mountain Meadows should now be closed.[7] The inaccurate but generally forthright inscription on the bronze tablet read:

> In this vicinity September 7th, 1857, occurred one of the most lamentable tragedies in the history annals of the West. A company of about 140 emigrants from Arkansas and Missouri led by Captain Charles Fancher, enroute to California, was attacked by white men and Indians. All but 17 small children were killed. John D. Lee, who confessed participation as leader, was legally executed here March 23rd, 1877. Most of the emigrants were buried in their own defense pit. This monument was reverently dedicated September 10, 1932, by the Utah Pioneer Trails and Landmarks Association and the people of Southern Utah.[8]

Theology teacher John T. Woodbury's dedication prayer moved people profoundly. "How many times since have I wished that that prayer might have been preserved, with all its richness of tone and inflection, upon a tape recorder!" Brooks recalled. "When it was finished, we were all welded into one great unity. We were humbled before the enormity of what had been done here; we were lifted by a hope and a desire that we should help to right the wrong. At least, we felt that we would each resolve that our lives would be cast upon a higher plane. Gone were all thoughts of bitterness, or revenge, or scorn." An obvious but unnoted problem was "the scandalous fact that this mass grave had been neglected for nearly eight decades."[9]

The dedication ceremony had double meaning for the young widow. Will Brooks, the recently widowed local postmaster, invited Juanita and her son to ride to the event in his car. He was not looking for a wife, he warned his guest that evening, "but when I do start, *you'd* better watch out." Despite an age difference of seventeen years and the older man's shortcomings—he was short, bald, and rotund and had false teeth—the couple wed in May 1933 and enjoyed a long and successful marriage.[10]

THE STORY SHE WAS BORN TO TELL

Juanita Brooks began collecting material on the massacre in 1933. She thought it could be easily done, but, she said, "the more I found, and the more people I talked to, the harder it has become." John D. Lee was "nothing to me, only I'd like to see the Devil get his dues, and I think if ever a man was wronged, he has been."[11] For the rest of her life, Brooks wrestled with "the story she was born to tell," as she came to view her work on Mountain Meadows.[12] No one in her generation was better equipped to tell the story of the massacre. Brooks not only possessed a first-rate intellect, but she had grown up in the waning days of the Mormon frontier and knew the culture inside and out. She was intimate with men who had been at the massacre; her grandfather had even told her stories about it.

With encouragement from scholar Nels Anderson, she began collecting and copying southern Utah diaries in 1934, and she was soon directing about a dozen women who helped to locate and transcribe local documents and oral histories. By 1936 she was a salaried employee of the Works Progress Administration (WPA), and she would later collect similar materials for the prestigious Huntington Library. Her close association with these records gave her an encyclopedic knowledge of southern Utah's history and people.[13]

Brooks did not join the cult of personality that had grown up around Brigham Young. Instead she "held a lifelong grudge against him for having sent her ancestors into an impoverished exile on the ragged edge of the Mormon empire," a not uncommon perspective among descendants of southern Utah's hardscrabble pioneers. More than most of her contemporaries, Brooks recognized Young's human failings and was especially aware of his callous treatment of his most loyal followers, which generated a deep anger. Brooks's favorite story told how Brigham Young's daughter visited St. George to tell the poverty-stricken women there they must retrench. After the lavishly dressed woman spoke, one of the sisters asked, "What do you want us to retrench from, the bread or the molasses?" While Brooks accepted Brigham Young's prophetic calling, she repudiated the heroic perfection of the man who dominated so much of Utah history.[14]

Over the years Brooks's native honesty won her countless friends and admirers. As her philosopher friend Sterling McMurrin observed, she was "entirely without vanity, certainly a woman without guile." Brooks was slight and thin, and she was always embarrassed by what she regarded as her homely appearance, but "she was a most uncommon woman draped in a very common exterior."[15]

She was also absolutely fearless, a trait she instilled in her children. One night her son Karl was walking home from a horror movie when he heard moans coming from a bush by the side of the road. Terrorized, he ran home and told his mother what had happened. She insisted they return to the bush, where they found an elderly woman injured in a fall.[16]

No amount of intimidation or character assassination could shake Brooks's passionate commitment to the truth. The long story of her contentious relationship with powerful male LDS church leaders evokes a female David confronting a modern corporate Goliath. She passionately stated her resolve: "I feel sure that nothing but the truth can be good enough for the church to which I belong."[17]

RECORDS THAT WILL BE PRICELESS: BROOKS AND DALE MORGAN

Brooks acquired a copy of John Higbee's "Bull Valley Snort" massacre account in September 1936. By 1940 she had Nephi Johnson's affidavit, and she used the two documents as part of "Sidelights on the Mountain Meadows Massacre," a paper she presented to the Utah Academy as her "first unwitting step into a dense and tangled thicket."[18] To guide her through the thicket, she relied on Dale L. Morgan, a native Utahn who was just beginning his career as one of the most talented historians of the American West.

Meningitis had left Morgan deaf at the age of fourteen. After graduating from the University of Utah with an art degree, he joined the Utah WPA Historical Records Survey. By 1940 he was state supervisor of the Utah Writers' Project, for which he oversaw publication of *Utah: A Guide to the State.* Morgan began exchanging documents with Brooks, who predicted, "Not only are you to become Utah's top historian, but you are to leave the state a collection of records that will be priceless." Morgan saw Brooks as a living remnant of the pioneer era, while she accepted Morgan as her mentor, and their lively correspondence provided intellectual stimulation unavailable in St. George. An unbeliever who wrote prolifically on the fur trade and overland emigration, Morgan never completed the history of Mormonism he long dreamed of writing, but his advice contributed profoundly to Brooks's development as a historian. He flooded her with references and source materials, including the results of his patient work in the National Archives and his transcription of Jacob Hamblin's journal.[19]

Morgan's insights guided Brooks as she struggled to tell the story of Mountain Meadows. Arguably, he charted a careful course that kept Brooks's book within the safe confines of Charles Penrose's defense, a strategy that would prevent LDS authorities from revoking her membership in the church she loved.[20] Brooks and Morgan openly discussed the "great divide" of their religious differences. Morgan was an admitted atheist, whereas Brooks found her grandfather's testimony of Joseph Smith compelling: "[It] made me quiver inside." She felt it was possible "to contact God direct," and she told Morgan of spiritual manifestations that bound her to the LDS church. "I like it and need it," she wrote, adding that she maintained her membership for the sake of her children, "but I refuse to surrender my intellectual independence to it." A mutual friend identified their bond: they both loved the truth.[21]

Dale Morgan introduced Brooks to Charles Kelly, who was one of Mormonism's most militant critics and had recently published the *Journals of John D. Lee.* Kelly shared Brooks's fascination with Mountain Meadows but none of her affection for the LDS church or her insight into its history and ways. Kelly was working on his own history of the massacre, but despite their differences, the two established a mutual respect. A notorious curmudgeon, Kelly eventually grew so fond of Brooks he "would have put her name on the license plates." Brooks used Kelly's work to try to enlist the support of LDS authorities for her own research, pointing out that the church would do well to support her balanced account rather than wait for the publication of a work by a rabid "Mormon eater" like Kelly.[22]

In April 1945 Blanche Knopf, wife of publisher Alfred A. Knopf, invited Brooks to submit a Mountain Meadows manuscript to her husband's firm. The offer encouraged Brooks to work on a book seriously and prompted her to search for affidavits by eight massacre eyewitnesses taken in 1909 by St. George jurist David H. Morris. The judge had invited Brooks to look at the affidavits, but each time she called to see them he was sick or did not want to show the documents in the presence of his children. After his death Morris's daughter was "so shocked by the story, that she took them in to Salt Lake, since she didn't want to trust them to the mail," and gave them to Apostle David O. McKay.[23]

Brooks made two unsuccessful attempts to talk with Elder McKay about the affidavits. An appointment was abruptly canceled when McKay's secretary learned what Brooks wanted. Having traveled more than three hundred miles to meet with him, Brooks was not about to tolerate such treatment. She asked for another appointment and offered to wait indefinitely, but she was turned away. Joseph Anderson, secretary to the First Presidency, finally promised to do what he could and asked Brooks to return the next morning. At this meeting Anderson said he and President J. Reuben Clark had read the affidavits. Clark had decided not to give them to her. While Brooks and Anderson talked, the affidavits lay between them on the table in "a large brown envelope, so old that it was cracking." The most difficult aspect of this encounter for Brooks to understand was "not so much the refusal to show the affidavits as the consistent and repeated refusal to discuss the question." Driven by her belief that she "MUST get these accounts written by men who actually participated in that thing," Brooks tried several stratagems to dislodge the papers, but none worked.[24] Ironically, this wonderfully competent historian later located copies of most if not all of these documents, though apparently she was unaware of her success.

Such encounters, including a sympathetic interview with the current prophet, George Albert Smith, made it clear to Brooks that she could expect no support from church leaders, but for fifteen years she tried to persuade them to endorse her interpretation of the massacre. She even briefly considered allowing church officials to censor her manuscript. A Rockefeller Foundation grant from The Huntington Library provided much-needed encouragement, and Brooks forged ahead. Interesting as it was, she wrote to a friend, the massacre was "such a ghastly thing that I shall be glad and relieved to feel that it is finally done."[25]

If You Can Trust Me Enough: Brooks and the Lee Family

As John D. Lee had anticipated, for generations his family suffered for his deeds. Legend said Brigham Young had cursed the family, but two of Lee's remarkable granddaughters were determined to set things right. For decades, Edna Lee Brimhall and Ettie Lee lobbied LDS church leaders and Utah historians to take a new look at their grandfather. Brimhall and Anthon H. Lee visited the office of Anthony Ivins of the LDS First Presidency on July 28, 1931. Ivins described what he had seen at their grandfather's execution. Brimhall and Lee explained their objections to the handling of Mountain Meadows in church historian Joseph Fielding Smith's *Essentials of Church History*. After reading Smith's account of Lee's excommunication, Ivins commented, "I don't know where he got his authority to say that." He began paging through some of the volumes arrayed across an entire wall of his large office. When Ivins finished, he confirmed an old Lee family tradition. According to the records, Lee "was never in anything but good standing in the Mormon Church." Brimhall asked if there might be other documents pertaining to the question. Ivins waved his arm across the books with a sweeping gesture and said, "Lady, this is the church library. These are the church records. Everything is here."[26]

Juanita Brooks received a note from Miss Ettie Lee of Los Angeles in November 1946 offering her documentary material that "should be used if the *true* John D. Lee is to be introduced to the reading public." Brooks replied immediately, praising Lee and noting that her own grandfather had been at the massacre. "If you can trust me enough to let me see your material," Brooks wrote, "I shall be glad." Ettie Lee, a single woman who had taught English in Los Angeles junior high schools since 1914, had grown rich investing in real estate during World War II. She marshaled her large fortune and larger family to support Brooks's work.[27]

As her book progressed, Brooks crossed swords with Kate B. Carter, the powerful president of the Daughters of Utah Pioneers. The families of pioneer diarists sometimes asked Brooks, "Why did you put that in?" about the contents of the documents she copied. "I didn't put it in," Brooks responded. "I *left* it in." She was appalled when Kate Carter told Brigham Young University faculty members that she purged documents of controversial passages before publication. "I never allow anything into print that I think will be injurious to my church," Carter insisted, "or that will in any way reflect discredit upon our pioneers."[28] Brooks directly challenged such duplicity when she published an article called "Let's Preserve Our Records" in 1948. "The first requirement in the preservation of the documents is that they should stand *absolutely unchanged*," she wrote. Legend has it that Carter excised and destroyed all references to Mountain Meadows in documents that came into her possession. Brooks may have heard that Carter boasted of burning the critical minutes of the September 6, 1857, Stake High Council meeting in Cedar City, which voted to destroy the Fancher party.[29]

HER TERRIFYING MESSAGE: THE BOOK

Brooks had completed the third draft—"from the first page to the last"—of her Mountain Meadows manuscript by July 1948. Alfred Knopf's firm had lost interest, but writer Wallace Stegner offered to do whatever he could to recommend the book to publishers. After its rejection by Houghton Mifflin, Stegner submitted Brooks's work to Stanford University Press. In the meantime Brooks and Dale Morgan toured southern Utah and visited Mountain Meadows. Stanford accepted the book in February 1949 but failed to notify the author because it did not have the funds to schedule its publication. Brooks made inquiries, and director Donald Bean told her if the Lee family could guarantee the purchase of a thousand copies, the press was ready to offer a formal contract. With Ettie Lee's support and after many petty negotiations, the press agreed to publish the book.[30]

The Mountain Meadows Massacre appeared in November 1950. Even before Brooks had seen a copy, her friend Dr. Joseph Walker wrote from Los Angeles praising the book and offering a liberal contribution if Brooks needed "a bullet-proof brassiere, or to buy wings with which to flee." Charles Kelly sent his compliments and offered a nice cave in the cliffs if she needed to escape from the wrath of the LDS church. Fawn Brodie, whose biography of Joseph Smith had made her a pariah to most Mormons, admired "the delicacy, dispassionateness, and understatement with which you have handled a potentially lurid and sensational problem." Praising its objectivity and thoroughness, Dale Morgan put it "among the most cherished books in [his] library." Even more impressive were laudatory reviews by distinguished scholars. Brooks had proved herself a skilled historian, wrote Henry Nash Smith. "Her courage and devotion to truth are even more remarkable. Whatever stigma may be cast upon the Mormons by the revelation that some of them were responsible for the crime is more than offset by Miss Brooks's demonstration that the society shaped by the Church can foster scholarly probity of a high order."[31]

As Smith predicted, Brooks's book ultimately had a positive impact on the public's perception of the LDS church and finally explained to devout members not only what had happened but why. As Levi Peterson said, the book's style "was simple and muted, unemphatic almost to a fault, as if she had been loath to express her terrifying message." Brooks's great skill as a historian was evident on every page, and although the careful methodology produced a slow-paced narrative, the final effect was extraordinary, "for with an utter integrity it gave shape to an electrifying drama."[32]

Under Dale Morgan's guidance, Brooks had crafted what was actually a very conservative historical work that went not an inch beyond the available evidence. She carefully presented each of the eyewitness accounts she had collected, noting their differences but not venturing to speculate on the many contradictions among the sources. Ironically, her account of the events leading up to the massacre and its immediate aftermath did not vary substantially from the traditional LDS view Franklin Richards and Charles Penrose had crafted in the 1880s. She dated the massacre to September 11, accepted the story of Haslam's ride and Young's September 10, 1857, letter to Isaac Haight, and left Wilford Woodruff's account of Lee's first report to Brigham Young unchallenged. Brooks's interpretation exonerated Brigham Young of ordering the massacre, but she charged Young and George A. Smith with creating the social conditions that resulted in mass murder. What raised the wrath of loyal Mormons was the massive evidence she presented that Young's cover-up of the crime made him an accessory after the fact, and that he stage managed the sacrifice of John D. Lee. High-ranking LDS church officials especially resented her descriptions of actions that made them appear to be authoritarian bureaucrats obsessed with suppressing the truth.

If the book had a historical Achilles' heel, it was Brooks's reliance on the testimony of murderers and her sympathetic treatment of Lee. "She was a fan of John D. Lee," her son conceded. "She worshipped him."[33] Her portrait of Lee was arguably too kind. Brooks used "carefully selected details" to evoke sympathy for the man and his fellow participants. This was a reaction against the vilification of Lee in standard LDS sources, and also a result of Brooks's empathy for the burden his family carried and her personal experience on the Mormon frontier. The book contained little information on the victims and repeated many of the slanderous tales of their depredations that were embedded in southern Utah folklore. Brooks's unquestioning acceptance of Lee's account of the massacre also led her to believe his most ingenious lies—that the Paiutes led the attack, that they had forced his hand, and that they were ultimately to blame for the atrocity. Brooks nevertheless concluded: "The final responsibility must rest squarely upon the Mormons."[34]

Despite its minor flaws, Brooks's work was both a masterful history and a profoundly courageous act. She reserved her most biting comments for the contemporary church authorities whose pettiness had made her work so much more difficult. She censured David O. McKay and Reuben Clark for their humiliating denial of access to the Morris affidavits. She challenged Joseph Fielding Smith's vigorous condemnation of the participants. Smith, she charged, had consciously distorted the truth in *Essentials in Church History* when he repeated Bancroft's statement that the massacre "was the crime of an individual, the crime of a fanatic of the worst stamp." As church historian, Smith was custodian of records containing abundant evidence to the contrary. Even the most superficial research would reveal that the statement was utterly ridiculous. It appeared that once they had "taken a stand and put forth a story, the leaders of the Mormon church . . . felt that they should maintain it, regardless of all the evidence to the contrary." "In their concern to let the matter die, they do not see that it can never be finally settled until it is accepted as any other historic incident, with a view only to finding the facts," Brooks concluded. "To shrink from it, to discredit any who try to inquire into it, to refuse to discuss it, or to hesitate to accept all the evidence fearlessly is not only to keep it a matter of controversy, but to make the most loyal followers doubt the veracity of their leaders in presenting other matters of history."[35]

SILENCE, TOTAL AND ABSOLUTE

Brooks's challenges to powerful men in the LDS church did not go unnoticed. Frank H. Jonas, a University of Utah political science professor, wrote to key members of the LDS church's historical establishment—Joseph Fielding Smith, Milton R. Hunter, Preston Nibley, and Levi Edgar Young—to gauge their reaction to *The Mountain Meadows Massacre*. Each said they had not read the book. Nibley confessed he could not find anyone at LDS headquarters who had, but this did not prevent Smith and Hunter from denouncing it. Smith put Brooks's book in a class with works by Vardis Fisher, Maureen Whipple, and Fawn Brodie. Hunter echoed the sentiment and argued that the church as a whole was free from blame for the massacre. Hunter made the unlikely claim that his mentor, Herbert Bolton, had advised him to stay away from subjects like the massacre, as such small incidents were "parts of history which should be forgotten." Surveying the First Council of the Seventy, Hunter learned that none of them had read it. But he could not understand why Brooks or anyone claiming to be a good Mormon would spend time "digging into stuff like the Mountain Meadow Massacre when there are so many wonderful achievements that have taken place in Utah."[36]

While returning from a speaking assignment with Joseph Fielding Smith, historian Brigham Madsen asked the apostle what he thought of Brooks's book. "Very bad!" Smith exploded, "very bad!" Madsen recalled, "That ended the conversation."[37]

Brooks took such negative reactions in stride and wrote to a friend, "You think I have done an evil thing; I believe sincerely that I have done a wholesome thing and done the church I love a service." She had long feared the LDS church would excommunicate her for the book, but a year after its publication she told Charles Kelly that Mormon officials responded to her work "by silence, total and absolute. Not a word anywhere. My local people, the bishop and the president of the Stake, and all the authorities here never refer to the book—they evade it with the delicacy and solicitude they might show to a mother who has given birth to a monster child. No one among the higher ups will admit that he has read it—as near as I can tell, few have."[38]

The ostracism she and her husband faced from her church and community "was subtle but devastating," and the experience left her ambivalent about Mormonism.

She resented the arrogance of the church's power in Utah, but she did not want to break her lifelong ties to her religion, and she longed for its acceptance. Despite many failures, she repeatedly tried to win the approval of church leaders. She sent Apostle Stephen L. Richards a copy of her book late in 1951 and tried to persuade him that her interpretation of the massacre was correct. Richards said he could not understand how a member "with a record of devotion and service such as you enjoy, should desire to recreate such a sad chapter in the history of southern Utah." Why did Brooks continue to reach for such an unattainable goal? Her biographer concluded that she wanted the LDS church to share the shame her native country had always borne alone. For justice's sake, she wanted "no less than an official admission that Brigham Young and his colleagues in Salt Lake had helped create the bellicose atmosphere from which the massacre devolved." She wanted it known that their treatment of John D. Lee was a "great injustice, and that their successors had perpetuated that injustice to the latest moment."[39]

Over the years Juanita Brooks adapted to her peculiar situation. At The Huntington Library in October 1954, she told scholar A. C. Lambert about her experiences in the LDS Historian's Office. "They still try to hold things out on me, but I have nailed them on so many things that I'm not afraid of them any more,—and that's an interesting feeling to have,—it makes quite a difference in my inner life." She had resolved the conflict between her religious leaders and her duties as a historian. "I don't quarrel with them; I don't fight them, I don't criticize them; I can just laugh at them for many of the silly little things they do."[40]

Norman Eatough rented a house from the Brooks family while teaching at Dixie College in 1964, and Juanita acted as his de facto landlord. He returned home one day to find Brooks picking pecans. "She didn't have a ladder, so she just shinnied up the tree in her dress and started throwing pecans down," he recalled. "It was a little embarrassing, but I can personally vouch that she wore her garments." He recalled how Brooks handled her son's predawn irrigation turn: "She was quite a sight in a dress, with a shovel over her shoulder, knee high rubber boots, and carbide miners lamp on a leather strap around her forehead." Eatough said, "I tried to take the shovel away from her and send her home one night about 1:00 A.M. I might just as well have tried to take a chick from an eagle's nest." He sensed "that Juanita longed for acceptance from members of the community that she could not get. She was very faithful to the church, but ostracized from it. I think she handled the cold shoulders she received quite well. I suppose she had no other choice."[41]

Shortly after publication of *The Mountain Meadows Massacre*, Warner Brothers expressed interest in making a movie based on it. Dale Morgan joked, "No one yields to me in admiration for your book, but if I had been asked to pick out the least likely candidate for a movie among the books published in 1950, *The Mountain Meadows Massacre* would have figured prominently in my ruminations." When Clark, then second-in-command in the First Presidency and a politically influential former ambassador, learned of the project, he successfully lobbied his connections in the movie business to cancel the production. (The LDS church's file on Morgan reveals that Clark had previously undercut the Guggenheim Foundation's 1949 grant to support Morgan's projected multivolume history of Mormonism.) Even before Clark killed the movie project, Brooks declined to participate. "From the first I had my doubts about what kind of picture they could make of it," she wrote, "and when I saw what the scenario writer had outlined, I knew at once that I wanted nothing to do with it. If he had read my book at all, there was little evidence of the fact."[42]

Nobody Can Forgive Murder

If she could please neither Salt Lake nor Hollywood, a singular act of courage won Brooks the respect and admiration of the people of northern Arkansas. On September 4, 1955, the Richard Fancher Society dedicated a monument to the victims and survivors of Mountain Meadows on the courthouse square in Harrison, Arkansas. J. K. Fancher invited Brooks to speak at the ceremony, and the Utah State Historical Society helped to fund her trip. The massacre had created deep-seated hostility against the LDS church that persisted in the Arkansas hills. One Fancher recalled that Mormon bashing was a favorite sport at family reunions. Brooks's courage in bringing a message of truth and reconciliation to such a hostile audience was a measure of her character. It was a task no male LDS authority had ever attempted.

Five hundred people gathered on a Sunday morning to sing, pray, and listen to speeches. The local paper wrote that Brooks would give the Mormon version of the massacre, and when the crowd broke for lunch, she was lonely and disconsolate. Brooks suggested to J. K. Fancher, "Don't you guess I'd better go to a cafe and get my dinner?" Fancher insisted she join the meal. He watched a "very sweet inspiring smile come over [her] face, and [her] feeling of loneliness and fear seemed to vanish." After the box lunch, a local historian recounted the grim details of the massacre, and Masons unveiled the marker, an imposing granite shaft. An eight-year-old great-great-granddaughter of Alexander Fancher laid a wreath of flowers on the monument, and Brooks prepared to deliver the most important speech of her life before a crowd that included four sons of Triphenia Fancher and Fancher family members from forty states.[43]

In her published remarks, Brooks began with a verse from Proverbs, "And with all thy getting, get understanding," but a witness to the speech recalled that her first words were, "Nobody can forgive murder."[44] Her directness won over the audience immediately. She characterized the massacre as one of the most despicable mass murders in history. She told of Nephi Johnson and his horrific death, of the bitter history that led up to the crime, and of the tragedy "of fine men who now became murderers, and for their children who for four generations now have lived under that shadow." She had loved her grandfather, Dudley Leavitt, but she had to accept that he had participated in an awful crime. She quoted Socrates, "To understand is to forgive all," and invited the people to attend a memorial service at Mountain Meadows on the centennial of the massacre. "May God help us all," she concluded, "as we strive for understanding and brotherhood."[45]

"Your coming has done much to establish a spirit of love and forgiveness," Fancher later wrote her. "The Mormon Church owes you much because now the people in this section feel much better toward the Mormon people." Brooks was "the public voice, otherwise silent, of confession and contrition for the most shameful deed in Mormon history." Her courage initiated a long process of reconciliation between the descendants of the participants and the victims of Mountain Meadows. But southerners have a long memory: in 1956 the mountain communities in northwestern Arkansas organized a wagon train that trekked from Harrison to Berryville to commemorate the Fancher party.[46] Despite Brooks's best efforts, a lingering bitterness—and a refusal to forget—remained alive in the Ozarks.

It Is from the Devil: Vindication

For more than two decades after the publication of *The Mountain Meadows Massacre*, Juanita Brooks remained vitally concerned with the event and its legacy. Shortly after her speech in Arkansas, The Huntington Library published *A Mormon Chronicle: The Diaries of John D. Lee, 1848–1876*, which Brooks had edited with nominal help from Robert Glass Cleland. The book won the Award of Merit from the American Association for State and Local History, and *Time* magazine praised it as "one of the most extraordinary documents ever written by an American." The *Deseret News* refused to print Olive Burt's favorable review, and Burt stalked the office "mumbling to herself and out loud to anybody who [would] listen—Cowards! Cowards! Cowards!"[47]

Brooks was unable to gather support in Utah for a centennial commemoration of the massacre, but she focused her disappointment on a persistent crusade to mark the site appropriately.[48] She turned her attention to writing a biography of John D. Lee that presented her evolving interpretation of the massacre. Lee's journals provided tremendous insights into the aftermath of the event, and Brooks was pleased to find that the new material she was constantly uncovering consistently confirmed her view of southern Utah history.

Once again her work created a controversy that brought her into conflict with the most powerful men in her church. The battle began when Ettie Lee reported the reinstatement of John D. Lee. Temple worker Merrit L. Norton had presented the family's request, and on April 20, 1961, the First Presidency and the Quorum of the Twelve authorized the restoration of Lee's membership and temple blessings. Norton was baptized for his dead grandfather, and on May 9 Apostle Ezra Taft Benson officiated in the endowment and sealing ceremonies at the Salt Lake Temple. Ettie Lee told Brooks the authorities advised her to give the information only to members of the Lee family to avoid "undue publicity." Brooks had already heard the news from five different sources—"Like a fire in the grass, it got out of control"—and she was ecstatic.[49]

Brooks felt the reinstatement was a tacit admission by the highest LDS authorities that her indictment of Brigham Young was correct. She immediately wrote her publisher, Arthur H. Clark, Jr., that the restoration was an event she had not expected to live to see. She wanted to insert a terse announcement in her Lee biography, but she asked Clark to wait to add the information until she could secure approval for its publication, for she did not dare to use it without official consent. Brooks could foresee no harm in publishing it, but the subsequent controversy resulted in yet another ordeal.

Brooks learned through Lee family members that the new prophet, David O. McKay, did not want this confidential information to appear in her book. He threatened to rescind Lee's reinstatement if Brooks persisted in publicizing it. Brooks felt McKay might well excommunicate her for publishing forbidden information, but she did not believe he would be so petty as to revoke Lee's restoration. She was confident it was only a bluff. Brooks proposed leaving the notice out of the initial publication, but she insisted she would include it in subsequent editions. At his request, Brooks met with Apostle Delbert E. Stapley at LDS headquarters in Salt Lake. "Like a broken victrola record," she recalled, the apostle repeated McKay's threat, while Brooks expressed her conviction that God had delayed the book's publication so that it could include this information. Outraged, the apostle slammed his fist on the table and said, "IT IS FROM THE DEVIL!" She finally agreed to omit the notice from the first printing, but, she said, "more than that I would not promise."[50]

Brooks met with the Lee family in Phoenix to sort out the controversy, and in an acrimonious debate lasting through what she described as a "horrible, horrible" July afternoon, the family pleaded with her "NOT to do this terrible thing." When all the Lees had said their piece, Brooks told them she could bear as fervent a testimony as anyone there, but since "I had put in seventeen years of my life working around this subject . . . I had a right to include in it what I wished." It was "MY book, not theirs." To each emotional appeal, Brooks replied, "Sorry, the answer is NO." She had already informed the family that the second edition with the notice of Lee's reinstatement would quickly follow the first. On her return to Utah she wrote to her publisher to confirm their plan to print two hundred copies of the first edition dated 1961 and then immediately release a second printing dated 1962 that ended with the news of Lee's rehabilitation.[51] The controversy made the first edition of the Lee biography a prized collector's item but resulted in no retaliation against either Juanita Brooks or John D. Lee.

John Doyle Lee: Zealot, Pioneer Builder, Scapegoat appeared in November 1961. The biography represented the culmination of Brooks's long struggle to bring Lee "out of the shadows and present him in his true light as a zealot, frontiersman, colonizer, and loyal member of his church." Historians criticized Brooks's use of invented dialogue and her lack of documentation, but the *San Francisco Chronicle* deemed her book "the most towering biography ever written about any character of the American West." Leonard Arrington praised it as "inherently significant and interesting, scholarly and simply and superbly written[.] *John Doyle Lee* is surely one of the finest biographies yet written of a Westerner."[52]

Brooks revised *The Mountain Meadows Massacre* for the University of Oklahoma Press in 1962, noting proudly that subsequent research had validated the first edition's conclusions. She revised the book again for the fourth printing in 1970, adding more detail to the Author's Statement. The revision reconsidered the Indian role in the massacre as well as Brigham Young's September 1, 1857, meeting with the Paiute chiefs. It noted the discovery of Malinda Cameron's Indian depredations claim and lowered the estimated number of victims to fewer than one hundred. Brooks decried the scandalous neglect that persisted at Mountain Meadows. Highway signs marking the meadows repeatedly disappeared, and by January 1966 the access road had deteriorated so much it was impossible for any car to reach the site of the wagon fort. Brooks made a passionate appeal to "do what needs to be done" to improve access. "Respect for the bodies of those buried there," she wrote, "would seem to demand that much." Her final comments—since ignored by a new generation of Mormon historians—resolutely placed the blame where it belonged: "white men, not Indians, were chiefly responsible."[53]

A historian's professional and personal conclusions often differ, as was the case with Brooks's final assignment of responsibility for the massacre at Mountain Meadows. In the last revision of her book, she stressed the importance of Young's manipulation of the Indian leaders and the military orders placing "each man where he was to do his duty." She retained her original conclusion that the existing evidence did not prove that Brigham Young and George A. Smith specifically ordered the massacre, but it showed they "set up social conditions that made it possible." In a private letter to Roger B. Mathison of the University of Utah library, she went much further: she had "come to feel that Brigham Young was directly responsible for this tragedy."[54] John D. Lee, she believed, would make it to heaven before Brigham Young.[55]

Having reached her own conclusions in the matter, she let it rest. Even before publication of the last edition of *The Mountain Meadows Massacre*, Brooks apparently lost interest in pursuing Brigham Young's involvement in the massacre. In 1968 she wrote, "I had long ago resolved that I would not tell this story again." Her friend and fellow historian Karl Larson cataloged St. George Temple papers that were shipped to church headquarters about November 1964. He found a considerable amount of Mountain Meadows material Brooks had never seen. Larson alerted her to its existence, but she "didn't seem overly interested" in the documents. During the 1970s, historian Charles S. Peterson told Brooks about a remarkable 1857 Dimick Huntington document he had come across in the LDS Archives, but Brooks did not care to track it down. Apparently, a friend noted, she did not want to travel that road again.[56]

To Relish the Victory: A Fading Light

As she grew older, Brooks tired of her struggle with her religious leaders over the nature of truth, but to the end of her career she remained "the minstrel of the Mountain Meadows massacre." Inevitably her integrity and the quality of her work won the respect and love of thousands of her fellow Saints. Even the institutional LDS church eventually confirmed her belief that time would prove her work was in the best interest of her faith. When the University of Utah awarded Brooks an honorary doctorate, Wendell J. Ashton, director of public communications for the LDS church, wrote, "I have long admired your fairness, your thoroughness, your courage, and your skill as a writer in giving to us some of our finest literature in Utah history." She was not too old to appreciate her vindication in November 1974 when the church's retail book outlet, Deseret Book, invited her to autograph one hundred copies of *The Mountain Meadows Massacre.*[57]

Progressive senility dimmed the brightest light in Mormon history. Brooks returned to St. George from Salt Lake in 1977 to care for her centenarian mother, but as she approached her own eightieth birthday, Brooks was in need of care herself. Although her body betrayed her, she continued to work and humbly accept the awards honoring her many contributions. The papers she donated to the Utah State Historical Society ultimately occupied seventeen feet of shelf space. With the dedicated help of editors Trudy McMurrin and Richard Howe, her autobiography, *Quicksand and Cactus: A Memoir of the Southern Mormon Frontier*, appeared in fall 1982 and won the Mormon History Association's Best Book award. Her family struggled to care for her, but her condition worsened, and in 1985 she moved to a nursing home where she soon fell into a semicoma. Juanita Brooks died on August 26, 1989, and was laid to rest next to Will Brooks in the St. George cemetery.[58]

Since it was republished in 1962, Brooks's masterpiece, *The Mountain Meadows Massacre*, has never been out of print. Her vast body of work left a legacy that will be remembered as "forever courageous, intelligent, and kind."[59] The most orthodox Mormon historians now point to her as the best interpreter of the massacre.[60] Often misrepresenting her conclusions, they promote the notion that her analysis represents the last word on the subject—a claim Brooks herself would certainly reject—and express the vain hope that the grim story of Mountain Meadows has finally been laid to rest.

Epilogue

The Ghosts of
Mountain Meadows

The Past is not dead; it is not even past.
—WILLIAM FAULKNER

By 1877 it appeared the curse of the Almighty had fallen over the place where one hundred twenty men, women, and children fought and died in 1857 and "so much wrong had been done in the name of religion." Legend tells that around the cairn that marked their grave "the ghosts of the slaughtered emigrants meet nightly at the springs, and with phantom-like stillness, but with perfectness of detail, act over in pantomime the cruelties and horrors connected with the massacre."[1] The dead at Mountain Meadows are long past human suffering, but every attempt to lay to rest the troublesome questions surrounding their fate has failed. The ghosts of Mountain Meadows still haunt the American past.

ONLY BECAUSE: AFTER JUANITA BROOKS

Even after Juanita Brooks's pathbreaking work, LDS historians had a difficult time confronting the darkest episode in their culture's past. Kenneth Stampp wrote that the work of Leonard Arrington, "a distinguished Mormon historian, illustrates the pain that this event has caused those who have written about the Mormon War." Arrington served as LDS church historian from 1972 to 1982. Stampp pointed out that his most noted work, *Great Basin Kingdom*, failed to mention the massacre and found his account in *The Mormon Experience*, written with Davis Bitton, brief and vague. Arrington's much-praised biography of Brigham Young commended Brooks's study as complete and dependable but ignored her most significant conclusions and laid the blame for the massacre on the Indians and the emigrants. Arrington and his colleagues had complete access to the Brigham Young papers but ignored—and sometimes distorted—evidence at their fingertips.[2]

That Mormonism's official historians have been less than forthright about the most horrible event in its past is hardly surprising. After Brigham Young's death, the men in the church historian's office carefully released records that would absolve their prophet of any guilt and lay the blame on Indians and local authorities. When necessary they suppressed evidence that implicated Young, such as the Dimick Huntington journal. Official church histories assigned responsibility to one man—John D. Lee—and denounced him as a monster who defied God's will and brought shame to his people. To this day LDS church leaders blame a large part of Mormon country for the crime, leaving a bitter legacy for the descendants of the participants. The cover-up of Young's involvement was a remarkably successful endeavor, for it is hard to find a modern history that fails to absolve the Mormon leader of any responsibility for the massacre. Yet the traditional explanation poses an untenable paradox—that Brigham Young was aware of "every sparrow" that fell in Utah Territory but for more than a dozen years knew nothing of the worst crime to take place during his service as territorial governor, Indian superintendent, and commander in chief of the militia.

Mormonism's critics addressed the subject with equal ineptitude. William Wise published *Massacre at Mountain Meadows: An American Legend and a Monumental Crime* in 1976, a study based entirely on Brooks's work yet one that ungraciously accused her of bias. Wise apparently never set foot in Utah and failed to use the resources of the state's many archives, and his circumstantial argument that Brigham Young ordered the massacre roused the ire of the Mormon historical community. Arrington led the charge, denouncing Wise's book as "an excellent model of what careful scholarship is not."[3]

In a rebuttal to Wise, Arrington rehearsed a strange collection of excuses before LDS religious educators in 1977. The massacre happened, he said, only because of the Utah War, only because of the taunts of the Missouri Wild-cats, and "only because of the Haun's Mill Massacre and the exterminating order of Governor Boggs." There was "absolute proof that Brigham Young and the Church itself were not involved in the massacre and its planning." The atrocity, he argued, "was an action of the militia and was regarded as a military exercise. We should separate the Church and its role from the massacre itself."[4]

Arrington warned about a possible television series that might require church educators to devote more time to the subject than "it warrants in our history." In the wake of the success of the *Roots* miniseries, the Columbia Broadcasting System planned to make a film based on Wise's book. The specter of the worst episode in its history playing to a national television audience prompted the LDS First Presidency to ask Arrington to do a background study on Mountain Meadows. The authorities wanted the report in four days, and he worked through a weekend to complete it. This proved to be the first and only time Arrington received a direct request to do research for the

First Presidency during his ten years as official church historian.[5] Historical department staff wrote letters outlining problems the network would face in dealing with the massacre as a historical event, and church officials apparently called on influential members to exert additional pressure. Although the script was completed and filming scheduled, producer David Susskind and CBS abandoned the project.[6]

Prestigious Mormon scholars continued to blame the massacre on vicious Paiutes well into the 1990s. Ronald K. Esplin and Dean C. Jessee, two prominent Brigham Young University professors, responded to an article in an Arkansas magazine in 1984. "Then there were the Indians," they wrote, who launched the attack and "demanded the cooperation of Mormon settlers. It was only then, fearful of alienating their Indian allies, that the Mormons became involved." Responding to this critique, Bob Lancaster argued it was absurd for the professors "to pretend that John D. Lee didn't plan and co-ordinate the attack on the wagon train."[7] Yet in 1996 the state-sponsored "Official Centennial History" of Utah claimed the Fancher party "abused" the Paiutes, and that the tribe "dogged" the wagon train from Fillmore, a location far from their homelands. This account claimed, "In part, the Utah militiamen massacred the Arkansans to help their allies and to avoid possible retaliation from them."[8] In other words, the Indians made them do it.

Such Great Emotion: Lee and Loving

As she lay dying in a St. George rest home, Juanita Brooks's long campaign to secure proper maintenance and marking of the historic sites at Mountain Meadows at last evoked a response. Ironically, it was a group of committed outsiders, both Mormon and non-Mormon, that finally compelled local citizens and the state of Utah to bring an end to more than one hundred thirty years of the unconscionable neglect of a vast mass grave and a major national historic site.

Several lives converged at Mountain Meadows in 1988. Aerospace engineer Ronald E. Loving began investigating how his own family fit into the history of the West, a topic that had long intrigued him. Loving's mother visited Visalia, California, the home of some of their pioneer ancestors, and discovered that her family was related to the dead of Mountain Meadows. Loving learned he was a descendant of John Fancher and a great-great-grandnephew of Alexander Fancher. The more he learned, the more Loving became fascinated with the story.

On February 25, 1987, Utah writer Lee Oertle sent a letter of inquiry to J. E. Dunlap, publisher of the *Harrison Daily Times* in Arkansas who had an interest in the Mountain Meadows massacre. Oertle had investigated the story for years in an unsuccessful effort to demonstrate that participants and victims had known each other before the massacre. His letter led to a meeting at Mountain Meadows in July 1988 that brought together a remarkable set of people and eventually had far-ranging consequences.[9]

Thirteen people met at the meadows on July 23, 1988. They included four Mormons—Lee Oertle, historian Morris Shirts, and John D. Lee descendant Irene Wait and a friend—and eight outlanders with family ties to the Fancher party—J. K. and Genevieve Fancher, Ron and Donna Loving, Leland and Vi Jordan, and Dan and Ada Hacklethorn. An unidentified Indian from Salt Lake also chanced by the old monument. Everyone in the group assumed the Indian was someone else's guest, but no one ever asked his name. The group met to survey the site, discuss the errors on the 1932 bronze plaque that both misidentified victims and upset Lee family members, and, as J. K. Fancher wrote, "establish dialogue after 131 years of hostile feeling." From this meeting came "the idea for a new monument to correct some errors and to make a new statement on the massacre."[10]

Afterward Ron and Donna Loving traveled to Lee's Ferry, where the John D. Lee family organization had held annual reunions for years. As Loving and his wife read the text of the historical monument at the ferry, a Lee family member asked them from which of John D.'s many wives they descended.

"I'm not a Lee," said Loving.

"Well, who are you?"

"I'm a Fancher." Loving's answer evoked considerable surprise. He was soon introduced to Verne Lee, president of the organization.[11] So began an extraordinary friendship. Verne Lee, a California entrepreneur, had made a lifelong study of his infamous ancestor. Like many of John D. Lee's descendants who remained devout Latter-day Saints, Verne Lee's family history was a troubling legacy that prompted him to learn everything he could about the story of Mountain Meadows. As a young missionary, Apostle Harold B. Lee (who claimed not to be related to John D.) spoke with him for an hour after pointedly asking about his ancestry. The apostle assured him, "You have nothing to be ashamed of," though at the time the young man had only a vague idea what the future prophet was talking about.[12]

Together, Lee and Loving accomplished miracles. Loving contacted former Secretary of the Interior Stewart Lee Udall, John D. Lee's great-grandson. Hoping to enlist the support of the LDS church, Udall arranged a meeting with Gordon B. Hinckley, first counselor in the First Presidency, who, because of the incapacity of Ezra Taft Benson, was effectively running the LDS church. A lifelong church employee, Hinckley possessed consummate organizational skills, a genius for public relations, and a long-standing personal interest in Mormon history. As part of his many duties, Hinckley had written several faith-promoting histories of his religion without mentioning Mountain Meadows. In the early 1980s he was a key figure in the Mark Hofmann forgery scandals and personally managed the secret purchase and suppression of documents that proved to be fraudulent.[13] Despite such complications, Hinckley was the perfect spokesperson for the church on Mountain Meadows. During a 1989 meeting with the committee now organized as the Mountain Meadows Association, Hinckley assured Lee, Loving, Udall, and Judge Roger V. Logan, Jr., of Arkansas that he would support their effort to build an appropriate monument at Mountain Meadows. President Hinckley made only one request: "No movies."[14]

The 1988 meeting at the meadows produced parallel efforts to create a monument, one by Utahns and one by Fancher and Lee descendants. Powerful Utah civic leaders had long opposed doing anything about the sorry state of the Mountain Meadows site, but once they learned that the new monument had official LDS church support, they quickly co-opted the effort. Nonetheless, Ron Loving and Verne Lee were instrumental in starting the movement that culminated in 1990 with the dedication of a handsome granite memorial listing the names of the victims and survivors. The $300,000 monument on a hilltop overlooking the meadows was financed by the state of Utah and private contributions.

Several thousand spectators attended the formal dedication program held at Cedar City. The evening before the ceremony, selected relatives of participants and victims watched President Gordon Hinckley replace the plaque on the rock cairn at the site of the wagon battle.

The four-hundred-voice Iron County Mountain Meadows Choir opened the formal dedication ceremony on the campus of Southern Utah State College in Cedar City on Saturday, September 15, 1990. State senator Dixie Leavitt conducted and Arkansans J. E. Dunlap, J. K. Fancher, Jr., and Judge Logan, a relative of almost two dozen massacre victims, gave opening remarks. "I cannot do honor to the people that I am attempting to memorialize unless I tell you a little about them and their suffering," he said. Generations of his family had kept alive the memory of Mountain Meadows with a very special sense of loss. Logan first heard the tale from his great-grandfather, who had been raised in the same home as Sarah Dunlap Lynch, the blind survivor. Sarah's mother died "holding her in her arms at Mountain Meadows," and the eighteen-month-old toddler was so badly wounded that her arm withered and atrophied. Another little girl "woke up screaming because of what happened at Mountain Meadows," Judge Logan recalled. "It is easy to see why such great emotion and strong opinion would arise in this situation; why for generations emigrant families remembered what happened."[15] Following Logan's powerful remarks, Paiute tribal elder Clifford Jake conducted a moving prayer ceremony. Brigham Young University president Rex Lee, a John D. Lee descendant, called on relatives of participants and then of victims to stand.

Hinckley took the podium, representing "a people who have suffered much." No matter how much one might study Mountain Meadows, he said, the event defied understanding, but this convocation was a miracle that would bless present and future generations. Although Hinckley's speech seemed to be building to an acknowledgment of the LDS church's role in the massacre, he admitted he had not come to apologize. Some non-Utahns in the audience, already offended at the tight security surrounding the ceremony, were dismayed. Verne Lee gave the benediction. After the prayer, buses took participants to the meadows, where the site of the monument on the north side of Dan Sill Hill offered a sweeping view of the meadows. The impressive granite monument designed by Michael Lee listed some of the names of the men, women, and children killed at or near Mountain Meadows.[16]

The text engraved in the granite was not so impressive. A committee led by LDS museum director Glen Leonard devised wording that relied on the passive voice in an attempt not to assign blame.

IN MEMORIUM

In the valley below, between September 7 and 11, 1857,
a company of more than 120 Arkansas emigrants led
by Capt. John T. Baker and Capt. Alexander Fancher was attacked
while en route to California. This event is known in history
as the Mountain Meadows Massacre.

The explanatory markers at the memorial were equally vague about what happened in the valley, and the description of the Old Spanish Trail was simply incorrect. The desire of the monument committee to create new markers that did not "point blame" resulted in vaguely worded text that identified the event as a massacre. Although the committee's motives were noble, the wording again subtly shifted accountability to the Indians—for in the popular mind, who else was responsible for massacres in the American West?

Three years later two hundred members of the John D. Lee family met at a three-day reunion in St. George to "close the book" on the Mountain Meadows massacre. The family conducted LDS temple ordinances, including endowments and sealings, for the murdered Arkansans. The Lee family had talked about doing something like this for more than sixty years, one member said. "We thought it was very important for members of our family to do this work, but even among the Lees there has been some strong feelings and prejudice surrounding the Mountain Meadows Massacre. It's taken a lot to get us to this point, but what we've done here today has been good for us, and I think it represents closure for the whole church on this terrible tragedy."[17]

YOU MUST DO SOMETHING

Since Brigham Young's time, the memory of Mountain Meadows has refused to die. After the dedication of the 1990 monument, even nature seemed to conspire to keep the story alive. In February 1998 frost and a mild earthquake toppled the polished granite markers on Dan Sill Hill listing the victims' names. The state of Utah, which had assumed responsibility for the monument but never budgeted sufficient funds to maintain it, "just seemed to sit on their thumbs about fixing it," Fancher descendant Ron Loving complained. After months of delay, concerned descendants took action. "We're not in business to stir things up," said Loving, "but this is something the emigrant families will not let die." Loving invited interested parties to St. George in

September 1998, where they reconstituted the Mountain Meadows Association to make sure that the monument would be properly restored and accurately commemorated.[18]

The evasive wording on the 1990 markers had drawn the ridicule of outsiders, including *New York Times* reporter Timothy Egan, who called the Dan Sill Hill plaques the most cryptic historical markers in the West. The markers at the site "of the worst carnage ever inflicted on a single band of overland emigrants in the entire nineteenth century" did nothing to answer questions about what happened. In an essay titled, "Bad Things Happen in the Passive Voice," historian-gadfly James W. Loewen noted that use of the term "massacre," while appropriate, "guarantees that most tourists will infer that Native Americans did the grisly work."[19]

Local authorities in Utah were unmoved by the criticism. "Because of the political sensitivity, the religious overtones and all the baggage that goes with the monument, state parks is not going to pursue any more interpretation of the site," said the local state park director. "What I hear from people is that this has caused enough sorrow, let it be," he continued. "Our position is there are a lot of historical books out there that someone could read if they want to know more. We're not interested in stirring the pot."[20]

Following news reports of the re-formation of the Mountain Meadows Association, Gordon B. Hinckley, now president of the LDS church, felt compelled to visit Mountain Meadows on October 9, 1998. In April 1965 the LDS church had acquired ownership of two and a half acres on Magotsu Creek at the site of the wagon siege from Ezra and May Lytle, whose family had owned it for generations. The parcel included the 1932 monument marking the site of the army burials of 1859. "I was shocked by what I found, I must confess it," President Hinckley later said. "The wall of the cairn was beginning to slip in the direction of the small stream in the gully. The weeds were tall. There was an ugly barbed-wire fence around this site. I knew that the church owned this ground. I said to myself, 'You must do something to make this a more beautiful and attractive and lasting memorial.'"[21]

By the end of the month Hinckley had called Ron Loving and asked him to arrange a meeting with concerned people. On October 30, 1998, Hinckley met with Loving, Donald Baker, and Burr Fancher, relatives of the victims, several John D. Lee descendants, landowner Kent Bylund, the local district ranger for the Forest Service (which owned 7.5 acres at the site), Dr. Glen Leonard of the LDS church museum, and history professors Gene Sessions and Lawrence Coates. Hinckley said he was embarrassed and ashamed at the run-down condition of the 1932 memorial and expressed his appreciation of the feelings of their kin for the dead. "We owe them respect," he said. "That land is sacred ground." He had already started plans to build a fitting memorial that would show proper reverence for the dead, "something special" that would stand for centuries. The prophet did not care about the cost and expressed his willingness to spend as much as $200,000 to build a respectable memorial.[22]

President Hinckley made "a remarkable historic statement, something that has never been uttered publicly by a leader of the Mormon church," Ron Loving recalled. "No one knows fully what happened at Mountain Meadows," Hinckley said. "I don't, nor can it be explained, but we express our regrets over what happened there and we all need to put this behind us." Burr Fancher felt Hinckley came as close to apologizing for the massacre as he could. The Mormon leader promised to share any historical evidence in the possession of the LDS church. "If I knew of any new information, I'd tell you," Fancher recalled Hinckley saying. "We need to eliminate the hatred."[23]

Hinckley proved as good as his word. Toward the end of the hour-long meeting he joked, "I am an old man, I'm almost 90. I don't know how much longer I have left, it can't be long." He said, "We must get this finished within a year. Can we do this?" He asked to keep the discussions private, but the meeting left some participants wondering if it really happened.[24] Even more striking was the speed with which Hinckley's vision was carried out. The association collaborated with LDS church architects to design a handsome monument that re-created Carleton's 1859 cairn, lacking only the inscribed cedar cross and the biblical quotation that had provoked Brigham Young to destroy the original monument in 1861. One hundred fifty volunteers from the Enterprise Fourth Ward began work at the site on May 17, 1999. Thirty-four children from the ward between the ages of one and sixteen, representing the children killed during the massacre, stood in silence at the grave. "Whoever thought to see such a sight," one participant recalled, "Mormons weeping for the victims from Arkansas." With substantial help from local volunteers, the site of the wagon battle and Carleton's cairn was transformed by late summer.[25]

VOICES OF THE DEAD

President Hinckley's conciliatory vision had unforeseen consequences. Some relatives of the victims claimed the LDS church promised not to do any "intrusive" archaeological work. Ron Loving said, "We do not want those bodies disturbed and the church is honoring that request."[26] However, replacing the 1932 monument required digging footings, which necessitated a careful archaeological survey to try to locate the 1859 army burials. The church contracted with Brigham Young University to manage the investigation. The Mountain Meadows Association spent thousands of dollars on an expensive and unproductive ground-penetrating radar survey. It failed to locate anything of significance or any ground disturbances that might indicate the siege defenses that were used as graves. The landowner refused to let the association survey the upper meadows where the great majority of the dead may be buried, but he did permit a model plane with an infrared camera to take pictures. They also failed to show evidence of soil disturbances.[27]

Ron Loving's autocratic management style and a feeling that the Mountain Meadows Association catered too much to the interests of the LDS church led to disagreements among association members and officials. By July 1999 the dissidents had formed the Mountain Meadows Monument Foundation, Inc., to support unrestricted public access to the monuments and to protect the site from encroachment, abandonment, and neglect, goals it shared with the existing association. Under the leadership of Scott and Burr Fancher, however, the foundation supported greater public awareness of the massacre's historical significance and federal management of the site.[28]

Archaeologists from the U.S. Forest Service, the Army Corp of Engineers, and Brigham Young University made numerous visits to the site of Carleton's cairn next to Magotsu Creek without locating any physical evidence of burials. Respect for the desires of family members, which were often contradictory and precluded significant test excavations, restricted the investigators' ability to conduct a thorough archeological survey. Micro-core samples produced no results, and the limited analysis concluded "that any remains that had not washed down the ravine had most likely dissolved leaving only traces of calcium and phosphorus deposits," recalled local landowner and project coordinator Kent Bylund.[29]

When digging began on August 3, 1999, Bylund examined every bucket of dirt the backhoe operator removed. The highly experienced excavator worked slowly, but the second or third bucket unearthed thirty pounds of human skeletal remains. Bylund immediately called LDS church headquarters and was told to halt the excavation. The next day the county sheriff, LDS church officials, and Mountain Meadows Association members descended on the site. As the landowner, the LDS church representatives again called in Brigham Young University to do the archaeological work. Believing that Ron Loving and the Mountain Meadows Association accurately represented the wishes of the descendants, they let Loving make many of the key decisions. At his request, the discovery was not to be announced until he could notify relatives of the dead. Loving subsequently threatened to sue the state Division of History if it did not guarantee in writing that the state would abide by several conditions of secrecy, including that "none of the contents of the [archaeological] report, in part or in whole, is released to anyone."[30]

Brigham Young University archaeologists spent two tedious days meticulously recovering more remains. "It was a very humbling, spiritual experience," said Washington County sheriff Kirk Smith, who witnessed the excavation. "It just really touched me deeply. I saw buttons, some pottery, and bones of adults and children. But the children—that was what really hit me hard."[31]

Mormon officials initially supported Loving's plan to rebury the bones quietly within forty-eight hours, but state archaeologist Kevin Jones informed them that Utah law required a permit to remove the remains. The permit mandated the filing of an archaeological report of the excavation based on current standards of scientific rigor that would identify each individual for proper reburial and estimated age, sex, race, stature, health condition, and cause of death. Brigham Young University received a permit on August 6 and project manager Shane Baker contracted with the University of Utah forensic anthropology laboratory to assist with the required forensic analysis. Ultimately the lab identified the remains of at least twenty-eight individuals, including three children whose ages were estimated to be between three and nine years.[32]

The project became public knowledge when the *St. George Spectrum* broke the story on August 13, 1999, and the Associated Press produced a report that appeared in the Sunday *New York Times*. The Associated Press story noted that Brigham Young University researchers were "examining the fragile bones for sex and age of pioneers and evidence of disease or trauma."[33] The news produced anger and disbelief among relatives of the dead, particularly in Arkansas.

On learning that archaeologists planned to delay reburial of the skulls until they could complete the forensic analysis, a few descendants of the victims persuaded Utah governor Leavitt to order the return of all remains for reburial. "It would be unfortunate if this sad moment in our state's history, and the rather good-spirited attempt to put it behind us, was highlighted by controversy," Leavitt wrote in an e-mail message to state officials. The governor's attempt to avoid controversy was futile. The *Salt Lake Tribune* later charged that Leavitt violated state law and his actions "may be another sad chapter in the massacre's legacy of bitterness, denial and suspicion."[34]

The Book of the Past Is Closed

On a brilliantly sunny Friday afternoon in September 1999, several hundred people from Arkansas, Oklahoma, Texas, New Mexico, Arizona, and California gathered at Mountain Meadows. They came to rebury the remains of their ancestors and relatives. Descendants of John D. Lee and other massacre participants joined in the memorial. That morning members of the Mountain Meadows Association installed two signs on the pathway to the granite marker on Dan Sill Hill that finally gave an honest account of what happened at the site in 1857. The Reverend Stanton Cram of the Friendship Baptist Church in Springdale, Arkansas, pastor to descendants of massacre victims and the husband of Virginia Fancher, conducted and preached a memorial service. Ron Loving placed the event in its modern context. Judge Roger Logan read a roll call of the known victims and gave an eloquent memorial to the dead. Representing John D. Lee descendants, Stewart Udall read his poem expressing the sorrow that afflicted all those connected with the massacre. Descendants deposited the remains of the dead in a vault located at the spot where the remains were discovered, and relatives placed soil from historic locations in Arkansas in the new grave.[35]

On September 11, 1999, the one hundred forty-second anniversary of the massacre at Mountain Meadows, more than one thousand people arrived for the monument dedication. Despite claims that the Paiute tribe declined to participate in the ceremony, Paiute Tribe of Utah chair Geneal Anderson says she was not invited to the event. Anderson had been a guest at the 1990 dedication and was "really uncomfortable" when Mormon speakers suggested that Paiutes should join them in asking forgiveness for their role in the massacre. "Somebody asked me afterwards how many Paiutes were involved," Anderson recalled. "I said, 'That's your history, not ours.'" She added, "They still call us wagon-burners."[36]

The LDS church televised the service by satellite throughout Utah and at Mormon chapels in Harrison, Berryville, Springdale, Huntsville, and Fort Smith, Arkansas. Except for local congregations that participated as volunteers and choir members, virtually everyone in attendance had a personal connection to the events of 1857. LDS officials conducted the services. To the puzzlement of non-Utahns, who recognized that the organist had begun playing "Scotland the Brave," the local choir broke into "We Thank Thee Oh God for a Prophet" to greet President Gordon B. Hinckley.

"Never in my wildest dreams did I think we'd get to this point," Ron Loving, president of the Mountain Meadows Association, told the crowd. "It is as if a dam of pent-up emotion and interest has been released. The truth of the massacre is being talked about freely, and there has been such an outpouring of feeling." He called for the site to be dedicated to healing. "It is hallowed ground. It is neutral ground. It is a place where only love and tolerance and understanding should be brought. Leave everything else behind. And no one should leave here without love in their hearts."[37]

Shirley H. Pyron, president of the Carroll County Historical Society, spoke with dignity and firmness of the feelings and memories of the families in Arkansas who lost loved ones at the meadows. She recalled how grief mingled with outrage as news reached Arkansas that the bodies of the dead had been "left where they fell without burial." Even the passage of time failed to ease the pain, but now "the tide of bitterness has been stemmed with friendship" because of the hard work and courage of men like Verne Lee and Ron Loving. In conclusion, Pyron made note of unfinished business: "My hope is the resting place of the other emigrants will be properly located and marked so they can never be forgotten again."[38]

President Hinckley followed with a personal statement on his experiences at what he called a sacred place. "My dear friends," he began. "This is an emotional experience for me. I come as a peacemaker. This is not a time for recrimination or the assigning of blame. No one can explain what happened in these meadows 142 years ago. We may speculate, but we do not know. We do not understand it. We cannot comprehend it. We can only say that the past is long since gone. It cannot be recalled. It cannot be changed. It is time to leave the entire matter in the hands of God." The Mormon leader recalled how he had first seen Mountain Meadows with his father some fifty years earlier. "We visited this place. There was no one else around. My father said nothing. I said nothing. We simply stood here and thought of what occurred here in 1857. The rock cairn was here. Weeds rustled in the breeze. We walked back to our car without speaking. We knew this ground was hallowed, and we were reverent and respectful."[39]

Hinckley described how he had worked with the Mountain Meadows Association to build an appropriate memorial. "We have spent a very substantial amount of money on what has been accomplished here," he said. "We have not spared expense to do it right and in a fashion that will remain through the years." Great effort and cost had gone into bringing electricity and water to the site and making it attractive, accessible, and secure. Hinckley pledged, "We intend to maintain this memorial and keep it attractive. I am an old man now, in my 90th year. I am grateful that I have had the opportunity to further this effort."[40]

"I sit in the chair that Brigham Young occupied as president of the church at the time of the tragedy," he continued. To this point, President Hinckley's remarks focused on conciliation and forgiveness, but some in the audience noted a sudden change in the tone of his homily. "I have read very much of the history of what occurred here. There is no question in my mind that he was opposed to what happened. Had there been a faster means of communication, it never would have happened and history would have been different." The president then read a statement inserted in the sermon at the direction of attorneys for the Corporation of the President of the LDS church. "That which we have done here must never be construed as an acknowledgment of the part of the church of any complicity in the occurrences of that fateful day." Few of those familiar with Mormon history had expected the prophet to make an outright apology, but many were surprised to hear the church leader make such an explicit and legalistic denial of any accountability. Despite this, he acknowledged, "We have a moral responsibility. We have a Christian duty to honor, to respect and to do all feasible to remember and recognize those who died here. May this cairn stand as a sacred monument to honor all of those who fell, wherever they might have been buried in these Mountain Meadows." If anyone had any remaining doubts about Hinckley's hope that his good efforts had finally laid the matter to rest, he stated his case unambiguously: "Let the book of the past be closed."[41]

Despite the desire of the LDS church to put the matter to rest, questions about Mountain Meadows persisted. In February 2000, after five years as the church's president, Gordon Hinckley granted his first interview with the *Salt Lake Tribune*. The *Tribune* asked Hinckley about the Mountain Meadows massacre. "I've never thought for one minute as I've read the history of that tragic episode that Brigham Young had anything to do with it. And it was a local decision and it was tragic. We can't understand it in this time, but none of us can place ourselves in the moccasins of those who lived there at the time," the prophet said. "But it occurred. Now, we're trying to do something that we can to honorably and reverently and respectfully remember those who lost their lives there." Asked who was to blame for the massacre, President Hinckley said, "Well, I would place the blame on the local people."[42]

MEN DID NOT GATHER HERE BY CHANCE: CONCLUSIONS

Late in life, Juanita Brooks described her first visit to Mountain Meadows and its broad sage-covered plain. "Men did not gather here by chance or mere hearsay," she thought as she contemplated the desolate site. "If they were here, they had come because they were ordered to come. And whatever went on was done because it had been ordered, not because individuals had acted upon impulse."[43] Today local ranchers have restored the once-desolate meadow to a degree of its former lushness. Cows and mule deer range the fields, and groves of lindens and cottonwoods stand amid the ranch houses and vacation homes scattered across the face of this historic and haunted place. It is not ghosts that haunt Mountain Meadows but rather enduring questions that many would prefer never to ask let alone answer.

No one should doubt or discredit Gordon B. Hinckley's sincere efforts to memorialize the unfortunate families who died at Mountain Meadows or his noble work to resolve the dilemma it poses for his church and his people. Yet as Dixie National Forest archaeologist Marian Jacklin observed, the attempt to end the enduring controversy of Mountain Meadows in 1999 was futile. "This whole episode didn't answer anything," she said. "It just asked more questions." Scott Fancher, president of the Mountain Meadows Monument Foundation in Arkansas, expressed the concerns of many outside Utah. "We're doubtful with the church in control this will ever be completely put to rest," he said. Arkansas governor Mike Huckabee joined the foundation's call for federal stewardship of the emigrant mass graves at Mountain Meadows.[44]

The evidence that has come to light since Juanita Brooks ended her work validates many but not all of her conclusions about causes and effects of the Mountain Meadows massacre. Sticking strictly to the evidence she had at hand, Brooks arrived at four findings. First, although Brigham Young did not specifically order the massacre, he and George A. Smith "set up social conditions which made it possible." Second, the Fancher party met disaster "due to a most unhappy combination of circumstances," including their own provocative behavior. Third, Young "was accessory after the fact, in that he knew what had happened, and how and why it happened." He knew that the men most responsible for the massacre had acted out of loyalty to him and his cause, and "he would not betray them into the hands of their common 'enemy.'" Fourth, LDS church leaders sacrificed John D. Lee when it became "impossible to acquit him without assuming a part of the responsibility themselves."[45]

New research confirms most of these conclusions, but I would dispute several of Brooks's points. A fuller understanding of the Fancher party discredits the tales of their depredations. Just as today a defense attorney might defame the victim in a rape case, such stories were designed to prove the murdered dead got what they deserved. It is remarkable that transparent lies concocted by, as Jacob Forney said in 1859, "*bad men,* for a bad purpose," should be so thoroughly discredited by the earliest investigators yet repeated so often by well-meaning people. Dale Morgan alerted Brooks in 1941 to the likelihood that the emigrant atrocity stories had been "set afloat by Mormons to further their alibi of the Massacre's having been perpetrated by Indians." Morgan had never been satisfied with tales that the company included a large contingent of maniacal Missourians. Even sixty years ago it was well established that the Fancher party came not from the scene of Mormon ordeals in Missouri and Illinois but from Arkansas.[46] Mormon historians seldom considered the likelihood that after committing mass murder, the killers of Mountain Meadows slandered their prey to justify their crimes. As historian David White wrote in 1998, "Rarely have victims been so pervasively vilified by unproved charges that are still often repeated unquestioningly today."[47]

The historic record of the 1850s validates that the Fancher party came into typical conflicts with local Utahns over cattle, grass, food, and culture, but that same evidence indicates they generated no more friction than any typical emigrant company and did no more than assert their rights as American citizens. Several events—the murder of Parley Pratt, the arrival of his overwrought and vengeful widow in Salt Lake in July 1857 amid war hysteria, and the inflammatory exhortations of Mormon leaders—support Brooks's belief that unfortunate circumstance played a part in the fate of the emigrants. Yet a ruthless commitment to revenge as a religious principle, ritualized in the temple ceremony's Oath of Vengeance as a personal vow to avenge the blood of the prophets, played a larger role than did mere happenstance. Brooks never saw Dimick Huntington's journal and its evidence that the atrocity was not a tragedy but a premeditated criminal act initiated in Great Salt Lake City. Although she lacked the documentation presented here that links Brigham Young to facilitating the murders, Brooks used abundant and unmistakable evidence from "the most impeccable Mormon sources" to establish that he was an accessory to murder after the fact. In trying to protect himself and the men directly responsible for a brutal crime, Brigham Young spun a web of lies that still entangles his church and its leaders.

Mountain Meadows was a crime of true believers. As Guy Bishop has noted, Eric Hoffer's analysis of the type of personality drawn to mass movements is especially relevant to understanding early Mormons.[48] Hoffer's definition of the "True Believer" described John D. Lee so precisely that Lee might well have been a prototype for Hoffer's work. The mind-set that led decent men to commit a horrific crime is not a quaint historical artifact but an enduring reality. "I am haunted by that story," historian Melvin T. Smith said of Mountain Meadows. "Not only because my people and my church were involved, but because as a true believer I could understand how they could do it; and because I sense that I might have been involved, as the true believer I was, had the time and circumstances been right."[49]

In 1857 John Hyde identified Brigham Young's great failing as a leader: he believed the end justifies the means.[50] Joseph Smith bequeathed his followers a troublesome legacy, the conviction that it was "the Kingdom or nothing" and the belief that any act that promoted or protected God's work was justified. Some have tried to dismiss Mountain Meadows as an isolated event, an aberration in the otherwise inspiring history of Utah and Mormonism, but it was much more a fulfillment of Smith's radical doctrines. Brigham Young's relentless commitment to the Kingdom of God forged a culture of violence from Joseph Smith's theology that bequeathed a vexatious heritage to his successors. Early Mormonism's peculiar obsession with blood and vengeance created the society that made the massacre possible if not inevitable. These obsessions had devastating consequences for Young's own family. In New York in 1902, William Hooper Young, the prophet's grandson, slit the abdomen of an alleged prostitute and wrote the words "Blood Atonement" in his father's apartment.[51]

The ultimate question about Mountain Meadows is whether it was the result of an unfortunate chain of circumstances or a calculated act of vengeance. The surviving record contains enough unanswered questions to keep historians wondering for generations, but a strict reading of the evidence supports the following conclusions.

Having virtually no military or political weapons to resist federal authority, Brigham Young resolved to use his Indian allies "to stop all emigration across the continent." Dimick Huntington's journal reveals that Young betrayed his sworn oath of office when, as Utah's Indian superintendent and territorial governor, he "gave" the Paiute chiefs the emigrants' cattle on the southern road to California. He encouraged his Indian allies to attack the Fancher party to make clear to the nation the cost of war with the Mormons. Young had already sent George A. Smith south to make sure local leaders provided the Paiutes with the encouragement and support needed to create a violent incident. After learning from Stewart Van Vliet that the government's intentions were not as demonic as he had feared, Young sent orders south with James Haslam to stop the events he had set in motion. Or perhaps Young merely wanted to ensure that he could blame whatever happened in southern Utah on the Indians, who he expected would, as he said, "do as they please." His manipulation of the Paiutes immediately before the massacre substantiates Juanita Brooks's private judgment that he "was directly responsible for this tragedy."[52]

After the massacre, when the surviving children made it clear that Mormons had orchestrated the murders and events outran his ability to control the situation, Brigham Young resolved to shield the perpetrators from justice. As governor and superintendent of Indian affairs for Utah Territory, it was his duty to protect American citizens and prosecute their murderers. Claiming that Brigham Young had nothing to do with Mountain Meadows is akin to arguing that Abraham Lincoln had nothing to do with the Civil War.

For faithful Mormons faced with troubling new evidence, the most reasonable historical interpretation of the massacre might be to argue that while Brigham Young may have connived to encourage a violent incident on the road to California, he did not foresee the outcome. Perhaps he failed to anticipate the results of his gift of other people's cattle to the Paiute chiefs or to appreciate the depth of fanaticism in southern Utah. He inadvertently may have set in motion an unfortunate chain of events in which one thing led to another, but he could not know that zealots would interpret his words as license to murder. Such a defense might plead that Brigham Young immediately regretted the consequences of his acts but was compelled to conceal them to protect his church and its members.

Yet his own words reveal that both before and after the massacre, Brigham Young recognized the likely result of his acts. He was fully aware that the Indians would kill innocent people. Before meeting with the Paiute chiefs, Young told Wilford Woodruff that the United States had forced the Mormons to go to war before they could civilize the Lamanites so "they would have some Judgment & not kill women & Children."[53] Twenty years after Mountain Meadows Young reasoned, "If I were to say, 'Kill this man,' I myself would be a murderer; or to say, 'Take such a person's money,' I would be a highwayman."[54] His request to be arrested in 1859 indicates that he fully grasped the meaning and implications of being an accessory to murder.

For Brigham Young and his religion, the haunting consequences of mass murder at Mountain Meadows are undeniable. Like many great crimes of power, the criminals expected to get away with it. Young's confidence was justified, for he was never indicted for any act connected to Mountain Meadows—and the only legal charge ever brought against him for these murders was drawn at his own request. But he could never escape the conviction of most of his contemporaries that he had masterminded an atrocity. Even if he burned every incriminating piece of evidence and persuaded every believing resident in Utah Territory to swear that he had nothing to do with the horror at Mountain Meadows, Brigham Young could not change the past. He knew the full truth of his complicity in the crime. The Mormon prophet acted with the certainly that he was the instrument of God's will, but he initiated the sequence of events that led to the betrayal and murder of one hundred twenty men, women, and children.

Anyone studying the Mountain Meadows massacre must finally confront two questions: what happened and why. We will never know all the details of this "awful tale of blood," but its causes and effects are not an impenetrable mystery. Those who pretend that the event is beyond comprehension apparently prefer not to understand it. Yet such questions demand answers. Some of the following conclusions are admittedly beyond historical proof, but they are simple and consistent with the evidence, which extends far beyond what was available to Juanita Brooks. They rest on a personal conviction that the tales of poisoned springs and murdered chickens are fabricated propaganda. These long-dead people were innocent victims of a terrible crime who had the misfortune to be at the wrong place at the wrong time and whose memory continues to be gratuitously slandered by baseless and ridiculous legends.

The party from Arkansas was probably doomed from the moment the Mormons learned of the death of Parley Pratt and the approach of an American army. The emigrants fell victim to Brigham Young's decision to stage a violent incident that would demonstrate his power to control the Indians of the Great Basin and to stop travel on the most important overland roads. Then there is the curious letter Brigham Young sent to Isaac Haight the day before the massacre directing his military commanders *not* to kill passing emigrants. Such an odd injunction suggests that until Young's meeting with Captain Van Vliet, there were standing orders to attack every emigrant party in southern Utah.

Even before the Fancher party left Salt Lake, George A. Smith was on his way to southern Utah to arrange their destruction at a remote and lonely spot. If he did not give explicit orders to "use them up," he made sure the region's military and religious leaders knew what was expected of them, much as four years later Brigham Young could direct the desecration of Carleton's cairn without uttering a word. After camping with the Fancher party at Corn Creek, Smith invented the tale of the poisoned spring to provide a motive for murder and sent Silas S. Smith south to rouse the population.

One of the puzzles of the Mountain Meadows story is, why the Fancher party? It was no mystery to the press in California, for less than a month after the massacre a newspaper noted, "The blow fell on these emigrants from Arkansas, in retribution of the death of Parley Pratt."[55] John D. Lee explained, "As this lot of people had men amongst them that were supposed to have helped kill the Prophets in the Carthage jail, the killing of all of them would be keeping our oaths and avenging the blood of the prophets."[56] At Mountain Meadows the killers fulfilled their sacred vows of vengeance.

Manipulation of the historical record will forever obscure many of the details of what really happened during that long ago September in 1857, yet the destruction of key documents and the manufacturing of evidence to manipulate history stand as an indictment rather than a vindication of the guilty. All this evidence did not vanish because it exonerated Mormon leaders. "Virtually every letter sent from church regional presidents to Brigham Young is archived in Utah," journalist Timothy Egan noted recently. But Isaac Haight's critical September 7, 1857, letter to Young, alerting him to events "that could lead to a war that could crush the church, has disappeared."[57]

The destruction of "so much evidence, including relevant pages from the journals of many settlers," the Paiute tribal history notes, "testifies to many Native Americans and their sympathizers that much of the official history cannot be considered complete or truthful."[58] Citing the compelling evidence of Dimick Huntington's journals, "one of the few key Mormon documents that was not destroyed," David White concluded that Brigham Young incited the Indians to plunder the emigrants, making the initial murders attributable to Young's prior actions. The Mormon leader, White reasoned, "cannot escape responsibility for setting the stage for the tragedy."[59]

"Mormons are still hard put to confront the massacre," observed Juanita Brooks biographer Levi Peterson. "If good Mormons committed the massacre, if prayerful leaders ordered it, if apostles and a prophet knew about it and later sacrificed John D. Lee, then the sainthood of even the modern church seems tainted. Where is the moral superiority of Mormonism, where is the assurance that God has made Mormons his new chosen people?" he asked. "For many Mormons, these are intolerable questions and they arouse intolerable emotions."[60]

In the face of such complexities, the sincere efforts of Mormon leaders to bring healing to the subject are admirable, but their hope that "the book of the past is closed" is futile without an acceptance of the religion's role in this event, as other faiths have learned. The Methodist church has acknowledged its complicity in the "foul and dastardly" massacre of Indians at Sand Creek led by its "Fighting Parson," Col. John Chivington, and the Roman Catholic church decreed A.D. 2000 a year of atonement for its treatment of Jews.

As a religion claiming direct divine inspiration, the LDS church is caught on the horns of an insoluble dilemma. Its leaders cannot admit that the Lord's anointed inspired, executed, and covered up a mass murder, and as long as modern prophets deny that the LDS church had "any complicity in the occurrences of that fateful day," they can never come to terms with the truth. The church's doctrine of repentance dictates that without acknowledging sin, there can be no forgiveness. There is, ultimately, no easy way for the Latter-day Saints to resolve the problems posed by this awful tale until they admit their historic responsibility for a terrible crime. The faith must accept its role, open all of its records on the subject, acknowledge its accountability, and repent—or learn to live with the guilt. Church leaders might wish until the end of time that the matter could be forgotten, but history bears witness that only the truth will lay to rest the ghosts of Mountain Meadows.

Addendum

On January 22, 2002, a National Park Service volunteer at Lee's Ferry, Arizona, discovered a lead sheet allegedly inscribed by John D. Lee. It was buried under several inches of debris near the fireplace inside Lee's Ferry Fort on the Colorado River. Mormon historians almost universally denounced the "Dead Lee Scroll" as a forgery, as did experts brought in to evaluate the plate. "Although it is not possible to 'positively' eliminate Lee as the author of the writing on the lead scroll," forensic authority George Throckmorton concluded, "the evidence is overwhelming that John D. Lee did NOT inscribe the lead plate with either the words, or the name 'J. D. Lee.'" The National Park Service is undertaking an isotopic analysis of the lead sheet that may resolve the controversy. While the scroll appears to be a hoax, the spelling, syntax, and sentiments are vintage John Doyle Lee.

AT THE PAHREAH

I HAV NOW LIVE LONGER THAN

ECCPECTED THO I AM NOW ILL—I DO

NOT FEAR ATHORITY FOR THE TIME IS

CLOSING AND AM WILLING TO TAK

THE BLAME FOR THE FANCHER—

COL. DANE—MAJ. HIGBY AND ME—ON ORDERS

FROM PRES YOUNG THRO GEO SMITH

TOOK PART—I TRUST IN GOD—I HAVE NO

FEAR—DEATH HOLD NO TEROR—LORD HAV

MERCI ON THIS RESLESS SOUL—

BY MY OWN HAND—

J. D. LEE—JAN 11-1872

Appendix

Victims of the Massacre

Historians will never produce a complete or definitive list of the men, women, and children murdered at Mountain Meadows, unless the list Jacob Hamblin reported receiving from the Paiute leader who took it from one of the Fancher party's last survivors miraculously survived. Nonetheless, relatives of the victims, in particular Judge Roger Logan of Harrison, Arkansas, have compiled an exhaustive accounting of the dead and survivors of Mountain Meadows drawn from the best sources. These names are inscribed on the monument dedicated next to Utah Highway 18 on the top of Dan Sill Hill in 1990. Ages and spelling have been corrected to reflect the best current information. Those believed killed at or near the Mountain Meadows were

> William Allen Aden, 19
> George W. Baker, 27
> Manerva A. Beller Baker, 25
>   Mary Levina, 7
> Wards of George and Manerva Baker
>   Melissa Ann Beller, 14
>   David W. Beller, 12
> John T. Baker, 52
>   Abel, 19
> John Beach, 21
> William Cameron, 51
> Martha Cameron, 51

Tillman, 24

Isom, 18

Henry, 16

James, 14

Martha, 11

Larkin, 8

William Cameron's niece

Nancy, 12

Allen P. Deshazo, 20

Jesse Dunlap, Jr., 39

Mary Wharton Dunlap, 39

Ellender, 18

Nancy M., 16

James D., 14

Lucinda, 12

Susannah, 12

Margerette, 11

Mary Ann, 9

Lorenzo Dow Dunlap, 42

Nancy Dunlap, 39

Thomas J., 17

John H., 16

Mary Ann, 13

Talitha Emaline, 11

Nancy, 9

America Jane, 7

William M. Eaton

Silas Edwards

Alexander Fancher, 45

Eliza Ingrum Fancher, 32

Hampton, 19

William, 17

Mary, 15

Thomas, 14

Martha, 10

Sarah G., 8

Margaret A., 8

James Mathew Fancher, 25

Frances "Fanny" Fulfer Fancher[1]

Robert Fancher, 19

Saladia Ann Brown Huff

    William

    Elisha

    Two other sons

John Milum Jones, 32

Eloah Angeline Tackitt Jones, 27

    Daughter

Newton Jones

Lawson A. McEntire, 21

Josiah (Joseph) Miller, 30

Matilda Cameron Miller, 26

    James William, 9

Charles R. Mitchell, 25

Sarah C. Baker Mitchell, 21

    John, infant

Joel D. Mitchell, 23

John Prewit, 20

William Prewit, 18

Milum L. Rush, 28

Charles Stallcup, 25

Cynthia Tackitt, 49

    Marion, 20

    Sebron, 18

    Matilda, 16

    James M., 14

    Jones M., 12

Pleasant Tackitt, 25

Armilda Miller Tackitt, 22

Richard Wilson

Solomon R. Wood, 20

William Wood, 26
Others unknown

Other names associated with the caravan included

George D. Basham
(Tom?) Farmer
(Thomas?) Hamilton
(James C.?) Haydon
David?) Hudson
Laffoon family
(Charles H.?) Morton family
Poteet family
Poteet brothers[2]
(John Perkins?) Reed
(Alf?) Smith
(Mordecai?) Stevenson

The following children survived and were returned to their families in northwestern Arkansas in September 1859.

Children of George and Manerva Baker
  Mary Elizabeth, 5
  Sarah Frances, 3
  William Twitty, 9 months
Daughters of Jesse and Mary Dunlap
  Rebecca J., 6
  Louisa, 4
  Sarah Ann., 1
Daughters of Lorenzo Dow and Nancy Dunlap
  Prudence Angeline, 5
  Georgia Ann, 18 months
Children of Alexander and Eliza Fancher
  Christopher "Kit" Carson, 5
  Triphenia D., 22 months

Daughter of Peter and Saladia Huff
    Nancy Saphrona [Cates], 4
Son of John Milum and Eloah Jones
    Felix Marion, 18 months
Children of Jos. and Matilda Miller
    John, Calvin, 6
    Mary, 4
    Joseph, 1
Sons of Pleasant and Armilda Tackitt
    Emberson Milum, 4
    William Henry, 19 months

No survivors remained in Utah.

This memorial erected September 1990
by the State of Utah
and the families and friends of
those involved and those who died.

The Lost Victims of Mountain Meadows

For generations, families all across America have wondered what happened to relatives who vanished on their way west during the great overland emigrations of the nineteenth century. A large body of folklore, perhaps supported in some cases by fact, linked these disappearances to the murders in southern Utah in 1857. News of the discovery of human remains at Mountain Meadows in August 1999 "triggered a flood of requests to BYU and the state from people wanting to know if their family roots could be traced to Mountain Meadows."[3]

In addition to the dozen speculative identifications and the eighty victims identified by name and memorialized at Mountain Meadows, historical sources point to other possible unnamed victims:

- Fifty-three-year-old Horace Moffitt and his wife, Phebe Merriam, a son, and two daughters, headed west to California from Michigan, and were later "supposed to have been killed in the Mountain Meadow massacre."[4]
- At Fort Bridger the Fancher party allegedly picked up a troublesome "Dutchman," probably a northern European emigrant who may have had medical training. Mention of the man in early newspaper reports and in some of the most reliable Mormon sources suggests he may well have existed. By all accounts, the man insisted on insulting the Mormons.[5]
- In 1883 J. P. Dunn reported a Utah tradition that a Missourian who had been held at Beaver "for some alleged offense" joined the party and "urged them to hurry beyond the power of the Mormons."[6]
- Carole A. Lange of Mabton, Washington, reports that her family legends tell that her ancestor, James Wilson Powers, died at Mountain Meadows.[7]
- As noted, other early reports suggest that an unknown number of apostate Mormons joined the Fancher train and died with them.

Cathy L. Starr of Simsbury, Connecticut, reported the surprising result of a Young Woman's Association service project in the Hartford Stake of the LDS church. Mormon volunteers spent a hot June day in 1999 restoring the community cemetery in Bloomfield. "One of our young women was clearing the brush from the front of a hidden grave monument when the words 'Mountain Meadow' caught her eye. She tore at the underbrush to reveal the stone, which reads, 'Wm E. Cooper, June 4, 1828. He and wife were murdered in Mountain Meadow Massacre—Utah, Sept. 11, 1857.'"[8]

NOTES

PREFACE

1. Brewer, "The Massacre at Mountain Meadows," 513/1.
2. Stenhouse, *The Rocky Mountain Saints*, 458; Buchanan, *Massacre at Mountain Meadows*, Serial 1033, 76; Smith, *Essentials in Church History*, 511.
3. Gates, *Brigham Young*, 24.
4. Brooks, *Mountain Meadows Massacre*, 219.
5. Roberts, *Comprehensive History*, 4:139–40.
6. Ibid., 4:139.
7. Stampp, *America in 1857*, 205.
8. Hallwas and Launius, eds., *Cultures in Conflict*, 1–7, 139.

PROLOGUE: THE MOUNTAIN MEADOW

1. Dixie Forest archaeologist Marion Jacklin described Paiute use of Mountain Meadows to the author on 10 June 1996.
2. Spence and Jackson, eds., *The Expeditions of John Charles Frémont*, 2:692–95. Many early sources referred to "the Mountain Meadow," but standard usage is now "Mountain Meadows."
3. Hafen and Hafen, eds., *Old Spanish Trail*, 354.
4. George Washington Bean's comment comes from Brooks, "The Mountain Meadows," 139.
5. Halleck to Whiting, 6 November 1900, Special Collections, Harold B. Lee Library, Brigham Young University (hereafter BYU Library), reporting what Paiutes told him in 1858. Punctuation corrected.

CHAPTER 1

1. Pratt, "Eleanor McLean and the Murder of Parley P. Pratt," 225.
2. Eleanor Pratt, Account of the death of Parley P. Pratt, 59.
3. "Murder of Parley P. Pratt," *Millennial Star*, 4 July 1857, 418.
4. Pratt, "Eleanor McLean," 225–26; Bancroft, *History of Utah*, 546n6.
5. "Murder of Parley P. Pratt," *Millennial Star*, 4 July 1857, 428.
6. Tyler, *Freedom's Ferment*, 25, 101; Cross, *The Burned-over District*, 3, 6–7, 82, 145.
7. Smith, *History of the Church*, 1:4–7, 11, 75–78. For Smith's career as a necromancer, see Quinn, *Early Mormonism and the Magic World View*, 30–66.
8. Young, Three Weeks in Brigham Young's Office, [9]; Brooks, *John Doyle Lee*, 30.
9. *Doctrine and Covenants*, Section 132, Introduction.
10. Ibid., Section 57:1.
11. "Murder of Parley P. Pratt," *Millennial Star*, 4 July 1857, 419, 420, 432.
12. Pratt, "Eleanor McLean," 227–32.
13. Ibid., 232–34; "Sad Story of Presbyterianism," *The Mormon*, 14 March 1857, 2/6. Many sources list McLean as Pratt's tenth wife, but Van Wagoner, *Mormon Polygamy*, 46, states she was the twelfth.
14. *Doctrine and Covenants*, Sections 52:2, 57:1–3.
15. Roberts, *Comprehensive History*, 1:321, 324.
16. *Book of Mormon*, 1 Nephi, 12:23, 3 Nephi 20:13–28; Smith, *Essentials in Church History*, 112, 114–15, 117–18; Roberts, *Comprehensive History*, 1:260.
17. McConkie, *Mormon Doctrine*, 146–47. Although never given official sanction by the LDS church, for a generation this topical discussion of theology and belief defined orthodox Mormonism. For the current doctrinal reference the LDS church released in 1992, see Ludlow, ed., *Encyclopedia of Mormonism*. Apostle Bruce McConkie's 1958 discussions of race, marriage, theocracy, blood atonement, and the Kingdom of God represented traditional Mormon views more accurately.

18. *Doctrine and Covenants*, Sections 58:52, 63:29, 64:27–28; *Evening and Morning Star*, cited in LeSueur, *The 1838 Mormon War*, 18.

19. John S. Higbee, Affidavit, 24 March 1839, Johnson, ed., *Mormon Redress Petitions*, 461–63.

20. LeSueur, *The 1838 Mormon War*, 16, 24, 28, 32–35; Schindler, *Orrin Porter Rockwell*, 39.

21. Schindler, *Orrin Porter Rockwell*, 30, 34–35.

22. Bishop, ed., *Mormonism Unveiled*, 57, 60.

23. Roberts, *Comprehensive History*, 1:474–76, 479. Parley Pratt was charged with murder for his role at Crooked River. Ibid., 500. Boggs's "extermination order" remained in effect until 1976 when Gov. Christopher Bond rescinded it with an apology to the Mormon people. See Schindler, *Orrin Porter Rockwell*, 49n62.

24. Schindler, *Orrin Porter Rockwell*, 50–51.

25. Roberts, *Comprehensive History*, 1:482. Allegedly the "nits make lice" comment was repeated at Mountain Meadows. See Brooks, *Mountain Meadows Massacre*, 5.

26. Johnson, *Mormon Redress Petitions*, 266–68; 274–78, 478–88, 490–91. William Palmer, in an undated letter to Harold B. Lee, stated that Samuel Knight was at Haun's Mill.

27. For the end of the Missouri conflict, see Schindler, *Orrin Porter Rockwell*, 41–46, 53–57.

28. William Bateman, Samuel White, and William Young signed the Nauvoo "scroll petition" to Congress for redress of their Missouri losses. For statements by men who were probably at Mountain Meadows in 1857, see Johnson, *Mormon Redress Petitions*, 166–67, 175–76, 442.

29. McConkie, *Mormon Doctrine*, 488; *Doctrine and Covenants*, Sections 56:3, 63:5–6, 105:6, 131:21.

30. McConkie, *Mormon Doctrine*, 381.

31. Roberts, *Comprehensive History*, 2:9, 11; Bancroft, *History of Utah*, 140–41.

32. Brodie, *No Man Knows My History*, 271–74. While it may be impossible to prove Joseph Smith sent Rockwell to kill Boggs, a church newspaper called the shooting a "noble deed." See Quinn, *Mormon Hierarchy: Origins of Power*, 113.

33. Roberts, *Comprehensive History*, 2:59; and Bancroft, *History of Utah*, 146–47. At the start of the Mexican War in 1846, the U.S. Army had only 637 officers and 5,925 men. See Heitman, *Historical Register*, 2:282. The regular army did not have lieutenant generals.

34. Higbee History and Stories, 52; Isaac C. Haight, Journals, 1842–1850, 3, 12. Both at Special Collections, Southern Utah University.

35. Brodie, *No Man Knows My History*, 300; *Doctrine and Covenants*, Section 132:4, 16, 20, 27.

36. W. Wyl, quoted in Brodie, *No Man Knows My History*, 297.

37. Arrington, *Brigham Young: American Moses*, 100.

38. Stanley, *The Archer of Paradise*, 163–64.

39. Smith, Jr., *History of the Church*, 6:408.

40. "The Government of God," *Times and Seasons*, 15 July 1842, 3:856/2.

41. Jessee, *The Papers of Joseph Smith*, 2:447.

42. See First Presidency Secretary Michael Watson to Bagley, 29 January and 26 August 1998, copies in author's possession.

43. Smith, Jr., *History of the Church*, 6:276, 365; "Religion and Politics," *Times and Seasons*, 15 March 1844, 5:470/2, 477/1.

44. Bigler, *Forgotten Kingdom*, 35 passim. Klaus J. Hansen was the first to recognize the significance of the Council of Fifty in *Quest for Empire*.

45. Dan. 2:35.

46. "History of Joseph Smith," *Deseret News*, 9 July 1856, 187; Quinn, *Mormon Hierarchy: Origins of Power*, 124; Smith, ed., *An Intimate Chronicle*, 122, 129, 154; Compton, *In Sacred Loneliness*, 6, 240, 634.

47. *Nauvoo Expositor*, 7 June 1844, 2/2, 2/3; and Quinn, *Mormon Hierarchy: Origins of Power*, 139.

48. Roberts, *Comprehensive History*, 2:236–37, 243; Cook, *William Law*, 55.

49. Hallwas and Launius, eds., *Cultures in Conflict*, 175–78, 182.

50. Smith, *History of the Church*, 6:545–49, 554–55.

51. Ibid., 6:612–22; Bishop, ed., *Mormonism Unveiled*, 153.

52. *Doctrine and Covenants*, 135:7.

53. Isaac C. Haight, Journal, 16; Schindler, *Orrin Porter Rockwell*, 128; Smith, *History of the Church*, 6:627–28.

54. Arrington, *Brigham Young*, 11, 34, passim. The leading biographies of Brigham Young are Stanley P. Hirshson's *The Lion of the Lord* and Leonard J. Arrington's *Brigham Young: American Moses*. The first is a critical study drawn largely from nineteenth-century newspapers. The second is a defense based on secondary sources and careful selections from LDS Archives. Neither book does justice to its subject.

55. Jenson, *LDS Biographical Encyclopedia*, 1:8–10.

56. Ibid., 1:10–11; and Quinn, *Mormon Hierarchy: Origins of Power*, 63–66.

57. For the succession crisis, see Quinn, *Mormon Hierarchy: Origins of Power*, 144–185, 648.

58. Bagley, "'Every Thing Is Favourable!'", 185–209. For an overview of the Great Western Measure, see Bagley, ed., *The Pioneer Camp of the Saints*, 39–61.

59. Bishop, ed., *Mormonism Unveiled*, 165, 169–70; and Brooks, *John Doyle Lee*, 73–74.

60. Brooks, *John Doyle Lee*, 17–27. For Lee's own story, see Bishop, ed., *Mormonism Unveiled*, 36–40, 43–46, 50–53, 76.

61. Bishop, ed., *Mormonism Unveiled*, 62–63, 81; Brooks, *John Doyle Lee*, 41–42.

62. Ludlow, ed., *Encyclopedia of Mormonism*, glossary. See Brooks, *John Doyle Lee*, 42–43, for Lee's blessing.

63. Bishop, ed., *Mormonism Unveiled*, 173; Quinn, *Mormon Hierarchy: Origins of Power*, 528–530.

64. For the temple rites, see Homer, "'Similarity of Priesthood in Masonry,'" 42–63.

65. Bishop, ed., *Mormonism Unveiled*, 169; Brooks, *John Doyle Lee*, 43. Second anointings are now performed only rarely for the highest LDS authorities.

66. The Mormon Temple "Oath of Vengeance," A. C. Lambert Collection, Special Collections, University of Utah (hereafter Marriott Library). In 1849 William Smith claimed "1,500 Salt Lake Mormons" had vowed in the Nauvoo Temple to "avenge the blood of Joseph Smith on this nation" and "carry out hostilities against this nation." See Smith, "Remonstrance," Serial 581, 1–2. The oath was removed from the temple ceremony in 1927.

67. Bishop, ed., *Mormonism Unveiled*, 160.

68. Verne Lee reported his family tradition to the author on 2 August 1996.

69. Seventies Minutes, 9 December 1847, General Church Minutes, MS 2737, Box 100, LDS Archives; Bishop, ed., *Mormonism Unveiled*, 132, 166.

70. Bigler and Bagley, eds., *Army of Israel*, 71.

71. Isaac C. Haight, Journal, 38; Jenson, *LDS Biographical Encyclopedia*, 1:40.

72. Quinn, *Mormon Hierarchy: Extensions of Power*, 238–39, 748, 749. As noted, the minutes of the Council of Fifty, which would date Young's ordination as king, are not available to scholars.

73. Thomas Bullock, Minutes, 24 September 1848, cited in Esplin, "'A Place Prepared,'" 85.

CHAPTER 2

1. Stegner, *The Gathering of Zion*, 202.

2. Olney Papers, Journal, 11 August 1842, Fd 8, Beinecke Library.

3. Bigler, *Forgotten Kingdom*, 142.

4. Holeman to Lea, 28 November 1851 and 29 March 1852, Buchanan, *The Utah Expedition*, Serial 956, 129, 140.

5. Bishop, ed., *Mormonism Unveiled*, 257.

6. Bailey, ed., "Lt. Sylvester Mowry's Report," 344.

7. Knowlton, Reminiscences, California Historical Society, 1:68.

8. See Entry 1593, P. H. Ferguson, in Mattes, *Platte River Road Narratives*, 473.

9. For Mormon-Indian relations in this period, see Christy, "Open Hand and Mailed Fist"; O'Neil and Layton, "Of Pride and Politics."

10. *Doctrine and Covenants*, Section 3:19–20; McConkie, *Mormon Doctrine*, 478; *Book of Mormon*, 2 Nephi, 5:21. Current editions of *The Book of Mormon* have changed "white" to "pure."

11. Brigham Young, 9 August 1857, *Journal of Discourses*, 5:128.

12. Brigham Young, 13 September 1857, *Journal of Discourses*, 5:236.

13. *Book of Mormon*, 1 Nephi, 12:23; 3 Nephi, 20:16, 19, 28; *Doctrine and Covenants*, Sections 49:24, 87:5. Early Mormons referred to American Indians as "Ephraim" and the "Stick of Joseph" (based on Ezekiel 37:16–19); as the "remnant of the house of Jacob" (based on Isaiah 10:20–21 and Micah 5:7–8); as the "remnant of the seed of Jacob" or the "remnant of the seed of Joseph" (based on Alma 46:23); or as "Manassa" or "Manasseh." This reflected their belief that the Indians were "a mixture of the tribes of Ephraim, Manasseh and Judah." See Roberts, *A New Witness for God*, 3:82.

14. Crawley, ed., *The Essential Parley P. Pratt*, 24, quoting Pratt's 1838 "*Mormonism Unveiled.*"

15. Hallwas and Launius, eds., *Cultures in Conflict*, 105–6.

16. Smith, Jr., *History of the Church*, 4:401.

17. Quinn, *Mormon Hierarchy: Origins of Power*, 649.

18. Pratt, *Proclamation of the Twelve Apostles*, 2–3, 5–6, 8–9, 11–13.

19. Smith, ed., *An Intimate Chronicle*, 371, 375. The Ute tribe was generally referred to as the "Utahs" in early sources.

20. Bagley, ed., *The Pioneer Camp of the Saints*, 243–44. Bigler's *Forgotten Kingdom*, 63–85, includes an excellent discussion of Mormon-Indian relations.

21. For native populations in 1847, see Lewis, "Native Americans in Utah," in Powell, ed., *Utah History Encyclopedia*, 390. For more, see D'Azevedo, ed., *Handbook of North American Indians: Great Basin*, 338–40, 530–33.

22. O'Neil, "A History of the Ute Indians of Utah until 1890," 26. For the best work on the subject, see Cuch, ed., *A History of Utah's American Indians*.

23. Day to Lea, 2 January 1852, in Buchanan, *The Utah Expedition*, Serial 956, 130–31. Van Hoak, "Waccara's Utes," 309–30, provides a brilliant analysis of the Ute equestrians.

24. Padilla, "Kanosh," in Powell, ed., *Utah History Encyclopedia*, 297; and Walker, "Toward a Reconstruction of Mormon and Indian Relations," 31.

25. O'Neil and Alley, "The Southern Paiutes," in Papanikolas, ed., *The Peoples of Utah*, 45.

26. Palmer, "Pahute Indian Homelands," 91, 98.

27. Journal History, 7 May 1849. The Journal History is a daily scrapbook of Mormon history consisting of journals, letters, and articles extracted from church records by Andrew Jenson and others.

28. Brooks and Cleland, eds., *A Mormon Chronicle*, 1:108.

29. Brooks, "Indian Relations on the Mormon Frontier," 23, 29.

30. Morgan, *Provo: Pioneer Mormon City*, 44–46.

31. Christy, "Open Hand and Mailed Fist," 224–26; O'Neil, "A History of the Ute Indians of Utah until 1890," Appendix B; Bagley, ed., *Frontiersman*, 152–57.

32. Brigham Young, 31 August 1856 and 28 July 1866, *Journal of Discourses*, 4:41, 11:264.

33. Smart and Smart, eds., *Over the Rim*, 20, 45, 126, 181.

34. Ibid., 90, 92, 94, 95, 108, 179, 183, 188.

35. Jenson, *LDS Biographical Encyclopedia*, 1:37–42. Novelist Helen Hunt Jackson saw Smith on a train in about 1874 and left a lurid description of the "scarlet magnate." See Jackson, *Bits of Travel at Home*, 17, 25–26.

36. Brooks, *John Doyle Lee*, 154.

37. Shirts, "The Iron Mission," in Powell, ed., *Utah History Encyclopedia*, 275–76. Shirts noted that more than half of the Deseret ironworkers were involved in the Mountain Meadows massacre.

38. Brigham Young, 13 May 1851, cited in Brooks, "Indian Relations on the Mormon Frontier," 6.

39. O'Neil, "The Walker War," 178; Brimhall, *The Workers of Utah*, 16; Hafen, ed., *The Mountain Men and the Fur Trade*, 339–50; Gunnison, *The Mormons*, 149.

40. Alexander, *Utah, the Right Place*, 114.

41. Statement, M. S. Martenas, Brigham Young Collection, LDS Archives. Slave trader Wallace Bowman publicly accosted Brigham Young in Provo and boasted he had four hundred Mexicans "awaiting his orders." Mormons disguised as Indians allegedly killed Bowman. See Green, ed., *Fifteen Years among the Mormons*, xi, 274–75.

42. O'Neil, "A History of the Ute Indians of Utah until 1890," 29.

43. Bigler, *Forgotten Kingdom*, 75–81, 88. Charles Wandell claimed Wakara "demanded a white squaw to help fill up his wick-e-up; but he died very suddenly by devouring, as is supposed, an innocent bowl of bread and milk!" See Argus, "Open Letter to Brigham Young," *Daily Utah Reporter*, 12 September 1870, 2/1–2.

44. Brooks, "Indian Relations on the Mormon Frontier," 10–11.

45. Brooks, ed., *Journal of the Southern Indian Mission*, 29–30.

46. Brimhall, *The Workers of Utah*, 16.

47. Stegner, *The Gathering of Zion*, 46.

48. Jenson, *LDS Biographical Encyclopedia*, 4:748–49.

49. Secretary of State, *Register of Officers and Agents . . . on the Thirtieth of September, 1855*, 90.

50. Smart and Smart, eds., *Over the Rim*, 226; Brooks and Cleland, eds., *Mormon Chronicle*, 2:255n53.

51. For a comprehensive reevaluation of this subject, see Jones, *The Trial of Don Pedro León Luján*.

52. Jones, *Forty Years among the Indians*, 53. For an overview of Indian slavery, see Jones, "'Redeeming the Indian.'"

53. Brooks, ed., *Journal of the Southern Indian Mission*, 68. Utah Indians often referred to Brigham Young as "Big Um," "Big Captain," or the "Big Mormon Chief."

54. Young to Manypenny, 30 September 1854, in Morgan, "Washakie and the Shoshoni," 26:165.

55. Euler, *The Paiute People*, 24–26; Alley et al., *Nuwuvi*, 32–33, 44–45; Smith to St. Clair, 25 November 1869, Historian's Office Journal, LDS Archives. Frémont said nothing of killing Paiutes. Kit Carson had hostile encounters with Paiute bands again in 1847 and 1848.

56. Hurt to Young, 31 March 1856, O'Neil and Layton, "Of Pride and Politics," 247.

57. Judd, Account of settlement of Santa Clara, Utah, Huntington Library. Settlers relocated Harmony three times and called some of these settlements New Harmony. "Harmony" is used to refer to all locations.

58. Morgan, "The Administration of Indian Affairs in Utah, 1851–1858," 397.

59. Jacob Hamblin's journal used the name Tonaquints "as they call themselves after the Indian name of the stream" they lived along, the present Santa Clara.

60. Brooks and Cleland, eds., *Mormon Chronicle*, 1:283.

61. Cuch, ed., *History of Utah's American Indians*, 127.

62. "Enos Punished for Stealing" and "Kanosh's Visit to the Piedes," *Deseret News*, 16 July 1856, 148/1–2; Shelton Affidavit, LDS Archives; Gunnison, *The Mormons*, x–xi, xiii.

63. Journal of Jacob Hamblin, 43; Little, *Jacob Hamblin*, 45–47; Alley et al., *Nuwuvi*, 72.

64. Brooks, ed., *Journal of the Southern Indian Mission*, 68.

65. Bailey, ed., "Lt. Sylvester Mowry's Report," 344. Mowry's report appears grossly inflated. Jacob Hamblin said "that to his certain knowledge in 1855 there were but three guns in the whole tribe," wrote Maj. James Carleton in 1859. "I doubt if they had many more in 1857." See Carleton, *Special Report*, Serial 4377, 12.

66. Mormon militia officer William Wall passed through Mountain Meadows in late 1857 and reported "if he had had command of the emigrant party he believes he could have whipt one thousand Indians." See Smith to Lyman, 6 January 1858, LDS Archives.

67. *Deseret News*, 30 July 1853, quoted in Fielding, *Unsolicited Chronicler*, 88.

68. Brigham Young to Walker, Chief of the Utahs, 24 March 1854, Brigham Young Collection.

69. Carvalho, *Incidents of Travel and Adventure in the Far West*, 193.

70. Bigler, "Garland Hurt, the American Friend of the Utahs," 155. For a report from the LDS mission to Indian Territory, see "Cherokee Nation," *Deseret News*, 8 April 1857, 35/4–36/1.

71. Brooks, ed., *Journal of the Southern Indian Mission*, 33, 123.

72. Bigler, *Forgotten Kingdom*, 97–98; Jenson, "The Salmon River Mission," 156–57. The name is now often spelled Lemhi, but early sources used *The Book of Mormon* spelling, Limhi.

73. Brooks, "Indian Relations on the Mormon Frontier," 21.

74. William Horne Dame, Papers, LDS Archives. Punctuation added.

75. Young to Cannon, 7 January 1857, *Western Standard*, 21 February 1857, 2/5.

CHAPTER 3

1. Langworthy, *Scenery of the Plains, Mountains and Mines*, 80.

2. "The Mormons, No. 3," *Oregonian*, 8 May 1852, 1.

3. Brigham Young, 6 October 1857, *Journal of Discourses*, 5:296.

4. Brooks, ed., *On the Mormon Frontier*, 1:238.

5. Ibid. See also Harwell, ed., *Manuscript History of Brigham Young*, 35–36. Young's experience still defines the role of prophet in the LDS church.

6. Brigham Young, 26 July 1857, *Journal of Discourses*, 5:75–76, 77.

7. *Doctrine and Covenants*, 136:1. This is Brigham Young's only canonized revelation.

8. *Daily Tribune*, 30 August 1877; Dwyer, *The Gentile Comes to Utah*, 97.

9. Brigham Young, 21 September 1856, *Journal of Discourses*, 4:55–56; Kenney, ed., *Wilford Woodruff's Journal*, 6 October 1856, 4:464.

10. *Doctrine and Covenants*, 134:1, 5; 38:22.

11. Jensen, "The Common Law of England in the Territory of Utah," 6, 7, 10–11.

12. Cannon, "'Mountain Common Law,'" 312.

13. Jensen, "The Common Law of England in the Territory of Utah," 10–12, 17, 18, 25; Christian, Dictation, 1886, Bancroft Library. For an excellent overview of the subject, see Homer, "The Judiciary and the Common Law in Utah Territory."

14. Brigham Young, 1 August 1852, *Journal of Discourses*, 1:361–62.

15. Justus Morse affidavit, in Hardy, *Solemn Covenant*, 366.

16. Smith, Jr., *History of the Church*, 5:135; *Deseret News*, 9 November 1856, 291. For a modern apostle's revealing essay on "lying for the Lord" see Oaks, "Gospel Teachings about Lying," 13–19.

17. Allen, "The Unusual Jurisdiction," 133, 134; Bancroft, *History of Utah*, 487.

18. Furniss, *The Mormon Conflict*, 41–42.

19. Quinn, *Mormon Hierarchy: Extensions of Power*, 226, 260.

20. For a study of this dichotomy, see Bigler, *A Winter with the Mormons*.

21. Beadle, *Life in Utah*, 171.

22. Brigham Young, 13 September 1857, *Journal of Discourses*, 5:232.

23. "Celebration of July Fourth," *Deseret News*, 9 July 1856, 140/3.

24. Fillmore, *Report of Messrs. Brandebury, Brocchus, and Harris*, Serial 640, 10.

25. Ibid., 6, 11.

26. Ibid., 6, 11–12; Furniss, *The Mormon Conflict*, 26–28.

27. Holeman to Lea, 29 March 1852, in Morgan, "Washakie and the Shoshoni," 25:187–88.

28. Jedediah M. Grant sermon of 2 March 1856, *Deseret News*, 12 March 1856, 4/2.

29. Furniss, *The Mormon Conflict*, 40–44.

30. Gunnison, *The Mormons*, 156; Mowry, Letters to Bicknall, 17 September 1854 and 27 April 1855, Utah State Historical Society.

31. Journal History, 11 December 1854; Blair, Reminiscences and Journals, 20 and 30 December 1854.

32. Brigham Young, 18 February 1855, *Journal of Discourses*, 2:183.

33. Fielding, *Unsolicited Chronicler*, 234–35, 243, 273–74.

34. Young to Walker, 24 March 1854, Brigham Young Collection, LDS Archives.

35. Furniss, *The Mormon Conflict*, 41–42.

36. Bancroft, *History of Utah*, 488, 490; Brooks, ed., *On the Mormon Frontier*, 2:583–84.

37. Furniss, *The Mormon Conflict*, 54–58.

38. Bigler, "Garland Hurt," 151, 155–57.

39. Hurt to Manypenny, 2 May 1855, Brooks, "Indian Relations on the Mormon Frontier," 16–17.

40. "From the East to the Pacific, and the Land Sharks of Utah," *Deseret News*, 13 July 1854, 64.

41. Shaw, *Eldorado*, 74; "Justice on the Plains," *Alta California*, 10 September 1854, 2/4.

42. Buchanan, *Massacre at Mountain Meadows*, Serial 1033, 130–31.

43. Hurt to Elliott, 4 October 1856, and Hurt to Manypenny, 30 March 1857, Morgan, "The Administration of Indian Affairs in Utah, 1851–1858," 401, 403.

44. O'Neil and Layton, "Of Pride and Politics," 248.

45. Campbell, *Establishing Zion*, 143; "Council from the First Presidency," *Deseret News*, 9 July 1856, 141/4; Young to Lyman, 1 June 1855, Arrington, *Charles C. Rich*, 187.

46. "Mass Meeting," *Deseret News*, 12 March 1856, 8/1–2.

47. Hyde, *Mormonism: Its Leaders and Designs*, 51.

48. Brigham Young sermon of 31 August 1856, *Deseret News*, 17 September 1856, 220/2.

49. Bigler, *Forgotten Kingdom*, 102, 121.

50. Browne, "The Utah Expedition," 364; Brooks, ed., *On the Mormon Frontier*, 2:627.

51. Brigham Young sermon of 2 March 1856, *Deseret News*, 12 March 1856, 2/2.

52. *Deseret News*, 28 November 1855, cited in Cannon, "The Mormon War," 13.

53. Brigham Young sermon of 16 March 1856, *Deseret News*, 26 March 1856, 19/1.

54. "From the East to the Pacific, and the Land Sharks of Utah," *Deseret News*, 13 July 1854, 64.

55. Brigham Young, September 21, 1856, *Journal of Discourses*, 4:52.

56. "The Utah Judges," *Philadelphia American*, reprinted in *Millennial Star*, 3 July 1852, 298. For the best account of Grant's life and the Mormon Reformation, see Sessions, *Mormon Thunder*.

57. Sessions, *Mormon Thunder*, 220–21.

58. "Great Reformation," *Deseret News*, 24 September 1856, 228/2.

59. Sessions, *Mormon Thunder*, 203–4, 209, 212.

60. Ibid., 221.

61. McConkie, *Mormon Doctrine*, 87–88. McConkie insisted "there is not one historical instance of so-called blood atonement" in modern times.

62. *Doctrine and Covenants*, 132: 19, 20, 26, 27.

63. Ludlow, ed., *Encyclopedia of Mormonism*. 1:131; Brooks and Cleland, eds., *Mormon Chronicle*, 1:129n143. In the 1950s official LDS commentary on such doctrines was more forthright. An apostle noted that those who understood blood atonement "could and did use their influence to get a form of capital punishment written into the laws of various states of the union so that the blood of murderers could be shed." See McConkie, *Mormon Doctrine*, 86–88. Beheading was an execution option in Utah until 1888.

64. Brigham Young, 21 September 1856 and 8 February 1857, *Journal of Discourses*, 4:53, 219–20.

65. Brooks and Cleland, eds., *Mormon Chronicle*, 1:98–99, contains the Council of Fifty's discussion about whether to behead Ira West in public or in secret.

66. Kenney, ed., *Wilford Woodruff's Journal*, 18 December 1857, 5:140.

67. Grant sermons of 12 March 1854 and 21 September 1856, in Sessions, *Mormon Thunder*, 127, 211.

68. Bishop, ed., *Mormonism Unveiled*, 279, 281–82.

69. Dalton, ed., *History of Iron Country Mission and Parowan*, 331.

70. James H. Martineau Record, quoted in Backus, *Mountain Meadows Witness*, 93.

71. Bishop, ed., *Mormonism Unveiled*, 251, 276–78.

72. Sessions, *Mormon Thunder*, 237, 238, 245, 250–51.

73. Ibid., 255, 257.

74. Quinn, *Mormon Hierarchy: Extensions of Power*, 753. After a six-month suspension, Young restored the sacrament on 6 April 1857. Ibid., 754.

75. Hendrix to Young, 23 June 1860, Brigham Young Collection, LDS Archives.

76. Brooks, ed., *On the Mormon Frontier*, 1:314.

77. John Steele on Lee, Beckwith, Shameful Friday, 184; Beadle, *Western Wilds*, 309.

78. Brown, *Journal of the Southern Indian Mission*, 30; Beckwith, Shameful Friday, 184.

79. William Wall, Report, 24 April–11 May 1853, Utah State Archives. Punctuation added.

80. Brown, ed., *Journal of the Southern Indian Mission*, 91, 118–19.

81. Hicks, Life History, 29.

CHAPTER 4

1. Elizabeth Baker Terry, "Survivor of a Massacre," described the camp at Caravan Spring, a few miles south of Harrison, Ark. A marker commemorates the 1857 emigrants.

2. Although the word had been used as early as the Revolution, "cowboy" would not enter the American vernacular until the 1880s.

3. Most names and ages of Fancher party members are from the 1999 "Memorial Service at the Reinternment of Remains of Victims of the Mountain Meadows Massacre" (cited as Memorial Program). Working with the late Utah historians Morris Shirts and Lee Oertle, Judge Roger V. Logan, Jr., of Harrison, Arkansas, assembled the original version of this authoritative roster, "Mountain Meadows Memorial Program," for the dedication of the 1991 memorial.

4. Fancher, *Westward with the Sun*, 212, 220–22, 242–43.

5. Fancher, *The Fancher Family*, 95–96. Studies by Paul L. Blair, Paul B. Fancher, Ronald E. Loving, and Lesley Wischmann preserve much Fancher history. Lyon, "Massacre of Fancher Family Recalled," and McClelland, "The Fancher Family Remembers," are also useful. Burr Fancher's *Westward with the Sun* contains a wealth of Fancher lore, and the author wishes to thank Dr. Fancher and J. K. Fancher of Harrison, Ark., for many insights into the family.

6. W. B. Flippin described the Tutt-Everett War in Berry, *The History of Marion County*, 65–70.

7. Alexander Fancher's 1850 Power of Attorney at the Carroll County, Arkansas, Historical Society dates his departure for California.

8. McArthur, *Arkansas in the Gold Rush*, 26, 101–13, 150–53, 161.

9. Bell, "Log of the Texas-California Trail, 1854," 209; McCoy, *Historic Sketches of the Cattle Trade*, 26–27. Demke, *The Cattle Drives of Early California*, indicates this price was exaggerated.

10. Dillon, ed., *California Trail Herd*, 17, 19, 22, 25, 36–37.

11. The following quotes are from Temple to Dear Wife, 11 May and 2 June 1850, Oregon State Historical Society, punctuation corrected.

12. On 21 May 1850, Fleming G. Hearn wrote, "We passed two New *Graves* this morning not more than two miles apart. I ascertained that one of them was shot by an old man from Arkansas, it appears the old man had his family with him and that this young Wilkerson insulted one of his daughters, for which this crime was committed. I saw his shirt with the blood upon it also a tinpan filled with blood." See Hearn, A Journal for 1850, 17–18. Micajah Littleton reported the boy's grave marker read, "killed by a man for making too free with his daughter." See Mattes, *The Great Platte River Road*, 78.

13. For William Bedford Temple's grave, see Littleton, Diary of overland journey, 1 July 1850, 23.

14. Peck, Diary of Washington Peck, 1–4 November 1850.

15. Ibid., 5 December 1850.

16. Loving, "The Fanchers of California," 1.

17. Parker, *Life and Adventures*, 43–45 described early Visalia, while Loving's "The Fanchers of California" recounts the family's experiences in the gold rush.

18. Based on family traditions, Burr Fancher described an 1854 overland trip in *Westward with the Sun*, 245–47.

19. Brooks, *John Doyle Lee*, 372. Burr Fancher located and photographed the inscription.

20. "From the East to the Pacific, and the Land Sharks of Utah," *Deseret News*, 13 July 1854, 64/3.

21. For Mormons in the California cattle trade, see "Departing Missionaries," *Deseret News*, 13 May 1857, 77/2; Campbell, *Report upon the Pacific Wagon Roads*, Serial 1008, 56.

22. Atkinson, "Cattle Drives from Arkansas to California," 54.

23. Stampp, *America in 1857*, describes the world and nation in this critical year.

24. Furniss, *The Mormon Conflict*, 75–76. See William P. MacKinnon's forthcoming *At Sword's Point* for an examination of the pivotal role this petition played in prompting federal action.

25. Stenhouse, *The Rocky Mountain Saints*, 427.

26. Members of the 1857 emigration described the missing families in the *Daily Alta California*: "The Immigrant Massacre," 17 October, 1/1; and "Letter from Angel's Camp," 1 November 1857, 1/3.

27. Contemporary newspaper articles provide detailed data about the Arkansas trains. From the *Arkansas State Gazette and Democrat*, see "Extract from a letter [from] Carroll Co.," 18 February 1858, 2/2; "How Not to Do It," 18 February 1858, 2/1; and "Public Meeting of the People of Carroll County," 27 February 1858, 3/1.

28. Brooks, *John Doyle Lee*, 202.

29. "The Immigrant Massacre," *Daily Alta California*, 17 October 1857, 1/1.

30. Memorial Program.

31. Ronald E. Loving located depositions taken in 1860 that describe the Arkansas emigrants in Papers Pertaining to the Territory of Utah, 1849–1870, at the National Archives. Judge Roger V. Logan, Jr., published the affidavits (with some transcription errors) in "New Light on the Mountain Meadows Caravan" in 1992. These documents, cited as 1860 Affidavits, provide invaluable information.

32. Holt, "One of the Baker Families," 160–62. Fred Baker of New Market, Ala., was the source of the Jack Baker stories.

33. "Extract from a letter [from] Carroll Co.," *Arkansas State Gazette and Democrat*, 18 February 1858, 2/2.

34. Parker, *Life and Adventures*, 53; and *Recollections of the Mountain Meadows Massacre*, 4.

35. Mitchell, "The Mountain Meadows Massacre—An Episode on the Road to Zion," cited as Sarah Baker Mitchell Memoir; John H. Baker deposition, 22 October 1860, in 1860 Affidavits.

36. John H. Baker and Mary Baker depositions; *Arkansas State Gazette and Democrat*, 18 February 1858, 2/2; *Daily Alta California*, 1 November 1857, 1/3. Nephi Johnson testified that the Fancher party brought the first longhorn cattle to Utah. See Bishop, ed., *Mormonism Unveiled*, 352, 364.

37. "Mountain Meadow Massacre," *Fort Smith Elevator*, 20 August 1897, 2/3; "The Mountain Meadow Massacre," *Daily Arkansas Gazette*, 1 September 1875, 3/1.

38. Joseph B. Baines and William C. Beller, 1860 Affidavits.

39. James Deshazo deposition, 23 October 1860, 1860 Affidavits.

40. Parker, *Recollections of the Mountain Meadows Massacre*, 5.

41. Logan, "The Mountain Meadows Massacre," 26; Mary Baker and William C. Beller, 1860 Affidavits. P. K. Jacoby told of his travels with the party in "Lee's Victims: The Families Murdered at Mountain Meadows," *San Jose Pioneer*, 21 April 1877, 1/5–6.

42. Historians often refer to the Baker-Fancher party, but this work calls it the Fancher party.

43. "Lee's Victims: The Families Murdered at Mountain Meadows," *San Jose Pioneer*, 21 April 1877, 1/6.

44. Malinda Cameron Scott Thurston charged in 1877 that "Mormons, under the authority of Brigham Young," killed eleven of her relatives and captured four more. Thurston said George Baker "was the captain of the company." Her Indian depredation case dragged on for almost thirty-five years. See Thurston statements in the National Archives, cited hereafter as Thurston Claim.

45. Logan, *Mountain Heritage*, 27; Parker, *Recollections of the Mountain Meadows Massacre*, 12; Fielding Wilburn and F. M. Rowan, 1860 Affidavits.

46. Fielding Wilburn and F. M. Rowan, 1860 Affidavits. The Poteet family survived the trip. See McEuen, *The Legend of Francis Marion Poteet and the Mountain Meadows Massacre*.

47. "Public Meeting," *Arkansas State Gazette and Democrat*, 27 February 1858, 3/1.

48. "How Not to Do It," *Arkansas State Gazette and Democrat*, 18 February 1858, 2/1.

49. Martha Elizabeth Baker Terry in Greenhaw, "Survivor of a Massacre," *Arkansas State Gazette and Democrat*, 4 September 1938, cited as Elizabeth Baker Terry Memoir.

50. Memorial Program; Logan, "New Light on the Mountain Meadows Caravan," 236–37.

51. Parker, *Life and Adventures*, 58, and *Recollections*, 12; Deposition, 2 May 1911, in Thurston Claim, 8; "Letter from Angel's Camp," *Daily Alta California*, 1 November 1857, 1/3.

52. For the Cherokee Trail, see Fletcher, Fletcher, and Whiteley, eds., *Cherokee Trail Diaries*; Whiteley, *The Cherokee Trail*; McArthur, *Arkansas in the Gold Rush*, 101–13.

53. Thomas J. to Elizabeth Litton, 19 June 1857, Atkinson, "Cattle Drives from Arkansas to California," 54–55.

54. Parker, *Life and Adventures*, 59–60. More reliably, S. B. Honea reported that on 20 June 1857 "Rappaho Indians" on the Arkansas River raided "the company of Captain Henry of Texas, who lost 151 head of cattle." See "More Outrages!!" *Los Angeles Star*, 24 October 1857, 2.

55. Apostle Wilford Woodruff noted that these Cheyenne raiders "stole 800 fat cattle" from the army. "Some said that they believed that those Indians who stole the cattle were half mormon." See Kenney, ed., *Wilford Woodruff's Journal*, 6 September 1857, 5:89–90.

56. "Lee's Victims," *San Jose Pioneer*, 21 April 1877, 1/6; Parker, *Life and Adventures*, 59–60.

57. John S. Baker, Affidavit, 27 December 1912; *John S. Baker v. the United States and the Cheyenne Indians*. In 1899 the U.S. court of claims awarded Baker $686.

58. "Mormon Immigrants," *Alta California*, 13 November 1856, 2/5. For trail conditions in 1857, see Browne, "The Utah Expedition," 366–67. For Frank King's report of meeting the Fancher party at South Pass, see Gibbs, *The Mountain Meadows Massacre*, 12–13.

59. Stenhouse, *"Tell It All,"* 325.

60. "Lee's Victims," *San Jose Pioneer*, 21 April 1877, 1/5–6.

61. "Dreadful Persecution of Mrs. McLean," *Millennial Star*, 4 July 1857, 429; Stanley, *The Archer of Paradise*, 333.

62. "Sad Story of Mormonism," *New Orleans Bulletin*, in *The Mormon*, 14 March 1857, 2/7; "Dreadful Persecution of Mrs. McLean," *Millennial Star*, 4 July 1857, 429–30.

63. "Murder of Parley P. Pratt," *Millennial Star*, 4 July 1857, 425.

64. Erastus Snow, Journals, March 1857.

65. "The Murder of the Mormon Pratt," *New York Herald*, 31 May 1857.

66. "The Killing of Pratt—Letter from Mr. McLean," *Daily Alta California*, 9 July 1857, 2/1.

67. "The Assassination of President P. P. Pratt," *Western Standard*, 3 July 1857, 2/2.

68. "The Killing of Pratt—Letter from Mr. McLean," *Daily Alta California*, 9 July 1857, 2/1.

69. Stanley, *The Archer of Paradise*, 301–3, 326–30.

70. Journal History, 13 May 1857.

71. "The Killing of Pratt—Letter from Mr. McLean," *Daily Alta California*, 9 July 1857, 2/1.

72. Ibid.

73. Journal History, 29 August 1859, quoting Eleanor McLean letter from the *New York Mormon*.

74. "The Assassination of President P. P. Pratt," *Western Standard*, 3 July 1857, 2/3.

75. Eleanor J. McComb Pratt to Erastus Snow, 14–15 May 1857, LDS Archives.

76. Ibid.

77. Pratt, Account of the death, LDS Archives, 53, 55, 57–58.

78. Carter, ed., *Heart Throbs of the West*, "Journal of Philip Margetts," 6:400.

79. "The Assassination of President P. P. Pratt," *Western Standard*, 3 July 1857, 2/2–3.

80. "The Killing of Pratt—Letter from Mr. McLean," *Daily Alta California*, 9 July 1857, 2/1.

Chapter 5

1. Browne, "The Utah Expedition," 364. For the origins of the conflict, see Poll and MacKinnon, "Causes of the Utah War Reconsidered," 16–44.

2. Tyler to Buchanan, 27 April 1857, in Auchampaugh, *Robert Tyler*, 180–81.

3. Ibid.; Moore, ed., *The Works of James Buchanan*, 10:152–54.

4. Poll, "Thomas L. Kane and the Utah War," 117–18.

5. Wilford Woodruff, 22 February 1857, "Discourse," *Deseret News*, 4 March 1857, 411/2.

6. Hurt to Forney, 4 December 1857, in Buchanan, *Massacre at Mountain Meadows*, Serial 1033, 94–95; Haight, "From Cedar City, Utah Territory," *Western Standard*, 24 April 1857, 3/3–4.

7. Bigler, *Forgotten Kingdom*, 131–32.

8. Furniss, *The Mormon Conflict*, 14, 46; Wheat, *Mapping the Transmississippi West*, 2:169n44; Alexander, *Utah, the Right Place*, 121.

9. Furniss, *The Mormon Conflict*, 57–59. The court records were allegedly returned to federal officials in 1858. Interestingly, the Department of Justice files for Utah Territory before 1870 cannot be found in the National Archives.

10. Brooks, ed., *On the Mormon Frontier*, 2:621–22.

11. Browne, "The Utah Expedition," 363.

12. For Drummond's 30 March 1857 letter to Attorney General J. S. Black and its effect, see Buchanan, *The Utah Expedition*, Serial 956, 212–14; Furniss, *The Mormon Conflict*, 55–57.

13. Arrington, *The Mormons in Nevada*, 25.

14. "Manufacturing Pistols and Gunpowder," *Deseret News*, 12 May 1858, 50/2.

15. Brigham Young, "Remarks," *Deseret News*, 15 April 1857, 44/4.

16. Arrington, *Charles C. Rich*, 205; "Letter from San Bernardino," *San Francisco Bulletin*, 12 November 1857, 2/3.

17. "Militia of Utah," *Deseret News*, 8 April 1857, 37/1–3; "Minutes," *Deseret News*, 15 April 1857, 43/3; "Head Quarters Nauvoo Legion," *Deseret News*, 15 April 1857, 48/2–3.

18. Bigler, "The Crisis at Fort Limhi, 1858," 130.

19. Bigler, *Forgotten Kingdom*, 137–39, 143–44; Brigham Young, "Remarks," *Deseret News*, 15 April 1857, 45/1; "Excursion to Fort Limhi," *Deseret News*, 3 June 1857, 108/4–109/3.

20. Bigler, "Garland Hurt," 163.

21. Bigler, "The Crisis at Fort Limhi, 1858," 133.

22. Bluth, "The Salmon River Mission," 906; "Excursion to Fort Limhi," *Deseret News*, 3 June 1857, 109/1.

23. Abraham Zundel, Diary, 1856–1858, 5; Shurtliff, Life and Travels, 19.

24. Clark, Israel Justus Clark's Journal, 147–48; Bluth, "The Salmon River Mission," 813–14, 906.

25. Young and Kimball, "Remarks," *Deseret News*, 10 June 1857, 107–8.

26. George A. Smith, 31 May 1857, *Journal of Discourses*, 4:332; Journal History, 10 June 1857.

27. Furniss, *The Mormon Conflict*, 63, 70; Cooley, ed., *Diary of Brigham Young*, 50.

28. Browne, "The Utah Expedition," 367; Furniss, *The Mormon Conflict*, 96–97.

29. Douglas, *Remarks*, 12–13.

30. Scott to Adjutant General et al., 28 May 1857; Lay to Harney, 29 June 1857, Buchanan, *The Utah Expedition*, Serial 956, 4, 7; Browne, "The Utah Expedition," 365.

31. Burr, Journal 1857–58, 24 June 1857; Furniss, *The Mormon Conflict*, 61.

32. Kenny, ed., *Wilford Woodruff's Journal*, 5:69; Schindler, *Orrin Porter Rockwell*, 246–47. How Eleanor Pratt crossed the 1,100-mile trail so quickly was long a mystery, but Thomas, ed., *Elias Smith's Journal,* 23 July 1857, provides the answer.

33. "The 24th of July," *Deseret News*, 29 July 1857, 165/4; Historical Department Journals, LDS Archives, 20–24 July 1857; Browne, "The Utah Expedition," 368.

34. Brigham Young, 13 September 1857, *Journal of Discourses*, 5:227–28. No known 1847 source reports Young's prophecy.

35. Heber C. Kimball, 26 July 1857, *Journal of Discourses*, 5:95, 96.

36. Cooley, ed., *Diary of Brigham Young*, 54; Kenney, ed., *Wilford Woodruff's Journal*, 5:70.

37. Kenney, ed., *Wilford Woodruff's Journal*, 5:71; Eleanor J. Pratt, Account of the death of Parley P. Pratt, 55, 57; Historical Department Journals, LDS Archives. Pratt read her story of the murder to Woodruff on 24 August, but the surviving version now in LDS Archives may be a revised account composed in April 1860 at the request of George A. Smith. See Pratt, "Eleanor McLean," 254.

38. Pratt, Account of the death of Parley P. Pratt, 27, 40–42.

39. Ibid.

40. "Murder of Parley P. Pratt," *Millennial Star*, 4 July 1857, 428.

41. Young to N. V. Jones, 4 August 1857, Brigham Young Collection, LDS Archives, 764.

42. Young to Hamblin, 4 August 1857; D. B. Huntington, Journal, 1857; Higbee, To My Family, Mountain Meadows File, LDS Archives, 2.

43. Brigham Young, August 2 1857, *Journal of Discourses*, 5: 98–99.

44. Brigham Young, "Remarks," 13 September 1857, *Deseret News*, 228/3–4; 229/1–3.

45. Young to Cannon, Young to Jones, 4 August 1857; Young to Eldredge, Young to Appleby, 8 August 1857, Brigham Young Collection, LDS Archives.

46. Young to Loveland and the Brethren, 15 August 1857, Brigham Young Collection, LDS Archives, 795–96.

47. George A. Smith, 2 August, *Journal of Discourses*, 5:110.

48. Journal History, 3 August 1857; Historical Department Journals, 3 August 1857.

49. "Interview with Brigham Young," *Deseret News*, 12 May 1877.

50. Mowry, Letters to Bicknall, 17 September 1854, Utah State Historical Society.

51. Wells to Dame, 1 August 1857, Palmer Collection, Southern Utah University.

52. "Diary of George A. Smith," in Jarvis, *Ancestry, Biography, and Family of George A. Smith*, 215; Brooks, *Mountain Meadows Massacre*, 31–32.

53. Alter and Dwyer, eds., "Journal of Captain Albert Tracy," 62.

54. Young to Brunson, Haight et al., 2 August 1857, Brigham Young Collection, LDS Archives, 732. Young and Smith later swore they only restricted selling grain for animals, not food for people.

55. Young to S. Smith, Richards, and Partridge, 4 August 1857, Brigham Young Collection, LDS Archives, 747.

56. "Diary of George A. Smith," in Jarvis, *Ancestry*, 215; George A. Smith sermon of 13 September 1857, *Deseret News*, 23 September 1857, 227/1.

57. Brooks, *Mountain Meadows Massacre*, 35.

58. Elias Morris, Statement, 2 February 1892, Mountain Meadows File, LDS Archives. John D. Lee claimed Samuel Lewis was at Mountain Meadows, but Krenkel, ed., *The Life and Times of Joseph Fish*, 55–57, reveals he was among the scouts sent to guard the eastern passes.

59. "Diary of George A. Smith," in Jarvis, *Ancestry*, 216; James Martineau Record, 1855 to 1860, 23–24; and George A. Smith, *Deseret News*, 23 September 1857, 227/1.

60. Ibid.; Journal of Rachel Andora Woolsey Lee, BYU typescript, 47.

61. Martineau, "Trip to the Santa Clara," *Deseret News*, 23 September 1857, 227/3–4. The "leap" was named for Peter Shirts, the "jump up" for Isaac Haight, and the "twist" for Jacob Hamblin.

62. Ibid., 227/4; George A. Smith, *Deseret News*, 23 September 1857, 227/1.

63. Smith, ed., *Six Decades in the Early West*, 26; Wells to Dame, 13 August 1857, Palmer Collection, Southern Utah University.

64. Martineau, "Trip to the Santa Clara," *Deseret News*, 23 September 1857, 227/4; and George A. Smith, *Deseret News*, 23 September 1857, 227/1–2.

65. Ibid., 227/1; Bishop, ed., *Mormonism Unveiled*, 222–23.

66. Ibid., 223–24.

67. Ibid., 224; "Lee's Last Confession. His Version of the Mountain Meadows Massacre," *San Francisco Daily Bulletin Supplement*, 24 March 1877, 1/2, (hereafter "Lee's Last Confession").

68. Carleton, *Special Report*, Serial 4377, 9.

69. Brooks, *Mountain Meadows Massacre*, 63–64.

70. Bishop, ed., *Mormonism Unveiled*, 225.

71. Jacob Hamblin Journal, 36–37.

72. Young to Allen and Young to Haight, 4 August 1857, Brigham Young Collection, LDS Archives, 742, 745–46.

73. Brooks, *Mountain Meadows Massacre*, 34–35. Less than a year later Young's letters to Haight and Allen fell into the hands of newspaper correspondent Albert G. Browne, who thought they "add to the light which has already been thrown on the Santa Clara massacre." "It appears Brigham Young did not consider Elder Allen a man of sufficient ability for the work which he intended should be performed at his mission." Browne called Jacob Hamblin "a man without conscientious scruple or physical fear." See "Letter from the Utah Army," *New York Daily Tribune*, 7 July 1858.

74. Journal of Jacob Hamblin, 37.

75. "Diary of George A. Smith," in Jarvis, *Ancestry*, 217–18.

76. John D. Lee Trials Transcript, Papers of W. L. Cook, Library of Congress, 254. Cited as Lee Trials Transcript.

77. Smith to St. Clair, 25 November 1869, LDS Archives, 941.

78. Brigham Young and Heber C. Kimball, 2 August 1857, *Journal of Discourses*, 5:99-100, 132.

79. Madsen, *Gold Rush Sojourners*, 31; Unruh, *The Plains Across*, 303–12. The longer overlanders stayed in Utah, the less they enjoyed their sojourn among the Mormons. Most visitors agreed with John Hawkin Clark's 1852 observation: Salt Lake "cost nothing to get in, but a great deal to get out."

80. Except where noted, the following quotes in this section are from the manuscript minutes of Brigham Young's 16 August 1857 sermon, Brigham Young Collection, LDS Archives. To capture Young's original speech, I used Watt's original transcription rather than his corrections.

81. Brigham Young, 9 August 1857, *Journal of Discourses*, 5:127.

82. As noted, these statements are from Brigham Young's unpublished 16 August 1857 sermon. Young's threat was exaggerated. John D. Unruh's definitive study, *The Plains Across*, 185, estimated Indians killed about thirty-seven emigrants in 1856–57 out of an estimated 14,500 who traveled to the West Coast. Unruh did not attribute the Fancher party deaths to Indians.

83. This concludes material from Brigham Young's 16 August 1857 discourse.

84. D. B. Huntington, Journal, 1857, 4. Subsequent quotes are from Huntington's journal.

85. Ibid., 8–9, 23–25.

86. Young, 16 August 1857 Minutes, Brigham Young Collection; D. B. Huntington, Journal, 1857, 10–13

87. Morgan, "Washakie and the Shoshoni," 27:65n105; Ackley, "Across the Plains in 1858," 223n4.

88. D. B. Huntington, Journal, 1857, 10–13; Hurt to Forney, 4 December 1857, in Buchanan, *Massacre at Mountain Meadows*, Serial 1033, 96–97.

89. "Scalping a Woman on the Plains," *San Francisco Bulletin*, 19 September 1857, 2/2, Typescript, California State Library. Not long after, this Mrs. Holloway died in Napa City, "quietly mad." See Morgan, *The Humboldt*, 212–13.

90. "More Mormon Massacres," *Daily Alta California*, 1 November 1857, 2/2.

91. *The California Farmer*, 30 October 1857, 128/1-2.

92. "More Mormon Atrocities," *San Francisco Herald*, 11 November 1857, 3/2, from Charles Kelly typescript of McLeod's statement of 9 November 1857 in the California State Library.

93. "Perils of the Plains," *San Francisco Herald*, 21 October 1857, 2/4.

94. Kenney, ed., *Wilford Woodruff's Journal*, 26 August 1857, 5:83, 84.

CHAPTER 6

1. Myres, ed., *Ho for California!* 103, 106, 117. For more on defecting Mormons in 1857, see entries 1598, 1602, 1605, 1610, and 1614 in Mattes, *Platte River Road Narratives*.

2. Browne, "The Utah Expedition," 367; Journal of Frederick H. Burr, 24 June 1857.

3. "Letter from Angel's Camp," *Alta California*, 1 November 1857, 1/3.

4. "Lee's Victims," *San Jose Pioneer*, 21 April 1877, 1/6, mentioned "the Reeds from Missouri, comprising Reed senior and his family, and his son and family." The 1990 Memorial Program listed John Perkins Reed among the victims, although the specific identification was dropped from the 1999 program.

5. Gibbs, *The Mountain Meadows Massacre*, 12; for Cecil's birth, see Shirley McFadzean to author, 12 February 1997, copy in author's possession.

6. Stenhouse, *The Rocky Mountain Saints*, 424, 427–28, 456; and *"Tell It All,"* 324–25. Eli Kelsey was Fanny Stenhouse's source.

7. For the "Dutchman," see *Los Angeles Star*, 7 November 1857, 2/2; Whitney, *History of Utah*, 2:800; Hawley, Autobiography, 15.

8. "The Immigrant Massacre," *Daily Alta California*, 17 October 1857, 1/1. The witnesses said the party included a group of Missourians, but they knew nothing about them.

9. Brigham Young, 26 July 1857, *Journal of Discourses*, 5:75, 78.

10. "The Late Horrible Massacre," *Los Angeles Star*, October 17, 1857, 2/2.

11. Journal History, 20 July 1857; Historical Department Journals, July–August 1857, LDS Archives.

12. Furniss, *The Mormon Conflict*, 46; Landon to Burr, 18 September 1857, in Buchanan, *The Utah Expedition*, Serial 956, 122–23.

13. For the 3 August date, see Historical Department Journals, August 1857; Malinda Cameron Scott Thurston Thompson's 15 October 1877 deposition and her 2 May 1911 statement in Record Group 123, Indian Depredation Claim 8479, National Archives, cited as Thurston Claim. She made these statements at 48 and 83 years of age. Other sources give 4 and 5 August as the date the Fancher party arrived in Salt Lake.

14. Brown, Journal, 4 August 1857, Huntington Library. This statement indicates the war policy of refusing to sell supplies to emigrants was more strictly enforced than previously recognized.

15. Stenhouse, *"Tell It All,"* 326.

16. Gibbs, *Lights and Shadows of Mormonism*, 211; Whitney, *History of Utah*, 2:790; "Mormon Murders," *Salt Lake Tribune*, 26 November 1874, cited in Fielding and Fielding, *The Trials of John D. Lee*, 17.

17. Bancroft, *History of Utah*, 547.

18. Kenney, ed., *Wilford Woodruff's Journal*, 1 August 1857, 5:71; "An Open Letter to Brigham Young," *Daily Corinne Reporter,* 15 July 1871, 2/3. If the widow Pratt actually made such a charge, it was false.

19. Parker, *Life and Adventures*, 62. In *Recollections of the Mountain Meadows Massacre*, 8–9, Parker wrote that Baker's train "was almost threatened in my presence."

20. Young to Cannon, 4 August 1857, Brigham Young Collection, LDS Archives, 736.

21. *Deseret News*, 12 May 1877. The story appeared in Bancroft, *History of Utah*, 547, and has been repeated as gospel ever since.

22. Depositions of 15 October and 18 December 1877 and 2 May 1911, in Thurston Claim, 4, 11. Wilford Woodruff apparently noted the Scott murder in his journal on 9 August 1857: "[Some emigrants had] killed each other. The survivers asked Thomas Dunn if they would be taken up for it. He said no if they would keep on doing so." Coates, The Fancher-Baker Train, 11, reported the 10 August birth of a baby girl to Mrs. Scott.

23. Carleton, *Special Report*, Serial 4377, 3; Bancroft, *History of Utah*, 547.

24. For a powerful example of the usefulness of such an approach, see "Chronology, 1857" in White, ed., *News of the Plains and the Rockies*, 4:215–26.

25. For Leach, see his 22 December 1856 affidavit and Jackson, *Wagon Roads West*, 143.

26. Jenson, *LDS Biographical Encyclopedia*, 3:131–32. Johnson described Leach's road building in his autobiography, typescript in author's possession, 2, 4, 5. Note that this document differs from The Life Sketch of Nephi Johnson (From His Diary) now in LDS Archives. The location of Johnson's actual diary is not known. Johnson's rank comes from Muster Rolls, 10 October 1857, Nauvoo Legion, Utah State Archives, 3346.

27. Flint, "Diary of Dr. Thomas Flint," 39, 48.

28. Ibid., 53, 58.

29. Utah territorial law dictated that anyone who "shall swear, by the name of God, or Jesus Christ, in any manner using their names profanely," could be fined five dollars "or be imprisoned at the discretion of the court." See Morgan, *The State of Deseret*, 178.

30. McQuarrie to Lund, Mountain Meadows File, LDS Archives.

31. John Fancher descendant Ronald E. Loving developed this theory in "Captain John Baker," 2. Burr Fancher arrived at the same conclusion. See Fancher, *Westward with the Sun*, 249.

32. "Argus," quoted in Stenhouse, *The Rocky Mountain Saints*, 432.

33. P. M. Warn statement in "The Late Horrible Massacre," *Los Angeles Star,* 17 October 1857, 2/4.

34. *Deseret News*, 23 January 1856, cited in Brooks, *Mountain Meadows Massacre*, 21–22.

35. Smith Deposition, 30 July 1875, Brooks, *Mountain Meadows Massacre*, 288–89.

36. P. M. Warn statement, "The Late Horrible Massacre," *Los Angeles Star,* 17 October 1857, 2/4.

37. J. G. McQuarrie told Wood's story to Will Lund. See Mountain Meadows File, LDS Archives.

38. See the notices by Aden's brother and father in the *Valley Tan*, 8 June 1859 and 3 August 1859, 4/2; Gibbs, *The Mountain Meadows Massacre*, 12; and Dr. S. B. Aden to Young, 14 March 1859, cited in Moorman and Sessions, *Camp Floyd and the Mormons*, 130, but not now available at LDS Archives.

39. Diary of Samuel Pitchforth, 15 and 17 August 1857, 50, 51; Bigler, *Forgotten Kingdom*, 166. Bigler located Pitchforth's daily diary, which is the only known contemporary LDS record that mentions the Fancher party before the massacre.

40. Arrington, Fox, and May, *Building the City of God*, 64–68; Brooks, ed., *Journal of the Southern Indian Mission*, 126. See 164–65 in Brooks for the Robinson deed consecrating their property in Pinto.

41. Browne, "The Utah Expedition," 362.

42. Brigham Young, 16 September 1855, *Journal of Discourses*, 3:6; Arrington, Fox, and May, *Building the City of God*, 71; Derry, "Autobiography of Elder Charles Derry," 425.

43. Parley P. Pratt and Brigham Young, 27 March 1853, *Journal of Discourses*, 1:83, 85.

44. "The Emigrant Massacre" and "Topics of the Day," *San Francisco Herald*, 15 October 1857, 2/1–2. The article confused Orson Hyde with the actual mail carrier, William Hyde.

45. Discursive Remarks, Utah State Historical Society.

46. "More Outrages on the Plains!!" *Los Angeles Star*, 24 October 1857, 2; "The Late Outrages on the Plains," *Los Angeles Star*, 7 November 1857, 2/2. This company approximated the size of the Fancher party, and two-thirds of its members were women and children.

47. Kenney, ed., *Wilford Woodruff's Journal*, 5:82; "Letter from San Bernardino," *San Francisco Bulletin*, 12 November 1857, 2/3; Mathews to Young, 7 October 1857, Brigham Young Collection, LDS Archives; Lyman, *San Bernardino*, 350, 362.

48. "The Late Horrible Massacre," *Los Angeles Star*, October 17, 1857, 2/2. As it approached San Bernardino in October, Dukes's train "consisted of seventy-one souls; Men, 27; women, 17; children 22." See "Letter from San Bernardino," *San Francisco Bulletin*, 12 November 1857, 2/3.

49. Ray to *Mountaineer*, 4 December 1859, unprocessed item, LDS Archives, 1–2. According to George A. Smith, Dr. John A. Ray was in England when the events he reported allegedly occurred. Ray provided his account in December 1859 at the request of Albert Carrington, editor of the *Deseret News*, as LDS leaders reacted to national pressure to explain the massacre.

50. Bigler, "Garland Hurt," 154, 157.

51. "Argus," in Stenhouse, *The Rocky Mountain Saints*, 433.

52. Ray to *Mountaineer*, 4 December 1859, LDS Archives, 3.

53. LDS Historian's Office Journal, 25 August 1857.

54. Smith to St. Clair, 25 November 1869, LDS Archives. Smith wrote in 1869 that the emigrants increased their guard from eight to ten men.

55. Carleton, *Special Report*, Serial 4377, 2–3.

56. Ray to *Mountaineer*, 4 December 1859, LDS Archives, 2.

57. "The Late Horrible Massacre," *Los Angeles Star*, 17 October 1857, 2/2-3. Emigrants later denounced this account of the massacre by Christian, William Mathews's son-in-law.

58. Forney, "Annual Report" in Serial 1023, *Message from the President*, 1859, 1:738. See also Buchanan, *The Utah Expedition*, Serial 956.

59. Elizabeth Brittain Knowlton, Reminiscences, 1857–1907, 1:75. Punctuation added.

60. Smith to Stenhouse, 15 April 1859, LDS Archives, 764–65.

61. Smith to St. Clair, 25 November 1869, LDS Archives.

62. Roberts, *Comprehensive History*, 4:147n118; Lee Trials Transcripts, 429.

63. Smith to St. Clair, 25 November 1869; Ray to *Mountaineer*, 4 December 1859, LDS Archives, 4.

64. Carleton, *Special Report*, Serial 4377, 3; Smith to St. Clair, 25 November 1869, LDS Archives; Brooks, *Mountain Meadows Massacre*, 51, 254; and Gibbs, *Lights and Shadows of Mormonism*, 238.

65. Carleton, *Special Report*, 3; Ray to *Mountaineer*, 4 December 1859, LDS Archives, 4.

66. Vital Statistics, Proctor Hancock Robison, Ancestral File, Family History Library.

67. Utah Stake Minutes, General Meetings 1855-1860, 27 September 1857, LDS Archives.

68. "The Late Horrible Massacre," *Los Angeles Star*, 17 October 1857, 2/2.

69. Ibid.; Ann Gordge Lee, Autobiography, BYU Library, 4–5. Mrs. Lee also claimed that she roamed the West with Geronimo and Billy the Kid. She accused the Mormons themselves of poisoning the wells; one of the Arkansans' children "took a drink of the water and died in a few minutes." The Mormons would not give the emigrants "lumber to make a Coffin for the Child."

70. Forney's Report, Brooks, *Mountain Meadows Massacre*, 255.

71. Flint, "Diary of Dr. Thomas Flint," 53; and Kelly, Utah's Black Friday, 13.

72. Brooks, *Mountain Meadows Massacre*, 48.

73. "Letter from San Bernardino," *San Francisco Bulletin*, 12 November 1857, 2/3.

74. Hallwas and Launius, eds., *Cultures in Conflict*, 292.

75. William McBride, Report, 24 June 1851, Territorial Militia Records, ST-27, Reel 3, Document 1,328, Utah State Archives.

76. Author's conversations with Floyd A. O'Neil and Dennis Defa, 9 June 1996.

77. Forney to Greenwood, August 1859, Buchanan, *Massacre at Mountain Meadows*, Serial 1033, 76.

78. Esplin and Jessee, "The Mormon Reaction," 26; Alexander, *Utah, the Right Place*, 130.

79. Jacob Hamblin, Journals and Letters, BYU Library, 46. Hamblin's "daybook" was the source for the edited version of Hamblin's journal long held at LDS Archives. Smith's comment appears to be the reason a page was cut from the LDS Archives copy of the document.

80. "Diary of George A. Smith," in Jarvis, *Ancestry*, 217; S. S. Smith testimony, Lee Trials Transcripts, 380, 396–97; Lockley, *The Lee Trial*, 22. George A. Smith may have invented the story. Perhaps he devised the poison story to provide a motive for the anticipated "Indian" attack; at least his reworking of the tale over almost two decades makes his role suspect. Such an interpretation fits into the long human tradition of projecting one's own worst sins—in this case, poisoning Indians—onto one's enemies.

81. Bigler first made this observation in *Forgotten Kingdom*, 167. My averages are slightly different. Altitudes are from the Utah Map of State Roads.

82. Robert Kershaw testimony, Lee Trials Transcripts, 260–61; Dunn, *Massacres of the Mountains*, 254. See also Kelly, Utah's Black Friday, 14.

83. McQuarrie to Lund, Mountain Meadows File, LDS Archives.

84. Autobiography of John Pierce Hawley, Community of Christ Archives, 15.

85. Utah Stake Minutes, 30 August 1857, 668–69, LDS Archives. Smith's comment on the Danites is basically accurate. After 1838 LDS church internal security had no formal organization and was replaced by a loose fraternity of "b'hoys" that included Porter Rockwell, Bill Hickman, Eph Hanks, and Howard Egan. Also called "Destroying Angels," Samuel Clemens described them as "Latter-Day Saints who are set apart by the Church to conduct permanent disappearances of obnoxious citizens." See Clemens, *Roughing It*, 1:110.

86. Utah Stake Minutes, 30 August 1857, 671. Punctuation added. Blackburn specifically identified emigrants as "our enemies."

87. Kenney, ed., *Wilford Woodruff's Journal*, 5:82–83, 87.

88. "Diary of George A. Smith," in Jarvis, *Ancestry*, 217. The day before the attack at Mountain Meadows, Sunday, 6 September 1857, the LDS Historical Office Journal recorded that Smith spent part of the day "writing letters to Wm. H. Dame." The letters do not survive in LDS Archives.

89. Jacob Hamblin—Journals and Letters, 46–47.

90. D. B. Huntington, Journal, 1857–1859, 13–14; Journal History, 1 September 1857; and Smith, *Accounts of Brigham Young*, Serial 1128, 97.

91. D. B. Huntington, Journal, 1857–1859, 13–15; and Cooley, ed., *Diary of Brigham Young*, 71.

92. See The Fancher-Baker Train, 14, by Lawrence G. Coates, professor of history at the LDS church's Ricks College, now part of Brigham Young University.

93. Kenney, ed., *Wilford Woodruff's Journal*, 26 August 1857, 5:84.

94. Wheeler, "The Late James Gemmell," 334. For evidence from the Brigham Young papers that Gemmell was aware of "what Conversation took place" in that fateful meeting, see chapter 15.

95. On 11 September 1857, D. B. Huntington submitted a voucher for lodging Indians visiting the superintendent of Indian affairs at Salt Lake between 8 August and 1 September, indicating that the Paiutes left the city soon after their meeting with Young. See Brooks, *John Doyle Lee*, 203.

96. Smith, ed., *Six Decades in the Early West*, 27. The next line, "this company was afterwards massacred at Mountain Meadows," reveals that the entry was composed after the fact, perhaps to support Smith's testimony at the Lee trial. Yet the document provides one of the few credible dates to track the travels of the Fancher party, and the journals of Smith and Rachel Lee both indicate that the Arkansans reached Mountain Meadows on 6 September.

97. Silas Smith testimony, Lee Trials Transcripts, 380.

98. Argus, in Stenhouse, *The Rocky Mountain Saints*, 432–34.

99. Baskin, *Reminiscences of Early Utah*, 112, citing testimony of James McGuffie. Gibbs, *The Mountain Meadows Massacre*, 17–18, told the story with different details.

100. Leany, Sr., to Steele, 17 February 1883, John Steele Papers, BYU Library.

101. Krenkel, ed., *The Life and Times of Joseph Fish*, 59, 69.

102. Hawley, Autobiography, Community of Christ Archives, 16.

103. Moorman and Sessions, *Camp Floyd and the Mormons*, 134.

104. Elvira Martineau Johnson, in Brimhall, Gleanings Concerning John D. Lee, 33. His daughter recalled that James Martineau "would cry about it whenever he spoke of" the massacre.

105. For these orders, see Samuel Knight's account in Abraham H. Cannon, Journal, 15 June 1895, 19:98; and Nephi Johnson to Anthon H. Lund, 18 March 1910, Mountain Meadows File, LDS Archives. Knight believed his orders "could not be disobeyed without imperiling his own life."

106. Rogerson, The Guilt of John D. Lee, Mountain Meadows File, LDS Archives, 4.

107. Higbee, To My Family, Mountain Meadows File, LDS Archives, 2.

108. Gibbs, *The Mountain Meadows Massacre*, 18. Bishop Philip Klingensmith saw "three or four [emigrants] at the mill getting grist done with some wheat that they had bought from Mr. Jackson." He apparently excommunicated Walker. See Backus, *Mountain Meadows Witness*, 112.

109. Alexander, review of David L. Bigler's *Forgotten Kingdom*, 421.

110. McQuarrie to Lund, Mountain Meadows File, LDS Archives.

111. Charles Willden affidavit, Mountain Meadows File, LDS Archives. Historian Donald Moorman apparently had access to an earlier and more complete version of this collection than the one now available, since many of the items he cited cannot be located at LDS Archives.

112. Brimhall, Gleanings Concerning John D. Lee, 31.

113. Brooks, *Mountain Meadows Massacre*, 56. Local historian William Palmer told Parry's story decades after the event.

114. Morris statement in Mountain Meadows File, LDS Archives; "Lee's Last Confession," 1/2.

115. Sudweeks, Laban Morrill History, 8.

116. Moorman's *Camp Floyd and the Mormons* contains a virtual catalog of southern Utah's Mountain Meadows lore collected by LDS historians in the late nineteenth century. In commenting on the manuscript of *Blood of the Prophets*, Moorman's editor, Gene Sessions, wrote, "The great mass of such tales came forth in the aftermath of the event and simply cannot be corroborated in the contemporary record."

117. White, ed., *News of the Plains and the Rockies*, 4:218–19. White referred to stories told by Brooks, Carleton, and Moorman.

118. Gibbs, *Lights and Shadows of Mormonism*, 238.

119. Brooks, *Mountain Meadows Massacre*, 108.

120. Elias Morris statement in Mountain Meadows File, LDS Archives.

121. Bishop, ed., *Mormonism Unveiled*, 218–21, 226. Lee dated this meeting to both a Saturday and Sunday night "about" 7 September, which was actually the Monday the attack began. If it took place at all, the meeting at the mill occurred before Lee began threshing his grain on 31 August. See Diary of Rachel Andora Woolsey Lee, BYU Typescript, 47.

122. Nephi Johnson to Anthon H. Lund, March 1910, Mountain Meadows File, LDS Archives.

123. Brimhall, Gleanings Concerning John D. Lee, 28.

124. Campbell to Jenson, 24 January 1892, Moorman and Sessions, *Camp Floyd and the Mormons*, 132–33. Moorman also cited an 1896 Samuel Knight affidavit. Like many sources Moorman apparently saw at LDS Archives, these documents are not in the current collection.

125. Bishop, ed., *Mormonism Unveiled*, 226, 243. Lee later made Shirts "suffer for being a coward" and extracted further vengeance in his memoir. Shirts told Mahonri Steele that Lee hated him because he refused to help kill the emigrants. See Beckwith, "Why John D. Lee Called . . . Carl Shirts, a Coward," in Shameful Friday, Huntington Library.

126. John Higbee, Statement, Mountain Meadows File, LDS Archives.

127. Moorman and Sessions, *Camp Floyd and the Mormons*, 43, citing John C. Chatterley to Andrew Jenson, 18 September 1919, LDS Archives. This document cannot be located at LDS Archives.

128. Hawley, Autobiography, Community of Christ Archives, 16. Hawley's memoir was written years later in Iowa after his conversion to the Reorganized Church of Jesus Christ of Latter Day Saints (RLDS, Community of Christ since 6 April 2001). Its chronology is confusing, but his account indicates that the charge that the emigrants boasted of killing Joseph Smith preceded them. John D. Lee listed Hawley as a participant in the massacre.

129. Ibid.

130. Ibid.

131. Brooks, *Mountain Meadows Massacre*, 52, citing Cedar Ward Records at LDS Archives.

132. Diary of Rachel Woolsey Lee, Huntington Library, 55. This diary contradicts Lee's later accounts and provides the best contemporary evidence of the date of Lee's initial attack on the emigrants, but it is difficult to interpret. The entry reads "Decr 5," although it falls between entries dated August and Sunday, "6 Sept." The bottom of the page is torn. The complete text is "Decr 5th [6?] the threshers have completed thrashing all the wheat at this place which amounted to 1000 Bushels. Sunday the thrashing machine ret [tear]. Bro: J. D. Lee went on an expedition South [tear]." The BYU typescript of Rachel Lee's diary transcribed the date as 5, but Brooks, *Mountain Meadows Massacre*, 66, dated the entry to 6 September.

133. William Rogers statement, *Valley Tan*, 29 February 1860, 3/2.

134. Brimhall, Gleanings Concerning John D. Lee, 31.

135. Benjamin Platt's account, from Gibbs, *The Mountain Meadows Massacre,* 57.

136. Moorman and Sessions, *Camp Floyd and the Mormons*, 130–31; Gibbs, *The Mountain Meadows Massacre*, 21.

137. Lyford, *The Mormon Problem*, 295. Sources differ on when the emigrants reached Mountain Meadows. Bancroft, *History of Utah*, 549, dated the party's arrival to 5 September. Charles Wandell believed the emigrants took five days to reach the meadows. The militia set out in pursuit, "intending to make the assault at the 'Clara Crossing'." See Stenhouse, *The Rocky Mountains Saints*, 435.

138. See Lt. John G. Chandler's map in Wheat, *Mapping the Transmississippi West*, 4:29.

139. Today's Iron Springs is northwest of Cedar City, but in 1859 Pvt. Tommy Gordon referred to "Iron or Cold Springs" about twenty miles west of Cedar City on Little Pinto Creek. See Cardon, "Mountain Meadows Burial Detachment," 145–46. Pinto Road now bypasses Hamblin's ranch. The Page Ranch, settled by Robert Ritchie in 1858, is on the National Register of Historic Places.

140. Flint, "Diary of Dr. Thomas Flint," 58.

141. Bishop, ed., *Mormonism Unveiled*, 279.

142. Carleton, *Special Report*, Serial 4377, 5, 6.

143. See "Mountain Meadow Massacre," *Deseret News*, 1 December 1869, for "'Cane Spring' in the Mountain Meadows." For the geography, see Cradlebaugh, *Utah and the Mormons*, 17–18.

144. Many reports state that the emigrants camped for several days before the attack, but given the distance and Jesse N. Smith's placing it in Paragonah on 3 September, the earliest date the Fancher train could have arrived at Mountain Meadows is 6 September 1857.

145. Cradlebaugh, *Utah and the Mormons*, 17; and Rogers statement, *Valley Tan*, 29 February 1860, 3/2.

CHAPTER 7

1. Cradlebaugh, *Utah and the Mormons*, 17–18. Had all the raiders been Paiutes, this would have been the end of a typical foray. The reports of Judge John Cradlebaugh and Bvt. Maj. James Carleton of their 1859 investigations are among the earliest and best sources on the events at Mountain Meadows.

2. Sarah Baker Memoir, 15. A ghostwriter apparently helped Mrs. Mitchell compose this article at age eighty-five. Names and ages of the child survivors are from the Memorial Program. For Sarah Baker's statement on the credibility of these young witnesses, see page 150.

3. Cradlebaugh, *Utah and the Mormons*, 18; Carleton, "Special Report," Serial 4377, 4.

4. Bishop, ed., *Mormonism Unveiled*, 239. Lee denied leading the initial attack, but Jacob Hamblin, Nephi Johnson, John Higbee, Orson W. Huntsman, and Apostles Charles Penrose, Anthony Ivins, and Orson Whitney reported Lee led the assault. Like the Mormons, the Paiute chiefs claimed they "were not there when the attack commenced." See Cradlebaugh, *Utah and the Mormons*, 17.

5. Jacob Hamblin, in Carleton, *Special Report*, Serial 4377, 4.

6. Rachael Hamblin, in Ibid., 5.

7. "Lee's Last Confession," 1/3.

8. Nancy Saphrona Huff Cates, "The Mountain Meadow Massacre: Statement of One of the Few Survivors," *Daily Arkansas Gazette*, 1 September 1875, 3/1. Cited as Nancy Huff Memoir.

9. Rebecca Dunlap Evans, "Mountain Meadow Massacre . . . Related by One of the Survivors," *Fort Smith Elevator*, 20 August 1897, 2/1-3. Cited as Rebecca Dunlap Memoir.

10. "'Children of the Massacre' May Meet in Reunion," *Arkansas Sunday Post-Dispatch*, late September 1895, transcribed by Anna Jean Backus from BYU microfilm.

11. Fancher, *Westward with the Sun*, 255; Sarah Baker Memoir; Elizabeth Baker Memoir. Sarah Baker was three and Martha Elizabeth Baker was five years old in 1857.

12. Bishop, ed., *Mormonism Unveiled*, 228. The absence of known white casualties suggests they left the assault to their allies. Lee may have joined the attack, for he later showed off bullet holes in his shirt and straw hat. See "Lee's Last Confession," 1/3; Bishop, ed., *Mormonism Unveiled*, 326–27, 361.

13. Bishop, ed., *Mormonism Unveiled*, 227; Nephi Johnson to Anthon H. Lund, 18 March 1910, Mountain Meadows File, LDS Archives; Cradlebaugh, *Utah and the Mormons*, 17. Clem is called Lemuel in Lee's journals.

14. Bishop, ed., *Mormonism Unveiled*, 226–28.

15. Jacob Hamblin, in Carleton, *Special Report*, Serial 4377, 5; Rogers statement, *Valley Tan*, 29 February 1860, 2/4.

16. Elias Morris, statement, 2 February 1892, Mountain Meadows File, LDS Archives, 2–3; Laban Morrill testimony, Gibbs, *The Mountain Meadows Massacre*, 48–49. Morris recalled that those who "opposed severe measures were John Morris, Laban Morrill, Hopkins, Pugmire, Elias Morris and others." Kate Carter, longtime president of the Daughters of Utah Pioneers, boasted that she burned the original minutes of this Stake High Council meeting.

17. Elias Morris, statement, 2 February 1892, Mountain Meadows File, LDS Archives, 2–3.

18. Gibbs, *The Mountain Meadows Massacre*, 48; Sudweeks, Laban Morrill History, 10.

19. Klingensmith testimony, Backus, *Mountain Meadows Witness*, 115. Klingensmith testified this meeting took place *before* the Fancher party reached Cedar City.

20. John Frederick Nash, Notebook, MS 4581, LDS Archives. Oddly, no copy of Haight's letter survived; Nash's version may be derived from James Haslam's testimony.

21. For Haslam's account, see Penrose, "Testimony of James Holt Haslam," 84–104. Haslam later served as a trusted employee of Brigham Young. The last chapter of Collins's *Great Western Rides* gives a colorful account of the trip.

22. Hurt to Forney, 4 December 1857, Buchanan, *Massacre at Mountain Meadows*, Serial 1033, 95, confirms that the story of Haslam's ride was not, as one historian put it, "a mere trick of the first presidency." See Bancroft, *History of Utah*, 568.

23. See Tom and Holt, "The Paiute Tribe of Utah," in Cuch, ed., *A History of Utah's American Indians*, 131–39.

24. Carleton, *Special Report*, Serial 4377, 10.

25. "Lee's Last Confession," 1/3. In *Mormonism Unveiled*, 229, Lee said the messenger "was either [Capt. Eliezar] Edwards or [George] Adair."

26. Higbee statement, Brooks, *Mountain Meadows Massacre*, 227.

27. "Lee's Last Confession," 1/3.

28. Ibid. Lee dated their arrival to Wednesday in *Mormonism Unveiled*, 228.

29. Bishop, ed., *Mormonism Unveiled*, 227–28. Lee's list of participants, mostly Indian missionaries, excluded his friends and included personal enemies who were not involved. Ranks are from Muster Rolls, 10 October 1857, Utah State Archives, 3346.

30. James Pearce testimony, Lee Trials Transcripts, 276.

31. Carleton, *Special Report*, Serial 4377, 7.

32. At Mountain Meadows on 14 September 1990, a brief video clip captured LDS apostle Gordon Hinckley saying "seventy-three volunteers from town" were present at the massacre, a number that appears in no source I have seen. See Larry Warren, KUTV, Mountain Meadows News Stories, 1989–1992, videotape in author's possession.

33. Cradlebaugh, *Utah and the Mormons*, 17.

34. "Interview with the Chief of the Beavers," clipping from *San Francisco Morning Call*, 3 August 1875, Ichel Watters Papers, Utah State Historical Society.

35. Brooks, *Mountain Meadows Massacre*, 247; Joel White testimony, Lee Trials Transcripts, 155; Higbee's 1896 "To My Family" statement in Mountain Meadows File, LDS Archives.

36. Moorman and Sessions, *Camp Floyd and the Mormons*, 132, citing a list no longer in the LDS Archives files.

37. Feargus O'Connor Willden Papers, Marriott Library, 4.

38. Wheeler, *Preliminary Report*, 37. Lee named Joe, Tom, Moquetus, and Bill as Indian participants.

39. Forney's Report, Brooks, *Mountain Meadows Massacre*, 255; Gibbs, *The Mountain Meadows Massacre*, 50.

40. Kane, Diary of Colonel Thomas L. Kane, Huntington Library.

41. Smith to John Lyman, 6 January 1858, Typescript, Historian's Office Letterbook, 509–10.

42. Cradlebaugh, *Utah and the Mormons*, 18.

43. Reacting to articles on Mountain Meadows in the *Arkansas Times* in 1984, two BYU history professors claimed southern Utah Mormons "were greatly outnumbered by Indians." See Esplin and Jessee, "The Mormon Reaction," 26. Utah Indian Superintendent Jacob Forney's December 1859 report in "Report of the Secretary of the Interior," in Buchanan, *Message*, Serial 1060, 733, reveals otherwise.

44. "Interview with the Chief of the Beavers," in Watters Papers, Utah State Historical Society. "Mericat" was Mormon-Indian patois for "American."

45. "Lee's Last Confession," 1/3.

46. Ibid.

47. Johnson's accounts contain minor contradictions. These details come from his March 1910 letter to Anthon H. Lund, Mountain Meadows File, LDS Archives, 4.

48. Johnson statement, Brooks, *Mountain Meadows Massacre*, 224.

49. "Lee's Last Confession," 1/3; Higbee statement, Brooks, *Mountain Meadows Massacre*, 228; and "Mountain Meadows: A Review," *San Francisco Daily Bulletin Supplement*, 24 March 1877, 1/6–7.

50. "Lee's Last Confession," 1/3; Rebecca Dunlap Memoir, 2/1.

51. Bishop, ed., *Mormonism Unveiled*, 230; "'Children of the Massacre,'" *Arkansas Sunday Post-Dispatch*, September 1895.

52. Higbee statements, Mountain Meadows File, LDS Archives; Brooks, *Mountain Meadows Massacre*, 227–28.

53. "Mountain Meadow Massacre," *Sacramento Daily Record*, 1 January 1875, McGlashan and McGlashan, eds., *From the Desk of C. F. McGlashan*, 141. See also "Mountain Meadows: A Review," *San Francisco Daily Bulletin Supplement*, 24 March 1877, 1/7.

54. "Lee's Last Confession," 1/3; Higbee statement, Brooks, *Mountain Meadows Massacre*, 228.

55. Josiah Rogerson, "The Guilt of John D. Lee," in Mountain Meadows File, LDS Archives, 5.

56. Morris to Jenson, 2 February 1892, Mountain Meadows File, LDS Archives, 3–4.

57. Brooks, *Mountain Meadows Massacre*, 80.

58. Ibid., 89, 229; Penrose, "Testimony of James Holt Haslam," 102–3. Lee claimed he only learned of Haslam's mission after the massacre. See "Lee's Last Confession," 1/2.

59. Klingensmith statement, Brooks, *Mountain Meadows Massacre*, 239. Bishop Klingensmith never explained if "headquarters" was in Parowan or Salt Lake.

60. Handwritten orders from Dame, D. H. Wells, and Brigham Young survive in William Dame's papers, but his collection contains no orders related to the massacre.

61. Bishop, ed., *Mormonism Unveiled*, 233–34; "The Late Horrible Massacre," *Los Angeles Star*, 17 October 1857, 2/2-3. Dame told Powers he had received an express from the besieged train at 2:00 A.M. on 9 September 1857 asking for assistance. Dame said "the attack on the train commenced on Monday, the 14th of September." "The Late Horrible Massacre," 2/3. This is the best evidence that the massacre occurred a week after the accepted date, but documentary support for the 11 September 1857 date is convincing.

62. This site was called Iron Creek, Little Pinto Creek, Iron Spring, or Cold Spring. *Mormonism Unveiled*, 235, called it Richards Springs, but it was actually named after homesteader Robert Ritchie, who settled on Little Pinto Creek in 1858.

63. Klingensmith statement, Brooks, *Mountain Meadows Massacre*, 239.

64. Remington, "Utah Militia Records," 152. Juanita Brooks guessed that every married massacre participant had received temple endowments. See Brooks to Lambert, 30 September 1957, A. C. Lambert Collection, Marriott Library.

65. Bishop, ed., *Mormonism Unveiled*, 235; "Lee's Last Confession," 1/3. The moon was 83 precent of full on 7 September 1857 and was still 40 percent of full on 11 September. See Oertle, "Mountain Meadows Today," 4.

66. Gibbs, *The Mountain Meadows Massacre*, 28; McGlashan and McGlashan, eds., *From the Desk of C. F. McGlashan*, 141–42; and Dunn, *Massacres of the Mountains*, 257–58, all tell different stories about Aden's mission. McGlashan placed the murder at Pinto, as did Sumner Howard, while Josiah Gibbs placed it at "Leachy spring" about seventeen miles from Mountain Meadows.

67. "Lee's Last Confession," 1/3. Brooks, *Mountain Meadows Massacre*, 71–72, 97–100, combined the stories of the Fancher party messengers. Beginning with John D. Lee, LDS writers credited Aden's murder as the immediate cause of the massacre, since it revealed the Mormon role in the assault. This begs the question: would the emigrants have surrendered if they had certain knowledge that Mormons had killed Aden?

68. Bishop, ed., *Mormonism Unveiled*, 230–31.

69. Ibid. It is impossible to know how much of Lee's story is true. Lee claimed Indians asked him for ammunition to kill the boys, but he told them, "I would kill the first one that made an attempt to injure them. By this act I was able to save the boys."

70. "Lee's Last Confession," 1/3; Carleton, *Special Report*, Serial 4377, 7.

71. Furniss, *The Mormon Conflict*, 105–6; Hammond, ed., *The Utah Expedition*, 54.

72. Cooley, ed., *Diary of Brigham Young*, 78; Van Vliet to Pleasanton, 16 September 1857, in Buchanan, *The Utah Expedition*, Serial 956, 25; Furniss, *The Mormon Conflict*, 106.

73. Brigham Young, 6 September 1857, *Journal of Discourses*, 5:211.

74. Brooks, ed., *On the Mormon Frontier*, 2:636.

75. Van Vliet to Pleasanton, 16 September 1857, in Buchanan, *The Utah Expedition*, Serial 956, 24–25.

76. Bancroft, *History of Utah*, 505–9, 543.

77. Van Vliet to Floyd, 20 November 1857, in Floyd, "Annual Report of the Secretary of War," Serial 920, 37–38; Brigham Young, 13 September 1857, *Journal of Discourses*, 5:232.

78. Penrose, "Testimony of James Holt Haslam," 91–94. At the second John D. Lee trial, Haslam said he arrived at Young's office at 11:00 A.M., not at daybreak. See Penrose, *The Mountain Meadows Massacre*, 44.

79. Hamilton G. Park Statement, October 1906, Mountain Meadows File, LDS Archives.

80. For the text of Young's letter to Haight, see Brooks, *Mountain Meadows Massacre*, 63, citing "Church Letter Book, No. 3," 827–28. In July 1996 I examined the letter on microfilm at LDS Archives. It is out of sequence, falling between two letters dated 7 September 1857 on pages 825 and 829, but this is not uncommon in the letterbook. Reliable sources such as John Hawley confirm that southern Utah militia leaders immediately acted on its instructions.

81. Penrose, *The Mountain Meadows Massacre*, 48; Brooks, *Mountain Meadows Massacre*, 63–65.

82. White, ed., *News of the Plains and the Rockies*, 4:221–22.

83. Young to Denver, 12 September 1857, in Buchanan, *The Utah Expedition*, Serial 956, 184, 205–8.

84. Young to Van Vliet, 11 September 1857, in Floyd, "Annual Report of the Secretary of War," Serial 920, 36–37.

85. Brigham Young, 13 September 1857, *Journal of Discourses*, 5:236.

86. Ibid.

87. Kenney, ed., *Wilford Woodruff's Journal*, 13 September 1857, 5:97.

88. Van Vliet to Pleasanton, 16 September 1857, in Buchanan, *The Utah Expedition*, Serial 956, 24–25.

89. Young to Jeter Clinton, 12 September, Brigham Young Collection, LDS Archives, 839–40.

CHAPTER 8

1. Edwards, Affidavit, 14 May 1924, Utah State Historical Society.

2. Nephi Johnson statement, Brooks, *Mountain Meadows Massacre*, 224.

3. John W. Bradshaw testimony, Lee Trials Transcripts, 239.

4. Johnson statement, Brooks, *Mountain Meadows Massacre*, 224. Johnson testified in 1876 that he reached Hamblin's ranch between 12:00 and 1:00 A.M., but he probably arrived at the meadows earlier. See Bishop, ed., *Mormonism Unveiled*, 340.

5. Bishop, ed., *Mormonism Unveiled*, 232–33; "Lee's Last Confession," 1/3–4.

6. Bishop, ed., *Mormonism Unveiled*, 243. Lee's claim of unanimous support is dubious.

7. Johnson statement, Brooks, *Mountain Meadows Massacre*, 224; Bishop, ed., *Mormonism Unveiled*, 237.

8. Beadle, *Western Wilds*, 500; Lyford, *The Mormon Problem*, 296–302; Brooks, *Mountain Meadows Massacre*, 99. This letter indicates that no "Dutchman" survived to tell of William Aden's murder.

9. "More Outrages on the Plains!!" *Los Angeles Star*, 24 October 1857, 2/3.

10. "The Late Horrible Massacre," *Los Angeles Star*, 17 October 1857, 2/4.

11. P. M. Warn said that mail carrier Bill Hyde joined the Mathews–Tanner train two days out of San Bernardino. See "Later from the South," *Alta California*, 27 October 1857, 1/4.

12. Those familiar with manuscript emigrant journals know how easily a Mormon glancing at the diary could have misread "Milum" for "William" and "Caldwell" for "Carroll." Basil Parker made a similar mistake when he wrote that the widow Tackitt had "a daughter married to William [actually, Milum] Jones." See Parker, *Recollections of the Mountain Meadows Massacre*, 5. The best expert, Judge Roger V. Logan, Jr., assured the author on 25 March 1996 that there was no William Jones of Missouri with the emigrants.

13. Lyford, *The Mormon Problem*, 298. Journalist C. F. McGlashan described the "forlorn hope" of the Fancher party in 1875, but he made the phrase famous in his *History of the Donner Party*.

14. Bishop, ed., *Mormonism Unveiled*, 237.

15. Klingensmith statement, Brooks, *Mountain Meadows Massacre*, 240.

16. Bishop, ed., *Mormonism Unveiled*, 235–36, 239.

17. William Edwards, Affidavit, 14 May 1924, Utah State Historical Society.

18. "Lee's Last Confession," 1/4.

19. Bishop, ed., *Mormonism Unveiled*, 237. Nephi Johnson claimed he was looking for his horse and witnessed the massacre from a hill. Old-timer Orson Huntsman said "15 white men armed" were concealed with the Indians. See Mountain Meadow Massacre, Davis Papers, Sutter's Fort Historical Museum, 3. With remarkable consistency, survivors Elizabeth Baker, Sarah Frances Baker, Rebecca Dunlap, and Christopher Fancher recalled seeing disguised white men wash paint from their faces in the stream at Hamblin's ranch after the massacre.

20. Bishop, ed., *Mormonism Unveiled*, 364; Beckwith, *Shameful Friday*, 23–25. His son-in-law said James Magnum, an alleged massacre participant, "Refused to act. . . . Just refused; said he wouldn't." Ibid., 259.

21. Brooks, *Mountain Meadows Massacre*, 73; Bishop, ed., *Mormonism Unveiled*, 240.

22. Nancy Huff Memoir, 3/1.

23. Klingensmith statement, Brooks, *Mountain Meadows Massacre*, 240.

24. "Cedar City," *Deseret News*, 2 December 1856, 309/3.

25. Amasa Lyman, Journal 1857–63, Typescript, BYU, 89; Cedar Stake Journal, 1856–1859, LDS Records, Palmer Collection, Southern Utah University.

26. Heber C. Kimball, 16 August 1857, *Journal of Discourses*, 4:375.

27. Rebecca Dunlap Memoir, 2. Lee claimed that a man carried the flag, but Dunlap's specific identification must be trusted over the story of a convicted murderer.

28. Bancroft, *History of Utah*, 553; "Lee's Last Confession," 1/4; Bishop, ed., *Mormonism Unveiled*, 239–40. In *Mormonism Unveiled*, Lee said the emigrants were burying "two men of note among them."

29. Anne Hoag testimony, Lee Trials Transcripts, 192; punctuation corrected.

30. Rebecca Dunlap Memoir, 2/1.

31. Fancher, *Westward with the Sun*, 257; author's telephone conversation notes, 6 March 1996. Sam Fancher of Kingston, Arkansas, recalled that Alexander Fancher "had been shot in the throat and couldn't talk too good. Said to his nephew, 'Lord God, Rob, no.' Rob said, 'What did he say?' John D. Lee said, 'He's just talking to his maker.'" Author's conversation notes, 25 March 1996.

32. See Knight's account in Abraham H. Cannon, Journal, 15 June 1895, 19:99, Marriott Library.

33. Sarah Baker Memoir, 15; Elizabeth Baker Memoir, 6.

34. "Lee's Last Confession," 1/4; Bishop, ed., *Mormonism Unveiled*, 240–41.

35. Higbee statement, Brooks, *Mountain Meadows Massacre*, 230.

36. "Lee's Last Confession," 1/4. Sources disagree on who gave the order. Most sources agree that Higbee "gave the signal to fire by shooting off his pistol," but his friends such as Daniel Macfarlane blamed

White or Klingensmith. Higbee said "it was Major Lee's orders whoever gave them." See Brooks, *Mountain Meadows Massacre*, 231, 236; Rebecca Dunlap Memoir, 2/2; George W. Adair in McKay, Diary, 27 July 1907.

37. Beckwith, Shameful Friday, 69; Bishop, ed., *Mormonism Unveiled*, 241.

38. Klingensmith statement, Brooks, *Mountain Meadows Massacre*, 240–41.

39. Backus, *Mountain Meadows Witness*, 136–38.

40. Westwood and Rohrbacher, *Yesteryear's Child*, 22–23. Phoebe Westwood recalled that this horrible experience caused her grandfather "to leave the Mormons and return to the Anglicans. He eventually served in Utah Territory during the Civil War under the name of Darius West, believing he had a price on his head for apostasy."

41. "Mountain Meadows," *San Francisco Daily Bulletin Supplement*, 24 March 1877, 1/6.

42. Diary Excerpts of Francis M. Lyman, 21 September 1895.

43. Bancroft, *History of Utah*, 553; Brooks, *Mountain Meadows Massacre*, 231.

44. Nancy Huff Memoir, 3. Although only four years old at the time, Nancy Huff wrote, "The scenes and incidents of the massacre were so terrible that they were indelibly stamped on my mind, notwithstanding I was so young."

45. Carleton, *Special Report*, Serial 4377, 13.

46. "'Children of the Massacre,'" *Arkansas Sunday Post-Dispatch*, September 1895. Tackitt later revisited "the fatal Meadows, the only one of the survivors who ever beheld the scene of the massacre since the awful day of death." Ibid.

47. William Young testimony, Lee Trials Transcripts, 217. Young claimed he was "a sick man" during the massacre and observed it from afar, but he could only have seen what he testified to if he participated in the attack.

48. Carleton, *Special Report*, 6–7; Memorial Program.

49. Rebecca Dunlap Memoir, 2. Jacob Hamblin was miles away, marrying Priscilla Leavitt in Great Salt Lake City, on 11 September 1857.

50. Young, *Wife No. 19*, 248. With more drama than credibility, Ann Eliza Young claimed Lee shot a girl clinging to his son and another "who had drawn a dagger to defend herself."

51. Beadle, *Western Wilds*, 499. Beadle is not an impeccable source, but he accurately reported Utah lore. For all his use of gruesome detail, Beadle claimed his massacre accounts were "imperfectly told—for I dare not sketch its foulest details."

52. "Klingensmith," *Salt Lake Daily Tribune*, 4 August 1881, 2/3.

53. Samuel Knight account in Abraham H. Cannon, Journal, 15 June 1895, 19:99.

54. Backus, *Mountain Meadows Witness*, 139–40.

55. Beadle, *Western Wilds*, 494, 500.

56. "Mountain Meadows," *San Francisco Daily Bulletin Supplement*, 24 March 1877, 1/8.

57. Ibid., 1/7.

58. Bishop, ed., *Mormonism Unveiled*, 241.

59. Memorial Program.

60. Knight and M'Murdy testimony, Bishop, ed., *Mormonism Unveiled*, 331, 336, 339.

61. Bishop, ed., *Mormonism Unveiled*, 241–42; Bancroft, *History of Utah*, 554.

62. "Lee's Last Confession," 1/4.

63. Bishop, ed., *Mormonism Unveiled*, 242–43.

64. "Lee's Last Confession," 1/4.

65. Collins R. Hakes statement, Mountain Meadows File, LDS Archives.

66. "Mountain Meadows," *San Francisco Daily Bulletin Supplement*, 24 March 1877, 1/7.

67. David O. McKay, Diary, 27 July 1907, Special Collections, Marriott Library.

68. Carleton, *Special Report*, Serial 4377, 11.

69. Rebecca Dunlap Memoir, 2/3.

70. Drewer to Clauds, Camp Floyd, 31 March 1859, Caroline Parry Woolley Collection, Southern Utah University.

71. Kenney, ed., *Wilford Woodruff's Journal*, 29 September 1857, 5:102.

72. Sarah Baker Memoir, double page.

73. Elizabeth Baker Memoir, 6.

74. Bishop, ed., *Mormonism Unveiled*, 242. Lee also said the Indian "caught her about one hundred feet from the wagon, and plunged his knife through her." See "Lee's Last Confession," 1/4.

75. Joseph Lee statement, Brimhall, Gleanings Concerning John D. Lee, 38.

76. Walker, James Gemmell's Narrative, BYU Library, 47.

77. Nancy Huff Memoir, 3.

78. Susan Brownmiller reported rapes associated with mass murders at Camp Grant in Arizona, My Lai in Vietnam, and pogroms in Russia. She also accepted Roberts's anecdotal reports of the rape of LDS women in Missouri that have no documentary support. See Brownmiller, *Against Our Will*, 101–5, 121, 124–26, 151.

79. Brooks, *Mountain Meadows Massacre*, 105–6; Carleton, *Special Report*, Serial 4377, 13; Bishop, ed., *Mormonism Unveiled*, 366–67; Walker, James Gemmell's Narrative, [1], 48.

80. Diary Excerpts of Francis M. Lyman, 21 September 1895. After years of research, I believe Johnson's simple statement is the most significant new evidence to appear since Juanita Brooks completed her work on Mountain Meadows. The original Lyman diaries are in the possession of the First Presidency of the LDS church and are not available to scholars.

81. Novak, "Mountain Meadows Forensics," *Salt Lake Tribune*, 21 January 2001, AA5.

82. Novak and Kopp, "Osteological Analysis of Human Remains," Table 4; Novak, "Mountain Meadows Forensics," *Salt Lake Tribune*, 21 January 2001, AA5; Smith, "Forensic Analysis Supports Tribe's Claim of Passive Role," *Salt Lake Tribune*, 21 January 2001, A6.

83. Novak, "Mountain Meadows Forensics," *Salt Lake Tribune*, 21 January 2001, AA5; Novak and Kopp, "Osteological Analysis of Human Remains," 49.

84. Smith, "Forensic Analysis Supports Tribe's Claim of Passive Role," *Salt Lake Tribune*, 21 January 2001, A1; Novak, "Mountain Meadows Forensics," *Salt Lake Tribune*, 21 January 2001, AA5.

85. Novak, "Mountain Meadows Forensics," *Salt Lake Tribune*, 21 January 2001, AA5; Carleton, *Special Report*, Serial 4377, 7.

86. Brooks, *Mountain Meadows Massacre*, 225, 231; Bishop, ed., *Mormonism Unveiled*, 244.

87. Bishop, ed., *Mormonism Unveiled*, 243; "Lee's Last Confession," 1/5.

88. Halleck to Whiting, 6 November 1900, BYU Library.

89. Bishop, ed., *Mormonism Unveiled*, 244.

90. Nephi Johnson statement, Brooks, *Mountain Meadows Massacre*, 225.

91. Bishop, ed., *Mormonism Unveiled*, 247; "Lee's Last Confession," 1/5.

92. Klingensmith statement, Brooks, *Mountain Meadows Massacre*, 241.

93. Bishop, ed., *Mormonism Unveiled*, 243. Lee said there were sixteen survivors.

94. Rebecca Dunlap Memoir, 2; Nancy Huff Memoir, 3.

95. Carleton, *Special Report*, Serial 4377, 6.

96. Rebecca Dunlap Memoir, 2; Elizabeth Baker Memoir, 6/4; Beckwith, Shameful Friday, 22.

97. Bishop, ed., *Mormonism Unveiled*, 245; "Lee's Last Confession," 1/4. Most accounts indicate the massacre happened not long before sundown. Lee wrote that these speeches and oaths took place on both Friday evening and Saturday.

CHAPTER 9

1. P. M. Warn statement in "The Late Horrible Massacre," *Los Angeles Star*, 17 October 1857, 2/3.

2. Bishop, ed., *Mormonism Unveiled*, 245.

3. "Lee's Last Confession," 1/5; Bishop, ed., *Mormonism Unveiled*, 245–46. Mormon historians have maintained since 1884 that the debate over whether to report the massacre proved that Brigham Young did not order it.

4. David O. McKay Diary, 27 July 1907, Marriott Library, 29.

5. Rebecca Dunlap Memoir, 2/2.

6. "The Late Horrible Massacre," *Los Angeles Star*, 17 October 1857, 2/2-3.

7. "More Outrages on the Plains!!" *Los Angeles Star*, 24 October 1857, 2/2.

8. "The Late Outrages on the Plains," *Los Angeles Star*, 7 November 1857, 2/1-2.

9. Smith-McKnight report, 6 August 1858, in Brooks, *Mountain Meadows Massacre*, 243.

10. Abraham H. Cannon, Journal, 15 June 1895, 19:99, Marriott Library.

11. Samuel Pollack testimony, Lee Trials Transcripts, 231.

12. "Lee's Last Confession," 1/5; Bishop, ed., *Mormonism Unveiled*, 247.

13. Nephi Johnson testimony, Gibbs, *The Mountain Meadows Massacre*, 51.

14. Bishop, ed., *Mormonism Unveiled*, 247–48.

15. Ibid., 247–50; Brooks, *John Doyle Lee*, 221.

16. Carleton, *Special Report*, Serial 4377, 3, 5–6; Nancy Huff Memoir, 3; Rebecca Dunlap Memoir, 2/2; Brooks, *John Doyle Lee*, 216.

17. Carleton, *Special Report*, Serial 4377, 3, 5–6.

18. Ibid., 13–14; Memorial Program.

19. Elizabeth Baker Memoir, 6; Brooks, *John Doyle Lee*, 225; Carleton, *Special Report*, Serial 4377, 14.

20. Nancy Huff Memoir, 3/1.

21. "The Federal Government and Utah," *Southern Vineyard*, 29 May 1858, 2/1.

22. Bishop, ed., *Mormonism Unveiled*, 244. Lee said he could not spare the time to describe the fate of these men but hinted he might do so "hereafter." Lee was in the hereafter before he could tell his version of this story.

23. *Alta California*, 27 October 1857, 1/4; "The Late Horrible Massacre," *Los Angeles Star*, 17 October 1857, 2/3. Lyford, *The Mormon Problem*, 301, named the Young brothers.

24. "More Outrages on the Plains!!" *Los Angeles Star*, 24 October 1857, 2/3.

25. Carleton, *Special Report*, Serial 4377, 12, 13.

26. Lynch affidavit, 27 July 1859, Buchanan, *Massacre at Mountain Meadows*, Serial 1033, 82–83.

27. Lyford, *The Mormon Problem*, 296–300.

28. Rogerson, "The Guilt of John D. Lee," in Mountain Meadows File, LDS Archives, 11–12.

29. Carleton, *Special Report,* Serial 4377, 13.

30. "The Late Horrible Massacre," *Los Angeles Star*, 17 October 1857, 2/3.

31. Ibid.; John Ward Christian Dictation, Beaver City, Utah, [1886], Bancroft Library. Christian said several people told him the party went through the meadows at night to prevent the gentiles from learning of the massacre, "but some of them might deny it now."

32. Lyman, *Francis Marion Lyman: Apostle*, 36–37.

33. Cedar Stake Journal, 1856-1859, LDS Records, Palmer Collection.

34. Penrose, "Testimony of James Holt Haslam," 95–96. The only known copy of Young's letter is the clerk's retained copy in the Brigham Young Collection at LDS Archives.

35. Diary of Rachel Woolsey Lee, Huntington Library.

36. Bishop, ed., *Mormonism Unveiled*, 249.

37. Diary of Benjamin Platt, BYU Library, 6 (spelling corrected); Anne Hoag testimony, The Lee Trial, W. L. Cook Papers, Library of Congress, 191; Gibbs, *The Mountain Meadows Massacre*, 57. Platt told Gibbs the Indians "made no oral demonstration of victory."

38. Brooks, *Mountain Meadows Massacre*, xix–xx.

39. Hurt to Forney, 4 December 1857, in Buchanan, *Massacre at Mountain Meadows*, Serial 1033, 95–96.

40. "The Late Horrible Massacre," *Los Angeles Star*, 17 October 1857, 2/2–3.

41. Ibid.

42. Ibid.

43. Brooks, *Mountain Meadows Massacre*, 122.

44. "More Outrages on the Plains!!" *Los Angeles Star*, 24 October 1857, 2/2.

45. Ibid.; Farnsworth, Dictation, Bancroft Library.

46. "More Outrages on the Plains!!" *Los Angeles Star*, 24 October 1857, 2/2.

47. Ibid.; Deposition, 28 February 1896, Welch v. the United States and the Ute Tribe, Indian Depredations Case No. 9239, 2 (cited as Welch Claim).

48. Hurt to Forney, 4 December 1857, Buchanan, *Massacre at Mountain Meadows*, Serial 1033, 95. Brigham Young's denunciation of Arapeen on 20 September 1857 as a "squaw" indicates Ammon was not the only Indian leader reluctant to follow his orders.

49. Martineau, Parowan Stake Record, 26–27. The Parowan Ward Records, cited in Brooks, *Mountain Meadows Massacre*, 116, date the attack at Beaver to 10 September 1857. No members of the Parowan militia were at Mountain Meadows, suggesting that William Dame held them in reserve to deal with the Dukes and Turner trains.

50. Parowan Ward Records, cited in Brooks, *Mountain Meadows Massacre*, 113, 116.

51. Martineau, "Trip to the Santa Clara," *Deseret News*, 23 September 1857, 227/4; "More Outrages on the Plains!!" *Los Angeles Star*, 24 October 1857, 2/2–3. Shirts and Carter turned back before they reached the agreed-upon destination, with Shirts "stealing a horse."

52. "Mountain Meadow," *Chicago Daily Inter-Ocean*, 18 September 1876.

53. "More Outrages on the Plains!!" *Los Angeles Star*, 24 October 1857, 2/2–3.

54. Carleton, *Special Report*, Serial 4377, 3.

55. Brooks, *Mountain Meadows Massacre,* 122. For Young's alleged instructions to Hamblin, see Hendrix to Young, 23 June 1860, Brigham Young Collection, LDS Archives.

56. Brooks, *Mountain Meadows Massacre*, 121, dated the theft on the Muddy River to 7 October. The 12 April 1858 petition of Turner, Welch, Anderson, Doake, and Bingham in the Welch Claim dated it to 3 October 1857.

57. "More Outrages on the Plains!!" *Los Angeles Star*, 24 October 1857, 2/2–3; "The Late Ourtages on the Plains—Another Account, " *Los Angeles Star*, 31 October 1857, 2/1–2. J. Ward Christian, LDS justice of the peace in San Bernardino, took this statement, which was published over the names of William Webb and others. Webb swore, "I never signed that statement," and it was "unqualifiedly false." See "The Late Outrages on the Plains—Further Particulars," *Los Angeles Star*, 7 November 1857, 2/2.

58. "Letter from San Bernardino," *San Francisco Bulletin*, 12 November 1857, 2/3.

59. Peyton Welch testimony, 6 June 1903, Abstract of Evidence, Welch Claim, 20. In 1910 the court awarded Welch damages of $1,135 for the theft of his cattle. See Thurston Claim, 51–52.

60. "More Outrages on the Plains!!" *Los Angeles Star*, 24 October 1857, 2/3.

61. Unpublished note to Carleton's Report, from Mountain Meadows File, LDS Archives.

62. "More Outrages on the Plains!!" *Los Angeles Star*, 24 October 1857, 2/3.

63. See Cooley, ed., *Diary of Brigham Young 1857*, 80–83. Printed copies of this document dated 5 August 1857 exist, but Young's diary reveals he did not ask Daniel H. Wells to write the declaration of martial law until 29 August. No contemporary record mentions seeing the August proclamation, which was probably misdated due to a printer's error.

64. "The Late Outrages on the Plains—Further Particulars," *Los Angeles Star*, 7 November 1857, 2/1.

65. Ibid., 2/2.

66. Bishop, ed., *Mormonism Unveiled*, 270–71.

67. Hendrix to Young, 23 June 1860, Brigham Young Collection, LDS Archives. Mormon sources only name "Mr. Lane, one of the emigrant stockowners," but S. B. Honea identified Joseph Lane as "one of our company." See "More Outrages on the Plains!!" *Los Angeles Star*, 24 October 1857, 2/2.

68. Hendrix to Young, 23 June 1860, Brigham Young Collection, LDS Archives.

69. Mormon sources give three dates for Tutsegabit's ordination. Huntington dated the event to 10 September. Writing to William Dame on 13 September, George A. Smith said, "We ordained Tutsegabbotts an Elder this Evening." Diarist Wilford Woodruff recorded Tutsegabit's ordination on 16 September 1857, the date followed here.

70. Huntington, Journal, 1857, LDS Archives, 20 September 1857. Arapeen was Wakara's successor. Like Kanosh, Arapeen was closely allied with the Mormons, but his career suggests he was a double agent. Havoc followed in Arapeen's wake as he told his Mormon patrons one thing and his Indian allies another.

CHAPTER 10

1. Nephi Johnson statement, Brooks, *Mountain Meadows Massacre*, 225–26.

2. "More Outrages on the Plains!!" *Los Angeles Star*, 24 October 1857, 2/2.

3. "The Late Horrible Massacre," *Los Angeles Star*, 17 October 1857, 2/4.

4. Backus, *Mountain Meadows Witness*, 155, 158.

5. Carleton, *Special Report*, Serial 4377, 4, 8, 11; Bishop, ed., *Mormonism Unveiled*, 250; Lockley, *The Lee Trial*, 17.

6. Brooks, *Mountain Meadows Massacre*, 124; Bishop, ed., *Mormonism Unveiled*, 257.

7. Brooks and Cleland, eds., *Mormon Chronicle*, 1:148, 158, 320–21n26. Receipts 755 and 756 to Benjamin Platte for "$18.50 from John D. Lee for stock in March 1858" and to John D. Lee for $150 in the Perpetual Emigration Fund records appear to be for these donations.

8. Beadle, *Western Wilds*, 501.

9. Bishop, ed., *Mormonism Unveiled*, 250; author's interview notes with Charles S. Peterson, 11 January 1995. Historian Ronald Barney also reported the tradition.

10. Carleton, *Special Report*, Serial 4377, 7, 11–12.

11. Lynch affidavit, 27 July 1859, Buchanan, *Massacre at Mountain Meadows*, Serial 1033, 82.

12. Journal of Jacob Hamblin, 1854–1859, Utah State Historical Society, 41.

13. Hendrix to Young, 23 June 1860, Brigham Young Collection, LDS Archives.

14. Crampton, ed., "F. S. Dellenbaugh of the Colorado," 242; Bishop, ed., *Mormonism Unveiled*, 270.

15. Brooks and Cleland, eds., *Mormon Chronicle*, 1:161; "Mountain Meadows," *San Francisco Daily Bulletin Supplement*, 24 March 1877, 1/7; Carleton, *Special Report*, Serial 4377, 11–12.

16. Bishop, ed., *Mormonism Unveiled*, 251.

17. Journal of Rachel Andora Lee, BYU typescript, 48. Lee returned to Harmony on 17 October, sick with "Horse Distemper," probably the virus that afflicted many Mormons that fall, including Brigham Young.

18. Smith, *Thales Hastings Haskell*, 24; Little, *Jacob Hamblin*, 46.

19. Brooks, *John Doyle Lee*, 223.

20. Ibid., 372–76; Buchanan, *Massacre at Mountain Meadows*, Serial 1033, 96, 82; Beadle, *Life in Utah*, 184.

21. 27 September 1857, Utah Stake Minutes, General Meetings 1855-1860, LDS Archives, 690–91 (946 in holograph). Punctuation added.

22. Armstrong's 30 September 1857 report, Brooks, *Mountain Meadows Massacre*, 143.

23. Brigham Young, 26 July 1857, *Journal of Discourses*, 5:76–77.

24. Bishop, ed., *Mormonism Unveiled*, 252; Brigham Young, 4 October 1857, *Journal of Discourses*, 5:293.

25. This statement suggests why Haight's 7 September 1857 letter to Young has vanished.

26. Bishop, ed., *Mormonism Unveiled*, 252.

27. Ibid., 253–54; "Lee's Last Confession," 1/5.

28. Kenney, ed., *Wilford Woodruff's Journal*, 29 September 1857, 5:102.

29. Bigler, *Forgotten Kingdom*, 174–77; Kenney, ed., *Wilford Woodruff's Journal*, 5:102–3. Woodruff made no entry for 28 September, the day Lee probably arrived in Salt Lake.

30. Historian's Office Journal, 28 and 29 September 1857, Typescript, LDS Archives; Bishop, ed., *Mormonism Unveiled*, 254.

31. Klingensmith statement, Brooks, *Mountain Meadows Massacre*, 241–42.

32. Backus, *Mountain Meadows Witness*, 157; Brooks, *John Doyle Lee*, 340.

33. Bishop, ed., *Mormonism Unveiled*, 255–56.

34. Brooks, *John Doyle Lee*, 224–25. Brooks had "little doubt that the amounts of all the articles were greatly exaggerated."

35. Brooks, *Mountain Meadows Massacre*, 286. Young dictated at least four draft answers to this question, and one reply differed in interesting details from the final deposition. After "considerable conversation," Lee "commenced to give me a detail of the massacre." Young "told him to stop, "~~as I had heard from various others enough to sicken the heart of any man, and so I utterly refused to hear any of his details~~." See Mountain Meadows File, LDS Archives.

36. Hurt, 24 October 1857, Buchanan, *The Utah Expedition*, Serial 956, 206–8.

37. Ibid., 205–8; Browne, "The Utah Expedition," 373.

38. Bigler, "Garland Hurt," 166; Hicks, Life History, 32.

39. Furniss, *The Mormon Conflict*, 101.

40. Hammond, ed., *The Utah Expedition*, 6.

41. Alexander to Cooper, 3 September 1857, Buchanan, *The Utah Expedition*, Serial 956, 20; Furniss, *The Mormon Conflict*, 105.

42. Furniss, *The Mormon Conflict*, 112, 115; Browne, "The Utah Expedition," 369.

43. Browne, "The Utah Expedition," 369; Furniss, *The Mormon Conflict*, 139–40, 162–63.

44. Alexander to Cooper, 9 October 1857, Buchanan, *The Utah Expedition*, Serial 956, 31–32.

45. Alter and Dwyer, eds., "Journal of Captain Albert Tracy," 23.

46. Wells to Taylor, 4 October 1857, Buchanan, *The Utah Expedition*, Serial 956, 56–57.

47. Schindler, *Orrin Porter Rockwell*, 255–57.

48. Alexander, *Utah, the Right Place*, 129; J. P. Terry, Autobiography, BYU Library, 2.

49. Furniss, *The Mormon Conflict*, 109, 144–45; Schindler, *Orrin Porter Rockwell*, 261–62.

50. Journal History, 14 October 1857; Wells to Smith, 17 October 1857, Lot Smith Papers, University of Arizona; Young to Wells et al., 17 October 1857, Reel 5, Brigham Young Papers, Marriott Library.

51. Furniss, *The Mormon Conflict*, 113–15.

52. Ibid., 115-16.

53. Wells to Young, 8 and 15 November 1857, Brigham Young Papers, Marriott Library. Bigler, *Forgotten Kingdom*, 156.

54. Furniss, *The Mormon Conflict*, 74; Browne, "The Utah Expedition," 372; Johnston to McDowell, 5 November 1857, and Clarke to Porter, 28 November 1857, in Buchanan, *The Utah Expedition*, Serial 956, 47, 104.

55. Browne, "The Utah Expedition," 371–73.

56. "More Outrages on the Plains!!" *Los Angeles Star*, 24 October 1857, 2/1; Brooks, *The Mountain Meadows Massacre*, 128, 131; Ginn, Mormons and Indian Wars, Utah State Historical Society; Jacob Hamblin Journal, 42–43.

57. Jacob Hamblin Journal, 44–49.

58. Clark, "A Trip across the Plains in 1857," 210–211, 215–17.

59. Brigham Young, 4 October 1857, *Journal of Discourses*, 5:293.

60. Vindex, "Mountain Meadows Massacre," 3.

61. Haight, Journal 2, January 1858, 18; Brooks, ed., *On the Mormon Frontier*, 2:649; Brooks, *John Doyle Lee*, 227–28.

62. Young to Cox, 4 December 1857, Brigham Young Collection, LDS Archives, 932.

63. Journal History, 15 December 1857.

64. Browne, "The Utah Expedition," 477.

65. Furniss, *The Mormon Conflict*, 146; Brooks and Cleland, eds., *Mormon Chronicle*, 1:141.

66. Haight, Journal 2, 26 December 1857, 17. Lee had Emma Batchelor's portrait made on 2 January and his own taken again on 16 January 1858.

67. Brooks and Cleland, eds., *Mormon Chronicle*, 1:141.

68. Bishop, ed., *Mormonism Unveiled*, 313–14.

69. Brooks and Cleland, eds., *Mormon Chronicle*, 1:318n8; Smith, *Accounts of Brigham Young*, Serial 1128, 96–102. Lee's copies of the accounts at the Huntington Library listed different amounts from those in the government report. See Brooks, *Mountain Meadows Massacre*, 151-53n11.

70. Brooks and Cleland, eds., *Mormon Chronicle*, 1:143, 146.

71. Ibid., 1:146.

Chapter 11

1. Stampp, *America in 1857*, 213, 221–22, 237–38; *Deseret News*, 6 January 1858, 349/1; Browne, "The Utah Expedition," 476.

2. Caroline Barnes Crosby, Journal, 30 September 1857, Utah State Historical Society.

3. Warren to Lyman, 6 October 1857, Amasa Lyman Papers, LDS Archives.

4. Lyman, *San Bernardino*, 318, 361–62; "Rumored Massacre on the Plains," *Los Angeles Star*, 3 October 1857, 2/3.

5. "Horrible Massacre of Emigrants!!" *Los Angeles Star*, 10 October 1857, 2/2.

6. "The Late Outrages on the Plains—Another account, " *Los Angeles Star*, 31 October 1857, 2/1.

7. "The Late Outrages on the Plains—Further Particulars," *Los Angeles Star*, 7 November 1857, 2/3.

8. "Horrible Massacre of Emigrants!!" *Los Angeles Star*, 10 October 1857, 2/2.

9. "The Federal Government and Utah," *Southern Vineyard*, 29 May 1858, 2/1–2.

10. "Massacre of Emigrants to California," *Western Standard*, 23 October 1857, 2/3.

11. Journal History, 12 December 1857, 2–3. The *Alta California*, 27 October 1857, 1/5, charged that Wall was a Danite and "one of the biggest rascals alive." Wall later claimed he had a noose placed around his neck before someone pointed out he had not been in Utah at the time of the massacre. See Lyman, *San Bernardino*, 389.

12. "Public Meeting," *Los Angeles Star*, 17 October 1857, 2/4.

13. Ibid.; "The Duty of the Government," *Los Angeles Star*, 17 October 1857, 2/1.

14. *San Francisco Herald*, 17 October 1857, 2/1.

15. *San Francisco Bulletin*, 27 October 1857, cited in Brooks, *Mountain Meadows Massacre*, 146–47.

16. *El Clamor Público*, 17 October 1857, 2/1. See "Horrorosa Carniceria," *El Clamor Público*, 17 October 1857, 1/1, for a Spanish translation of George Powers's story.

17. Woodruff Collection, item dated 6 September 1857, box 1, fd 10, LDS Archives.

18. Smith to Dame, 12 August [*sic*] 1857, William Horne Dame Papers, LDS Archives. This information is in a postscript added on "Sunday evening," 13 September. Smith claimed, "The Quarter Master [Van Vliet] returns without contracting for a single article, as he is plainly told that the troops will not be allowed to enter this valley."

19. Jenson, *LDS Biographical Encyclopedia*, 2:371.

20. "Extract from a letter written by Elder Samuel W. Richards," in Woodbury, Journal, 20 November 1857, Huntington Library.

21. "Interesting from Carson Valley," *Alta California*, 8 October 1857, 1.

22. Burns, *The Jesuits and the Indian Wars of the Northwest*, 164–65; Dunbar and Phillips, eds., *The Journals and Letters of Major John C. Owen*, 189–93.

23. Stott, *Search for Sanctuary*, 44, 48.

24. For an alternative interpretation of Young's strategy, see Sessions and Stathis, "The Mormon Invasion of Russian America."

25. Clark to HQ, 1 January 1858, Mackall to Steptoe, 12 January 1858, and Steptoe to Mackall, 25 February 1858, in Floyd, "Report of the Secretary of War," Serial 975, 335–36, 338–39.

26. Campbell, *Establishing Zion*, 90–91; Lyman, *San Bernardino*, 350, 383, 390–91.

27. Kenney, ed., *Wilford Woodruff's Journal*, 5:115.

28. Lyman, *San Bernardino*, 414–15.

29. Mildred Brown, History of Justus Wellington Seeley II, Special Collections, BYU Library.

30. Incidents in the Life of Sarah Elizabeth Dunn Thornton, Hammond Family Papers, Special Collections, BYU Library. Thornton recalled the apostles as "Orson Pratt, Orson Hyde, John Bull, and George Q. Cannon." At the time only Pratt and Hyde were apostles.

31. Skinner, Autobiography, LDS Archives, 15–16. Skinner was a juror in a John D. Lee trial.

32. 19 December 1857, Cedar Stake Journal, 1856-1859, LDS Records, Palmer Collection, Southern Utah University Library.

33. Letter to the Editor, *Los Angeles Star*, 12 December 1857. Orson Hyde is said to have laid a similar curse on Carson Valley.

34. *Deseret News*, 6 January 1858, 349; and Brooks and Cleland, eds., *Mormon Chronicle*, 1:141.

35. Smith to John Lyman, 6 January 1858, Typescript, Historian's Office Letterbook, 509–10.

36. Young to Wells et al., 17 October 1857, Reel 5, Brigham Young Papers, Marriott Library.

37. Bigler, *Forgotten Kingdom*, 183–84; Brooks, ed., *On the Mormon Frontier*, 2:652.

38. Bertrand, *Memoires d'un Mormon*. Chappius translation in Donald R. Moorman Collection.

39. Bigler, *Forgotten Kingdom*, 184. Bigler was the first to recognize the significance of this unique military organization.

40. Derry, "Autobiography," 431.

41. Furniss, *The Mormon Conflict*, 96, 164–66; "The Slander of Gov. Cumming," *Valley Tan*, 1 March 1859, 1/3–4.

42. Browne, "The Utah Expedition," 371; Furniss, *The Mormon Conflict*, 164–66.

43. Floyd, "Report of the Secretary of War," Serial 956, 6, 7; Browne, "The Utah Expedition," 374.

44. Extracts from the Diary of Maj. Fitz-John Porter, Porter Papers, Library of Congress, 2–3.

45. Young to Johnston, 26 November 1857, Buchanan, *The Utah Expedition*, Serial 956, 110–11.

46. Extracts from the Diary of Maj. Fitz-John Porter, Porter Papers, Library of Congress, 3. A noted Mormon historian found Johnston's reaction "churlish" and "not conducive to polite intercourse." See Roberts, *Comprehensive History*, 4:310. The messengers gave the salt to Indians who smuggled it into the army camp and sold it for $2.50 per pound. Despite "the tenderest care of experienced hostlers and veterinary surgeons," Brigham Young later informed Colonel Alexander that his mule "succumbed to age and aggravated grief." Ibid., 4:309–10.

47. Browne, "The Utah Expedition," 475; Furniss, *The Mormon Conflict*, 169–70.

48. Poll, "Thomas L. Kane and the Utah War," 11.

49. Diary of Colonel Thomas L. Kane, Huntington Library. Punctuation added. Kanosh was on his way to Salt Lake with Jacob Hamblin when the events he described to Kane allegedly occurred.

50. Stott, *Search for Sanctuary*, 50; Kenney, ed., *Wilford Woodruff's Journal*, 5:168; Roberts, *Comprehensive History*, 4:346.

51. Brooks, ed., *On the Mormon Frontier*, 2:652–53. Samuel Sirrine, writing as "Achilles," charged that Porter Rockwell castrated apostate Henry Jones for incest with his mother. Rockwell allegedly shot Jones and slit his mother's throat when they later tried to escape to California. See Schindler, *Orrin Porter Rockwell*, 255, 290n15.

52. Smith to Dame, 3 February [March] 1858, Dame Papers. As with other George A. Smith letters, its content reveals it is misdated. Wilford Woodruff wrote a lengthy letter to Kane on 4 March 1858, no copy of which is known to survive, "giving a reason of our hope and faith and the cause of our defending ourselves. . . . [I]t contained 6 pages of fools cap." See Kenney, ed., *Wilford Woodruff's Journal*, 5:173.

53. Journal History, 24 April 1859, 5; Roberts, *Comprehensive History*, 4:347; Kenney, ed., *Wilford Woodruff's Journal*, 5:208–9.

54. Brooks, ed., *On the Mormon Frontier*, 2:653n23. Webster defined "b'hoy" as a "gang member, rowdy."

55. Roberts, *Comprehensive History*, 4:348–49.

56. Journal History, 8 March 1858.

57. Lansdale, Journal, Beinecke Library, 49; Shurtliff, Life and Travels, Idaho Historical Society, 26, 27. Page numbers are from Bigler typescripts in the author's possession.

58. Powell and Jackson statements, "Report of the Secretary of War," Serial 975, 80–81. For an LDS account of their dealings with the Nez Perces, see Bluth, "The Salmon River Mission," 905–6.

59. Diary of Samuel Pitchforth, 10 March 1857, BYU Library,.

60. Clark, Copy of Israel Justus Clark's Journal, David L. Bigler Journal Collection, 149.

61. Bluth, "The Salmon River Mission," 911.

62. Bigler, "The Crisis at Fort Limhi, 1858," 127–31. Much of my interpretation of the Utah War is derived from this article and Bigler's *Forgotten Kingdom*.

63. Ibid., 186–87.

64. Isaac Bullock to Young, 18 August 1857, Brigham Young Collection, LDS Archives.

65. Ficklin to Porter, 15 April and 21 April 1858, in Floyd, "Report of the Secretary of War," Serial 975, 68–70, 79; Extracts from the Diary of Maj. Fitz-John Porter, Porter Papers, Library of Congress, 29. See Furniss, *The Mormon Conflict*, 159, for the whiskey.

66. Healy, J. W. Powell and Fort Lemhi, Montana Historical Society; Thrapp, *Encyclopedia of Frontier Biography*, 3:1168–69.

67. Powell Statement, "Report of the Secretary of War," Serial 975, 80–81; Bluth, "The Salmon River Mission," 905.

68. Healy, J. W. Powell and Fort Lemhi, Montana Historical Society.

69. Journal History, 8 March 1858; "Indian Outrage," *Deseret News*, 17 March 1858, 13/1.

70. Bluth, "The Salmon River Mission," 911.

71. Young to Kane, 9 March 1858, in Floyd, "Report of the Secretary of War," Serial 975, 87–88.

72. Brigham Young, 13 September 1857, *Journal of Discourses*, 5:231.

73. Extracts from the Diary of Maj. Fitz-John Porter, Porter Papers, Library of Congress.

74. Roberts, *Comprehensive History*, 4:355–56; Furniss, *The Mormon Conflict*, 181.

75. Extracts from the Diary of Maj. Fitz-John Porter, Porter Papers, Library of Congress, 11; Brooks, ed., *On the Mormon Frontier*, 1:177.

76. Furniss, *The Mormon Conflict*, 182.

77. Cumming to Johnston, 15 April 1858, in Floyd, "Report of the Secretary of War," Serial 975, 92–93.

78. Journal History, 13 April 1858.

79. Cumming to Johnston, 15 April 1858, in Floyd, "Report of the Secretary of War," Serial 975, 93–96. Interestingly, the court records—and the Department of Justice records for Utah Territory before 1870—do not survive in the National Archives.

80. Stenhouse, *The Rocky Mountain Saints*, 393.

81. Cumming to Johnston, 15 April 1858, in Floyd, "Report of the Secretary of War," Serial 975, 93.

82. "Another Murder by Indians," *Deseret News*, 14 April 1858, 35/2.

83. Forney to Cumming, 21 April 1858; Magraw and Bridger to Porter, 28 April 1858, in Floyd, "Report of the Secretary of War," Serial 975, 78, 82.

84. Dickinson to Gordon, 16 April 1858, Bancroft Library; Extracts from the Diary of Maj. Fitz-John Porter, Porter Papers, Library of Congress, 10.

85. Smith to Stenhouse, Provo, 7 June 1858, Historian's Office Letterbook, LDS Archives, 521.

86. Wells to Young, 24 April 1858, CR 1234/1, Box 43, Folder 9, LDS Archives. It is not clear why Cumming canceled his plans to investigate the massacre immediately after assuming office.

87. "An Interview with Alfred Cumming," *Salt Lake Tribune*, 1 November 1876, 4/4.

88. Furniss, *The Mormon Conflict*, 192–95.

89. Brooks, ed., *On the Mormon Frontier*, 2:654.

90. Stott, *Search for Sanctuary*, 44, 57, 235–37.

91. David L. Bigler typescript of Abraham Zundel, Diary, 1856–1858, 21; original at LDS Archives.

92. Arrington, *Brigham Young*, 265–67; "Instructions," *Deseret News*, 14 April 1858, 34/4.

93. Powell and McCulloch to Floyd, 3 July 1858, in Floyd, "Report of the Secretary of War," Serial 975, 175–76.

94. Furniss, *The Mormon Conflict*, 201–02.

95. Ashton, *Voice in the West*, 97; Browne, "The Utah Expedition," 570–71; Moorman and Sessions, *Camp Floyd and the Mormons*, 105.

96. Furniss, *The Mormon Conflict*, 227; Arrington, *Brigham Young*, 267; Cumming to Cass, Utah Territorial Papers, National Archives, 208.

CHAPTER 12

1. See *San Francisco Bulletin*, "Another Anti-Mormon Volunteer Company," 26 January 1858, 3/2; "Anti-Mormon Military Company at Watsonville," 27 January 1858, 2/1; and "More Volunteers for the Mormon War," 5 January 1858, 2/1, which reported the spontaneous formation of volunteer companies at Visalia, Jackson, and Cacheville.

2. "The Murders at Mountain Canon Confirmed," *Alta California*, 27 October 1857, 1/2–5.

3. See the military records of these units and Letters Received, Adj. Gen. W. C. Kibbe, in the California State Militia Records, and "The National Guard in California 1849–1880 (Part 1)," California State Library, 22, 206–9.

4. Mitchell to Sebastian, 31 December 1857, Buchanan, *Massacre at Mountain Meadows*, Serial 1033, 42–43; Memorial Program.

5. "Extract from a letter [from] Carroll Co. [dated 5 January 1858]," *Arkansas State Gazette and Democrat*, 18 February 1858, 2/2.

6. "Public Meeting of the People of Carroll County," *Arkansas State Gazette and Democrat*, 27 February 1858, 3/1.

7. Historian's Office Journal, 22 April 1859, Typescript, LDS Archives, 104.

8. "Massacre of Emigrants to California," *Congressional Globe*, 18 March 1858, 1176–77, and 19 March 1858, 1187. Secretary of War Floyd filed his report later in the month, but no record of it can be located in the National Archives.

9. Thomas Bullock Journal, May–June 1858, BYU Library; Furniss, *The Mormon Conflict*, 210.

10. Young to Cumming, 8 May 1858, cited in Furniss, *The Mormon Conflict*, 189–90.

11. Browne, "The Utah Expedition," 361.

12. Cumming to Smith, 24 September 1858, Canning and Beeton, eds., *The Genteel Gentile*, 94.

13. "An Interview with Alfred Cumming," *Salt Lake Tribune*, 1 November 1876, 4/4; "Important News from Salt Lake," *San Francisco Bulletin*, 19 May 1859, 2/1.

14. Holmes, ed., *Covered Wagon Women*, 7:249–50.

15. Journal History, 24 April 1859, 2.

16. Arrington, *Brigham Young*, 279; Historian's Office Journal, 18 June 1858, LDS Archives, 13.

17. Little, *Jacob Hamblin*, 46, 59–60.

18. Brooks, *John Doyle Lee*, 242.

19. George A. Smith "journalizes as follows," in Journal History, 29 July 1858.

20. Hendrix to Young, 23 June 1860, Brigham Young Collection, LDS Archives.

21. Brooks and Cleland, eds., *Mormon Chronicle*, 1:178–80.

22. Smith-McKnight report, 6 August 1858, Brooks, *Mountain Meadows Massacre*, 242–44.

23. William Horne Dame, Papers, LDS Archives; Journal History, 12 August 1859.

24. Brooks, *John Doyle Lee*, 255; Minutes of an Investigation of William H. Dame, 8 August 1858, LDS Archives. Brooks suggested the discussions centered on who would bear responsibility for the massacre. She concluded, "Perhaps the contradictory nature of the orders" to both preserve peace with the Indians and spare the emigrants "was the subject for the long controversy." See Brooks, *John Doyle Lee*, 243–44.

25. Isaac C. Haight, Journal No. 2, 12 August 1858, Southern Utah University.

26. A complete list of the signers appears in Brooks, *Mountain Meadows Massacre*, 169.

27. William Horne Dame, Papers, LDS Archives.

28. Smith to Young, 17 August 1858, Brooks, *Mountain Meadows Massacre*, 244–48.

29. Ibid., 181, 247; Roberts, *Comprehensive History*, 4:164, 166.

30. "A Portion of Mormondom Exposed," *San Francisco Daily Evening Bulletin*, 25 April 1859, 1/1.

31. "The Death of Peter McAuslan," *Sutter County Farmer*, 25 December 1908, 7/6; Chamberlain and Wells, *History of Sutter County*, 660. On the escort's return, Capt. Isaac Lynde met the Shepherd train, which had been attacked by a party that included "at least three white men, painted and disguised as Indians." See Buchanan, *Massacre at Mountain Meadows*, Serial 1033, 35, 37.

32. Mix to Forney, 4 March 1858; Forney to Mix, 22 June 1858; Forney to Denver, 18 March 1859; Forney to Greenwood, August 1859, in Buchanan, *Massacre at Mountain Meaodws*, Serial 1033, 42–45, 53, 75.

33. Young to Dame and Haight, 3 August 1858, Brigham Young Collection, LDS Archives, 316.

34. Hamblin to Forney, 9 December 1858, and Cumming to Anderson, 14 February 1859, *Valley Tan*, 15 February 1859, 2/1.

35. Brooks and Cleland, eds., *Mormon Chronicle*, 1:199, 209. The child was Christopher Carson Fancher.

36. Young to S. B. Aden, 27 April 1859 and 12 July 1859, MS 2736, Box 5, Folder 5, LDS Archives, 185. Young posted the notice in the *Deseret News*, 27 April 1859, 61/3.

37. Moorman and Sessions, *Camp Floyd and the Mormons*, 106–7; "The Democracy and Mormon Eniquity," *San Francisco Bulletin*, 17 June 1859, 2/2.

38. Furniss, *The Mormon Conflict*, 208–9; Wilson to Thompson, 4 and 28 March 1859, in Buchanan, *Massacre at Mountain Meadows*, Serial 1033, 100, 102.

39. "Letter from Great Salt Lake," *San Francisco Bulletin*, 27 April 1859, 1/1.

40. Young to Kane, 14 January 1859, Winther, ed., *The Private Papers and Diary of Thomas Leiper Kane*, 60–61.

41. *Valley Tan*, 5 April 1859, 2/3-3/1. Cradlebaugh complained that the article in the 16 March 1859 *Deseret News*, 9/1–4, purporting to be his charge to the grand jury was "*incorrect.*" He gave the paper "the *substance* of the charge . . . embracing *truthfully* what I did say." Ibid., 22 March 1859, 2/3.

42. "Letter from Provo City, U.T.," *San Francisco Bulletin*, 19 April 1859, 3/3-4; *Valley Tan*, 5 April 1859, 3/1.

43. Gemmell to Little, 14 October 1872, Brigham Young Collection, LDS Archives.

44. "Discharge of the Grand Jury," *Valley Tan*, 5 April 1859, 2/4 ; "District Court, 2nd Judicial District," *Deseret News*, 16 March 1859, 16/2-4; "Letter from Great Salt Lake," *San Francisco Bulletin*, 27 April 1859, 1/1.

45. "Correspondence between the judges of Utah and the Attorney General or President," in Buchanan, *Utah Territory*, Serial 1031, 29, 32, 41.

46. Statements Regarding Soldiers and Judge Cradlebaugh, Collected Materials Relative to the Church Historian's Office, LDS Archives. The size of this collection is a measure of the efforts the LDS church made to counter Cradlebaugh's investigation.

47. Moorman and Sessions, *Camp Floyd and the Mormons*, 110–12, 115.

48. "Discharge of the Grand Jury," *Valley Tan*, 29 March 1859, 3/3–5.

49. Journal History, 13 April 1859, Brooks, *Mountain Meadows Massacre*, 248–51.

50. Cradlebaugh, *Utah and the Mormons*, 16–17.

51. William H. Rogers Statement, *Valley Tan*, 29 February 1860, Brooks, *Mountain Meadows Massacre*, 266.

52. James Lynch, Affidavit, 29 July 1859, Buchanan, *Massacre at Mountain Meadows*, Serial 1033, 83–84; Lynch's statement in the *San Francisco Bulletin*, 31 May 1859, 3/3.

53. Brooks, *Mountain Meadows Massacre*, 267; Lynch, Affidavit, 29 July 1859, 81; *San Francisco Bulletin*, 31 May 1859, 3/3.

54. National Archives typescript of "Will Ask Aid for Those He Saved: Captain J. C. Lynch Tells of the Mountain Meadow Horror—Will Ask for Congressional Appropriation," *Arkansas Gazette*, 5 June 1908, copy in author's possession.

55. *San Francisco Bulletin*, 31 May 1859, 3/3.

56. Brooks, *Mountain Meadows Massacre*, 269; Brooks and Cleland, eds., *Mormon Chronicle*, 1:210–12. Charles Kelly, in *Journals of John D. Lee*, 203, indicated sixteen pages were missing from Lee's 1859 diary at this point.

57. Discursive Remarks, Utah State Historical Society. This photostat of a manuscript acquired some thirty years ago is written in an old-fashioned hand on 38 lined foolscap pages. The "Mountain Medow Massacre" account covers pages 15 to 34. The last section, "The United States Forgery Case!" ends in midsentence. The Donald R. Moorman Collection, Special Collections, Weber State University, contains a 21-page typescript of the document. Moorman may have acquired the item from his friend, LDS church historian Joseph Fielding Smith.

58. This ends citations from Discursive Remarks. John D. Lee and his family told strikingly similar tales until he was convicted of murder in 1876. See the *Salt Lake Daily Herald*, 1 January 1875, account published as "Rachel's Story as Recorded by Wells Spicer," in Bailey, *A Tale of the "Unkilled,"* 59–63.

59. Curtis E. Bolton statement, Historian's Office Journal, 4 May 1859, LDS Archives.

60. James Lynch, Affidavit, 29 July 1859, and Forney, 29 September 1859, in Buchanan, *Massacre at Mountain Meadows*, Serial 1033, 82, 88.

61. Forney, reports and letters. Ibid., 45, 53, 79, 88.

62. James Lynch, Affidavit, 29 July 1859. Ibid., 82, 84.

63. Rogers statement, Brooks, *Mountain Meadows Massacre*, 270.

CHAPTER 13

1. Porter to Campbell, 19 April 1859, RG 393, Part 1, Old Military Records, Department of Utah Letter Book, vol. 2, National Archives, 183–84, 188; Carleton, *Special Report*, Serial 4377, 1.

2. Haight, Journal 2, 23; Forney to Mix, 30 May 1859, Buchanan, *Massacre at Mountain Meadows*, Serial 1033, 60. Kanosh's report of a child survivor between fourteen to seventeen years old was incorrect.

3. Kelly, ed., *Journals of John D. Lee*, 204, 207, 209; Rogers statement, Brooks, *Mountain Meadows Massacre*, 272–73.

4. Brooks, *Mountain Meadows Massacre*, 272–73, 277–78.

5. Ibid., 271; Hamblin, Affidavit, 3 June 1859, LDS Archives; Cardon, "Mountain Meadows Burial Detachment, 1859," 145; Carleton, *Special Report*, Serial 4377, 15–16.

6. Campbell to Porter, 6 July 1859, in Buchanan, *Massacre at Mountain Meadows*, Serial 1033, 15.

7. Brewer to Campbell, 6 May 1859, Ibid., 16–17.

8. Cradlebaugh, *Utah and the Mormons*, 17; Gemmell to Little, 14 October 1872, Brigham Young Collection, LDS Archives; Carleton, *Special Report*, Serial 4377, 9–10.

9. Dame to Smith, 18 May 1859, LDS Archives, cited in Pease, "William Horne Dame," 130.

10. Ibid., 15.

11. Campbell to Porter, 6 July 1859, in Buchanan, *Massacre at Mountain Meadows*, Serial 1033, 16; Carleton, *Special Report*, Serial 4377, 12.

12. Brewer, "The Massacre at Mountain Meadows," 513–14. Dr. Brewer recalled meeting the emigrants at Ash Hollow, north of the probable route of the Arkansas parties.

13. A tracing of the Prince map is in RG 94, Record and Pension File 751395, National Archives. See Backus, *Mountain Meadows Witness*, 110, for a reproduction.

14. Carleton, *Special Report*, Serial 4377, 16; Cardon, "Mountain Meadows Burial Detachment," 145.

15. Shelton, Diary, 20 May 1859, LDS Archives; Carleton, *Special Report*, Serial 4377, 4–5, 11.

16. Manuscript copy of Carleton's Report, Mountain Meadows File, LDS Archives, Josiah Rogerson Lee Trial Materials, LDS Archives, 7.

17. Carleton, *Special Report,* Serial 4377, 15; Shelton, Diary, 20 May 1859, LDS Archives. The granite marker has long since disappeared.

18. Cradlebaugh, *Utah and the Mormons*, 17, 20, 22; Rogers statement, Brooks, *Mountain Meadows Massacre*, 277. The next month the U.S. attorney general ordered "that the military should not be used in protecting the Courts."

19. A song that long outlasted their stay expressed the soldiers' conclusions about what they had seen at Mountain Meadows:

> Uncle Sam is bound to see
> This bloody matter through.
> The soldiers will be stationed
> Throughout this Utah land,
> All for to find these murderers out
> And bring them to his hand.
> By order of their president
> This awful deed was done.
> He was the leader of the Mormon church,
> His name was Brigham Young.

See Cheney, ed., *Lore of Faith & Folly*, 158. According to folklorist Olive W. Burt, in Utah this song "was sung only clandestinely for many, many years."

20. Isaac C. Haight, Journal 2, 29 May 1859, Southern Utah University, 24.

21. Cradlebaugh to Buchanan, 3 June 1859, *San Francisco Bulletin*, 24 June 1859, 3/4.

22. Robinson, "The Utah Expedition," 335–36; Dale L. Morgan typescript of John Wolcott Phelps Diary, Juanita Brooks Papers, Special Collections, Marriott Library.

23. Carleton, "The Mormons as a People," 550–51.

24. Ibid.

25. Carleton to Mackall, 24 June 1859, RG 393, National Archives. Thanks to Durwood Ball for sharing this item.

26. Statements Regarding Soldiers and Judge Cradlebaugh, Collected Materials Relative to the Church Historian's Office, May–June 1859 re MMM, LDS Archives.

27. Shelton, Affidavit, 3 June 1859, Historian's Office Unprocessed Documents, May–June 1859, LDS Archives.

28. Hamblin, Affidavit, 3 June 1859, Collected Materials Relative to the Church Historian's Office, LDS Archives. However truthful the rest of his tale, Jacob Hamblin dated this conversation to 1 May 1859, but the army did not reach Santa Clara until a week later.

29. Hamblin, Affidavit, 17 June 1859, LDS Archives.

30. Furniss, *The Mormon Conflict*, 217; Larson and Larson, eds., *Diary of Charles Lowell Walker*, 63; Alter and Dwyer, eds., "Journal of Captain Albert Tracy," 68.

31. Kenney, ed., *Wilford Woodruff's Journal*, 23 March 1859, 5:313; Whitney, *History of Utah*, 1:717; Brooks, ed., *On the Mormon Frontier*, 2:694.

32. Kenney, ed., *Wilford Woodruff's Journal*, 22 April 1859, 5:329.

33. Ibid., 5:330; Journal History, 24 April 1859.

34. Journal History, 24 April 1859.

35. Ibid.

36. Forney to Mix, 4 May 1859, in Buchanan, *Massacre at Mountain Meadows*, Serial 1033, 57–58. For his reasons for holding back the names of the suspects, see Forney to Greenwood, 22 September 1859, ibid., 86. For Forney's report, see Brooks, *Mountain Meadows Massacre*, 260–65.

37. Smith, Arrest Warrants for Brigham Young, May 1859, LDS Archives.

38. Ibid.

39. Ibid.

40. Journal History, 12 May 1859; Smith and Burton, Executed Warrant, LDS Archives. The latter contains a draft of Young's affidavit and the executed warrant. No trace of the case or its disposition survives in Probate Court Criminal and Civil Case Docket, Series 3944, Reel 2, Utah State Archives, or in any other court record I have examined or that is known to the state archivist or court officials.

41. Author's conversation with archivist Robert Kvasnicka, National Archives, March 1996.

42. In the midst of this controversy, Dimick Huntington's 1857–59 journal was deposited on 24 May 1859 in the Church Historian's Office. If any court in the American West (excepting, of course, one of Utah's probate courts) had seen the evidence it contained, the only debate among the jurors would have been when, where, and how high to hang Brigham Young.

43. Forney to Greenwood, 10 August 1859 and 22 September 1859, in Buchanan, *Massacre at Mountain Meadows*, Serial 1033, 74, 86. For Wilson's defense of his actions, see Buchanan, *Utah Territory*, Serial 1031, 29, 32, 39–42, 55–56, 61.

44. Historian's Office Journal, 25 May 1859, Typescript, LDS Archives, 132.

45. Kenney, ed., *Wilford Woodruff's Journal*, 5:389–90; Forney to Greenwood, 2 November 1859, in Buchanan, *Massacre at Mountain Meadows*, Serial 1033, 91.

46. "Highly Important Letter" and "Affairs in Utah," *Deseret News*, 29 June 1859, 133/1–2.

47. Porter to Dotson, 27 June 1859, Fort Crittenden Letter Book, National Archives, 2:250.

48. Dotson to Cradlebaugh, 3 June 1859, *San Francisco Bulletin*, 24 June 1859, 2/4.

49. Cradlebaugh, *Utah and the Mormons,* 25.

50. Denver to Delaney, 4 March 1859, in Buchanan, *Massacre at Mountain Meadows*, Serial 1033, 51.

51. Young to Eldredge, 5 May 1859, G. R. Bailey collection, copy in author's possession. William C. Mitchell, grandfather of the Dunlap orphans, was one of the commissioners.

52. In the Matter of the . . . Mountain Meadows Children, Utah State Archives.

53. Forney's report, 29 September 1859, in Buchanan, *Massacre at Mountain Meadows*, Serial 1033, 89.

54. Johnston to Adjutant General, 27 June 1859, Fort Crittenden Letter Book, National Archives, 2:251–52.

55. Buchanan, *Massacre at Mountain Meadows*, Serial 1033, 62–63, 65–66.

56. *Valley Tan*, 6 July 1859, 2/1. The paper noted that P. E. Fund debts were "like Sinbad's old man of the sea—very difficult to be got rid of."

57. Porter to Fancher, 6 July and 21 July 1859, Fort Crittenden Letter Book, National Archives, 2:261, 273–74.

58. Lynch affidavit, 27 July 1859, Buchanan, *Massacre at Mountain Meadows*, Serial 1033, 81; Carleton, *Special Report*, Serial 4377, 14; "'Children of the Massacre,'" *Arkansas Sunday Post-Dispatch*, September 1895; Sarah Baker Memoir.

59. Rogers statement, Brooks, *Mountain Meadows Massacre*, 269. The eye disease, which eventually blinded Sarah Dunlap, was perhaps conjunctivitis caused by the wind, sand, and glare of southern Utah. James Lynch later claimed Dunlap told him "one of the butchers ran up and shot her in the right arm, on her dead mothers breast, and the flash of the gun injured her eyesight." See Parker, *Recollections of the Mountain Meadows Massacre*, 31.

60. Forney to Greenwood, 25 July 1859, August 1859, and 29 September 1859, in Buchanan, *Massacre at Mountain Meadows*, Serial 1033, 71–72, 79, 89.

61. As noted, John D. Lee reported the number in a sermon on 27 September 1857, while Hamblin told Carleton the emigrants "had all been killed off . . . except seventeen children."

62. "'Children of the Massacre,'" *Arkansas Sunday Post-Dispatch*, September 1895.

63. Memorial Program.

64. Brooks, *Mountain Meadows Massacre*, 104–5; Brooks, *John Doyle Lee*, 372.

65. Holmes, ed., *Covered Wagon Women*, 7:251–52.

66. Historian's Office Letterbook, 30 June 1859, Typescript, LDS Archives, 790.

67. Forney to Greenwood, 2 November 1859, Buchanan, *Massacre at Mountain Meadows*, Serial 1033, 91. Forney did not adopt Tackitt.

68. Cannon to Young, 13 December 1859, Brigham Young Collection, LDS Archives; Young, 12 April and 24 May 1860, Letters to William H. Hooper, Western Americana Collection, Beinecke Library.

69. Cannon to Young, 13 December 1859, Brigham Young Collection, LDS Archives.

70. Greenwood to Henry, 13 December 1859, in Buchanan, *Massacre at Mountain Meadows*, Serial 1033, 99.

71. "'Children of the Massacre,'" *Arkansas Sunday Post-Dispatch*, September 1895.

72. "The Mountain Meadows Massacre," *San Francisco Bulletin*, 31 May 1859, 3/3.

73. "Mountain Meadows," *San Francisco Bulletin Supplement*, 24 March 1877, 1/8. This story was attributed to "a most estimable lady" who tended the children in Salt Lake. Jacob Forney listed "John Sorough" as one of the surviving children, but William C. Mitchell correctly identified the boy as John Calvin Miller. See Mitchell to Greenwood, 27 April 1860, Letters Received, Bureau of Indian Affairs, National Archives.

74. Cradlebaugh, *Utah and the Mormons*, 20.

75. Greenwood to Mitchell, 23 July 1859, and Mitchell to Greenwood, 4 October 1859, in Buchanan, *Massacre at Mountain Meadows*, Serial 1033, 69–70, 90.

76. Baskin, *Reminiscences of Early Utah*, 142–43.

77. Fancher, *The Fancher Family*, 96. Family tradition says that Kit saw his father murdered, "and after the massacre, while herding sheep, found one of the wives of a Mormon wearing his murdered mother's cape."

78. Logan, "New Light on the Mountain Meadows Caravan," 228, 234, 236; Thurston deposition, 2 May 1911, 5.

79. Elizabeth Baker Memoir, 6; Sarah Baker Memoir.

80. "Extract from a letter to this office," *Arkansas State Gazette and Democrat*, 24 September 1859, 2/4.

81. Remarks of Judge Roger V. Logan, Jr., 15 September 1990, LDS Archives.

82. Smith to Young, 17 August 1858, Brooks, *Mountain Meadows Massacre*, 248; Brooks, *John Doyle Lee*, 253; Moorman and Sessions, *Camp Floyd and the Mormons*, 142, citing Historian's Office Journal, 13 April 1859.

83. Brooks and Cleland, eds., *Mormon Chronicle*, 1:213; Haight, Journal 2, 31 July 1859, Special Collections, Southern Utah University, 24; photo "J. M. Higbee, Mayor 1867–1871," Special Collections, Southern Utah University.

84. Brooks and Cleland, eds., *Mormon Chronicle*, 1:214, 219; Brooks, *John Doyle Lee*, 252. Lee's second attorney was Hosea Stout.

85. Marion Jackson Shelton, Diary, 21 September 1859, LDS Archives.

86. Cradlebaugh and Sinclair to Buchanan, 16 July 1859, "Correspondence between the judges of Utah and the Attorney General or President," in Buchanan, *Utah Territory*, Serial 1031, 20.

87. Ibid., 21; Brigham Young Office Journal, 2 September 1859, 78, 86; Young to Kane, 17 September 1859, Brigham Young Collection, LDS Archives.

88. "The Mountain Meadows Massacre—Affected Inquiry into It," *San Francisco Bulletin*, 28 October 1859, 3/4, from a transcription in the California State Library's Mormon file.

89. Baskin, *Reminiscences of Early Utah*, 118, 122.

90. Cannon to Young, 13 December 1859, Brigham Young Collection, LDS Archives.

91. Historian's Office Journal, 8 December 1859, Typescript, LDS Archives, 88.

92. Young to Kane, 15 December 1859, Brigham Young Collection, LDS Archives, 325–28. Kane sent the attorney general Young's 15 December 1859 letter to show to the president. Kane preserved all "the great man's letters," and he asked Black to return the original. See Kane to Buchanan, 15 January 1860, Papers of Jeremiah Sullivan Black, Manuscripts Division, Library of Congress, 54008, 54010.

93. Young to Kane, 15 December 1859, Brigham Young Collection, LDS Archives, 325–28.

94. Furniss, *The Mormon Conflict*, 208, 210.

95. See Young to Hicks, 16 February 1869, Brigham Young Collection, LDS Archives; Arrington, *Brigham Young*, 279–81.

96. "An Interview with Alfred Cumming," *Salt Lake Tribune*, 1 November 1876, 4/4.

97. Stenhouse, *The Rocky Mountain Saints,* 445.

98. Ibid.

99. Long, *The Saints and the Union*, 19, 24; Brigham Young, 10 March 1860, *Journal of Discourses*, 8:363.

100. Moorman and Sessions, *Camp Floyd and the Mormons*, 276.

101. Historian's Office Journal, 12 May 1861, LDS Archives. For the story of the murder of Sgt. Ralph Pike, who had smashed Spencer's skull in a grazing dispute, see Schindler, *In Another Time,* 100–2. Spencer stood trial for the murder in 1889 and was found not guilty, but the presiding judge said, "If this is not a case of murder, speaking from a practice of over 23 years, then I have never seen one in a court of justice."

102. Spencer, Father's Trips to St. George, Special Collections, Southern Utah University Library; Greenwood, ed., *Brigham Young's Excursions into the Settlements*, 97.

103. Brooks and Cleland, eds., *Mormon Chronicle*, 1:313.

104. Ibid., 1:313–14.

105. Kenney, ed., *Wilford Woodruff's Journal*, 25 May 1861, 5:577. According to Woodruff, Brigham Young "said it should be vengeance is mine and I have taken a little."

106. Brooks, *Mountain Meadows Massacre*, 183. George F. Price's company of California Volunteers restored the monument in May 1864. It lasted until about 1870, when it was again torn down. When Lorenzo Brown saw the monument on 1 July 1864, someone had written below the Bible verse, "Remember Hauns Mill and Carthage Jail." See Brooks, *John Doyle Lee*, 266.

CHAPTER 14

1. Whitney, *History of Utah*, 2:623; Baskin, *Reminiscences of Early Utah*, 5–6.

2. Ibid., 83–84. DeWolfe never published his editorial, for the *Valley Tan* ceased publication after printing William Rogers's statement.

3. Townsend, *The Mormon Trials at Salt Lake City,* 27.

4. Brodie, ed., *The City of the Saints*, 378–79.

5. Clemens, *Roughing It*, 111, 143–44.

6. Bishop, ed., *Mormonism Unveiled*, 259.

7. Brooks, *John Doyle Lee*, 257–58, 262–63, 268–69; Anderson, *Desert Saints*, 192. As president of the Harmony Branch, Lee held a post equivalent to bishop, but he never actually served as a bishop.

8. Brooks, *John Doyle Lee*, 271; Brooks and Cleland, eds., *Mormon Chronicle*, 2:6.

9. Brooks, *John Doyle Lee*, 269–72.

10. Bigler, *Forgotten Kingdom*, 199.

11. Kenney, ed., *Wilford Woodruff's Journal*, 31 December 1860, 5:529.

12. Bigler, *Forgotten Kingdom*, 201–4; Schindler, *Orrin Porter Rockwell*, 315–16. As outrageous as the charge of castration sounds, Brooks explained the Mormon attitude: "If it were necessary to emasculate a man

who was corrupting the morals of the community, it would serve as a warning to others that such things would not be tolerated here." See Brooks, *John Doyle Lee*, 153.

13. Anderson, *Joseph Morris*, 94, 128; Bigler, *Forgotten Kingdom*, 212.

14. Dwyer, *The Gentile Comes to Utah*, 107–9.

15. Long, *The Saints and the Union*, 67–70.

16. Ibid., 74; Bernhisel to Young, 11 July 1862, Brigham Young Collection, LDS Archives.

17. Alexander, *Utah, the Right Place*, 147; Long, *The Saints and the Union*, 10, 47–48, 70–72.

18. Bigler, *Forgotten Kingdom*, 224–28.

19. Schindler, "The Bear River Massacre," 302. For the best history of the event, see Madsen, *The Shoshoni Frontier and the Bear River Massacre*.

20. Kenney, ed., *Wilford Woodruff's Journal*, 11 and 31 December 1861, 5:606, 617.

21. Smith, *Accounts of Brigham Young*, Serial 1128, 1–7.

22. Ibid., 2–3; Bernhisel to Young, 12 January 1862, Brigham Young Papers, Marriott Library.

23. Brooks, *Mountain Meadows Massacre*, 153–54.

24. Smith, *Accounts of Brigham Young*, Serial 1128, 101–2. This list is sometimes used to identify Indians who participated in the massacre.

25. Bernhisel to Young, 24 March 1862, Brigham Young Papers, Marriott Library. Although "April 15, 1862 Answered" is written on Bernhisel's letter, no reply survives in the Brigham Young Collection at LDS Archives.

26. Bernhisel to Young, 11 July 1862, Brigham Young Collection, LDS Archives.

27. Brigham Young, Letter to John Fitch Kinney, 2 November 1863, Western Americana Collection, Beinecke Library. Young refused to pay Moses his agreed-upon fee.

28. Cradlebaugh, *Utah and the Mormons*, 21; Arrington, *Brigham Young*, 269. Arrington gave no source for this information.

29. Young to Rossé, 4 March 1863, Brigham Young Collection, Utah State Historical Society.

30. Brigham Young, 8 March 1863, *Journal of Discourses*, 10:109–10.

31. Bishop, ed., *Mormonism Unveiled*, 217, 258. Lee was replaced as judge in March 1859. See Brooks, *John Doyle Lee*, 262.

32. Brooks, *On the Ragged Edge*, 77; and *Mountain Meadows Massacre*, 164–65. Carleton's 1859 report identified Leavitt as a likely massacre participant, but the government never reindicted him, suggesting he may have secretly cooperated with federal investigators.

33. Brooks, *Mountain Meadows Massacre*, 165; Lyman, *San Bernardino*, 419–20. Woods's rank comes from Muster Rolls, 10 October 1857, Nauvoo Legion, Utah State Archives, 3346.

34. Baskin, *Reminiscences of Early Utah*, 13, 164.

35. Bigler, *Forgotten Kingdom*, 247–53. Eveline Brooks Auerbach heard "terrible cries" the night Robinson was murdered. Her mother recognized one of the killers "but dared not tell." See Ogden, ed., *Frontier Reminiscences*, 51–52.

36. Connor to Carter, 23 October 1866, copy in author's possession.

37. Whitney, *History of Utah*, 2:153; Baskin, *Reminiscences of Early Utah*, 28.

38. Baskin, *Reminiscences of Early Utah*, 15–16, citing "Talk with Brigham Young," *New York Evening Post*, 7 November 1867.

39. Baskin, *Reply by R. N. Baskin*, 16, 25–26; Alexander, *Utah, the Right Place*, 153.

40. Sherman to Young, Telegram, 10 April 1866, and Young to Sherman, 11 April 1866, Brigham Young Collection, LDS Archives. Punctuation added. Sherman's threat was a bluff. He had his "hands full with the Indians, and the conflict of the races in the South, without begging any new cause of trouble," he told his brother. "We should attempt nothing with the Mormons until the railroad is finished as far as Fort Bridger." See Thorndike, ed., *The Sherman Letters*, 288.

41. Brigham Young, 23 December 1866, *Journal of Discourses*, 11:281–82. Most Americans doubted that Young was as sensitive as he claimed. Had he been president, the Mormon leader told journalist Samuel Bowles with "an almost demon-like spirit," he would have put the Confederate diplomats captured on the British ship *Trent* "where they would never peep." While Bowles had been "quite disposed to be incredulous"

on such matters, he "could not help thinking of the Mountain Meadows Massacre." See Bowles, *Across the Continent*, 113.

42. Larson, *Erastus Snow*, 571.

43. Hicks, Life History, 45; Hicks to Young, 4 December 1868, Brigham Young Collection, LDS Archives. See *Deseret News*, 8 January 1867, for Young's sermon.

44. Hicks to Young, 11 October 1867, Brigham Young Collection, LDS Archives; Hicks, Life History, 44–45.

45. Hicks to Young, 4 December 1868, Brigham Young Collection, LDS Archives.

46. Young to Hicks, 16 February 1869, Brigham Young Collection, LDS Archives. See Arrington, *Brigham Young*, 281, for a less-than-forthright interpretation of Young's letter to Hicks.

47. Ibid.

48. Hicks, Life History, 44.

49. George W. Gibbs, Affidavit, 21 July 1914, Mountain Meadows File, LDS Archives. No such letter to Haight is to be found in the Brigham Young Collection at LDS Archives.

50. Ashworth, The Autobiography of William B. Ashworth, 101.

51. Brooks and Cleland, eds., *Mormon Chronicle*, 2:100–2.

52. Ibid., 122–23; see Brimhall, Gleanings of John D. Lee, 10, for Bishop Pace's name.

53. Hicks, "Some Startling Facts," *Salt Lake Tribune*, 20 August 1874, 2/3.

54. Journal History, 9 September 1877, citing the *Deseret News*.

55. Larson, *Erastus Snow*, 571; George Armstrong Hicks, Scrapbook, 1887–1925, LDS Archives. The scrapbook consists of letters and newspaper articles on beet farming, Republican politics, polygamy, the Civil War, and astrology, but it does not contain Brigham Young's 1869 letter. For an interpretation of the Hicks-Young correspondence that characterized Hicks as "a nuisance" and his letters as "insolent," see Bitton, "'I'd Rather Have Some Roasting Ears,'" 214–16.

56. Muster Rolls, 10 October 1857, Nauvoo Legion, Utah State Archives, 3346.

57. Spencer to E. Snow, 26 March 1867, Brigham Young Collection, LDS Archives. It is not clear if Snow or Young ever replied to this letter. Beadle, *Western Wilds*, 497, wrote that a St. George schoolteacher named Spencer "died of grief and remorse for his share of the act."

58. Autobiography of John Hawley, Community of Christ Archives.

59. "The Real Criminals," *Salt Lake Tribune*, 29 July 1875, 4/4.

60. Obituary, *San Bernardino Times*, 9 February 1877; typescript copy by E. Leo Lyman in author's possession. The Mormon church excommunicated Apostle Lyman on 12 May 1870.

61. Young, *Wife No. 19*, 251.

62. "Journal of George Cannon Lambert," in Carter, ed., *Heart Throbs of the West*, 9:329–30. Lambert regretted not hearing Lee's story, for later he was "called to hunt up and publish all the facts connected with that sanguinary affair" as part of the Charles Penrose investigation.

63. Lockley, *The Lee Trial*, 23.

64. Peterson, "Life in a Village Society, 1877-1920," 86.

65. Ann Gordge Lee, Autobiography, BYU Library, 11. For many reasons Ann Lee's story is literally unbelievable. She told a blood-chilling version of the massacre and described all the classic tales of southern Utah blood atonement and several new stories. She also claimed to have wandered the West with Geronimo and Billy the Kid. As noted, persuasive evidence indicates that all of the seventeen children saved from the massacre were rescued. By her own account, Lee married Gordge when she was thirteen years old. See J. Golden Kimball, Diary, 23 October 1897, Kimball Papers, Marriott Library.

66. Hicks, Life History, 42–43. Hicks claimed Lee's wives confessed to their husband they had all slept with his sometime son-in-law, Richard "Rattle Snake Dick" Darling.

67. Rogerson, "The Guilt of John D. Lee," in Mountain Meadows File, LDS Archives, 9.

68. Affidavit of Hezekiah E. Duffin, LDS Archives.

69. Joseph Fielding Smith to Brimhall, 10 October 1930, Gleanings Concerning John D. Lee, 10.

70. Baskin, *Reminiscences of Early Utah*, 138–39.

71. Roberts, *Comprehensive History*, 5:259–61.

72. Young, *Wife No. 19*, 289; Hance, A biographical sketch of John Varah Long, 83–84.

73. Walker, *Wayward Saints*, 101–4. Brigham Young's 12 September 1857 letter to Clinton was ill-considered, but Young had made similarly provocative remarks in public the same day.

74. Roberts, *Comprehensive History*, 5:260, 262, 264; Walker, *Wayward Saints*, 5–8, 153–66.

75. Peterson, *Utah's Black Hawk War*, 8, 13–15, 383.

76. Roberts, *Comprehensive History*, 5:305; Walker, *Wayward Saints*, 232–34.

77. "Revenge of an Outlawed Husband," *The World: New York*, 23 November 1869, 1/6–2/1.

CHAPTER 15

1. Newton, *Hero or Traitor*, 11, 15–17.

2. "Wandell's Lecture," *Salt Lake Tribune*, 31 January 1873, 3/3.

3. Wandell to Joseph Smith III, 26 September 1874, Typescript, Community of Christ Archives, 2.

4. Stenhouse, *The Rocky Mountain Saints*, 431–34; and Stenhouse, *Tell It All*, 326.

5. Wandell to Joseph Smith III, 26 September 1874, Typescript, Community of Christ Archives, 2.

6. "Wandell's Lecture," *Salt Lake Tribune*, 31 January 1873, 3/3; *Carson State Register*, 12 February 1871, 2/4, referencing an 11 February 1871 issue of the *Utah Reporter* that is no longer available.

7. Joseph C. Walker, History of the Mormons in the Early Days of Utah, 58.

8. Beadle, *Western Wilds*, 503, 514.

9. "A Second Interview with Brigham Young, Jr.," *Philadelphia Morning Post*, 1 November 1869, 1/4.

10. "Mountain Meadow Massacre," *Deseret Weekly News*, 1 December 1869, 3/1–3. Brooks, *Mountain Meadows Massacre*, 213, identified Cannon as the article's author, but the text is derived from a George A. Smith letter. As noted, Cannon had learned in 1858 that Mormons "did the job." See Newton, *Hero or Traitor*, 44, 81n95.

11. Buchanan, *A Good Time Coming*, 181.

12. *Salt Lake Tribune*, 27 July 1875, cited in Dwyer, *The Gentile Comes to Utah*, 100–1.

13. Morgan to Brooks, 7 September 1942, Box 1, Folder 1, Brooks Papers, Marriott Library.

14. Rogerson to J. H. Smith, 22 May 1911, Mountain Meadows File, Folder 21, LDS Archives.

15. Rogerson, "The Guilt of John D. Lee," Mountain Meadows File, LDS Archives, 9.

16. Argus, "Lee and the Mountain Meadow Massacre," *Carson State Register*, 12 February 1871, 2/4, quoting from an 11 February 1871 issue of the *Utah Reporter*.

17. The "forged letter" story is told in several variations in the Caroline Parry Woolley Collection, Southern Utah University.

18. Brooks, *John Doyle Lee*, 288; Brooks and Cleland, eds., *Mormon Chronicle*, 2:135–36.

19. Brimhall, Gleanings Concerning John D. Lee, 21, 23.

20. Brooks and Cleland, eds., *Mormon Chronicle*, 2:143–44. "It is strange," noted Brooks, that Lee himself provided all the information about his excommunication known to her. William Lund of the LDS Church Historian's Office told Brooks they had no copy of "Carrington's letter nor any minutes" describing the action. Ibid., 2:256.

21. Staker, ed., *Waiting for the World's End*, 302; Brooks and Cleland, eds., *Mormon Chronicle*, 2:146–47.

22. Brooks and Cleland, eds., *Mormon Chronicle*, 2:150, 168, 258n70; Rogerson to J. H. Smith, 22 May 1911, Mountain Meadows File, LDS Archives. The prophet's nephew said he saw Brigham Young refuse to shake hands with Lee in September 1865 and asked why he lied to him about the massacre. See Young, "Reminiscences of John R. Young," 85. This recollection may be based on an actual event, but the 1865 date is questionable.

23. Brooks and Cleland, eds., *Mormon Chronicle*, 2:151–52.

24. Ibid., 2:152–53.

25. Ibid., 2:153–54.

26. Ibid., 2:154, 165.

27. Edna Lee Brimhall, Joseph Lee, Thomas S. Kimball, and E. W. Richardson statements in Brimhall, Gleanings Concerning John D. Lee, 15, 38, 43, 44, 45.

28. Argus, "Lee and the Mountain Meadow Massacre," *Carson State Register*, 12 February 1871, 2/4, quoting from an 11 February 1871 issue of the *Utah Reporter.*

29. Backus, *Mountain Meadows Witness*, 177, 181, 188–89, 191, 196–97, 203, 214, 220.

30. "Klingensmith . . . Murdered by Mormons," *Salt Lake Tribune*, 4 August 1881, 2/3; "Remarks on the Lee Trial," *Salt Lake Tribune*, 29 July 1875, 4/3; Brooks and Cleland, eds., *Mormon Chronicle*, 1:319n17.

31. "Klingon Smith" affidavit, Brooks, *Mountain Meadows Massacre*, 238–41.

32. Ibid.

33. Whitney, *History of Utah*, 2:782, 801.

34. Brooks and Cleland, eds., *Mormon Chronicle*, 2:164–65.

35. Brooks, *Mountain Meadows Massacre*, 190, quoting Frederick Dellenbaugh.

36. Brooks and Cleland, eds., *Mormon Chronicle*, 2:174, 175, 176–77.

37. Ibid., 2:175; Rusho, *Lee's Ferry*, 13, 18–20, 34.

38. Dellenbaugh, *A Canyon Voyage*, 195, 210–12.

39. Kelly, ed., "Captain Francis Marion Bishop's Journal," 237–38.

40. Beaman, "The Cañon of the Colorado, . . . Glimpses of Mormon Life," 592–93.

41. Crampton, ed., "F. S. Dellenbaugh of the Colorado," 242.

42. Brooks and Cleland, eds., *Mormon Chronicle*, 2:200–1, 259n81. If this letter exists at LDS Archives it is not available to scholars.

43. Beadle, *Life in Utah*, 185.

44. Brooks and Cleland, eds., *Mormon Chronicle*, 2:203; see Beadle, *Western Wilds*, 302–7 for Beadle's account of "the remarkable story told me by Major *John Doyle Lee.*"

45. Higbee History and Stories, Special Collections, Southern Utah State University, 10.

46. Woolley Collection, Southern Utah University. It is not clear what motivated Young to restore Haight's blessings.

47. Brooks, "Lee's Ferry at Lonely Dell," 290.

48. Brooks and Cleland, eds., *Mormon Chronicle*, 2:336–38.

49. J. A. Little to Reynolds, 27 November 1872, Brigham Young Collection, LDS Archives.

50. See, for example, the references to Missourians in the twentieth-century memoirs of Elizabeth Baker Terry and her sister, Sarah Baker Mitchell, which do not appear in earlier survivor accounts. Much of the prosecution's strategy in the first Lee trial appears to be an attempt to validate stories told in the Stenhouse books.

51. Stenhouse, *The Rocky Mountain Saints*, 424, 427–28, 434; Stenhouse, "*Tell It All*," 325. *Rocky Mountain Saints* introduced the term "Missouri Wild-cats."

52. *Los Angeles Star*, 7 November 1857, 2/2. Lee trial prosecutor Robert N. Baskin in *Reply by R. N. Baskin*, 15–16, argued that the "Wild Cats" were actually the Dukes company.

53. "More Outrages on the Plains!!" *Los Angeles Star*, 24 October 1857, 2/2.

54. Moorman and Sessions, *Camp Floyd and the Mormons*, 133. Based on the childhood memories of Francis Fawcett Hayes, this fable does not stand up to the most basic analysis.

55. Bigler, *Forgotten Kingdom*, 191, 309–13; Schindler, *Orrin Porter Rockwell*, 357–59. Bigler demonstrates that the defense relied on perjured testimony and fabricated 1857 journals to win the acquittal of Sylvanus Collett in his subsequent trial for these killings.

56. Brooks and Cleland, eds., *Mormon Chronicle*, 2:174; Pusey, *Builders of the Kingdom*, 117; Alexander, *Utah, the Right Place*, 175–77.

57. "The People's Column," *Salt Lake Tribune*, 8 November 1872.

58. Dwyer, *The Gentile Comes to Utah*, 98.

59. Young to Secretary of War Belknap, 21 May 1872, Brigham Young Collection, LDS Archives.

60. Bates to Williams, 24 October 1872, and Hawley to Williams, 20 November 1872, Mountain Meadows Massacre, National Archives Microfilm Publication; Waters, *Life among the Mormons and a March to Their Zion*, 191.

61. Baskin, *Reminiscences of Early Utah*, 36–37, 57–58.

62. Stenhouse, *The Rocky Mountain Saints*, 456–57.

63. Cannon to Young, 10 and 12 December 1872, Brigham Young Collection, LDS Archives.

64. Baskin, *Reply by R. N. Baskin*, 27, 28; Bigler, *Forgotten Kingdom*, 281–85.

65. Baskin, *Reminiscences of Early Utah*, 59.

66. Alexander, *Utah, the Right Place*, 176; Whitney, *History of Utah*, 2:783; Dwyer, *The Gentile Comes to Utah*, 99.

67. Whitney, *History of Utah*, 2:782–83.

68. Tomblin to Young, 12 July 1871, Brigham Young Collection, LDS Archives.

69. Wheeler, "The Late James Gemmell," 332–34; "Career of Montana Pioneer Is Rival of Monte Cristo's," *Dillon Tribune*, undated article in author's possession, courtesy of Elaine White. Gemmell's gravestone in Sheridan, Montana, gives his birth date as 4 February 1814. Virtually all Utah sources spell his last name "Gammell."

70. Elizabeth Mahala Hendricks, Family History Library; Journal History, 19 October 1851 and 14 September 1850; Joseph C. Walker, History of the Mormons in the Early Days of Utah, 42.

71. Ibid., 53; Journal History, 24 February 1856. Hosea Stout met "James M. Gammell returning from a trading tour some 600 miles S.E." On 23 January 1855 he told Stout that Indians had killed "a small party of Whites" near Devils Gate. See Brooks, ed., *On the Mormon Frontier*, 2:519, 549.

72. Walker, History of the Mormons in the Early Days of Utah, 44–56; *Western Standard*, 3 July 1857, 2/2.

73. I. N. Hinckley, Diary, 21 July 1857, LDS Archives; Wheeler, "The Late James Gemmell," 334; Walker, History of the Mormons in the Early Days of Utah, 45–46; Bennion, Diary, Book 2, October 1857.

74. "Letter from Provo City, U.T.," *San Francisco Bulletin*, 19 April 1859, 3/3-4, and *Valley Tan*, 5 April 1859, 3/1; Walker, History of the Mormons in the Early Days of Utah, 1, 45–48.

75. Gemmell to Little, 14 October 1872, Brigham Young Collection, LDS Archives. Gemmell did not indicate how he answered the investigator's questions.

76. Ibid.

77. Photograph of James Gemmell's headstone in the Sheridan, Montana, cemetery provided to the author by Elaine White of Whitefish, Montana. The headstone dates Gemmell's flight to 1857, an obvious error.

78. Gemmell to Little, 14 October 1872, Brigham Young Collection, LDS Archives.

CHAPTER 16

1. See Brimhall, Gleanings Concerning John D. Lee, 40–41, for Samuel B. Tenney's account of the first Lee-Stokes meeting. Pratt Pace, 62, tells a variant of the story.

2. Brooks, *John Doyle Lee*, 52–53, 110, 116–7, 119, 259.

3. Brimhall, Gleanings Concerning John D. Lee, 41. J. S. McFate told of a healing of his son, Joe. Ibid., 47. For a similar story, see James E. Taylor's account of Lee's healing of his sister in Brooks, *Mountain Meadows Massacre*, 203.

4. William Henry Solomon, Journal, 15 March 1873, LDS Archives, 69.

5. Hicks, Life History, 43.

6. Alexander, *Utah, the Right Place*, 176–77.

7. Stokes, "Arrest of John D. Lee," in Bishop, ed., *Mormonism Unveiled*, 293–96.

8. Hakes, To Whom it May Concern, 24 April 1916, BYU Library.

9. Ibid.

10. Beadle, *Western Wilds*, 490.

11. Bishop, ed., *Mormonism Unveiled*, 297–99.

12. Ibid., 299–301.

13. Brimhall, Gleanings Concerning John D. Lee, 22.

14. Schindler, "125 Years of Comment," *Salt Lake Tribune*, 14 April 1996, A18.

15. Bancroft, *History of Utah*, 565n46; Beadle, *Western Wilds*, 526.

16. Whitney, *History of Utah*, 2:786–87; Brooks, *Mountain Meadows Massacre*, 195.

17. Historian's Office Journal, 14 July 1875, Typescript, LDS Archives, 69.

18. Fielding, *Trials of John D. Lee*, 65; "Lee and the Priesthood," *Salt Lake Tribune*, 18 July 1875, 1/2.

19. Lockley, *The Lee Trial*, 8–9. Lockley printed only the preamble and conclusion of Lee's confession but summarized its main points. No source appears to reproduce the entire confession.

20. Beadle, *Western Wilds*, 504; Whitney, *History of Utah*, 2:789; Lockley, *The Lee Trial*, 54.

21. "City Jottings," *Salt Lake Tribune*, 27 July 1875, 2/2; Macfarlane, *Yours Sincerely, John M. Macfarlane*, 64–66, 96–97, 169–72. Macfarlane, a stepson of Isaac Haight, was indicted in 1859 for participating in the massacre. He composed the Christmas hymn, "Far, Far Away on Judea's Plains."

22. Lockley, *The Lee Trial*, 6, 10; Whitney, *History of Utah*, 2:789–90.

23. Lockley, *The Lee Trial*, 6; Brooks, *Mountain Meadows Massacre*, 191.

24. Beadle, *Western Wilds*, 507; Fielding, *Trials of John D. Lee*, 122.

25. Lockley, *The Lee Trial*, 15–17; Brooks, *Mountain Meadows Massacre,* 192; F. E. Lockley to E. M. C. Lockley, 26 July 1875, Lockley Collection, Huntington Library, 2.

26. Lee Trials Transcripts, 240.

27. Lockley, *The Lee Trial*, 24, 25, 28.

28. Brooks, *John Doyle Lee*, 337–38; Historian's Office Journal, 29 July 1875, Typescript, LDS Archives, 73; "The Lee Trial," *Salt Lake Tribune*, 30 July 1875, 1/2. Brooks, *Emma Lee*, 84, told a different version of the story.

29. Boreman Papers, Typescript, Utah State Historical Society, 10.

30. Beadle, *Western Wilds*, 510.

31. Lee Trials Transcripts, 292–96.

32. Lockley, *The Lee Trial*, 30. The argument "the Indians made us do it" would be repeated with dramatic detail in Lee's memoir and in all subsequent participant statements, despite the fact that their Mormon allies tightly controlled and probably outnumbered the Paiutes.

33. Whitney, *History of Utah*, 2:804, dismissed these fears as "malicious falsehoods."

34. "Interview with the Chief of the Beavers," *San Francisco Morning Call*, from clippings in Ichel Watters Papers, Utah State Historical Society. Pe-be-ats was leader of the Qui-ump-uts band of Paiutes when the Mormons founded Beaver in 1856. Pe-be-ats was known as Beaverats and may be the man the *Call* interviewed in 1876. See Palmer, "Pahute Indian Homelands," 92–93.

35. F. E. Lockley to E. M. C. Lockley, 31 July 1875, Lockley Collection, Huntington Library, 3.

36. Lee Trials Transcripts, 306; Whitney, *History of Utah*, 2:799. Lee's claim that he tried to save the surviving emigrants lacks credibility, but he may have felt he had avenged the blood of the prophets in the initial attack. Lee said the Paiutes called him "Yaw Guts"—crybaby—when he "cried with sorrow when [he] saw that [he] could not pacify the savages." See Bishop, ed., *Mormonism Unveiled*, 227, 229. The Paiutes said they gave Lee the nickname when he cried over lost cattle.

37. "The Mountain Meadows Slaughter," newspaper dispatch dated 29 July 1875, Watters, Papers, Utah State Historical Society; Wells Spicer's opening statement, Lee Trials Transcripts, 327.

38. Lockley, *The Lee Trial*, 31, 33.

39. Ibid., 35; Whitney, *History of Utah*, 2:800; Baskin, *Reminiscences of Early Utah*, 145. Baskin thought Hoops's testimony revealed he was not only "a false witness, but a fool as well."

40. Clipping from *San Francisco Morning Call*, Watters Papers, Utah State Historical Society.

41. Lockley, *The Lee Trial*, 49–50.

42. Baskin, *Reminiscences of Early Utah*, 135–36.

43. Lockley, *The Lee Trial*, 39–42.

44. Beadle, *Western Wilds*, 512–13.

45. Ibid., 514; newspaper extracts from Lockley, *The Lee Trial*, 54, 56, 57, 62, 63.

46. "Brigham's Great Crime," *Salt Lake Tribune*, 10 August 1875; Fielding, *Trials of John D. Lee*, 194.

47. Ashworth, Autobiography, Utah State Historical Society, 102; Brooks, *Mountain Meadows Massacre*, 193.

48. Bishop, ed., *Mormonism Unveiled*, 267.

49. Pusey, *Builders of the Kingdom*, 122–23; Jenson, *LDS Biographical Encyclopedia*, 1:42; Kelly, *Utah's Black Friday*, 191; Brooks and Cleland, eds., *Mormon Chronicle*, 2:355.

50. "Argus," quoted in Stenhouse, *The Rocky Mountain Saints*, 435–37; Baskin, *Reminiscences of Early Utah*, 148; Brooks, *Mountain Meadows Massacre*, 219.

51. Brooks and Cleland, eds., *Mormon Chronicle*, 2:369, 378, 380, 382.

52. Ibid., 2:370, 375, 389, 391, 396, 397, 401.

53. Whitney, *History of Utah*, 2:803–4; Spears to Pierpoint, 21 January 1876, Mountain Meadows Massacre, National Archives Microfilm Publication.

54. Interview with S. W. Crowe, 18 September 1886, copy in author's possession.

55. Amorah Lee Smithson statement in Brimhall, Gleanings Concerning John D. Lee, 26–27.

56. Webb, Interviews with Living Pioneers, 1935, LDS Archives, 29–30.

57. Bishop, ed., *Mormonism Unveiled*, 267.

58. Brooks and Cleland, eds., *Mormon Chronicle*, 2:436, 449, 452.

59. Dwyer, *The Gentile Comes to Utah*, 101.

60. Cannon to Young, 31 March 1876, Brigham Young Collection, LDS Archives.

61. Cannon to Young, 2 April and 27 April 1876, Brigham Young Collection, LDS Archives.

62. Howard to Ferris, 27 May 1876, Mountain Meadows Massacre, National Archives Microfilm Publication.

63. Baskin, *Reminiscences of Early Utah*, 56.

64. Krenkel, ed., *The Life and Times of Joseph Fish, Mormon Pioneer,* 59–60.

65. Baskin, *Reminiscences of Early Utah*, 136.

66. Whitney, *History of Utah*, 2:804–5; Brimhall, Gleanings Concerning John D. Lee, 26; Brooks, *John Doyle Lee*, 358; Brooks, *Emma Lee*, 88.

67. J. D. Lee to Rachel Lee, 12 October 1876, John D. Lee Collection, Huntington Library; Whitney, *History of Utah*, 2:805; Bishop, ed., *Mormonism Unveiled*, 267–68.

68. J. D. Lee to Emma B. Lee, 21 September 1876, John D. Lee Collection, Huntington Library.

69. "Lee Interviewed," *Salt Lake Tribune*, 14 September 1876, 2/2.

70. Boreman Papers, Typescript, Utah State Historical Society, 12; Arrington, "Crusade against Theocracy," 1–45.

71. LDS authorities used these tactics to win the acquittal of Sylvanus Collett in his 1878 trial for the Aiken party murders of 1857. See Bigler, *Forgotten Kingdom*, 309–13.

72. "The Lee Trial," *Salt Lake Tribune*, 12 September 1876, 1/2; Brimhall, Gleanings Concerning John D. Lee, 23, 27; Bishop, ed., *Mormonism Unveiled*, 33.

73. Baskin, *Reminiscences of Early Utah*, 137.

74. "Blood-Atoners Testify," *Salt Lake Tribune*, 16 September 1876, Fielding, *Trials of John D. Lee*, 217; Whitney, *History of Utah*, 2:817; Brooks, *John Doyle Lee*, 360.

75. Boreman Papers, Typescript, Utah State Historical Society, 12.

76. J. D. Lee to Rachel Lee, 24 September 1876, John D. Lee Collection, Huntington Library. Lee had particular reason to despise Wells; Louisa Free, one of Lee's favorite wives, divorced him and married Wells in 1849. See Brooks and Cleland, eds., *Mormon Chronicle*, 1:118n32.

77. Wells to Young, Lee Trial Telegrams, 14 September 1876, LDS Archives.

78. Beadle, *Western Wilds*, 515; Bishop, ed., *Mormonism Unveiled*, 303.

79. Whitney, *History of Utah*, 2:805–6; and Bishop, ed., *Mormonism Unveiled*, 268.

80. Bishop, ed., *Mormonism Unveiled*, 303.

81. Young to Brunson, 2 August 1857, and Young to Haight, 10 September 1857, Brigham Young Collection, LDS Archives; the affidavit is in Brooks, *Mountain Meadows Massacre*, 284–86.

82. Collected material concerning the Mountain Meadows Massacre, Folder 5, Josiah Rogerson Trial Materials, LDS Archives; Dwyer, *The Gentile Comes to Utah*, 102.

83. Lockley, *The Lee Trial*, 55; Baskin, *Reminiscences of Early Utah*, 114.

84. For evidence and testimony of the second Lee trial, see Bishop, ed., *Mormonism Unveiled*, 302–78.

85. Beadle, *Western Wilds*, 517; Kelly, ed., *Journals of John D. Lee*, 243.

86. Brooks, *Mountain Meadows Massacre*, 196–97. No such letters to Hamblin or Johnson are available at LDS Archives.

87. Whitney, *History of Utah*, 2:819–21; Brooks, *Mountain Meadows Massacre*, 198.

88. Kelly, ed., *Journals of John D. Lee*, 242–43.

89. Boreman Papers, Utah State Historical Society, 12–13; Hamblin testimony, Bishop, ed., *Mormonism Unveiled*, 366–67; Beadle, *Western Wilds*, 516.

90. Hamblin testimony, Bishop, ed., *Mormonism Unveiled*, 375–76.

91. Brooks, *Mountain Meadows Massacre*, 198; Beadle, *Western Wilds*, 516; Wells to Young, Lee Trial Telegrams, 15 September 1876, LDS Archives.

92. Bishop, ed., *Mormonism Unveiled*, 218; Kelly, ed., *Journals of John D. Lee*, 242.

93. W. F. Lee statement in Brimhall, Gleanings Concerning John D. Lee, 22, 23; Whitney, *History of Utah*, 2:821.

94. *Los Angeles Star*, 23 September 1877, 1/1; Bishop, ed., *Mormonism Unveiled*, viii.

95. Correy statement in Brimhall, Gleanings Concerning John D. Lee, 50–51,

96. J. D. Lee to Emma B. Lee, 21 September 1876, John D. Lee Collection, Huntington Library.

97. Baskin, *Reminiscences of Early Utah*, 113–14. Roberts described Bates's subsequent moral decline in *Comprehensive History*, 5:607.

CHAPTER 17

1. John Amasa Lee to L. W. Peterson, 4 August 1938, Mountain Meadows File, LDS Archives.

2. Brimhall, Gleanings Concerning John D. Lee, 28.

3. Diary Excerpts of Francis M. Lyman, 21 September 1895.

4. Whitney, *History of Utah*, 2:822–23. The exact requirements for a proper blood atonement are not clear, but simply being shot apparently fell short.

5. "Attorney Howard's Strategy Examined," 20 September 1876, *Salt Lake Tribune*, Fielding, *Trials of John D. Lee*, 233.

6. Nelson and Howard to Taft, 22 September 1876, Dwyer, *The Gentile Comes to Utah*, 103; Mountain Meadows Massacre, National Archives Microfilm Publication.

7. Howard to Taft, 4 October 1876, Dwyer, *The Gentile Comes to Utah*, 104.

8. Ibid; Devins to Bates, 16 April 1877, Dwyer, *The Gentile Comes to Utah*, 103–6.

9. Cannon to Young, 11 January 1877, Brigham Young Collection, LDS Archives.

10. Dwyer, *The Gentile Comes to Utah*, 105–7, 110–11.

11. Ibid, 105–6.

12. Ibid., 111; Bishop, ed., *Mormonism Unveiled*, 32.

13. Stewart to Young, 10 March 1877, Brigham Young Collection, LDS Archives.

14. Lee and Corry affidavits, Brimhall, Gleanings Concerning John D. Lee, 21, 50–51.

15. Bishop, ed., *Mormonism Unveiled*, 289–90.

16. Emma B. Lee to J. D. Lee, 12 November 1876, John D. Lee Collection, Huntington Library.

17. J. D. Lee to Rachel Lee, 17 October 1876, John D. Lee Collection, Huntington Library. This collection also contains Lee's February 1877 interpretation of "Idaho Bill's Dream."

18. J. D. Lee to H. P. Lee, 17 October 1876, John D. Lee Collection, Huntington Library; "Lee's Last Confession," 1/4–5. Press reports called Sloan William Fancher, but Lee's letters refer to him as Charles. Christopher "Kit" Carson Fancher actually died in Arkansas in 1873. See Fancher, *The Fancher Family*, 96. Their portraits suggest the two men bore a striking resemblance.

19. J. D. Lee to J. W. Baxter, 10 November 1876 and 21 January 1877, John D. Lee Collection, Huntington Library. Lee specifically stated that seventeen children survived the massacre.

20. J. D. Lee to Nate Hanson, 31 October 1876, John D. Lee Collection, Huntington Library. Hanson and Sloan were tried for robbing a stage on 21 September 1876. See Fielding, *Trials of John D. Lee*, 237.

21. J. D. Lee to Rachel Andora Lee, 12 October 1876, John D. Lee Collection, Huntington Library.

22. Bishop, ed., *Mormonism Unveiled*, 290.

23. J. D. Lee to Rachel Lee, 29 September 1876 and 12 October 1876; J. D. Lee to Emma B. Lee, 9 December 1876, John D. Lee Collection, Huntington Library.

24. Kelly, ed., *Journals of John D. Lee*, 201; Brimhall, Gleanings Concerning John D. Lee, 27.

25. Bishop, ed., *Mormonism Unveiled*, 74, 260. Three manuscript John D. Lee journals are located at LDS Archives: one covering May 1844 to November 1846; one running from February to August 1846; and the 1850 to 1853 Iron Mission journal, published as Larson, ed., "Journal of the Iron County Mission," *Utah Historical Quarterly*, 1952. Like other Mormon pioneers, Lee may have provided them to the Church Historian's Office to be used to compile the Manuscript History of the Church, which summarized his 1846 Mormon Battalion journal. Other Lee journals are said to be in the possession of the First Presidency.

26. Amorah Lee Smithson to J. D. Lee, 9 February 1877, and J. D. Lee to Emma B. Lee, 9 December 1876, John D. Lee Collection, Huntington Library. This appears to be the 1859 journal Charles Kelly published in *Journals of John D. Lee*, but Nancy Lee Dalton to J. D. Lee, 27 January 1877, called it "your family record," perhaps the genealogy preserved at the Huntington Library.

27. Bishop's family eventually sold Lee's journals to the Huntington Library. Along with journals Juanita Brooks collected from the family, they were edited by Brooks and Robert Glass Cleland and published in 1955 as *A Mormon Chronicle: The Diaries of John D. Lee, 1848–1876*. Virtually every document mentioned in the 1876 and 1877 John D. Lee letters appears to have been published or can be located in an archive.

28. J. D. Lee to Emma B. Lee, 9 December 1876, John D. Lee Collection, Huntington Library.

29. "The Reported Confession of John D. Lee," typescript of *Arkansas Gazette*, 24 March 1877.

30. *Beaver Square Dealer*, 20 March 1877, cited in Whitney, *History of Utah*, 2:825–26. Whitney noted that Lee's first confession contradicted the stories in Bishop's *Mormonism Unveiled*.

31. "The Reported Confession of John D. Lee," *San Francisco Call*, 6 March 1877. Lee said that his attorney had possession of his statement on 12 September 1875. See Brooks and Cleland, eds., *Mormon Chronicle*, 2:362. Charles Kelly claimed Lee wrote a private confession for his family, which Amorah Lee Smithson preserved for years until one of her daughters ultimately destroyed it. See Kelly, ed., *Journals of John D. Lee*, 201–2. An honest account of the massacre by John D. Lee would be invaluable if unlikely.

32. To Prest Young, 22 March 1877, Telegrams 1877, Brigham Young Collection, LDS Archives.

33. Beadle, *Western Wilds*, 504. The widely reprinted Bishop confession intially appeared in the *New York Herald*, the *San Francisco Chronicle*, and as "Lee's Story!" *Salt Lake Tribune*, 25 March 1877, 1/2–4. The Howard confession appeared as "The Confession!" *Salt Lake Tribune*, 28 March 1877, 1/1–5; and as as "Lee's Last Confession," *San Francisco Daily Bulletin Supplement*, 24 March 1877, 1/2 (the version used in this book). Howard said his edited version of the confession would "in no way interfere" with his plans to prosecute other participants. Beadle, *Western Wilds*, 519–23, includes parts of both confessions.

34. Brooks, *John Doyle Lee*, 365–66.

35. Beadle, *Western Wilds*, 307; Whitney, *History of Utah*, 2:825.

36. Fuller, "John D. Lee. Preparations for His Execution," *New York Herald*, 21 March 1877.

37. Brooks, *John Doyle Lee*, 370–71; Henrie, *Descendants of John Doyle Lee*, 668–69.

38. Whitney, *History of Utah*, 2:826.

39. Instructions to Lt. Patterson in Journeying to M.M., National Archives. The copy of Lt. George T. T. Patterson's orders of 20 March 1877 at the LDS Archives suggests that someone in the official party gave the confidential orders to the LDS church.

40. Bancroft, *History of Utah*, 569–70.

41. Beadle, *Western Wilds*, 524; "John D. Lee," *San Francisco Daily Bulletin Supplement*, 24 March 1877, 1/1; Whitney, *History of Utah*, 2:826–27. Lee was shot across Magotsu Creek from the ruins of the Carleton monument in an area that today is an unpaved parking lot.

42. "Shooting of Lee!" *Salt Lake Tribune*, 30 March 1877, 4/2–4.

43. Rogerson to Dougall, 22 March 1877, Telegrams 1877, Brigham Young Collection, LDS Archives; Deposition by Collins R. Hakes, Mountain Meadows File, LDS Archives; Whitney, *History of Utah*, 2:826.

44. "John D. Lee," *San Francisco Daily Bulletin Supplement*, 24 March 1877, 1/1.

45. Brimhall, Gleanings Concerning John D. Lee, 21.

46. "Shooting of Lee!" *Salt Lake Tribune*, 30 March 1877, 4/3-4; Whitney, *History of Utah*, 2:826; Bishop, ed., *Mormonism Unveiled*, 386–87. W. W. Bishop assembled his account of Lee's execution from the newspapers, which fairly consistently report this last speech.

47. Bishop, ed., *Mormonism Unveiled*, 387–88.

48. Whitney, *History of Utah*, 2:828–29; "Lee's Execution: Second Dispatch," *Salt Lake Tribune*, 24 March 1877.

49. "John D. Lee," *San Francisco Daily Bulletin Supplement*, 24 March 1877, 1/1

50. Bishop, ed., *Mormonism Unveiled*, 291–92.

51. "Shooting of Lee!" *Salt Lake Tribune*, 30 March 1877, 4/4.

52. Brimhall, Gleanings Concerning John D. Lee, 14. In 1931 Apostle Anthony Ivins told Brimhall he was sent with two others "to be present at the execution of John D. Lee."

53. Ivins to Welch, 16 October 1922, LDS Archives. Lee's execution produced more attempts to blackmail Brigham Young. "Unless you *very bountifully reward me*," L. L. Wilson of Illinois threatened, "[I will release information that could] result in the *extermination* of you & *your followers*." Wilson repeated one of the prophet's favorite phrases: "Mr. Young 'a word to the wise is sufficient.'" See Wilson to Young, April 1877, Brigham Young Collection, LDS Archives.

54. Amorah Smithson, 18 February 1930, Brimhall, Gleanings Concerning John D. Lee, 27–28.

55. Ibid., 35.

56. Brooks, *John Doyle Lee*, 12; and Roberts, *Comprehensive History*, 5:607.

57. Bishop, ed., *Mormonism Unveiled*, v-vi, 34. For an example of the exploitive confessions, see *The Mountain Meadows Massacre, with the Life, Confession and Execution of John D. Lee*, copy in Special Collections, Marriott Library.

58. Bishop, ed., *Mormonism Unveiled*, 74.

59. Ibid., 213–14, 379–82. The book included Lee's last letter to his family; William Stokes's account of Lee's arrest; the Young and Smith affidavits; the 1857 declaration of martial law; Brigham Young's reports to Indian commissioner James Denver; and his 14 September 1857 letter to William Dame. It contained samples of the second trial testimony of Daniel Wells, Laban Morrill, Joel White, Samuel Knight, Samuel McMurdy, Nephi Johnson, and Jacob Hamblin, followed by the "names of assassins" and an account of Lee's execution. Later editions included a "Life of Brigham Young."

60. Roberts, *Comprehensive History*, 4:152; Juanita Brooks Papers, Marriott Library.

61. Bishop, ed., *Mormonism Unveiled*, viii, 33, 34, 144, 192. The book does contain several puzzling errors. For example, Lee implied that he witnessed the 8 August 1844 speeches of Brigham Young and Sidney Rigdon, when he was actually in Kentucky at the time.

62. Rogerson, "A review of John D. Lee's life and confessions," in Mountain Meadows File, LDS Archives, 1. Bishop acknowledged Patterson's help in Bishop, ed., *Mormonism Unveiled*, 35.

63. Lucinda C. Lee and Evans Coleman, Brimhall, Gleanings Concerning John D. Lee, 14, 26.

64. Calder to J. W. Young, 31 March 1877, Telegrams 1877, Brigham Young Collection, LDS Archives.

65. Young to Hayes, 31 March 1877, Telegrams 1877, Brigham Young Collection, LDS Archives.

66. Larson and Larson, eds., *Diary of Charles Lowell Walker*, 1:457; Taylor, *The Kingdom or Nothing*, 258.

67. Taylor, *The Kingdom or Nothing*, 258. Taylor's colorful speculations are not widely accepted but do reflect rumors and newspaper reports current at the time.

68. Bennett to Young, 21 March 1877, Telegrams 1877, Brigham Young Collection, LDS Archives.

69. Beadle, *Western Wilds*, 523.

70. "Interview with Brigham Young," *New York Herald*, 6 May 1877; reprinted in *Deseret News*, 12 May 1877, 2/5.

71. Ibid. Young's report of Rich's advice is the only known source of the story.

72. "Interview with Brigham Young," *Deseret News*, 12 May 1857.

73. McIntyre and Barton, eds., *Christopher Layton*, 136.

74. Arrington, *Brigham Young*, 292–93, citing Werner, *Brigham Young*, 452.

75. Alexander, *Utah, the Right Place*, 177.

76. Brooks and Cleland, eds., *Mormon Chronicle*, 2:449; Arrington, *Brigham Young*, 390; Bush, "Brigham Young in Life and Death," 99n72, 100–3.

77. Werner, *Brigham Young*, 459; Arrington, *Brigham Young*, 398–99. Hirshson, *Lion of the Lord*, 320, 374n65, cited *Deseret News*, 5 September 1877, as the first source of the "Joseph, Joseph" quote.

78. "Last Moments of President Brigham Young," *Deseret News*, 31 August 1877, 2/2.

79. Hirshson, *Lion of the Lord*, 319. Dr. Lester E. Bush dismissed rumors that Young was poisoned in "Brigham Young in Life and Death," 92–103.

CHAPTER 18

1. Penrose, *The Mountain Meadows Massacre*, 76–77.

2. Stenhouse, *The Rocky Mountain Saints*, 447.

3. Young, *Wife No. 19*, 251–52.

4. Stenhouse, *The Rocky Mountain Saints*, 455; Gregory, ed., "Journal of Stephen Vandiver Jones," 106; Brimhall, Gleanings Concerning John D. Lee, 23, 24; Bringhurst statement, Mountain Meadows File, LDS Archives. As noted, Brigham Young authorized Haight's rebaptism in March 1874.

5. Elizabeth Baker Terry Memoir; Naylor, "The Mormons Colonize Sonora," 325–27, 330, 332.

6. The Life and Religion of George Calvin Williams, LDS Archives. Williams's correspondence with John Taylor does not survive; LDS Archives to author, 24 January 1997.

7. Naylor, "The Mormons Colonize Sonora," 338, 340; A. H. Cannon Diary, 2 May 1895, cited in Moorman and Sessions, *Camp Floyd and the Mormons*, 305n99. Williams was "reinstated by proxy" in the LDS church on 21 March 1936. (Citing scriptures such as 1 Co. 15:29, Mormons perform posthumous temple ordinances including baptism and the endowment ceremony. Most "temple work" is conducted by proxy for the dead, on the theory that these blessings can be accepted or rejected in the afterlife.) Ten days later ordinances were performed for Williams in the Mesa, Arizona, LDS temple. See the Life and Religion of George Calvin Williams, LDS Archives.

8. Brooks, *Mountain Meadows Massacre*, 212.

9. "Klingensmith: He Is Supposed to Have Been Murdered by Mormons," *Salt Lake Tribune*, 4 August 1881, 2/3, based on a report in the *Pioche Record*.

10. "A Far-fetched Assumption," *Deseret News*, 16 August 1881.

11. Backus, *Mountain Meadows Witness*, 231, 234–35.

12. Gibbs, *Lights and Shadows of Mormonism*, 235.

13. Seegmiller, "Personal Memories of the United Order of Orderville," 161. For Higbee's years as mayor, see photo 00174 0153, Special Collections, Southern Utah University.

14. Pendleton, "The Orderville United Order of Zion," 142–43.

15. Gould, Statement, Juanita Brooks Papers, Utah State Historical Society. Brooks never used this, which might reflect her view of its reliability. A note indicates southern Utah chronicler Mrs. Luella Adams Dalton took the dictation from Sam Gould and had him sign it. The statement also appears in the Nels Benjamin Lundwall Papers, LDS Archives.

16. Ibid.

17. Ibid.

18. Higbee statement, in Brooks, *Mountain Meadows Massacre*, 226–35. Higbee's account was so confusing that Brooks puts him in two places—the meadows and Parowan—on Thursday night. Ibid., 80.

19. Brooks, *Mountain Meadows Massacre*, 230–31. The story that Lee let the men decide if they would kill their victims is suspect. It is unlikely that the Paiutes would use firearms to kill unarmed victims, and forensic evidence indicates most of the males were shot. See Novak, "Mountain Meadows Forensics," *Salt Lake Tribune*, 21 January 2001.

20. Brooks, *Mountain Meadows Massacre*, 231, 234.

21. Ibid., 231–32, 233.

22. "Echo of Mountain Meadow," *Salt Lake Tribune*, 28 February 1896, 8. Higbee was also apparently exonerated at an LDS church trial. Brooks saw an affidavit with a long list of signatures in the St. George Temple absolving Higbee of all blame and reinstating him "in full fellowship in the church." See Brooks, *Mountain Meadows Massacre*, 86.

23. "1896 J M Higbee trial," 15 June 1896, Mountain Meadows File, LDS Archives. Andrew Corry, one of the jurors who condemned John D. Lee, witnessed Higbee's statement.

24. Ibid.

25. Ibid; Rogerson, The Guilt of John D. Lee, Addendum, Mountain Meadows File, LDS Archives, 8.

26. See Collins, *Great Western Rides*, for an outsider who accepted much of Palmer's local lore but bridled at believing that the Paiutes were responsible for the violence.

27. Penrose, *The Mountain Meadows Massacre*, 5, 6. For another Penrose 1884 apologia, see *Blood Atonement, as Taught by the Leading Elders*, a similar pamphlet in which Penrose attempted to explain the problematic doctrine of blood atonement.

28. Penrose, *The Mountain Meadows Massacre*, 7; Godfrey, "Charles W. Penrose and His Contributions to Utah Statehood," 359.

29. Lambert of the *Deseret News* was also "called upon to hunt up and publish all the facts" about Mountain Meadows. See Lambert, "Journal of George Cannon Lambert," 9:330.

30. Richards, Diary, 25 and 26 February 1882, MS 2737, Box 16, Folder 5, LDS Archives.

31. Rogerson, "The Guilt of John D. Lee," in Mountain Meadows File, LDS Archives, 18. Capitalization in the original.

32. Ibid., 1, 5–6, 14, 18; Historical Department Journals, Typescript, LDS Archives, 111.

33. Newspaper clipping and McKay to Dame, 10 October 1878, Dame Papers, LDS Archives.

34. Jenson, *LDS Biographical Encyclopedia*, 1:532.

35. Rogerson, Addendum to the Guilt of John D. Lee, Mountain Meadows File, LDS Archives, 4, 5.

36. Ibid., 3–5.

37. Ibid.

38. Ibid.

39. Ibid., 6, 7; Letter to the *Deseret News*, Dame Papers, LDS Archives.

40. Penrose, *The Mountain Meadows Massacre*, 7, 8, 9, 12, 31.

41. Ibid., 38, 40, 44–47.

42. Ibid., 48, 51–56.

43. Ibid.

44. The Mountain Meadows File at LDS Archives contains several holograph Woodruff statements and affidavits on Mountain Meadows. Published affidavits are found in Penrose, *The Mountain Meadows Massacre*, 51–55.

45. Penrose, *The Mountain Meadows Massacre*, 67–68, 78, 80.

46. Vindex, *Mountain Meadows Massacre*, 1, 3.

47. Birney, *Zealots of Zion*, 138.

48. Brooks, *Mountain Meadows Massacre*, 216.

49. Ellsworth, "Hubert Howe Bancroft and the *History of Utah*," 104–8, 113–15, 120, 121. Bancroft's histories were collaborative endeavors. J. M. Stone, one of Bancroft's disgruntled writers, charged that Richards furnished most of the text of *History of Utah*. Richards provided a very influential draft history, but manuscript evidence indicates Bancroft, Alfred Bates, and Edward P. Newkirk wrote the final book. Ibid., 118.

50. Bancroft, *History of Utah*, 543–45, 549, 568.

51. Jenson, *Autobiography*, 197–98. In 1890 the First Presidency consisted of Wilford Woodruff, George Q. Cannon, and Joseph F. Smith.

52. Ibid., 198; Bitton and Arrington, *Mormons and Their Historians*, 47–48, 176. The authors are correct about the fate of Rogerson's papers. As for this author, the secretary to the First Presidency wrote, in rejecting a request to see these materials: "In connection with several affidavits which are in possession of the Church, these items have for some time been restricted from purposes of research." See Watson to Bagley, 20 September 2000, copy in author's possession.

53. Bitton and Arrington, *Mormons and Their Historians*, 76–77, 81.

54. Roberts, *Comprehensive History*, 4:139.

55. Ibid., 4:141, 144–47, 149–50, 154–55, 159; for responsibility, see 160–80; for the Lee trial, see 5:604–7.

56. "Josiah F. Gibbs Loses Fellowship in Church," *Salt Lake Tribune*, 23 May 1908, 7/11; Alter, *Early Utah Journalism*, 74, 177.

57. Gibbs, *Lights and Shadows of Mormonism*, 12–15, 228.

58. Ibid., 208–9, 233, 238.

59. Rogerson, The Guilt of John D. Lee, Mountain Meadows File, LDS Archives, 1, 14.

60. White, ed., *Church, State, and Politics*, 668.

61. Rogerson to First Presidency, 28 April 1911, Mountain Meadows File, LDS Archives.

62. Rogerson to First Presidency, 10 August 1911, Mountain Meadows File, LDS Archives. The aphorism is from "The Mountain Meadows," Box 1, Folder 11, Brooks Papers, Marriott Library.

63. Rogerson to First Presidency, 10 August 1911, Mountain Meadows File, LDS Archives.

64. Morgan to Brooks, 24 February 1949, Box 1, Folder 4, Brooks Papers, Marriott Library.

65. See Mountain Meadows File, Collected Material Concerning the Mountain Meadows Massacre, MS 2674, LDS Archives.

66. Bitton and Arrington, *Mormons and Their Historians*, 64–65.

67. Baskin, *Reply by R. N. Baskin*, 15, 16, 22, 21.

68. Bitton and Arrington, *Mormons and Their Historians*, 65.

69. Baskin, *Reply by R. N. Baskin*, 29.

70. Tom and Holt, "The Paiutes," in Cuch, ed., *A History of Utah's American Indians*, 139–40; Alley et al., *Nuwuvi*, 72.

71. Holt, *Beneath These Red Cliffs*, 43–44.

72. Brooks, "Indian Relations on the Mormon Frontier," 25–26.

73. Papanikolas, ed., *The Peoples of Utah*, 48.

74. Topping, ed., *Gila Monsters and Red-Eyed Rattlesnakes*, 116.

75. Holt, *Beneath These Red Cliffs*, 40–41.

76. Papanikolas, ed., *The Peoples of Utah*, 49.

77. See the interviews with Paiutes in Cuch, ed., *A History of Utah's American Indians*, 134–36. For Adair's story, see David O. McKay Diary, 27 July 1907, Marriott Library.

78. Clifford Jake, interview with author, Paiute Tribal Headquarters, Cedar City, Utah, 29 November 1995.

79. Martineau, *Southern Paiutes*, xiii, 62. Johnny Jake of the Indian Peak Band recalled that Isaac Hunkup was involved in the massacre. The Mormons told the Paiutes they could have all the loot "except the round yellow stuff (gold). They said, 'It was no good for the Indians.'"

80. Kelly, Utah's Black Friday, 194.

81. Karl Brooks, author interview notes, 12 January 1996, St. George, Utah. Tom and Holt, "The Paiutes," in Cuch, ed., *A History of Utah's American Indians*, 141, note that some of the original residents of the core Paiute homeland on the Santa Clara moved to the Moapa reservation or to Cedar City.

82. Anthon Lee, Statement, from Brimhall, Gleanings Concerning John D. Lee, 2.

83. Grant to McClintock, 15 February 1929; Ivins to McClintock, 26 February 1929; "Arizonans Hear Mormon's Plea," 5 March 1929; in McClintock clipping file, Phoenix Public Library. Lee's name is still attached to the site of his farm at Lee's Ferry, now a popular departure point for Grand Canyon raft tours.

84. Peterson, *Juanita Brooks*, 219.

85. Heath, ed., *In the World*, 738.

86. Rex E. Lee affidavit, 3 April 1931, Brimhall, Gleanings Concerning John D. Lee, 48–50.

87. Krenkel, ed., *The Life and Times of Joseph Fish*, 57–58.

88. Alva Matheson's recollections in author's possession. See also Matheson, John D. Lee and the Chaffin Mill, Special Collections, Southern Utah State University, for a version without the rape story. Matheson wrote that Lee killed one of the surviving orphans and buried him at the mill. On 27 June 1997 Matheson told the author and historian Steven Heath he had found the child's skeleton. He closed and dedicated the grave in a secure location. Matheson has an Allen pepperbox revolver he believes Joseph Smith used in the Carthage jail, which John M. Higbee allegedly found on the body of "Charles" Fancher. Smith's pistol is actually in the LDS Church Museum of History and Art in Salt Lake. Many of Matheson's massacre stories lack credibility, but they accurately reflect local legends.

89. Author's notes of telephone conversation with Bill Walker, 29 January 1997.

90. Edwards, Affidavit, 14 May 1924, Utah State Historical Society; Jenson, *LDS Biographical Encyclopedia*, 3:623–24.

91. William Edwards, Ancestral File, Family History Department, LDS Church.

92. Elizabeth Baker Terry Memoir, 6; Lee, "Some Descendents of John Twiddy Baker," 6–7.

93. Newton, "Death at Mountain Meadows," *Arkansas Gazette*, September 1959, 2D.

94. Sarah Baker Mitchell Memoir.

Chapter 19

1. Brooks, *Quicksand and Cactus*, 215–16. The following quotations are from this memoir.

2. This concludes quotations from Brooks, *Quicksand and Cactus*, 215–16, 227–29.

3. Peterson, "Life in a Village Society, 1877–1920," 91.

4. Peterson, *Juanita Brooks*, 50–53, 63, 68, 76–80. This chapter relies heavily on Levi Peterson's award-winning biography.

5. Ibid., 44, 102.

6. Ibid., 84; Beckwith, Shameful Friday, 476–78; McMurrin interview, 4 February 1986, Utah State Historical Society, 2. Palmer gave Sterling McMurrin "a detailed account of the opposition that he first encountered from the church in his efforts to save the graves."

7. Palmer, Monument Dedication, 10 September 1932, Mountain Meadows Massacre Subject File, Utah State Historical Society.

8. Brooks, *Mountain Meadows Massacre*, 221.

9. Peterson, *Juanita Brooks*, 84–85.

10. Ibid., 85–87, 89. See also Brooks, *Uncle Will Tells His Story*.

11. "The Mountain Meadows," in Brooks Papers, Marriott Library, University of Utah.

12. Karl Brooks, author interview notes, 12 January 1996, St. George, Utah.

13. Peterson, *Juanita Brooks*, 100, 103, 144–45.

14. Ibid., 246.

15. McMurrin interview, 4 February 1986, Utah State Historical Society, 7.

16. Karl Brooks, author interview notes, St. George, Utah, 12 January 1996.

17. Brooks, *Mountain Meadows Massacre*, xxvi.

18. Peterson, *Juanita Brooks*, 114–15.

19. Ibid., 120–21. Morgan noted that the pages describing the massacre had been ripped from Hamblin's transcribed journal.

20. Historian Douglas Alder shared this perceptive observation with the author. For evidence, see Morgan's letters in the Brooks and Morgan Papers, Marriott Library.

21. Peterson, *Juanita Brooks*, 124, 170–71; Todd Berens interview, 17 September 1985, Utah State Historical Society, 5.

22. Berens interview, 12–13; Peterson, *Juanita Brooks*, 121, 167.

23. Peterson, *Juanita Brooks*, 158–59.

24. Brooks, *Mountain Meadows Massacre*, 217–18; Peterson, *Juanita Brooks*, 159–61, 167–68, 176. J. Reuben Clark recorded that Flora Morris Brooks of St. George deposited the Johnson affidavit on 13 June 1942. "She said this affidavit was made by Nephi Johnson and left with her father, D. H. Morris." She "felt it should not be left to be handed about among relatives, etc., but should be put in a place of safe keeping. I told her I would have it deposited in the Historian's Office with Elder Joseph Fielding Smith." See Mountain Meadows File, LDS Archives. Peterson, *Juanita Brooks*, 176, reported, "There were only three affidavits, two by Nephi Johnson (one of which Brooks already possessed) and one by Samuel Knight."

25. Peterson, *Juanita Brooks*, 161, 175, 179.

26. Brimhall, Gleanings Concerning John D. Lee, 14–15.

27. Peterson, *Juanita Brooks*, 181–82.

28. Brooks, "Jest a Copyin'—Word f'r Word," 384; Peterson, *Juanita Brooks*, 185.

29. Brooks, "Let's Preserve Our Records," 263; David Whittaker and Ronald Esplin, author conversation notes, 17 January 1997, Provo, Utah. Carter told Russell R. Rich she felt "innocent people of today might suffer" if the contents of the minute book became known, so she "cast it into the fireplace and watched it burn." Rich noted that the minutes "probably could have cleared up much confusion and contradiction." See Rich, The Mountain Meadows Massacre, 9.

30. Peterson, *Juanita Brooks*, 192–93, 197, 199–200.

31. Ibid., 205, 208, 209.

32. Ibid., 205.

33. Karl Brooks, author interview notes, 12 January 1996, St. George, Utah.

34. Peterson, *Juanita Brooks*, 207; Brooks, *Mountain Meadows Massacre*, 95.

35. Peterson, *Juanita Brooks*, 207–08; Brooks, *Mountain Meadows Massacre,* 217–18.

36. Peterson, *Juanita Brooks*, 209; Juanita Brooks Papers, Marriott Library.

37. Madsen, *Against the Grain*, 212–13.

38. Peterson, *Juanita Brooks*, 210, 218.

39. Pulsipher, "Personal Glimpses of Juanita Brooks," 276; Peterson, *Juanita Brooks*, 219–20.

40. Conversation Notes, 8 October 1954, A. C. Lambert Collection, Marriott Library, 3–4.

41. Norman Eatough, 14 October 1996, e-mail to author and LDS-BOOKSHELF Internet list.

42. Peterson, *Juanita Brooks*, 217, 218; Quinn, *J. Reuben Clark: The Church Years*, 170, 308n41.

43. Peterson, *Juanita Brooks*, 237–39.

44. Burr Fancher, conversation notes with author, 6 March 1996 and 12 September 1998.

45. Brooks, "An Historical Epilogue," 71–80.

46. Ibid.

47. Peterson, *Juanita Brooks*, 241–42.

48. Ibid., 255.

49. Brooks to Jesse Udall, 23 June 1961; Brooks to Lambert, 11 December 1961, A. C. Lambert Collection, Marriott Library.

50. Peterson, *Juanita Brooks*, 274–75.

51. Ibid., 273–77; Brooks to Cooley, 1 February 1969. Art Clark of Cedar City, a John D. Lee descendant, reports that his family has a John D. Lee journal account of the Mountain Meadows massacre. It allegedly states that a cryptic message from Brigham Young arrived *before* the massacre: "Brethren, do your duty." Lee descendants Cameron Norton and Marcus Buckley took the journal to LDS church headquarters in about 1957 as part of the effort to restore Lee's blessings. Church officials returned it with instructions never to show it to anyone. "No one," Clark told archivist Janet Seegmiller, "will ever see it." Author's conversation notes, Southern Utah University, 21 October 1999.

52. Brooks, *John Doyle Lee*, 12; Peterson, *Juanita Brooks*, 281, 282.

53. Brooks, *Mountain Meadows Massacre*, xxiv, 222.

54. Ibid., xviii, 219; Brooks to R. B. Mathison, 21 November 1968, Brooks Papers, Marriott Library, 2.

55. Karl Brooks, author interview notes, 12 January 1996, St. George, Utah.

56. Brooks to Mathison, 21 November 1968, Brooks Papers; Norman Eatough, 5 and 14 October 1996, e-mail to the author and LDS-BOOKSHELF Internet mailing list; Charles S. Peterson, interview with author, 11 January 1996. Peterson recalled he saw a document different from Huntington's Journal, 1857 Aug–1859 May, MS 1419-2, LDS Archives.

57. Peterson, *Juanita Brooks*, 395, 400. Despite this, as late as 1975 a Deseret Book clerk told a customer seeking a copy of *The Mountain Meadows Massacre* to look "in fiction where it belongs." See Peterson, "Juanita Brooks: Historian as Tragedian," 49.

58. Peterson, *Juanita Brooks*, 400, 408, 417, 420–21, 423.

59. Ibid., 422.

60. For a recent example that claims Brooks "exonerates Brigham Young from direct responsibility" for the Mountain Meadows Massacre, see Davis Bitton's Summer 2000 article, "'I'd Rather Have Some Roasting Ears,'" 196–222.

EPILOGUE

1. Bishop, ed., *Mormonism Unveiled*, 35; Bancroft, *History of Utah*, 570.

2. Stampp, *America in 1857*, 362–63. Compare historian Ronald Esplin's account of the George Hicks affair in Arrington, *Brigham Young*, 281, with the story told in this volume.

3. Arrington, review of *Massacre at Mountain Meadows*.

4. Arrington, "Vistas in Church History," 21.

5. Ibid.; Arrington, *Adventures of a Church Historian*, 155. Perhaps because of its intended audience and the tight deadline, Arrington's "Background Report on John D. Lee and the Mountain Meadows Massacre" was filled with factual errors. Like earlier polemics, it blamed the victims and the Paiutes. It was not Arrington's finest work.

6. Author's personal conversations with Gene Sessions and Harold Schindler, the *Salt Lake Tribune's* television critic at the time; Louise Degn, "Juanita Brooks" videotape.

7. See Esplin and Jessee, "The Mormon Reaction," 26; and Bob Lancaster's response, 30–31. Among other causes, in 1994 Esplin blamed the "disgraceful conduct" of some of the emigrants and the demands of "young Indian braves" that whites join in the atrocity. See Esplin, "Tragedy in the Meadows," 30, 32.

8. Alexander, *Utah, the Right Place*, 130–31, 133.

9. J. K. Fancher, "Healing Process over Mountain Meadows," *Harrison Daily Times*, 8 April 1989, 8.

10. J. K. Fancher, "Who Was the Indian at Meeting?" *Harrison Daily Times*, 6 September 1991.

11. Ronald E. Loving, e-mail message to author, 16 June 1998.

12. Author's notes of conversation with Verne Lee, 12 December 1995.

13. Hinckley's role in the Hofmann affair is described in Sillitoe and Roberts, *Salamander*.

14. Author's interviews with participants. Incredibly, Ronald Loving wrote, "I have an agreement with President Hinckley to try and stop any book writing, TV, and movies [about the massacre] from being presented to the general public." See Loving to Bagley, 15 November 1995, copy in author's possession. In a later communication, Loving indicated he had agreed to stop *inaccurate* information.

15. Judge Roger V. Logan, Jr., 1990 Monument Dedication Remarks, LDS Archives.

16. Author's notes of the dedication services. "Dan Sill Hill" may be a corruption of the original name, Dan's Hill.

17. Sappington, "Lee, Fancher Families Close Book on Massacre," *St. George Spectrum*, 16 October 1993, quoted in the *Cactus Flat Lee Quarterly*, November 1993, 1, 7. In 1989 Verne Lee heard a fellow family member ask of the Fancher party, "Well, didn't they get what they deserved?" "The Fancher Train—1857," ibid., June 1989, 1.

18. Smith, "Mountain Meadows Marker," *Salt Lake Tribune*, 29 September 1998, A1.

19. Egan, *Lasso the Wind*, 111; Loewen, *Lies across America*, 94.

20. Smith, "Mountain Meadows Marker," *Salt Lake Tribune*, 29 September 1998, A5.

21. Wadley, "Monument Instills Healing," *Deseret News*, 12 September 1999, 1; Glen Leonard to Will Bagley, 2 February 2001, copy in author's possession.

22. Loving, Minutes of Salt Lake City Meeting, 30 October 1998; Bylund to Bagley, summary of 30 October 1998 meeting, 1 March 2001, copy in possession of the author.

23. Bylund to Bagley, 1 March 2001; Loving, Minutes of Salt Lake City Meeting, 30 October 1998; author's personal communications with meeting participants. According to Kent Bylund's notes, President Hinckely asked Glen Leonard, "Is this true, are we holding anything back?" Leonard said there were certain sensitive items that were not available to the public. Hinckley told him, "By all means let them see it, we have nothing to hide." Leonard does not recall such a conversation.

24. Ibid.; and Bylund to Bagley, summary of 30 October 1998 meeting, 1 March 2001.

25. Bylund to Smith, 19 June 1999, e-mail to LDS-BOOKSHELF Internet list, copy in author's possesion.

26. Havnes and Webb, "Massacre Victims Will Get a 'Fitting' Memorial," *Salt Lake Tribune*, 1 April 1999, B2. The LDS church attempted to address the concerns of family members, but the project coordinator does not recall that the church made such an unworkable commitment.

27. Bylund to Bagley, 1 March 2001.

28. Burr Fancher to Wilson et al., 27 November; Scott Fancher to Bagley, 21 July 1999; Smith, "Bones of Contention," *Salt Lake Tribune*, 12 March 2000, A16; *Newsletter*, November 1999, Mountain Meadows Monument Foundation, Inc., 1. Copies in author's possession.

29. Bylund to B. Fancher, 28 August 1999, copy in author's possession. The core samples came within inches of the burials.

30. Ibid.; Baker to Bagley, 21 February 2001; Smith, "Bones of Contention," *Salt Lake Tribune*, 12 March 2000, A16. Copies in author's possession. Association officials later claimed they merely wanted to

keep the news quiet until they could notify relatives of the victims, but most relatives learned of the discovery in press reports twelve days after the discovery.

31. Foy, "Bones from 1857 Massacre Unearthed," *New York Times*, 15 August 1999, 22.

32. Smith, "Bones of Contention," *Salt Lake Tribune*, 12 March 2000, A16–17; Novak and Kopp, "Osteological Analysis," 8, Table 4.

33. Foy, "Bones from 1857 Massacre Unearthed," *New York Times*, 15 August 1999, 22.

34. *Newsletter*, November 1999, Mountain Meadows Monument Foundation, 1; Smith, "Bones of Contention," *Salt Lake Tribune*, 12 March 2000, A1, A16–17.

35. Mountain Meadows Association, Program of the Memorial Service at the Re-internment of Remains of Victims of the Mountain Meadows Massacre.

36. Smith, "Forensic Analysis Supports Tribe's Claim," *Salt Lake Tribune*, 21 January 2001.

37. Wadley, "Monument Instills Healing," *Deseret News*, 12 September 1999, 1.

38. Author's notes of Shirley H. Pyron's remarks, 11 September 1999.

39. Hinckley, Remarks (LDS Public Relations Department press release of Gordon B. Hinckley's remarks and dedicatory prayer).

40. Ibid. The LDS church did not report its outlay for the project, but in October 1998 Hinckley had estimated the monument could cost as much as $200,000. See Loving, Minutes of Salt Lake City Meeting, 30 October 1998.

41. Hinckley, Remarks; Hart, "'Let the book of the past be closed,'" *Church News*, 18 September 1999, 3, 8–9; personal conversations with officers of the MMA. LDS church attorneys apparently feared an apology would lead to wrongful-death lawsuits.

42. "Transcript of the Interview with Gordon B. Hinckley, February 26, 2000," *Salt Lake Tribune*, at http://www.sltrib.com/2000/Feb/02262000/utah/29446.htm.

43. Brooks, *Quicksand and Cactus*, 250, 255.

44. Smith, "Bones of Contention," *Salt Lake Tribune*, 12 March 2000, A16.

45. Brooks, *Mountain Meadows Massacre*, 219–20.

46. Morgan to Brooks, 7 September 1942, Brooks Papers, Marriott Library.

47. White, ed., *News of the Plains and the Rockies*, 4:219.

48. Bishop, *Henry William Bigler*, ix, 160–61; Hoffer, *The True Believer*.

49. Smith, "Faithful History," 66.

50. Hyde, *Mormonism*, 49. H. H. Bancroft considered most apostates vile traitors but praised John Hyde. See White, ed., *News of the Plains and the Rockies*, 3:242, 243.

51. Quinn, *Mormon Hierarchy: Extensions of Power*, 721. See also *New York Times*, 19, 20, 21 September 1902. Kent Larson provided William Hooper Young's name.

52. Karl Brooks, author interview notes, 12 January 1996, St. George, Utah.

53. Kenney, ed., *Wilford Woodruff's Journal*, 5:84.

54. "Interview with Brigham Young," *Deseret News*, 12 May 1877, 2/4.

55. "Horrible Massacre of Emigrants!!" *Los Angeles Star*, 10 October 1857, 2/2.

56. Bishop, ed., *Mormonism Unveiled*, 221.

57. Egan, *Lasso the Wind*, 118.

58. Cuch, ed., *A History of Utah's American Indians*, 138.

59. White, ed., *News of the Plains and the Rockies*, 4:213–14. White's introduction to Carleton's report includes a revealing time line outlining "who knew what, and when they knew it."

60. Peterson, "Juanita Brooks," 52.

APPENDIX

1. Fulfer did not accompany her husband to California and probably survived the massacre.

2. McEuen, *The Legend of Francis Marion Poteet and the Mountain Meadows Massacre*, reveals that no Poteets died at Mountain Meadows, although they were among the emigrants who traveled through southern Utah in 1857.

3. Smith, "Bones of Contention," *Salt Lake Tribune*, 12 March 2000, A16–17.

4. Daniels, *History of the Town of Oxford*, 616.

5. For references to this problematic "Dutchman," see Henry Mogridge's statement in the *Los Angeles Star*, 7 November 1857, 2/2; and Autobiography of John Hawley, Community of Christ Archives, Independence, Missouri. Elisha Hoops testified that he met a "German doctor" when he camped with the Fancher party at Corn Creek. See Whitney, *History of Utah*, 2:800.

6. Dunn, *Massacres of the Mountains*, 254. See also Kelly, Utah's Balck Friday, 14.

7. Lange family information on file at Special Collections, Southern Utah University.

8. Cathy L. Starr to Dennis B. Neuenschwander, 23 November 1999, copy in author's possession.

BIBLIOGRAPHY

The bibliography is arranged in sections as follows: Books, Theses, and Dissertations; Articles; Newspapers; Manuscripts; Survivor Accounts; Government Documents; Internet Sources, Compact Disks, and Video-tapes.

BOOKS, THESES, AND DISSERTATIONS

Alexander, Thomas G. *Utah, the Right Place: The Official Centennial History*. Salt Lake City: Gibbs Smith, 1995.

Allen, James B., and Glen M. Leonard. *The Story of the Latter-day Saints*. Salt Lake City: Deseret Book Co., 1976.

[Alley, John R., et al]. *Nuwuvi: A Southern Paiute History*. Salt Lake City: Inter-Tribal Council of Nevada, 1976.

Alter, J. Cecil. *Early Utah Journalism: A Half Century of Forensic Warfare, Waged by the West's Most Militant Press*. Salt Lake City: Utah State Historical Society, 1938.

Anderson, C. LeRoy. *For Christ Will Come Tomorrow: The Saga of the Morrisites*. Logan: Utah State University Press, 1981. 2d ed., *Joseph Morris and the Saga of the Morrisites*, 1988.

Anderson, Nels. *Desert Saints: The Mormon Frontier in Utah*. Chicago: University of Chicago Press, 1942.

Arrington, Leonard J. *Adventures of a Church Historian*. Urbana: University of Illinois Press, 1998.

———. *Brigham Young: American Moses*. New York: Alfred A. Knopf, 1984.

———. *Charles C. Rich: Mormon General and Western Frontiersman*. Provo: Brigham Young University Press, 1974.

———. *Kate Field and J. H. Beadle: Manipulators of the Mormon Past*. Salt Lake City: Center for Studies of the American West, 1971.

———. *The Mormons of Nevada*. Las Vegas, Nev.: Las Vegas Sun, 1979.

Arrington, Leonard J., and Davis Bitton. *The Mormon Experience: A History of the Latter-day Saints*. New York: Random House, 1980.

Arrington, Leonard J., Feramorz Y. Fox, and Dean L. May. *Building the City of God: Community and Cooperation among the Mormons*. Salt Lake City: Deseret Book Co., 1976.

Ashton, Wendell J. *Voice in the West: Biography of a Pioneer Newspaper*. New York: Duell, Sloan & Pearce, 1950.

Auchampaugh, Philip G. *Robert Tyler, Southern Rights Champion*. Duluth, Minn: H. Stein, Printer, 1934.

Backus, Anna Jean. *Mountain Meadows Witness: The Life of Bishop Philip Klingensmith*. Spokane, Wash.: Arthur H. Clark, 1995.

Bagley, Will, ed. *Frontiersman: Abner Blackburn's Narrative*. Salt Lake City: University of Utah Press, 1992.

———. *The Pioneer Camp of the Saints: The 1846 and 1847 Trail Journals of Thomas Bullock*. Spokane, Wash.: Arthur H. Clark, 1997.

———. *Scoundrel's Tale: The Samuel Brannan Papers*. Spokane, Wash.: Arthur H. Clark, 1999.

Bailey, Lynn R. *A Tale of the "Unkilled": The Life, Times, & Writings of Wells W. Spicer*. Tucson: Westernlore Press, 1999.

Bancroft, Hubert Howe. *History of Utah, 1540–1886*. San Francisco: History Company, 1889.

Barry, Louise. *The Beginning of the West: Annals of the Kansas Gateway to the American West, 1540–1854*. Topeka: Kansas State Historical Society, 1972.

Baskin, Robert N. *Reminiscences of Early Utah*. Salt Lake City: By the author, 1914.

————. *Reply by R. N. Baskin to Certain Statements by O. F. Whitney in His History of Utah Published in 1916.* Salt Lake City: Lakeside Printing Co., 1916.

Beadle, John Hanson. *Life in Utah; or, the Mysteries and Crimes of Mormonism, being an Exposé of the Secret Rites and Ceremonies of the Latter-day Saints, with a Full and Authentic History of Polygamy and the Mormon Sect from Its Origin to the Present Time.* Philadelphia: National Publishing Co., 1870.

————. *Western Wilds, and the Men Who Redeem Them.* Cincinnati: Jones Brothers & C., 1879.

Bennett, Richard E. *Mormons at the Missouri.* Norman: University of Oklahoma Press, 1987.

Berry, Earl. *The History of Marion County.* Little Rock: Marion County Historical Association, 1977.

Bertrand, Louis A. *Memoires d'un Mormon.* Paris: E. Jung-Treuttel, 1862. [Translated by Gaston Chappius, Donald R. Moorman Collection, WA 86 5, Weber State University, Ogden, Utah.]

Bigler, David L. *Forgotten Kingdom: The Mormon Theocracy in the American West, 1847–1896.* Spokane, Wash.: Arthur H. Clark, 1998.

————. *A Winter with the Mormons: The 1852 Letters of Jotham Goodell.* Salt Lake City: Tanner Trust, 2001.

Bigler, David L., and Will Bagley, eds. *Army of Israel: Mormon Battalion Narratives.* Spokane, Wash.: Arthur H. Clark, 2000.

Birney, Hoffman. *Zealots of Zion.* Philadelphia: Penn Publishing Co., 1931.

Bishop, M. Guy. *Henry William Bigler: Soldier, Gold Miner, Missionary, Chronicler: 1815–1900.* Logan: Utah State University Press, 1998.

Bishop, William, ed. *Mormonism Unveiled; or the Life and Confessions of the Late Mormon Bishop, John D. Lee.* St. Louis: Bryan, Brand & Co., 1877.

Bitton, Davis, and Leonard J. Arrington. *Mormons and Their Historians.* Salt Lake City: University of Utah Press, 1988.

Bowles, Samuel. *Across the Continent: A Summer's Journey to the Rocky Mountains, the Mormons, and the Pacific States, with Speaker Colfax.* Springfield, Mass.: Samuel Bowles & Company; New York: Hurd & Houghton, 1866.

Brewer, Dr. Charles. *Retribution at Last: A Mormon Tragedy in the Rockies.* Cincinnati: Editor Publishing Co., 1899. [Fiction.]

Brimhall, George W. *The Workers of Utah.* Provo, Utah: Enquirer Company, 1889. Reprint Provo, Utah: George W. Brimhall Family, 1950, 1951.

Brodie, Fawn. *No Man Knows My History: The Life of Joseph Smith the Mormon Prophet.* New York: Alfred A. Knopf, 1945. 2d ed., 1973.

————, ed. *The City of the Saints and Across the Rocky Mountains to California, by Richard F. Burton.* New York: Alfred A. Knopf, 1963.

Brooks, Juanita. *John Doyle Lee: Zealot, Pioneer Builder, Scapegoat.* Glendale, Calif.: Arthur H. Clark, 1961. Reprint Salt Lake City: Howe Brothers, 1982.

————. *Emma Lee.* Logan, Utah: Utah State University Press, 1984.

————. *The Mountain Meadows Massacre.* Stanford, Calif.: Stanford University Press, 1950. Reprint Norman: University of Oklahoma Press, 1962. Third revision, fourth printing, 1970. First paperback edition, with a foreword by Jan Shipps, 1991.

————. *On the Ragged Edge: The Life and Times of Dudley Leavitt.* Salt Lake City: Utah State Historical Society, 1972.

————, ed. *Journal of the Southern Indian Mission: The Diary of Thomas D. Brown.* Logan: Utah State University Press, 1972.

————, ed. *On the Mormon Frontier: The Diary of Hosea Stout.* 2 vols. Salt Lake City: University of Utah Press, 1964.

————. *Quicksand and Cactus: A Memoir of the Southern Mormon Frontier*. Salt Lake City: Howe Brothers, 1982.

————. *Uncle Will Tells His Story*. Salt Lake City: Taggart & Co., 1970.

Brooks, Juanita, and Robert Glass Cleland, eds. *A Mormon Chronicle: The Diaries of John D. Lee, 1848–1876*. 2 vols. San Marino, Calif.: The Huntington Library, 1955. Reprint Salt Lake City: University of Utah Press, 1983.

Brownmiller, Susan. *Against Our Will: Men, Women and Rape*. New York: Simon and Schuster, 1975.

Buchanan, Frederick Stewart. *A Good Time Coming: Mormon Letters to Scotland*. Salt Lake City: University of Utah Press, 1988.

Burns, Robert Ignatius, S.J., *The Jesuits and the Indian Wars of the Northwest*. New Haven: Yale University Press, 1966.

Campbell, Eugene E. *Establishing Zion: The Mormon Church in the American West, 1847–1869*. Salt Lake City: Signature Books, 1988.

Canning, Ray R., and Beverly Beeton, eds. *The Genteel Gentile: Letters of Elizabeth Cumming, 1857–58*. Salt Lake City: Tanner Trust Fund and University of Utah Library, 1977.

Cannon, George Q. *Writings from the Western Standard*. Liverpool: George Q. Cannon, 1864.

Cannon, M. Hamlin. "The Mormon War: A Study in Territorial Rebellion." M.A. thesis, George Washington University, 1938.

Carleton, James Henry. *The Mountain Meadows Massacre by Brevet Major James Henry Carleton*. Spring Grove, Minn.: Five Quail Books, 1995.

Carter, Kate B., ed. *Heart Throbs of the West*. 12 vols. Salt Lake City: Daughters of Utah Pioneers, 1939–54.

————. *Our Pioneer Heritage*. 20 vols. Salt Lake City: Daughters of Utah Pioneers, 1961–77.

————. *Treasures of Pioneer History*. 6 vols. Salt Lake City: Daughters of Utah Pioneers, 1955–60.

Carvalho, Solomon Nuñes. *Incidents of Travel and Adventure in the Far West with Colonel Fremont's Last Expedition*. New York: Derby & Jackson, 1856.

Chamberlain, William H., and Harry L. Wells. *History of Sutter County, California*. Oakland, Calif.: Thompson & West, 1879.

Cheney, Thomas E., ed. *Mormon Songs from the Rocky Mountains: A Compilation of Mormon Folksong*. Salt Lake City: University of Utah Press, 1981.

Cheney, Thomas E., with Austin E. Fife and Juanita Brooks, eds. *Lore of Faith & Folly*. Salt Lake City: University of Utah Press, 1971.

Clark, Robert A., ed. *The Mountain Meadows Massacre: A Special Report by Brevet Major James Henry Carleton*. Spokane: Arthur H. Clark, 1995.

Clemens, Samuel. *Roughing It*. 2 vols. 1871; Author's National Edition. New York: Harper & Brothers, 1913.

Collins, Dabney Otis. *Great Western Rides*. Denver: Sage Books, 1961.

Compton, Todd. *In Sacred Loneliness: The Plural Wives of Joseph Smith*. Salt Lake City: Signature Books, 1997.

Cook, Lyndon W. *William Law*. Orem, Utah: Grandin Book Co., 1994.

————, ed. *Aaron Johnson Correspondence*. Orem, Utah: Center for Research on Mormon Origins, 1990.

Cooley, Everett L., ed. *Diary of Brigham Young 1857*. Salt Lake City: Tanner Trust Fund, 1980.

Corle, Edwin. *Desert Country*. New York: Duell, Sloan & Pearce, 1941.

Cradlebaugh, John. *Utah and the Mormons: Speech of Hon. John Cradlebaugh, of Nevada, on the Admission of Utah as a State. Delivered in the House of Representatives, February 7, 1863*. Privately printed, 1863.

Crawley, Peter L., ed. *The Essential Parley P. Pratt*. Salt Lake City: Signature Books, 1990.

Cross, Whitney R. *The Burned-over District: The Social and Intellectual History of Enthusiastic Religion in Western New York, 1800–1850*. Ithaca: Cornell University Press, 1950.

Cuch, Forrest, ed. *A History of Utah's American Indians*. Salt Lake City: Utah State Division of Indian Affairs/Utah State Division of History, 2000.

Dalton, Luella Adams, ed. *History of the Iron Country Mission and Parowan, the Mother Town*. 2d ed. Provo: Simon K. Benson, n.d.

Daniels, George F. *History of the Town of Oxford, Massachusetts, with Genealogies and Notes on Persons and Estates*. Oxford: By the author and the town of Oxford, Massachusetts, 1892.

D'Azevedo, Warren L., ed. *Handbook of North American Indians: Great Basin*. Washington, D.C.: Smithsonian Institution Press, 1986.

DeLafosse, Peter, ed. *Trailing the Pioneers*. Logan: Utah State University Press, 1994.

Dellenbaugh, Frederick S. *A Canyon Voyage*. New York: Putnam, 1908. Reprinted Tucson, University of Arizona Press, 1991.

———. *The Romance of the Colorado River*. New York: Putnam, 1909.

Demke, Siegfried G. *The Cattle Drives of Early California*. San Gabriel, Calif.: Prosperity Press, 1985.

Desgranges, Danièle. *Autopsie d'un massacre*. Paris: Éditions Phébus, 1990. [Fiction]

Dillon, Richard H., ed. *California Trail Herd: The 1850 Missouri-to-California Journal of Cyrus C. Loveland*. Los Gatos, Calif.: Talisman Press, 1961.

The Doctrine and Covenants of The Church of Jesus Christ of Latter-day Saints. Salt Lake City: The Church of Jesus Christ of Latter-day Saints, 1921.

Dunbar, Seymour, and Paul C. Phillips, eds. *The Journals and Letters of Major John C. Owen, 1850–1871*. New York: Edward Eberstadt, 1927.

Dunn, J. P., Jr. *Massacres of the Mountains: A History of the Indian Wars of the Far West, 1815–1875*. New York: Harper & Brothers, 1886. Reprint New York: Archer House, n.d.

Dwyer, Robert Joseph. *The Gentile Comes to Utah: A Study in Religious and Social Conflict (1862–1890)*. Washington, D.C.: Catholic University of America Press, 1941.

Egan, Timothy. *Lasso the Wind: Away to the New West*. New York: Alfred A. Knopf, 1998.

Erskine, Gladys Shaw. *Broncho Charlie: A Saga of the Saddle*. New York: Thomas Y. Crowell, 1934. [Story of Pony Express rider Billy Tate, who "got away."]

Euler, Robert C. *The Paiute People*. Phoenix: Indian Tribal Series, 1972.

———. *Southern Paiute Ethnohistory*. Salt Lake City: Department of Anthropology, University of Utah, 1996.

Fancher, Burr. *Westward with the Sun*. Bend, Ore.: Fancher & Associates, 1999.

Fancher, Paul Buford. *Richard Fancher (1700–1764) of Morris County, New Jersey [and] Richard Fancher's Descendants 1764–1992*. Roswell, Ga.: W. H. Wolfe Associates, 1993.

Fancher, William Hoyt. *The Fancher Family*. Milford, N.H.: The Cabinet Press, 1947.

Fielding, Robert Kent. *Unsolicited Chronicler: An Account of the Gunnison Massacre, Its Causes and Consequences*. Brookline, Mass.: Paradigm Publications, 1993.

Fielding, Robert Kent, and Dorothy S. Fielding. *The Tribune Reports of the Trials of John D. Lee for the Massacre at Mountain Meadow*. Higganum, Conn.: Kent's Books, 2000.

Folk, Edgar E., and George A. Lofton. *The Mormon Monster or, the Story of Mormonism*. Chicago: Fleming H. Revell, 1900.

Fletcher, Patricia K. A., Jack Earl Fletcher, and Lee Whiteley, eds. *Cherokee Trail Diaries*. Caldwell, Idaho: Caxton Printers, 1999.

Freeman, Judith. *Red Water.* New York: Pantheon Books, 2002. [Fiction.]

Furniss, Norman F. *The Mormon Conflict, 1850–1859.* New Haven: Yale University Press, 1960.

Garner, Hugh, ed. *A Mormon Rebel: The Life and Times of Frederick Gardiner.* Salt Lake City: Tanner Trust Fund, University of Utah Library, 1993.

Garr, Arnold K., Donald Q. Cannon, and Richard O. Cowan. *Encyclopedia of Latter-day Saint History.* Salt Lake City: Deseret Book Co., 2000.

Gates, Susa Young. *Brigham Young: Patriot, Pioneer, Prophet.* Salt Lake City: KSL Radio, 1929.

Gibbons, Francis M. *Brigham Young: Modern Moses/Prophet of God.* Salt Lake City: Deseret Book Co., 1981.

Gibbs, Josiah. *Kawich's Gold Mine: An Historical Narrative of Mining in the Grand Canyon of the Colorado, and of Love and Adventure Among the Polygamous Mormons of Southern Utah.* Salt Lake City: Century Printing Co., 1913. [Fiction.]

———. *Lights and Shadows of Mormonism.* Salt Lake City: Salt Lake Tribune Publishing Co., 1909.

———. *The Mountain Meadows Massacre.* Salt Lake City: Salt Lake Tribune Publishing Co., 1910.

Green, Nelson Winch, ed. *Fifteen Years among the Mormons: Being the Narrative of Mrs. Mary Ettie V. Smith* [Mary E. Coray]. New York: H. Dayton, 1858. Reprinted as *Mormonism: Its Rise, Progress, and Present Condition. Being the Narrative of Mrs. Mary Ettie V. Smith, of Her Residence and Experience of Fifteen Years with the Mormons; Containing a Full and Authentic Account of Their Social Condition—Their Religious Doctrines, and Political Government.* Hartford: Belknap & Bliss, 1870.

Greenwood, Jean S., ed. *Brigham Young's Excursions into the Settlements.* Salt Lake City: Daughters of Utah Pioneers, 1994.

Gunnison, John W. *The Mormons, or, Latter-day Saints, in the Valley of the Great Salt Lake.* Philadelphia: Lippincott, Grambo & Co., 1852. Enlarged edition, 1860.

Hafen, LeRoy R., ed. *The Mountain Men and the Fur Trade of the Far West.* 10 vols. Glendale, Calif.: Arthur H. Clark, 1965–72.

———. *The Utah Expedition, 1857–1858: A Documentary Account of the United States Military Movement under Colonel Albert Sidney Johnston, and the Resistance by Brigham Young and the Mormon Nauvoo Legion.* Glendale, Calif.: Arthur H. Clark, 1958.

Hafen, LeRoy R., and Ann W. Hafen, eds. *Old Spanish Trail: Santa Fé to Los Angeles, with extracts from contemporary records and including the diaries of Antonio Armijo and Orville Pratt.* Glendale, Calif.: Arthur H. Clark, 1954.

Hallwas, John E., and Roger Launius, eds. *Cultures in Conflict: A Documentary History of the Mormon War in Illinois.* Logan: Utah State University Press, 1995.

Hammond, Otis G., ed. *The Utah Expedition, 1857–1858: Letters of Capt. Jesse A. Gove, 10th Inf., U.S.A., of Concord, N.H., to Mrs. Gove, and Special Correspondence of the New York Herald.* Concord: New Hampshire Historical Society, 1928.

Hansen, Klaus J. *Quest for Empire: The Political Kingdom of God and the Council of Fifty in Mormon History.* East Lansing: Michigan State University Press, 1967.

Hardy, B. Carmon. *Solemn Covenant: The Mormon Polygamous Passage.* Urbana: University of Illinois Press, 1992.

Harwell, William S., ed. *Manuscript History of Brigham Young, 1847–1850.* Salt Lake City: Collier's, 1997.

Heap, Gwinn Harris. *Central Route to the Pacific.* Edited by LeRoy R. Hafen and Ann W. Hafen. Glendale, Calif.: Arthur H. Clark, 1957.

Heath, Harvard. *In the World: The Diaries of Reed Smoot.* Salt Lake City: Signature Books, 1997.

Heitman, Francis B. *Historical Register and Dictionary of the United States Army, from Its Organization, September 29, 1789, to March 2, 1903.* 2 vols. Washington, D.C.: Government Printing Office, 1903. Reprint Urbana: University of Illinois Press, 1965.

Henrie, Manetta Prince. *Descendants of John Doyle Lee, 1812–1877.* Provo, Utah: n.p., 1960.

Hickman, William A., and J. H. Beadle. *Brigham's Destroying Angel: Being the Life, Confession, and Startling Disclosures of the Notorious Bill Hickman, the Danite Chief of Utah.* New York: Geo. A. Crofutt, 1872.

Hirshson, Stanley P. *The Lion of the Lord: A Biography of Brigham Young.* New York: Alfred A. Knopf, 1969.

History of the Mountain Meadows Massacre, Butchery in Cold Blood of 134 Men, Women and Children by Mormons and Indians, September, 1857, Also a Full and Complete Account of the Trial, Confession and Execution of John D. Lee, The Leader of the Murderers, Illustrated by a True Likeness of John D. Lee. For Distribution with Their Celebrated Picture of Mountain Meadows. San Francisco: Pacific Arts Press, 1877.

Hoffer, Eric. *The True Believer: Thoughts on the Nature of Mass Movements.* New York: Harper & Row, 1951. Reprint Alexandria, Va.: Time-Life Books, 1980.

Holmes, Kenneth L., ed. *Covered Wagon Women: Diaries & Letters from the Western Trails, 1840–1890.* 11 vols. Glendale, Calif.: Arthur H. Clark, 1983–93.

Holt, Ronald L. *Beneath These Red Cliffs: An Ethnohistory of the Utah Paiutes.* Albuquerque: University of New Mexico Press, 1992.

———. "Beneath These Red Cliffs: The Utah Paiutes and Paternalistic Dependency." Ph.D. dissertation, University of Utah, 1987.

Hyde, John. *Mormonism: Its Leaders and Designs.* New York: Fetridge, 1857.

[Jackson, Helen Hunt.] H. H. *Bits of Travel at Home.* Boston: Roberts Brothers, 1894.

Jackson, W. Turrentine. *Wagon Roads West: A Study of Federal Road Surveys and Construction in the Trans-Mississippi West, 1846–1869.* Berkeley: University of California Press, 1952.

Jarvis, Zora Smith. *Ancestry, Biography, and Family of George A. Smith.* N.p.: By the family, 1962.

Jenson, Andrew. *Autobiography of Andrew Jenson.* Salt Lake City: Deseret News Press, 1938.

———. *Latter-day Saint Biographical Encyclopedia.* 4 vols. Salt Lake City: Andrew Jenson History Co., 1901.

Jessee, Dean C. *The Papers of Joseph Smith.* 2 vols. Salt Lake City: Deseret Book, 1989, 1992.

Johnson, Clark V., ed. *Mormon Redress Petitions: Documents of the 1833–1838 Missouri Conflict.* Provo: Bookcraft, 1992.

Journal of Discourses. 26 vols. London: Latter-Day Saints Book Depot, 1854–86.

Jones, Daniel W. *Forty Years among the Indians: A True and Thrilling Narrative of the Author's Experiences among the Natives.* Salt Lake City: Juvenile Instructor Office, 1890.

Jones, Sondra. *The Trial of Don Pedro León Luján: The Attack against Indian Slavery and Mexican Traders in Utah.* Salt Lake City: University of Utah Press, 2000.

Kelly, Charles, ed. *Journals of John D. Lee, 1846–47 & 1859.* Salt Lake City: Western Printing Company, 1938. Reprint Salt Lake City: University of Utah Press, 1984.

Kelly, Charles, and Hoffman Birney. *Holy Murder: The Story of Porter Rockwell.* New York: Minton, Balch & Co., 1934.

Kelly, Charles, and Dale L. Morgan. *Old Greenwood: The Story of Caleb Greenwood, Trapper, Pathfinder, and Early Pioneer.* Georgetown, Calif.: Talisman Press, 1965.

Kenney, Scott G., ed. *Wilford Woodruff's Journal.* 10 vols. Midvale, Utah: Signature Books, 1983.

King, David S. *Mountain Meadows Massacre: A Search for Perspective.* Washington, D.C.: Potomac Corral, the Westerners, 1970.

Klare, Normand. *The Final Voyage of the Central America, 1857: The Saga of a Gold Rush Steamship, the Tragedy of Her Loss in a Hurricane, and the Treasure Which Is Now Recovered.* Spokane, Wash.: Arthur H. Clark, 1992.

Kraut, Ogden. *Blood Atonement*. Salt Lake City: Kraut's Pioneer Press, n.d.

Krenkel, John H., ed. *The Life and Times of Joseph Fish, Mormon Pioneer*. Danville, Ill.: Interstate Printers & Publishers, 1970.

Lair, Jim. *The Mountain Meadows Massacre: An Outlander's View*. Harrison, Ark.: Carroll County Historical and Genealogical Society, 1986.

Lamar, Howard R. *The Far Southwest 1846–1912: A Territorial History*. New Haven: Yale University Press, 1966. Revised edition, Albuquerque: University of New Mexico Press, 2000.

———, ed. *The Reader's Encyclopedia of the American West*. New York: Thomas Y. Crowell Company, 1977. Reissued as *The New Encyclopedia of the American West*. New Haven: Yale University Press, 1998.

Lancaster, Bob. *The Jungles of Arkansas*. Fayetteville: University of Arkansas Press, 1989.

Langworthy, Franklin. *Scenery of the Plains, Mountains and Mines: or a Diary kept upon the Overland Route to California, by way of the Great Salt Lake*. Ogdensburgh, N.Y.: J. S. Sprague, Bookseller; Hitchcock & Tillotson, Printers, 1855.

Larson, Andrew Karl. *Erastus Snow: The Life of a Missionary and Pioneer for the Early Mormon Church*. Salt Lake City: University of Utah Press, 1971.

———. *"I Was Called to Dixie," the Virgin River Basin: Unique Experiences in Mormon Pioneering*. St. George: By the author, 1961.

Larson, Andrew Karl, and Katharine Miles Larson, eds. *Diary of Charles Lowell Walker*. 2 vols. Logan: Utah State University Press, 1980.

Lee, John D. *Mormonism Unveiled*. See Bishop, William.

———. *The Mountain Meadows Massacre, with the Life, Confession and Execution of John D. Lee*. Philadelphia: Barclay & Co., 1877. [This pamphlet has pages numbered 19 to 46, lurid plates, and this variant title on its title page: *The Life and Confession of John D. Lee, the Mormon. With a Full Account of the Mountain Meadows Massacre and Execution of Lee. Helpless Women and Children Butchered in Cold Blood by Merciless Mormon Assassins.*]

LeSueur, Stephen C. *The 1838 Mormon War in Missouri*. Columbia: University of Missouri Press, 1987.

Lindsay, Robert. *A Gathering of Saints: A True Story of Money, Murder and Deceit*. New York: Simon and Schuster, 1988.

Little, James A. *Jacob Hamblin: A Narrative of His Personal Experiences as a Frontiersman, Missionary to the Indians and Explorer*. Salt Lake City: Juvenile Instructor, 1881. 2d ed., Deseret News, 1909. Reprinted as *Jacob Hamblin among the Indians*. Salt Lake City: General Board of the Young Men's Mutual Improvement Association, 1945.

[Lockley, Frederic]. *The Lee Trial*. Salt Lake City: Tribune Printing Co., 1875.

Loewen, James W. *Lies across America: What Our Historic Sites Get Wrong*. New York: New Press, 1999.

Logan, Roger V., Jr., ed. *Mountain Heritage: Some Glimpses into Boone County's Past after One Hundred Years*. Harrison, Ark.: Harrison Junior Chamber of Commerce, 1969.

Long, E. B. *The Saints and the Union: Utah Territory during the Civil War*. Urbana: University of Illinois Press, 1981.

Ludlow, Daniel, ed. *Encyclopedia of Mormonism*. 4 vols. New York: Macmillan, 1992.

Lyford, C. P. *The Mormon Problem: An Appeal to the American People*. New York: Phillips & Hunt, 1886.

Lyman, Albert R. *Francis Marion Lyman: Apostle*. Delta, Utah: Melvin A. Lyman, 1958.

Lyman, Edward Leo. *San Bernardino: The Rise and Fall of a California Community*. Salt Lake City: Signature Books, 1996.

McArthur, Priscilla. *Arkansas in the Gold Rush*. Little Rock: August House, 1986.

McConkie, Bruce R. *Mormon Doctrine*. Salt Lake City: Bookcraft, 1958.

McCoy, Joseph G. *Historic Sketches of the Cattle Trade of the West and Southwest.* Edited by Ralph P. Bieber. Glendale: Arthur H. Clark, 1939. Reprint Lincoln: University of Nebraska Press, 1985.

McEuen, Douglas. *The Legend of Francis Marion Poteet and the Mountain Meadows Massacre: History of the Poteet Family.* Pleasanton, Tex: Zabava Printing, 1996.

Macfarlane, L. W. *Yours Sincerely, John M. Macfarlane.* Salt Lake City: By the author, 1980.

McGlashan, C. F. *History of the Donner Party.* Truckee, Calif.: Crowley and McGlashan, 1879.

McGlashan, M. Nona, and Betty H. McGlashan, eds. *From the Desk of C. F. McGlashan.* Truckee, Calif.: Truckee Historical Society, n.d.

McIntyre, Myron W., and Noel R. Barton, eds. *Christopher Layton: Colonizer, Statesman, Leader.* Salt Lake: Christopher Layton Family Organization, 1966.

MacKinnon, William P., ed. *At Sword's Point: A Documentary History of the Utah War of 1857–1858.* Spokane, Wash.: Arthur H. Clark, forthcoming.

Madsen, Brigham D. *Against the Grain: Memoirs of a Western Historian.* Salt Lake City: Signature Books, 1998.

———. *Gold Rush Sojourners in Great Salt Lake City, 1849 and 1850.* Salt Lake City: University of Utah Press, 1983.

———. *The Shoshoni Frontier and the Bear River Massacre.* Salt Lake City: University of Utah Press, 1985.

Manderscheid, Lorraine Richardson, ed. *Some Descendants of John Doyle Lee.* Belleview, Wash.: Family Research and Development, 1996.

Martineau, LaVan. *Southern Paiutes.* Las Vegas: KC Publications, 1992.

Mattes, Merrill J. *The Great Platte River Road.* Lincoln: Nebraska State Historical Society, 1969. Second edition, Lincoln: Bison Books, 1978.

———. *Platte River Road Narratives.* Urbana: University of Illinois Press, 1988.

Marquardt, H. Michael, and Wesley P. Walters. *Inventing Mormonism: Tradition and the Historical Record.* Salt Lake City: Smith Research Associates, 1994.

Maxwell, William Audley. *Crossing the Plains, Days of '57.* San Francisco: Sunset, 1915.

Metcalf, A. *Ten Years before the Mast: Shipwrecks and Adventures at Sea! Religious Customs of the People of India and Burmah's Empire; How I Became a Mormon and Why I Became an Infidel!* Elk Horn, Malad Valley, Idaho: n.p., 1881.

Moore, John Bassett, ed. *The Works of James Buchanan, Comprising His Speeches, State Papers, and Private Correspondence.* 11 vols. New York: Antiquarian Press, 1960.

Moorman, Donald R., and Gene A. Sessions. *Camp Floyd and the Mormons: The Utah War.* Salt Lake City: University of Utah Press, 1992.

Morgan, Dale L. *The Humboldt: Highroad of the West.* New York: Farrar & Rinehardt, 1943.

———. *The State of Deseret.* Logan: Utah State University Press, 1987.

Morgan, Dale L., and Federal Writers' Projects of the Works Progress Administration. *Provo: Pioneer Mormon City.* Portland, Ore.: Binfords & Mort, 1942.

Myres, Sandra L., ed. *Ho for California! Women's Overland Diaries from the Huntington Library.* San Marino: The Huntington Library, 1980.

Newton, Marjorie. *Hero or Traitor: A Biographical Study of Charles Wesley Wandell.* Independence, Mo.: John Whitmer Historical Association, 1992.

Ogden, Annegret S., ed. *Frontier Reminiscences of Eveline Brooks Auerbach.* Berkeley, Calif.: Friends of the Bancroft Library, 1994.

Ogle, Sandra K. *The Miller Family in California.* Baltimore: Gateway Press, 1985.

O'Neil, Floyd A. "A History of the Ute Indians of Utah until 1890." Ph.D. dissertation, University of Utah, 1973.

Papanikolas, Helen Z. *The Peoples of Utah*. Salt Lake City: Utah Historical Society, 1976.

Parker, Basil G. *The Life and Adventures of Basil G. Parker: An Autobiography*. Plano, Calif.: Fred W. Reed, American Printer, 1902.

———. *Recollections of the Mountain Meadows Massacre*. Plano, Calif.: Fred W. Reed, American Printer, 1901.

Pease, Harold W. "The Life and Works of William Horne Dame." M.A. thesis, Brigham Young University, 1971.

Penrose, Charles W. *Blood Atonement, as Taught by the Leading Elders of the Church of Jesus Christ of Latter-day Saints*. Salt Lake City: Juvenile Instructor Office, 1884.

———. *The Mountain Meadows Massacre: Who Were Guilty of the Crime?* Salt Lake City: Juvenile Instructor Office, 1884.

———. "Testimony of James Holt Haslam." In *Supplement to the Lecture on the Mountain Meadows Massacre: Important Additional Testimony Recently Received*. Salt Lake City: Juvenile Instructor Press, 1885.

Peterson, Levi. *Juanita Brooks: Mormon Woman Historian*. Salt Lake City: University of Utah Press and Tanner Trust Fund, 1988.

Peterson, Ruth. *Across the Plains in '57: The Story of Peter Campbell and a train of immigrants as told by Nancy Campbell Lowell, a member of the party*. San Francisco: Grand Parlor [Natives Daughters of the Golden West], 1936.

Powell, Allen Kent, ed. *Utah History Encyclopedia*. Salt Lake City: University of Utah Press, 1994.

Pratt, Parley. *Proclamation of the Twelve Apostles of the Church of Jesus Christ of Latter-day Saints to All the Kings of the World, to the President of the United States of America; to the Governors of the Several States, and to the Rulers and People of All Nations*. New York: Pratt and Brannan, 1845; Liverpool: Wilford Woodruff, 1845.

Purple, Samuel S. *In Memoriam. Edwin R. Purple. Born, 1831, Died, 1879*. New York: Privately printed, 1881.

Pusey, Merlo J. *Builders of the Kingdom: George A. Smith, John Henry Smith, George Albert Smith*. Provo: Brigham Young University Press, 1981.

Quinn, D. Michael. *Early Mormonism and the Magic World View*. Salt Lake City: Signature Books, 1987. 2d ed., 1998.

———. *J. Reuben Clark: The Church Years*. Provo: Brigham Young University Press, 1983.

———. *The Mormon Hierarchy: Extensions of Power*. Salt Lake City: Signature Books, 1997.

———. *The Mormon Hierarchy: Origins of Power*. Salt Lake City: Signature Books, 1994.

Rea, Ralph R. *The Mountain Meadows Massacre and Its Completion as a Historic Episode*. Harrison, Ark.: n.p., 1957.

Rice, William B. *The Los Angeles Star*. Edited by John W. Caughey. Berkeley: University of California Press, 1947.

Roberts, Brigham H. *A Comprehensive History of The Church of Jesus Christ of Latter-day Saints*. 6 vols. Salt Lake City: Deseret News Press, 1930.

———. *A New Witness for God*. Salt Lake City: George Q. Cannon, 1895.

Rusho, W. L. *Lee's Ferry: Desert River Crossing*. Third edition. Salt Lake City and St. George: Tower Productions, 1998.

Schindler, Harold M. *In Another Time: Sketches of Utah History*. Logan: Utah State University Press, 1998.

———. *Orrin Porter Rockwell: Man of God, Son of Thunder*. Salt Lake City: University of Utah Press, 1966. 2d ed., 1983.

Sessions, Gene A. *Mormon Thunder: A Documentary History of Jedediah Morgan Grant*. Urbana: University of Illinois Press, 1982.

Shaw, David Augustus. *Eldorado; or, California as Seen by a Pioneer, 1850–1900*. Los Angeles: B. R. Baumgardt & Co., 1900.

Sheffer, H. Henry, III, and Sharyn R. Alger. *"The Mountain Meadows Massacre": The Oppression of the Saints*. Apache Junction, Ariz.: Norseman Publications, 1995.

Sherman, William T. *Memoirs of General William T. Sherman*. 2 vols. New York: D. Appleton, 1876.

Sillitoe, Linda, and Allen Roberts. *Salamander: The Story of the Mormon Forgery Murders*. Salt Lake City: Signature Books, 1988.

Smart, William B., and Donna T. Smart, eds. *Over the Rim: The Parley P. Pratt Exploring Expedition to Southern Utah, 1849–1850*. Logan: Utah State University Press, 1999.

Smith, Albert E. *Thales Hastings Haskell: Pioneer—Scout—Explorer—Indian Missionary, 1847–1909*. Salt Lake City: By the author, 1964. [See also Haskell's autobiographical sketch in Daughters of Utah Pioneers Lesson Committee, *An Enduring Legacy*. 12 vols. Salt Lake City: Daughters of Utah Pioneers, 1978–90, 2:231–32.]

Smith, George D., ed. *An Intimate Chronicle: The Journals of William Clayton*. Salt Lake City: Signature Books, 1991.

———. *Faithful History: Essays on Writing Mormon History*. Salt Lake City: Signature Books, 1992.

Smith, Joseph, Jr. *History of the Church*. 7 vols. Edited by Brigham H. Roberts. Salt Lake City: Deseret News Press, 1932.

Smith, Joseph Fielding. *Essentials in Church History*. Salt Lake City: Desert News Press, 1922.

Smith, Oliver R., ed. *Six Decades in the Early West: The Journal of Jesse Nathaniel Smith*. Provo: Jesse N. Smith Family Association, 1970.

Spence, Mary Lee, and Donald Jackson, eds. *The Expeditions of John Charles Frémont*. Vol. 1. Chicago: University of Illinois Press, 1970.

Staker, Susan, ed. *Waiting for the World's End: The Diaries of Wilford Woodruff*. Salt Lake City: Signature Books, 1993.

Stampp, Kenneth M. *America in 1857: A Nation on the Brink*. New York: Oxford University Press, 1990.

Stanley, Reva Holdaway. *A Biography of Parley P. Pratt, the Archer of Paradise*. Caldwell, Idaho: Caxton Printers, 1937.

Stegner, Wallace. *The Gathering of Zion*. New York: McGraw-Hill, 1964.

Stenhouse, T. B. H. *The Rocky Mountain Saints: A Full and Complete History of the Mormons, from the First Vision of Joseph Smith to the Last Courtship of Brigham Young*. New York: D. Appleton, 1873.

Stenhouse, Mrs. T. B. H. [Fanny]. *"Tell It All": The Story of a Life's Experience in Mormonism, an Autobiography*. Hartford, Conn.: A. D. Worthington & Co., 1873.

Stott, Clifford L. *Search for Sanctuary: Brigham Young and the White Mountain Expedition*. Salt Lake City: University of Utah Press, 1984.

Taylor, Samuel W. *The Kingdom or Nothing: The Life of John Taylor, Militant Mormon*. New York: Macmillan, 1976.

———. *Nightfall at Nauvoo*. New York: Macmillan, 1971.

Tea, Roy D., ed. *"The Southern Route" of the Forty-Niners: Salt Lake City South to Los Angeles*. Salt Lake City: Utah Crossroads Chapter, Oregon-California Trails Association, 1999.

Thomas, Sarah C., ed. *Elias Smith's Journal*. 3 vols. Salt Lake City: By the family, 1984.

Thorndike, Rachel Sherman, ed. *The Sherman Letters: Correspondence between General Sherman and Senator Sherman from 1837 to 1891*. New York: Charles Scribner's Sons, 1894. Reprint New York: Da Capo Press, 1969.

Thrapp, Dan L. *Encyclopedia of Frontier Biography.* 4 vols. Glendale, Calif.: Arthur H. Clark, 1988, 1994.

Topping, Gary, ed. *Gila Monsters and Red-Eyed Rattlesnakes: Don Maguire's Arizona Trading Expeditions, 1876–1879.* Salt Lake City: University of Utah Press, 1997.

Townsend, George Alfred. *The Mormon Trials at Salt Lake City.* New York: American News Co., 1871.

Tullidge, Edward W. *Life of Brigham Young; or, Utah and Her Founders.* New York: Tullidge & Crandall, 1876.

Tyler, Alice Felt. *Freedom's Ferment: Phases of American Social History from the Colonial Period to the Outbreak of the Civil War.* Minneapolis: University of Minnesota Press, 1944. Reprint New York: Harper & Row, 1962.

Unruh, John D., Jr. *The Plains Across: The Overland Emigrants and the Trans-Mississippi West, 1840–1860.* Urbana: University of Illinois Press, 1979.

Van Deusen, Increase Mcgee. *The Mormon Endowment; A Secret Drama, or Conspiracy, in the Nauvoo Temple, in 1846.* Syracuse: N. M. D. Lathrop, 1847.

Van Wagoner, Richard S. *Mormon Polygamy: A History.* Salt Lake City: Signature Books, 1989.

Vindex. *Mountain Meadows Massacre: Review of Elder Penrose's exculpatory address delivered Oct. 26th, 1884, in Twelfth Ward Meeting House.* Salt Lake City: n.p., 1884.

Walker, Ronald W. *Wayward Saints: The Godbeites and Brigham Young.* Urbana: University of Illinois Press, 1998.

Waters, W. E. *Life among the Mormons and a March to Their Zion: To which is added a chapter on the Indians and Mountains of the West, by an Officer of the U.S. Army.* New York: Moorhead, Simpson & Bond, 1868.

Werner, M. R. *Brigham Young.* New York: Harcourt, Brace, 1925.

Westwood, Phoebe Louise, and Richard W. Rohrbacher. *Yesteryear's Child: Golden Days & Summer Nights.* Stockton, Calif.: Heritage Books, 1993.

Wheat, Carl I. *Mapping the Transmississippi West.* 5 vols. in 6. San Francisco: Institute of Historical Cartography, 1957–63.

Wheeler, George M., and D. W. Lockwood, *Preliminary Report upon a Reconnaissance through Southern and Southeastern Nevada, made in 1869.* Washington, D.C.: Government Printing Office, 1875.

White, David A., ed. *News of the Plains and the Rockies, 1803–1865.* Vol. 3, *Missionaries, Mormons, 1821–1864; Indian Agents, Captives, 1832–1865.* Spokane, Wash.: Arthur H. Clark, 1997. Vol. 4, *Warriors, 1834–1865; Scientists, Artists, 1835–1859.* Spokane, Wash.: Arthur H. Clark, 1998.

White, Jean Bickmore, ed. *Church, State, and Politics: The Diaries of John Henry Smith.* Salt Lake City: Signature Books and Smith Research Associates, 1990.

Whiteley, Lee. *The Cherokee Trail: Bent's Fort to Fort Bridger.* Denver: Denver Posse of Westerners, 1999.

Whitney, Orson F. *History of Utah.* 4 vols. Salt Lake City: George Q. Cannon, 1892–1904.

———. *Popular History of Utah.* Salt Lake City: George Q. Cannon, 1916.

Winther, Oscar Osburn, ed. *The Private Papers and Diary of Thomas Lieper Kane: A Friend of the Mormons.* San Francisco: Gelber-Lilientahl, 1937.

Wischmann, Lesley. *The Descendants of Richard Fancher and Patsy Gray Bynum.* Larami, Wyo.: Wischmann Genealogy Services, 1995.

Wise, William. *Massacre at Mountain Meadows: An American Legend and a Monumental Crime.* New York: Crowell, 1976.

Wixom, Hartt. *Hamblin: A Modern Look at the Frontier Life and Legend of Jacob Hamblin.* Springville, Utah: Cedar Fort, 1996.

Young, Ann Eliza Webb. *Wife No. 19, or the Story of a Life in Bondage.* Hartford, Conn.: Dustin, Gilman & Co., 1875.

Young, Brigham. *A series of instructions and remarks by President Brigham Young at special council, Tabernacle, March 21, 1858.* Salt Lake City: n.p., 1858.

ARTICLES

Ackley, Richard Thomas. "Across the Plains in 1858." Edited by Dale L. Morgan. *Utah Historical Quarterly* 9:3–4 (1941): 190–228.

Alexander, Thomas G. Review of David L. Bigler's *Forgotten Kingdom*. *New Mexico Historical Review* 74:4 (October 1999): 420–21.

Allen, James B. "The Unusual Jurisdiction of County Probate Courts in the Territory of Utah." *Utah Historical Quarterly* 36:2 (Spring 1968): 132–42.

Alter, J. Cecil. "The Mormons and the Indians." *Utah Historical Quarterly* 12 (January–April 1944): 49–67. [Summarizes Indian-related material in the early *Deseret News*.]

Alter J. Cecil, and Robert J. Dwyer, eds. "Journal of Captain Albert Tracy." *Utah Historical Quarterly* 13 (1943): 1–119.

Arrington, Leonard J. "Crusade against Theocracy: The Reminiscences of Judge Jacob Smith Boreman of Utah, 1872–1877." *Huntington Library Quarterly* 24:1 (November 1960): 1–45.

———. Review of William Wise, *Massacre at Mountain Meadows. Brigham Young University Studies* (Summer 1977): 82.

———. "Vistas in Church History." *The First Annual Church Educational System Religious Educators Symposium: Transcripts of Addresses and Abstracts of Presentations* (August 1977): 17–21.

Atkinson, J. H. "Cattle Drives from Arkansas to California in the Decade before the Civil War." *Pulaski County Historical Review* 16 (March 1968): 53–56.

Bagley, Will. "'Every Thing Is Favourable! And God Is On Our Side': Samuel Brannan and the Conquest of California." *Journal of Mormon History* 23:2 (Fall 1997): 185–209.

Bailey, Lynn R., ed. "Lt. Sylvester Mowry's Report on His March in 1855 from Salt Lake City to Fort Tejon." *Arizona and the West* 7 (Winter 1965): 329–45.

Baker, R. P. "Arkansans in the Mountain Meadow Massacre." *Arkansas Family Historian* 20:1 (March 1982): 38–39. [Lists Arkansas 1850 census information on victims.]

Beaman, E. O. "The Cañon of the Colorado, and the Moquis Pueblos: A Wild Boat-Ride through the Cañons and Rapids—A Visit to the Seven Cities of the Desert—Glimpses of Mormon Life." *Appleton's Journal* 9:268 (9 May 1874): 592–93.

Bell, James G. "Log of the Texas-California Trail, 1854." Edited by J. Evetts Haley. *Southwestern Historical Quarterly* 35:3 (January 1932): 208–37.

Bigler, David L. "The Crisis at Fort Limhi, 1858." *Utah Historical Quarterly* 35:2 (Spring 1967): 121–36.

———. "Garland Hurt, the American Friend of the Utahs." *Utah Historical Quarterly* 62:2 (Spring 1994): 149–70.

Bitton, Davis. "'I'd Rather Have Some Roasting Ears': The Peregrinations of George Armstrong Hicks." *Utah Historical Quarterly* 68:3 (Summer 2000): 196–222.

Bitton, Davis, and Maureen Ursenbach, eds. "Riding Herd: A Conversation with Juanita Brooks." *Dialogue* 9:1 (Spring 1974): 11–33.

Blair, Alma. "The Haun's Mill Massacre." *Brigham Young University Studies* 13 (Autumn 1972).

Bluth, John V. "The Salmon River Mission: An Account of Its Origin, Purpose, Growth and Abandonment." *Improvement Era* 3:11 (September 1900): 801–15; and 3:12 (October 1900): 900–13.

Brooks, Juanita. "An Historical Epilogue [Speech Given at the Dedication of a Monument Honoring the Victims of the Massacre at the Mountain Meadows]." *Utah Historical Quarterly* 24 (January 1956): 71–80.

———. "Indian Relations on the Mormon Frontier." *Utah Historical Quarterly* 12 (January-April 1944): 1–48.

———. "Jest a Copyin'—Word f'r Word." *Utah Historical Quarterly* 37:4 (Fall 1969): 375–95.

———. "Lee's Ferry at Lonely Dell." *Utah Historical Quarterly* 25 (October 1957): 283–95.

———. "Let's Preserve Our Records." *Utah Humanities Review* 2:3 (July 1948): 259–63.

———. "The Mountain Meadows: Historic Stopping Place on the Spanish Trail." *Utah Historical Quarterly* 35:2 (Spring 1967): 137–43.

——— "A Place of Refuge." *Nevada Historical Society Quarterly* 14:1 (Spring 1971): 13–24.

[Browne, Albert G.] "The Utah Expedition: Its Causes and Consequences." *Atlantic Monthly* 3:17–19 (March, April, May 1859): 361–584.

Burt, Olive. "Murder Ballads of Mormondom." *Western Folklore* 28:2 (April 1959): 141–56.

Bush, Lester E. "Brigham Young in Life and Death: A Medical Overview." *Journal of Mormon History* 5 (1978): 92–103.

Cannon II, Kenneth L. "'Mountain Common Law'—The Extralegal Punishment of Seducers in Early Utah." *Utah Historical Quarterly* 51:4 (Fall 1983): 308–27.

Cardon, A. F. "Mountain Meadows Burial Detachment, 1859: Tommy Gordon's Diary." *Utah Historical Quarterly* 35:2 (Spring 1967): 143–46.

Cheesman, David W. "By Ox-team from Salt Lake to Los Angeles, 1850." Edited by Mary E. Foy. *Publications of the Historical Society of California* 14 (1930): 271–338.

Child, John K. "The Mountain Meadows Massacre—A Summary Appraisal." *The First Annual Church Educational System Religious Educators Symposium: Transcripts of Addresses and Abstracts of Presentations* (August 1977): 46–48.

Christy, Howard A. "Open Hand and Mailed Fist: Mormon-Indian Relations in Utah, 1847–52." *Utah Historical Quarterly* 46:3 (Summer 1978): 216–35.

———. "'What Virtue There Is in Stone' and Other Pungent Talk on the Early Utah Frontier." *Utah Historical Quarterly* 59:3 (Summer 1991): 300–19.

Clark, William. "A Trip across the Plains in 1857." Edited by Louis Bernhard Schmidt. *Iowa Journal of History and Politics* 20:2 (April 1922): 163–223.

Coates, Lawrence G. "Brigham Young and Mormon Indian Policies: The Formative Period, 1836–1851." *Brigham Young University Studies* 18:3 (Spring 1978): 428–52.

Cooley, Everett L. "A Brigham Young Letter to George Q. Cannon, 1859." *Brigham Young University Studies* 25:3 (Summer 1985): 106–9.

Cottam, Walter P. "Man as a Biotic Factor Illustrated by Recent Floristic and Physiographic Changes at the Mountain Meadows, Washington County, Utah." *Ecology* 10:4 (October 1929): 361–63.

Cottam, Walter P., and George Stewart. "Plant Succession as a Result of Grazing and of Meadow Desiccation by Erosion Since Settlement in 1862." *Journal of Forestry* 38 (August 1940): 613–26.

Crampton, C. Gregory, ed. "F. S. Dellenbaugh of the Colorado: Some Letters Pertaining to the Powell Voyages and the History of the Colorado River." *Utah Historical Quarterly* 37 (Spring 1969): 214–43.

Cureton, Gilbert. "The Cattle Trail to California, 1840–1860." *Historical Society of California Quarterly* 35:2 (June 1953): 99–109.

Derry, Charles. "Autobiography of Elder Charles Derry." *Journal of History* 1:3–4 (July–October 1908): 259–91, 423–45.

Ellsworth, S. George. "Hubert Howe Bancroft and the History of Utah." *Utah Historical Quarterly* 22:2 (April 1954): 99–124.

"The Emigrant Caravan." *Chambers's Journal of Popular Literature, Science, and Art* (25 March 1876).

Esplin, Ronald K. "'A Place Prepared': Joseph, Brigham and the Quest for Promised Refuge in the West." *Journal of Mormon History* 9 (1982): 85–111.

———. "Tragedy in the Meadows." *Mormon Heritage Magazine* 1 (May–June 1994): 28–35.

Esplin, Ronald K., and Dean C. Jessee. "The Mormon Reaction." *Arkansas Times* 10:11 (July 1984): 25–30.

Fletcher, Jack, and Patricia Fletcher. "The Cherokee Trail." *Overland Journal* 13 (Summer 1995): 21–33.

Flint, Thomas. "Diary of Dr. Thomas Flint: California to Maine and Return, 1851–1855." *Annual Publications of the Historical Society of Southern California* (Los Angeles: The Historical Society of Southern California, 1923).

Godfrey, Kenneth W. "Charles W. Penrose and His Contributions to Utah Statehood." *Utah Historical Quarterly* 64:4 (Fall 1996): 357–71.

Gregory, Herbert E., ed. "Journal of Stephen Vandiver Jones." *Utah Historical Quarterly* 16–17 (1948–49): 19–174.

Groesbeck, Kathryn D. "The Mountain Meadows Massacre." *True West* (March–April 1959): 14–16, 44–47.

Healy, John T. "An Adventure in the Idaho Mines." Edited by Clyde McLemore. *Frontier and Midland: A Magazine of the West* 18:2 (Winter 1937–38). Reprinted as *Sources of Northwest History no. 26*. Missoula: Montana State University.

"History of John Mount Higbee." *Higbee Family Magazine* 2:1 (1957): 118–22. Palmer Collection, Special Collections, Sherratt Library, Southern Utah University.

Holt, Jack Baker. "One of the Baker Families of Carroll (Boone) County Arkansas." *Boone County Historian* 5:3 (Fall 1982): 160–66.

Homer, Michael W. "The Judiciary and the Common Law in Utah Territory, 1851–61." *Dialogue: A Journal of Mormon Thought* 21:1 (Spring 1988): 97–108.

———. "'Similarity of Priesthood in Masonry': The Relationship between Freemasonry and Mormonism." *Dialogue: A Journal of Mormon Thought* 27:3 (Fall 1994): 1–113.

Irving, Gordon. "The Law of Adoption: One Phase of the Development of the Mormon Concept of Salvation, 1830–1900." *Brigham Young University Studies* 14:3 (Spring 1974): 291–314.

Irwin, Ray W. "The Mountain Meadows Massacre." *Arkansas Historical Quarterly* 9 (Spring 1950): 1–32.

Jensen, Jerrold S. "The Common Law of England in the Territory of Utah." *Utah Historical Quarterly* 60:1 (Winter 1992): 4–26.

Jenson, Andrew. "The Salmon River Mission." In *The Bannock State*, 150–62. Salt Lake City: n.p., 1890.

Jones, Sondra. "'Redeeming the Indian': The Enslavement of Indian Children in New Mexico and Utah." *Utah Historical Quarterly* 67:3 (Summer 1999): 220–41.

Kelly, Charles, ed. "Captain Francis Marion Bishop's Journal." *Utah Historical Quarterly* 15 (1947): 159–238.

Lambert, George Cannon. "Journal of George Cannon Lambert." In *Heart Throbs of the West*, 9:269–324. Salt Lake City: Daughters of Utah Pioneers, 1948.

Lancaster, Bob. "Blood on the Meadows: The Murder of a Saint Triggers a Wagon-Train Massacre." *Arkansas Times* 10:7 (March 1984): 28–95.

———. "Mormons Wage a Holy War: Those Tragically Massacred included 120 Arkansas Emigrants." *Arkansas Times* (15 September 1994): 40–43.

Larson, Gustive O., ed. "Journal of the Iron County Mission, John D. Lee, Clerk." *Utah Historical Quarterly* 20 (April, July, October 1952): 2:109–34; 3:253–83; 4:353–83.

Lee, Verne R. "New Mountain Meadows Monument Planned." *Utah State Historical Society Newsletter* (June 1990).

———. "A Visit with Some Descendents of John Twiddy Baker." *Journal of the Mountain Meadows Association* 1:2 (August 1991): 2–8.

Logan, Roger V., Jr., "The Mountain Meadows Massacre." In *Mountain Heritage: Some Glimpses Into Boone County's Past After One Hundred Years*, edited by Roger V. Logan, Jr., 25–31. Harrison, Ark.: Harrison Junior Chamber of Commerce, 1969.

———. "New Light on the Mountain Meadows Caravan." *Utah Historical Quarterly* 60:3 (Summer 1992): 224–37.

Loving, Ronald E. "Captain John Baker." *Mountain Meadows Newsletter* 1:2 (June 1990): 2.

———. "The Fanchers of California." *Mountain Meadows Newsletter* 1:2 (June 1990).

MacKinnon. William P. "125 years of Conspiracy Theories: Origins of the Utah Expedition of 1857–58." *Utah Historical Quarterly* 52:3 (Summer 1984): 212–30.

Matheson, Alva, ed. "Survivor of Haun's Mill Massacre." In *Cedar City Reflections*, 212–13. Cedar City: Southern Utah State College Press, 1974.

Morgan, Dale L. "The Administration of Indian Affairs in Utah, 1851–1858." *Pacific Historical Review* 17 (November 1948): 383–409.

———. "Washakie and the Shoshoni." *Annals of Wyoming* 25–27 (pt. 1, July 1953; pt. 2, January 1954; pt. 3, July 1954; pt. 4, April, 1955; pt. 5, October 1955).

Munkres, Robert L. "Indian-White Conflict before 1870: Cultural Factors in Conflict." *Journal of the West* 10 (July 1971): 439–73.

Naylor, Thomas H. "The Mormons Colonize Sonora." *Arizona and the West* 20:4 (Winter 1978): 325–42.

Oaks, Dallin H. "Gospel Teachings about Lying." *Clark Memorandum* [of the J. Rueben Clark School of Law, Brigham Young University] (Spring 1994): 13–19.

Oertle, V. Lee. "Mountain Meadows Today." *Carroll County Historical Society Quarterly* 34 (Spring 1988): 3–6.

Olesen, B. G. "Mountain Meadows Revisited." *The Branding Iron: Los Angeles Westerners Corral*, no. 194 (Winter 1993): 112.

O'Neil, Floyd A. "The Walker War." *Utah Historical Quarterly* 39:2 (Spring 1971): 178.

O'Neil, Floyd A., and Stanford J. Layton. "Of Pride and Politics: Brigham Young as Indian Superintendent." *Utah Historical Quarterly* 46:3 (Summer 1978): 236–50.

Palmer, William R. "Pahute Indian Homelands." *Utah Historical Quarterly* 6 (July 1933): 88–102.

Pendleton, Mark A. "The Orderville United Order of Zion." *Utah Historical Quarterly* 7 (October 1939): 141–59.

Peterson, Charles S. "Life in a Village Society, 1877–1920." *Utah Historical Quarterly* 49:1 (Spring 1981): 78–96.

———. "A Portrait of Lot Smith—Mormon Frontiersman." *Western Historical Quarterly* 1:4 (October 1970): 393–414.

Peterson, Levi S. "Juanita Brooks: Historian as Tragedian." *Journal of Mormon History* 3 (1976): 47–54.

Poll, Richard. "Thomas L. Kane and the Utah War." *Utah Historical Quarterly* 61 (Spring 1993): 112–35.

Poll, Richard, and William P. MacKinnon. "Causes of the Utah War Reconsidered." *Journal of Mormon History* 20:2 (Fall 1994): 16–44.

Pratt, Steven. "Eleanor McLean and the Murder of Parley P. Pratt." *Brigham Young University Studies* 15:2 (Winter 1975): 225–56.

Pulsipher, Ernest. "A Few Personal Glimpses of Juanita Brooks." *Utah Historical Quarterly* 55:3 (Summer 1987): 268–77.

Read, B. M. "Ben Ficklin 1849 and the Pony Express." *Virginia Military Institute Alumni Review* (Summer 1973): 13–14.

Remington, Gordon. "Utah Militia Records at the Family History Library." *Genealogical Journal* 19:3–4 (1991): 144–51.

Robinson, John C. "The Utah Expedition." *Magazine of American History* (April 1884): 335–36.

Schindler, Harold. "The Bear River Massacre: New Historical Evidence." *Utah Historical Quarterly* 67:4 (Fall 1999): 300–8.

Seegmiller, Emma Carroll. "Personal Memories of the United Order of Orderville, Utah." *Utah Historical Quarterly* 7 (October 1939): 160–200.

Sessions, Gene A., and Stephen W. Stathis. "The Mormon Invasion of Russian America: Dynamics of a Potent Myth." *Utah Historical Quarterly* 45:1 (Winter 1977): 22–35.

Smith, Melvin T. "Faithful History: Hazards and Limitations." *Journal of Mormon History* 9 (1982): 61–69.

Swanson, Budington. "Murders in the Meadows." *Pioneer West* (September 1979): 26–58.

Van Hoak, Stephen. "Waccara's Utes: Native American Equestrian Adaptions in the Eastern Great Basin, 1776–1876." *Utah Historical Quarterly* 67:4 (Fall 1999): 309–30.

Walker, Ronald W. "Toward a Reconstruction of Mormon and Indian Relations, 1847–1877." *Brigham Young Univesity Studies* 29 (Fall 1989): 23–42.

Wheeler, William F. "The Late James Gemmell." *Contributions to the Historical Society of Montana* 2 (1896): 331–36.

Whittaker, David J. "Mormons and Native Americans: A Historical and Bibliographical Introduction." *Dialogue: A Journal of Mormon Thought* 18:4 (Winter 1985): 33–64.

Widtsoe, John A. "Was Brigham Young Responsible for the Mountain Meadows Massacre?" *Improvement Era* 54:8 (August 1951): 558–59, 589.

Williams, David A. "President Buchanan Receives a Proposal for an Anti-Mormon Crusade, 1857." *Brigham Young University Studies* 14:1 (Autumn 1973): 103–5.

Winkler, Albert. "The Circleville Massacre: A Brutal Incident in Utah's Black Hawk War." *Utah Historical Quarterly* 55:1 (Winter 1987): 4–21.

Young, John A. "Reminiscences of John R. Young." *Utah Historical Quarterly* 24 (January 1930): 83–85.

Zamonski, Stanley W., and Teddy Keller. "Battle Axes of the Lord." *Denver Westerners Monthly Roundup* 17 (April 1961): 5–17.

NEWSPAPERS

Arkansas Post-Dispatch

Arkansas State Gazette and Democrat

Carson Daily State Register

Chicago Daily Inter-Ocean

Chicago Sunday Tribune

Church News [LDS]

Congressional Globe

Daily Alta California

Daily Corrine Reporter

Daily Memphis Avalanche

Deseret Evening News

Deseret News

El Clamor Público

Fort Smith Elevator

Frank Leslie's Illustrated Newspaper

Harrison Daily Times

Latter-day Saints' Millennial Star

Los Angeles Star

Mountain Meadow Newsletter

Oregonian

Nauvoo Expositor

New York Daily Tribune

New York Herald

New York Mormon

New York Times

New York World

Philadelphia Morning Post

Provo Daily Herald

Sacramento Union

Saints' Herald

Salt Lake Tribune

San Bernardino Times

San Francisco Daily Bulletin

San Francisco Daily Evening Bulletin

San Francisco Herald

San Francisco Morning Call

San Jose Pioneer

St. George Daily Spectrum

Southern Vineyard

Sutter County Farmer

American Weekly

Times and Seasons

Union Vedette

Utah Reporter

Valley Tan

Western Standard

SURVIVOR ACCOUNTS

Cates, Nancy Huff. Letter in "The Mountain Meadow Massacre: Statement of one of the Few Survivors." *Daily Arkansas Gazette*, 1 September 1875, 66:240, 3/1.

"'Children of the Massacre' May Meet in Reunion." Undated 1895 article from the *Arkansas Sunday Post-Dispatch*, transcribed by Anna Jean Backus from BYU microfilm. [At LDS Historian's Office on 30 September 1985, Andrew Kimball showed F. D. Richards a copy of this article from a "St. Louis paper."]

Evans, Rebecca Dunlap. "Mountain Meadow Massacre . . . Related by One of the Survivors." *Fort Smith Elevator*, 20 August 1897, 2/1–3.

Mitchell, Sallie [Sarah Francis] Baker. "The Mountain Meadows Massacre—An Episode on the Road to Zion." *American Weekly*, 1 September [?] 1940.

Terry, Elizabeth Baker. Memoir. In Clyde R. Greenhaw, "Survivor of a Massacre: Mrs. Betty Terry of Harrison Vividly Recalls Massacre of Westbound Arkansas Caravan in Utah More than 80 Years Ago." *Arkansas Gazette*, 4 September 1938, Sunday Magazine Section, 6.

Manuscripts

Anonymous. Discursive Remarks. MSS A 628, Utah State Historical Society. The USHS catalog lists this item as: "38 pages, photocopy of manuscript. Summary: An anonymous series of essays addressing Mormons and Mormonism in the 19th century. Examines such topics as the Mountain Meadows Massacre, 'Mormon morality' and practices, and the Forgery Case against some Mormons in 1858. Written apparently by a non-Mormon living in Salt Lake City, Utah. The manuscript is incomplete." A typescript is in the Donald Moorman papers at Weber State University, suggesting that Moorman might be the source of the USHS photostat. This item is obviously written by several Mormon writers. The author of the "Mountain Medow Massacre" section is almost certainly John D. Lee.

Arrington, Leonard J. Papers. Charles C. Rich Research Files, MS 4212, LDS Archives.

———. Transcripts of Jacob S. Boreman Papers at The Henry E. Huntington Library. A 61–2, Utah State Historical Society.

Ashworth, William B. The Autobiography of William B. Ashworth. MS B As3, Utah State Historical Society.

Beckwith, Frank. Shameful Friday: A Critical Study of the Mountain Meadow Massacre. HM 31255, 1935, Henry E. Huntington Library, San Marino, Calif.

Bennion, John. Diary, Book II, July 1857–September 1862. "In Army of S. [F.] D. Richards from Sept. 27 to Oct. 25, 1857 as Captain." Typescript. MS B-16, Box 3, Fd. 5, Utah State Historical Society.

Berens, Todd I. Interview with Levi Peterson, 17 September 1985. A 2721, Utah State Historical Society.

Bigler, David L. Typescript Journal Collection. In author's possession.

Bigler, Jacob G., to Priesthood Quorum Presidents, Nephi, Utah, 23 December 1856. Minute Books of the Mass Quorum of Seventies. Microfilm copy, Special Collections, Brigham Young University Library.

Black, Jeremiah Sullivan. Papers. Manuscripts Division, Library of Congress.

Blair, Paul L. The Fanchers of Clay County, Illinois. Copy in author's possession.

Blair, Seth Millington. Reminiscences and Journals, 1851–1868. MS 1710, Folder 1, LDS Archives.

Boreman, Jacob S. Papers. Henry E. Huntington Library.

Brimhall, Edna Lee. Gleanings Concerning John D. Lee: A compilation of "gleanings" from the 1930s. From a 1958 copy presented to the author by Verne R. Lee.

Brooks, Juanita. Collection. B-103, Utah State Historical Society.

———. Papers. MS 486, Manuscripts Division, Marriott Library, University of Utah. Consists mostly of Dale Morgan's letters to Brooks.

Brown, Lorenzo. Journal. FAC 558, Mormon File, Henry E. Huntington Library.

Brown, Mildred. History of Justus Wellington Seeley II. MSS 946, Special Collections and Manuscripts, Brigham Young University Library.

Browne, Albert G. Scrapbook of Clippings from the *New York Daily Tribune* covering the Utah Expedition of 1857–58: With a Letter Written to the *Tribune* from Camp Scott in 1858 Concerning Indians, Mormons and U.S. Army in Utah Territory. Manuscripts Division, Marriott Library, University of Utah.

Burr, Frederick H. Journal, 1857–58. Typescript and Index in David L. Bigler Journal Collection, 1965; original at Beinecke Library, Yale Collection of Western Americana.

Cannon, Abraham H. Journal, Vol. 19, MS 3, Manuscripts Division, Marriott Library, University of Utah.

Carleton, James Henry. Letter to Mackall, 24 June 1859, RG 393, National Archives.

Cedar Stake Journal, 1856–59. LDS Records, Palmer Collection, Special Collections, Sherratt Library, Southern Utah University.

Christian, John Ward. Dictation of Jno. Ward Christian, Beaver City, Utah, [1886]. MSS P-F 52, Bancroft Library, Dale Morgan typescript in McQuown Papers, MS 143, Manuscripts Division, Marriott Library, University of Utah.

Church Historical Department. Journals, 1844–90. CR 100 1, LDS Archives.

Clark, Mary Jane. Copy of Israel Justus Clark's Journal. David L. Bigler Journal Collection.

Coates, Lawrence G. The Fancher-Baker Train: From Salt Lake to Mountain Meadows, unpublished article. Copy in Special Collections, Browning Library, Dixie College, St. George, Utah.

Cropper, Thomas Waters. Autobiography. MSS 654, Special Collections and Manuscripts, Brigham Young University Library.

Crosby, Caroline Barnes. Diaries. Vault Manuscript B 89, Utah State Historical Society.

Crowe, S. W. Interview with S. W. Crowe, 18 September 1886. Typescript of an endsheet inscription in D. H. Prosworth's copy of an 1878 edition of *Mormonism Unveiled*. Courtesy of Ken Sanders. Copy in author's possession.

Dame, William Horn. Papers. Vault MSS 55, Special Collections and Manuscripts, Brigham Young University Library. Copies in MS 2041, LDS Archives; and Utah State Historical Society.

Dame, William Horn, to George A. Smith, 18 May 1859. Church Historian's Office Letterbook, LDS Archives.

Daughters of Utah Pioneers. Collection, 1828–1963. MS 8795, Reel 9, LDS Archives.

Davis, Charles. Mountain Meadow Massacre, Journal entries 11–14 October 1927. Davis Papers, Sutter's Fort Historical Museum, Sacramento, Calif.

Derry, Charles. Autobiography of Charles Derry. Holograph manuscript, RG 25 f98, History Department/Commission Records, Community of Christ Archives, ms. pp. 106–18.

Dickinson, J. H., to W. A. Gordon, Camp Scott, 16 April 1858. MSS 68, Bancroft Library.

Douglas, N., to George T. T. Patterson. Letter, 20 March 1877, Fort Cameron, Utah. MS 6568, LDS Archives. Lieutenant Patterson's orders to escort John D. Lee to his execution.

Drewer, Thomas, to Dr. Abram Clauds, Camp Floyd, 31 March 1859. Partial transcription "of the Contents of a Letter from Camp Floyd Utah Territory" in the Paul C. Rohloff Mormon Collection. Copy in Caroline Parry Woolley Collection, Special Collections, Gerald R. Sherratt Library, Southern Utah University.

Duffin, Hezekiah E. Affidavit. 3 May 1950. Aberdeen Idaho, MS d 3066, LDS Archives.

Edwards, William. Affidavit, 14 May 1924, MS A 1112, Utah State Historical Society.

Emery, George W. Governor's Message to the Legislative Assembly of the Territory of Utah, Salt Lake City, Utah Territory, 15 January 1878. Special Collections and Manuscripts, Brigham Young University Library.

Evans, David. Papers. MIC A 1136, Utah State Historical Society.

Fancher Family File, Carroll County Historical Society, Berryville, Ark. This file includes the Alexander Fancher Power of Attorney to James Fancher, 19 April 1850; and John S. Baker's Affidavit, 27 December 1912.

Fancher, J. Polk, to Mary Anne Campbell Lowell, 36 November 1915. California State Library.

Farnsworth, Philo T. Dictation, Beaver City, Utah, [1886?]. MSS P-F 51, Bancroft Library, Dale Morgan typescript in McQuown Papers, MS 143, Manuscripts Division, Marriott Library, University of Utah.

Fish, Joseph. History of Enterprise and Its Surroundings. Special Collections, Browning Library, Dixie College, St. George, Utah.

Forney, Jacob. In the Matter of the Estate and Guardianship of Mountain Meadows Children. Utah State Archives.

Fuller, E. N. Lee execution reports from *New York Herald*. MS 2924, LDS Archives.

Ginn, John I. Mormons and Indian Wars [Dale L. Morgan typescript]. MS A 77–1, Utah State Historical Society.

Gould, Sam. Statement. Juanita Brooks Papers, Box 25, Folder 15, Utah State Historical Society.

Grant, G. D. Seventies Minutes, 9 December 1847. Edyth Romney Typescripts, General Church Minutes, MS 2737, Box 100, LDS Archives.

Hafen, Arthur Knight. A Sketch of the Life of Samuel Knight. Daughters of Utah Pioneers Document 3355, Cedar City Public Library.

Haight, Isaac C. Journals, 1842–1850 and August 1852–February 1862. Typescript, Special Collections, Sherratt Library, Southern Utah University.

Hakes, Collins Rowe. To Whom it May Concern: And Especially My Own Family, 24 April 1916. MSS 466, Special Collections and Manuscripts, Brigham Young University Library. This and other versions are in LDS Archives.

Halleck, H. L., to W. E. D. Whiting, 6 November 1900. MSS 65, Special Collections and Manuscripts, Brigham Young University Library.

Hamblin, Jacob. Affidavits, 3 and 16 June 1859. Collected Materials Relative to the Church Historian's Office, MS 5020, Box 4, LDS Archives.

———. Jacob Hamblin—Journals and Letters. Special Collections, Amer M270.1 H17, Special Collections and Manuscripts, Brigham Young University Library.

———. Journal of Jacob Hamblin, 1854–59. Typescript, MS A 567-1, Utah State Historical Society.

Hance, Irma Watson. A biographical sketch of John Varah Long: his diaries, writings, lectures and notes. ACCN 278, Special Collections, Marriott Library, University of Utah.

Harker, Joseph. Journal. David L. Bigler typescript in author's possession; holograph original, MS 1560, LDS Archives.

Hart, Richard. Papers. Accession 1251, Box 55, Folders 2 and 8, Manuscripts Division, Marriott Library, University of Utah.

Hawley, John Pierce. Autobiography. P13.F317, Community of Christ Archives, Independence, Mo.

Healy, John. J. W. Powell and Fort Lemhi Told by Johnny Healy. Montana Historical Society.

Hearn, Fleming G. A Journal for 1850. MS 6014, Oregon State Historical Society, 17–18.

Hendrix, George F., to Brigham Young, 23 June 1860. Brigham Young Collection, MS 1234, LDS Archives.

Hicks, George Armstrong. The Life History of George Armstrong Hicks Written by Himself Containing the principle events of a life among the poor of Utah and the "Saints" generally [1877]. Family transcription with spelling and punctuation corrections by Kent V. Marvin, Mary Ann Loveless, and Karen Kenison, 1997. Copy provided to the author by Dawn Nodzu.

———. Scrapbook, 1887–1925, MS 8805, LDS Archives.

Higbee History and Stories. Special Collections, Sherratt Library, Southern Utah University.

Hinckley, Gordon B. Dedicatory Prayer, 15 September 1990. Mountain Meadows Memorial Dedication Ceremonies File, M0-2-2, Special Collections, Sherratt Library, Southern Utah University.

———. Remarks and Dedicatory Prayer, Mountain Meadows Monument Rededication, 11 September 1999. LDS Public Affairs draft. Copy in author's possession.

———. Remarks, 15 September 1990. Mountain Meadows Memorial Dedication Ceremonies File, M0-2-2, Special Collections, Sherratt Library, Southern Utah University.

Hinckley, Ira Nathaniel. Diary, March 1857–June 1858. MS 13687, LDS Archives.

Hubbard, Lester. Papers. "The Mountain Meadows Massacre." Audiotape of southern Utah ballad. MS 158, Manuscripts Division, Marriott Library, University of Utah.

Huntington, Dimick Baker. Journal. 1857 August–1859 May. MS 1419-2, LDS Archives.

Huntington, Oliver Boardman. Journal. A 858-2, Utah State Historical Society.

Huntsman, Orson W. Statement on Mountain Meadows Massacre. Box 89, Palmer Collection, Special Collections, Sherratt Library, Southern Utah University.

Hurt to Manypenny, 30 March 1857. Microfilm Publication 234, roll 898; Records of the Bureau of Indian Affairs, 75, National Archives.

Ivins, Anthony Woodward, to Mrs. G. T. Welch, 16 October 1922. MS D 4222, LDS Archives.

Journal History. Family and Church History Department of The Church of Jesus Christ of Latter-day Saints, Salt Lake City, Utah.

Judd, Zadoc Knapp. Account of settlement of Santa Clara, Utah, 27 March 1891. Mormon File, Henry E. Huntington Library, San Marino, Calif.

Kane, Thomas Leiper. Diary of Colonel Thomas L. Kane. Mormon File, FAC 515, Henry E. Huntington Library, San Marino, Calif.

———. Papers. MS 8829, LDS Archives.

Kelly, Charles. Collection. MSS B-114, Utah State Historical Society.

———. Collection. Utah's Black Friday: History of the Mountain Meadows Massacre of 1857. Charles Kelly Collection, MS 100, Manuscripts Division, Marriott Library, University of Utah.

Kimball, J. Golden. Papers, 1883–1938. MS 662, Manuscripts Division, Marriott Library, University of Utah.

Kimball, Stanley B. "Love, Marriage, Romance, and Sex on Mormon Trails, 1831–68." Unpublished article in the author's possession.

Knowlton, Elizabeth Brittain. Reminiscences, 1857–1907. 2 vols. Vault MS 128, California Historical Society.

Lambert, A. C. Collection. MS 35, Boxes 23, 35, 36, Manuscripts Division, Marriott Library, University of Utah.

Lansdale, R. H. Journal. Yale Collection of Western Americana, Yale University, typescript in David L. Bigler Journal Collection.

Leach, James. Affidavit on the Southern Route, 22 December 1856. RG 233, Records of the U.S. Congress, Territorial Papers, Utah, 1852–72, National Archives.

Leany, William, Sr., to John Steele, 17 February 1883. John Steele Papers. Vault MSS 528, Box 1, Folder 30, Special Collections and Manuscripts, Brigham Young University Library.

Lee, Ann Gordge. Autobiography. MSS SC 1706, Special Collections and Manuscripts, Brigham Young University Library.

———. Autobiography. Variant biography given to a Salt Lake City policeman in 1915. Copy in author's possession.

Lee, John D. Collection. B116-1, Utah State Historical Society.

———. Collection. Henry E. Huntington Library, San Marino, Calif.

———. Trial Papers. Clerk of the Court, District Court for Beaver County, Fifth District of Utah, Beaver City.

———. Trial Transcripts. W. L. Cook Papers, Manuscripts Division, Library of Congress.

Rachel Lee. Journal. Henry E. Huntington Library, San Marino, Calif.

———. Journal of Rachel Andora Woolsey Lee. Typescript, Brigham Young University Library, 1970.

Lee, Rex E. Remarks, 15 September 1990. Mountain Meadows Memorial Dedication Ceremonies File, Mo-2-2, Special Collections, Sherratt Library, Southern Utah University.

Lee, Verne R., and Ronald E. Loving. The Fancher Train of 1857. Typescript in Material on Fancher Emigrant Party of 1857, MSS A 4289, Utah State Historical Society.

Littleton, Micajah. Diary of Overland Journey from Independence to California, May to October 1850. James Littleton Collection. MS Box 230, Folder 3, California State Library.

Lockley, Frederic E. Collection, including Letters to Elizabeth Metcalf Campbell Lockley, 1869–1904. Box 6, Henry E. Huntington Library, San Marino, Calif.

Logan, Judge Roger, Jr. Mountain Meadows Association, 1991. MS 13429, LDS Archives.

———. Remarks of Judge Roger V. Logan, Jr., at the dedication of the Mountain Meadows Massacre Memorial, September 15, 1990, Cedar City, UT. MS 13069, LDS Archives.

Loving, Ronald E. Material on Fancher Emigrant Party of 1857. MSS A 4289, Utah State Historical Society.

Lowell, Nancy Campbell. Recollections. Compiled by Ruth Peterson as Across the Plains in '57. Typescript, 1931, California Historical Society Library.

Lundwall, Nels Benjamin. Papers, 1884–1969. MS 8193, LDS Archives.

Lyman, Francis M. Diary Excerpts of Francis M. Lyman, 1892–96. The original diaries are in possession of the First Presidency of the LDS church and are not available to the public. A Lyman family transcription can be found on the *New Mormon Studies CD-ROM: A Comprehensive Resource Library.*

McClintock, James H. Clipping File. Phoenix Public Library, Phoenix, Ariz. Courtesy W. L. Rusho.

McKay, David O. Diary, 27 July 1907. MS 668, Manuscripts Division, Marriott Library, University of Utah.

McMurrin, Sterling. Interview with Levi Peterson, 4 February 1986. A 2766, Utah State Historical Society.

Martineau, James H. The Mountain Meadow catastrophy [sic]. MS 163, LDS Archives.

———. Parowan Stake Record. Typescript, Palmer Collection, Special Collections, Sherratt Library, Southern Utah University.

———. Record, 1855 to 1860. Typescript, Box 90, Folder 4, Palmer Collection, Special Collections, Sherratt Library, Southern Utah University.

Martineau, James H., to F. E. Eldredge, 23 July 1907. James Martineau Papers, MSS 467, Special Collections and Manuscripts, Brigham Young University Library.

Matheson, Alva. John D. Lee and the Chaffin Mill. Special Collections, Sherratt Library, Southern Utah University.

Moorman, Donald R. Papers. Special Collections, Stewart Library, Weber State University.

Morgan, Dale L. Collection. MSS B-40, Utah State Historical Society.

———. Papers. Bancroft Library. Microfilm copy at Special Collections, University of Utah.

Mountain Meadows Association. "Mountain Meadows Memorial Dedication Program." Cedar City: Mountain Meadow Memorial Steering Committee, 1990.

———. "Memorial Service at the Re-internment of Remains of Victims of the Mountain Meadows Massacre [at] Mountain Meadows Emigrant Campsite." Harrison, Ark.: Harrison Daily Times Print Shop, 1999. [Contains a revised list of victims and survivors. Cited as Memorial Program.]

Mountain Meadows File, Collected Material Concerning the Mountain Meadows Massacre. MS 2674, LDS Archives.

Mountain Meadows Massacre Reference Microfilm. National Archives Microfilm Publication NNO-170A-3015, National Archives.

Mowry, Sylvester. Letters to Edward Bicknall, 1853–1855. MSS A 15, Utah State Historical Society.

Novak, Shannon, and Derinna Kopp. "Osteological Analysis of Human Remains from the Mountain Meadows Massacre." Draft. Provo: Office of Public Archaeology, Brigham Young University, 2000.

Olney, Oliver H. Papers. WA MSS 364. Yale Collection of Western Americana, Beinecke Library.

Palmer, William R. Collection. Special Collections, Sherratt Library, Southern Utah University.

———. The Paiute Indians, March 1954 lesson, Sons of Utah Pioneers. Typescript. LDS Library.

Palmer, William R., to Harold B. Lee. Copy of undated letter in author's possession.

Parkin, Max H. Papers. Accession 1539, Box 71, Folder 1, Manuscripts Division, Marriott Library, University of Utah.

Peck, Washington. Diary of Washington Peck, 1850. Typescript, OCTA Manuscripts, Mattes Library, National Frontier Trails Center, Independence, Mo.

Pitchforth, Samuel. Diary of Samuel Pitchforth, 1857–1868. Typescript. Mor M270.1 P68d, Special Collections and Manuscripts, Brigham Young University Library.

Platt, Benjamin. Diary of Benjamin Platt, 1856–1863. Typescript. BX 8670.M82 vol. 15. Brigham Young University Library, 1947.

Poll, Richard D. Collection. Ms 674, Manuscripts Division, Marriott Library, University of Utah.

Porter, Fitz-John. Papers. Manuscripts Division, Library of Congress. Includes Extracts from the Diary of Maj. Fitz-John Porter, container 53.

Pratt, Eleanor J. McComb. Account of the death of Parley P. Pratt, ca. 1857. MS 525, LDS Archives.

Pratt, Eleanor J. McComb, to Erastus Snow. 14–15 May 1857. MS 2099, LDS Archives.

Quong, Terrence O. The Mountain Meadows Massacre Revisited: Conflicting Accounts. Independent Study in History for California State University, Dominguez Hills, March 1997. Copy in author's possession.

Ray, John A., to Mountaineer re MMM, 4 December 1859. Unprocessed item, LDS Archives.

Rich, Charles C. Journal. MS 889, LDS Archives.

Rich, Russell R. The Mountain Meadows Massacre. Annotated copy in Max H. Parker Papers, Accession 1539, Box 71, Folder 1, Manuscripts Division, Marriott Library, University of Utah.

Richards, Jane. Reminis[c]ences of Mrs. F. D. Richards, San Francisco, 1880. Bancroft Library, Utah and the Mormons Collection, MS 8305, Reel 2, LDS Archives.

Rogerson, Josiah, to W. B. Dougall, 22 March 1877. MS 1234, Box 46 Folder 15: Telegrams 1877, Brigham Young Papers, 1801–77, LDS Archives.

Selected documents relating to the Mountain Meadows Massacre, [Paul C. Richards National Archives Material, ca. 30 August 1966]. MS 8502, LDS Archives.

Shelton, Marion Jackson. Affidavit. Unprocessed Documents, Church Historian's Office Journal, May–June 1859, LDS Archives.

———. Diary, March 1858–June 1859. MS 1412, fd. 1, LDS Archives.

Sherman, William T., to Brigham Young. Telegram, 10 April 1866. MS 1234, Brigham Young Collection, LDS Archives.

Shirts, Morris A. Mountain Meadows Massacre—Another Look. Special Collections, Browning Library, Dixie College.

Shurtliff, Lewis W. Life and Travels. Idaho Historical Society. Typescript in David L. Bigler Journal Collection.

Skinner, James. Autobiography. MS 6587, LDS Archives.

Smith, Elias, and Robert T. Burton. Draft Arrest Warrant for Brigham Young, May 1859. Collected Materials Relative to the Church Historian's Office, MS 5020, Box 4, LDS Archives.

———. Executed Warrant for the Arrest of Brigham Young, 12 May 1859. Unprocessed Documents, Church Historian's Office, LDS Archives.

Smith, George A., to John Lyman. Letter, 6 January 1858. Typescript, Church Historian's Office Letterbook, MS 2737, Box 26, Folder 3, 508–9.

Smith, George A., to T. B. H. Stenhouse. Provo, 7[?] June 1858. Historian's Office Letterpress Copybooks, CR 100 38, Reel 2, LDS Archives, 521.

————. 15 April 1859. Typescript, Church Historian's Office Letterbook, MS 2737, 26:4, LDS Archives, 764–65.

Smith, George A., to Mr. St. Clair, 25 November 1869. Typescript Collection CR 100/38, vol. 2, MS 2737, LDS Archives, 941–49.

Smith, Lot. Papers. AZ 186, Special Collections, University of Arizona.

Snow, Erastus. Journals, 1837–March 1857. Originals in LDS Archives, typescript in D. Michael Quinn Papers, Uncat. WA MS.98, Beinecke Library, Yale University. Although dated Journals 1837–March 1857, the microfilm copy of Snow's journals at LDS Archives ends in 1852.

Solomon, William Henry. Journal, 1873–1874; 1879–1893. MS 14808, LDS Archives.

Spencer, Clarissa Young. Father's Trips to St. George. Special Collections, Sherratt Library, Southern Utah University.

Statements Regarding Soldiers and Judge Cradlebaugh. Collected Materials Relative to the Church Historian's Office, May–June 1859 re MMM. MS 5020, box 4, LDS Archives.

Steele, John. Papers. Vault MSS 528, Special Collections and Manuscripts, Brigham Young University Library. Includes William Strong, Statement, Box 2, Folder 8.

Sudweeks, Joseph. Laban Morrill History. Mor M278 A1a #285, Special Collections and Manuscripts, Brigham Young University Library.

Temple, William Bedford. Letters, 11 May and 2 June 1850, MSS 1508, Oregon Historical Society.

Terry, James Parshall, 1830–1918. Autobiography, 1880–1905. MSS SC 1698. Special Collections and Manuscripts, Brigham Young University Library.

Utah Stake Minutes, General Meetings 1855–1860. Typescript. MS 2737, Box 53, Folder 4, LDS Archives.

Utah Territorial Militia Records, 1849–1877. Series 2210, Utah State Archives.

Walker, Joseph C. History of the Mormons in the Early Days of Utah. Joseph C. Walker Papers. MSS 1461, Box 2, Folders 11 and 12, Special Collections and Manuscripts, Brigham Young University Library. Includes James Gemmell's Narrative.

Wandell, Charles W. Correspondence, in Henry A. Stebbins Papers. P24, f28, Community of Christ Library–Archives, Independence, Mo.

Watters, Ichel. Papers. A 1588, Utah State Historical Society.

Wells, Daniel H. Lee Trial Telegrams, 14, 15, 20 September 1876. CR 1234/1, Box 43, Folder 20, LDS Archives.

Willden, Feargus O'Connor. Papers. Accession 1292, Manuscripts Division, Marriott Library, University of Utah.

Williams, George Calvin. The Life and Religion of George Calvin Williams. Typescript, MS 13382, LDS Archives.

Woodbury, John Stillman. Journal, 1851–1857. FAC 507, Mormon File, Henry E. Huntington Library, San Marino, Calif.

Woolley, Carolyn Parry. Collection. Special Collections, Sherratt Library, Southern Utah University. Includes "I Would to God," Parry's biography of her grandfather, Isaac Haight.

Young, Brigham. Collection. MS 1234, LDS Archives.

————. Collection. B-93, Utah State Historical Society. Includes a typescript of the Brigham Young office journal, Three Weeks in Brigham Young's Office.

————. Collection. MS 566, Special Collections, Marriott Library, University of Utah.

————. Letter to John Fitch Kinney, 2 November 1863. WA MSS S-172 Y84, Western Americana Collection, Beinecke Library.

————. Office Journal. Unprocessed item, LDS Archives.

Zundel, Abraham. Diary, 1856–1858. Typescript in David L. Bigler Journal Collection; original at LDS Archives.

INTERVIEWS

Alder, Douglas. Interview notes. Dixie College, St. George, Utah, 11 January 1996.

Backus, Anna Jean. Telephone conversation notes. 9 May and 3 September 1996.

Brooks, Karl. Interview notes. Dixie College, St. George, Utah, 12 January 1996.

Coates, Larry. Interview notes. 30 August 1995, LDS Archives.

Fancher, Burr. Telephone conversation notes, 6 March 1996.

Fancher, Sam. Telephone conversation notes, 25 March 1996.

Hinckley, Gordon B. "Transcript of the Interview with Gordon B. Hinckley, February 26, 2000." *Salt Lake Tribune*, at http://www.sltrib.com/2000/Feb/02262000/utah/29446.htm.

Jake, Clifford. Interview notes, tape, and transcriptions. Paiute Tribal Headquarters, Cedar City, Utah, 29 November 1995.

Logan, Judge Roger V., Jr. Interview notes. Boone County Courthouse, Harrison, Ark., 25 March 1996.

————. Telephone conversation notes, 21 May 1995.

Peterson, Charles S. "Chas." Interview notes. St. George, Utah, 11 January 1996.

Whittaker, David, and Ronald Esplin. Interview notes. Provo, Utah, 17 January 1997.

GOVERNMENT DOCUMENTS

A bill for the relief of Malinda Thurston and Nancy Littleton. H.R. 3945, 45th Cong., 2d sess.

Baker, John S. John S. Baker v. the United States and the Cheyenne Indians. Indian Depredation Case File 1262, Record Group 123, Records of the U.S. Court of Claims, National Archives, Washington, D.C.

Buchanan, James. *Message of the President of the United States, Communicating, in compliance with a resolution of the Senate, information in relation to the massacre at Mountain Meadows, and other massacres in Utah Territory*. 36th Cong., 1st sess., Senate Exec. Doc. 42, Serial 1033. Washington, D.C.: Government Printing Office, 1860. Cited as *Massacre at Mountain Meadows*.

————. *The Utah Expedition. Message of the President of the United States, Transmitting Reports from the Secretaries of War, of the Interior, and of the Attorney General, relative to the military expedition ordered into the Territory of Utah*. 35th Cong., 1st sess., House Exec. Doc. 71, Serial 956. Washington, D.C.: Government Printing Office, 1858.

————. *Utah Territory. Message of the President of the United States, Communicating, in compliance with a resolution of the House, copies of correspondence relative to the condition of affairs in the Territory of Utah*. 36th Cong., 1st sess., House Exec. Doc. 78, Serial 1031. Washington, D.C.: Government Printing Office, 1860.

California State Militia Records. California State Archives, Sacramento.

California State Library. "The National Guard in California 1849–1880 (Part 1)." Compiled with the Assistance of the Works Projects Administration from Records in the Adjutant General's Office of California and the California State Library, 1940.

Campbell, Arthur H. *Report upon the Pacific Wagon Roads, Constructed under the direction of the Hon. Jacob Thompson, Secretary of the Interior, in 1857–'58–'59*. 35th Cong., 2d sess., House Exec. Doc. 108, 1859, Serial 1008.

Carleton, James Henry. "The Mormons as a People." In Maj. George W Davis, Leslie J. Perry, and Joseph W. Kirkley, eds., *The War of the Rebellion: A Compilation of the Official Records of the Union and the Confederate Armies*. Ser. 1, vol. 50, pt. 1, Serial 3583. Washington, D.C.: Government Printing Office, 1897.

———. *Report on the Subject of the Massacre at the Mountain Meadows, in Utah Territory . . . by Brevet Major James Henry Carleton, U. S. Army, and Report of the Hon. William C. Mitchell relative to the seventeen surviving children*. Little Rock: True Democrat Steam Press, 1860.

———. *Special Report of the Mountain Meadow Massacre, by J. H. Carleton, Brevet Major, United States Army, Captain, First Dragoons*. 57th Cong., 1st sess., House Exec. Doc. 605, Serial 4377.

Cowan, B. R. *Ute, Pai-ute, Go-si Ute, and Shoshone Indians*. 43d Cong., 1st sess., House Exec. Doc. 157. Washington, D.C.: Government Printing Office, 1874.

Denver, James. "Report of the Commissioner of Indian Affairs . . . for the Year 1857." In *Message of the President of the United States*. 35th Cong., 2d sess., Senate Exec. Doc. 1, Serial 974. Washington, D.C.: William A. Harris, Printer, 1858.

Fillmore, Millard. *Report of Messrs. Brandebury, Brocchus, and Harris, to the President of the United States*. 32d Cong., 1st sess., House Exec. Doc. 25, Serial 640. Washington, D.C.: Government Printing Office, 1852.

Floyd, John B. "Annual Report of the Secretary of War." 35th Cong., 1st sess., Senate Exec. Doc., Serial 920.

———. "Report of the Secretary of War." *Message of the President of the United States*. 35th Cong., 2d sess., Senate Exec. Doc. 85, Serial 975. Washington, D.C.: William A. Harris, 1858.

Forney, Jacob. "Annual Report." In *Report of the Secretary of the Interior, Office of Indian Affairs, New Mexico, Utah, Oregon and Washington Superintendencies*. 35th Cong., 1st sess., Senate Exec. Doc. 2, Serial 1023, 1859.

———. Annual Report. In *Message from the President of the United States*, 36th Cong., 1st sess., House Exec. Doc. 10, Report of the Secretary of the Interior, Serial 956. Washington: George W. Bowman, 1860.

Fort Crittenden Letter Books, RG 393, Old Military Records, Department of Utah, Series 5029, National Archives.

Howard, Sumner, to Attorney General Alphonso Taft, 4 October 1876. National Archives Microfilm Publication NNO-170A-3015, Mountain Meadows Massacre Reference Microfilm, Source-Chronological Files: Utah, Department of Justice, Record Group 60, National Archives.

Muster Rolls, 10 October 1857, Companies A to H, 4th Battalion, Tenth Regiment of Infantry, Iron County Brigade, Nauvoo Legion, Series 3346, Utah State Archives.

Nelson, William, and Sumner Howard to Attorney General Alphonso Taft, 23 September 1876. National Archives Microfilm Publication NNO-170A-3015, Mountain Meadows Massacre Reference Microfilm, Source-Chronological Files: Utah, Department of Justice, Record Group 60, National Archives.

Papers Pertaining to the Territory of Utah, 1849–1870. Records of the United States Senate, Record Group 46, National Archives, Washington, D.C. Also available on microfilm as Roll 15, Territorial Papers of the United States, Senate 1789–1873, Utah, 31 December 1849–11 June 1870. Affidavits gathered in Arkansas in 1860 from surviving relatives of massacre victims.

Probate Court Criminal and Civil Case Docket. Series 3944, Reel 2, Utah State Archives.

Probate Court Record Book A, Salt Lake County Estates, 1852–1869. Series 3372, Reel 1, Box, 1, Utah State Archives.

Secretary of State. *Register of Officers and Agents, Civil, Military, and Naval, in the Service of the United States on the Thirtieth of September, 1855*. Washington, D.C: A.O.P. Nicholson, 1855.

Smith, Caleb B. *Accounts of Brigham Young, Superintendent of Indian Affairs in Utah Territory*. 37th Cong., 2d sess., House Exec. Doc. 29, 1862, Serial 1128. Washington, D.C: Government Printing Office, 1862.

Smith, William. *Remonstrance of William Smith et al., of Covington, Kentucky, against the Admission of Deseret into the Union.* 31st Cong., 1st sess., House Misc. Doc. 43, Serial 581, 1849.

Thurston, Malinda Cameron Scott. Depositions in support of H.R. 1459 and H.R. 3945, 18 December 1877. Record Group 123, Indian Depredation Claim 8479, Thurston v. the United States and the Ute Indians, National Archives.

———. Malinda Thurston, Joel Scott, Frederick Arnold, and Andrew Wolf statements, 2 May 1911. Record Group 123, Indian Depredation Claim 8479, Thurston v. the United States and the Ute Indians, National Archives.

Utah Territorial Legislature. *Acts, Resolutions and Memorials, passed at the Several Annual Sessions of the Legislative Assembly of the Territory of Utah, from 1851 to 1870 Inclusive.* Salt Lake City: Joseph Bull, 1870.

Utah Territorial Militia. Correspondence 1849–1875. A-384, Utah State Historical Society.

Utah Territorial Papers. Utah Territory, vol. 1, 1853–1859. National Archives

Wall, William. Report, 24 April –11 May 1853. Doc. 243, Ser. 2210, Reel 4, Territorial Militia Records, Utah State Archives.

Welch, Peyton Y. v. the United States and the Ute Tribe. Record Group 205, Records of the Court of Claims Section (Justice), Indian Depredations Case No. 9239, National Archives.

Young, Brigham, to William Wall, 25 April 1853. Doc. 236, Series 2210, Reel 4, Territorial Militia Records, Utah State Archives.

INTERNET SOURCES, COMPACT DISKS, AND VIDEOTAPES

Degn, Louise. "Juanita Brooks." Videotape of "Dimension Five" episode. KSL-TV, ca. 1980.

Eatough, Norman. E-mail to author and LDS-BOOKSHELF Internet mailing list.

Family History Library, search engine at *http://www.familysearch.org.*

KUTV, Salt Lake City, Utah. Mountain Meadows news stories with outtakes, 1990–92. Video in possession of the author.

Loving, Ronald E. Minutes of Salt Lake City Meeting about the Old Monument Held in the LDS Church Administration Building, 30 October 1998. Posted in 2001 at *http://www.mtn-meadows-assoc.com/ Meetin_Notes/Oct30meeting.htm.* Copy in author's possession.

Mountain Meadows Association Website. *http://www.mtn-meadows-assoc.com.*

New Mormon Studies CD-ROM: A Comprehensive Resource Library. Salt Lake City: Smith Research Associates, 1998.

INDEX